Feminist and Queer Information Studies Reader

This title is number 4 in the Litwin Books Series on Gender and Sexuality in Information Studies, Emily Drabinski, Series Editor.

Also in the series:

Number 1: *Out Behind the Desk: Workplace Issues for LGBTQ Librarians*, edited by Tracy Nectoux

Number 2: *Make Your Own History: Documenting Feminist and Queer Activism in the 21st Century*, edited by Lyz Bly and Kelly Wooten

Number 3: *Feminist Pedagogy for Library Instruction*, by Maria Accardi

Forthcoming:

Ephemeral Material: Queering the Archive, by Alana Kumbier

Queers Online: LGBT Digital Practices in Libraries, Archives, and Museums, Edited by Rachel Wexelbaum

Feminist and Queer Information Studies Reader

Patrick Keilty and Rebecca Dean, Editors

Litwin Books
Sacramento, California

Published by Litwin Books, 2013
P.O. Box 188784
Sacramento, CA 95818
http://litwinbooks.com

This book is printed on acid-free paper meeting all present ANSI standards for archival preservation.

Cover design by Jennifer Hennesy

Layout by Martin K. Wallace

Index by Lynley Wheaton

Library of Congress Cataloging-in-Publication Data

Feminist and queer information studies reader / editors: Patrick Keilty and Rebecca Dean.
　　pages cm. -- (Litwin Books series on gender and sexuality in information studies ; 4)
　Includes bibliographical references and index.
　Summary: "Gathers existing research along with new scholarship on the intersection of gender and sexuality and information use"--Provided by publisher.
　ISBN 978-1-936117-16-1 (alk. paper)
　1. Women's studies. 2. Feminism. 3. Sexual minorities. 4. Gays. I. Keilty, Patrick editor of compilation. II. Dean, Rebecca, 1982- editor of compilation.
　HQ1180.F428 2013
　　305.42--dc23
　　　　　　　　　　　　　　　　　　　　　　　　　　　2013008438

Contents

Acknowledgements ... ix

Foreword
~ Sandy Stone ... xii

Introduction
~ Patrick Keilty ... 1

Part One
Information as Gendered Labor ... 11

   The Bride Stripped Bare to Her Data:
Information Flow + Digibodies
~ Mary Flanagan ... 13

   Essentialism and Care in a Female-Intensive Profession
~ Melodie J. Fox and Hope A. Olson ... 48

   Reflections on Meaning in Library and Information Studies:
A Personal Odyssey through Information, Sexuality, and Gender
~ Alvin M. Schrader ... 62

Part Two
Cyborgs and Cyberfeminism ... 99

   Feminist Theories of Technology
~ Judy Wajcman ... 101

   Cyborg Feminism and the Methodology of the Oppressed
~ Chela Sandoval ... 117

   Developing a Corporeal Cyberfeminism:
Beyond Cyberutopia
~ Jessica E. Brophy ... 137

Part Three
Online Environment — 161

Going On-line:
Consuming Pornography in the Digital Era
~Zabet Patterson — 163

Avatars and the Visual Culture of Reproduction on the Web
~Lisa Nakamura — 182

"OH NO! I'M A NERD!"
Hegemonic Masculinity on an Online Forum
~Lori Kendall — 227

Part Four
Information Organization — 249

How We Construct Subjects: A Feminist Analysis
~Hope A. Olson — 251

Queer Theory and the Creation of Contextual Subject Access Tools for Gay and Lesbian Communities
~D. Grant Campbell — 290

Paraphilias:
The Perversion of Meaning in the Library of Congress Catalog
~Melissa Adler — 309

Administrating Gender
~Dean Spade — 324

Part Five
Information Extraction, Information Flow — 351

On Torture: Abu Ghraib
~Jasbir K. Puar — 353

Tacit Subjects
~Carlos Ulises Decena — 384

A Tapestry of Knowledge:
Crafting a New Approach to Information Sharing
~Sherilyn M. Williams and Pamela J. McKenzie — 406

Sharing Economies and Value Systems on the Nifty Archive
~Mica Ars Hilson — 431

Table of Contents

Part Six
Archive — 441

  Police/Archives
    ~Steven Maynard — 443

  The Brandon Archive
    ~Judith Halberstam — 473

  Love and Lubrication in the Archives, or rukus!
  A Black Queer Archive for the United Kingdom
    ~Ajamu X, Topher Campbell, and Mary Stevens — 502

  "Welcome Home"
  An Exploratory Ethnography of the Information
  Context at the Lesbian Herstory Archives
    ~Danielle Cooper — 526

  Accessing Transgender //
  Desiring Queer(er?) Archival Logics
    ~K. J. Rawson — 542

  In the Archives of Lesbian Feelings:
  Documentary and Popular Culture
    ~Ann Cvetkovich — 561

Part Seven
Performance — 599

  How I Learned to Stop Worrying and Love the Rape Kit
    ~Aliza Shvarts — 601

  Joe Orton, Kenneth Halliwell and the Islington Public Library:
  Defacement, Parody and Mashups
    ~D. Grant Campbell — 620

  Becoming Dragon:
  A Transversal Technology Study
    ~micha cárdenas — 640

  GRIDs, Gay Bombs, and Viral Aesthetics:
  Queer Technologies' Networked Assemblages
    ~Zach Blas — 662

Afterword
　~Leah A. Lievrouw　　　　　　　　　　　　　　　　679
Author Bios　　　　　　　　　　　　　　　　　　　683
Index　　　　　　　　　　　　　　　　　　　　　689

Acknowledgements

This book saw its genesis in the especially conducive environments of the UCLA Departments of Information Studies and Women's Studies (now Gender Studies), where we had the privilege to study information, technology, gender, and sexuality as graduate students. We owe the completion of this project, in no small measure, to the commitments of these departments' faculties and students to issues of social justice, interdisciplinary scholarship, and critical studies. We are extravagantly indebted to them for creating a rialto of common lending, borrowing, and exchange.

We also owe a lot to the personal participation of others. In particular, Sandra Harding's generosity continues to amaze and inspire us. She set aside invaluable time to teach us the process of editing our first book—a humbling experience from someone we so deeply admire. Sandra personifies the ideal advisor: patient, thoughtful, clear, useful, encouraging, and knowledgeable. Without Sandra, we would not have known where to begin. She has advised us throughout this project, from its inception to its completion. We can only hope to emulate her example in our future advisory roles.

Other intellectual and moral support came from Zach Blas, Joseph Bristow, Clara Chu, Ron Day, Johanna Drucker, Mary Flanagan, Dustin Friedman, Jonathan Furner, Anne Gilliland, Grace Hong, David Kim, Andrew Lau, Gregory Leazer, Leah Lievrouw, Mary Niles Maack, Lilly Nguyen, Liladhar Pendse, James Schultz, Katie Shilton, Sandy Stone, Liza Taylor, Sharon Traweek, Jillian Wallace, Michael Wartenbe, Vivian Wong, Laura Wynholds, and Juliet Williams. Martin Weiss, in his capacity as interim chair of the Library and Information Science Program at the University of Pittsburgh, helped to pay the fees required for reprinting several of the essays contained in this volume. Without such support, the fate of this book would have been, at best, uncertain. Emily Drabinski, our series editor, continued to remind us of the importance of this project. With a keen editorial eye, Emily gave a stylistic scrubbing to several essays—but it would be impossible to innumerate her many contributions. Special thanks go to Matthew Schuman, whose support has been deeply uplifting, particularly at moments of low-ebb—when the preponderance of graduate work and the academic job market was upon us.

We cannot heap enough praise on Rory Litwin, our publisher. Along with Martin, Rory set funds aside to pay for many of the permission fees. More than that, however, he gave us the time, space, and intellectual freedom to develop this book fully. The field of Information Studies has been vastly improved by the many contributions, broad in scope, his press has made. Perhaps no other publisher would have treated us so favorably, been so committed to our project, and trusted us to determine its content. We could not have found a more suitable publisher for the audience, subject, and quality of this book. We are profoundly lucky to have Litwin Books as a platform for many important political, social, cultural, and historical works.

Finally, this book is a palimpsest of previously published and unpublished material. The borrowings from previously published materials, in order of appearance, are as follows:

Flanagan, Mary. "The Bride Stripped Bare to Her Data: Information Flow + Digibodies." In *Data Made Flesh: Embodying Information*, edited by Robert Mitchell and Phillip Thurtle, 153-180. New York: Routledge, 2004.

Wajcman, Judy. "Feminist Theories of Technology." *Cambridge Journal of Economics* 34, no.1 (2010): 143-152. doi:10.1093/cje/ben057.

Sandoval, Chela. "New Sciences: Cyborg Feminism and the Methodology of the Oppressed." In *The Cyborg Handbook*, edited by Chris Hables Gray, 407-421. New York: Routledge, 1995.

Brophy, Jessica. "Developing a Corporeal Cyberfeminism: Beyond Cyberutopia." *New Media & Society* 12, no.6 (2010): 929-945. doi:10.1177/1461444809350901.

Patterson, Zabet. "Going On-Line: Consuming Pornography in the Digital Era." In *Porn Studies*, edited by Linda Williams, 104-123. Durham, NC: Duke University Press, 2004.

Nakamura, Lisa. "Avatars and the Visual Culture of Reproduction on the Web." In *Digitizing Race: Visual Cultures of the Internet*, 131-170. Minneapolis: University of Minnesota Press, 2008.

Kendall, Lori. "'OH NO! I'M A NERD!': Hegemonic Masculinity on an Online Forum." *Gender & Society* 14, no.2 (2000): 256-274. doi:10.1177/089124300014002003.

Olson, Hope. "How We Construct Subjects: A Feminist Analysis." *Library Trends* 56, no. 2 (2007): 509-541.

Campbell, D. Grant. "Queer Theory and the Creation of Contextual Subject Access Tools for Gay and Lesbian Communities." *Knowledge Organization* 27, no. 3 (2000): 122-131.

Acknowledgements

Spade, Dean. "Administrating Gender." In *Normal Life: Administrative Violence, Critical Trans Politics, and the Limits of the Law*, 137–169. New York: South End Press, 2011.

Puar, Jasbir K. "On Torture: Abu Ghraib." *Radical History Review* 93 (2005): 13–38. doi:10.1215/01636545-2005-93-13.

Decena, Carlos Ulises. "Tacit Subjects." *GLQ: A Journal of Lesbian and Gay Studies* 14, no. 2–3 (2008): 339–359.

X, Ajamu; Campbell, Topher; Stevens, Mary. "Love and Lubrication in the Archives, or rukus!: A Black Queer Archive for the United Kingdom." In "Special Section on Queer Archives." Edited by Rebecka Sheffield and Marcel Barriault. Special issue, *Archivaria* 68, no. 7 (2010): 271–294.

Rawson, K. J. "Accessing Transgender // Desiring Queer(er?) Archival Logics." In "Special Section on Queer Archives." Edited by Rebecka Sheffield and Marcel Barriault. Special issue, *Archivaria* 68, no. 7 (2010): 123–140.

Maynard, Steven. "Police/Archives." In "Special Section on Queer Archives." Edited by Rebecka Sheffield and Marcel Barriault. Special issue, *Archivaria* 68, no. 7 (2010): 159–182.

Halberstam, Judith. "The Brandon Archive." In *In A Queer Time and Place: Transgender Bodies, Subcultural Lives*. New York: New York University Press, 2005: 22–46.

Cvetkovich, Ann. "In the Archive of Lesbian Feelings: Documentary and Popular Culture." *Camera Obscura* 17, no. 1 (2002): 107–147.

Shvarts Aliza. "How I Learned to Stop Worrying and Love the Rape Kit." *Extensions: The Online Journal of Embodiment and Technology* 6 (October, 2011): http://www.extensionsjournal.org/the-journal/6/how-i-learned-to-stop-worrying-and-love-the-rape-kit.

cárdenas, micha. "Becoming Dragon: A Transversal Technology Study." *CTHEORY* April 29, 2010. http://ctheory.net/articles.aspx?id=639.

Foreword

When I was twelve, I would secretly commandeer my dad's ancient Remington typewriter and bang out long philosophical screeds. At that age I was so enamored of European philosophers that I always wrote as if I were translating myself out of the German. You can imagine how awful that was. Of course, it wasn't the philosophers' style that I admired: it was their translators', though I didn't know it. It never occurred to me that between my crazy young brain and the minds of the scholars and thinkers I thought I loved, there was an invisible machine. Later, of course, via a constellation of discourses that included critical and cultural studies, came the idea that invisible machines were everywhere, and that an important work of scholarship was to make them visible.

This has a moral dimension. When in the latter part of the 20th Century the epistemic shit hit the fan, few disciplines escaped; the rift between TradAcs (Traditional Academics) and young discourse shredders for whom disciplinary reflexivity was an obvious and inescapable consequence of their research created tectonic shifts in the scholarly landscape. Queer discourses arrived at that fortuitous time when cracks and declivities were appearing in scholarship's vertical face, and feisty, energetic queer scholars wasted no time with their wedges and pitons.

This collection is about Queer Studies and Information Science. For the purposes of this little essay, let's take Information Science (I.S.) to mean a scholarly inflection of *apophenia*, or our hardwired need to find patterns where no pattern may exist; and let's take a Queer inflection of I.S. to mean our attempt to show that establishing those patterns isn't value-free but in practice is a working implementation of *Forbidden Planet*, with its insanely powerful monsters from the id.[1] I can get away with this only because the editors follow on with a thoughtful and carefully nuanced overview of the nascent field which is the subject of this collection, but, since I can, I'm going

---

1   *Forbidden Planet*, directed by Fred M. Wilcox (Culver City, CA: Metro-Goldwyn-Mayer, 1956).

Foreword

to lumber on and take advantage of our different approaches to scholarship and its pleasures.

In elucidating a Queer methodology we're fortunate in having, in some respects, shoulders to stand on: for example, beginning in the latter half of the 20th Century, work on developing inquiries grounded in reflexivity, such as James Clifford's anthropologies of anthropologists;[2] also, a large part of the Strong Programme in the Sociology of Technology and Innovation (for methods only, since to that worthy group the idea of Queer would have been utterly alien); and of course the pioneers of cultural studies and its many ramifications, race and ethnicity studies, gay and lesbian studies, transgender studies, academic feminism, and cyberfeminism. The concept of Queer both embraces and extends all of those, and adds to them a nasty variant of the episteme-wrangling originated by the philosopher-poets of what used to be called High Theory: that is, using a specific unanticipated aspect or subset of language to subvert the structures of that selfsame language (or, in another sense, using *parole* or more precisely *écriture* to attack *langue*), thereby undermining the way meaning is made by turning the process of making meaning back on itself. This ontic masochism, like figure/ground inversion in astronomy, has the felicitous effect of setting off in high relief the structures that power embeds in language and which subtly distort the processes by which meaning is finally produced. Queer Studies took that rarefied practice, turned it upside-down, shook it out, democratized it, scuffed it up, and packaged it like a hammer in a hardware shop, so that anyone with a mind to can pick it up and bash away at the discourse of their choice. Of course, this has certain problems of its own—think A. Q. Khan passing out plans for nuclear weapons—but space is limited here, so let's move on.

Queering applies the *uncanny valley* effect to discourses that may have nothing to do with vision. In the uncanny valley effect, CGI humans that approach the quality of appearing "human" to a degree exquisitely close to but still not exactly "human" evoke a sense of creepiness and revulsion. Semioticians will note that it's all about extremely fine degrees of difference. The effect works with any ethnicity and so doesn't seem to be about "otherness" as we customarily frame it. For our purposes, the work of this collection is about mapping the effect onto a discourse, and it's also about the creepiness. We do want a target discourse to feel creepy. The eventual goal is to get practitioners of that discourse to wonder *why* it feels creepy.

I'm not sure it's critical to know what Information Science actually is, though. In practice, it's huge: I.S. sprawls across disciplines like a drunken senator. As you can tell from the breadth of interests, approaches, and styles

---

2   See, for example, *On the Edges of Anthropology: Interviews* (Chicago: Prickly Paradigm Press, 2003).

represented here, it may be that the only way to identify an I.S. issue is by Justice Potter Stewart's remark that he knew it when he saw it.

Why a Queer-inflected Information Science? Well, there's the theoretical and there's the pragmatic. In the theoretical we reflect on the changes in discourses which might come about because of resonances we were able to create between topics near the heart of I.S. and insurgent discourses which do their work at the periphery, but which, if they are good, inevitably burrow in and create disturbance at the center. In the pragmatic, perhaps we reflect on how being intimate with these discourses can advance our prospects for employment. We don't usually talk much about the second one, but nevertheless it's there.

Because the folks who assembled this anthology address the former, and to excellent effect, I'm going to concentrate on the latter. It is my considered opinion that the multiple intersections of Queer Studies and Information Science may be the key sites which, by virtue of their centrality vis-à-vis communication technologies—those utterly pervasive discourses by means of which we build the experiential world (and my twelve-year-old self adds *menschenbild*, the personal world)—will in the immediate future have profound effects on global cultural formations. You—the people reading this collection—will be among those with their hands on those levers. As the presumptive heirs of one of the only scrappy disciplines left standing, it behooves us all to peer myopically (which, after all, is the only way we can do it) down the corridor of time to get an idea of what our field may be like.

Of course the first thing we see is radical change: change that affects us, and probably more profoundly than many other fields. Put simply, we're entering a time of contraction. Rather than encouraging one to take risks, times like that tend to make one more conservative. There will be fewer resources and more pressure. So here are a few suggestions for surviving in a fresh discipline like Queer Studies or the recent incarnation of Information Science in the coming academic climate, and I doubt they are the ones you expect:

- Your job is to find your voice. That is your only job. Everything else follows. This sounds simple. It isn't. The rest of the world, and most certainly the academic world, exists to try to distract you from it.

- Find your ideal audience and play to it. Your ideal audience may not be in your department; it may not even be in your institution. In fact, it may exist only in your imagination. No matter; play to it anyway, because in pitching yourself that high, you give yourself creative scope to make your very best work. You are also assuring that, no matter where it is, how localized or scattered, your

Foreword

audience has a chance to find you. This may cost you in the short run, but if you remain true, you won't regret it.

The standard argument against this is that you must get tenure first, before you do anything else. Keep in mind, then, that, precisely because she followed the suggestions listed here—or possibly because she wrote them—the author of this essay was given tenure over the objections of her own department. Believe me, that's awkward, but don't let anyone try to tell you it's impossible.

- Even poor institutions are bursting with resources, but you have to learn to look for them with different eyes. The system is designed for scarcity, so think playfully instead. Bottoms of stairwells can be cornucopias of equipment, since staff clearing out old stuff frequently stash it there until it can be moved or picked up. Grab it. Seek out useless spaces: closets, utility rooms, storage rooms. Occupy them. Don't ask permission; just set up whatever you need to and get on with the work. Eventually someone will complain, and then you have to think fast. In guerrilla pedagogy it's much better to apologize than to ask.

- Don't be scared by credentialing. Don't forget that none of the people who created Queer Studies had a degree in Queer Studies. This is key. Things have originary moments. Be alert for them. If you see a chance for a radical break from Queer Studies or Information Science themselves, don't hesitate to exploit it. If the direction your work takes you doesn't fit the existing naming conventions, create your own. Name joyously and with abandon. Find variations on existing names. Or just make shit up. Don't get stuck in other peoples' discourses unless you really want to.

- This may not make sense to you at this point, but remember it anyway: viral infection beats collisions of power, and, when virally subverting institutions, you win not by winning, but by not losing. When shit closes in and the situation seems hopeless, change the terms of engagement.

- Most of all, beware of people who analyze postmodernity from within the modernist paradigm. You will recognize that Queer Studies at its best is a postmodern discourse: from a modernist perspective, its language is unintelligible—as is every truly new discipline.

And there you have it—a few cranky words from a crabby old theoretician about a spanking new assemblage of discourses. I now gratefully turn you over to saner voices and calmer thoughts about the same topic. May you enjoy this anthology, and the fruitful discussions that I know will arise from the crosstalk, harmonies and dissonances among the articles in it.

Just remember: no guts => no galaxy.

~Sandy Stone

Introduction

This book arrives many decades after the profession and field of library science had been spun out into a variety of intellectual directions, and reconstituted as schools or departments of "information science" or "information studies." As library school students, we learn about the impact of the computational boom of the 1950s and, resulting from it, the introduction of faculty into library schools from a wide variety of disciplines, including mathematics (later, computer science), communications, and behavioral sciences, to name a few. We learn, too, about the influence on the profession of the early European documentalist and internationalist movements, and about a genealogy that traces these movements to contemporary hypertext and hypermedia systems used by libraries. And, if we are lucky, we learn about Suzanne Briet, a little known French librarian, who entered the professional class when she became one of the first of three women appointed as professional librarians at the *Bibliothèque Nationale de France* in 1924.

Briet took up many of the pressing issues of librarianship in her day: internationalization, institutionalization, and advancements in technology. She was, of course, not alone in these endeavors, but, unlike many of her predecessors, Briet brought a deep understanding of culture to librarianship, documentalism, and technology. In doing so, Briet showed that technology and culture were deeply connected. "She saw society and, therefore, culture, as being re-shaped by technology," writes Michael Buckland. "The techniques of documentation in aiding and shaping intellectual work were, in her view, both a symptom of, and contributing force within the 'industrialization' of knowledge workers. We can now see, in the impact of computers and telecommunications, how right she was."[1]

Briet also challenged her predecessors' emphasis on fixed forms of documents, suggesting instead, as Ron Day has it, "an unlimited horizon of

---

1 Michael Buckland, "A Brief Biography of Suzanne Renée Briet," in *What is Documentation? English Translation of the Classic French Text*, by Suzanne Briet, trans. and ed. Ronald E. Day and Laurent Martinet with Hermina G. B. Anghelescu, (Lanham, MD: Scarecrow, 2006), 3.

physical forms and aesthetic formats for documents and an unlimited horizon of techniques and technologies (and of 'documentary agencies' employing these) in the service of multitudes of particular cultures."[2] Thus, starting with Briet, library and information studies begins to broaden its understanding of information to include the variety of cultural evidence.

Her thirty year career at the *Bibliothèque Nationale* often put Briet in close contact with major French thinkers of the day, including scientists, historians, linguists, and philosophers, which had a significant impact on her philosophy. Briet embraced modernity and science, but she also made a difference to modernism and science by introducing cultural methods and concerns, especially semiotics, to librarianship and documentalism. "Her modernist perspective, combined with semiotics," writes Buckland, "deserves attention now because it is different from, and offers an alternative to, the scientific, positivist view that has so dominated information science and which is increasingly questioned."

Feminist and Queer Information Studies Reader extends Briet's project by presenting cultural methods and concerns within information studies, particularly as they relate to gender and sexuality. As library science has incorporated computer and behavioral sciences, so too has it come to incorporate many of their epistemological traditions, from the enormously popular studies of bibliometrics to a presupposition of technology as merely instrumental, merely used. Such a presupposition insists on a conception of people as "users"—a word that simultaneously reflects the influence of both applied and behavioral sciences. While the word "culture" gets attached to a wide variety of scientific scholarship across the field, much of it bares little resemblance to "cultural studies" as they are understood in the humanities and humanistic social sciences. Instead, we find that the field of information studies continues to be dominated by the scientific positivism Briet sought to counter.

This drastically brief history of methodology in the field may come as a surprise to those of us unfamiliar with the current trend of scholarship within information studies, the field that often trains librarians. Many of our colleagues in the humanities see libraries, along with archives and museums, as carriers of culture, great modernist systems that allow for the preservation, storage, and retrieval of cultural artifacts. This history might seem especially surprising for those of us who know so many culturally minded librarians. How many librarians had significant humanistic training in college? How many have artistic careers on the side? How many find themselves daily, as a result of their profession, on the front lines of so many cultural and social battles, including the USA PATRIOT Act, technology policy, copyright law, immigration, homelessness, disability issues, and intellectual freedom, to

---

2   Ronald E. Day, preface to *What is Documentation?* by Suzanne Briet.

name a few. On this last point, noteworthy in a book on feminist and queer issues, some librarians have been indefatigable defenders of access to books with LGBT content, particularly in the midst of the Culture Wars of the late twentieth century. It should come as no surprise, then, that librarians formed the nation's first LGBT professional organization in 1970, at the beginning of the gay liberation era. So it seems ironic that this great cultural profession should lack cultural methods and concerns—particularly queer concerns—as an academic discipline.

In recent years, however, a number of scholars, particularly those with the benefit of cultural studies as undergraduates, have begun engaging humanistic methods and concerns within information studies. Increasingly, these scholars, many of them junior faculty and graduate students, suggest that information studies and cultural studies must inform each other and be brought into critical conversation. For those of us who adhere to the political-intellectual commitments of feminism and queer studies, it often means turning to the traditions of feminist and post-colonial studies of science and technology, and, of course, to cyberfeminism—which has an early presence in this book.

We also cannot help but sense that the disciplinary divide within information studies—which coarsely sees cultural inquiry on one side, scientific positivism on the other—at least partly owes to gender stratification that privileges the latter over the former. Some of the evidence for this might come from the way in which departments dominated by women—education, nursing, social welfare, women's physical education, home economics, and, of course, library science—which began around 1900 as separate, unequal institutions, low in status and prestige, struggled in large academic environments with little support, only to be terminated by academic administrators in the mid-late twentieth century, when they were no longer useful, or did not generate the kind of research money universities began increasingly to expect. If these departments persevered, they did so without economic rewards, prestige, or power. In times of budgetary crises, these departments were the first ones targeted for closure.[3]

The incorporation of applied and behavioral scientists, who brought with them the potential for large research funds, may have been as much financially motivated as it was intellectually motivated at a time, in the latter part of the twentieth century, when many of the nation's library schools closed due to university budget cuts. Among the most noteworthy closures were the library schools at the University of Chicago, the University of Southern California, the University of California, Berkeley, and Columbia

---

[3] Maresi Nerad, *The Academic Kitchen: A Social History of Gender Stratification at the University of California, Berkeley* (Albany: State University of New York Press, 1999).

University.[4] During this time, the applied and behavioral sciences, fields dominated by men, had achieved increasing economic reward, prestige, and power, while women's departments were on the decline.

A corollary to this can be seen in the romantic comedy *Desk Set*, which Mary Flanagan analyzes in an essay that serves as the opening to the first section of this book. Flanagan's essay, "The Bride Stripped Bare to Her Data: Information Flow + Digibodies," examines several media examples that depict data, technological change, and information in ways that tie them directly to women's bodies. In the film, the main character, Bunny Watson, played by Katharine Hepburn, is a reference librarian at a large corporation. Spencer Tracy plays Richard Sumner, an early computer scientist who has been hired to introduce a computer, "EMERAC," always personified as a temperamental "girl," into the all-women reference library. Remarking on the troublingly sexist depictions of women in the film, Flanagan writes:

> Unexpectedly, it is Bunny's methodological and meticulous, almost machinelike command of knowledge that allows her to beat the very machines sent to replace her. Her knowledge is vast, crisp, and helpful at all times. At the same time the EMERAC is installed in the reference area (with a new female operator), one is installed in Payroll and promptly generates pink slips for everyone in the company. Still, Bunny beats the machine in an uncanny way, saving the day with her genuine human knowledge, her way of connecting events and facts in a sensible order; she becomes a metaphoric "bride" defeating the efficient machines of her bachelor suitor. The machine spins out of control, while Bunny remains cool and knowledgeable. In the end, Bunny shares her space with the machine yet controls it; she is then enfolded into a new and seemingly more equitable heterosexual relationship.[5]

Contributing to this sexist narrative, Richard repeatedly insists that EMERAC can only make a mistake "if the human element makes a mistake first." For Richard, EMERAC is a flawless system for retrieving knowledge, while the "human element," nearly always gendered female, functions as the unstable variable of knowledge retrieval, in need of computational improvement. (Noteworthy, too, is how Richard genders EMERAC's role to retrieve knowledge as female, always for the purpose of male consumers.) Thus, the film creates a dichotomy in which the method of the computer—privileged by

---

4   Larry J. Ostler, Therrin C. Dahlin, and J. D. Willardson, *The Closing of American Library Schools: Problems and Opportunities* (Westport, CT: Greenwood, 1995).

5   Mary Flanagan, "The Bride Stripped Bare to Her Data: Information Flow + Digibodies," in *Data Made Flesh: Embodying Information*, ed. Robert Mitchell and Phillip Thurtle (New York: Routledge, 2004), 153–54.

the corporation's financially conscious, all-male executives—displaces the method of the erroneous (and female) human.

It is, of course, not a coincidence that this film, which is set in the midst of the computational boom of the 1950s, depicts the incorporation of computer technologies into a library at the same time library schools began incorporating applied scientists into their programs, as a way to improve (or even "save") librarianship.[6] The incorporation of emerging and heavily rewarded applied and behavioral sciences into library schools has meant that the balance of power within these programs began to tilt toward scientific and behaviorist, often positivist, modes of inquiry. These modes of inquiry, and their economic rewards, frequently displaced cultural and humanistic inquiry at conferences, in academic journals, on the academic job market, and in tenure and promotion.

Yet, as Sandra Harding has shown, these Western scientific modes of inquiry do not serve well the constituents of feminism, critical race theory, post-colonialism, and queer studies. While scientific positivist methods have delivered some benefits to some of these constituents, they were not designed to respond to the needs of these constituents, let alone to the distinctive needs and desires of people in different classes, races, ethnicities, sexualities, and cultural groups around the globe. "They have been designed," Harding shows, "to respond primarily to the needs of states, militaries, and corporations," the design and management of which these constituents have systematically been excluded.[7] One way for information studies to better serve the constituents of feminism, critical race theory, post-colonialism, and queer theory is to engage with cultural inquiry and humanistic methods. Doing so recognizes and extends Briet's understanding that information, technology, and culture are deeply connected. Like Briet, we embrace much advancement in information technology, while acknowledging that the field must engage with cultural and humanistic modes of inquiry if we are to understand the connection between information, technology, and culture. Thus, this book does not serve as a polemic against the advancements of applied sciences so much as it seeks to improve upon their modes of inquiry and analysis.

This book serves as an antidote to the marginalization of cultural and humanistic inquiry by presenting a collection of essays that represent feminist and queer interventions into information scholarship. We do not intend for

---

[6] This is not to suggest that computer technologies have not vastly improved the profession. They certainly have improved on the documentalist and internationalist goals of librarianship—though, one should probably resist the hyperbolic/apocalyptic rhetoric of salvation that comes with cyberutopia.

[7] Sandra Harding, ed., *The Postcolonial Science and Technology Studies Reader* (Durham, NC: Duke University Press, 2011), 12.

the *Reader* to represent a definitive collection. Space limitations allow us only to highlight certain interventions, and as a result, we have had to omit some of the most fruitful essays within the field. We do not intend for this collection to serve as an all-encompassing course reader. Instead, we hope that instructors who use our reader for class will supplement these essays with ones they have found useful over the years, or that suit the specific audience or topic of their class.

This collection acknowledges that often our concerns with race, gender, sexuality, socio-economic status, and other identity-fracturing, identity-constituting discourses too often ignore each other. The assumption that these concerns are separate from each other neglects the reality of their "intersection."[8] These axes of identity interrelate, operating on multiple and simultaneous levels, contributing to systemic social inequality. We must be aware, however, that the metaphor of "intersection" retains the false impression that somehow racial relations and gender relations operated simultaneously but separately before they intersected. The metaphor also gives the false impression that there are only two possible axes. Furthermore, it is not enough simply to acknowledge that multiple axes of identity intersect. Instead, we must seek to understand how these axes function together and interrelate to co-constitute each other, especially within institutions and systems of power that oppress people. Finally, this collection acknowledges that these axes, such as race, class, gender, and sexuality, are both descriptive and analytic terms. According to Harding, they designate "both something 'out there' in social relations and also a kind of analytic framework invoked to explain diverse manifestations of such social relations."[9]

In this collection, we consider "information" in a broad sense, not as something always in a fixed form, and not simply as data or something always able to be quantifiably measured. We understand that such a broad definition of information lends itself to a particularly nebulous understanding of information studies. We recognize that there are productive and counter-productive qualities to such an ever-changing, ever-expanding definition—much in the way the humanities have broadened what constitutes a "text." Early in library school, students are asked to define "information"; the answer is, of course, always situational, always contingent. This collection of essays reflects various contexts in which information phenomena occur.

The structure of this collection flows from the topics of the essays we have selected. Rather than choosing essays that fit a particular structure, we chose essays—some previously published, some unpublished—that we felt reflected the broad array of interventions being made within information studies,

---

[8] Kimberlé Crenshaw et al. eds., *Critical Race Theory: The Key Writings That Formed the Movement* (New York: New Press, 1995).

[9] Harding, *The Postcolonial Science and Technology Studies Reader*, 13.

or that might speak to an information studies audience but have yet to do so. Readers hoping to find the traditional subfields of information studies will be disappointed. This owes, in part, to the fact that many of these essays do not fit within the boundaries of the field as they are presently defined; and we had no intention of imposing those boundaries on them.

This is not to say that traditional areas of inquiry are absent from this collection. Some of these areas will be immediately identifiable to readers, such as archives or information organization, each of which have their own section in this collection by virtue of the fact that a burgeoning amount of feminist and queer work has lately emerged from them. Some traditional areas, such as information seeking or information policy, will not be immediately identifiable by simply glancing at the Table of Contents. But for the careful reader, interested in making connections between information scholarship, feminism, and queer studies, traditional areas of study reveal themselves in the process of reading. Indeed, part of the joy in creating (and reading) a collection such as this is to see just how many feminist and queer authors have something to say to information scholars, and, conversely, how many information scholars speak to feminism and queer studies. Many of these essays examine encounters with information phenomena and technology that do not lend themselves easily to the scientific and behaviorist modes of description that have long dominated the field of information studies.

For example, while Zabet Patterson, a scholar of contemporary art and digital media, likely did not write with an information studies audience in mind, her essay, "Going On-Line: Consuming Pornography in the Digital Era," nevertheless reveals how theories of desire can help us better understand human-computer interaction and information seeking in the case of viewing pornography online. In her essay, "Avatars and the Visual Culture of Reproduction," Lisa Nakamura, a scholar of Asian American studies, considers the increasing medicalization of pregnancy and its social networking on the Internet as part of the technologizing of the body, as women search online for reproductive health information. In his essay, "Administrating Gender," Dean Spade, a professor of law, examines the consequences for trans people of gender reclassification policies within government administrative agencies, such as the Department of Motor Vehicles, Medicaid, the US Census Bureau, and the Centers for Disease Control. In her essay, "On Torture: Abu Ghraib," Jasbir Puar, a scholar of women's and gender studies, whose talk at UCLA partly inspired this book, discusses the extraction of national security information from the body in the process of torture at Abu Ghraib—a process, Puar reveals, fraught with homoeroticism and homonationalism. In his essay, "Tacit Subjects," Carlos Ulises Decena, a professor of Latino and Caribbean studies, proposes the concept of tacit subjects to suggest that gay men and those close to them may be complicit in relegating information about a person's sexuality to the realm of what is tacit and/or understood, revealing the collaborative nature of identity and personal information.

Finally, this collection concludes with a set of essays that examine performance as it relates to feminist and queer issues within information studies. In her essay, "How I Learned to Stop Worrying and Love the Rape Kit," Aliza Shvarts, a scholar of performance studies, examines the ethical issues that surround the process of evidence recovery in the rape kit, which requires an invasive extraction of bodily "data" of sexual violence, taken from an already violated body, that government officials archive for later retrieval. In his essay, "Joe Orton, Kenneth Halliwell, and the Islington Public Library," Grant Campbell, a scholar of information and media studies, uses a famous incident of library vandalism to explain how traditional libraries have a problematic relationship to current Web trends, particularly large-scale digitization of library collections and the growing use of mash-up for informational and parodic purposes.

As our acknowledgements page indicates, this book saw its genesis in the especially conducive environments of the UCLA Departments of Information Studies and Women's Studies (now Gender Studies), where we had the privilege to study information, technology, gender, and sexuality as graduate students. The essays contained herein represent a small collection of work that we found intellectually sustaining and galvanizing in our time there. Both departments provided many opportunities for intellectual engagement that left an indelible impression on our academic and political work. UCLA's Information Studies Department has become particularly well known for its commitment to cultural studies within the field. It is one of the few departments that extends Briet's documentalist project by engaging cultural concerns and humanistic methods for addressing the social, political, economic, and historical context of information and technology. We owe the completion of this project to the path the faculty and students in UCLA's Information Studies Department have forged, according to Ron Day, "in engaging social critiques that push against social norms and against the, at best, apolitical boundaries of so-called library and information science."[10] As we leave UCLA to begin our careers, we hope this book honors the critical and cultural work being done there.

~Patrick Keilty
Pittsburgh, PA

---

10 Ronald Day, "The Self-Imposed Limits of Library and Information Science: Remarks on the Discipline, on the Profession, on the University, and on the State of 'Information' in the US at Large Today," *InterActions: UCLA Journal of Education and Information Studies* 6, no. 2 (2010): article 6, http://escholarship.org/uc/item/0jr2h7w5.

Bibliography

Briet, Suzanne. *What is Documentation? English Translation of the Classic French Text*. Translated and edited by Ronald E. Day and Laurent Martinet, with Hermina G. B. Anghelescu. Lanham, MD: Scarecrow, 2006.

Buckland, Michael. "A Brief Biography of Suzanne Renée Briet." In Briet, *What is Documentation?*, 1-8.

Crenshaw, Kimberlé, Neil Gotanda, Gary Peller, and Kendall Thomas, eds. *Critical Race Theory: The Key Writings That Formed the Movement*. New York: New Press, 1995.

Day, Ronald E. Preface to *What is Documentation?* by Suzanne Briet, v-x.

———. "The Self-Imposed Limits of Library and Information Science: Remarks on the Discipline, on the Profession, on the University, and on the State of 'Information' in the US at Large Today." *InterActions: UCLA Journal of Education and Information Studies* 6, no. 2 (2010): article 6. http://escholarship.org/uc/item/0jr2h7w5.

Flanagan, Mary. "The Bride Stripped Bare to Her Data: Information Flow + Digibodies." In *Data Made Flesh: Embodying Information*. Edited by Robert Mitchell and Phillip Thurtle, 153-180. New York: Routledge, 2004.

Harding, Sandra, ed. *The Postcolonial Science and Technology Studies Reader*. Durham, NC: Duke University Press, 2011.

Nerad, Maresi. *The Academic Kitchen: A Social History of Gender Stratification at the University of California, Berkeley*. Albany: State University of New York Press, 1999.

Ostler, Larry J., Therrin C. Dahlin, and J. D. Willardson. *The Closing of American Library Schools: Problems and Opportunities*. Westport, CT: Greenwood, 1995.

Part One
Information as Gendered Labor

The Bride Stripped Bare to Her Data:
Information Flow + Digibodies

Mary Flanagan[1]

In a class I taught in 2001 entitled "New Technologies and Communications Media," I presented excerpts from a twentieth-century film in order to foster discussion of the cultural position of information historically within the Western imaginary. The romantic comedy, *Desk Set*, depicts a research library in the center of the large "Federal" corporation, and is perhaps the first film depicting an IBM-like "EMERAC" machine as it spews out the credits.[2] Katherine Hepburn plays Bunny Watson, the head of the all-female reference division of the company, a woman who can spontaneously answer any question asked of her or find the answer almost as quickly. From reciting "By the shores of Gitche Gurnee" by Longfellow to answering inquisitive calls about which issue of the *New York Times* contained which report, she is an information maven. However, Spencer Tracy arrives as the character Richard Sumner, an "efficiency engineer," seemingly determined to replace the human knowledge of the research division with the overstuffed, ballroom-sized IBM computer.

Bunny's troubled romantic relationship with her boss, Mike Cutler, puts gender politics of the workplace at the forefront of the romantic comedy, and the film is rife with troubling sexist remarks and behavior. Every time the

---

1 Editors' note: this paper was previously published as a chapter in *Data Made Flesh: Embodying Information*, ed. Robert Mitchell and Phillip Thurtle, (New York: Routledge, 2004), 153–180.

2 Although the name EMERAC is a fictional name play on the real ENIAC activated at University of Pennsylvania in 1946, the real IBM logo plays a prominent role in *Desk Set*, especially in the credits sequence; see Pheobe Ephron, Henry Ephron and William Merchant, *Desk Set*, directed by Walter Lang (1957; Los Angeles, CA: Twentieth Century Fox, 2004), DVD.

women know the answer to a difficult query, the narrative counters this "untraditional" knowledge by reinscribing the feminine: the female characters seem to be always applying lipstick, ordering dresses, watering plants, or showing each other their new clothes for the upcoming dance. In this way, although there is an attempt to depict a "single-woman work culture" in the 1950s, this culture is focused around their interactions with men.[3]

Unexpectedly, it is Bunny's methodological and meticulous, almost machinelike command of knowledge that allows her to beat the very machines sent to replace her. Her knowledge is vast, crisp, and helpful at all times. At the same time the EMERAC is installed in the reference area (with a new female operator), one is installed in Payroll and promptly generates pink slips for everyone in the company. Still, Bunny beats the machine in an uncanny way, saving the day with her genuine human knowledge, her way of connecting events and facts in a sensible order; she becomes a metaphoric "bride" defeating the efficient machines of her bachelor suitor. The machine spins out of control, while Bunny remains cool and knowledgeable. In the end, Bunny shares her space with the machine yet controls it; she is then enfolded into a new and seemingly more equitable heterosexual relationship.

Desk Set is one of many media examples that depicts data, technological change, and information in ways which tie them directly to women's bodies. Although Bunny is allowed to possess knowledge and information, her dangerous knowledges are tamed by bouts of overemphasized femininity. Bunny repeatedly costumes herself in the film; she holds up glamorous gowns, hoping to transform herself literally at "the ball"—while underneath, keeping her "suits" of knowledge for the domain of the anonymous reference call. Although *Desk Set*'s Bunny ultimately triumphs over technology, images of women today produced by our technologically driven media forms are not necessarily invoking such images of equity and mastery, and are still conspicuously bound up in a heterosexual system of representation.

Representing data is not only a big business and the focus of countless classic professions; as we see from this example of filmic representation of the role of data, the practice has political and cultural implications and has historically been tied to the representation of women's bodies. With the emergence of contemporary ways of gathering, storing, and defining information, the complex relationship between information and the human body has evolved in interesting ways. Virtual bodies tend toward the hyperreal—characters such as (my favorite), Lara Croft from the *Tomb Raider* series, Kasumi in *Dead or Alive 2*, or Sarah Kerrigan in the *Starcraft* games are all, in one way or another, hyperreal, exaggerated

---

3   The characters also display an ambiguity about what a shift to marriage would mean.

"hyperbodies."[4] These hyperbodies seem to be slowly giving way to even more "realistic" representations as technology permits and audiences consume. Digital media are now working toward building a unique aesthetic for perfection—note the most suprahuman model yet created, the "down-to-the-eyelash-follicle-perfect" rendering of the brilliant and beautiful Dr. Aki Ross in the 2001 film *Final Fantasy: The Spirits Within*. From virtual sets for television which create 3-D backgrounds in real time, to virtual newscasters and characters themselves, the field of information design as an area of graphic design has quickly evolved into an area of biological design. Information today is enacting its own etymology: information, from the Greek word *morph*; in Latin "morph" became "form," to the Latin *informare*: to bring something into form.

As mentioned in previous essays by myself and others, computationally rendered graphics and the systems, machines, and traditions that produce them are powerful yet problematic for a number of reasons.[5] Virtual spaces are conscious creations produced by a numeric process, a process produced primarily through programming code. N. Katherine Hayles has noted that "even though information provides the basis for much of contemporary U.S. society, it has been constructed never to be present in itself."[6] But a symbolic system that has allowed computer code to come into an existence of its own is indeed taking shape. The merging of data production with digital media has much significance and immediately conjures up questions from the domain of semiotics. In fact, the dictionary definition of "virtual" was possibly written by the founder of the American branch of modern semiotics, Charles Sanders Peirce.[7] Bodies are acting as conduits for information; with the general move to make bodies perfect yet believably "realistic," strange eruptions occur, signaling gaps within our current system of signs.

---

4 Mary Flanagan, "Mobile Identities, Digital Stars, and Post-Cinematic Selves," *Wide Angle: Issue on Digitality and the Memory of Cinema* 21, no. 1 (1999): 77-93, doi:10.1353/wan.1999.0002.

5 Vivian Sobchack and Scott Bukatman offer criticisms of computer graphics images in the collection *Meta-Morphing: Visual Transformation and the Culture of Quick Change* (Minneapolis: University of Minnesota Press, 2000). In my own essays, I specifically look at systems that produce 3-D space; see "Navigating the Narrative in Space: Gender and Spatiality in Virtual Worlds," *Art Journal* 59, no. 3 (Fall 2000): 74-85, doi:10.2307/778029.

6 N. Katherine Hayles, *How We Became Posthuman: Virtual Bodies in Cybernetics, Literature, and Informatics* (Chicago: University of Chicago Press, 1999), 25.

7 Peter Skagestad, "Peirce, Virtuality, and Semiotics," paper included in the published proceedings of the Twentieth World Congress of Philosophy, *Paideia: Philosophy Educating Humanity*, Boston, MA, August 1998, http://www.bu.edu/wcp/Papers/Cogn/CognSkag.htm.

This chapter explores the evolution of electronic media representation of information, from charts and graphs which represent data, to information's new form: virtual and organic flesh. Our connection with and interfaces to the computer change daily. Among human-computer interface (HCI) researchers, computer-generated "personalities" are seen as the evolutionary form of the icons used in next-generation graphical user interfaces.[8] In this essay, I want to explore the nodal points around which information bodies can be organized, and their system of signs. However, the essay focuses not on language but on the embodied code of virtual characters. I map this embodied data through phenomena—the world's first virtual newscaster, Ananova, a character-based live information interface, Motorola's Mya data service, and Syndi, the "celebrity portal" search engine that purports a subjective search experience through a character—to explore the ramifications of data embodiment. Specifically, in this chapter, I look to virtual characters developed to represent data and news in online environments as the site of a monumental shift in digital cultural consciousness. Where older models such as those represented in *Desk Set* contain data in the female form, present embodiments have left the real female body behind in a significant way. Embodied data through phenomena such as virtual newscasters and other data agents are becoming commonplace, but what are the implications of making information biological? If our data must now be embodied, what is the impact on how we understand data in the form of human bodies, especially female-shaped bodies that act as conduits for information flow? What is the role of the female in this representation, and what are the social implications of embodied data?

Duchamp, Technology, and Gender

A representational review is in order to reflect on the visual coupling of woman and technology, bodies and codes, for it is at the female body that the formation and contestation of digibodies is occurring. Notions of the machinistic successes of the nineteenth-century industrial revolution resulted in shifts in art, such as that produced by cubists and futurists, to the industrio-sexo-mechanical metaphors churned out by Marcel Duchamp. Duchamp, one of the influential thinkers of the time, represented the shift from the industrial to postindustrial Western cultures repeatedly in his work through the figure of woman. After his groundbreaking "Nude Descending a Staircase #2" (1912), Duchamp expressed ideas about time, work, and technological innovation in his artwork, and throughout his career veered away from representational forms (in this, he furthered Delaroche's proposal, for Duchamp believed that

---

[8] Daniel Gross, "Merging Man and Machine: The Future of Computer Interfaces Evolving in Japan," *Computer Graphics World* 14, no. 5 (May 1991): 47–51.

representational forms themselves were dead).[9] Problematic as Dadaist and Surrealist representations of women were, there are a number of similarities between contemporary cultural change and the shift that occurred in the earlier part of the twentieth century. In trying to read our current semiotic shift, I look to Duchamp because he also briefly broke the system of representation between gender, the body, and technology. If de Saussure established semiotics as a system of signs within society and focused meaning as defined by the relationships of one sign to another, and if Peirce described the science of signification and the sign as an "object," Duchamp was the radical who turned popular semiotic conventions upside down, moving away from both representation and cultural references, breaking the link between his works and the "objects" they supposedly represented.

Scholars have debated the nature of historical and contemporary linkages between the figure of woman and technology. For example, as Andreas Huyssen notes in his book *After the Great Divide: Modernism, Mass Culture, Postmodernism*, technology and woman have historically been linked: "As soon as the machine came to be perceived as a demonic, inexplicable threat and as harbinger of chaos and destruction... Woman, nature, machine had become a mesh of significations which all had one thing in common: otherness."[10] We can also look ahead and see how negative images of women played out in Weimar Germany's technological and industrial shift.[11] In twentieth-century culture struggling to find a place for photography and film within the traditional arts, it was in part through Duchamp's challenges to artistic definitions and institutions that it became possible to contextualize the creative act using mechanical reproduction paradigms—especially in the 1920s, when there was a major shift in both technology and in visible/virtual culture.

At around nine feet high and over five feet wide, Duchamp's famous 1923 painting *The Bride Stripped Bare by Her Bachelors, Even* depicted "the bride" as an engine to symbolize twentieth-century progress (see Figure 1). "*The Large*

---

9 French history painter Paul Delaroche is particularly remembered for his much-quoted remark, on seeing the Daguerreotype, that "from today, painting is dead!" However, he was a staunch supporter of photography, particularly the Daguerreotype; see Robert Leggat, *A History of Photography: From Its Beginnings Till the 1920s* (1995; web, 1999), http://www.mpritchard.com/photohistory/history/delaroch.htm.

10 Andreas Huyssen, "The Vamp and the Machine: Fritz Lang's Metropolis," in *After the Great Divide: Modernism, Mass Culture, Postmodernism* (Bloomington: Indiana University Press, 1986), 70.

11 Klaus Theweleit's study of Weimar Germany—a text I find myself returning to again and again for the proliferation of images of women and technology—is truly formidable; see Klaus Theweleit, *Male Fantasies*, trans. Chris Turner, vol. 2, *Women, Floods, Bodies, History* (Minneapolis: University of Minnesota Press, 1987).

Glass," as it is also called, is considered to be his most major work and took eight years to evolve.[12] As Jean François Lyotard noted in his book, *TRANS/formers*, although Duchamp's ideas are inspired by technology and image making materials such as time lapse photography, he continued to move away from representational form—as Lyotard calls it, Duchamp worked in an "a-cinematic" form.[13]

Although Duchamp's bride is all about desire, women, and machines, the visual representation in the work itself is far from typical. Although the bride is a self-sustaining mechanical character in perpetual motion, her nine bachelors, who, in Duchamp's notes on the work, are said to survive on coal and the fuel of sexual tension, are positioned below their mistress. In her domain atop the painting, the bride issues her commands, orders, and authorizations, acting as a kind of motor; Duchamp's bride could be read as erotic, and she is in complete control. She is both passive (allowing herself to be stripped) and in control as an active (moving and desiring) subject, inhabiting an electric space that Lyotard claims is "transcribed in a plastic way: the Bride-machine is not placed in the same space as the Bachelor workshop," but rather in the space of electronics.[14] The large, cloudlike shape at the top of the glass is the halo of the bride, a type of veil, an access point or network in which the bachelors desire to participate. Unlike digital characters, which are "powered" by logical code, the mechanical bride of Duchamp is fueled by "love gasoline."[15]

The idea that this bride is passive through her permitting herself to be stripped, and active because she is desiring and controlling, is important, for such discussion positions the bride in a duality: she is in total control, has her own electronic, erotic autonomy, and is not bound by stereotypical representation. Machines, bodies, and time are blended together and fused with concepts of gender roles and their relationship to information. The technological woman, the mechanical bride, like the Internet, is self-generating, bringing about technological change.

Duchamp's work is read through both its visual representation on the glass, as well as in various notes and boxes, which contain calculations,

---

12   Dalia Judovitz, *Unpacking Duchamp: Art in Transit* (Berkeley: University of California Press, 1995), 52.

13   Jean-Fransois Lyotard, *Duchamp's TRANS/formers*, trans. Ian McLeod (Venice, CA: Lapis, 1990), 161.

14   Ibid. 144.

15   As Francis Naumann notes in his exposé article about Marcel Duchamp's intimate life, Duchamp rather imagined himself as one of his *Large Glass* bachelors, and many years after the work was completed, he found the bride: surrealist sculptor Maria Martins; see Francis Naumann, "Marcel & Maria," *Art in America* 89, no. 4 (April 2001): 99.

Fig. 1. Marcel Duchamp, *The Bride Stripped Bare By Her Bachelors, Even (The Large Glass)*, 1915-1923. Oil, varnish, lead foil, lead wire, and dust on two glass panels, 109 1/4" x 69 1/4". Succession Marcel Duchamp, ARS, N.Y. / ADAGP, Paris. Reprint permission courtesy of ARS.

scribbles, theories, and other information which mediates the experience of viewing the glass so that, according to Duchamp, the experience of the piece aesthetically will be interrupted. As he noted, the painting itself "must not be 'looked at' in the aesthetic sense of the word. One must consult the book, and see the two together."[16]

The erotic logic of such an artificial and mechanical system is both anti-representational and illogical; Duchamp makes many notes in his "The Green Box" about his "hilarious" picture, noting that rather than an image, the work is the whole of an illogical process and antirepresentational presentation. As Tzara argued, "The beginnings of Dada were not the beginnings of an art, but of a disgust" with traditional art forms.[17] Like the Internet's tendency toward hiccupping downloads and the now popularly described "lag" phenomenon of the Internet experience, Duchamp called his *Large Glass* a "delay in glass," playing with moments of "in between time."[18]

Read within his play of logic, Duchamp's vision of the coupling of technology within a consciously marked gendered construction offers an interesting position on the combination of woman and machine. Valued for his play with gender, Duchamp bridges the problematic mind/body split by foregoing representation of the mind or the body, moving to a third, conceptual space.[19] In this way, Duchamp avoids scripting both negative representations variously depicted as phallocentric or patriarchal, and he also avoids locating the

---

16 Duchamp, in Pierre Cabanne, *Dialogues with Marcel Duchamp*, trans. Ron Padgett (New York: Da Capo, 1988), 42–43. To the artist, the ideas presented in the work were more important than the realization of the work, especially Duchamp's interest in the fourth dimension which he explores with the tactile love metaphor between bride and bachelors.

17 "Tristan Tzara: Lecture on Dada. (1922)," in *The Dada Painters and Poets: An Anthology*, trans. and ed. Robert Motherwell (Cambridge, MA: Harvard University Press, 1981), 250. Similar to other Dada artists, Duchamp worked with logical systems towards the abolition of logic.

18 Judovitz, *Unpacking Duchamp*, 60.

19 Many artists and art historians value Duchamp because of his exploration of gender. In the "In a Different Light" show organized by curator Lawrence Rinder and artist Nayland Blake, the curators focus on Duchamp's work as they track queer sensibilities through various art movements; see Michael Duncan, "Queering the Discourse: Gay and Lesbian Art, University Art Museum, Berkeley, California," *Art in America* 83, no. 7 (July 1995): 27–31. The authors of the exhibition catalog argue that Duchamp, more than other artists, "opened a space for queers to formulate points of resistance to the monolithic structure of culture;" see also Nayland Blake, Lawrence Rinder, and Amy Scholder, eds., *In a Different Light: Visual Culture, Sexual Identity, Queer Practice* (San Francisco: City Lights Books, 1995), 14.

figure of woman as a passive innocent that we cannot represent. Some of Duchamp's analysts, however, raise questions about his depiction of women. Lyotard argued that "the whole Duchamp affair goes via women" and asks, "[s]hall we say that women are the principle of the a-mechanizing cunning, that they have no soul ... their bodies being mechanically reducible ... won't that be their whole morality: either married or prostituted?"[20] He goes on to argue that, in his work and in his masquerade as Mademoiselle Rrose Sélavy, Duchamp goes beyond sex by reconciling sexual difference.[21]

Duchamp's conceptual erotic, dimensional machines are not based in representation but in delay: the bride is neither naked nor clothed, leaving us in an in-between state where "there is no art, because there are no objects."[22] Reading Duchamp clues us into the possibilities of the absence of representation; it confuses other semiotic systems, disrupts the formal models we use to create meaning, and opens up a third space for the digibody.

The New Woman: Prototype Digibodies

The Bride can represent for us progress, technology, desire, and control. Duchamp's bride both is passive and yet, controlling "progress." But in the next century after this monumental work, with subtler, nonmechanical technological change influencing every aspect of our everyday lives, the conceptualization of gender and technology has manifested in a way closely related to Duchampian thought. Researchers around the globe are looking to computer-generated "personalities" as the next evolutionary form of the graphical user interface. Humanlike faces are already beginning to replace buttons and icons (think of the Microsoft prototypical paper clip). At National Taiwan University, researchers are designing personal secretaries for PDAs by scanning real human faces to make the virtual secretaries more appealing; researchers note that they "want to go for a friendly interface" (see Figure 2).

VR communications agents put a skin on our current fascination with stock and business news and helpful applications, and at the time of this writing, digital agents and news sources have all been depicted as female. Rather than doling out commands to her bachelors in Duchamp's painting, these brides have instead manifested as 3-D graphic characters on the World Wide Web, doling out news and other kinds of always-updated streaming information. While Duchamp resisted the aesthetic to convey his fascination with information and the symbolic, this century's digital characters collapse the real and the virtual into one system, foreclosing any possibility of critical distance in our interactions with them. Moreover, interactive design has

---

20 Lyotard, *Duchamp's TRANS/formers*, 114.
21 Ibid. 115.
22 Ibid. 20.

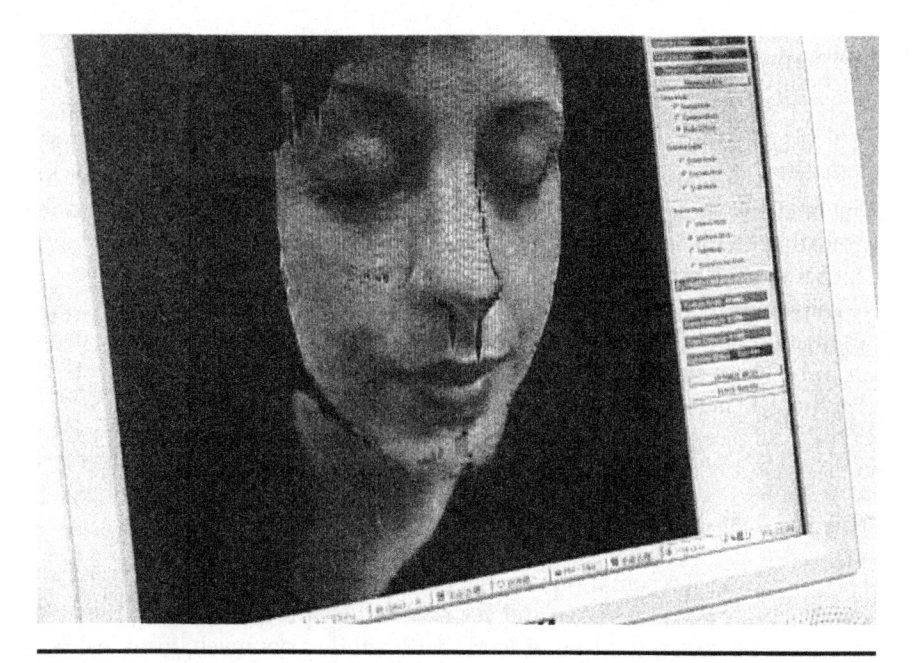

Fig. 2. National Taiwan University scan of human faces (face of Mary Flanagan) (2001). Created in custom software. Screen capture taken by Mary Flanagan. Courtesy CML lab, directed by Ming Ouhyoung.

taught us that critical distance is precisely the thing designers are taught to avoid, especially at the interface.

To understand the phenomenon of digital characters within the context of interactivity and service functions (as opposed to, say, game characters that carry a related yet different set of concerns), we should briefly look at the current state of the merging of broadcasting, information design, and visualization, for these are the areas that traditionally have provided information flow and established representational norms of the information itself.[23] Outlets for this material include broadband, Web, and mobile computing solutions, all of which compete for users' time and attention.

As a discipline, information design historically has investigated different issues than media forms such as broadcasting, news or the traditional areas of film and print—instead of telling stories in time, information designers need to depict stories in space—and generally, this space has been a flatland that graphic designers have worked to dimensionalize. Leading information design guru Edward Tufte is one of the innovators in visualizing information in graphic form so that everything from day-to-day matters to important

---

23   See note 3.

security systems are easily understood, arguing that through good information design we are able to "change the way people see."[24] Interfaces, like signs in semiotics, stand for other things: icons and indices give way to the heart of the content. A sign does not function as a sign unless it is understood by the user as a sign, however. In computer applications, this system relies on a rich tradition of graphic design to create understandable user interfaces.

Information design is nowhere more significant than in the interface between humans and computers. Historically, interface surfaces have been unreal: imaginary buttons, unnatural keyboards, molded extensions of our palm, and stick controllers. Many designers agree with Donald Norman, a leading design specialist, that user interfaces should blend with the task in order to make tools, the apparatus of production invisible and keeps technology as the means and not the goal. Accordingly, computer interfaces should not call attention to themselves; characteristic buzzwords include "intuitive," "adaptive," "supportive," and "easy to use." Norman admits, however, that there may be no natural relationship between one design and other designs or objects. In other words, design is a purely artificial ideal, and interfaces are sites of artifice designed with human physiology, cognition, and habit in mind.

It should not come as a surprise, then, that the latest computer interfaces, or portals, are artificial computer generated characters. Digital hosts are manifestations of digibodies, following on the emphasis on game characters and pop culture animations.[25] Part material and part symbolic, virtual characters, be it a mobile or Web-based network, are now hosting everything from cell phones to game shows to DVDs. Here, we should turn to real world examples of this embodied data manifest in interactive virtual characters.

Syndi

Especially in the area of information retrieval, virtual characters put a human face on the front of real time, up-to-date flows of data. Not only are they the conduits for a flood of information, but they are also a flow of signs, representing and reinforcing our myths, stories, and ideologies. Signifying uncertainty about the meaning of embodiment, these characters represent a shift in digital cultural consciousness. "As the net cools, information begins to self-organize. Applications become attention windows. Attention

---

24 Michael H. Martin, "The Man Who Makes Sense of Numbers: Yale Professor Edward Tufte Dazzles Business People by Making Rational the Data that Rule Their Work Lives," *Fortune, October* 27, 1997, paragraph 4.

25 See, for example, Horipro's 1996 launch of virtual persona Kyoko Date and more recent incarnations of characters such as Cyber Lucy, the virtual host of the children's game show *Wheel 2000*.

windows become celebrity portals." So begins a conversation with Peter Seidler, Chief Creative Officer of Razorfish as he discussed the company's research effort, a search engine with "subjectivity."[26] Seidler wrote a cover story for *Artbyte* in 1999, "My Syn," which detailed the abilities of Syndi, a proposed "celebrity portal" search engine created by Razorfish.[27] Syndi is able to learn about the necessities, tastes, and interests of users (see Figure 3). Unlike her ancestors, text boxes or strings of data, Syndi is a three-dimensional polygonal model, taking the form of a woman with pulled back brown hair, huge green eyes and a long, tanned, thin face.

Fig. 3. Jim Anderson, *Syndi* (1999). September/October issue of *Artbyte Magazine*, Courtesy of Artbyte Magazine.

Syndi, if built, would be one of the first "native" species of cyberspace. Working on specific tasks based on detailed personal user profiles, these agents come from a long line of traditional "AI" projects began in the 1950s and 1960s from programs such as the Eliza and Julia engines. As her creators note, "Syndi's existence depends on her capacity to fit into her environment" and she appears the way she does because "commodification creates a need for distinction."[28] In this way, the agents are distinguished only by their constructions, not by their abilities or services.

It is significant that the female databodies like Syndi are generally composite bodies: by composite bodies I mean a mixture of presumed "normal" female characteristics (combined with supermodel and superbody styling) and constructed with presupposed racial characteristics. We could look to many historical markers in order to contextualize markers of

---

26   Peter Seidler, "A Few Thoughts," High Ground Design, 2000, http://www.highgrounddesign.com/design/dcessay995.htm.
27   Peter Seidler, "Syndi: Your Celebrity Portal: A User's Manual," *ArtByte*, September/October, 1999, 51–54.
28   Seidler, "A Few Thoughts," paragraph 3.

race in representation, but I choose a rather recent set of circumstances because this example had significant impact on graphic design and advertising, two major vectors along which virtual characters were created. The work of influential designer Tibor Kalman (1949-1999) and his design house M&Co. are essential in order to contextualize the creation of digital characters. This group created many influential works in Benetton's spinoff magazine *Colors*, which pushed an editorial emphasis on shocking images and politics.

Many M&Co. and *Colors* images pushed the boundaries on race representation in the early 1990s, especially layouts such as the "What if . . . ?" spread from Issue #4, "Race," in 1993.[29] Using digital imaging programs, *Colors* changed the races of several iconic men and women. Queen Elizabeth was made to look black and Spike Lee white, and Kalman offered readers an Asian Pope John Paul II. These experiments investigated the taboo of racial switching and performance, setting standards for pop culture, advertising, and media that we still see today in digital character creation. For example, many digital stars, including Lara Croft, have ambivalent racial composite faces, hair, bodies, and skin color, with a problematic tendency toward a "Caucasian blend." This composite takes on more significance as we begin to see the role of the construction, of the artificial, in ideologies that construct these characters. Even though the intent of Kalman's group was to cause readers to reflect on racial inequity, the *Colors* overall effect was to depoliticize the representation of racial hybridity. In the realm of graphic design, race became a design element with this use of morphing and imaging technologies. In turn, digital characters reflect this apolitical representational practice.

To return to digital characters and the creation of the character Syndi, we are tempted to understand Syndi's personality. Her makers say her "brand attributes" control what she appears to feel like for the user, and she is intended to evolve: her makers focusing on her subjective evolution of consciousness and beyond, to the domains of the "digital superconsciousness." However, she has not evolved very far—information about Syndi after the interview with Seidler is very difficult to find, even in her native habitat, but her design speaks to the overall goals and desires of dot.com entrepreneurs.

Seidler's article did not address the naming of the Razorfish character, but Syndi's name could be a reference to Pat Cadigan's 1991 cyberpunk novel *Synners*. In *Synners*, Visual Mark and Gina are "synners," that is, synthesizers who work together to create immersive music videos through a direct neural connection to cyberspace. At last, Visual Mark finds a way to download himself into the network and "lose the meat." Mark becomes the first net-born synth-human, existing only in

---

29 The "Tiborocity: Design And Undesign by Tibor Kalman 1979-1999" exhibit at the New Museum of Contemporary Art in New York featured these controversial images; see *Colors* no. 4, Race issue, Spring 1993.

cyberspace.[30] Cyberpunk fiction has long predicted artificially created network beings. Syndi offers users a similar promise of the escape of the flesh. Although she wears a halo suspiciously close to Duchamp's bride, hers is a cloud of zeros and ones as her veil, her neck ringed with strings of binaries, black and white, zeros and ones . . . a human genotype: the genetic code of the digital character, worn closely as she gazes at her bachelor-users. Unlike Duchamp's bride, however, Syndi's makers offer us a representational body to go with her networked dataconsciousness.

Ananova

The world's first functioning virtual newscaster, Ananova, is the "human" face serving a real-time information and news system. A little more realistic in design functionality and commercial expectations, Ananova appeared on the Internet on April 19, 2000 with her enthusiastic, "Hello World! Here is the news and this time it's personal."[31] Ananova was designed to be the interface for real-time news, and she can also handle transactions.

Although the choice to use a female face for the conduit of information was not informed by rigorous research—Ananova says they decided to make their bot female "because people tend to respond better to getting information from a woman . . ."—her face is a composite of what designers thought were attractive and useful features: useful, because they function within technical constraints. For example, the character's mouth had to be large in order to showcase the company's innovative lip synch technology on screens of all sizes, and her clothing is said to be "figure hugging" in order to "make her easier to animate." The choice to give Ananova a bright shock of green hair was made in order to make her stand out on advertising as well as on mobile devices such as WAP phones.[32]

Ananova news services are similar to any online news service (such as international competitor CNN.com), and can be browsed in a similar fashion or can be read, with theme music and images, by the Ananova character. She comes in low and high bandwidth streams to your desktop in pixelly chunks, slowly reading the news to users. The "personalized" aspects do not come from the agent but rather from the user, who can customize his or her news

30 Pat Cadigan, *Synners*, 10th ed. (New York: Four Walls Eight Windows, 2001).
31 Alexander MacLeod, "Barbara Walters Meets Posh Spice Online: This Virtual Anchor's Emotions are Tailor-Made For Each Story (And She Can't Bug the Boss For a Raise!)," *Chistian Science Monitor*, April 24, 2000, http://www.csmonitor.com/2000/0424/p7s1.html.
32 Orange Personal Communications Services, "Designing Ananova," *Ananova,Internet Archive* Way Back Machine archival version, February 17, 2009, http://web.archive.org/web/20090217151157/http://ananova.com/about/story/sm_128668.html.

preferences. Although she has received marriage proposals and fan mail (as well as generating a large movement of "Ananova lookalike" groups on the web), the value of the human head to read news to users from the Internet remains unknown.

Mya

Mya "debuted" in March 2000 in an advertising spot during the annual Oscars, slipping over the video screen in her hip silver jumpsuit to the event. Mya is a 24-hour, voice-driven digital personal assistant that reads out websites over user's mobile telephones. Motorola gained much publicity for their 60-second commercial in which they promoted their fashionable cyber guide to the vast Infobahn. Visually seamless, digibodies like Mya appear quite realistic, although as a visual representation only pops up in advertising— while using the Mya service, the character is still a computer-generated, disembodied voice. However, the quest for ultra-realism in images of Mya is strong: Mya was created and was fashioned after a human model hired by media makers Digital Domain. Visual effects supervisor and animation director Fred Raimondi notes that he first focused on realistic hair and cloth "but not necessarily a photo-realistic woman," instead focusing on aspects we normally look for as clues that the character is computer generated, such as hair and clothes modeling and rendering.

Logging into a Mya demo online, we hear a slightly mechanically buzzing young woman's voice tell us dreamily, "My world is a world without boundaries without limits" (said without a comma, as well).[33] For now, Mya's is a real voice, but mechanically enhanced to give the illusion of the digital. Mya is, by far, the best-rendered and most self-assured of the digibodies, and her voice, human or not, is the most haunting; in fact it is her voice that is the most researched and promoted for wireless WAP systems.

Although she does not appear powerless, writer Tobey Grumet calls Mya "virtually submissive" because she is created only to serve users.[34] Mya "isn't a Web browser, this is someone who can speak to you" says Geoffrey Frost, a VP at Motorola.[35] The company decided to "give her a face, a name and a

---

33 Editor's note: in the original 2004 publication of this paper, the Mya demo was attributed to the Motorola website, http:www.motorola.com/MIMS/ISG/voice/ mayademo/mayademo.htm. At the time of this publication it is no longer available.

34 Tobey Grumet, "Digital Dame," Technology Watch, *Popular Mechanics*, November 2000, 36.

35 David Barboza, "Motorola Hopes a Computer-Generated Character Will Link the Real World with the Virtual One," Technology, *New York Times* online edition, April 25, 2000, http://www.nytimes.com/2000/04/25/business/media-business -advertising-motorola-hopes-computer-generated-character-will-link.html.

personality.... [H]umanize her."[36] The creation myth extends to her production team: "It was so exciting for me to finally see the cloth tests, for instance. It was kind of like meeting God, because you've never seen it before," said her art director.[37]

Although an ultrarealistic look in images of these women characters is very strong, after seeing several one can begin to see a definite trend in their representation. All of the digibodies found online or under design are women, and all either sport short or severely pulled-back hairstyles. Animation details, such as hair, eyes, and movement, are key areas where artists work especially hard to make a convincing digibody. In Mya's case, her creators noted that it was very difficult to create her in a way that she looked "alive." They focused on movement and her eyes, noting that she needed specular highlights and eye blinks to bring her to life.

Repetition is key to believing in virtual characters. Judith Butler notes that "[a]s in other ritual social dramas, the action of gender [and sexuality] requires a performance that is repeated. This repetition is at once a reenactment and re-experiencing of a set of meanings already socially established; and it is the mundane and ritualized form of their legitimization."[38] Repetition not only legitimizes and naturalizes the character's gender, but also reestablishes our relationship of power with the virtual character and allows the virtual body to function as a "material-semiotic object," that is, naturalizing the function and visibility of the body into one presence.[39] Therefore, Mya's appearances at events such as the Oscars and her ubiquitous mobility make her a "real girl" by virtue of sheer repetition (a mantra without boundaries without limits as advertising and media infiltrate into cars, phones, mobile phones, and clothing), and through the merging of the material and technological. Whether or not the real body plays into the picture, data embodied through Ananova, Syndi, and Mya, as well as other digital bodies that embody information flow, fascinate us.

Looking at these characters through a semiotic lens, we run into some rather difficult questions. If the images of bodies stand for "real" human bodies as interface experts claim, and the ideas they convey are data, or news,

---

36 Iain Blair, "Say Hello to Motorola's Mya," *Post Industry*, April 28, 2000, *Internet Archive* Way Back Machine archival version, July 16, 2001, http://web.archive.org/web/20010716210239/http://www.postindustry.com/article/mainv/0,7220,109815,00.html, paragraph 2.

37 Ibid. paragraph 11.

38 Judith Butler, *Gender Trouble: Feminism and the Subversion of Identity*, 10th ed. (New York: Routledge, 1999), 178.

39 Donna J. Haraway, *Modest_Witness@Second_Millenium.FemaleMan_Meets_OncoMouse: Feminism and Technoscience* (New York: Routledge, 1997).

how is the meaning of the data associated with these bodies? What do they construct? One immediately looks to all newscasting and storytelling forms wherein the human body stands as a transmitter to the receivers. A data body is not just data—when virtual bodies are created and represented they acquire additional meanings. Signs, the popular saying goes, are never innocent.

This indicates that there are three separate and simultaneous "writings" of the character in virtual spaces: one is the animation embodied as the character itself, one is realized through interacting with the character, and one is witnessed through the character's curious voice. How does the visual regime cope with the addition of voice to these virtual characters? The role of the human sounding voice and its synchronization with the digibodies onscreen has become an important aspect of virtual characters and hosts. Since the invention of the telephone, women's voices have been the standard, "soothing" voice of information, and virtual female bodies are still acting in this role. Whether it is the frequency range or social allusion to woman as providing helpful services remains a question, for the popularity of women's voices embedded in mechanical devices includes most subway systems, airline recordings, and the like. What is not in question, however, is the haunting, surreal quality voices have, and in particular, the recorded or synthesized voices of virtual characters. Although most computer game characters have short dialogue lines and grunts, virtual hosts are always talking: offering weather updates, stock tips, and round the world news.[40] In his book, *A Lover's Discourse*, French philosopher Roland Barthes explores the idea of texts that speak, and the speaking voice itself is preserved within written media. He asserts, "we do not know who is speaking; the text speaks, that is all." For Barthes, the text is enough; the living quality we assign to voice is simply another fiction. To him, the voice is the terrain of death and signals absence, the past, silence—the living quality of the voice is a false illusion:

> *It is characteristic of the voice to die. What constitutes the voice is what, within it, lacerates me by dint of having to die, as if it were at once and never could be anything but a memory. This phantom being of the voice is what is dying out, it is that sonorous texture which disintegrates and disappears. I never know the loved being's voice except when it is dead, remembered, recalled inside my head. . . .*[41]

---

40 Their constancy makes this author wish for fast forward buttons: for me, the nonlinearity of digital media has been a blessing of time. Skimming has taken on new meaning with the ability to cover multiple windows and multiple news sources on one desktop in a matter of seconds.

41 Roland Barthes, *A Lover's Discourse: Fragments*, trans. Richard Howard (New York: Hill and Wang, 1978), 114.

By reading Barthes, we understand that voice can be tragic, for it refers to a once living or vanished object, leaving a recording to remain in a dying state, only in human—or computer—memory. As a result, virtual characters' voices are specters, created from data alone, and thus they refuse the human aspect of speaking and transfer it to an a-human space.[42] Perhaps the "unreal-ness" gives the subject a breathing space, room to acknowledge inadequacies and lacks through the lack in the virtual character. Or perhaps the virtual voice acts to further jar the semiotic system away from assigning symbols to signs.

Here I am reminded of the African American women who were brought into studios to dub in the singing voice of white stars in popular Hollywood films of the 1940s.[43] Although Hollywood tried to problematically eliminate the representation of the African American female body, it seems that digital entertainment goes even further, working to efface all women's bodies. Swapping representational practices and effacing bodies has always held political consequence.

Mappings

As fascinating as they are, Mya, Ananova, and Syndi are only part of a much larger system of encoding the virtual woman. From striptease Web news programs (stripping and nude women reading the Webcasts at NakedNews.com) to geographical and medical imaging, the human body undergoes multiple mappings.[44] Although realistic digital agents command WAP devices such as phones and even automobiles, these same devices can also track the body; as new technologies enhance our ability to monitor and locate human bodies around the world, and this ability does have an impact on the physical body. The use of surveillance, global positioning systems (GPS), and health, bank, and credit records to chart human movement is widespread and not as shocking or outrageous to citizens as one might expect. Taipei and other large, international cities have long had automatic "speeding-ticket" cameras trained on major streets. The use of Internet cookies is also widespread; as artist David Rokeby notes in his description of his 2001 installation

---

42 Animated characters are only identified by voice when shown in noninteractive form such as cinema or major television programs; online characters and game characters' voice talents are rarely identified and publicized. Films such as *Toy Story* and *Ants*, and programs such as *The Simpsons* clearly identify the voices of the actors.

43 Patricia Mellencamp, "Making History: Julie Dash," *Frontiers: A Journal of Women Studies* 15, no. 1 (1994): 76–102, http://www.jstor.org/stable/3346614. Julie Dash's *Illusions* is a sensitive film that addresses the issues of race, gender, and feminism.

44 Tamsen Tilson, "Bare Fact: News Site is a Real Hit," *Variety*, February 5, 2001, 32.

"Guardian Angel," a work that uses surveillance to track, record, and recognize human faces:

> Cookies are convenient. It is strangely pleasant to be recognized on arrival at a web-site you have used before. I shop on-line. I fill in forms in exchange for free software. I use my bank's debit card for purchases (though I swore I never would!) . . . It is highly inconvenient not to "trust" on-line corporate entities.[45]

GPS systems, and surveillance systems, have implications for certain kinds of bodies over others: mapping the body in space and time has particular significance for women. "Nannycams" and networked pornography have made the surveillance and/or webcam primarily the domain of the image of woman. This kind of voyeurism has taken hold with reality television, as well as god games such as *Dungeon Keeper* or *The Sims*, and the proliferation of webcams. Whether it is because users are attempting to find themselves reflected in others, or they are interested in the feeling of connection that comes from such voyeuristic acts, the female body lies at the center of such interaction. Brian Curry, founder of the webcam company Earthcam.com, notes that in a few hours of watching webcammed situations, voyeurs "create an affinity with the people they're looking at."[46]

As in space, a second mapping occurs within the body. Although we can encode data to create female forms such as our example agents, there has been a long tradition of "mapping" the interior of the human body. Control paradigms, subjectivity, and imaging technologies have traditionally reduced the category of "woman" to symptomatic images. For example, studies of Charcot's nineteenth century images of "hysterical" women to the recent "visible woman" project explored by Kate O'Riordan and Julie Doyle in their essay, "Virtually Visible: Female Cyberbodies and the Medical Imagination," show problematic historical and contemporary medical representations of the body through new digital imaging technologies such as CT and MRI.[47] In the visible woman project, the first phase of identification is to orient and segment the human body data points. Normative notions of gender both mark and form the imaged body. O'Riordan and Doyle argue that the body is represented through its relationship to technologies, but do not incorporate an experience of the flesh. In addition, many women artists explore this

---

45 David Rokeby, "Works: Guardian Angel (2001)," last modified November 27, 2010, http://www.davidrokeby.com/angel.html.
46 Chris Taylor, "Looking Online," *Time*, June 26, 2000, 60.
47 Kate O'Riordan and Julie Doyle, "Virtually Visible: Female Cyberbodies and the Medical Imagination," in *Reload: Rethinking Women in Cyberculture*, ed. Mary Flanagan and Austin Booth (Cambridge, MA: MIT Press, 2002), 239–260.

interior body mapping as a particular concern for women. Montreal-based artist Char Davies has produced a series of images known as the *Interior Body Series* and in her VR (virtual reality) work extends her exploration to include bodily organs, blood vessels and bones. In a way, she is turning the gaze of medical imaging upside down by creating the interior of the body as an aesthetic rather than material object.

Third, the rise in popularity of digital characters has coincided with an increased fascination with bodies and body parts on the part of the medical establishment, which desires to map the body genetically. In February 2001, scientists announced the completion of the human genome. Even though the 20,000–40,000 human genes are closer genetically to fruit flies than to other creatures, we rush to have our own DNA trademarked in an effort to achieve immortality. In the sequencing phase, researchers identified the approximately 3.5 billion chemical letters (A, C, G, T) that make up human DNA, comprising "the most important, most wondrous map ever produced by humankind."[48] If biology is now information, then information design must also be considered as an organic endeavor. Although the study of morphologic form (e.g., the anatomical forms of organisms) is no longer a popular discipline, the study of biological information in DNA or RNA is the heart of present biological interest. Although entertainers and media producers seek to turn data into human bodies, research scientists such as those working on the human genome project seek to turn the body into data. Information has substituted for form as the preferred key to the fundamental problems of biology.

The human genome project is problematic for many because of the privacy, social, and modification issues that are inherent to such an undertaking. Most striking are issues raised by genetic screening, and the ideas of "norms" created by such prospects. Bioethical issues such as how we think about normality and abnormality arise instantaneously. And again, women are at the center of this debate, "because of their central role in reproduction and caregiving"; women are affected "differently but also more significantly than men by the information emerging" from the results of the Human Genome Project, potentially devaluing their roles.[49] With new possibilities arising from the ability to alter our genetic code, we need to look at the inevitable transformation of human kind in light of the virtual revolution in the critical

---

48   Quote of U. S. President Bill Clinton, from CNN Online, "Human Genome to Go Public," February 9, 2001, http://archives.cnn.com/2001/HEALTH/02/09/genome.results/index.html.

49   See Mary B. Mahowald et al., "The New Genetics and Women," *Milbank Quarterly: A Journal of Public Health and Health Care Policy* 72, no. 2 (1996): 240. http://www.jstor.org/stable/3350248.

light that authors such as N. Katherine Hayles, Robert Cook-Deegan, and others propose.[50]

Virtual "Breakups," Virtual Desire

We have considered how we trace bodies in space, peer at them internally, and design and track them numerically with genetic code. Digibodies are mapped with the desires of their creators, and their creators are on a quest for a great Real. What is this Real? How do we know it when we encounter it? And why this desperate need to know, to look at the face of the Real? The balance between real and unreal is perhaps nowhere more striking than in the realm of VR experiences. To look at databodies in order to understand them in a larger cultural context we must examine their construction and their "femaleness," as these data conduits; the fact that almost all examples are inscribed as female makes obvious the significance of gender in this type of information representation and user relationship. With the possibility of deconstructing and reconstructing the bodies, the way in which an understanding of gender is drawn out, mapped, and manifested in these networked characters is essential.

Images of women's bodies, fictional or otherwise, have pervaded popular media for a century of North American culture. The body's surface has been written and inscribed in media and popular culture: segmented, distorted and distended for selling consumer goods through sexual enticement. Bodies evolve into datasets: even in animation the face and body are segmented to create "talking heads." The moving parts are conceptually and technically separated from the lesser-moving aspects of the head and body. The Internet's incorporation of bodies, however—from pornography to online games to news sites—has a particular significance for women's bodies.

First, let us explore the means of production of digital images. These segments that create virtual characters are not simply components of a whole, but discrete parts in and of themselves. As an everyday example, the ubiquitous Adobe Photoshop logo has, for almost the last decade, always included the long-clichéd eye collage on its box, and the eye as its famous application icon. In 2001, the photographic eye and associated collage was switched to a nonphotographic representation. Such a shift in this particular year is important, for it showed the current sense of fluidity between photographic and computer-generated imagery. Digital media has quickly and directly

---

50 N. Katherine Hayles, *How We Became Posthuman: Virtual Bodies in Cybernetics, Literature, and Informatics* (Chicago: Chicago University Press, 1999); Robert Cook-Deegan, *The Gene Wars: Science, Politics, and the Human Genome* (New York: W.W. Norton, 1994); Necia Grant Cooper, ed., *The Human Genome Project: Deciphering the Blueprint of Heredity* (Mill Valley, CA: University Science Books, 1994).

dispensed with photographic images as the primary focus for representation, instead investigating the depth, manipulatibility, and maneuverability of 3-D and vector based images.[51] In other words, artificial signs that have no link to the visible, "natural" world are replacing our previous preferences for photorealism. It is not only logos or packaging which have signaled this shift from the photographic, from the whole to its parts. Software applications themselves have increasingly offered users not only control of images but of image parts in both time and space. The use of layers, symbols, and other elements easily separated and individualized has been an invaluable part of each software upgrade in the most popular programs. In addition, and perhaps more importantly, segmentation has become a philosophy in processes related to media production and object oriented programming, software segmenting objects, elements, and processes, allowing us to create believable scenes asynchronously.

At National Taiwan University's computer science department, an innovative project utilizes simple photos of the human in order to "bring the virtual character to life." Movement was one of the first focal areas in popular software packages, so relatively untrained users could, for example, create inverse kinematic animation to simulate human movement without parsing stream after stream of real user body data. At NTU, teams use custom software to choose areas such as the mouth, eyes, and face of simple 2-D photographs and use algorithms to mathematically control the 2-D image so that it can be lip synched to voice information. Consequently, not only is a former whole segmented, proportioned, and divided, but the focus remains on these segmented elements. The digibody—its movement, voice, and expressions—can be created mathematically from a simple photograph. This process, however, is being superceded by accurate 3-D modeling and scanning techniques that offer us a new body while losing the referential link to the material world through alternating a few data points.

Virtual bodies are easily mastered and in many examples in computer games show that one can derive great pleasure from controlling virtual bodies. Web sites with controllable characters create a tension between dichotomies such as inside and outside, knowing and controlling, recognition and anonymity, mastery and submission, and this tension continues to draw users back with a desire to interact. The interaction with the characters is ritualized—we are told when to click, generally we repeat actions such as opening and closing windows, and our roles are limited, defined. The characters

---

51 Early CD-ROMs featured important work such as "I Photograph to Remember"; such photoreal media would unlikely be produced today. See Pedro Meyer, "Some Background Thoughts," *I Photograph to Remember*, May 5, 2001, http://www.pedromeyer.com/galleries/i-photograph/work.html.

quickly become a familiar interface while possessing seemingly infinite sequences or combinations of logical elements. Based on the fragment, the layer, and the repeated action, sequence or word, their role is to generate and maintain a system of expectations.

Virtual information service scenarios are quite unlike television news programs. TV news traps the anchors in the "head and shoulders" frame, rarely allowing movement. However, US TV news conventions dictate establishing shots of the set, and this exposes the apparatus of the production that produces the illusion. Virtual newscasts, however, efface the means of production. We do not see a real woman behind the voice of Mya, for example; we do not see the development of the character or the context of its production. The processes and code are hidden, or if they are exposed they are bound ritualistically in "behind the scenes" movie clips and special "making of" add on products. This effacement is counter to Duchamp's proposition in *The Large Glass*; Duchamp's bride woman is not a doll, for dolls can have moving parts hidden from view: ". . . if the woman in the top of the Glass was in separate parts, her construction did not make a mystery about it."[52] When the digibodies do not have evidence of the labor that goes into their development and the bodies are segmented into products themselves, they become fetishes.

Two models offer examples for virtual body fetishism: the Marxist commodity fetish and a psychoanalytic model. First, Marx claims that a commodity's form mystifies the labour, the actual work involved in an object's production, so that the object acquires mystical (if distorted) properties and becomes a "commodity object." Because virtual stars are products created by the latest technology, delivered on hot commercially important computer objects, this approach offers us one way to look at virtual desire. Second, the user's desire of the virtual character can be read as a form of sexual fetishization. Like Barthes's comparison of a reader to a lover, a participant who desires to control, devour, and name the object of desire, the interest in virtual bodies from consumers is sustained from the appeal of the unanticipated and mysterious or by focusing on parts in order to control, comprehend, and conquer. Both of these approaches classify the fetish as an object possessing a special energy and power. The role of fetishism, particularly the fetishization of the woman, in digital media is of great interest to any critical understanding of this new landscape, for digibodies are created from discreet elements and are positioned within a command and control paradigm of desire. Thus what is proposed here is that the means of this particular kind of 3-D artifact production allows the body to be thought of as segmented and zoned. The breaking up of the female body into discrete elements, i.e., the creation of the image of woman as series of objects, is in terms of fetishistic scopophilia,

---

52 Lyotard, *Duchamp's TRANS/formers*, 182.

focusing on the object or body part used for sexual enjoyment. The fetish is a specificity—as Haraway terms it, the "thing-in-itself." It signals, above all else, perfection, isolation, and containment.

As the databodies are both objects in and of themselves and simultaneously self-referential, we must wonder about this seemingly enclosed system that serves to abstract and yet manifest them again, forever a process of regurgitation and digestion. Barthes' effective stretching of semiotics to include images, codes, and cultural systems prefigures cyborg methodologies and allows us to examine this hybrid creature—a creature we can define as one not of materiality or even as a human and machine combination, but rather one of referential and non-referential elements. Digibodies, constructed from text, create a text-based shape: ". . . the text itself . . . can reveal itself in the form of a body, split into fetish objects, into erotic sites."[53] Yet the resemblance to the physical human tempts us to draw this link. We measure characters at first on their proximity to the real: her movement is realistic, or her hair is not very realistic; then we move inwards, tripping down a chain of code signifiers. Whatever body part is chosen by animators as significant or nomadic, or thought by the audience as realistic or not, the character is replaced by a series of costume objects which become mobile disguises, fetishes. Even if the fetish is based on a "natural" phenomenon—a birthmark, for example—it positions participants into an artificial situation. By the very nature of its artifice the fetish erases the means of production of its own illusion.

The act of seeing the body in discreet pieces has its roots in the desire that Jean Baudrillard discusses as seduction. Seduction is founded upon the artificial; and while Baudrillard is problematic for feminists, his work offers an interesting argument for our desire to watch, control, and interact with digibodies. For Baudrillard, the shift from the real to the hyperreal occurs when representation gives way to simulation, and he insists that women's power relies on their capacity for artifice, disguise and seduction.[54]

Virtual characters—specifically online news and game characters—are popular, hyperreal pleasures. Such popular manifestations of pleasure are not founded on classic ideas of "quality art," but rather popular desires. Roland Barthes differentiates between desire and pleasure in *The Pleasure of the Text* (1975) and insists that current consumer culture lives for desire (to him, the absence of pleasure); he then compares popular pleasures to sexual desire, and our postmodern experience of them akin to a kind of sample or demo, hallmark notions of the digital age: "I impose upon the fine surface:

---

53 Roland Barthes, *A Barthes Reader*, ed. Susan Sontag (New York: Hill and Wang, 1995), 410.
54 Jean Baudrillard, "Fatal Strategies," in *Jean Baudrillard: Selected Writings*, ed. Mark Poster (Stanford: Stanford University Press, 1988).

I read on, I skip, I look up, I dip in again."[55] The segmentation, control, and maneuverability of VR characters, their surfaces, are navigated in a ballet of pieces, moments, fragments. Whether playing games like *The Sims* or *Black and White*, or simply just getting the news, humans are mesmerized by virtual characters: their movement, their unchanging steadiness in the face of our distractions beg the question of what interaction could bring to them. We click all over them like ants to honey, wanting them to react and offer stock quotes, a fast news fix, a protest, a wink. Sometimes, they react too slowly, voices steady, appearing calm, effacing the processing and framerates that generate them wherever, whenever we want them. These agents are also constructed by the surroundings in which they are birthed into their digital universe, on the frontier, organisms that are extensions of the network itself. And they are real, but a kind of real we are not accustomed to categorizing.

We users have a particular fascination with exposing the Real, of seeing behind the scenes, uncovering detail. Reality has become dislocated, homeless, and it floats free as a hyperreality is created in its place, able to exist through the breakup of the body parts while the seduction of the partial ensnares the users. But what is a way to reject the formation of the body as a fetish or commodity object, if our way of discovering the body object is still through a visible system? The female digibody has become a pure signifier which does not carry meaning beyond its appearance—or does it? The idea of gender as performative, rather than a naturalized or inherent biological entity, is useful when considering gender and the digibody. With virtual personae, the character and creator are indeed separated, and the relationship is open to change, multiplicity, and radical identity shifts. But a curious thing happens with digital characters: the manifestation of the female characters are so far down the chain of signification that their connection to any real female body becomes blurred. Here, Barthes' study of Bunraku theater is a useful resource for our examination of virtual characters, for he examines the idea of performed gender within artificial surroundings and character-agents external to the flesh body. Barthes' notes that men playing women characters in Bunraku do not "copy Woman" but rather work to signify her; their performance is "not bogged down in the model, but detached from its signified; femininity is present to read, not to see."[56] The conjoining of both sign and passivity thus create the figure of woman as a semiotic figure, an ideal woman agent.

---

55 Roland Barthes, *The Pleasure of the Text*, trans. Richard Miller (New York: Noonday, 1975), 11–12.
56 Roland Barthes, *The Empire of Signs*, trans. Richard Howard (New York: Hill and Wang, 1982), 53.

Social Implications of Embodied Data

The question of the Real continues with the investigation of gender, for both are inextricably intertwined. The semiotic distance Barthes proposes does not address issues of culture, and historical context. In further discussion of theatre, Barthes insists that the use of a "real" woman in the role of a woman character would actually be detrimental, for this would appear as an attempt at realistic representation and would lose the possibility for true "expressivity."[57] From a feminist perspective, however, such a copy of woman is problematic for it is created and defined by media creators within a cultural context of patriarchy; under such careful control, it seems as though there will be limited innovations and changes to the power structure; to the ways in which the digital woman is created, packaged, and the kinds of powers she will truly possess. Claims that female digibodies have, in fact, a slim indexical link to the idea of woman suggest that if these images are not really like real women, they do not have to be taken seriously.

Digital characters, however, are in fact encoding methods that inscribe both gender and cultural norms. If we compare them to the way we generate letters to form words, the equivalent tie is between the word and the idea. This gap, Barthes proposes, is like theatre in which characterizing "Woman" transcends nature and image to become an idea, "and as such, she is restored to the classifying function and to the truth of her pure difference."[58] This brings us to the key point in thinking about women digital characters: media makers continue to create eruptions such as Ananova's green hair, reminding us with such markers and eruptions that these characters are digital, that is, distinct from the real. Do we desire the markers of difference on virtual characters?[59] Such markers have helped avoid the inevitable questions about representation and virtual characters; game makers, for example, easily dismiss stereotypical depictions of women in games because they are, after all, fictional, exaggerated characters. The social implications of embodied data have the potential to be politically reductive. *Tomb Raider* fans note, for example, that if one were "to see women built like this in real life . . . it would be

---

57 Ibid. 89.
58 Ibid. 91.
59 I am very much informed while writing this article by the computer science students at NTU (mostly male), many of whom have images of cute Japanese girls as their monitor background images. In this case, the image of woman is twice removed: first, by her "Japanese" ethnic differentiator, very much a desirable "other" in the eyes of young Taiwanese men. Then, the images themselves; the photos make them all look a little plastic, a bit too shiny and smooth, much like Mya's artificial lighting. In fact, since I could not tell if the stars were real humans or not, I had to ask. To some of the students, it did not really matter.

kind of scary."[60] This kind of discursive distance has kept games and game characters in the realm of either the joke (i.e., Lara Croft is as exaggerated as a blowup doll) or the technology fetish (the graphic technology that produces the character is in itself the interest). But what happens when this critical distance is erased, the markers of difference elided by a new type of life form? This process is beginning to develop with the *Final Fantasy* film, for example, and will continue to be perfected.

The nature of the digital medium is peculiar: at once it is networked and fluid, yet at the same time individual, tailored, and fetishistic. It seems that virtual characters are based on Western, human norms of acting, conventions of news giving, and conversations. As her Oscar debut suggests, even Mya wants to be on a talk show. Barthes would argue for us to embrace the plastic, embrace the artifice, and be one with the code.

Code Shapes

With the rise of digital media and its capacity for interactive systems, information design at the interface has become an important site for meaning creation, especially to interface gurus Ben Schneiderman, Donald Norman, and Jacob Neilson, among many other high-tech industryworkers and consumers of digital products. A visual interface surrounds almost every user of technology, creating a semiotic horne for all users, ideally meeting their task, entertainment, and social needs. Interfaces must be easy to use, even "intuitive." Systems and interfaces, however, can be created more or less usable for regular consumers. For idealistic interface guru Donald Norman, the human is clearly the preferable system: "We are analog beings trapped in a digital world, and the worst part is, we did it to ourselves."[61] Norman explores what he calls "the horrible mismatch between requirements of these human-built machines and human capabilities." He cites a long list of dichotomies between machines and humans: "Machines are mechanical, we are biological. Machines are rigid and require great precision and accuracy of control. We are compliant. We tolerate and produce huge amounts of ambiguity and uncertainty, very little precision and accuracy . . . Analog and

---

60 Sarah Baig, "Quote of the Day: True Love; Possible Justification for Liking Video Game Babes? Or Argument Against It?," *IGN for Men*, February 16, 1999, *Internet Archive* Way Back Machine archival version, February 4, 2000, http://web.archive.org/web/20000204165611/http://formen.ign.com/news/12182.html, paragraph 3.

61 Donald Norman, *The Invisible Computer: Why Good Products Can Fail, the Personal Computer Is So Complex, and Information Appliances Are the Solution* (Cambridge, MA: MIT Press, 1998), 1.

biological."[62] Digital systems still do not excel in processing ambiguity and imprecise situations.

The interface research conducted at Xerox PARC during the 1970s established most of the visual and functional conventions of present graphic user interfaces, and these conventions helped make the screen reality into a lived reality.[63] New media theorist Terry Harpold notes, "[a] subtle thing happens when everything is visible: the display becomes reality."[64] In other words, the distance between the real and the virtual, much discussed in cybercircles, collapses into itself. The creation of digital characters and digibodies makes the display the object of our desire. New creatures are created from texts, and by virtue of their computational environment, are machines of the eventual erasure of the symbolic. From the physical aspects of the computer (keyboard, mouse) to the internal interfaces (Web page, application graphical user interface) computers offer themselves through signs. When we write text, for example, that will appear in a book such as the one you are holding, the signs we produce to create ideas are a common currency. In the computer, ASCII text represents the letters in the word "sign" (already a meta sign) as "115 105 103 110." This chain of signifiers continues down the line in the various processes a program runs via the processor. However, an interesting thing happens when we reach through the operating system to machine code. At the machine code level, things are different: machine code exists and controls in and of itself, a place where the sign system is replaced by impulses, 0s and 1s, jolts. It is a place, to use Baudrillard's words, where "truth, reference and objective causes have ceased to exist."[65]

If we consider data and information, even computer code, as texts, Barthes might suggest we derive our pleasure from the collision of a text's figurative aspects with its informative functions. No longer does an object have to be material to exist. We follow an object oriented programming model here: at the simple invocation of an instance of an object—Plato's shadow, if you will,

---

62   Ibid. 15.
63   The attribution of the interface always causes a lively argument; here I am backed up by Patrick J. Lynch in his paper, "Visual Design for the User Interface Part 1: Design Fundamentals," *Journal of Biocommunication* 21, no. 1 (1994): 22-30.
64   Editor's note: the original 2004 publication of this paper attributed this statement to Terry Harpold in his presentation "Thickening Space: On Reading and the 'Visible' Interface" at the Fourth International Digital Arts & Culture Conference in 2001; in fact Harpold is quoting David Canfield Smith, Charles Irby, Ralph Kimball, Bill Verplank, and Eric Harslem, "Designing the Star User Interface," *Byte*, April 1982, 260; see http://www.guidebookgallery.org/articles/designingthestaruserinterface.
65   Jean Baudrillard, *Simulations*, trans. Paul Foss, Paul Patton, and Philip Beitchman (New York: Semiotext(e), 1983), 6.

in relationship to the object—the object exists, even if only in code. Thus although Harpold sites a problematic shift at the graphic itself, perhaps the root of the issue lies at a much more conceptual level. Code is shaping our consciousness and our culture.

Uncertain signs are unstable territories, and we work to fix them to the familiar. Good examples of this principle come from N. Katherine Hayles's observations that along with the mechanization of language, there has been a one-to-one correspondence with language to action or object; unlike computer actions, which can, through their abstract association with a particular text or action perform the insignificant to the monumental with the touch of a button (such as the "send" on a fiery email) typewriter keys or printing press blocks, are directly related to the script they produce.[66] However, virtual portals are appearing all over the Internet. They represent a critical moment of the virtual age; Arthur and Marilouise Kroker write that we are in an era "typified by a relentless effort on the part of the virtual class to force a wholesale abandonment of the body, to dump sensuous experience into the trash bin, substituting instead a disembodied world of empty data flows" (see Figure 4).[67]

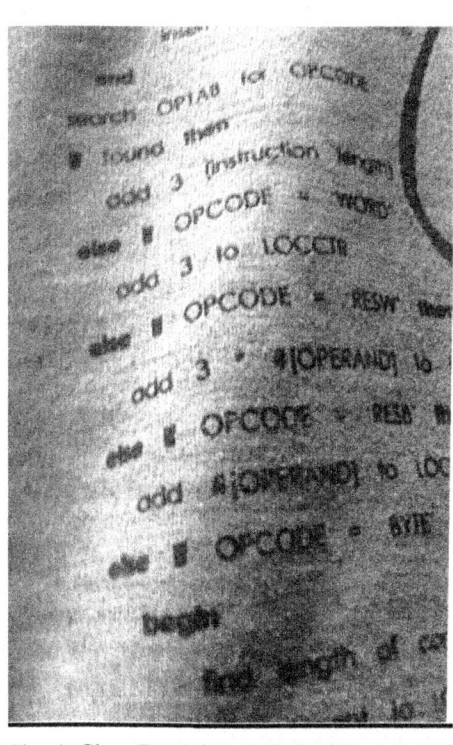

Fig. 4. Chen Dung Yun's clothing is covered with code, showing the tension between the physical and the code environment. 2001. Photograph by Mary Flanagan with the cooperation of CML lab, directed by Ming Ouhyoung.

The move toward mobility of information means the shape of the machine must better adapt to our own bodies, to complete the merger of network and embodiment. In fact, our desire for the latest information, our wish to have a

---

66 N. Katherine Hayles, "Virtual Bodies and Flickering Signifiers," *October* 66 (Fall 1993): 69–91.
67 Arthur Kroker and Marilouise Kroker, "Code Warriors," in *The Cybercultures Reader*, ed. David Bell and Barbara M. Kennedy (London: Routledge, 2000), 98.

personal helper, our secret dream of the "genie in the bottle" manifests online; we are living in an age when that which "was previously mentally projected, which was lived as a metaphor in the terrestrial habitat is from now on projected, entirely without metaphor, into the absolute space of simulation."[68] In this case, the blurring of the virtual body with these bride bodies by their means of distribution and task (erupting off of our desktops from websites with news for us in little boxes) can tell us a great deal about our relationship with virtual characters and desire. For as technology has taken a shape, it has taken a shape the creators of the technology desire, morphed into a form (information), creating a body.

There are several implications of this shift. First, these pleasurable character/services offered by industry equate women's bodies with service and ubiquity; these women are "scattered into x number of places, that are never gathered together into anything she knows of herself."[69] The ubiquity poses the question about the social importance of ubiquity and access, and the more accessible, the less valuable. Another implication of this trend is towards the loss of the body, which numerous writers continue to postulate. The body's racial, aged, and sexual categories are interconnected, but in virtual characters, these combinations are constructed as personality features rather than historical or culturally specific categories. Rather than focus on this erasure, however, this essay asks more about the virtual body and its own lived reality and its consequences on biological women's bodies.

Who is this third creature, this creature of code? Bukatman has called digitally created bodies a "literal hollowness," creatures of mathematical persuasion that are as deep as a surface, not as an interior. In his analysis, all elements of the image are reduced to digital bits, which are reformed before our eyes as the masquerade of the solid, of the real, while there is, in fact, "nothing inside."[70] But perhaps nothing has turned into "the thing-in-itself;" like the relationship of puppet performer and puppet, perhaps our virtual puppets have ". . . no more strings. No more strings, hence no more metaphor, no more Fate; since the puppet no longer apes the creature, man is no longer a puppet in divinity's hands, the *inside* no longer commands the

---

68 Jean Baudrillard, *The Ecstasy of Communication*, ed. Sylvére Lotringer, trans. Bernard Schutze and Caroline Schutze (New York: Semiotext(e), 1988), 16.

69 Luce Irigaray, *The Speculum of the Other Woman*, trans. Gillian C. Gill (Ithaca, NY: Cornell University Press, 1985), 227; see also the science fiction novel *Virtual Girl* by Amy Thompson, who chronicles an AI's attempt to reconcile her computational and human aspects in a female body.

70 Scott Bukatman, "Taking Shape: Morphing and the Performance of Self," in *Meta-Morphing: Visual Transformation and the Culture of Quick-Change*, ed. Vivian Carol Sobchack (Minneapolis: University of Minnesota Press, 2000), 245.

outside."[71] Does the text have a human form; is it a figure, an anagram of the body? asks Barthes. Clearly, "information" has taken over where "form" used to suffice. This shift represents a semiotic transfer, a way in which the flow of information has become re-imagined and embodied. In *The Pleasure*, Barthes writes:

> *Text means tissue. We are now emphasizing, in the tissue, the generative idea that the text is made, is worked out in a perpetual interweaving; lost in this tissue – this texture – the subject unmakes himself, like a spider, dissolving in the constitutive secretion of its web.*[72]

I return now to N. Katherine Hayles's idea that information "is never present in itself." Perhaps the digital bodies discussed in this essay do have a presence in and of themselves. On the surface, these hyperbodies seem to be slowly giving way to more "realistic" representations as technology permits us to visualize more of the body than ever before. Digital media has been working toward creating multidimensional perfection. Blurring the real, their perfect bodies are unable to contain the strange eruptions of shiny plastic skin, of green hair, of almost slithering movement. Like melodrama and pornography before them, digibodies must manifest the excess of the perfect in hyperreal "bursts," a product of the overproduction of signs of the feminine and the virtual. Because of his apt writing about media personalities, Steven Whittaker might help us see that female digital characters turn into a kind of same-sex transvestite, so overproduced that they would become a kind of camp spectacle of a woman.[73]

Indeed, Baudrillard would describe this seduction of the collective consciousness, when we could be one not only with the data but with the digibodies, in terms of seduction: "There is no active or passive mode in seduction, no subject or object, no interior or exterior: seduction plays on both sides, and there is no frontier separating them."[74] The experience is undeniably exhilarating:

> *Anyway, feel a million flurries of now, a million intangibles of the present moment, an infinite permutation of what could be . . . the thought gets caught. . . . You get the picture. In the data cloud of collective consciousness, it's one of those issues that just seems to keep popping up.*[75]

---

71 Barthes, *The Empire of Signs*, 62; italics in original.
72 Barthes, *The Pleasure of the Text*, 64.
73 Steve Whitaker, "Face To Efface With The Pout," *Ctheory*, June 28, 2000, http://www.ctheory.com/article/a087.html.
74 Baudrillard, *Simulations*, 81.
75 Paul D. Miller (DJ Spooky), "Material Memories: Time and the Cinematic Image," *Ctheory*, May 2, 2001, http://www.ctheory.net/articles.aspx?id=135.

Without the link to the signified, digibodies are electric phantoms, almost haunted flesh, shells which have no link to the material or physical form of the sign. They are a semiotic flesh, a coded flesh, code changed to flesh, code itself. We are in a quest for perfection by way of the development of our noiseless music, through our data, our carefully scrubbed genes—our numeric flesh. The fields of human computer interaction, graphic design, genetic engineering, and computer science must confront the merger that has already happened between code and bodies; many of us no longer need look at the face of the real and know it, recognize it, and have no urge to look further, to assign extra meanings, signs, readings. We need new critical practices which recognize this new body form and to create ethics for this new body form. If our thoughts, actions, and communications have literally become digital signal and binary image, it is important that we look around us in the offline sense. Digital bodies can deny the situations of real bodies, real women, real class, and poverty issues in the focus on seduction.

Meanwhile, real physical bodies are reflecting the semiotic shift. Images of broken, pierced, incomplete, amputated, ruptured and fragmented "horrible" bodies proliferate in American culture just as our media strives to allow containment, control, and artificial perfection, a closed circuit where signs replicate and mutate into other phantom realities and pseudo lives. As Barthes noted:

> *Imagine an aesthetic (if the word has not become too depreciated) based entirely (completely, radically, in every sense of the word) on the pleasure of the consumer, whoever he may be, to whatever class, whatever group he may belong, without respect to cultures or languages: the consequences would be huge, perhaps even harrowing.*[76]

Acknowledgements

I would like to thank Meg Knowles for introducing me to *Desk Set*, Roy Roussel for reintroducing me to Barthes, Cal Clements for bringing in Duchampian dimensions, Frank Miller, the students at National Taiwan University for involving me in their digital embodiment projects: Perng Guo Luen, Carol Chia Ying Lee, Wei Ru Chen, Alex Wan-Chun Ma, I Chen Lin, Cindy, Super Yeh (Jeng Sheng), Wei Teh Wang (bearw), Murphy, Joyce, Jun Wei Yeh, Cindy Chi Hui Huang, Kan Li Huang, and Eugenia Yijen Leu and Professor Ming Ouhyoung for his warm welcome and invitation to visit NTU's Communications and Multimedia Laboratory, where this article was written.

---

76 Barthes, *Barthes Reader*, 413.

Bibliography

Barthes, Roland. *A Barthes Reader.* Edited by Susan Sontag. New York: Hill and Wang, 1995.

———. *A Lover's Discourse: Fragments.* Translated by Richard Howard. New York: Hill and Wang, 1978.

———. *The Empire of Signs.* Translated by Richard Howard. New York: Hill and Wang, 1982.

———. *The Pleasure of the Text.* Translated by Richard Miller. New York: Noonday, 1975.

Baudrillard, Jean. *The Ecstasy of Communication.* Edited by Sylvére Lotringer. Translated by Bernard Schutze and Caroline Schutze. New York: Semiotext(e), 1988.

———. "Fatal Strategies." In *Jean Baudrillard: Selected Writings*, 185–206. Edited by Mark Poster. Stanford: Stanford University Press, 1988.

———. *Simulations.* Translated by Paul Foss, Paul Patton, and Philip Beitchman. New York: Semiotext(e), 1983.

Blake, Nayland, Lawrence Rinder, and Amy Scholder, eds. *In a Different Light: Visual Culture, Sexual Identity, Queer Practice.* San Francisco: City Lights Books, 1995.

Bukatman, Scott. "Taking Shape: Morphing and the Performance of Self." In *Meta-Morphing: Visual Transformation and the Culture of Quick-Change*, 225–249. Edited by Vivian Carol Sobchack. Minneapolis: University of Minnesota Press, 2000.

Butler, Judith. *Gender Trouble: Feminism and the Subversion of Identity.* 10th ed. New York: Routledge, 1996.

Cabanne, Pierre. *Dialogues with Marcel Duchamp.* Translated by Ron Padgett. New York: Da Capo, 1988.

Cadigan, Pat. *Synners.* 10th ed. New York: Four Walls Eight Windows, 2001.

Colors no. 4, Race issue. Spring 1993.

Cook-Deegan, Robert. *The Gene Wars: Science, Politics, and the Human Genome.* New York: W. W. Norton, 1994.

Cooper, Necia Grant, ed. *The Human Genome Project: Deciphering the Blueprint of Heredity.* Mill Valley, CA: University Science Books, 1994.

Duncan, Michael. "Queering the Discourse: Gay and Lesbian Art, University Art Museum, Berkeley, California." *Art in America* 83, no. 7 (July 1995): 27–31.

Ephron, Pheobe, Henry Ephron and William Merchant. *Desk Set.* Directed by Walter Lang. Los Angeles: Twentieth Century Fox, 2004. Originally produced in 1957. DVD.

Flanagan, Mary. "Mobile Identities, Digital Stars, and Post-Cinematic Selves." *Wide Angle* 21, no. 1 (1999): 77-93. doi:10.1353/wan.1999.0002.

———. "Navigating the Narrative in Space: Gender and Spatiality in Virtual Worlds." *Art Journal* 59, no. 3 (Fall 2000): 74-85. doi:10.2307/778029.

Gross, Daniel. "Merging Man and Machine: The Future of Computer Interfaces Evolving in Japan." *Computer Graphics World* 14, no. 5 (May 1991): 47-51.

Grumet, Tobey. "Digital Dame." Technology Watch. *Popular Mechanics*. November 2000. 36.

Haraway, Donna J. *Modest_Witness@Second_Millenium.FemaleMan_Meets _OncoMouse: Feminism and Technoscience*. New York: Routledge, 1997.

Hayles, N. Katherine. *How We Became Posthuman: Virtual Bodies in Cybernetics, Literature, and Informatics*. Chicago: University of Chicago Press, 1999.

———. "Virtual Bodies and Flickering Signifiers." *October* 66 (Fall 1993): 69-91.

Huyssen, Andreas. "The Vamp and the Machine: Fritz Lang's Metropolis." In *After the Great Divide: Modernism, Mass Culture, Postmodernism*, 65-81. Bloomington: Indiana University Press, 1986.

Irigaray, Luce. *The Speculum of the Other Woman*. Translated by Gillian C. Gill. Ithaca, NY: Cornell University Press, 1985.

Judovitz, Dalia. *Unpacking Duchamp: Art in Transit*. Berkeley: University of California Press, 1995.

Kroker, Arthur and Marilouise Kroker. "Code Warriors." In *The Cybercultures Reader*, edited by David Bell and Barbara M. Kennedy, 96-103. London: Routledge, 2000.

Leggat, Robert. *A History of Photography: From Its Beginnings Till the 1920s*. Web version of the 1995 UK edition, 1999. http://www.mpritchard.com/photohistory/history/delaroch.htm.

Lynch, Patrick J. "Visual Design for the User Interface Part 1: Design Fundamentals." *Journal of Biocommunication* 21, no. 1 (1994): 22-30.

Lyotard, Jean-Fransois. *Duchamp's TRANS/formers*. Translated by Ian McLeod. Venice, CA: Lapis, 1990.

Mahowald, Mary B., Dana Levinson, Christine Cassel, Amy Lemke, Carole Ober, James Bowman, Michelle Le Beau, Amy Ravin, and Melissa Times. "The New Genetics and Women," *Milbank Quarterly: A Journal of Public Health and Health Care Policy* 72, no. 2 (1996): 239-283. http://www.jstor.org/stable/3350248.

Martin, Michael H. "The Man Who Makes Sense of Numbers: Yale Professor Edward Tufte Dazzles Business People by Making Rational the Data that Rule Their Work Lives." *Fortune*, October 27, 1997, 273-276.

Mellencamp, Patricia. "Making History: Julie Dash." *Frontiers: A Journal of Women Studies* 15, no. 1 (1994): 76–102, http://www.jstor.org/stable/3346614.

Miller, Paul D. "Material Memories: Time and the Cinematic Image," *Ctheory*, May 2, 2001. http://www.ctheory.net/articles.aspx?id=135.

Naumann, Francis. "Marcel & Maria." *Art in America* 89, no. 4 (April 2001): 98–111.

Norman, Donald. *The Invisible Computer: Why Good Products Can Fail, the Personal Computer Is So Complex, and Information Appliances Are the Solution.* Cambridge, MA: MIT Press, 1998.

O'Riordan, Kate, and Julie Doyle. "Virtually Visible: Female Cyberbodies and the Medical Imagination." In *Reload: Rethinking Women in Cyberculture*, edited by Mary Flanagan and Austin Booth, 239–260. Cambridge, MA: MIT Press, 2002.

Seidler, Peter. "Syndi: Your Celebrity Portal: A User's Manual." *ArtByte*. September/October 1999, 51–54.

Skagestad, Peter. "Peirce, Virtuality, and Semiotic." Paper included in the published proceedings of the Twentieth World Congress of Philosophy, *Paideia: Philosophy Educating Humanity*, Boston, MA, August 1998. http://www.bu.edu/wcp/Papers/Cogn/CognSkag.htm.

Smith, David C., Charles Irby, Ralph Kimball, Bill Verplank, and Eric Harslem. "Designing the Star User Iterface." *Byte*. April 1982, 242–282.

Taylor, Chris. "Looking Online." *Time*, June 26, 2000, 60.

Theweleit, Klaus. *Male Fantasies*. Vol. 2, *Women, Floods, Bodies, History*. Translated by Chris Turner. Minneapolis: University of Minnesota Press, 1987.

Thompson, Amy. *Virtual Girl*. New York: Ace, 1993.

Tilson, Tamsen. "Bare Fact: News Site is a Real Hit." *Variety*, February 5, 2001.

Tzara, Tristan. "Tristan Tzara: Lecture on Dada. (1922)." In *The Dada Painters and Poets: An Anthology*, translated and edited by Robert Motherwell, 246–251. Cambridge, MA: Harvard University Press, 1981.

Whitaker, Steve. "Face To Efface With The Pout." *Ctheory*. June 28, 2000. http://www.ctheory.net/articles.aspx?id=130.

Essentialism and Care in a Female-Intensive Profession

Melodie J. Fox and Hope A. Olson

In library and information studies (LIS), we have not yet reached a transcendent state of postfeminism. We have addressed the obvious issues such as the occupational segregation that disadvantaged women striving for management positions face—although we still have work to do, there is general agreement that it needs to be done, and change is gradually happening. We now face more complex and systemic issues that relate to things like our mission, even our personal epistemic stances and our epistemology/ies as a profession, all of which are highly gendered. Feminists have long understood systemic issues like those related to the status of librarianship; feminist theory is rich with theoretical angles we have not tried, and it makes sense in the inevitably gendered context of a female-intensive profession.

Traditionally, LIS has used two strategies to address women's issues: 1) an assertive, direct approach, drawn primarily from liberal feminism, demanding opportunities and compensation equal to that of men; or 2) a revalorization of women's "special" abilities, especially in regard to service and caring drawn primarily from relational feminism. Both of these feminisms have been questioned as to their essentializing of women. This article examines the work of two feminist thinkers, describes how their work can be applied in LIS, and suggests how they can guide us toward alternative perspectives. Gayatri Chakravorty Spivak is a feminist, postcolonial theorist who writes in the rich and dense prose of critical theory, and Joan Tronto is a feminist professor of political science and women's studies who writes about ethics and care. Spivak constructs her feminist and postcolonial perspectives on the surprisingly robust foundation of poststructuralism whereas Tronto saw poststructuralists as denying any overriding form of ethics.[1] The two are an

---

1 Joan C. Tronto, *Moral Boundaries: A Political Argument for an Ethic of Care* (New York: Routledge, 1993), 149.

unlikely pair to be linked together, but they both offer pertinent ideas to help us address issues in LIS. At the core of these issues is a recognition that we can strengthen our female-intensive profession, but questions arise around the means and the risks. Should we demand an even playing field? Or a garden? Should we revalorize buns and sensible shoes? Should we evoke identity politics? Should we re-establish the profession along feminist principles? And what about the possibility of tumbling into the sinkhole of essentialism? An important concern when addressing questions from a feminist perspective is the risk of essentializing women, making them homogeneous. However, to express "women's" issues, it is necessary to generalize and it is politically advantageous to present a united front even though it is recognized that women and our issues are not homogeneous. Spivak presented the concept of "strategic essentialism" as a possible solution.[2]

Essentialism

What is *essentialism*? Diana Fuss, in her *Essentially Speaking: Feminism, Nature & Difference*, describes it as "A belief in the *real, true essence* of things, the *invariable and fixed* 'whatness' of a given entity."[3] Her subtitle suggests the conflicting stances of feminine traits appearing due to how girls are nurtured in a gendered society vs. feminine traits as biologically innate in women by nature of their sex. Is femininity learned or is it innate? If it is innate then it is also unchanging: "invariable and fixed," immutable.

Ashcroft, Griffiths, and Tiffin consider essentialism in a postcolonial world, describing it as "the assumption that groups, categories or classes of objects have one or several *defining features exclusive to all members of that category*."[4] That is, essence is *independent* of context.

In Aristotelian thought, innate, immutable, independent characteristics constitute the essence of a thing and thereby define it. An essentialist view of women, for example, would say that in spite of some difference there are one or more characteristics that all women everywhere hold in common and these characteristics cannot be changed. Hence, essentialism suspends women in the status quo like an insect in amber.

---

2   Gayatri Chakravorty Spivak, "Criticism, Feminism, and the Institution (an interview by Elizabeth Grosz)," 1984, in *The Post-Colonial Critic: Interviews, Strategies, Dialogues* (New York: Routledge, 1990), 11. Many of Spivak's works are more readily available in collections than in their original form. In such cases, we include two dates. The first date is for the original, and the second date and pagination are for the reprint in a collection.

3   Diana Fuss, *Essentially Speaking: Feminism, Nature, and Difference* (New York: Routledge, 1989), xi.

4   Bill Ashcroft, Gareth Griffiths, and Helen Tiffin, *Key Concepts in Post-Colonial Studies*, (London: Routledge, 1998), 77.

	Innate, Immutable, Independent Truths	Groups by defined by common characteristics	Members of groups displaying defining traits
Aristotelian problem of universals	Universals	Particulars	Individuals
Aristotle on the definition of things	Essences	Classes	Things
Example	Essence *of* woman representing essential characteristics "nurturance, empathy, supportiveness, non-competitiveness"	Women	Cleopatra, Hildegard von Bingen, Golda Meir, Margaret Thatcher, Mother Teresa, Sarah Palin, Gloria Steinem, your mother, my aunt, the lady across the street, each woman working retail at the mall, etc.

Fig. 1. On essences, universals, particulars, classes, and individuals

Essentialism is closely related to the problem of universals in the Aristotelian tradition. Universals, particulars, and individuals form a hierarchy: "Things are particulars and their qualities are universals. So a universal is the property predicated of all the individuals of a certain sort or class."[5] That is, particulars are groups of individuals sharing one or more characteristics, and universals define particulars by representing those characteristics. Universals, particulars, and individuals make up the hierarchy that grows from formal logic. So universals are similar to Aristotelian essences in that we cannot perceive them empirically; we can only see individual or particular instances of them.

Classes are groups of entities that have one or more defining characteristics. The *Oxford English Dictionary* (*OED*) defines a class as a "number of individuals (persons or things) possessing common attributes, and grouped together under a general or 'class' name; a kind, sort, division." Like classes, particulars are defined by attributes or characteristics.

---

5 Anthony Flew, *A Dictionary of Philosophy*, 2nd rev. ed., (New York: Gramercy, 1979), 360.

Essences represent the *characteristics* that *define classes* in the same way that universals represent the characteristics that define *particular*. By representing these characteristics, *essences* are identifying the *characteristics* that are innate to individual things or people in a given *class;* these characteristics define the boundaries of the class. *Essences* impose definition through *hierarchical force,* "[t]he principle that the attributes of a class ... apply to all the subdivisions of the class."[6] Figure 1 is a framework devised to reflect essentialism and similar concepts, demonstrating the example of *women.*[7] Following the model of Aristotle's first syllogism:

> *Women are characterized by "nurturance, empathy, supportiveness, non-competitiveness."*
>
> *Margaret Thatcher is a woman.*
>
> *Therefore, Margaret Thatcher is nurturing, empathetic, supportive, and non-competitive.*

All of the women listed in Figure 1 and all other women contemporary and historic in all cultures would have the same defining characteristics. While the example is designed to illustrate how ludicrous essences/universals can be, it also shows how close essences/universals are to stereotypes.

In his predicables, Aristotle examined the difference between essential characteristics and accidental characteristics. The former are innate, immutable, independent characteristics that define groups of things, and the latter are not significant in establishing likeness because they can vary from one individual to another.[8] The characteristics that we may see in Margaret Thatcher as a ruthless, service-cutting, cutthroat competitive leader would be accidental rather than innate if we follow this logic. What characteristics of women could possibly encompass all of the individual women listed in Figure 1?

Essentialism and Feminism

"Women's essence is *assumed to be given and universal* and is usually, though not necessarily, identified with women's biological or 'natural' *characteristics*

---

6   Melvil Dewey, *Dewey Decimal Classification and Relative Index,* 22nd ed., (Dublin, OH: OCLC, 2003), lxix.

7   The genus-species relationship so widely used in hierarchical classifications and controlled vocabularies is similar.

8   For elaboration, see Michael Loux, "Kinds and Predications: An Examination of Aristotle's Theory of Categories," *Philosophical Papers* 26, no. 1 (1997): 3-28. doi:10.1080/05568649709506554.

... nurturance, empathy, supportiveness, non-competitiveness, and so on."[9] Such a definition of women did not seem to fit into a feminist agenda.

Essentialism and feminism have a rocky relationship. Without some class or grouping that can be called "women," it is difficult even to have a feminist argument. The thorny question of the validity or inadvisability of essentialism is the feminist version of the nature/nurture debate. Essentialism is embraced by some feminists who believe that essential "women's" qualities exist, and that women's positive characteristics are repressed or undervalued by our patriarchal structure. However, feminism from this perspective has been accused of excluding many women who do not fit the *essential characteristics*.

Primarily for that reason, essentialism was rejected by many feminists who believed that common characteristics are the result of social construction through social discourses and that systems, institutions, etc. should be made inclusive of all marginalized groups, but not homogenized. What does Spivak have to say? In her early career Spivak wrote, "essentialism is a trap. It seems more important to learn to understand that *the world's women do not all relate to the privileging of essence . . . in quite the same way.*"[10] Spivak is here setting up the epistemic position that our definition of some essence is constructed in a particular context; it is not universal. She established herself as an anti-essentialist, but a practical one:

> *. . . no rigorous definition of anything is ultimately possible. . . . [D]efinitions are necessary in order to keep us going, to allow us to take a stand. The only way I can see myself making definitions is in a provisional and polemical one:* <u>I construct my definition as a woman not in terms of a woman's putative essence but in terms of words currently in use.</u> *'Man' is such a word in common usage.*[11]

The logical progression from agreeing that definitions are necessary ends in Spivak's notion of "strategic essentialism." She knew that dabbling in essentialism is risky, but when interviewed by Elizabeth Grosz in 1984, Spivak said, "I think it's absolutely on target to take a stand against the discourses of essentialism, universalism. . . . But *strategically* we cannot."[12] On how to use strategic essentialism she said:

---

9 Elizabeth Grosz, "Sexual Difference and the Problem of Essentialism," in *The Essential Difference*, eds. Naomi Schor and Elizabeth Weed (Bloomington: Indiana University Press, 1994), 84.
10 Gayatri Chakravorty Spivak, "Feminism and Critical Theory," 1985, in *The Spivak Reader* (New York: Routledge, 1996), 68.
11 Ibid., 54, emphasis added.
12 Spivak, "Criticism, Feminism, and the Institution," 11.

> *You pick up the universal that will give you the power to fight against the other side, and what you are throwing away by doing that is theoretical purity. Whereas the great custodians of the anti-universal are obliged therefore simply to act in the interest of a great narrative, the narrative of exploitation, while they keep themselves clean by not committing themselves.*[13]

Spivak is committed to action and to agency as the ability to act, so the step to strategic essentialism followed logically. However, she met with criticism. Rey Chow wrote, "Isn't Spivak's argument for risking essentialism that the essentialist moment is the irreducible part of any discourse? And isn't 'naming' precisely the centering, the essentializing *act*?"[14]

Spivak reconsidered strategic essentialism in a 1989 interview, particularly objecting to continuing to sanction essentialism after the strategic activity was past, that is, in allowing essentialism to become entrenched which she said, "is the impossible risk of a lasting strategy."[15] And about strategy: "A strategy suits a situation; a strategy is not a theory."[16] So "I have then reconsidered my cry for a strategic use of essentialism."[17] That is, strategies are *ad hoc* ploys designed to address a specific concern. They are a poor match for the power of essentialism's innate, immutable, and independent essences. But we are still left with the problem of how to take action to remedy the thorny lingering issues that liberal and relational feminisms have been unable to address if we cannot define "women." Must we succumb to "the unavoidable usefulness of something [essentialism] that is quite dangerous"?[18]

Spivak reconsidered the risk and abandoned strategic essentialism. Looking back after four years she said: "You know, I gave a long interview [in 1989] . . . where I said that I no longer want to use it [strategic essentialism]. . . . So, as a phrase, I have given up on it. As to whether I have given up on it as a project, that is really a different idea."[19] What does that last sentence mean? What is she leaving open and why? Because she sees agency, the ability to act, as dependent on some class we can call women, Spivak must find a way to allow something that functions like strategic essentialism, but without the risks. To do this she deconstructs the boundary that separates agency and

---

13 Ibid., 12.
14 Rey Chow, "Ethics after Idealism," *diacritics* 223 (1993): 15.
15 Gayatri Chakravorty Spivak, "In a Word: Interview," by Ellen Rooney, 1989, in *Outside in the Teaching Machine*, (New York: Routledge, 1993), 3.
16 Spivak, "In a Word: Interview," 4.
17 Ibid., 5.
18 Ibid.
19 Gayatri Chakravorty Spivak, "An Interview with Gayatri Chakravorty Spivak," by Sara Danius and Stefan Jonsson, *boundary* 2 20, no. 2 (1993): 35.

anti-essentialism so that "bits of them float into each other's boundaries."[20] Spivak minimizes essences to bring our focus to agency to accomplish the work of feminism.

> Essences, it seems to me, are just a kind of content. All content is not essence. Why be so nervous about it? Why not demote the word 'essence,' because without a minimalizable essence, an essence as ce qui reste, an essence as what remains, there is no exchange. Difference articulates these negotiable essences. There is no time for essence/anti-essence. There is so much work to be done.[21]

Spivak subverts essence by making it negotiable, no longer immutable. She uses difference to name essences, and since essences require sameness they shrink into what remains: leftovers. This minimizing of essences opens up space for work—a space where we can exercise agency.

How do we take up our agency? Here is where she seems to speak almost directly to librarianship as she enjoins us to create culture. Librarians and allied professionals are not just the keepers of culture. Whether consciously or unconsciously, we shape the context that creates culture.

> I start with the assumption that men and women occupy different positions in the making of culture. Any discussion of culture that does not take this into consideration is symptom more than explanation. Women are either silenced or ventriloquial, not-quite-subjects who hold up the culture or, if conscientized, resist.[22]

The stereotypical shushing librarian silences herself as well as others, but she is not the essence of *librarian*. In reality she is not singular, but diverse and capable of agency. To follow Spivak, librarians must avoid becoming "ventriloquial" in favor of speaking out in our own voices. Instead of holding up the status quo we should become "conscientized" and resisting.

Are we really silenced or ventriloquial? Questions may answer this question: Who creates and maintains the standards that govern our practice? To what degree is defining what we do taken out of our hands and given over to vendors to revise our cataloging tools and run our approval plans? How much are we encouraged to take the homogenized product and use it without contextualizing it in the name of efficiency and economy?

The result of silence in the face of usurpation of professional judgment is, of course, deprofessionalization—loss of agency. The shushing, non-technical, sensible, helpful librarian cannot thrive without giving up the easy

---

20 Spivak, "In a Word: Interview," ix.
21 Ibid., 18.
22 Gayatri Chakravorty Spivak, "Acting Bits/Identity Talk." *Critical Inquiry* 18, no. 4, *Identities* (Summer, 1992), 775, http://www.jstor.org/stable/1343830.

suffering in silence or of repeating and, thus, reinforcing disadvantageous discourses that do not reflect her values. Spivak's assessment that there is a lot of work to do applies to librarianship in its position as a female-intensive profession that is becoming increasingly dependent on not only the services, but also the decisions of outside agencies. What kind of action can we take to reassert ourselves? Some of it is simple, for example, constructive complaining: when a time limit is put on answering reference questions; when the public catalog interface presents keyword searching as the default and hides references generated from authority records; when the coverage of a database excludes journals from small, independent publishers and societies; when jobs vacated by librarians are advertised as non-professional and filled accordingly. Other options take back agency rather than just resisting. Librarians can often make adjustments that contextualize their resources and services to fit their communities. There is work to do, but how do we go about it? The concept of an ethic of care originated by Carol Gilligan and reinterpreted by Joan Tronto offers one option.

Ethics of Justice and Care

The ethic of care also has had a fraught relationship with essentialism. Because a care orientation was first described as a feminine trait, the presumption followed that it was an immutable and therefore definitive part of being a woman. It originated in the 1980s as a response to the ascendancy of the purportedly masculine ethic of justice, as imagined first by John Rawls and then Lawrence Kohlberg, which went on to dominate moral philosophy starting in the late 1950s. Generally speaking, applying an ethic of justice to a moral dilemma means that the decision relies on a universal set of principles that govern morality or the domain that the dilemma inhabits. As a normative ethic, the ethic of justice represents a system where majority rules, goods are distributed equally, and all relationships are equally valuable, discounting special relationships such as familial, friendship or collegial. All decisions are based on universal rights and laws rather than the specific situation or other contextual details. Because Rawls's theory of justice was influenced by Kant's Doctrine of Virtue, his theory of morality did not include any sort of emotional consideration. Kohlberg's studies of moral development concluded that moral problem-solving by referring to universal principles, laws, or duty demonstrates attainment of the highest level of moral development,[23] and Kohlberg found that women rarely attained this level of reasoning. Kant's belief that women are not rational beings, consequently making them poor moral agents, trickled down from Rawls to Kohlberg.

---

23 Owen Flanagan and Kathryn Jackson, "Justice, Care, and Gender: The Kohlberg-Gilligan Debate Revisited," *Ethics* 97, no. 3 (1987): 622, doi:10.1086/292870.

Kohlberg's pronounced superiority of the ethic of justice prompted Carol Gilligan to challenge his conclusions.[24] She found that he had used mostly males as his subjects, who most often generated the responses that supported his interpretations. Gilligan, questioning Kohlberg's "universal" conclusions, believed that alternative and equally valid ways of moral problem-solving existed and conducted her own study to dispute what she perceived as the sexism of Kohlberg's study, as well as earlier conceptions of moral development by Freud and Piaget. Gilligan's results showed a different method of moral problem-solving indeed exists, a method that considers context rather than universal rules and values preservation of relationships over preservation of principle. This alternative view, she notes, most often exercised by women, garners little respect by the dominant, male-constructed ethos of justice. As she defines it, women depend on context, thus approaching problem-solving in a different way than the justice-oriented methods described by Kohlberg. Women consider situational factors such as responsibility and personal relationships rather than bowing to the rigidity of rights and universal rules. Gilligan labeled this alternative perspective an "ethic of care." Though her discussion points to male/female alignment with the ethics of justice and care, she later clarified that she believes that they represent two ways of looking at the same thing, rather than a physiological male/female difference; however, the language of her study points to an innate preference toward one or the other that falls along gendered lines. She insists

> . . . *justice and care perspectives are distinct orientations that organize people's thinking about moral problems in different ways; boys and men . . . tend to define and resolve moral problems within the justice framework, although they introduce considerations of care; and the focus on care in moral reasoning, although not characteristic of all women, is characteristically a female phenomenon in the advantaged populations that have been studied.*[25]

Women *characteristically* consider situational factors such as responsibility and personal relationships rather than bowing to the rigidity of rights and universal rules, and men *characteristically* rely on those rules in order to ensure equal treatment. This qualifier attempts to avoid the suggestion of essentialism, yet still hints at a gendered essence. However, Gilligan's addressing the issue of essentialism suggests that she was aware (and if not critics

---

24 Carol Gilligan, *In a Different Voice: Psychological Theory and Women's Development*, (Cambridge, MA: Harvard University Press, 1982).

25 Carol Gilligan, "Forum: Different Voice: Reply by Carol Gilligan," *Signs: Journal of Women in Culture and Society* 11, no. 2 (1986): 330, http://www.jstor.org/stable/3174055.

made her aware) that she was in danger of sliding into essentialism just as Spivak had warned. Gilligan had used the category of "women" strategically and encountered the danger of lingering essentialism.

Since the early 1980s when Gilligan's research took place, it could be argued that women have been employed in decision-making positions long enough to adapt themselves to a male-constructed, justice-oriented management style, yet Gilligan says, "the fact that educated women are capable of high levels of justice reasoning has no bearing on the question of whether they would spontaneously choose to frame moral problems in this way."[26] She also believes that the ethic of care can be learned, yet the suggestion that most women would automatically lean towards a care orientation implies that she believes it is innate.

Both ethical perspectives have earned criticism. Budd rightly says that the "easiest . . . rights and obligations to accept, and the least controversial, are those grounded in law."[27] When faced with a difficult moral decision, referring to a principle requires the least amount of consideration and deliberation. Deference to laws and principles removes responsibility from the decision-maker, making the policy or moral law the basis for the decision. The ethic of justice also has been deemed too one-dimensional to handle the complexity of reality. Gastil blames a "desire for neatness"[28] for the insistence on universality. He suggests the innate messiness of humankind complicates the notion of universal truth. He goes on to accuse Rawls, originator of the theory of justice, of being "more interested in the good society than in personal relationships."[29] The Milgram experiments illustrate an extreme example of the ethic of justice, where the participants disregarded the suffering of their "victims" in order to obey authority. The participant who decided to stop the "shocks" prioritized the relationship between him and the victim over following the commands of the experiment team, thus exercising the ethic of care. On the other hand, the ethic of care has been criticized as too vulnerable to relativism, or of creation of too many sets of different rules for different groups. Also, relationships with close family and friends may supersede care for others.[30] Despite the continued gendering of both ethics,

---

26 Gilligan, *In a Different Voice*, 328.
27 John M. Budd, "Toward a Practical and Normative Ethics for Librarianship," *Library Quarterly* 76, no. 3 (2006): 252, http://www.jstor.org/stable/10.1086/511140.
28 Raymond D. Gastil, "Beyond a Theory of Justice," *Ethics* 85, no. 3 (1975): 185, http://www.jstor.org/stable/2380046
29 Ibid., 187.
30 See Flanagan and Jackson, "Justice, Care, and Gender"; and Joan. C. Tronto, "Beyond Gender Difference: A Theory of Care." *Signs: Journal of Women in Culture and Society* 12, no. 4 (1987).

both Gilligan and Flanagan and Jackson admit that most people, male or female, incorporate both types of ethics into decision-making.[31]

Joan Tronto objects to Gilligan's theory as "dangerous," just as Spivak warned about "the unavoidable usefulness of something [essentialism] that is quite dangerous."[32] Tronto sees the danger in treating the ethic of care as a gendered phenomenon, which has been interpreted as a "difference" that implies subordination, and consequently, inferiority.[33] She examined Gilligan's data, believing that Gilligan found differences in social position rather than gender.[34] Tronto asserts that the innate ethic of care has social, rather than psychological origins. Women and minorities develop the ethic of care because social forces thrust them into caretaking roles. The social rather than physiological origin enables Tronto to endorse revision and development of Gilligan's idea to extend beyond male/female difference to a non-gendered, neutral theory of care that serves as an equally respected alternative, rather than a secondary, subordinate method. Tronto acknowledges many difficulties with the ethic of care, such as definitions of the boundaries of care and the appeal of the universal to help avoid difficult decisions. She believes that the ethic of care can be institutionalized, but only if those institutions can accept and implement a mindset that differs from the predominant viewpoint.

Ethic of Care in the Library

An ethical framework in librarianship rooted in justice is concerned with fair treatment and equitable access. All are treated equally, no matter the situation, but yet an ethic of care seems logical and right, given libraries' social mission. But what would it look like in practice? The characteristics of an ethic of justice in LIS include an emphasis on consistency, universality, and uncompromised commitment to rules and "best practices" developed independent of context or in a different context. Fairness in this context means the same treatment for all users, so the same system provides the same answers. An ethic of care includes willingness to hear another perspective, deeper delving to get at context, and bending of rules to endeavor to satisfy any user's need. Many have acknowledged the theoretical value of the ethic of care, but have dismissed it as unsatisfactory in practice because it is by definition, a contextual morality, not universal or impartial which makes application of it a whole lot of work. It involves "accommodating the needs of the self and

---

31 Gilligan, "Forum: Different Voice"; Flanagan and Jackson, "Justice, Care, and Gender."
32 Spivak, "In a Word: Interview," 5.
33 Tronto, "Beyond Gender Difference," 646–647.
34 Ibid., 649.

of others, of balancing competition and cooperation, and of maintaining the social web of relations in which one finds oneself,"[35] a lot to consider.

How can we apply this in libraries? Many issues can be addressed through the lens of an ethic of care: accommodating the needs of homeless people alongside other users; establishing reference collections that reflect a variety of epistemic perspectives; offering children's programming appropriate for the non-dominant cultures and languages of the community; allocating equitable funding for more recently established collections that are historically under-funded (for example, many area studies collections); valuing grey literature as sometimes the only resources for researching issues of society's margins; maintaining hours and circulation policies that accommodate people working more than one job—all of these concerns can be addressed through an ethic of care by taking care of the users and potential users of a given library's context and thus avoiding the homogenizing tyranny of the mainstream "universal."

Perhaps the greatest challenge is in the organization of information, which is usually performed away from users and far away from those who create and maintain our bibliographic tools. Information organization is held in thrall to bibliographic and authority control, the set of universal rules and regulations to which catalogers and users alike are required to defer in the interests of economy and efficiency.

Gendered or Not?

Librarianship since Dewey has been a female-intensive field; as of March 2011, men constituted roughly 20 percent of ALA membership.[36] So if the ethic of care is innate to women, as Gilligan suggests, why did an ethic of care not develop from the start in information organization? Perhaps it did in other areas, but historically speaking, the origins of our modern idea of bibliographic control and the tools of knowledge organization originated with Bacon, Hegel, Cutter, Dewey, Bliss, Richardson, Ranganathan, et al.—all men. Although Dewey championed women as ideal for librarianship, he considered them "handicapped," for the same reason that Tronto does, that society dictates the role of women. In discussing why women's salaries are lower, he lays blame on "circumstance, not necessarily of sex," yet goes on to say women must accept their lot, unless they are willing to gain the same business training, physical stamina and commitment level as

---

35 Ibid., 658.
36 American Library Association Office for Research & Statistics, *ALA Demographic Studies: March 2011*, p. 2, http://www.ala.org/ala/research/initiatives/membershipsurveys/ALA_Demographic_Studies_March2011.pdf.

men.[37] In other words, in order to be successful, women must become more like men. Even today, men with an MLIS degree still earn 8.3 percent more than women, mainly because they tend to take technology-related, management, or private industry jobs rather than care-oriented, front-line library jobs, an increase from 7.4 percent in 2008.[38] Whether the difference is physiological or merely characteristic, historically the patterns exist. Can librarianship take advantage of its female-intensiveness to assert an ethic of care in our practice? Can we apply that ethic creatively to really serve our communities? Can even library catalogs achieve an ethic of care while still maintaining the consistency that allows works to be accessed? Of course they can, but there is much work to do.

Bibliography

American Library Association Office for Research & Statistics. *ALA Demographic Studies: March 2011.* http://www.ala.org/ala/research/initiatives/membershipsurveys/ALA_Demographic_Studies_March2011.pdf.

Ashcroft, Bill, Gareth Griffiths, and Helen Tiffin. *Key Concepts in Post-Colonial Studies.* London: Routledge, 1998.

Budd, John M. "Toward a Practical and Normative Ethics for Librarianship." *The Library Quarterly* 76, no. 3 (2006): 251-269. http://www.jstor.org/stable/10.1086/511140.

Chow, Rey. "Ethics after Idealism." *diacritics* 223 (1993): 3-22.

Dewey, Melvil. *Dewey Decimal Classification and Relative Index.* 22nd ed. Dublin, OH: OCLC, 2003.

———. "Women in Libraries: How They Are Handicapped." *Library Notes* 1 (1886): 89-90.

Flanagan, Owen, and Kathryn Jackson. "Justice, Care, and Gender: The Kohlberg-Gilligan Debate Revisited." *Ethics* 97, no. 3 (1987): 622-637. doi:10.1086/292870.

Flew, Anthony. *A Dictionary of Philosophy.* 2nd rev. ed. New York: Gramercy, 1979.

Fuss, Diana. *Essentially Speaking: Feminism, Nature, and Difference.* New York: Routledge, 1989.

---

37 Melvil Dewey, "Women in Libraries: How They are Handicapped," *Library Notes* 1 (1886): 90.

38 Stephanie Maata, "Placements & Salaries Survey 2010: Growing Equity Gap," *Library Journal*, October 15, 2010, http://www.libraryjournal.com/lj/careers/salaries/887204-305/placements_salaries_survey_2010.html.csp.

Gastil, Raymond D. "Beyond a Theory of Justice." *Ethics* 85, no. 3 (1975): 183-194. http://www.jstor.org/stable/2380046.

Gilligan, Carol. "Forum: Different Voice: Reply by Carol Gilligan." *Signs: Journal of Women in Culture and Society* 11, no. 2 (1986): 324-333. http://www.jstor.org/stable/3174055.

———. *In a Different Voice: Psychological Theory and Women's Development.* Cambridge, MA: Harvard University Press, 1982.

Grosz, Elizabeth. "Sexual Difference and the Problem of Essentialism." In *The Essential Difference*, edited by Naomi Schor and Elizabeth Weed, 82-97. Bloomington: Indiana University Press, 1994.

Loux, Michael. "Kinds and Predications: An Examination of Aristotle's Theory of Categories." *Philosophical Papers* 26, no. 1 (1997): 3-28. doi:10.1080/05568649709506554.

Maata, Stephanie. "Placements & Salaries Survey 2010: Growing Equity Gap." *Library Journal*, October 15, 2010. http://www.libraryjournal.com/lj/careers/salaries/887204-305/placements_salaries_survey_2010.html.csp.

Spivak, Gayatri Chakravorty. "Acting Bits/Identity Talk." *Critical Inquiry* 18, no. 4, *Identities* (Summer, 1992), pp. 770-803. http://www.jstor.org/stable/1343830.

———. "Criticism, Feminism, and the Institution [an interview by Elizabeth Grosz]." 1984. In *The Post-Colonial Critic: Interviews, Strategies, Dialogues*, 1-17. New York: Routledge, 1990.

———. "Feminism and Critical Theory." 1985. In *The Spivak Reader*, 53-74. New York: Routledge, 1996.

———. "In a Word: Interview." By Ellen Rooney. 1989. In *Outside in the Teaching Machine*, 1-23. New York: Routledge, 1993.

———. "Interview with Gayatri Chakravorty Spivak." By Sara Danius and Stefan Jonsson. *Boundary 2* 20, no. 2 (1993): 24-50.

Tronto, Joan. C. "Beyond Gender Difference: A Theory of Care." *Signs: Journal of Women in Culture and Society* 12, no. 4 (1987): 644-663.

———. *Moral Boundaries: A Political Argument for an Ethic of Care.* New York: Routledge, 1993.

Reflections on Meaning in Library and Information Studies:
A Personal Odyssey through Information, Sexuality, and Gender

Alvin M. Schrader

My contribution to this book's framework of interrogation of gender, sexuality, and information attempts to capture the highlights of my personal journey in finding meaning in the broad, applied disciplinary domain of library and information studies encompassing both research and practice dimensions. These dimensions, research and practice, often seem more like divergent forks in thought and doing than merging streams. With some decidedly idiosyncratic elements, as any autobiographical account must be, the approach I try to portray here is emphatically not a template for others but merely indicative of one pathway of reflection. The measure of its value cannot be right or wrong, only whether it is heuristically fruitful. I leave that appraisal of robustness to readers.

My autobiographical borrowing of the grand metaphor "odyssey" may appear disproportionate or excessive, but I adopt it in the more modest sense of reflections on a long, uneven, and eventually emergent journey of cerebral scholarly travels, philosophical explorations, and emotional catharsis—though no less absorbing for me personally than Homer's tale. Other contributors to this volume can write more cogently about particular theories and epistemologies, in particular, perhaps, about deconstructionist approaches to sexual and gender identity and their regulation through state and institutional discourses and discursive practices, together with the insidious and subtle construction of heterosexual hegemonies.

Principles, Essences, and Influences

My approach has been grounded in and motivated by a lifelong search for core organizing principles and foundational essences, and a parallel questioning of the formative influences on my own values and beliefs. The challenge of critical engagement with ideas in order to articulate a coherent approach has involved searching and exploring—problematizing just about everything at one point or another, particularly dominant cultures, beliefs, and value systems. But infinite regress invites despair if not madness; conjectures, assumptions, and principles must be explicated for oneself and shared with others.

Formative influences and deep experiences are multi-layered and multi-faceted, fluid and in flux, and intermingling. Foremost among my own is my upbringing as a farm boy from central Alberta (Canada), raised with deep roots in nature, hard work and struggle, social justice and service to others, compassion for the marginalized and victimized, independence, freedom of expression, choice, and the power of education.

My interest in freedom of expression goes back to high school, where I learned about sexism and misogyny (watch the television series *Mad Men* to understand the culture in which I grew up); when racism, assorted other ethnic prejudices, and religious hatreds were ubiquitous; and when same-sex relationships were criminalized in almost every country in the world. I learned about unspeakable injustice everywhere over millennia, and in my own time, too. My high school principal vetoed as too controversial, and possibly anti-American, the cover sketch of our student newspaper depicting food, housing, education, health care, welfare support, and other social needs burning up in the fiery thrust of an ascending rocket. Perhaps the artwork was too crude.

But another layering was even more formative, and it does not make an appearance in traditional *CVs*, conference bios, or speaker introductions. What is not generally known about me is that I was born a criminal, and I remained a criminal for the first twenty-five years of my life. During that dark time, private parties of gay men and lesbians were dangerous and illegal, as were the possession of homosexually themed materials sent through the postal service; even more sinister was Canada's McCarthy-esque—but infinitely more secretive—campaign of police surveillance, intimidation, blackmail, entrapment, and otherwise systemic repression against (perceived) gay men and lesbians as national security risks, a campaign that included "fruit machine" research into ways of "detecting" homosexuals.[1]

---

1   Gary Kinsman and Patrizia Gentile, *The Canadian War on Queers: National Security as Sexual Regulation*, (Vancouver: UBC, 2010).

The state and its institutions had declared their hatred of me, had turned me into a fugitive, and I returned the favour, finding it even now difficult to set aside suspicion of society at large, police and politicians, chambers of commerce, and big media—not to mention, to be patient enough to temper my contempt for homophobic demagogues and polemicists of all religious and cultural persuasions.

And then it was another thirty-six years of outlaw existence before I became a full citizen of the country in which I was born and raised, with all of the rights and responsibilities of citizenship—if not always with all of the dignity and respect that it normally confers. I refer to two milestone events in the laws of Canada: the federal decriminalization of same-sex adult relationships in 1969; and the federal adoption of marriage equality in 2005. Along the way there were incremental, but piecemeal and hodgepodge, steps adopted at various governmental levels to prevent one form or another of sexual minority discrimination.

A third but broader milestone event should be recognized, the passage of the *Canadian Charter of Rights and Freedoms* in 1982, with its equality rights provisions (Section 15) coming into force three years later. Although many did not recognize it at the time, the *Canadian Charter* has come to have a profound impact on the rights and freedoms of sexual and gender minority Canadians. It is most unlikely that federal marriage equality in 2005 would have happened without the *Charter*'s foundational guiding principles.

It is also most unlikely that, without the pressure of court cases beginning to test the equality provisions of the *Canadian Charter*, another landmark would have occurred: the Canadian military's decision in 1992 to end its longstanding policy of barring gays and lesbians from the armed forces of Canada.[2] As an aside, a Canadian refugee board was recently ordered by the Federal Court to consider "Don't Ask, Don't Tell" in a US army deserter's application for refugee status in Canada.[3]

Even now, however, while I no longer feel like an outlaw, and while legally sanctioned discrimination abates domestically in my own country (with the important exception of the trans-identified communities), I am still humiliated every time I cross the border into the United States where I must present myself as a single traveller; and until 2003 I could not engage in "sodomy" in many American states without risk of arrest and public humiliation. Travelling to more than 80 other countries in the world is fraught with danger and, in far too many places, state-sanctioned violence, incarceration, and murder.

---

[2] Clyde H. Farnsworth, "Canada Ending Anti-Gay Army Rules," *New York Times*, October 11, 1991, http://www.nytimes.com/1991/10/11/world/canada-ending-anti-gay-army-rules.html.

[3] Ian Austin, "Canada: Court Orders Refugee Board To Consider 'Don't Ask, Don't Tell' in Army Deserter's Case," *New York Times*, November 21, 2009, A6.

And though legal sanction has taken great strides domestically, the scourge of public stigma will not allow me any time soon to walk hand in hand with a partner on the street, to kiss in a theater unless it were very dark, to lay side by side with bodies touching at the beach, to close-dance with a partner, or to embrace in front of other people's children—all widely accepted gestures of affection and love taken as "normal" within the dominant social norm of heteronormativity. As far as I know, *The New York Times* is still the only major US newspaper to regularly publish same-sex marriage and civil union announcements, even after almost a decade; *The Times* announced in August 2002 it would begin reporting gay couples' ceremonies, and did so the following month.[4]

Persistent social taboo around sexual and gender minorities makes it imperative to be cautious and wary with a partner in almost every conceivable public space in Canada—not to mention in the United States and even more so in the rest of the world. So although I am no longer criminalized and outlawed at home, I am still a social outcast, not of equal value in the eyes of many other Canadians. That reality compels every coming out, inevitable each time one meets someone new or decides to level with somebody they already know, to be approached as an act strained by uncertainty, risk, and even fear. The recent increase in media and public attention to suicide by gay teenagers due to bullying in the United States and Canada underscores the urgency of cause for alarm. And yet at the same time, prominent companies and religious groups are taking public stands in increasing numbers each and every day in both of our countries in support of the rights of sexual and gender minorities—lesbian, gay, bisexual, trans-gender, trans-identified, intersex, two-spirit, queer, and questioning (LGBTQ) citizens. To even list all of these businesses and faith organizations would fill a Manhattan phone book.

Nonetheless, homophobic actions and comments are ubiquitous, both locally and at the highest levels of political rhetoric and fearmongering, particularly in the United States. Social understanding and acceptance of sexual and gender minority communities are the next frontier awaiting critique and challenge, tied as they are to pervasive and often virulent misogyny that normalizes heterosexual dominance and male power and privilege in every important sphere of human behavior—in politics, government, the medical profession, hospitals, economics, religion, the media, and culture at large.

The real battle still to be broached today, however, is in our public schools and on the playgrounds, where glimpses of light are few in number. Legislation passed in California in 2011 to take effect by the 2013–2014 school year represents a landmark in this

---

4   "Times Will Begin Reporting Gay Couples' Ceremonies," *New York Times,* August 18, 2002, http://www.nytimes.com/2002/08/18/us/times-will-begin-reporting-gay-couples-ceremonies.html.

movement.[5] It is the first state in the country to add lessons about gays and lesbians to social studies classes in public schools and to ensure that textbooks and instructional materials used in public schools include the contributions and roles of sexual minorities.

Some incremental progress is being made in Canada. Most notably, a movement towards developing LGBTQ-inclusive school board policy has taken a strong hold in the province of British Columbia, and has even expanded to neighbouring Alberta. Efforts to ensure that the provincial curriculum is also inclusive of sexual minorities has been most directly evidenced in Ontario, Saskatchewan, and British Columbia. However, the Canadian Council of Ministers, which is the national voice for Canada's provincial ministers of education, has remained completely silent on the plight of sexual minorities in education.

This silence is all the more perplexing given the results of Egale Canada's recent national safe schools climate survey of 3,700 students across the country conducted between December 2007 and June 2009, which revealed that sexual and gender minorities are amongst the most at-risk groups of students in our schools today.[6]

In this context, I feel blessed to live in the City of Edmonton (Canada) with a resolutely gay-positive mayor. Since 2006, Mayor Stephen Mandel has held the Mayor's Pride Brunch, an annual fundraiser to support Camp fYrefly, a leadership camp for LGBTQ youth that was started two years earlier by Andre Grace and Kris Wells at the University of Alberta. He courageously declared at his second Brunch: "The health of the LGBTQ community is a barometer of the entire community."[7]

Many LGBTQ young people do not have support at home or at school, and certainly not at faith centers. Sexual and gender minority youth in suburban and rural areas are at even greater risk. Someone recently observed that being LGBTQ means growing up in a family that is not of the same minority.

Where can these young people turn for support, for safe space, for information, for materials that speak to their lives, for confidential access to materials through properly assigned subject headings, and for confidential

---

5   Judy Lin, "California Gay History Law: Jerry Brown Signs Landmark Bill," *Huffington Post*, July 14, 2011. http://www.huffingtonpost.com/2011/07/14/california-gay-history-law-jerry-brown_n_898745.html.

6   Catherine Taylor et al., *Every Class in Every School: The First National Climate Survey on Homophobia, Biphobia, and Transphobia in Canadian Schools. Final Report*, (Toronto: Egale Canada Human Rights Trust, 2011), http://egale.ca/wp-content/uploads/2011/05/EgaleFinalReport-web.pdf.

7   Stephen Mandel, "Remarks at the Mayor's Pride Brunch in Support of Camp fYrefly," (speech, Edmonton, Alberta, Canada, 2007).

reference service in answer to their questions? Many of them have nowhere else to go.

Librarians can play a critical role in LGBTQ-positive services and collections as part of their umbrella commitment to diversity. They can create safe places for diversity. They can turn pain into opportunity, tolerance into celebration and optimism. One excellent documentary guide for librarians was produced by Lynne Barnes.[8]

There are innumerable testimonies to the power of a positive role for librarians and libraries, but one example will suffice. At the 2007 Stonewall Book Awards, sponsored since 1971 by the American Library Association's Gay, Lesbian, Bisexual, and Transgendered Round Table, award winner Alison Bechdel (*Fun Home: A Family Tragicomic*) told us: "Libraries are so often how we learn about who we are, not family, etc." As a young teen, her feelings took her "to the symbolic world of language" in the library, and that in turn sent her back to feelings, and to people; and again to more books. She said it was a life-altering experience to learn of the category "lesbian," and then to discover that it was also a library subject heading! "We will never know," she said, "how many have found validation on the shelves of libraries and in LCSH [Library of Congress Subject Headings]."[9]

At the same time, many other library users have experienced indifference, silence, and even outright hostility by library staff. So what message are we giving to teenagers, children, their families, and friends, if we leave the life experiences of sexual minority youth *out* of our library collections and our services in schools and school libraries, public libraries, and the libraries of post-secondary institutions?

It is not that stereotypes are bad because they are false, it is because they are incomplete, taking instances for the whole. They under-represent human reality and reduce our collective complexity to simple-minded dichotomies.

Focus of Research, Teaching, Service, and Activism

The focus of my research, teaching, service, and advocacy in the broad domain of library and information studies has been asking questions and thinking critically about our disciplinary and professional identities. What is the nature of library and information studies positioned as a discipline

---

8 Lynne Barnes, *Reaching Out: Library Services for Lesbian, Gay, Bisexual, Transgender, and Questioning Youth*, (San Francisco: Friends of The San Francisco Public Library, 2004) DVD.

9 Alvin M. Schrader, "Challenging Silence, Challenging Censorship, Building Resilience: LGBTQ Services and Collections in Public, School and Post-Secondary Libraries," *Feliciter* 55, no. 3 (2009): 107–8, http://www.cla.ca/Content/NavigationMenu/Resources/Feliciter/PastIssues/2009/Vol55No3/.

versus as an occupational practice? What good do either the discipline or the practice do? How do we define and describe their respective disciplinary and professional identities? And how do we name them? What are the dominant values of each? What competencies and educational programs do we need for the professional practitioner? What is their public image? What principles should guide service delivery?

Core Concepts, Values, and Passions

At the heart of these principles of practice are several core values and passions: service to others, access as core function, recorded culture as the core domain, freedom of expression and human rights, language and naming and cultural construction, indexing and classification, and the power of the arts and literature. Informing all of these must be practice grounded in research of all kinds.

A Human and Social Enterprise

Foremost is a recognition of librarianship as a human and social enterprise grounded in the disciplinary base of library and information studies. Douglas Waples declared more than seventy-five years ago, "I take it no one has to argue any longer the fact that librarianship *is* primarily a social enterprise."[10]

Research-based Professional Practice

From my earliest days as a skeptic, I looked for evidence as the basis of beliefs, so it was serendipitous that I took several graduate courses in my Master of Library Science program at the University of Toronto from Professor Lloyd Houser, who decried the administrative mindset of practicing librarians. The monograph I co-wrote with him argued for the pursuit of a "scientific profession" and a research-based educational curriculum, as any graduate program should be.[11] We were motivated by impatience with 20th century reliance in both librarianship and its educational programs on tradition, authority, and relentless operational and managerial pragmatism, and our work was greeted with considerable controversy, assorted false charges of positivism and exaggeration, and even anger.

Today, almost thirty-five years later, research-based education and professional practice have become more prominent, but more emphasis in both on research is urgently needed. Echoing our stance, Stephen Abram recently

---

10 Emphasis in original; Douglas Waples, "The Graduate Library School at Chicago," *Library Quarterly* 1, no. 1 (1931): 30, http://www.jstor.org/stable/40039627.

11 L. Houser and Alvin M. Schrader, *The Search for a Scientific Profession: Library Science Education in the U.S. and Canada* (Metuchen, NJ: Scarecrow, 1978).

spoke in support of more user research: "You can't serve well what you don't understand."[12]

My own research has involved not only empirical work but also philosophical, theoretical, and historical modes of inquiry: logical and conceptual (definitional) analysis, bibliometrics, surveys, and interviews, and involving, variously, philosophical and historical analysis, conceptual and discourse analysis, qualitative analysis, and quantitative statistical analysis.

Recorded Culture as the Inclusive Domain of Professional Practice

Growing out of my own doctoral work, which analyzed disciplinary definitions of library science, information science, and their semantic relatives, was a broad conception of recorded materiality as the proper domain of professional practice, encompassing all symbolic records, all recorded discourses, all recorded forms of expressive communication, including fiction, the visual, puzzles and cartoons, and the barely factual—that is, beyond "information." Information as an organizing construct takes no account of disinformation, misinformation, lies, and other forms of human misanthropy; and it did not prevent 9/11 nor does it explain misogyny, homophobia, the disingenuous and fraudulent invasion of Iraq, Fox News watchers, or a myriad of other phenomena where ideology and culture trump mere information.

The reality that information is value-laden seems unacknowledged by advocates of the construct. Experience is also value-laden. Jeffrey Feldman has written about the central role in the human mind of "deep frames," encompassing one's moral worldview, core values, and underlying principles.[13] Framing is dedicated "to morality and truth: to communicating your values and principles and to framing facts as having a moral value and, often, an ethical imperative."[14]

The construct of "information" is severely reductionistic. But "information behavior," abbreviated from information seeking behaviour, explains even less and claims too much. Information and information behaviour do not make clear why people with the same information are regularly at great

---

12   Stephen Abram, "Worry: Part 1," 2006; reprinted *Sirsidynix Onesource*, 2 no. 2, (August 24, 2011): 4, http://www.imakenews.com/sirsi/e_article000523948.cfm?x=b11,0,w.

13   Jeffrey Feldman, *Framing the Debate: Famous Presidential Speeches and How Progressives Can Use Them to Change the Conversation (and Win Elections)* (Brooklyn: Ig, 2007).

14   George Lakoff, "Introduction: Framing Is About Ideas, and Ideas Matter," Introduction to *Framing the Debate: Famous Presidential Speeches and How Progressives Can Use Them To Change the Conversation (and Win Elections)*, by Jeffrey Feldman (Brooklyn: Ig, 2007), xi-xiii.

variance in how to interpret it and what it means. This is because information is itself constructed and processed within the far greater, all-encompassing umbrella of social context, which comprises every dimension of being human, alone and in the emergent complexity of relationships through time present, past, and future. Information is processed through a myriad of cultural lenses grounded in each human being's confluence of values, norms, beliefs, attitudes, and behaviors, compounded at every turn by their own individuality in values, norms, beliefs, attitudes, and behaviors. Cognitive linguistics scholar George Lakoff has argued that thinking is done unconsciously, with equally unconscious emotional and physiological responses, and the rational brain is the last to act on information.[15] Rachel Maddow put it more simply: "In a fight between fear and facts, fear will win."[16]

This interplay extends to and is illustrated by the world of reading and what reading means. Alberto Manguel explained the essential nature of reading as the relationship between reader and information:

> *The power of readers lies not in their ability to gather information, in their ordering and cataloguing capability, but in their gift to interpret, associate and transform their reading. . . . [K]nowledge lies not in the accumulation of texts or information, nor in the object of the book itself, but in the experience rescued from the page and transformed again into experience, in the words reflected both in the outside world and in the reader's own being.*[17]

At a broader level, the weakness of the information construct is underlined by waning use of the phrase "information society" and a concomitant turning to "knowledge society"—though this may well be abandoned in another decade or so in favour of something else again. "Information professional" could face the same fate. Whether "information science" will survive as a distinct and broader discipline divorced from librarianship, library science, and even library and information studies, remains to be seen.

It is important to recognize the inability of this triad of constructs—information behavior, information society, and information science—to explain satisfactorily what librarians do and to encompass the entire range of resources with which they perform their functions. These constructs ignore large parts of the reality that make up the domain of librarianship, for example, the entire realm of fiction in all formats and genres and entertainment in the forms of music, movies, and games.

---

15 David Moscrop, "Media's Language Stokes Culture of Fear," *Edmonton Journal*, August 12, 2011, A18.
16 Rachel Maddow, *The Rachel Maddow Show*, MSNBC, February 3, 2010.
17 Alberto Manguel, *The Library at Night* (Toronto: Knopf, 2006), 91.

The fundamental inadequacy of information constructs as explanatory principles is underscored by the equally fundamental absence of common definitions of meaning. Advocates for them frequently reveal ideology and emotion instead of critical engagement with ideas, eschewing the demands of thoroughly rigorous logical analysis.[18]

One of the crucial omissions from the information construct is the phenomenon of reading; information scholar-advocates have ignored it almost entirely. A closely related exclusion is the nature of the book, frequently undergirded by a deliberate ideology espoused by some graduate school professors: "If you are entering the profession, because you are inspired by a love of books, you are entering the wrong profession." There is an irony here in that great attention is often paid by these critics to the (sub-) discipline of human-computer interactions, with its own established acronym "HCI."

Of one thing I am confident: "Librarian" will endure because the term enjoys broad recognition in the world (even if not always a positive image), and "library" is a widely recognized "brand." Every other neologism has failed because of conceptual inadequacy, resulting in ubiquitous confusion among user communities and the public at large.[19]

Perhaps my prediction comes from an appreciation that librarians apprehend their role as encompassing much more complexity than the label "information" connotes. Lines from T.S. Eliot's famous poem "Choruses from 'The Rock'" come to mind:

> *Where is the wisdom we have lost in knowledge?*
> *Where is the knowledge we have lost in information?*[20]

The Construct of Unfettered Access Grounded in Freedom of Expression and Human Rights

Whoever, or whatever, controls the power to name controls the discursive practices of society and the voices that are allowed to be heard in the public domain. The principles of unfettered access to all recorded culture lead directly to a focus on the central role of human rights and freedom of expression in the work and value system of librarians. The profession requires a

---

18 Alvin M. Schrader, "Toward a Theory of Library and Information Science," (PhD diss., Indiana University–Bloomington, 1983); Alvin M. Schrader, "One Field or Two? A Definitional Analysis of the Relationship between Library Science and Information Science," 1995, ERIC ED 401908, December 1996, http://www.eric.ed.gov/ERICWebPortal/contentdelivery/servlet/ERICServlet?accno=ED401908.
19 Ibid.
20 T. S. Eliot, "Choruses from 'The Rock,'" in *Selected Poems* (London: Faber and Faber, 1954), 107.

human rights framework to function effectively for the common good. The profession also requires democratic forms of government to be truly effective.

Key implications of free speech rights are a belief in the general intelligence of people, and in the responsibility of every individual for their own access decisions and the consequences. In his inaugural address at the 2008 annual conference of CLA, incoming president Ken Roberts said:

> *We are one of the few professions whose professional values help to define exactly who we are and—by extension—why we must continue to exist and to thrive.*
>
> *We are the only profession whose value to society resides in a faith that people have the ability to make personal decisions that are good for them when—and if—they also have free and open access to all of the information that they might need.*[21]

Delegation of this responsibility to anyone else—or any "thing" else such as Internet filtering software or a movie rating system—is theoretically and morally impossible. It is recognized that children need "age-appropriate" access guidance, but beyond that, everyone—and especially teenagers—should have the widest possible access to knowledge and to sources of knowledge. Age of consent laws are deeply flawed and inconsistent both within and among nations—in one Canadian province the drinking age is 18 and in another 19, while in much of the United States it is 21.

In *Areopagitica* John Milton expressed the imperative of individual autonomy when he wrote:

> *And who shall silence all the airs and madrigals that whisper softness in chambers?*[22]

Perhaps more eloquently expressed, but his question echoed Roman poet Juvenal some fifteen hundred years earlier: "But who will guard the guardians themselves?"[23] Variant translations include: "Who watches the watchmen?" and, "Who guards the guards?"

At the same time, many fundamental questions are raised. In an age of postmodernist relativism, is it possible to argue for universal secular values?

---

21 Ken Roberts, "Keeping True to the Faith: Inaugural Address," *Feliciter* 54, no. 4 (2008): 144, http://www.cla.ca/AM/Template.cfm?Section=Vol_54_No_4&Template=/CM/HTMLDisplay.cfm&ContentID=8264.

22 John Milton, *Areopagitica: A Speech for the Liberty of Unlicensed Printing to the Parliament of England*, 1644, available from *Project Gutenberg*, 2006, http://www.gutenberg.org/files/608/608-h/608-h.htm.

23 Juvenal, *The Satires*, VI, line 347, ca 1st-2nd century CE, http://en.wikiquote.org/wiki/Juvenal.

Universal principles of law? Universal rights of children? Are the rights of the individual the only measure of a just society? What is the balance between individual rights and collective rights? Can multiculturalist discourse about the equality of cultures, with its oversimplification of identity and power, be reconciled with universal values? Can freedom be reconciled with security? Can freedom be reconciled with incitement to violence or genocide?

Here I must recognize my own cultural context. I am the cultural product of Canada and Canadian values, foremost among which is a deep belief in universal values; and indeed, fellow Canadian John Peters Humphrey was a prime architect of the Universal Declaration of Human Rights. To mark the 25th anniversary of Canada's Freedom to Read Week in 2009, which is sponsored by a myriad of free speech allies under the auspices of the Book and Periodical Council [Canada], some 25 individuals in the arts, sciences and other endeavours were invited to articulate for the annual magazine *Freedom to Read* what freedom of expression and freedom to read meant to them. I was fortunate to be among them:

> *While there is wide room for disagreement among Canadians about which values should be taken as universal, the categorical imperative for me is freedom of expression—that all voices should be heard; that silence is not golden and eliminating people does not eliminate ideas or truth; that communication with enemies and opponents is superior to killing them; that tolerance and generosity and choice are more powerful than torture and genocide; that violence is the antithesis of intellectual freedom; that the first casualty of war and murder is human freedom in all of its manifestations.*[24]

While self-serving and self-perpetuating authoritarian regimes around the world demonize as alien the values of social democracy and social justice because they appear to be Western in origin, most of them are nevertheless signatories to many international agreements such as the United Nations Universal Declaration of Human Rights and the United Nations Convention on the Rights of the Child. It is easy to dismiss the puerile arguments of deluded demagogues with their infinite capacity for brutality instead of empathy. What is more challenging is to reconcile and resolve the underlying tensions between freedom of expression and diversity, between universal values and cultural difference.

Implicit in this scaffolding of human rights for professional practice is a much greater need for professional knowledge of the relationship between expressive communication and the law and legal principles, and between expressive communication and economics. How does the law control the

---

24 Alvin M. Schrader, "Freedom of Expression and Freedom to Read," *Freedom to Read 2009*, 25 (2008), 8, http://issuu.com/thebpc/docs/kit2009.

circulation of cultural productions? When does creativity become criminal? When does creativity become obscenity? How does the law deal with cultural productions depicting violence, hate, and treason? And at the broader level of legal concepts, when a right is granted, does it also grant the rights essential to the exercise of that right? Without a right to receive information, is the right to free speech meaningless? And what are reasonable and justifiable limitations on freedom of expression in a democratic society?

We also need to do a better job of linking librarianship and human rights, as well as making stronger connections with human rights organizations whose mandates are like-minded. In this regard, the American Library Association is far ahead of other national library associations, but much leaves to be desired even in the United States at other levels of jurisdiction.

Deeper understanding of the economics of expressive communication is equally vital. What is the interplay between the cultural values of art, literature, and knowledge and the production, distribution, and "consumption" of the products and services that convey them to us? What balance should be sought between market forces and the public good? Between media monopoly and cultural diversity? Between competition and sharing? What social, legal, and regulatory policies should govern rival emerging media? The paucity of graduate courses for librarians in publishing, as well as in the history of the book and libraries, leaves the profession naive and uninformed about the broader contexts within which they serve their communities. At the very least, the profession is burdened with a legacy of ahistoricity, reductionist understandings of political economy, and blinkered visions of power relations. An example is the unthinking—some might say reckless, or even negligent—embrace of new digital technologies and the concomitant abandonment as well as the wholesale disposal of print, much as earlier librarians adopted successive iterations of microprint and threw out the paper originals; a corollary is the economic and accounting question as to what "asset" libraries acquire and own with their millions of dollars "invested" in digital subscriptions, particularly in the case of serials.

Culture, Language, Naming, Values, and Structures of Power

My approach to analysis in all areas of my research is to start always with language and naming. How is language constructed and used within cultures and across cultures, and how is it employed within structures of power and control? Language is never neutral: Who gets to name? Whose voices get to be heard in the public forum? Every naming, every representation of every idea, occurs within a culture. In this position I have been greatly inspired and guided by Stephen Toulmin:

Each of us thinks his own thoughts; our concepts we share with our fellow-men. For what we believe we are answerable as individuals; but the language in which our beliefs are articulated is public property.[25]

Words represent values, power, and social structures. Every word is a window into culture and identity. Every term is culturally constructed and constrained. But as Kathleen Parker observed, while language is limited, it is not meaningless: "The words we use to define and express ourselves are the foundations of cultural and social identity. John Stuart Mill put it this way: 'Language is the light of the mind.'"[26] And because these words—in their broadest form, writing—are public, the writing of words is a form of politics.

Multiple overlapping discourse communities—"publics and counterpublics" as characterized by discursive acts—illustrate the political nature of writing.[27] Counterpublics compete not just for attention but for social transformation; their tensions and clashes with the dominant cultural horizon always embody an awareness of subordinate status. In challenging social power and pursuing hierarchical transformation, counterpublics necessarily enter "the temporality of politics."[28]

Thus there is power in names and in naming. Words are power, because of their potential to persuade, to elicit, to influence, to evoke, to convince, to inspire, to encourage, and to affect in every other way the affective impulse in every human thought. At their worst, the power of words is used to manipulate, to control—to manufacture consent, in the title phrasing of Herman and Chomsky's most popular work.[29]

We must recognize that there is always a viewpoint, always a complex intermingling of collective and individual influences, always value-laden, and always limited. As Ludwig Wittgenstein wrote: "The limits of my language are the limits of my world."[30] And bell hooks has pointed out that there is no such thing as politically neutral

---

25 Emphasis in original; Stephen Toulmin, *Human Understanding: The Collective Use and Evolution of Concepts* (Princeton, NJ: Princeton University Press, 1972), 35.
26 Kathleen Parker, "Language Isn't Meaningless," *National Post*, August 23, 2007, A13.
27 Michael Warner, *Publics and Counterpublics* (Brooklyn: Zone, 2002).
28 Ibid, 124.
29 Edward S. Herman and Noam Chomsky, *Manufacturing Consent: The Political Economy of the Mass Media* (New York: Pantheon, 1988).
30 Ludwig Wittgenstein, *Tractatus logico-philosophicus*, (New York: Harcourt, Brace, 1922), 149; see also *Grand Strategy: The View from Oregon*, June 3, 2011, http://geopolicraticus.wordpress.com/2011/06/03/the-limits-of-my-language-are-the-limits-of-my-world/.

education;[31] elsewhere, she has argued, "There is no politically neutral intellectual work."[32]

Language, Naming, Categorizing, Indexing, and Classification

Every naming is in essence an act of categorizing, because it implies, and introduces corollary categories—if only, "not-this." Alberto Manguel has pointed out that "order begets order. Once a category is established, it suggests or imposes others, so that no cataloguing method, whether on shelf or on paper, is ever closed unto itself."[33]

There are innumerable examples of cultural constructions (and reconstructions) with which librarians are familiar through their services and collections: maps, calendars, colors, etiquette—especially eating habits and manners—, morality and immorality, mental disorders, gender, religions, "Western" values, economic value and gross national product, and book shelving arrangements in libraries.[34]

Of keen interest to our profession are library classification systems, disciplinary systems, Internet filtering and filtering categories, movie classification and rating systems, the V-chip for television, viewer advisories and warnings, parental advisories for rap music, and labelling systems for other media—including books!

The chapter headings in Alberto Manguel's 2006 book *The Library at Night* illustrate one way of constructing the many facets of 'library' as he perceives it: as myth, order, space, power, showdown, shape, chance, workshop, mind, island, survival, oblivion, imagination, identity, and home.[35]

Cultural Constructions of the Dominant

The confluence of politics and rhetoric gives rise to a never-ending cacophony of culturally determined namings that maintain and advance dominant value systems and social perspectives. Real power, to paraphrase John Ralston Saul, sits in the dominant structures of society, not in individuals.[36]

To suggest but a few namings that serve particular cultural and political agendas, either by vilifying or glorifying: "community standards," "family

---

31 bell hooks, *Outlaw Culture: Resisting Representations* (New York: Routledge, 1994), 4.
32 bell hooks, *Killing Rage; Ending Racism* (New York: Henry Holt, 1995) 239.
33 Manguel, *Library at Night*, 39.
34 Marilyn Waring, *Counting for Nothing: What Men Value and What Women Are Worth*, 2nd ed. (Toronto: University of Toronto Press, 1999).
35 Manguel, *Library at Night*.
36 Mark Abley, "Saul Searching," *Edmonton Journal*, June 22, 1997, F5.

values," "welfare babies," "special rights," "homosexual agenda," "homosexual lifestyle," "aliens," "left-wing media," globalization, the free market as freedom and consumer rights as human rights, terrorism, age of consent and "harmful to minors," age appropriate, offensive language, obscenity, pornography, undue exploitation of sex, media desensitization, or, for that matter, postmodernism. The cognitive models theory describes such social stereotypes as cases of metonymy, "where a subcategory has a socially recognized status as standing for the category as a whole, usually for the purpose of making quick judgments about people," defining dominant cultural ("normal") expectations, and drawing inferences.[37]

The preceding examples illustrate how terms—namings—represent values within culture and therefore privilege the exercise of power over it. Whether such nebulous catchall namings, such meanings, "mean" anything is irrelevant to their perpetrators. These terms are designed to ensnare, contain, marginalize, and silence those who offend the structures of power. These terms are deliberate strategies of naming by dominant groups to impose norms, values, expectations, and boundaries on all members of society. They are strategies of power and control over difference.

Some of these terms are coded language insinuating but never revealing deep motivations such as racism, ethnic hatred, misogyny, homophobia, religious prejudice, or any of a myriad of other attributes perceived to be inferior, to be the "Other." These terms ridicule, stigmatize, and stereotype. They serve to marginalize non-conforming identities and behaviors. They enable social exclusion, and in some social realms even criminalization of the Other.

Stereotypes are not wrong because they are inaccurate but because they are incomplete. That is the malice of linguistic binaries, particularly when political rhetoric becomes propaganda and brainwashing. "The homosexual agenda" and "the war on drugs" are examples of such linguistic politics.

Power and Fear of the Arts and Literature

Literature and other arts are so deeply contested because they are beyond the control and the power of dominant ideologies and identities. What is the nature of art and the imperative of artists? To speak truth to power? To unmask humanity? To make people feel good? To entertain them? To educate? To enlighten?

A primary threat of the arts and literature is a fear of empathy beyond dominant cultural constructions. In its most exaggerated form, this empathy overwhelms the (unexamined) self and an unstable sense of personal responsibility to consume the reader, viewer, or listener until she or he

---

[37] George Lakoff, *Women, Fire, and Dangerous Things: What Categories Reveal about the Mind* (Chicago: University of Chicago Press, 1987), 79.

becomes what was feared—the reader turns gay or transitions genders; the movie viewer commits murder; the CD listener becomes a satanist. Causality is assumed to be a simple linear pathway, such as the gradual social disintegration of the protagonist in Gustave Flaubert's *Madame Bovary*; Skip Wilson's famous quip said it best: "The devil made me do it!" It is the presumed power of desensitization in action. For Madame Bovary, it was romance literature.

Beyond the fictions perpetuated by fear of empathy are the alarmist claims about the dire social effects of media violence (copycat killings) and media desensitization. But compare the destructive force of the rhetoric ("collateral damage"; "ethnic cleansing") and the ultimate violence of state warfare when it is the first option instead of the last in international conflict resolution.

The fear that a mere reading, viewing, or listening will forever destroy a person's value and belief system lies at the heart of censorship. I explored this in *Fear of Words: Censorship and the Public Libraries of Canada*, published by the Canadian Library Association.[38]

It is true that empathy and vicarious experience are the real benefits of literature and the arts. Allan Stratton, winner of the Canadian Library Association's 2009 Young Adult Book Award for *Chanda's Wars*, said in his acceptance speech:

> *Maths and science are prized for being knowledge based. The study of literature, by contrast, is often seen as a frill or an entertainment. But literature is, in fact, the most necessary study of all. For it asks us to engage human emotions—for real. In so doing it develops empathy. Literature is a bridge across divides—a means to see ourselves in the Other and the Other in ourselves.*[39]

Is there a clear distinction between words and actions? At rhetorical extremes, can words incite violence, killing, and genocide? Can words be so offensive as to justify censorship? For example, should anything offensive to a particular religion be banned, such as the Mohammed Cartoons? In 2007, the press reported that Indian Muslims were pressuring the Indian government to expel Taslima Nasrin—herself a Muslim, a medical doctor, an author of controversial novels (*Shame; Split in Two*), critic of Islam, and an exile from her native Bangladesh—on the basis that, as spokesperson Bhaktipada Ghosh declared without a hint of irony: "Ours is a secular society. We cannot tolerate attacks on any religion here."[40]

---

38 Alvin M. Schrader, *Fear of Words: Censorship and the Public Libraries of Canada* (Ottawa, ON: Canadian Library Association, 1995).

39 Quoted by Lisa Doucet in 2011 e-mail communication with author, regarding Young Adult Book Award introduction, Canadian Library Association annual conference, Halifax, Nova Scotia, May 29, 2011.

40 Umarah Jamali, "Muslim Groups Press India To Expel Author," *Globe and Mail*, August 28, 2007, A11.

In the realm of sexual representation, enduring controversy surrounds the feasibility of a distinction between art and "pornography," between the erotic (art) and the pornographic (obscenity). In *The Year of Living Dangerously*, Peter Curtis asks, "Is that porn or art?" To which Bill Kwan responds, "If it's in focus, it's porn. If it's out of focus, it's art."[41]

If we look at "porn" versus "erotica" as a sort of two-term indexing system, it is clear why all formal indexing systems have inherent category problems. Complex concepts do not fit into simple compartments. Is all violence of the same kind? Is a punch the same as an execution? Is sex the same as nudity? I am reminded of a famous observation by Trinh T. Minh-Ha about porous categories: "Despite our desperate, eternal attempts to separate, contain, and mend, categories always leak."[42]

And because words represent values, children are a primary battleground in cultural and value conflicts, witness children's picture books with same-sex themes (or even sub-themes), or Israeli-Palestinian relations.[43] As Jonathan Dollimore points out, "Of the vulnerable groups censors have obsessed about the most—women, the lower orders, and children—the first two have been emancipated, but not children, or even adolescents."[44] Rhetoric about the harmful effects on the young of literature that dares to defy and rupture the mantra of social responsibility continues to dominate mainstream culture, not to mention the criminal law.

But as Oscar Wilde wrote in his Preface to *Picture of Dorian Gray*, "There is no such thing as a moral or an immoral book. Books are well written, or badly written. That is all."[45] And elsewhere in the novel, he declared: "The books that the world calls immoral are books that show the world its own shame."[46]

Citing Wilde and several other nonconforming artists down through the ages, Dollimore argued that to take art seriously is to recognize the dangers of both forbidden knowledge and dissident and transgressive attitudes. Art—some art—should be distrusted precisely because it ignores and scorns the triadic social responsibilities of instructing, delighting, and inspiring, of

---

41 *The Year of Living Dangerously*, motion picture, directed by Peter Weir (Hollywood, CA: MGM, 1982).

42 Trinh T. Minh-Ha, *Woman, Native, Other: Writing, Postcoloniality and Feminism* (Bloomington: Indiana University Press, 1989), 94.

43 PEN Canada, "PEN Canada Urges Reconsideration of Decision by Toronto District School Board Regarding *Three Wishes: Palestinian and Israeli Children Speak*" (press release, Toronto, March 16, 2006). http://www.pencanada.ca/media/ThreeWishes-16Mar06.pdf.

44 Jonathan Dollimore, *Sex, Literature and Censorship* (Cambridge, UK: Polity, 2001), 157.

45 Oscar Wilde, *Picture of Dorian Gray* (1891; repr., Westminster, MD: Modern Library, 2000), xv.

46 Ibid., 224.

beauty, wholesomeness, and health. Instead, it expresses "the unspeakable" and hints at "the unutterable" in human desire.[47] Art would unleash, deregulate, and destabilize human desire and its contradictions, even damage and corrupt us. Some art should therefore be distrusted by the political and cultural orthodoxies, a position originating with one of Western culture's most important philosophers, Plato.[48]

But the solution to this very old belief in the potential peril of art is not Plato's endorsement of censorship, which puts means above ends. In this privileging, ends are perforce betrayed. Censoring art in the name of protecting society ultimately fails, if not in one generation then in the next or the next or the next. Censorship cannot protect society from itself and its contraries. As an aside, in his denigration of "poetry," the paradox of Plato framing his expositions as story after story and story within story seems to have afforded him no ironical lesson in wit.

At the same time, Dollimore criticized the duplicity of whitewashing "high art" as never dangerous, never "prurient," never political, but always respectable, wholesome, and pure. He pointed out that:

> *A not inconsiderable virtue of Camille Paglia's Sexual Personae is the way it finds the western artistic canon to be pornographic and perverse at its heart. Time and again she finds a disturbing knowledge in the texts which have been tamed by those academics and critics who continue to censor literature even as they fight furiously to speak authoritatively on its behalf.*[49]

Words do have power. Let us use them wisely, and courageously, and to look within.

Research Programs

I have selected three research streams to put flesh to some of the principles and perspectives outlined above. Although fully aware of their reductionistic quality, for fun I have incorporated visualizations with tagclouds to represent quantitatively the linguistic shapes of these streams (Figures 1-3).[50] All three streams—Internet access and filtering, "Queering Libraries," and the "Digital Closet"—demonstrate the problems—and power—of naming and representation.

---

47 Dollimore, *Sex, Literature and Censorship*, 101.
48 Plato, *The Republic of Plato*, trans. Allan Bloom (New York: Basic, 1968), Book X.
49 Dollimore, *Sex, Literature and Censorship*, 106.
50 See *Wordle*, http://www.wordle.net/create.

Internet Access and Filtering

At just the time in the mid-1990s when unfettered Internet access was being called into question in the United States and Canada, and the American Library Association in particular had experienced a vicious public campaign against its support for uncensored access in libraries in a Resolution adopted by the American Library Association Council on July 2, 1997, it was my good fortune to be a member of the Executive Council of the Canadian Library Association.[51]

It was both an honor and a bit worrisome, therefore, to be asked to draft a position statement for the Canadian Library Association, which became the 1997 "Statement on Internet Access."[52] Also at the invitation of CLA, I co-wrote with Joanne Greiner, Edmonton Public Library, a brochure entitled "Have a Safe Trip! A Parent's Guide to Safety on the Internet" that was first distributed at the 1998 annual conference.[53] Later, in 2001 and early 2002, I was part of the Internet Manifesto Work Team for the Freedom of Information and Freedom of Expression Committee, which drafted the IFLA Internet Manifesto, subsequently adopted at the 2002 annual conference of the International Federation of Library Associations and Institutions in Glasgow, Scotland.[54]

The Canadian Library Association brochure "Have a Safe Trip!" described the fallacies and weaknesses of commercial software filters that still characterize almost all Internet censorware: they block words, phrases, subjects, and sites on the Web using certain keywords. Because the technology is programmed on the basis of exact match character recognition, regardless of what the marketing hype claims, filters cannot discriminate between genuinely unsuitable sites and innocent ones because blocking is context-free, for example, educational anti-smoking sites and even sites devoted to geology (smoking volcanoes) or magic (smoke and mirrors). In the same vein, homonyms, words that have a "double" meaning, will perforce be blocked; when

---

51 American Library Association, "Resolution on the Use of Filtering Software in Libraries," http://www.ala.org/ala/aboutala/offices/oif/statementspols/ifresolutions/resolutionuse.cfm.

52 Canadian Library Association, "Statement on Internet Access," 1997, last updated February 27, 2000, http://www.cla.ca/AM/Template.cfm?Section=Position_Statements&Template=/CM/ContentDisplay.cfm&ContentID=3048.

53 Canadian Library Association, "Have a Safe Trip! A Parent's Guide to Safety on the Internet," *Net Safe; Net Smart: Managing and Communicating About the Internet in the Library*, last modified August 2000, http://www.cla.ca/netsafe/netsafe.pdf.

54 International Federation of Library Associations and Institutions, "IFLA Internet Manifesto," 2002, http://www.ifla.org/en/publications/the-ifla-internet-manifesto.

one product blocked "couple" several years ago, the White House site disappeared because "couple" appeared there in a reference to the Clintons and the Gores. The same product also blocked the site for Super Bowl XXXI, because of news that a player had been sidelined due to a groin injury.

The brochure went on to argue that parents are "the best and most reliable Internet filter" for their own children. The values and skills of children are the major means to safeguard their wellbeing. Internet filters do not block all content that violates a particular family's values and beliefs. Testing shows that all Internet filters fail to block some sexually explicit sites or sites with illegal content, and they cannot adapt to the age and level of maturity of particular children. They do not help children learn to make independent judgments and to say no. Choices of words, ideas, and topics to be blocked may be driven by the product owner's personal values, ideology, and political agenda, leading to the exclusion of many sites that have information regarding sex education, environmentalism, homosexuality, abortion, or health-related issues such as breast cancer, among others.

Uncritical reliance on Internet filtering creates an urgent need for a more theoretically grounded perspective that takes account of the very essence of being human—the expressive communication that we call "language"—and its relationship to educational and cultural goals. Some insights into language come from three areas of foundational knowledge in library and information studies: intellectual freedom; indexing theory for information retrieval; and reader response theory.

In a nutshell, what these bodies of thought reveal is a whole set of intractable barriers that render perfect control over expressive content in any communications medium an impossible idea and ideal. These barriers issue from the unsolvable problems of ambiguity in language, indexing, and reading. And although significant advances are being made in natural language processing, the cognitive dimension of the human mind represents only one small part of what it means to be fully human and to experience the unknowable interplay between thinking, feeling, and intentionality indissolubly linked to the body and the senses. The reality is, then, that the locus of the problems associated with Internet content is social and political, not "technological".

Some filters also block or control access to chat rooms, e-mail, newsgroups and instant messaging—and now, social networking sites such as MySpace, YouTube, and Facebook. Other products block sites based on the site's rating, or block all sites that are not rated. And, some products block every site until it is identified as an approved site. Almost all filters use American English and spelling, which is fine if one is American. Filtering products require constant updating, since thousands of new sites are added daily.

What should concern us is young people who have access to only one view of the world, young people brought up with no knowledge of choice, no awareness of the rich diversity around them. We should focus on teaching them to be critical thinkers, and in turn adults should turn their energies and resources to the real problems of real children, to suffering and hunger, homelessness and health, education and caring. Society must abandon techno-ethics and recognize that the cultural, political, and ideological concerns arising from innovative technology cannot be solved by yet more technology. Bad ideas and bad images do not create bad kids. There are no reasonable grounds to fear contagion or uncritical acceptance of ideas if children have strong family values. The worst flaw of filters is that they give people a false sense of security.

The bottom line, then as it is now, is that filters block huge amounts of constitutionally protected information and sites, whether it is the United States or Canada or any other country under consideration, and all of this censorship is unknown to Internet users. This is because filters are software products relying almost exclusively on automation, not on human eyes and brains. They cannot evaluate content. Commercial filters are accountable to no one and transparent to no one. Trying to "censorproof" the Internet is doomed to failure, just as making library collections and information safe from complaints and challenges—that is, self-censoring acquisitions, classification, subject access, or shelving location—is theoretically unattainable and illusory.[55] "A truly great library contains something in it to offend everyone," declared Jo Godwin.[56]

What is most troublesome about this whole industry is that librarians and school administrators do not perform due diligence in adopting filter software products. They take at naive face value the vendors' claims to only block illegal content. So far as I am aware, no comprehensive testing is ever done.

In addition to my research into filtering efficacy, I realized that librarians in the late 1990s had available only anecdotal examples of other Internet policies in developing their own, so I initiated a project to create and maintain a Web-based resource guide to the Internet access policies of Canadian

---

[55] Alvin M. Schrader, "Censorproofing School Library Collections: The Fallacy and Futility," *School Libraries Worldwide* 2, no. 1 (1996): 71-94, http://www.iasl-online.org/pubs/slw/slwjan96.html; Alvin M Schrader, "Why You Can't 'Censorproof' Your Public Library: What Research Tells Us," *Public Library Quarterly* 16, no. 11 (1997): 3-30, http://www.tandfonline.com/doi/abs/10.1300/J118v16n01_02.

[56] Esther Lombardi, "Library quotes—What have writers said about libraries?," *About.com*, 2011, http://classiclit.about.com/od/litlibraries/a/aa_libraryquote.htm.

libraries in the public sector.[57] Current coverage includes public libraries, school libraries, and post-secondary libraries, as well as a section "Helpful Resources" that are published by Canadian authors or Canadian associations. This Web site collects links to approximately 250 Internet access policies adopted by Canadian public, school, and post-secondary libraries. The site also contains a list of the more than 60 variant terms used by Canadian libraries to refer to these policy statements, ranging from "Acceptable Use Agreement" and "Code of Conduct for Computer and Network Users" to "Principles in the Use of Information Technology."

Fig. 1. Tagcloud: Internet Filtering

The tagcloud visualization in Figure 1 captures the linguistic patterns in two of my texts that exemplify in general terms my articles and presentations in this area of research.[58] Prominent terms are Internet, filtering, library/

---

57 *Directory of Internet Access Policies of Canadian Libraries in the Public Sector*, Web site maintained by Alvin M. Schrader, 2001, http://www.ualberta.ca/~aschrade/internet/access.htm.

58 Alvin M. Schrader, "Internet Filters: Library Access Issues in a Cyberspace World" (presentation, IFLA/FAIFE Open Session Lecture, 65th IFLA Council and General Conference, August 25, 1999), http://archive.ifla.org/faife/papers/others/schrader.htm; Alvin M. Schrader, "Technology and the Politics of Choice: Information Literacy, Critical Thinking, and Intellectual Freedom" (presentation to ODYSSEY 2002—Bending the Light: Powerful Learning: A Conference for K-12 Educators and Administrators, Alberta Teachers Association Learning Resources

libraries, products/product, information, access, sites/site, url, software, human, indexing, content, filters, librarians, language, and technology.

Queering Libraries—Sexual and Gender Minority Library Services and Issues

"Queering Libraries" comes from a chapter I had the privilege of co-authoring with Kris Wells for a book edited by Ellen Greenblatt,[59] *Serving LGBTIQ Library and Archives Users: Essays on Outreach, Service, Collections and Access.*

My research in this area explores the challenges and issues of inclusive library services and collections in all sectors about and for those who identify as sexual minority or gender variant or LGBTQ—lesbian, gay, bisexual, transgendered, trans-identified, intersex, two-spirited, and queer or questioning individuals. One particular area of focus is on LGBTQ Canadian youth with limited resources in rural and smaller urban areas, including the myths, stereotypes, and barriers to inclusive collections. The research includes library strategies for supporting LGBTQ communities, starting with the need for a legal, ethical, and mission framework for dealing with sexual minority and gender identity issues.

In addition to this contribution, I was also greatly privileged to co-author a book with Kris Wells that was published simultaneously in English and French by the Canadian Teachers Federation in 2007 entitled *Challenging Silence, Challenging Censorship: Inclusive Resources, Strategies and Policy Directives for Addressing Bisexual, Gay, Lesbian, Trans-Identified and Two-Spirited Realities in School and Public Libraries.*[60]

I was particularly proud to have been the President of the Canadian Library Association in 2008, when a "Position Statement on Diversity and Inclusion" was brought to Executive Council for adoption that was initiated by Vice President Ken Roberts.[61] As far back as 1993, the American Library

---

Council, Kananaskis, Alberta, March 15, 2002), http://hdl.handle.net/10402/era.23393.

59 Alvin M. Schrader and Kristopher Wells, "Queering Libraries and Classrooms: Strategies to Build Inclusive Collections and Services for Sexual Minority and Gender Variant Youth," in *Serving LGBTIQ Library And Archives Users: Essays on Outreach, Service, Collections and Access,* ed. Ellen Greenblatt (Jefferson, NC: McFarland, 2011), 94–112.

60 Alvin M. Schrader and Kristopher Wells, *Challenging Silence, Challenging Censorship: Inclusive Resources, Strategies and Policy Directives for Addressing Bisexual, Gay, Lesbian, Trans-Identified and Two-Spirited Realities in School and Public Libraries* (Ottawa, ON: Canadian Teachers' Federation, 2007).

61 Canadian Library Association, "Position Statement on Diversity and Inclusion," May 25, 2008, http://www.cla.ca/AM/Template.cfm?Section=Position_Statements&Template=/CM/ContentDisplay.cfm&ContentID=4713.

Association adopted a specific policy on "Access to Library Resources and Services Regardless of Sex, Gender Identity, or Sexual Orientation."[62] Then, alarmed by extremist public discourse, the Association adopted further a "Resolution on Threats to Library Materials Related to Sex, Gender Identity, or Sexual Orientation" to counter legislative proposals that would restrict or prohibit access to materials related to sexual orientation within publicly-funded libraries.[63]

Parenthetically, all of this is a far cry from the reaction of some members of the American Library Association when the 1992 annual conference was held in San Francisco during the time of the gay pride parade. Its house organ, *American Libraries*, published a photograph on the cover of its July/August 1992 issue showing several people in the parade holding a blue and white sign that said "Gay and Lesbian Task Force, American Library Association" and featured two pairs of library-symbol figures holding hands. Then managing editor Leonard Kniffel recalled the subsequent backlash of fear and loathing by letter writers and callers:

> *The response to that cover was immediate and sharply divided between those who wanted to "puke" and those who applauded and called us "courageous." We received many letters and phone calls, more from the pukers than the supporters. We published 15 letters, spread over the next three issues. Readers began to feel they had to take sides. One reader called it a "happy, celebratory photograph," while another saw it as an example of ALA's "ceaseless advocacy of social issues."*[64]

In a letter published in the November issue, Cal Gough identified himself as one of the people on the cover and noted:

> *Gays and lesbians are not going to disappear from professional associations, or disappear from libraries, or disappear from families and communities everywhere — no matter how many magazines we're kept off the cover of or how many other ways some people try to deny, trivialize, or erase our existence.*

---

62 American Library Association, "Access to Library Resources and Services Regardless of Sex, Gender Identity, Gender Expression, or Sexual Orientation: An Interpretation of the Library Bill of Rights" (last updated 2008), http://www.ala.org/ala/aboutala/offices/oif/iftoolkits/glbttoolkit/glbttoolkit.cfm.

63 American Library Association, "Resolution on Threats to Library Materials Related to Sex, Gender Identity, or Sexual Orientation" (2005), http://www.ala.org/ala/aboutala/offices/oif/statementspols/ifresolutions/threats.cfm.

64 Leonard Kniffel, "Gay Doesn't Always Mean Happy. The First 100 Years. A Centennial Blog: Celebrating 100 Years of *American Libraries* Magazine" (January 29, 2007), http://blogs.ala.org/AL100.php?cat=240.

Apparently, the cover had not humiliated him. If you are reading, Cal, I invite you and all of the other dozen or so members whose faces are visible on that infamous cover, to add your recollections about how it affected your professional life—or didn't.

As well, the American Library Association is home to the Gay, Lesbian, Bisexual, and Transgendered Round Table, which was founded in 1970, long before the shameful 1992 backlash, as the Task Force on Gay Liberation, and considered to be the first such professional organization in the world.[65] Its many advocacy activities include annual book awards, programs at the annual conferences of the American Library Association, a quarterly newsletter, a clearinghouse of resources and a Web site of policies and information of special interest to LGBTQ persons.

Fig. 2. Tagcloud: Queering Libraries

The enduring power of literature and the arts to contribute to LGBTQ resilience, especially youth resilience, makes access to library resources and services critical. Paraphrasing Brent, a blogger and book reviewer: with so much ugliness and hatred directed at gender and sexual minorities, the easiest place to find beauty and love in the world is in words and literature.[66]

65 American Library Association—Gay, Lesbian, Bisexual, and Transgendered Round Table, (2011), http://www.ala.org/template.cfm?Section=glbtrt.
66 Brent, "Gay Teen Blogger/Book Reviewer Takes Librarians To Task Over LGBT Lit" (2010), http://Janettrumble.Wordpress.Com/2010/06/15/Gay-Teen-Bloogerbook-Reviewer-Takes-Librarians-To-Task-Over-Lgbt-Lit.

To represent the tagcloud for this research stream, I chose Part 1 of Schrader and Wells[67] and the text of a presentation I gave at the 2007 annual conference of the Pacific Northwest Library Association that was published in the Association's journal.[68] This tagcloud (Figure 2) shows the following prominent terms: library/libraries, school, LGBTQ, school/schools, public, gay, lesbian, access, librarians, Canadian, information, materials, youth/young, librarians, materials, sexual, and teachers.

The Digital Closet—Sexual and Gender Minority Internet Access and Filtering

This research stream is the opportune confluence of my research interests in Internet access and sexual and gender minority communities. I have characterized this area as the "digital closet" because several studies have documented systematic viewpoint discrimination against LGBTQ sites and information perpetrated by a number of commercial filters. The inspiration for my title phrase "the digital closet" comes from *The Celluloid Closet* by Vito Russo, a definitive analysis of Hollywood film images of gays and lesbians in more than 300 movies over 80 years of film-making.[69] Russo argued that invisibility has been the great enemy of truth about minority sexual orientation.

And that is precisely "the hidden agenda" of some, if not most, of the commercial filtering products. The Henry J. Kaiser Family Foundation commissioned a study of the blocking of health information sites for teens by seven commonly used filters (CyberPatrol, Symantec, BESS, SmartFilter, Websense, and AOL Parental Controls).[70] The study found that at even the least restrictive level, the filters incorrectly blocked approximately one in ten sites on safe sex, condoms, and health issues pertaining to lesbians and gays, despite the fact that less than 1% of general health sites were blocked.

At the most restrictive settings, however, the filters were found to have a major impact on access to health information: even 25% of general health sites were blocked, and for topics on sexual health, such as safe sex, the rates were as high as 50%.

---

67 Schrader and Wells, *Challenging Silence*, 2007.
68 Alvin M. Schrader, "'I Thought I'd Find Myself at the Library': LGBTQ Services & Collections in Public and School Libraries," *PNLA Quarterly* 72, no. 1 (2007): 4–9, http://www.pnla.org/quarterly/Fall2007/PNLA_Fall07.pdf.
69 Vito Russo, *The Celluloid Closet: Homosexuality in the Movies*, rev. ed. (New York: Harper & Row, 1987).
70 Henry J. Kaiser Family Foundation, *See No Evil: How Internet Filters Affect the Search for Online Health Information* (press release, 2002), http://www.kaiserhealthnews.org/daily-reports/2002/december/11/dr00015026.aspx.

But for lesbian and gay health information, 60% of the sites were blocked. These filters blocked sites such as: femalehealth.com, a female condom site; gayhealth.com; goaskalice.columbia.edu; hivchannel.com/prevention/safesex/; teenwire.com, Planned Parenthood's teen site; and youngwomenshealth.org/spherpes, Boston Children's Hospital's site because of information about herpes.

Many filters have subject categories that target sexual minority sites and information, for example, one of *CyberSitter*'s filtering categories is "Gay/Lesbian Topics"; American Family Filter (Bsafe) has a "Lifestyle" category that blocks information about "sexual lifestyles outside of marriage"; *CyberPatrol* has a sex education category; *Bess* has a category called "Sexual Materials" for sites with humor, innuendo, as well as educational and medical health information. And responding to criticism about blocking homosexual sites, a company representative from *CyberSitter* said, "We filter anything that has to do with sex. Sexual orientation [is about sex] by virtue of the fact that it has sex in the name."[71]

For those teenagers who just want to know more about themselves or acquaintances, blocking out access to information and to online communities is discriminatory; for those who are questioning their sexuality, it may well be disastrous. The recent launch by the American Civil Liberties Union, in partnership with Yale Law School, of a campaign "Don't Filter Me" is welcome, if tardy, news.[72] The campaign asks students to report school censorship of Web content geared towards LGBT communities, noting that, "Programs that block all LGBT content violate First Amendment rights to free speech, as well as the Equal Access Act. . . ." In the launch announcement, campaign staff attorney Joshua Block said:

> *Schools harm students by denying them vital information. Schools not only have a legal duty to allow students access to these sites, it is also*

---

71 Marjorie Heins, Christina Cho, and Ariel Feldman, *Internet Filters: A Public Policy Report*, 2nd ed. (New York: Brennan Center for Justice, 2006), http://www.fepproject.org/policyreports/filteringreport.html.

72 American Civil Liberties Union, "ACLU Launches 'Don't Filter Me' Initiative to Stop Unconstitutional Web Filtering of LGBT Content in Schools" (press release, February 15, 2011), http://www.aclu.org/lgbt-rights/aclu-launches-don-t-filter-me-initiative-stop-unconstitutional-web-filtering-lgbt-conten; Chris Hampton, "'Don't Filter Me' Interim Report, February 1, 2011–August 31, 2011," *New York: American Civil Liberties Union* (2011), http://www.aclu.org/files/assets/dontfilterme_report.pdf; Lisa Keen, "ACLU Steps Up Fight Against Overzealous School Internet Filters," *Keen News Service* (August 17, 2011), http://www.keennewsservice.com/2011/08/17/aclu-steps-up-fight-against-overzealous-school-internet-filters.

imperative that LGBT youth who are experiencing discrimination and bullying be able to access this information for their own safety.

The American Civil Liberties Union has declared September 28th as "Banned Websites Awareness Day" to raise awareness of these discriminatory software practices.[73]

As I mentioned above, filtering products both overblock and underblock at the same time on these and many other topics, with the result that millions of sites are incorrectly, and I would say, illegally, blocked.

Why all the problems with accurately identifying sites and subjects? As I also described above, human language and human indexing are at the core of the censorware challenges. It is the essential ambiguity of language itself, compounded by the ambiguities inherent therefore in indexing language, that explains censorware failure. Just as language is socially constructed, so too is the indexing of language. Indexing is, quite simply, the naming of information. It is easy to see that indexing languages—e.g., a thesaurus, or a library catalogue language such as LCC/LCSH and DDC—are cultural constructions, with all of the cultural baggage of their institutional creators. It is not just the indexing systems themselves, but every individual human act of indexing and cataloguing too, which is inevitably and unavoidably an exercise of judgement within a cultural framework.

Every language in the world, so far as I can tell, has a multitude of synonyms and euphemisms, puns and double entendres, words with multiple meanings (homographs, homonyms) such as "queen" and "curse" and "breast." And many homographs with a sexual meaning also have at least one meaning that is non-sexual in nature, words such as "gay," "cock," and "beaver," and of course I am only referring to their innocent forms, you understand! The variation and fluctuation in meaning will always lead to imprecise and variable descriptor terms and inherent category problems, especially when divorced from context.

The viewpoint discrimination built into many commercial filtering software products is not only unconstitutional in both the United States and Canada, it is a flagrant abuse of LGBTQ communities. Such products deny them access to information and Web sites that in many instances might save lives; they privilege dominant cultural traditions; and they help to perpetuate the social and political invisibility of gender and sexual minorities in both countries.

Internet blocking software is like performing brain surgery with a chainsaw. And in the case of Web content dealing with LGBTQ content, our brain

---

73 American Civil Liberties Union, "ACLU Marks Banned Websites Awareness Day with Report on LGBT Censorship in Schools" (press release, September 28, 2011), http://www.aclu.org/Lgbt-Rights/Aclu-Marks-Banned-Websites-Awareness-Day-Report-Lgbt-Censorship-Schools.

surgeon is also a homophobe. Third party software products make sexual minorities invisible, and feed our youth a conservative ideological bias rather than allowing them to develop their own value systems. This is a very poor model for teaching students to understand and respect democratic society and freedom of expression as a core human right. Internet filtering denies choice, and denial of choice is what censorship is all about.

Fig. 3. Tagcloud: The Digital Closet

American poet, essayist, and lesbian feminist Adrienne Rich explained the profound effects that the rendering of invisibility has on the human psyche:

> When those who have power to name and to socially construct reality choose not to see you or hear you . . . when someone with the authority of a teacher, say, describes the world and you are not in it, there is a moment of psychic disequilibrium, as if you looked into a mirror and saw nothing. Yet you know you exist and others like you, and that this is a game with mirrors. It takes some strength of soul—and not just individual strength, but collective understanding—to resist this void, this nonbeing, into which you are thrust, and to stand up, demanding to be seen and heard.[74]

---

74 Adrienne Rich, "Invisibility in Academe," in *Blood, Bread, and Poetry: Selected Prose 1979–1985* (New York: Norton, 1986), 199.

The tagcloud visualization in Figure 3 of this research stream, based on two selected texts, highlights the following terms: sites, Internet, filtering, filters, Web, language, content, products/product, software, information, sexual, access, blocked, and indexing.[75]

Epilogue: Transforming the Scholarly and Professional Culture of Library and Information Studies for Social Justice

All of the questions and issues raised about gender, sexuality, and information in this personal odyssey to find meaning in the discipline and profession through my teaching, research, service, and advocacy come back to fundamental world perspectives on humanity as reflected in and through our core values and our vision and goals for library and information studies. Much remains to be done.

Cultural transformation of the discipline and profession will have to be accompanied by yet another important project in the arsenal of social justice. Freedom from sexual oppression and harassment must also be linked to confronting misogyny and dismantling gendered privileges and rights. Unfortunately, sexism is still the popular weapon of homophobia. For example, the modern stereotype of male gayness, frequently defined as "sissy" or "effeminacy" and hence as weakness, is rooted in the heteronormative delusion of heterosexual male superiority, and in the harsh sexism of male privilege, power, and hegemony.[76]

There can be no hierarchy of oppression. If we fight against one form of injustice we must strive to fight against them all. Ignorance is based in fear that leads to violence.[77] And just as there is no hierarchy of oppression, there can be no hierarchy of equality and equality rights. Truth to power has many voices. We must let all of them in. So the larger struggle for a tolerable balance continues on many fronts for social democracy. The whole story of the odyssey through the myriad of countervailing forces awaits telling.

---

75 Alvin M. Schrader, "From Movie Codes to Web Filters—'Same Old, Same Old': Technologies to Suppress, Distort, Manipulate, Marginalize, and Silence LGBTQ Diversity" (presentation, Inside/OUT Speakers' Series, University of Alberta, Edmonton, Alberta, 2005); Alvin M. Schrader, "Internet Censorship of Lesbian, Gay, Bisexual, and Transgendered Information" (presentation, Conference on Sex and Gender Differences, Education, and Culture II, Edmonton, Alberta, 2007).

76 Russo, *Celluloid Closet*, 4.

77 Andre P. Grace, "Being, Becoming, and Belonging As a Queer Citizen Educator: The Places of Queer Autobiography, Queer Culture As Community, and Fugitive Knowledge" in *Proceedings of the 20th Annual Conference of the Canadian Association for the Study of Adult Education* (Quebec City: Laval University, 2001), 100-106.

I conclude this autobiographical odyssey with an eloquent and powerful declaration by celebrated Canadian author Timothy Findley. It is from an Afterword he wrote for the equally celebrated and equally Canadian author Margaret Laurence's 1974 novel *The Diviners*, one of the most popular Canadian works of all time, and one of the most vilified:

> *Books, like dreams, are essentially private realms. Nothing should be allowed to detract from each person's right to read a book privately and to interpret it freely in the light of what each person has experienced and knows of life.*[78]

Acknowledgments

I am deeply grateful to my dear colleagues Michael R. Brundin, Ali Shiri, and Kristopher Wells for their encouragement and reading of this work, and to my life partner Tony Thai for patience and persistence in helping me get it written.

Bibliography

Abley, Mark. "Saul Searching." *Edmonton Journal*, June 22, 1997, F5.

Abram, Stephen. "Worry: Part 1." 2006. Reprinted *Sirsidynix Onesource*, 2 no. 2 (August 24, 2011): 1–5. http://www.imakenews.com/sirsi/e_article000523948.cfm?x=b11,0,w.

American Civil Liberties Union. "ACLU Launches 'Don't Filter Me' Initiative to Stop Unconstitutional Web Filtering of LGBT Content in Schools." Press Release, February 15, 2011. http://www.aclu.org/lgbt-rights/aclu-launches-don-t-filter-me-initiative-stop-unconstitutional-web-filtering-lgbt-conten.

———. "ACLU Marks Banned Websites Awareness Day with Report on LGBT Censorship in Schools." Press Release, September 28, 2011. http://www.aclu.org/Lgbt-Rights/Aclu-Marks-Banned-Websites-Awareness-Day-Report-Lgbt-Censorship-Schools.

American Library Association. "Access to Library Resources and Services Regardless of Sex, Gender Identity, Gender Expression, or Sexual Orientation: An Interpretation of the Library Bill of Rights." First adopted 1993. Last updated 2008. http://www.ala.org/ala/aboutala/offices/oif/iftoolkits/glbttoolkit/glbttoolkit.cfm.

———. "Resolution on the Use of Filtering Software in Libraries." Adopted, July 2, 1997. http://www.ala.org/ala/aboutala/offices/oif/statementspols/ifresolutions/resolutionuse.cfm.

---

78 Timothy Findley, Afterword to *The Diviners*, by Margaret Laurence (1974; repr. Toronto: McClelland & Stewart, 1988), 539–40.

———. "Resolution on Threats to Library Materials Related to Sex, Gender Identity, or Sexual Orientation." 2005. http://www.ala.org/ala/aboutala/offices/oif/statementspols/ifresolutions/threats.cfm.

Barnes, Lynne. *Reaching Out: Library Services for Lesbian, Gay, Bisexual, Transgender, and Questioning Youth*. DVD. San Francisco: Friends of The San Francisco Public Library, 2004.

Canadian Library Association. "Have a Safe Trip! A Parent's Guide to Safety on the Internet." *Net Safe; Net Smart: Managing and Communicating About the Internet in the Library*. Last modified August 2000. http://www.cla.ca/netsafe/netsafe.pdf.

———. "Position Statement on Diversity and Inclusion." May 25, 2008. http://www.cla.ca/AM/Template.cfm?Section=Position_Statements&Template=/CM/ContentDisplay.cfm&ContentID=4713.

———. "Statement on Internet Access." Last updated February 27, 2000. http://www.cla.ca/AM/Template.cfm?Section=Position_Statements&Template=/CM/ContentDisplay.cfm&ContentID=3048.

Directory of Internet Access Policies of Canadian Libraries in the Public Sector. Site maintained by Alvin M. Schrader. 2001.http://www.ualberta.ca/~aschrade/internet/access.htm.

Dollimore, Jonathan. *Sex, Literature and Censorship*. Cambridge, UK: Polity, 2001.

Eliot, T. S. "Choruses from 'The Rock.'" In *Selected Poems*, 107–27. London: Faber and Faber, 1954.

Feldman, Jeffrey. *Framing the Debate: Famous Presidential Speeches and How Progressives Can Use Them to Change the Conversation (and Win Elections)*. Brooklyn: Ig, 2007.

Findley, Timothy. "Afterword" to *The Diviners*, by Margaret Laurence, 539–43. 1974. Reprint, Toronto: McClelland & Stewart, 1988.

Grace, Andre P. "Being, Becoming, and Belonging As a Queer Citizen Educator: The Places of Queer Autobiography, Queer Culture As Community, and Fugitive Knowledge." In *Proceedings of the 20th Annual Conference of the Canadian Association for the Study of Adult Education*, 100–106. Quebec City: Laval University, 2001.

Hampton, Chris. "'Don't Filter Me' Interim Report, February 1, 2011–August 31, 2011." New York: American Civil Liberties Union, http://www.aclu.org/files/assets/dontfilterme_report.pdf.

Heins, Marjorie, Christina Cho, and Ariel Feldman. *Internet Filters: A Public Policy Report*. 2nd ed. New York: Brennan Center for Justice, 2006. http://www.fepproject.org/policyreports/filteringreport.html.

Henry J. Kaiser Family Foundation. *See No Evil: How Internet Filters Affect the Search for Online Health Information*. Press Release, 2002. http://www.kaiserhealthnews.org/daily-reports/2002/december/11/dr00015026.aspx.

Herman, Edward S., and Noam Chomsky. *Manufacturing Consent: The Political Economy of the Mass Media*. New York: Pantheon, 1988.

hooks, bell. *Killing Rage; Ending Racism*. New York: Henry Holt, 1995.

———. *Outlaw Culture: Resisting Representations*. New York: Routledge, 1994.

Houser, L., and Alvin M. Schrader. *The Search for a Scientific Profession: Library Science Education in the U.S. and Canada*. Metuchen, NJ: Scarecrow, 1978.

International Federation of Library Associations and Institutions. "IFLA Internet Manifesto." 2002. http://www.ifla.org/en/publications/the-ifla-internet-manifesto.

Juvenal. *The Satires*. VI, line 347, ca 1st–2nd century CE. http://en.wikiquote.org/wiki/Juvenal.

Kinsman, Gary, and Patrizia Gentile. *The Canadian War on Queers: National Security as Sexual Regulation*. Vancouver: UBC Press, 2010.

Lakoff, George. "Introduction: Framing Is About Ideas, and Ideas Matter." Introduction to *Framing the Debate: Famous Presidential Speeches and How Progressives Can Use Them To Change the Conversation (and Win Elections)*, by Jeffrey Feldman, xi–xvii. Brooklyn: Ig, 2007.

———. *Women, Fire, and Dangerous Things: What Categories Reveal about the Mind*. Chicago: University of Chicago Press, 1987.

Manguel, Alberto. *The Library at Night*. Toronto: Knopf, 2006.

Milton, John. *Areopagitica: A Speech for the Liberty of Unlicensed Printing to the Parliament of England*. 1644. Available from *Project Gutenberg*. 2006. http://www.gutenberg.org/files/608/608-h/608-h.htm.

Minh-Ha, Trinh T. *Woman, Native, Other: Writing, Postcoloniality and Feminism*. Bloomington, IN: Indiana University Press, 1989.

Moscrop, David. "Media's Language Stokes Culture of Fear." *Edmonton Journal*, August 12, 2011, A18.

PEN Canada. "PEN Canada Urges Reconsideration of Decision by Toronto District School Board Regarding *Three Wishes: Palestinian and Israeli Children Speak*." Press release. Toronto, March 16, 2006. http://www.pencanada.ca/media/ThreeWishes-16Mar06.pdf.

Plato. *The Republic of Plato*. Translated, notes by Allan Bloom. New York: Basic, 1968.

Rich, Adrienne. "Invisibility in Academe." In *Blood, Bread, and Poetry: Selected Prose 1979–1985*, New York: Norton, 1986, 198–201.

Roberts, Ken. "Keeping True to the Faith: Inaugural Address." *Feliciter* 54, no. 4 (2008): 144–45. http://www.cla.ca/AM/Template.cfm?Section=Vol_54_No_4&Template=/CM/HTMLDisplay.cfm&ContentID=8264.

Russo, Vito. *The Celluloid Closet: Homosexuality in the Movies.* Rev. ed. New York: Harper & Row, 1987.

Schrader, Alvin M. "Freedom of Expression and Freedom to Read." *Freedom to Read 2009,* 25 (2008): 8–10. http://issuu.com/thebpc/docs/kit2009.

———. "Censorproofing School Library Collections: The Fallacy and Futility." *School Libraries Worldwide* 2 no. 1: (1996): 71–94. http://www.iasl-online.org/pubs/slw/slwjan96.html.

———. "Challenging Silence, Challenging Censorship, Building Resilience: LGBTQ Services and Collections in Public, School and Post-Secondary Libraries." *Feliciter* 55 no. 3 (2009): 107–8. http://www.cla.ca/Content/NavigationMenu/Resources/Feliciter/PastIssues/2009/Vol55No3/.

———. *Fear of Words: Censorship and the Public Libraries of Canada.* Ottawa, ON: Canadian Library Association, 1995.

———. "From Movie Codes to Web Filters—'Same Old, Same Old': Technologies to Suppress, Distort, Manipulate, Marginalize, and Silence LGBTQ Diversity." Presentation in the Inside/OUT Speakers' Series, University of Alberta, Edmonton, Alberta, 2005.

———. "Internet Censorship of Lesbian, Gay, Bisexual, and Transgendered Information." Presentation to the Conference on Sex and Gender Differences, Education, and Culture II, Edmonton, Alberta, 2007.

———. "Internet Filters: Library Access Issues in a Cyberspace World." Presentation at the IFLA/FAIFE Open Session Lecture, 65th IFLA Council and General Conference, August 25, 1999. http://archive.ifla.org/faife/papers/others/schrader.htm.

———. "'I Thought I'd Find Myself at the Library': LGBTQ Services & Collections in Public and School Libraries." *PNLA Quarterly* 72 no. 1 (2007): 4–9. http://www.pnla.org/quarterly/Fall2007/PNLA_Fall07.pdf.

———. "One Field or Two? A Definitional Analysis of the Relationship between Library Science and Information Science." 1995. ERIC ED 401908, December 1996. http://www.eric.ed.gov/ERICWebPortal/contentdelivery/servlet/ERICServlet?accno=ED401908.

———. "Technology and the Politics of Choice: Information Literacy, Critical Thinking, and Intellectual Freedom." Presentation to ODYSSEY 2002—Bending the Light: Powerful Learning: A Conference for K-12 Educators and Administrators, Alberta Teachers Association Learning Resources Council, Kananaskis, Alberta, March 15, 2002. http://hdl.handle.net/10402/era.23393.

———. "Toward a Theory of Library and Information Science." PhD diss., Indiana University (Bloomington), 1983.
———. "Why You Can't 'Censorproof' Your Public Library: What Research Tells Us." *Public Library Quarterly* 16, no. 11 (1997): 3–30. http://www.tandfonline.com/doi/abs/10.1300/J118v16n01_02.
Schrader, Alvin M., and Kristopher Wells. *Challenging Silence, Challenging Censorship: Inclusive Resources, Strategies and Policy Directives for Addressing Bisexual, Gay, Lesbian, Trans-Identified and Two-Spirited Realities in School and Public Libraries*. Ottawa, ON: Canadian Teachers' Federation, 2007.
———. "Queering Libraries and Classrooms: Strategies to Build Inclusive Collections and Services for Sexual Minority and Gender Variant Youth." In *Serving LGBTIQ Library And Archives Users: Essays on Outreach, Service, Collections and Access*, edited by Ellen Greenblatt, 94–112. Jefferson, NC: McFarland, 2011.
Taylor, Catherine, and Tracey Peter, *Every Class in Every School: The First National Climate Survey on Homophobia, Biphobia, and Transphobia in Canadian Schools. Final Report*. With T. L. McMinn, Sarah Paquin, Kevin Schachter, Stacey Beldom, Allison Ferry, and Zoe Gross. Toronto: Egale Canada Human Rights Trust, 2011. http://egale.ca/wp-content/uploads/2011/05/EgaleFinalReport-web.pdf.
Toulmin, Stephen. *Human Understanding: The Collective Use and Evolution of Concepts*. Princeton, NJ: Princeton University Press, 1972.
Waples, Douglas. "The Graduate Library School at Chicago." *Library Quarterly* 1, no. 1 (1931) 26–36, http://www.jstor.org/stable/40039627.
Waring, Marilyn. *Counting for Nothing: What Men Value and What Women Are Worth*. 2nd ed. Toronto: University of Toronto Press, 1999.
Warner, Michael. *Publics and Counterpublics*. Brooklyn: Zone, 2002.
Wilde, Oscar. *Picture of Dorian Gray*. 1891. Reprinted, 2000. Westminster, MD: Modern Library.
Wittgenstein, Ludwig. *Tractatus logico-philosophicus*. English-language trans. New York: Harcourt, Brace, 1922.
The Year of Living Dangerously. Motion picture. Directed by Peter Weir. Hollywood, CA: MGM, 1982.

Part Two

Cyborgs and Cyberfeminism

Feminist Theories of Technology

Judy Wajcman[1]

This article provides an overview of the various approaches to conceptualising the link between gender and technology, both past and present. In turning to this task, I should emphasise that feminist discussions have always taken diverse and overlapping forms. While standard accounts of feminist thought tend to present liberal, socialist and post-modern feminisms as distinct perspectives, in reality they did not develop as independent strands or in a simple chronological order. Moreover, like the field of science and technology studies (STS), feminist scholarship works across disciplines and is organised around core interests and problems resulting in a heterodox body of work. For our purposes here, I will, of necessity, present the different strands rather schematically in order to highlight their contrasting perspectives. However, what should emerge from this overview is an understanding of their interconnectedness, and the shared concern between earlier and more recent "technofeminist" theories to interrogate the gender power relations of the material world.[2]

I will begin by looking at how a feminist perspective shifts our understanding of what technology is, broadening the concept to include not only artefacts but also the cultures and practices associated with technologies. I then outline some early approaches that emphasised the role of technology in reproducing patriarchy, contrasting this with more recent cyberfeminist writings that see digital and biomedical technologies as offering possibilities for destabilising conventional gender differences. The essay will then examine the exciting body of work that has burgeoned at the intersection of feminist scholarship and STS over the past few decades. Such approaches focus on the mutual shaping of gender and technology, where there is no

---

1 Editors' note: this paper was previously published in *Cambridge Journal of Economics* 34, no. 1, (2010): 143–152, doi:10.1093/cje/ben057.
2 Judy Wajcman, *TechnoFeminism* (Cambridge, UK: Polity, 2004).

presumption that either gender or technology are pre-existing or that the relationship between them immutable. The resulting literature is generally more critical of technoscience than its forerunners while at the same time being aware of its potential to open up new gender dynamics.

Technology as Culture

What role does technology play in embedding gender power relations? Let us begin with the traditional conception of what technology is taken to be. In this view technology tends to be thought of in terms of industrial machinery and military weapons, the tools of work and war, overlooking other technologies that affect most aspects of everyday life. The very definition of technology, in other words, is cast in terms of male activities.

An initial challenge for feminists was to demonstrate that the enduring identification between technology and manliness is not inherent in biological sex difference. Feminist scholars have demonstrated how the binary oppositions in Western culture, between culture and nature, reason and emotion, hard and soft, have privileged masculinity over femininity.[3] The taken-for-granted association of men and machines is the result of the historical and cultural construction of gender. Similarly, the standard conceptions of innovation, production and work have been the subject of scrutiny. Just as feminist economists have redefined the discipline of economics to take account of unpaid domestic and caring work,[4] so too feminist scholars of STS have argued for the significance of everyday life technologies.[5] A revaluing of cooking, childcare and communication technologies immediately disrupts the cultural stereotype of women as technically incompetent or invisible in technical spheres.

It is salutary to be reminded that it was only with the formation of engineering as a white, male middle-class profession that "male machines rather than female fabrics" became the markers of technology.[6] During the

---

3 Sandra Harding, *The Science Question in Feminism* (New York: Cornell University Press, 1986).
4 N. Folbre, *The Invisible Heart: Economics and Family Values* (New York: New Press, 2001); Susan Himmelweit, "An Evolutionary Approach to Feminist Economics: Two Different Models of Caring" in *Toward a Feminist Philosophy of Economics*, ed. Drucilla K. Barker and Edith Kuiper (London: Routledge, 2003), 247–265.
5 Ruth Schwartz Cowan, "The 'Industrial Revolution' in the Home: Household Technology and Social Change in the Twentieth Century," *Technology and Culture* 17 (1976): 1–23; A. Stanley, *Mothers and Daughters of Invention* (New Jersey: Rutgers University Press, 1995).
6 Ruth Oldenziel, *Making Technology Masculine: Men, Women and Modern Machines in America* (Amsterdam: Amsterdam University Press, 1999), 26 *et seq.*

late nineteenth century, mechanical and civil engineering increasingly came to define what technology is, diminishing the significance of both artefacts and forms of knowledge associated with women. This was the result of the rise of engineers as an elite with exclusive rights to technical expertise. Crucially, it involved the creation of a male professional identity, based on educational qualifications and the promise of managerial positions, sharply distinguished from shop-floor engineering and blue-collar workers. It also involved an ideal of manliness, characterised by the cultivation of bodily prowess and individual achievement. At the same time, femininity was being reinterpreted as incompatible with technological pursuits. It was during and through this process that the term *technology* took on its modern meaning. The legacy is our taken-for-granted association of technology with men.

In common with mainstream STS, feminist writing has long identified the ways in which socio-technical relations are manifest not only in physical objects and institutions but also in symbols, language and identities.[7] Scientific facts and technological artefacts are treated as simultaneously semiotic and material. Such a broad notion of science and technology (technoscience) as a culture or "material-semiotic practice" enables us to understand how our relationship to technology is integral to the constitution of subjectivity for both sexes.[8] To continue with the example of engineering for a moment, here we see a classic case of an archetypal masculine culture, where mastery over technology is a source of both pleasure and power for the predominantly male profession.[9] Such images resonate with the world of computer hackers at MIT described by Sherry Turkle: "though hackers would deny that theirs is a macho culture, the preoccupation with winning and of subjecting oneself to increasingly violent tests make their world peculiarly male in spirit, peculiarly unfriendly to women."[10]

This is not to say that all women reject "geek culture," or that computer science is Universally coded as masculine. In Malaysia, for example, women are well represented among computer science students.[11] Sexual ideologies

---

7   M. McNeil, ed., *Feminist Cultural Studies of Science and Technology* (London: Routledge, 2007).

8   Donna J. Haraway, *Modest_Witness@Second_Millenium.FemaleMan_Meets _OncoMouse: Feminism and Technoscience* (New York: Routledge, 1997).

9   W. Faulkner and M. Lohan, "Masculinities and Technologies," *Men and Masculinities* 6, no. 4 (2004): 319-29; S. Hacker, *Pleasure, Power and Technology* (Boston: Unwin Hyman, 1989).

10 Sherry Turkle, *The Second Self: Computers and the Human Spirit* (London: Granada, 1984), 216.

11 V. Lagesen, "A Cyberfeminist Utopia? Perceptions of Gender and Computer Science Among Malaysian Women Computer Science Students and Faculty," *Science, Technology, & Human Values* 33, no. 1 (2008): 5-27.

are remarkably diverse and fluid, and for some men technical expertise may be as much about their lack of power as the realization of it. However, in contemporary Western society, the hegemonic form of masculinity is still strongly associated with technical prowess and power.[12] Different childhood exposure to technology, the prevalence of different role models, different forms of schooling, and the extreme gender segregation of the job market all lead to what Cockburn describes as "the construction of men as strong, manually able and technologically endowed, and women as physically and technically incompetent."[13] Entering technical domains therefore requires women to sacrifice major aspects of their feminine identity.

Notwithstanding the recurring rhetoric about women's opportunities in the new knowledge economy, men continue to dominate technical work. Women's employment in the information technology, electronics and communications (ITEC) sector is much lower than their participation in the workforce generally, and it is declining in most industrialized countries. In the UK, for example, fewer than one in five ITEC professionals and managers are female and this figure is even lower in IT strategy and software development roles.[14] This is consistent with the findings of the 2007 Skills Survey from Felstead et al., which found that men are more likely than women to be found in jobs that involve complex and advanced computer or computerised equipment use and "this gender imbalance has changed little between 1997 and 2006."[15] These sexual divisions in the labour market are proving intransigent and mean that women are largely excluded from the processes of technical design that shape the world we live in—a point to which I return below.

Labour market economists tend to explain such sex segregation in terms of differences in human capital, domestic responsibilities that fall disproportionately on women, and employment

---

12 Judy Wajcman, *Feminism Confronts Technology* (Cambridge, UK: Polity, 1991).

13 C. Cockburn, *Brothers: Male Dominance and Technological Change* (London: Pluto, 1983), 203.

14 Christina Evans et al., *Implementing Diversity Policies: Guiding Principles* (London: Royal Academy of Engineering, 2007). http://www.womenandtechnology.eu/digitalcity/servlet/PublishedFileServlet/AAABGWEJ/enterp_implementing_diversity_policies_2008.07.13-20.08.38.pdf.

15 Alan Felstead et al., *Skills at Work, 1986 to 2006* (Oxford: ESRC Centre on Skills, Knowledge and Organisational Performance, 2007), xii. This is also reflected in the gender pay gap in London—the highest in Britain—as a result of the dominance of the finance sector that targets graduates in mathematics, science and engineering; see Greater London Authority, *Women in London's Economy: Closing the Gap* (London: Greater London Authority, 2008). http://legacy.london.gov.uk/mayor/wile/docs/closing-the-gap.pdf.

discrimination.[16] In this framework, remedying the "gender deficit" is seen as a problem that can be overcome by a combination of different socialisation processes and equal opportunity policies. The strengths and limitations of equal employment opportunity policies have been much debated in recent decades.[17] Feminists have pointed out that the problem does not lie with women (their socialisation, their aspirations and values) and that we need to address the broader questions of whether and in what way technoscience and its institutions can be reshaped to accommodate women. Such critiques emphasise that, in addition to gender structures and stereotyping, engrained cultures of masculinity are still ubiquitous within these industries, causing many young women to reject careers and older women to leave the field. This is fundamentally because women are being asked to exchange major aspects of their gender identity for a masculine version, whilst there is no similar "degendering" process prescribed for men.

Technology as Gendered

Recognising the complexity of the relationship between women and technology, by the 1980s feminists were exploring the gendered character of technology itself. In Sandra Harding's words, feminist criticisms of science evolved from asking the "Woman question" in science to asking the more radical "science question" in feminism.[18] Rather than asking how women can be more equitably treated within and by science, the question became how a science apparently so deeply involved in distinctively masculine projects can possibly be used for emancipatory ends. Similarly, feminist analyses of technology were shifting from women's access to technology to examining the very processes by which technology is developed and used, as well as those by which gender is constituted. Both socialist and radical feminisms began to analyse the gendered nature of technical expertise, and put the spotlight on artefacts themselves. The social factors that shape different technologies came under scrutiny, especially the way technology reflects gender divisions and inequalities. The problem was not only men's monopoly of technology, but also the way gender is embedded in technology itself.

---

16 G. Becker, *A Treatise on the Family* (Cambridge, MA: Harvard University Press, 1991).

17 C. Bacchi, *The Politics of Affirmative Action* (London: Sage, 1996); Clem Herman and Juliet Webster, eds., "Information, Communication & Society," special issue, *Gender and ICT* 10, no. 3 (2007): 279–86. doi:10.1080/13691180701409739; S. Wyatt, F. et al., eds., *Technology and In/equality: Questioning the Information Society* (London: Routledge, 2000).

18 Harding, *Science Question in Feminism*, 29.

For radical feminism, women and men are fundamentally different and women's power, women's culture and women's pleasure are regarded as having been systematically controlled and dominated by men, operating through patriarchal institutions like medicine and militarism. Western technology, like science, is deeply implicated in this masculine project of the domination and control of women and nature. This approach has been particularly influential in relation to the technologies of human biological reproduction.[19] It is fuelled by the perception that the processes of pregnancy and childbirth are directed and controlled by ever more sophisticated and intrusive technologies. Radical feminists' strong opposition to the development of the new reproductive technologies (such as *in-vitro* fertilisation) during the 1980s reflected fears of patriarchal exploitation of women's bodies. There was a call for new technology based on female rather than male values.

These approaches took the debate about gender and technology beyond the use/abuse model, focusing on the political qualities of technology. Where liberal feminism sees the problem in terms of male control of neutral technologies, radical feminists argued that gender power relations are embedded more deeply within technoscience. This was also a forceful assertion of women's interests and needs as being different from men's and highlighted the way in which women are not always well served by current technologies. However, in representing women as inherently nurturing and pacifist, it tended to reinforce an essentialist view of sex difference. The historical and cultural specificity of our modern understanding of women as being radically other than men was overlooked.[20] Too often the result was a pessimistic portrayal of women as victims of patriarchal technoscience.

While radical feminism focused on women's bodies and sexuality, the core concern of Socialist feminism was the relationship between women's work and technology. Like many of my feminist contemporaries, I came to gender and technology studies from having been immersed in the 1970s' Marxist labour process debates about the technology of production. This literature provided a compelling critique of technological determinism, arguing that, far from being an autonomous force, technology itself is crucially affected by the antagonistic class relations of production. Technological revolution was understood to be a trait of capital accumulation processes. The socialist feminist approach began by revealing that the division of labour was also a sexual hierarchy, and that its gendered nature was not incidental. A crucial

---

19   G. Corea et al., *Man-Made Women: How New Reproductive Technologies Affect Women* (London: Hutchinson, 1985); P. Spallone and D. Steinberg, eds., *Made to Order: The Myth of Reproductive and Genetic Engineering* (London: Pergamon, 1987).
20   C. Merchant, *The Death of Nature: Women, Ecology and the Scientific Revolution* (New York: Harper and Row, 1980).

historical perspective was brought to bear on the analysis of men's monopoly of technology. Extensive research demonstrated that women's exclusion from technology was as a consequence of the male domination of skilled trades that developed during the Industrial Revolution.[21]

Socialist feminist frameworks, then, saw masculinity as embedded in the machinery itself, highlighting the role of technology as a key source of male power.[22] Instead of treating artefacts as neutral or value-free, social relations (including gender relations) are materialized in tools and techniques. Technology was seen as socially shaped, but shaped by men to the exclusion of women. While this literature did reflect an understanding of the historical variability and plurality of the categories of "women" and "technology," it was nevertheless pessimistic about the possibilities of redesigning technologies for gender equality. The proclivity of technological developments to entrench gender hierarchies was emphasised rather than the prospects they afford for change. In short, not enough attention was paid to women's agency. And it is precisely this rather negative register that provoked a reaction from a new generation of feminist scholars.

Moreover, by the late 1980s second-wave feminism had transformed itself in response to sustained critiques from black feminism, queer theory, post-modernism and post-colonial theory. A number of writers now refer to "post-feminism" or third-wave feminism to mark both an epistemological break, and to denote the period after the height of second-wave feminism.[23] This more recent work marks a shift away from a focus on equality to a focus on debates about differences between women, stressing that gender is connected to other axes of power such as race, colonialism, sexuality, disability and class. Rather than thinking of feminism, we need to think of feminisms as multiple and dynamic, and in the process of ongoing transformation.

Contemporary Approaches

If feminists of the 1980s were rather pessimistic about the prospects for women offered by the microelectronic revolution, there was a much more enthusiastic response to the dawn of the digital age. Sharing the optimism

---

21 Harriet Bradley, *Men's Work, Women's Work* (Cambridge, UK: Polity, 1989); Cockburn, *Brothers: Male Dominance*; R. Milkman, *Gender at Work: The Dynamics of Job Segregation During World War II* (Urbana: University of Illinois Press, 1987).

22 C. Cockburn, *Machinery of Dominance: Women, Men and Technical Know-How* (London: Pluto Press, 1985); M. McNeil, ed., *Gender and Expertise* (London: Free Association Books, 1987); Wajcman, *Feminism Confronts Technology*; Juliet Webster, *Office Automation: The Labour Process and Women's Work in Britain* (Hemel Hempstead, UK: Harvester Wheatsheaf, 1990).

23 Rosalind Gill, *Gender and the Media* (Cambridge, UK: Polity, 2007), 250-1.

of cyber-gurus from Manuel Castells to Nicholas Negroponte, feminist approaches of the 1990s and today are positive about the possibilities of information and communication technologies (ICTs) to empower women and transform gender relations.[24]

A common argument in this literature is that the virtuality of cyberspace and the Internet spell the end of the embodied basis for sex difference.[25] Cyberfeminists, for example Sadie Plant, see digital technologies as blurring of boundaries between humans and machines, and between male and female, enabling their users to choose their disguises and assume alternative identities.[26] Industrial technology may have had a patriarchal character, but digital technologies, based on brain rather than brawn, on networks rather than hierarchy, herald a new relationship between women and machines. Writers such as Plant are interested in revalorising the feminine, bringing woman's radical alterity, her difference, into being. For them, the Internet and cyberspace are seen as feminine media, providing the technological basis for a new form of society that is potentially liberating for women. According to this view, women, rather than men, are uniquely suited to life in the digital age.

The optimism of this post-feminist literature is best summed up by Donna Haraway's cyborg metaphor, conveying the idea that technology is fully part of all of us.[27] Because it is an aspect of our identity, an aspect of our embodiment, conceiving of ourselves as cyborgs provides a tool for transforming the gender relations of technoscience. Haraway notes the great power of science and technology to create new meanings and new entities, to make new worlds. She positively revels in the very difficulty of predicting what technology's effects will be and warns against any purist rejection of the "unnatural," hybrid, entities produced by biotechnology. Genetic engineering, reproductive technology and the advent of virtual reality are all seen as fun-

---

24   Manuel Castells, *The Rise of the Network Society* (Oxford: Blackwell, 1996); Nicholas Negroponte, *Being Digital* (Sydney: Hodder & Stoughton, 1995); E. Green and A. Adam, eds. "Editorial Comment," *Information, Communication & Society* 2, no. 4 (1999); S. Kemp and J. Squires, eds., *Feminisms: An Oxford Reader* (Oxford: Oxford University Press), 1998; G. Kirkup et al., *The Gendered Cyborg: A Reader* (London: Routledge, 2000).

25   M. Millar, *Cracking the Gender Code: Who Rules the Wired World?* (Toronto: Second Story, 1998); Sadie Plant, *Zeros and Ones: Digital Women in the New Technoculture* (London: Fourth Estate, 1998).

26   Plant, *Zeros and Ones*.

27   Donna J. Haraway, "A Manifesto for Cyborgs: Science, Technology, and Socialist Feminism in the 1980s," *Socialist Review* 80, (1985): 65–108; Haraway, *Modest _Witness*.

damentally challenging traditional notions of gender identity. As such, they mark a transformation in the relationship between women and technology.

Developments in digital technologies do call for some radical rethinking, both of the processes of technological innovation and of their impact on the culture and practices of everyday life. Haraway's groundbreaking work opened up new possibilities for feminist analyses to explore the ways in which women's lives are intimately entwined with technologies. In looking forward to what ICTs and biotechnologies may make possible, Haraway elabourates a new feminist "imaginary" different from the "material reality" of the existing technological order. Her writing has been particularly influential among feminist scholars within STS, epitomising the challenge to second-wave feminism's tendency to portray women as victims of technological change.

While Haraway is optimistic about the opportunities for radical political transformations opened up by developments in technoscience, too often her work has been read as an uncritical acceptance of everything digital. Such enthusiasm has tipped some post-modern commentators towards technological determinism—albeit of a celebratory rather than pessimistic bent. There is still a current in feminist literature on cyberculture that regards new digital technologies as a rupture from more established ones and downplays any continuity between them.

Certainly women have been actively engaged in constructing hybrid, transgendered identities through their consumption of new media. Diary writing on web logs, for example, is a popular activity among young women. However, the possibility and the fluidity of gender discourse in the virtual world are constrained by the visceral, lived gender relations of the material world. Even *Second Life* (an online virtual world with over two million registrations), which is widely seen, as promoting anti-establishment values, has become a major source of virtual pornography, apparently well suited to those with a taste for sadomasochistic forms of sex.[28] Such fantasy cyberworlds, then, are not necessarily comfortable cultural environments for women to inhabit. To move forward, we need to understand that technology as such is neither inherently patriarchal nor unambiguously liberating.

---

28 Shaowen Bardzell and Jeffrey Bardzell, "Sex-Interface-Aesthetics: The Docile Avatars and Embodied Pixels of Second Life BDSM" (paper, CHI conference, Montreal, Canada, April 22-27, 2006), http://www.ics.uci.edu/~johannab/sexual.interactions.2006/papers/ShaowenBardzell&JeffreyBardzell-SexualInteractions2006.pdf.

Technofeminism: Combining Feminism and STS

Over the last two decades, feminist writing within the field of STS has theorised the relationship between gender and technology as one of mutual shaping. A shared idea in this tradition is that technological innovation is itself shaped by the social circumstances within which it takes place. Crucially, the notion that technology is simply the product of rational technical imperatives has been dislodged. Objects and artefacts are no longer seen as separate from society, but as part of the social fabric that holds society together; they are never merely technical or social. Rather, the broad social shaping or constructivist approach treats technology as a sociotechnical product— a seamless web or network combining artefacts, people, organisations, cultural meanings and knowledge.[29] It follows that technological change is a contingent and heterogeneous process in which technology and society are mutually constituted.

Within mainstream STS, the ways in which technological objects may shape and be shaped by the operation of gender interests or identities has not been a central focus. Whilst innovations are seen as sociotechnical networks, it has been largely incumbent on feminists to demonstrate that gender relations inform these networks. After all, if "technology is society made durable," then gender power relations will influence the process of technological change, which in turn configures gender relations.[30] Women's systematic absence from the sites of observable conflict over the direction of technological developments is therefore as indicative of the mobilisation of gender interests as is the presence of other actors. Empirical research on everything from the microwave oven,[31] the telephone,[32] and the contraceptive pill,[33] to robotics

---

[29] Wiebe E. Bijker, Thomas P. Hughes, and Trevor Pinch, eds., *The Social Construction of Technological Systems* (Cambridge, MA: MIT Press, 1987); Edward J. Hackett et al., eds., *The Handbook of Science and Technology Studies*, 3rd ed. (Cambridge, MA: MIT Press, 2008); J. Law and J. Hassard, eds., *A Sociology of Monsters: Essays on Power, Technology and Domination* (London: Routledge, 1991); Donald MacKenzie and Judy Wajcman, *The Social Shaping of Technology*, 2nd ed. (Milton Keynes, UK: Open University Press, 1999).

[30] B. Latour, "Technology is Society Made Durable," in Law and Hassard, *A Sociology of Monsters*, 103.

[31] C. Cockburn and S. Ormrod, *Gender and Technology in the Making* (London: Sage, 1993).

[32] M. Martin, *'Hello Central?' Gender, Technology, and the Culture in the Formation of Telephone Systems* (Montreal: Mcgill-Queen's University Press, 1991).

[33] N. Oudshoorn, *Beyond the Natural Body: An Archaeology of Sex Hormones* (London: Routledge, 1994).

and software agents[34] has clearly demonstrated that the marginalisation of women from the technological community has a profound influence on the design, technical content and use of artefacts.

A social constructivist framework now has been widely adopted by feminist STS scholars.[35] In common with my own technofeminist theory, it conceives of technology as both a source and consequence of gender relations.[36] In other words, gender relations can be thought of as materialised in technology, and masculinity and femininity in turn acquire their meaning and character through their enrolment and embeddedness in working machines. Such a mutual shaping approach recognises that the gendering of technology affects the entire life trajectory of an artefact. Indeed, feminist research has been at the forefront of more general moves within STS to deconstruct the designer/user divide, and that between production and consumption, emphasising the connectedness of all phases of technological development.[37] The gendering of technologies can then be understood as not only shaped in design, but also shaped or reconfigured at the multiple points of consumption and use.

Let me again illustrate this by considering an economist's account of the impact of technologies on domestic labour. Avner Offer explains why some kinds of household appliances have diffused more rapidly than others by comparing "time-saving goods" (for example, cookers and washing machines) with "time-using goods" (such as radio and television).[38] However, the finding puzzles him that there is no direct link between timesaving appliances and the amount of time spent in housework. While he takes account of rising standards and class differences in housework, his model of consumption is not attuned to the gender relations of artefacts. Domestic appliances enter a domain heavily signified in terms of traditional sex roles, and are already imprinted with gendered agendas or "genderscripts" defining their appropriate

---

34 Lucy Suchman, "Feminist STS and the Sciences of the Artificial," in Hackett et al., *The Handbook of Science and Technology Studies*, 139–163.
35 A. Berg, "Digital Feminism," (PhD thesis, Norwegian University of Science and Technology, Trondheim, 1996); W. Faulkner, "The Technology Question in Feminism: A View from Feminist Technology Studies," *Women's Studies International Forum* 24, no. 1 (2001); M. Lie, ed., *He, She and IT Revisited: New Perspectives on Gender in the Information Society* (Oslo: Gyldendal Akademisk, 2003).
36 Wajcman, *TechnoFeminism*.
37 Ruth Schwartz Cowan, "The Consumption Junction: A Proposal for Research Strategies in the Sociology of Technology," in Bijker, Hughes, and Pinch, *The Social Construction of Technological Systems*, 261–280.
38 Avner Offer, *The Challenge of Affluence* (Oxford: Oxford University Press, 2006).

operators.[39] Indeed, individuals demonstrate their gender identity in part through their daily use of objects. To be feminine is to perform femininity, and the daily doing of housework continues to be pivotal to being a wife and mother.

Moreover, technological innovations often change the nature and meaning of tasks, as well as introducing novel practices. STS scholarship increasingly recognises that the social meanings of technology are contingently stabilised and contestable, that the fate of a technology depends on the social context and cannot simply be read off fixed sets of power arrangements. The "domestication" framework, in particular, has sensitised researchers to some of the complex processes at work in incorporating technologies into everyday life.[40] In line with social shaping principles, domestication foregrounds user agency in the way people continuously interpret, appropriate and use artefacts in their everyday lives.

Similarly, the concept of gender itself is now understood as a performance or social achievement, constructed in interaction.[41] Rather than conceiving of gender as fixed and existing independently of technology, the notion of performativity, or "gender as doing," sees the construction of gender identities as shaped together with the technology in the making. Thus, both technology and gender are products of a moving relational process, emerging from collective and individual acts of interpretation. It follows from this that gendered conceptions of users are fluid, and that the same artefact is subject to a variety of interpretations and meanings. The result is more nuanced feminist research that captures the increasingly complex intertwining of gender and technoscience as an ongoing process of mutual shaping over time and across multiple sites.

Conclusion

Feminist theories of technology have come a long way over the last quarter of a century. The intellectual exploration at the intersections of feminist scholarship and STS has enriched both fields immeasurably. While each has been characterised by diverse lines of argument over the last decades, the underlying continuities are all the more striking. Both fields foreground the way that

---

39 Cockburn and Ormrod, *Gender and Technology*; N. Oudshoorn, E. Rommes, and M. Stienstra, "Configuring the User As Everybody: Gender and Cultures of Design in Information and Communication Technologies," *Science, Technology & Human Values* 29, no. 1 (2004): 30–64.

40 L. Haddon, *Information and Communication Technologies in Everyday Life* (Oxford: Berg, 2004); R. Silverstone and E. Hirsch, *Consuming Technologies* (London: Routledge, 1992).

41 J. Butler, *Gender Trouble* (New York: Routledge, 1990).

people and artefacts co-evolve, reminding us that things could be otherwise, that technologies are not the inevitable result of the application of scientific and technological knowledge.

For me, the distinguishing insight of feminist STS or technofeminism is that gender is integral to this sociotechnical process: that the materiality of technology affords or inhibits the doing of particular gender power relations. Women's identities, needs and priorities are configured together with digital technologies. For all the diversity of feminist voices, feminist scholars share a concern with the hierarchical divisions marking relations between men and women.

Key to our analysis is the understanding that, while gender is embedded in technoscience, the relationship is not immutably fixed. While the design process is decisive, sociotechnical configurations exhibit different degrees of determination and contingency at different moments in their relationship. The capacity of women users to produce new, advantageous readings of artefacts is dependent on their broader economic and social circumstances.

Such a perspective redefines the problem of the exclusion of groups of people from technological domains and activities. Technofeminism exposes how the concrete practices of design and innovation lead to the absence of specific users, such as women. While it is not always possible to specify in advance the characteristics of artefacts and information systems that would guarantee more inclusiveness, it is imperative that women are involved throughout the processes and practices of technological innovation. STS provides a theory of the constitutive power of tools, techniques and objects to materialise social, political and economics arrangements. Drawing more women into design—the configuration of artefacts—is not only an equal employment opportunity issue, but is also crucially about how the world we live in is shaped, and for whom. We live in a technological culture, a society that is constituted by science and technology, and so the politics of technology is integral to the renegotiation of gender power relations.

Bibliography

Bacchi, C. *The Politics of Affirmative Action*. London: Sage, 1996.

Bardzell, Shaowen, and Jeffrey Bardzell. "Sex-Interface-Aesthetics: The Docile Avatars and Embodied Pixels of Second Life BDSM." Paper presented at CHI conference, Montreal, Canada, April 22-27, 2006. http://www.ics.uci.edu/~johannab/sexual.interactions.2006/papers/ShaowenBardzell&JeffreyBardzell-SexualInteractions2006.pdf.

Becker, G. *A Treatise on the Family*. Cambridge, MA: Harvard University Press, 1991.

Berg, A. "Digital Feminism," PhD thesis, Norwegian University of Science and Technology, Trondheim, 1996.
Bijker, Wiebe E., Thomas P. Hughes, and Trevor Pinch, eds. *The Social Construction of Technological Systems*. Cambridge, MA: MIT Press, 1987.
Bradley, Harriet. *Men's Work, Women's Work*. Cambridge, UK: Polity, 1989.
Butler, J. *Gender Trouble*. New York: Routledge, 1990.
Castells, Manuel. *The Rise of the Network Society*. Oxford: Blackwell, 1996.
Cockburn, C. *Brothers: Male Dominance and Technological Change*. London: Pluto, 1983.
———. *Machinery of Dominance: Women, Men and Technical Know-How*. London: Pluto Press, 1985.
Cockburn, C., and S. Ormrod. *Gender and Technology in the Making*. London: Sage, 1993.
Corea, G., R. D. Klein, J. Hanmer, H. B. Holmes, B. Hoskins, and M. Kishwar. *Man-Made Women: How New Reproductive Technologies Affect Women*. London: Hutchinson, 1985.
Cowan, Ruth Schwartz. "The Consumption Junction: A Proposal for Research Strategies in the Sociology of Technology." In Bijker, Hughes, and Pinch, *The Social Construction of Technological Systems*, 261-280.
———. "The 'Industrial Revolution' in the Home: Household Technology and Social Change in the Twentieth Century." *Technology and Culture* 17, (1976): 1-23.
Evans, Christina, Judith Glover, Yvonne Guerrier, and Cornelia Wilson. *Implementing Diversity Policies: Guiding Principles*. London: Royal Academy of Engineering, 2007. http://www.womenandtechnology.eu/digitalcity/servlet/PublishedFileServlet/AAABGWEJ/enterp_implementing_diversity_policies_2008.07.13-20.08.38.pdf.
Faulkner, W. "The Technology Question in Feminism: A View from Feminist Technology Studies." *Women's Studies International Forum* 24, no. 1 (2001): 79-95.
Faulkner, W., and M. Lohan. "Masculinities and Technologies." *Men and Masculinities* 6, no. 4 (2004): 319-29.
Felstead, Alan, Duncan Gallie, Frances Green, and Ying Zhou. *Skills at Work, 1986 to 2006*. Oxford: ESRC Centre on Skills, Knowledge and Organisational Performance, 2007.
Folbre, N. *The Invisible Heart: Economics and Family Values*. New York: New Press, 2001.
Gill, Rosalind. *Gender and the Media*. Cambridge, UK: Polity, 2007.
Greater London Authority. *Women in London's Economy: Closing the Gap*. London: Greater London Authority, 2008. http://legacy.london.gov.uk/mayor/wile/docs/closing-the-gap.pdf.

Green, E., and A. Adam, eds. "Editorial Comment." *Information, Communication & Society* 2, no. 4 (1999): v–vii.
Hacker, S. *Pleasure, Power and Technology*. Boston: Unwin Hyman, 1989.
Hackett, Edward J., Olga Amsterdamska, Michael Lynch, and Judy Wajcman, eds. *The Handbook of Science and Technology Studies*. 3rd ed. Cambridge, MA: MIT Press, 2008.
Haddon, L. *Information and Communication Technologies in Everyday Life*. Oxford: Berg, 2004.
Haraway, Donna J. "A Manifesto for Cyborgs: Science, Technology, and Socialist Feminism in the 1980s." *Socialist Review* 80 (1985): 65–108.
———. *Modest_Witness@Second_Millenium.FemaleMan_Meets_OncoMouse: Feminism and Technoscience*. New York: Routledge, 1997.
Harding, Sandra. *The Science Question in Feminism*. New York: Cornell University Press, 1986.
Herman, Clem, and Juliet Webster, eds. "Information, Communication & Society." Special issue, *Gender and ICT* 10, no. 3 (2007): 279–286. doi:10.1080/13691180701409739.
Himmelweit, Susan. "An Evolutionary Approach to Feminist Economics: Two Different Models of Caring." In *Toward a Feminist Philosophy of Economics*, edited by Drucilla K. Barker and Edith Kuiper, 247–265. London: Routledge, 2003.
Kemp, S., and J. Squires, eds. *Feminisms: An Oxford Reader*. Oxford: Oxford University Press, 1998.
Kirkup, G., L. Janes, K. Woodward, and F. Hovenden. *The Gendered Cyborg: A Reader*. London: Routledge, 2000.
Lagesen, V. "A Cyberfeminist Utopia? Perceptions of Gender and Computer Science Among Malaysian Women Computer Science Students and Faculty." *Science, Technology, & Human Values* 33, no. 1 (2008): 5–27.
Latour, B. "Technology is Society Made Durable." In Law and Hassard, *A Sociology of Monsters*, 103–31.
Law, J., and J. Hassard, eds. *A Sociology of Monsters: Essays on Power, Technology and Domination*. (London: Routledge, 1991).
Lie, M., ed. *He, She and IT Revisited: New Perspectives on Gender in the Information Society*. Oslo: Gyldendal Akademisk, 2003.
MacKenzie, Donald, and Judy Wajcman. *The Social Shaping of Technology*. 2nd ed. Milton Keynes, UK: Open University Press, 1999.
Martin, M. *'Hello Central?' Gender, Technology, and the Culture in the Formation of Telephone Systems*. Montreal: Mcgill-Queen's University Press, 1991.
McNeil, M., ed. *Feminist Cultural Studies of Science and Technology*. London: Routledge, 2007.
———. *Gender and Expertise*. London: Free Association Books, 1987.

Merchant, C. *The Death of Nature: Women, Ecology and the Scientific Revolution*. New York: Harper and Row, 1980.

Milkman, R. *Gender at Work: The Dynamics of Job Segregation During World War II*. Urbana: University of Illinois Press, 1987.

Millar, M. *Cracking the Gender Code: Who Rules the Wired World?* Toronto: Second Story, 1998.

Negroponte, Nicholas. *Being Digital*. Sydney: Hodder & Stoughton, 1995.

Offer, Avner. *The Challenge of Affluence*. Oxford: Oxford University Press, 2006.

Oldenziel, Ruth. *Making Technology Masculine: Men, Women and Modern Machines in America*. Amsterdam: Amsterdam University Press, 1999.

Oudshoorn, N. *Beyond the Natural Body: An Archaeology of Sex Hormones*. London: Routledge, 1994.

Oudshoorn, N., E. Rommes, and M. Stienstra. "Configuring the User As Everybody: Gender and Cultures of Design in Information and Communication Technologies." *Science, Technology & Human Values* 29, no. 1 (2004): 30–64.

Plant, Sadie. *Zeros and Ones: Digital Women in the New Technoculture*. London: Fourth Estate, 1998.

Silverstone, R., and E. Hirsch. *Consuming Technologies*. London: Routledge, 1992.

Spallone, P., and D. Steinberg, eds. *Made to Order: The Myth of Reproductive and Genetic Engineering*. London: Pergamon, 1987.

Stanley, A. *Mothers and Daughters of Invention*. New Jersey: Rutgers University Press, 1995.

Suchman, Lucy. "Feminist STS and the Sciences of the Artificial." In Hackett et al., *The Handbook of Science and Technology Studies*, 139–163.

Turkle, Sherry. *The Second Self: Computers and the Human Spirit*. London: Granada, 1984.

Wajcman, Judy. *Feminism Confronts Technology*. Cambridge, UK: Polity, 1991.

———. *TechnoFeminism*. Cambridge, UK: Polity, 2004.

Webster, Juliet. *Office Automation: The Labour Process and Women's Work in Britain*. Hemel Hempstead, UK: Harvester Wheatsheaf, 1990.

Wyatt, S., F. Henwood, N. Miller, and P. Senker, eds. *Technology and In/equality: Questioning the Information Society*. London: Routledge, 2000.

Cyborg Feminism and the Methodology of the Oppressed

Chela Sandoval[1]

> *We didn't cross the border, the border crossed us.*
>
> ~Chicana/o Slogan

> *If life is just a highway*
> *Then the soul is just a car*
> *And objects in the rear view mirror*
> *May appear closer than they are*
>
> ~Meatloaf

> *If we are imprisoned by language,*
> *then escape from that prison-house requires*
> *language poets.*
>
> ~Donna Haraway

What constitutes "resistance" and oppositional politics under the imperatives of political, economic, and cultural transnationalization? Current global restructuring is effecting the organizational formations not only of business, but of cultural economies, consciousness, and knowledge. Social activists and theorists throughout the twentieth century have been attempting to construct theories of opposition that are capable of comprehending, responding to, and acting back upon these globalizing forces in ways that renegotiate power on behalf of those Marx called the "proletariat," Barthes called the "colonized classes," Hartsock called "women," and Lorde called the "outsiders." If transnational corporations are generating "business strategy and its relation to political initiatives at regional, national, and local

---

[1] Editor's note: this paper was previously published as a chapter in *The Cyborg Handbook*, ed. Chris Hables Gray, (New York: Routledge, 1995), 407-421.

levels,"[2] then, what are the concurrent forms of strategy being developed by the subaltern—by the marginalized—that focus on defining the forms of oppositional consciousness and praxis that can be effective under first world transnationalizing forces?

Let me begin by invoking Silicon Valley—that great land of Lockheed, IBM, Macintosh, Hewlett Packard—where over 30,000 workers have been laid off in the last two years, and another 30,000 more await a similar fate over the year to come: the fate of workers without jobs, those who fear for their livelihood. I begin here to honor the muscles and sinews of workers who grow tired in the required repetitions, in the warehouses, assembly lines, administrative cells, and computer networks that run the great electronic firms of the late twentieth century. These workers know the pain of the union of machine and bodily tissue, the robotic conditions, and in the late twentieth century, the cyborg conditions under which the notion of human agency must take on new meanings. A large percentage of these workers who are not in the administrative sector but in labor-grade sectors are US people of color, indigenous to the Americas, or those whose ancestors were brought here as slaves or indentured servants; they include those who immigrated to the United States in the hopes of a better life, while being integrated into a society hierarchized by race, gender, sex, class, language, and social position. Cyborg life: life as a worker who flips burgers, who speaks the cyborg speech of McDonald's, is a life that the workers of the future must prepare themselves for in small, everyday ways. *My argument has been that colonized peoples of the Americas have already developed the cyborg skills required for survival under techno-human conditions* as a requisite for survival under domination over the last three hundred years. Interestingly, however, theorists of globalization engage with the introduction of an oppositional "cyborg" politics as if these politics have emerged with the advent of electronic technology alone, and not as a requirement of consciousness in opposition developed under previous forms of domination.

In this essay I propose another vision, wrought out of the work of cultural theorist and philosopher of science Donna Haraway, who in 1985 wrote the groundbreaking work on "Cyborg Feminism,"[3] in order to re-demonstrate what is overlooked in current cyborg theory, namely, *that cyborg consciousness can be understood as the technological embodiment of a particular and specific form*

---

2   Richard P. Appelbaum, "New Journal for Global Studies Center," *CORI: Center for Global Studies Newsletter* 1, no. 2 (May 1994).

3   Editors' note: using the title "Cyborg Feminism" here and elsewhere in this chapter, Sandoval is referring to Donna Haraway's essay "A Cyborg Manifesto: Science, Technology, and Socialist-Feminism in the Late Twentieth Century," in *Simians, Cyborgs, and Women: The Reinvention of Nature* (New York: Routledge, 1991), 149-181; see also note 13.

of oppositional consciousness that I have elsewhere described as "US third world feminism."[4] And indeed, if cyborg consciousness is to be considered as anything other than that which replicates the now dominant global world order, then cyborg consciousness must be developed out of a set of technologies that together comprise the methodology of the oppressed, a methodology that can provide the guides for survival and resistance under first world transnational cultural conditions. This oppositional cyborg consciousness has also been identified by terms such as "mestiza" consciousness, "situated subjectivities," "womanism," and "differential consciousness." In the interests of furthering Haraway's own unstated but obvious project of challenging the racialization and apartheid of theoretical domains in the academy, and in the interests of translation, of transcoding from one academic idiom to another, from "cyborgology" to "feminism," from "US third world feminism" to "cultural" and to "subaltern" theory, I trace the routes traveled by the methodology of the oppressed as encoded by Haraway in "Cyborg Feminism."

Haraway's research represents an example of scholarly work that attempts to bridge the current apartheid of theoretical domains: "white male poststructuralism," "hegemonic feminism," "postcolonial theory," and "US third world feminism." Among her many contributions, Haraway provides new metaphoric grounds of resistance for the alienated white male subject under first world conditions of transnationalization, *and thus the metaphor cyborg represents profound possibilities for the twenty-first century* (implications of hope, for example, for Jameson's lost subject which "can no longer extend its pro-tensions and re-tensions across the temporal manifold."[5] Under cyborg theory, computer "travel" can be understood as "displacing" the "self" in a similar fashion as the self was displaced under modernist dominations). An oppositional cyborg politics, then, could very well bring the politics of the alienated white male subject into alliance with the subaltern politics of US third world feminism. Haraway's metaphor, however, in its travels through the academy, has been utilized and appropriated in a fashion that ironically represses the very work that it also fundamentally relies upon, and this continuing repression then serves to reconstitute the apartheid of theoretical domains once again. If scholarship in the humanities thrives under the regime of this apartheid, Haraway represents a boundary crosser, and her work a rises from a place that is often overlooked or misapprehended under hegemonic understandings.

---

4 See Chela Sandoval, "US Third World Feminism: The Theory and Method of Oppositional Consciousness in the Postmodern World," *Genders* 10 (Spring 1991): 1-24, which lays the groundwork for articulating the methodology of the oppressed.

5 Fredric Jameson, "Postmodernism, or The Cultural Logic of Late Capitalism," *New Left Review* 146 (July-August 1984): 71.

I have argued elsewhere that the methodology of the oppressed consists of five different technologies developed in order to ensure survival under previous first world conditions.[6] The technologies which together comprise the methodology of the oppressed generate the forms of agency and consciousness that can create effective forms of resistance under postmodern cultural conditions, and can be thought of as constituting a "cyborg," if you like, or at least a "cyber" form of resistance.[7] The practice of this Cyber Consciousness that is US third world feminism, or what I refer to as a "differential postmodern form of oppositional consciousness" has also been described in terms that stress its motion; it is "flexible," "mobile," "diasporic," "schizophrenic," "nomadic" in nature. These forms of mobility, however, align around a field of force (other from motion itself) which inspires, focuses and drives them as oppositional forms of praxis. Indeed, this form of consciousness-in--opposition is best thought of as the particular field of force that makes possible the practices and procedures of the "methodology of the oppressed." Conversely, this methodology is best thought of as comprised of techniques-for-moving energy or better, as *oppositional technologies of power*: both "inner" or psychic technologies, and "outer" technologies of social praxis.

These technologies can be summarized as follows: 1) What Anzaldúa calls "la facultad," Barthes calls semiology, the "science of signs in culture," or what Henry Louis Gates calls "signifyin'" and Audre Lorde calls "deep seeing" are all forms of "sign-reading" that comprise the first of what are five fundamental technologies of this methodology. 2) The second, and well-recognized technology of the subaltern is the process of challenging dominant ideological signs through their "de-construction": the act of separating a form from its dominant meaning. 3) The third technology is what I call "meta-ideologizing" in honor of its activity: the operation of appropriating dominant

---

6   Chela Sandoval, *The Methodology of the Oppressed* (Minneapolis: University of Minnesota Press, 2000).

7   The term *cybernetics* was coined by Norbert Wiener from the Greek word *Kubernetics*, meaning to steer, guide, govern. In 1989 the term was split in two, and its first half "cyber" (which is a neologism with no earlier root) was broken off from its "control" and "govern" meanings to represent the possibilities of travel and existence in the new space of computer networks, a space, it is argued, that must be negotiated by the human mind in new kinds of ways. This cyberspace is imagined in virtual reality films like *Freejack*, *The Lawnmower Man* and *Tron*. But it was first termed "cyberspace" and explored by the science fiction writer William Gibson in his 1987 book *Neuromoncer*. Gibson's own history, however, passes through and makes invisible 1970s feminist science fiction and theory, including the works of Russ, Butler, Delany, Piercy, Haraway, Sofoulis, and Sandoval. In all cases, it is this Cyberspace that can also adequately describe the new kind of movement and location of differential consciousness.

ideological forms and using them whole in order to transform their meanings into a new, imposed, and revolutionary concept. 4) The fourth technology of the oppressed that I call "democratics" is a process of locating: that is, a "zeroing in" that gathers, drives, and orients the previous three technologies, semiotics, deconstruction, and meta-ideologizing, with the intent of bringing about not simply survival or justice, as in earlier times, but egalitarian social relations, or, as third world writers from Fanon through Wong, Lugones, or Collins have put it,[8] with the aim of producing "love" in a de-colonizing, postmodern, post-empire world. 5) Differential movement is the fifth technology, the one through which, however, the others harmonically maneuver. In order to better understand the operation of differential movement, one must understand that it is a polyform upon which the previous technologies depend for their own operation. Only through differential movement can they be transferred toward their destinations, even the fourth, "democratics," which always tends toward the centering of identity in the interest of egalitarian social justice. These five technologies together comprise the methodology of the oppressed, which enables the enactment of what I have called the differential mode of oppositional social movement as in the example of US third world feminism.

Under US third world feminism, differential consciousness has been encoded as "la facultad" (a semiotic vector), the "outsider/within" (a deconstructive vector), strategic essentialism, (a meta-ideologizing vector), "womanism" (a moral vector), and as "la conciencia de la mestiza," "world traveling" and "loving cross-cultures" (differential vectors).[9] Unlike westerners such as Patrick Moynihan who argue that "the collapse of Communism" in 1991 proves how "racial, ethnic, and national ties of difference can only ultimately divide any society,"[10] a differential form of oppositional

---

[8] For example, see Merle Woo, "Letter to Ma," in *This Bridge Called My Back: Writings by Radical Women of Color*, ed. by Cherríe Moraga and Gloria Anzaldúa (Watertown, MA: Persephone Press, 1981), 140-147; Maria Lugones, "Playfulness, 'World'-Travelling, and Loving Perception," *Hypatia: A Journal of Feminist Philosophy* 2, no. 2 (1987): 3-19, doi:10.1111/j.1527-2001.1987.tb01062.x; Patricia Hill Collins, *Black Feminist Thought: Knowledge, Consciousness, and the Politics of Empowerment* (Boston: Unwin Hyman, 1990); June Jordan, "Where is the Love?" in *Making Face, Making Soul: Creative and Critical Perspectives by Feminists of Color*, ed. by Gloria Anzaldúa (San Francisco: Aunt Lute Foundation, 1990), 174.

[9] It is through these figures and technologies that narrative becomes capable of transforming the moment, of changing the world with new stories, of meta-ideologizing. Utilized together, these technologies create trickster stories, stratagems of magic, deception, and truth for healing the world, like Rap and CyberCinema, which work through the reapportionment of dominant powers.

[10] Patrick Moynihan, interview, *MacNeil/Lehrer NewsHour*, PBS, November 1991.

consciousness, as utilized and theorized by a racially diverse US coalition of women of color, is the form love takes in the postmodern world.[11] It generates grounds for coalition, making possible community across difference, permitting the generation of a new kind of citizenship, countrywomen and men of the same psychic terrain whose lives are made meaningful through the enactment of the methodology of the oppressed.

Whether interfaces with technology keep cyborg politics in re-newed contestation with differential (US third world feminist and subaltern) politics is a question only the political and theoretical strategies of undoing apartheid—of all kinds—will resolve. The differential form of social movement and its technologies—the methodology of the oppressed—provide the links capable of bridging the divided minds of the first world academy, and of creating grounds for what must be considered a new form of transdisciplinary work that centers the methodology of the oppressed—of the subaltern—as a new form of post-western empire knowledge formation that can transform current formations and disciplinizations of knowledge in the academy. As we shall see in the following analysis of Haraway's theoretical work, the networking required to imagine and theorize "cyborgian" consciousness can be considered, in part, a technologized metaphorization of the forms of resistance and oppositional consciousness articulated during the 1970s under the rubric of US third world feminism. However, terms such as "difference," the "middle voice," the "third meaning," "rasquache," "la conciencia de la mestiza," "hybridity," "schizophrenia," and processes such as "minor literature" and "strategic essentialism" also call up and represent forms of that cyberspace, that other zone for consciousness and behaviour that is being proposed from many locations and from across disciplines as that praxis most able to both confront and homeopathically resist postmodern cultural conditions.

Donna Haraway: Feminist Cyborg Theory and US Third World Feminism

Haraway's essay "Manifesto for Cyborgs" can be defined in its own terms as a "theorized and fabricated hybrid," a textual "machine," or as a "fiction mapping our social and bodily reality," phrases which Haraway also calls upon in order to re-define the term "cyborg," which, she continues, *is a "cybernetic organism," a mixture of technology and biology, a "creature" of both "social*

---

[11] See writings by US feminists of color on the matter of love, including June Jordan, "Where is the Love?"; Merle Woo, "Letter to Ma"; Patricia Hill Collins, *Black Feminist Thought*; Maria Lugones, "Playfulness, 'World'-Travelling, and Loving Perception"; and Audre Lorde, *Sister Outsider* (Trumansburg, NY: Crossing Press, 1984).

reality" and "fiction."[12] This vision that stands at the center of her imaginary is a "monstrous" image, for Haraway's cyborg is the "illegitimate" child of dominant society and oppositional social movement, of science and technology, of the human and the machine, of "first" and "third" worlds, of male and female, indeed, of every binary. The hybridity of this creature is situated in relation to each side of these binary positions, and to every desire for wholeness, she writes, as "blasphemy" stands to the body of religion.[13] Haraway's blasphemy is the cyborg, that which reproaches, challenges, transforms, and shocks. But perhaps the greatest shock in her feminist theory of cyborg politics takes place in the corridors of feminist theory, where Haraway's model has acted as a transcoding device, a technology that insists on translating the fundamental precepts of US third world feminist criticism into categories that are comprehensible under the jurisdictions of Women's Studies.

Haraway has been very clear about these intellectual lineages and alliances. Indeed, she writes in her introduction to *Simians, Cyborgs and Women* that one primary aim of her work is similar to that of US third world feminist theory and methods, which is, in Haraway's words, to bring about "the break-up of versions of Euro-American feminist humanisms in their devastating assumptions of master narratives deeply indebted to racism and colonialism." (It might be noted there that this same challenge, when uttered through the lips of a feminist theorist of color, can be indicted and even dismissed as "undermining the movement" or as "an example of separatist politics"). Haraway's second and connected aim is to propose a new grounds for theoretical and political alliances, a "cyborg feminism" that will be "more able" than the feminisms of earlier times, she writes, to "remain attuned to specific historical and political positionings and permanent partialities without abandoning the search for potent connections."[14] Haraway's cyborg feminism was thus conceived, at least in part, to recognize and join the contributions of US third world feminist theorists who have challenged, throughout the 1960s, 1970s and 1980s what Haraway identifies as hegemonic feminism's "unreflective participation in the logics, languages, and practices of white humanism." White feminism, Haraway points out, tends to search "for a single ground of domination to secure our revolutionary voice."[15]

---

12 Donna Haraway, *Simians, Cyborgs, and Women: The Reinvention of Nature* (New York: Routledge, 1991), 150. Most quotations in this section are from this text, especially from chapters 8 and 9, "A Cyborg Manifesto: Science, Technology, and Socialist-Feminism in the Late Twentieth Century" and "Situated Knowledges: The Science Question in Feminism and the Privilege of Partial Perspective."

13 Ibid., 149.

14 Ibid., 1.

15 Ibid., 160.

These are thus strong ideological alliances, and so it makes sense that Haraway should turn to US third world feminism for help in modeling the "cyborg" body that can be capable of challenging what she calls the "networks and informatics" of contemporary social reality. For, she affirms, it has been "feminist theory produced by women of color" which has developed "alternative discourses of womanhood," and these have disrupted "the humanisms of many Western discursive traditions."[16] Drawing from these and other alternative discourses, Haraway was able to lay the foundations for her theory of cyborg feminism, yet she remains clear on the issue of that theory's intellectual lineages and alliances:

> *White women, including socialist feminists, discovered (that is were forced kicking and screaming to notice) the non-innocence of the category "woman." That consciousness changes the geography of all previous categories; it denatures them as heat denatures a fragile protein. Cyborg feminists have to argue that "we" do not want any more natural matrix of unity and that no construction is whole.*[17]

The recognition "that no construction is whole," however—though it helps—is not enough to end the forms of domination that have historically impaired the ability of US liberation movements to effectively organize for equality. And for that reason, much of Haraway's ongoing work has been to identify the additional technical *skills* that are necessary for producing this different kind of coalitional, and what she calls "cyborg," feminism.

To understand Haraway's contribution, I want to point out and emphasize her correlation of these necessary skills with what I earlier identified as the methodology of the oppressed. It is no accident that Haraway defines, names

---

16 Donna Haraway, "Ecce Homo, Ain't (Ar'n't) I a Woman, and Inappropriate/d Others: The Human in a Post-Humanist Landscape," in *Feminists Theorize the Political*, ed. Judith Butler and Joan Scott (New York: Routledge, 1992), 95.

17 Haraway, *Simians, Cyborgs, and Women*, 157. This quotation historically refers its readers to the impact of the 1970's US third world feminist propositions which significantly revised the women's liberation movement by, among other things, renaming it with the ironic emphasis "the white women's movement"; and perhaps all uncomplicated belief in the righteous benevolence of US liberation movements can never return after Audre Lorde summarized seventies' women's liberation by saying that "when white feminists call for 'unity'" among women "they are only naming a deeper and real need for homogeneity." By the 1980s the central political problem on the table was how to go about imagining and constructing a feminist liberation movement that might bring women together across and through their differences. Haraway's first principle for action in 1985 was to call for and then teach a new hoped-for constituency, "cyborg feminists," that "'we' do not want any more natural matrix of unity and that no construction is whole."

and weaves the skills necessary to cyborgology through the techniques and terminologies of US third world cultural forms, from Native American concepts of "trickster" and "coyote" being[18] to "mestizaje," or the category "women of color," until the body of the feminist cyborg becomes clearly articulated with the material and psychic positionings of US third world feminism.[19] Like the "mestiza consciousness" described and defined under US third world feminism which, as Anzaldúa explains, arises "on borders and in margins" where feminists of color keep "intact shifting and multiple identities" and with "integrity" and love, the cyborg of Haraway's feminist manifesto must also be "resolutely committed to partiality, irony, intimacy and perversity."[20] In this equivalent alignment, Haraway writes, feminist cyborgs can be recognized (like agents of US third world feminism) to be the "illegitimate offspring," of "patriarchal capitalism."[21] Feminist cyborg weapons and the weapons of US third world feminism are also similar with "transgressed boundaries, potent fusions and dangerous possibilities."[22] Indeed, *Haraway's cyborg textual machine represents a politics that runs parallel to those of US third world feminist criticism.* Thus, insofar as Haraway's work is influential in feminist studies, her cyborg feminism is capable of insisting on an alignment between what was once hegemonic feminist theory with theories of what are locally apprehended as indigenous resistance, "mestizaje," US third world feminism, or the differential mode of oppositional consciousness.[23]

This attempted alignment between US feminist third world cultural and theoretical forms and US feminist theoretical forms is further reflected in Haraway's doubled vision of a "cyborg world," which might be defined, she believes, as either the culmination of Euro-American "white" society in its drive-for-mastery, on the one hand or, on the other, as the emergence of

---

18 Haraway, *Simians, Cyborgs, and Women*, 199.
19 See Haraway's "The Promises of Monsters: A Regenerative Politics for Inappropriate/d Others," in *Cultural Studies*, ed. Lawrence Grossberg, Cary Nelson, and Paula A. Treichler (New York: Routledge, 1992), 328, where the woman of color becomes the emblematic figure, a "disturbing guide figure," for the feminist cyborg, "who promises information about psychic, historical and bodily formations that issue, perhaps from some other semiotic processes than the psychoanalytic in modern and postmodern guise" (Ibid., 306).
20 Haraway, *Simians, Cyborgs, and Women*, 151.
21 Ibid.
22 Ibid., 154.
23 US third world feminism recognizes an alliance named "indigenous mestizaje," a term which insists upon the kinship between peoples of color similarly subjugated by race in US colonial history (including but not limited to Native peoples, colonized Chicano/as, Blacks, and Asians), and viewing them, in spite of their differences, as "one people."

resistant "indigenous" world views of mestizaje, US third world feminism, or cyborg feminism. She writes:

> A cyborg world is about the final imposition of a grid of control on the planet, about the final abstraction embodied in Star Wars apocalypse waged in the name of defense, about the final appropriation of women's bodies in a masculinist orgy of war. From another perspective a cyborg world might be about lived social and bodily realities in which people are not afraid of their joint kinship with animals and machines, not afraid of permanently partial identities and contradictory standpoints.[24]

The important notion of "joint kinship" Haraway calls up here is analogous to that called for in contemporary indigenous writings where tribes or lineages are identified out of those who share, not blood lines, but rather lines of affinity. Such lines of affinity occur through attraction, combination, and relation carved out of and in spite of difference, and they are what comprise the notion of mestizaje in the writings of people of color, as in the 1982 example of Alice Walker asking US black liberationists to recognize themselves as mestizos. Walker writes:

> We are the African and the trader. We are the Indian and the Settler. We are oppressor and oppressed . . . we are the mestizos of North America. We are black, yes, but we are "white," too, and we are red. To attempt to function as only one, when you are really two or three, leads, I believe, to psychic illness: "white" people have shown us the madness of that.[25]

Mestizaje in this passage, and in general, can be understood as a complex kind of love in the postmodern world where love is understood as affinity-alliance and affection across lines of difference which intersect both in and out of the body. Walker understands psychic illness as the attempt to be "one," like the singularity of Roland Barthes' narrative love that controls all meanings through the medium of the couple-in-love. The function of mestizaje in Walker's vision is more like that of Barthes' prophetic love, where subjectivity becomes freed from ideology as it ties and binds reality. Prophetic love undoes the "one" that gathers the narrative, the couple, the race into a singularity. Instead, prophetic love gathers up the mexcla, the mixture-that-lives through *differential movement* between possibilities of being. This is the kind

---

24 Haraway, *Simians, Cyborgs, and Women*, 154. Haraway's contribution here is to extend the motion of "mestizaje" to include the mixture, or "affinity," not only between human, animal, physical, spiritual, emotional and intellectual being as it is currently understood under US third world feminism, but between all these and the machines of dominant culture too.

25 Alice Walker, "In the Closet of the Soul: A Letter to an African-American Friend," *Ms. Magazine* 15 (November, 1986): 32–35.

of "love" that motivates US third world feminist mestizaje, and its theory and method of oppositional and differential consciousness, what Anzaldúa theorizes as *laconsciencia de la mestiza*, or "the consciousness of the Borderlands."[26]

Haraway weaves such US third world feminist commitments to affinity-through-difference into her theory of cyborg feminism, and in doing so, begins to identify those skills that comprise the methodology of the oppressed, as indicated in her idea that the recognition of differences and their corresponding "pictures of the world" must not be understood as relativistic "allegories of infinite mobility and interchangeability."[27] Simple mobility without purpose is not enough, as Gayatri Spivak posits in her example of "strategic essentialism," which argues both for mobility *and* for identity consolidation at the same time. Differences, Haraway writes, should be seen as examples of "elaborate specificity" and as an opportunity for "the loving care people might take to learn how to see faithfully from another point of view."[28] The power and eloquence of writings by certain US feminists of color, Haraway continues, derives from their insistence on the "power to survive not on the basis of original innocence, (the imagination of a 'once-upon-a-time wholeness' or oneness), but rather on the insistence of the possibilities of affinity-through-difference." This mestizaje or differential consciousness allows the use of any tool at one's disposal (as long as its use is guided by the methodology of the oppressed) in order to both ensure survival and to remake the world. According to Haraway, the task of cyborg feminism must similarly be to "recode" all tools of "communication and intelligence," with one's aim being the subversion of "command and control."[29]

In the following quotation, Haraway analyzes Chicana intellectual Cherrie Moraga's literary work by applying a "cyborg feminist" approach that is clearly in strong alliance with US third world feminist methods. She writes:

> Moraga's language is not "whole"; it is self-consciously spliced, a chimera of English and Spanish, both conqueror's languages. But it is this chimeric monster, without claim to an original language before violation, that crafts the erotic, competent potent identities of women of color. Sister Outsider *hints at the possibility of world survival not because of her innocence, but because of her ability to live on the boundaries, to write without the founding myth of original wholeness, with its inescapable apocalypse of final return to a deathly oneness. . . . Stripped of identity, the bastard race teaches about the power of the margins and the*

---

26 Gloria Anzaldúa, *Borderlands: The New Mestiza* (San Francisco: Spinsters/Aunt Lute, 1987), 77.
27 Haraway, *Simians, Cyborgs, and Women*, 190.
28 Ibid.
29 Ibid., 175.

> *importance of a mother like Malinche. Women of color have transformed her from the evil mother of masculinist fear into the originally literate mother who teaches survival.*[30]

Ironically, US third world feminist criticism, which is a set of theoretical and methodological strategies, is often understood by readers, even of Haraway, as a demographic constituency only ("women of color," a category which can be used, ironically, as an "example" to advance new theories of what are now being identified in the academy as "postmodern feminisms"), and not as itself a theoretical and methodological approach that clears the way for new modes of conceptualizing social movement, identity, and difference. The textual problem that becomes a philosophical problem, indeed, a political problem, is the conflation of US third world feminism as a theory and method of oppositional consciousness with the demographic or "descriptive" and generalized category "women of color," thus depoliticizing and repressing the specificity of the politics and forms of consciousness developed by US women of color, feminists of color, and erasing the specificity of what is a particular *form* of these: US third world feminism.

By 1991 Haraway herself recognizes these forms of elision, and how by gathering up the category "women of color" and identifying it as a "cyborg identity, a potent subjectivity synthesized from fusions of outsider identities" (i.e. *Sister Outsider*), her work inadvertently contributed to this tendency to elide the specific theoretical contributions of US third world feminist criticism by turning many of its approaches, methods, forms and skills into examples of cyborg feminism.[31] Haraway, recognizing the political and intellectual implications of such shifts in meaning, proceeded to revise her position, and six years after the publication of "Cyborg Feminism" she explains that today, "I would be much more careful about describing who counts as a 'we' in the statement 'we are all cyborgs,'" Instead, she asks, why not find a name or concept that can signify "more of a family of displaced figures, of which the cyborg" is only one, "and then to ask how the cyborg makes connections" with other non-original people who are also "multiply displaced?"[32] Should we not be imagining, she continues, "a family of figures" who could "populate our imaginations" of "postcolonial, postmodern worlds that would not be quite as imperializing in terms of a single figuration of identity?"[33] These are important questions for theorists across disciplines who are interested in

---

30 Ibid., 175–76.
31 Ibid., 174.
32 Constance Penley and Andrew Ross, "Cyborgs at Large: Interview with Donna Haraway," in *Technoculture* (Minneapolis: University of Minnesota Press, 1991), 12.
33 Ibid., 13.

effective new modes of understanding social movements and consciousness in opposition under postmodern cultural conditions. Haraway's questions remain unanswered across the terrain of oppositional discourse, however, or rather, they remain *multiply answered and divided by academic terrain*. And even within feminist theory, Haraway's own cyborg feminism and her later development of the technology of "situated knowledges," though they come close, have not been able to effectively bridge the gaps across the apartheid of theoretical domains described earlier.

For example, if Haraway's category "women of color" might best be understood, as Haraway had earlier posited, "as a cyborg identity, a potent subjectivity synthesized from fusions of outsider identities and in the complex political-historical layerings of her biomythography,"[34] then why has feminist theory been unable to recognize US third world feminist criticism itself as a mode of cultural theory which is also capable of unifying oppositional agents across ideological, racial, gender, sex or class differences, even if that alliance and identification would take place under the gendered, "raced" and transnational sign "US third world feminism"? Might this elision be understood as yet another symptom of an active apartheid of theoretical domains? For, as I have argued, the nonessentializing identity demanded by US third world feminism in its differential mode creates what Haraway is also calling for, a mestiza, indigenous, even cyborg identity.[35]

We can see Haraway making a very similar argument for the recognition of US third world feminist criticism in her essay in *Feminists Theorize the Political*. Haraway's essay begins by stating that women who were "subjected to the conquest of the new world faced a broader social field of reproductive unfreedom, in which their children did not inherit the status of human in the founding hegemonic discourses of US society."[36] For this reason, she asserts, "feminist theory produced by women of color" in the United States continues to generate discourses that confute or confound traditional western standpoints. What this means, Haraway points out, is that if feminist theory is ever to be able to incorporate the visions of US third world feminist theory

---

34 Haraway, *Simians, Cyborgs, and Women*, 174.

35 We might ask why dominant theoretical forms have proven incapable of incorporating and extending theories of black liberation, or third world feminism. Would not the revolutionary turn be that theorists become capable of this kind of "strategic essentialism?" If we believe in "situated knowledges," then people of any racial, gender, sexual categories can enact US third world feminist practice. Or do such practices have to be transcoded into a "neutral" language that is acceptable to all separate categories, "differential consciousness," for example, or "cyborgology"?

36 Haraway, "Ecce Homo," 95.

and criticism, then the major focus of feminist theory and politics must make a fundamental shift to that of making *"a place for the different social subject."*[37]

This challenge to feminist theory—indeed, we can read it as a challenge to all social movement theory—represents a powerful theoretical and political shift, and if answered, has the potential to bring feminism, into affinity with such theoretical terrains as post-colonial discourse theory, US third world feminism, postmodernism, and Queer Theory.

How might this shift be accomplished in the domain of feminist theory? Through the willingness of feminists, Haraway proposes, to become "less interested in joining the ranks of gendered femaleness," to instead become focused on "gaining the INSURGENT ground as female social subject."[38] This challenge to Women's Studies means that a shift must occur to an arena of resistance that functions outside the binary divide male/female, for it is only in this way, Haraway asserts, that "feminist theories of gendered *racial* subjectivities" can "take affirmative AND critical account of *emergent, differentiating, self-representing, contradictory social subjectivities,* with their claims on action, knowledge, and belief."[39] Under this new form of what Haraway calls an "anti-racist," indeed, even an *anti-gender* feminism, Haraway asserts, "there is no place for women," only "geometries of difference and contradiction crucial to women's cyborg identities."[40]

It is at this point that Haraway's work begins to identify the specific technologies that fully align her theoretical apparatus with what I have called the methodology of the oppressed. How, then, might this new form of feminism, or what I would call this new form of oppositional consciousness, be brought into being? By identifying a set of skills that are capable of dis-alienating and realigning what Haraway calls the human "join" that connects our "technics" (material and technical details, rules, machines and methods), with our "erotics" (the sensuous apprehension and expression of "love"-as-affinity).[41] Such a joining, Haraway asserts, will require what is a savvy kind of "politics of articulation," and these are the primary politics that lay at "the heart of an anti-racist feminist practice"[42] that is capable of making "more powerful

---

37 Ibid. Emphasis mine.
38 Haraway, *Simians, Cyborgs, and Women,* 95. The new theoretical grounds necessary for understanding current cultural conditions in the first world and the nature of resistance is not limited to feminist theory, according to Haraway. She writes, "we lack sufficiently subtle connections for collectively building effective theories of experience. Present efforts—Marxist, psychoanalytic, feminist, anthropolitical—to clarify even 'our' experience are rudimentary" (Ibid., 173).
39 Ibid., 96. Emphasis mine.
40 Ibid., 171.
41 Haraway, "The Promises of Monsters," 329.
42 Ibid.

collectives in dangerously unpromising times."[43] This powerful politics of articulation, this new "anti-racist" politics that is also capable of making new kinds of coalitions, can be recognized, argues Haraway, by identifying the "skilled practices" that are utilized and developed within subaltern classes. Such skills, or technologies, what Haraway calls "the standpoints of the subjugated" are preferred, she writes, because

> *In principle they are least likely to allow denial of the critical and interpretive core of all knowledge. They are savvy to modes of denial through repression, forgetting, and disappearing acts — ways of being nowhere while claiming to see comprehensively. The subjugated have a decent chance to be on to the god-trick and all its dazzling — and therefore, blinding — illuminations. "Subjugated" standpoints are preferred because they seem to promise more adequate, sustained, objective, transforming accounts of the world. But HOW to see from below is a problem requiring at least as much skill with bodies and language, with the mediations of vision, as the "highest" technoscientific visualizations.*[44]

Haraway's theoretical work outlines the forms taken by the subjugated knowledges she identifies. These forms required, as she writes, "to see from below," are particular skills that effect "bodies," "language" and the "mediations of vision." Haraway's understanding of the nature of these skills cleaves closely to those same skills that comprise the methodology of the oppressed, which including the technologies of "semiotics," "deconstruction," "meta-ideologizing," "democratics," and "differential movement." It is these technologies that permit the constant, differential repositioning necessary for perception and action from what Haraway identifies as "the standpoints of the subjugated." Indeed, Haraway's essay on cyborg feminism identifies all five of these technologies (if only in passing) as ways to bring about what she hopes will become a new feminist methodology.

Of the first "semiotic" technology, for example, Haraway writes that "self knowledge requires a semiotic-material technology linking meanings and bodies . . . the opening of non-isomorphic subjects, agents, and territories to stories unimaginable from the vantage point of the cyclopian, self-satiated eye of the master subject."[45] Though Haraway does not identify the technologies of "deconstruction," or "meta-ideologizing" separately, these two interventionary vectors are implied when she writes that this new contribution to social movement theory, cyborg feminism, must find many "means of understanding and *intervening in the patterns of objectification* in the world." This means "decoding and transcoding plus translation and criticism: all

---

43   Ibid., 319.
44   Haraway, *Simians, Cyborgs, and Women*, 191; emphasis mine.
45   Ibid., 192.

are necessary." "Democratics" is the technology of the methodology of the oppressed that guides all the others, and the moral force of this technology is indicated in Haraway's assertion that in all oppositional activity, agents for change "must be accountable" for the "patterns of objectification in the world" that have now become "reality." In this effort to take responsibility for the systems of domination that now exist, Haraway emphasizes that the practitioner of cyborg feminism cannot be "about fixed locations in a reified body." This new oppositional actor must be "about nodes in fields" and "inflections in orientation." Through such mobilities, an oppositional cyborg feminism must create and enact its own version of, *"responsibility for difference in material-semiotic fields of meaning."*[46] As for the last technology of the methodology of the oppressed, called "differential movement," Haraway's own version is that cyborg feminism must understand "the impossibility of innocent 'identity' politics and epistemologies as strategies for seeing from the standpoints of the subjugated." Rather, oppositional agents must be "committed" in the enactment of all forms-of-being and all skills, whether those "skills" are semiotic, "decoding," "recoding" or "moral" in function, to what Haraway calls "mobile positioning and passionate detachment."[47]

I have argued that the "cyborg skills" necessary for developing a feminism for the twentieth century are those I have identified as the methodology of the oppressed. Their use has the power to forge what Haraway asserts can be a potentially "earthwide network of connections" including the ability to make new coalitions across new kinds of alliances by translating "knowledges among very different—and power-differentiated—communities."[48] The feminism that applies these technologies as "skills" will develop into another kind of science, Haraway asserts, a science of "interpretation, translation, stuttering, and the partly understood." Like the "science" proposed under the differential mode of consciousness and opposition—US third world feminism—cyborg feminism can become the science of those Haraway describes as the "multiple subject with at least double vision." Scientific "objectivity" under this new kind of science, writes Haraway, will mean an overriding commitment to a practice capable of facing down bureaucratic and administrative sciences, a practice of "objectivity" that Haraway calls "situated knowledges."[49] For, she writes, with the advent of US third world feminism and other forms of feminisms, it has become clear that "even the simplest matters in feminist analysis require contradictory moments and a wariness of their resolution." A scholarly and feminist consciousness-of-science, then,

---

46   Ibid., 195.
47   Ibid., 192.
48   Ibid., 187.
49   Ibid., 188.

of objectivity as "situated knowledges" means, according to Haraway, the development of a different kind of human relation to perception, objectivity, understanding, and production, that is akin to Hayden White and Jacques Derrida's use of the "middle voice," for it will demand the scholar's situatedness "in an ungraspable middle space."[50] And like the mechanism of the middle voice of the verb, Haraway's "situated knowledges" require that what is an "object of knowledge" also be "pictured as an actor and agent," transformative of itself and its own situation while also being acted upon.[51]

In other words, Haraway's situated knowledges demands a form of differential consciousness. Indeed, Haraway names the third part of her book *Simians, Cyborgs and Women*, "Differential Politics for Inappropriate/d Others." This chapter defines a coalescing and ever more articulated form of social movement from which "feminist embodiment" can resist "fixation" in order to better ride what she calls the "webs of differential positioning."[52] Feminist theorists who subscribe to this new postmodern form of oppositional consciousness must learn, she writes, to be "more generous and more suspicious—both generous and suspicious, exactly the receptive posture I seek in political semiosis generally. It is a strategy closely aligned with the oppositional and differential consciousness"[53] of US third world feminism.

It was previously assumed that the behaviors of oppressed classes depend upon no methodology at all, or rather, that they consist of whatever acts one must commit in order to survive, both physically and psychically. But this is exactly why the methodology of the oppressed can now be recognized as that mode-of-being best suited to life under postmodern and highly technologized conditions in the first world. For to enter a world where any activity is possible in order to ensure survival is also to enter a cyberspace-of-being and consciousness. This space is now accessible to all human beings through technology, (though this was once a zone only accessible to those forced into its terrain), a space of boundless possibilities where meanings are only cursorily attached and thus capable of reattaching to others depending upon the situation to be confronted. This cyberspace is Barthes' zero degree of meaning and prophetic love, Fanon's "open door of every consciousness," Anzaldúa's "Coatlique" state, and its processes are linked closely with those of differential consciousness.

To reiterate, the differential mode of oppositional consciousness finds its expression through the methodology of the oppressed. The technologies of semiotic reading, de-construction of signs, meta-ideologizing, and moral

---

50 Ibid., 111.
51 Ibid., 198.
52 Ibid., 196.
53 Haraway, "The Promises of Monsters," 326.

commitment-to-equality are its vectors, its expressions of influence. These vectors meet in the differential mode of consciousness, carrying it through to the level of the "real" where it can guide and impress dominant powers. Differential consciousness is itself a force which rhyzomatically and parasitically inhabits each of these five vectors, linking them in movement, while the pull of each of the vectors creates on-going tension and re-formation. Differential consciousness can be thus thought of as a constant reapportionment of space, boundaries, of horizontal and vertical realignments of oppositional powers. Since each vector occurs at different velocities, one of them can realign all the others, creating different kinds of patterns, and permitting entry at different points. *These energies revolve around each other, aligning and realigning in a field of force that is the differential mode of oppositional consciousness, a CyberConsciousness.*

Each technology of the methodology of the oppressed thus creates new conjunctural possibilities, produced by ongoing and transforming regimes of exclusion and inclusion. Differential consciousness is a crossing network of consciousness, a transconsciousness that occurs in a register permitting the networks themselves to be appropriated as ideological weaponry. This cyberspace-of-being is analogous to the cyberspace of computer and even social life in Haraway's vision, but her understanding of cyberspace is more pessimistic:

> *Cyberspace seems to be the consensual hallucination of too much complexity, too much articulation. . . . In virtual space, the virtue of articulation, the power to produce connection threatens to overwhelm and finally engulf all possibility of effective action to change the world.*[54]

Under the influence of a differential oppositional consciousness understood as a form of "cyberspace," the technologies developed by subjugated populations to negotiate this realm of shifting meanings are recognized as the very technologies necessary for all first world citizens who are interested in re-negotiating contemporary first world cultures with what we might call a sense of their own "power" and "integrity" intact. But power and integrity, as Gloria Anzaldúa suggests, will be based on entirely different terms then those identified in the past, when, as Jameson writes, individuals could glean a sense of self in opposition to the centralizing dominant power that oppressed them, and then determine how to act. Under postmodern disobediencies the self blurs around the edges, shifts "in order to ensure survival," transforms according to the requisites of power, all the while, under the guiding force of the methodology of the oppressed carrying with it the integrity of a self-conscious awareness of the transformations desired, and

---

54   Ibid., 325.

above all, a sense of the impending ethical and political changes that those transformations will enact.

Haraway's theory weds machines and a vision of first world politics on a transnational, global scale together with the apparatus for survival I call the methodology of the oppressed in US third world feminism, and it is in these couplings, where race, gender, and capital, according to Haraway, "require a cyborg theory of wholes and parts"[55] that Haraway's vision contributes to bridging the gaps that are creating the apartheid of theoretical domains. Indeed, the coding necessary to re-map the kind of "disassembled and reassembled postmodern collective and personal self"[56] of cyborg feminism must take place according to a guide capable of placing feminism in alignment with other movements of thought and politics for egalitarian social change. This can happen when being and action, knowledge and science, become self-consciously encoded through what Haraway calls "subjugated" and "situated" knowledges, and what I call the methodology of the oppressed, a methodology arising from varying locations and in a multiplicity of forms across the first world, and indominably from the minds, bodies, and spirits of US third world feminists who have demanded the recognition of "mestizaje," indigenous resistance, and identification with the colonized. When feminist theory becomes capable of self-consciously recognizing and applying this methodology, then feminist politics can become fully synonymous with anti-racism, and the feminist "subject" will dissolve.

In the late twentieth century, oppositional actors are inventing a new name and new languages for what the methodology of the oppressed and the "Coatlicue," differential consciousness it demands. Its technologies, from "signifyin'" to "la facultad," from "cyborg feminism" to "situated knowledges," from the "abyss" to "differance" have been variously identified from numerous theoretical locations. The methodology of the oppressed provides the schema for the cognitive map of power-laden social reality for which oppositional actors and theorists across disciplines, from Fanon to Jameson, from Anzaldúa to Lorde, from Barthes to Haraway, are longing.

Acknowledgements

This paper is dedicated to those who move in resistance to the "proper," and especially to Chicana feministas Yolanda Broyles-Gonzalez, Antonia Castaneda, Deena Gonzalez, Emma Perez, Gloria Anzaldúa, Shirley Munoz, Norma Alarcon, Ellie Hernandez, Pearl Sandoval, and Tish Sainz.

---

55 Haraway, *Simians, Cyborgs, and Women*, 181.
56 Ibid., 163.

Bibliography

Anzaldúa, Gloria. *Borderlands: The New Mestiza*. San Francisco: Spinsters/Aunt Lute, 1987.

Appelbaum, Richard P. "New Journal for Global Studies Center." *CORI: Center for Global Studies Newsletter* 1, no. 2 (May 1994).

Collins, Patricia Hill. *Black Feminist Thought: Knowledge, Consciousness, and the Politics of Empowerment*. Boston: Unwin Hyman, 1990.

Haraway, Donna. "Ecce Homo, Ain't (Ar'n't) I a Woman, and Inappropriate/d Others: The Human in a Post-Humanist Landscape." In *Feminists Theorize the Political*, edited by Judith Butler and Joan Scott, 86–100, New York: Routledge, 1992.

–––. "The Promises of Monsters: A Regenerative Politics for Inappropriate/d Others," In *Cultural Studies*, edited by Lawrence Grossberg, Cary Nelson, and Paula A. Treichler, with Linda Baughman and assistance from John Macgregor Wise, 295–337. New York: Routledge, 1992.

–––. *Simians, Cyborgs, and Women: The Reinvention of Nature*. New York: Routledge, 1991.

Jameson, Fredric. "Postmodernism, or The Cultural Logic of Late Capitalism." *New Left Review* 146 (July–August 1984): 53–92.

Jordan, June. "Where is the Love?" In *Making Face, Making Soul: Creative and Critical Perspectives by Feminists of Color*, edited by Gloria Anzaldúa, 174. San Francisco: Aunt Lute Foundation, 1990.

Lorde, Audre. *Sister Outsider*. Trumansburg, NY: Crossing Press, 1984.

Lugones, Maria. "Playfulness, 'World'-Travelling, and Loving Perception." *Hypatia: A Journal of Feminist Philosophy* 2, no, 2 (1987): 3–19. doi:10.1111/j.1527-2001.1987.tb01062.x.

Penley, Constance, and Andrew Ross, "Cyborgs at Large: Interview with Donna Haraway." In *Technoculture*, 1-20 Minneapolis: University of Minnesota Press, 1991.

Sandoval, Chela. *The Methodology of the Oppressed*. Minneapolis: University of Minnesota Press, 2000.

–––. "US Third World Feminism: The Theory and Method of Oppositional Consciousness in the Postmodern World." *Genders* 10 (Spring 1991): 1–24.

Walker, Alice. "In the Closet of the Soul: A Letter to an African-American Friend." *Ms. Magazine* 15 (November, 1986): 32–35.

Woo, Merle. "Letter to Ma." In *This Bridge Called My Back: Writings by Radical Women of Color*, edited by Cherríe Moraga and Gloria Anzaldúa, 140–147. Watertown, MA: Persephone Press, 1981.

Developing a Corporeal Cyberfeminism: Beyond Cyberutopia

Jessica E. Brophy[1]

> *There are no utopian spaces anywhere*
> *except in the imagination.*[2]
>
> ~Elizabeth Grosz

Many of the early discourses surrounding the internet were utopian in nature, claiming that the disembodied nature of online spaces creates an egalitarian online experience, devoid of the discrimination attributed to the embodied experience. Feminists, in particular, have been quick to assess the possibilities of gender bending,[3] online activism and connectivity,[4] though not all feminists have uncritically accepted the internet as a potentially utopian medium.[5]

This article recognizes the importance of exploring the feminist potentialities of disembodied and dislocated online interaction, yet calls for a more nuanced approach to understanding the role of the body and materialism in studies of the internet. Indeed, the purpose here is to encourage modification of existing frameworks for understanding the experience of the internet.

---

1   Editors' note: this paper was previously published in *New Media & Society* 12, no. 6 (2010): 929-945, doi:10.1177/1461444809350901.
2   Elizabeth Grosz, *Architecture from the Outside: Essays on Virtual and Real Space* (Cambridge, MA: MIT Press, 2001), 19.
3   B. Danet, "Text as Mask: Gender, Play, and Performance on the Internet," in *Cybersociety 2.0*, ed. S. Jones (Thousand Oaks, CA: Sage, 1998), 129-58.
4   Susan Hawthorne and Renata Klein, *Cyberfeminism: Connectivity, Critique and Creativity* (North Melbourne: Spinifex Press, 1999).
5   C. Kramarae, "Feminist Fictions of Future Technology," in Jones, *Cybersociety 2.0*, 100-28; C. Stabile, *Feminism and the Technological Fix* (New York: Manchester University Press, 1994).

Judith Butler and Elizabeth Grosz's arguments for placing embodiment and corporeality at the center of performativity are examined,[6] while also addressing the idea of articulation and Karen Barad's understanding of intra-agency.[7] Subsequently, the concept of liminality is developed and applied to cyberspace, not as the crossing of a "threshold" of a noncorporeal place, but as an experience of the intra-agency of body and medium. Drawing on these concepts, I advocate a version of cyberfeminism that rejects "leaving the body behind" while simultaneously rejecting a cyberfeminism based on viewing the medium as a simple extension of the body. In conclusion, I offer some suggestions for future research, including a call for more in-depth examination of the internet as a medium and its relation to our bodies.

Identifying Cyberutopia

Technological "progress" or the introduction of a new medium into the daily experience of social beings often brings with it a proliferation of rhetoric concerning the medium. The advent of the telegraph, the radio, the telephone, and the television—all these media introduced new discourses and impacted our understanding of the world. Often, the original purposes for which a medium is developed is reworked by its users; one ready example of this is the telephone, which originally was considered to be a tool for businessmen to facilitate their work and whose use was reformulated as a means to stay in touch or reconnect with friends or family.[8]

So it is with the internet, originally designed by the US military. Despite its origin as a highly limited-use medium "deeply embedded in masculine codes and values"[9] the internet now has global reach, with females comprising nearly half of all internet users in the United States.[10] Some of the rhetoric surrounding the internet, particularly in reference to gender and the inter-

---

6   Judith Butler, *Gender Trouble: Feminism and the Subversion of Identity* (New York: Routledge, 1999); Elizabeth Grosz, *Volatile Bodies: Toward a Corporeal Feminism* (Bloomington: Indiana University Press, 1994); and Grosz, *Architecture from the Outside*.
7   Karen Barad, "Posthumanist Performativity: Toward an Understanding of How Matter Comes to Matter," *Signs* 28, no. 3 (2003): 801-31.
8   Liesbet van Zoonen, "Gendering the Internet: Claims, Controversies and Cultures," *European Journal of Communication* 17, no. 1 (2002): 5-23.
9   Ibid., 6.
10   Deborah Fallows, *How Women and Men Use the Internet*, Pew Internet and American Life Project Report (Washington, DC: Pew Research Center, 2005), http://www.pewinternet.org/Reports/2005/How-Women-and-Men-Use-the-Internet.aspx.

net, has been utopian in nature. The internet is sometimes extolled as a space where one can *be* or *become* anyone. As Vivian Sobchack writes, "man's lived body ... in all its material facticity, its situatedness, its finitude, and its limitations, seemed to have been transubstantiated through textualization into the infinite possibility, receptivity, literality, and irresponsibility of the 'pure' sign."[11]

For some feminist scholars, the potential of the internet as a space to explore the "pure" sign has opened new vistas for personal exploration and growth. As Janet Morahan-Martin writes, online anonymity "frees individuals of social and physical restraints, and has allowed women to express parts of themselves that they might not otherwise in a safe environment, enabling them to explore new identities, heal inner wounds, and express sexuality."[12] In such discourses of liberation, the internet can be a place where differences and social contexts are erased, creating a true meritocracy or a utopian ideal. As Jenny Sunden notes in her discussion of the various types of cyberfeminism, one version of early cyberfeminism holds that on "the Internet among disembodied subjectivities, [a] feminist utopia could be realized."[13]

The cyberutopian theme relies primarily on the principle of disembodiment. Leaving behind the body—and its associated sex, gender, sexuality, race, ethnicity, religion, (dis)ability, and so on—frees the user to be judged solely on their online presence, which they are able to carefully construct. The internet is a space where one has the chance to "trade-in, remodel, or even leave behind the physical nature with which we are, in reality, burdened."[14] For feminists desiring a cyberutopia, the internet is an exciting "playground for the experimenting with gender symbols and identity, a space to escape from the dichotomy of gender and the boundaries produced by physical bodies."[15] The internet can be viewed as a gathering place for feminists and as a place to enact or perform gender subversions. It is a place where women—typically limited by their physicality and its associated bodily subjugation—can experiment with fewer social or bodily consequences.

Such cyberlibertarian rhetoric "draws on an abstract, disembodied concept of the individual that is far removed from the concrete day-to-day

---

11 Vivian Sobchack, *Carnal Thoughts: Embodiment and Moving Image Culture* (Los Angeles: University of California Press, 2004), 167.

12 Janet Morahan-Martin, "Women and the Internet: Promise and Perils," *CyberPsychology & Behavior* 3, no. 5 (2000): 683.

13 Jenny Sunden, "What Happened to Difference in Cyberspace? The (Re)turn of the She-Cyborg," *Feminist Media Studies* 1, no. 2 (2001): 215.

14 Nancy Paterson, "Cyberfeminism," 1998, http://www.vacuumwoman.com/CyberFeminism/cf.txt.

15 van Zoonen, "Gendering the Internet," 12.

practices which make individuality and forms of togetherness possible in the first place."¹⁶ This abstraction lays a foundation for a universal ground of interaction—a possible unifying force, encouraging solidarity and collective action. However, the same abstractions have within them the possibility of essentializing the concepts they represent. Women, in their multitude of site-specific social locations, become Woman. As Sunden warns in her essay on the She-Cyborg, any instance "where 'the meat' is left behind and the disembodied consciousness released from its earthly groundings . . . [will] repeat the classical patriarchal model."¹⁷

The work of Dennis Waskul and Mark Douglass illustrates the fluidity allowed users in online contexts.¹⁸ Through interviews and observation of users in online chat rooms, the authors demonstrate the importance of anonymity and disembodiment as related to users' production of "cyberselves." Despite the importance and attendant freedom proffered by anonymity and the nature of online interaction as a "hyperreal simulacrum of communication—neither real nor imaginary,"¹⁹ the authors also note that there are continual efforts by users to "test" other users' performances. Much effort is put forth in online interaction to "emplace" or "engender" users; that is, to establish with some sort of fixity a user's "a/s/l" or age, sex and location. To underestimate the importance of users' desires to emplace and engender other users is to potentially undermine efforts to address the material specificities of user's lives and the repercussions of the processes of representation.

The anonymous freedom to "try on" genders or sexualities without social recourse is often cited as one of the most liberating dimensions of life online; however, a user may reify and enact stereotypes, thereby reinforcing the normative understandings of gender, sexuality, race or ethnicity. This, in theory, can recreate and reify the same limiting norms which may have encouraged the user to experiment with gender and sexuality in the first place. In this way, lauding cyberspace as merely a disembodied utopian dream masks the processes and performances that re-create and re-enact oppressive normative social structures—*both* in cyberspace *and* in our shared bodily space. Adopting a cyberutopia that masks opportunities to understand the processes and performances of gender norms undermines feminist efforts to directly

---

16 Mihaela Kelemen and Warren Smith, "Community and its 'Virtual' Promises: A Critique of Cyberlibertarian Rhetoric," *Information, Communication & Society* 4, no. 3 (2001): 377.
17 Sunden, "What Happened to Difference in Cyberspace?," 216.
18 Dennis Waskul and Mark Douglass, "Cyberself: The Emergence of Self in On-line Chat," *The Information Society* 13 (1997): 375–97. doi:10.1080/019722497129070.
19 Waskul and Douglass, "Cyberself," 380.

address these normative practices, including "compulsory heterosexuality"[20] or "the tyranny of gender."[21]

A second danger of cyberutopia is that by separating a user from her or his site-specific socioeconomic location, all users are *assumed* to represent the dominant (sex, race, class, etc.)—what Lisa Nakamura calls "default whiteness."[22] Nakamura notes that many advocates of the internet as a liberatory space claim "if no one's body is visible while participating in cyberspace, theoretically racism and bigotry cannot exist at that time."[23] Ironically, many users experience heightened personal attacks and discrimination in cyberspace. Several scholars have studied the practice of "flaming" (a form of harassment) online, as well as cyber-stalking and sexual harassment online.[24] As Nakamura discusses, conversations about how the web can "'wipe out' race may obscure the fact that users do indeed possess bodies that are raced—bodies that are denied housing and discriminated against in job interviews and that suffer institutional forms of racism."[25] Users online are assumed white—and are often assumed male, middle-class, technologically savvy, and on US-based sites, Christian. The seduction of thinking of cyberspace as cyberutopia belies the reality of daily lived experiences outside of cyberspace.

Constructing users in cyberspace as "free" potentially relieves cyberfeminists of the burden of addressing the lived experiences of racism (or sexism, homophobia, and other forms of discrimination). As Nathan Stormer describes in his account of the mind/body dualism, some people seek to "distance themselves from the embodied world because it was well understood as a site of oppression. The often metaphysical claims of moral, intellectual, and spiritual equality speak to distinctly separate orders of things and discourses."[26] It is often easier to advocate a new space for "moral, intellectual, and spiritual equality" than it is to deal with discrimination and oppression in already-extant and occupied space. However, given the proliferation of activism and grassroots efforts aided by the internet, as well as the exchange

---

20 Adrienne Rich, *Blood, Bread, and Poetry* (New York: Norton, 1994).
21 Danet, "Text as Mask."
22 Lisa Nakamura, *Cybertypes: Race, Ethnicity, and Identity on the Internet* (New York: Routledge, 1999).
23 Nakamura, *Cybertypes*, 107.
24 See, for example, D. Bostdorff, "The Internet Rhetoric of the Ku Klux Klan: A Case Study in Web Site Community Building Run Amok," *Communication Studies* 55, no. 2 (2004): 340–61.
25 Nakamura, *Cybertypes*, 107.
26 Nathan Stormer, "Articulation: A Working Paper on Rhetoric and Taxis," *Quarterly Journal of Speech* 90, no. 3 (2004): 269. doi:10.1080/0033563042000255516.

of information via online interaction, it is important to note that there is not a simple and easy disassociation of online and off. Cyberfeminists should not understand cyberspace as a utopian *replacement* for the spaces of lived experiences, but rather as an *augmentation* of those spaces. These complex inter-relations should not be reduced to a bifurcation of online and offline where either is considered entirely separate from and unaffected by the other; rather, the material conditions of the offline world need to remain visible to scholars.

For example, the internet has been lauded as a resource for women's upward mobility, particularly in networking and career development.[27] While the internet may, in fact, offer (some) women new occasions for career development, this urge to view cyberspace as opening new vistas of opportunity makes several tenuous assumptions. First, the sliver of working women—and it is a sliver—who have or may benefit from networking or career development are benefiting only if we proscribe to a very narrow, individualized and liberal understanding of progress. Whether one is addressing the technology itself or the construction of "women's success," the underlying assumption is one of *progress*, or a constant linear movement. Such a narrow view does not question the *nature* of gendered labor and women's experiences. The "empowerment" in terms of career development for women is considered primarily from a highly individualized, liberal feminist understanding; and even those resources available for women in this narrow understanding are often questionable in worth to feminists. As Nancy Worthington notes, "the flexible nature of the Internet seems to offer a progressive alternative to traditional mainstream media's consistent devaluation of female labor . . . [but] the commercial nature of many Web sites often prevents fulfillment of that promise."[28] At the very least, cyberutopian positions do not address the negative impacts of technology for women's labor on a global scale.[29]

A further danger of cyberutopia is the reinforcement of the mind/body dualism. As Grosz discusses in her advocacy for a corporeal feminism,

> *Feminists and philosophers seem to share a common view of the human subject as a being made up of two dichotomously opposed characteristics: mind and body, thought and extension, reason and passion, psychology and biology. This bifurcation of being is not simply a neutral division of an otherwise all-encompassing descriptive field. Dichotomous thinking necessarily hierarchizes and ranks the two polarized terms so that one*

---

27 For a nuanced examination of this position, see R. Woodfield, *Women, Work and Computing* (Cambridge: Cambridge University Press, 2000).

28 Nancy Worthington, "Women's Work on the World Wide Web: How a New Medium Represents an Old Problem," *Popular Communication* 3, no. 1 (2005): 56.

29 See J. K. T. Basi, *Women, Identity and India's Call Centre Industry* (New York: Routledge, 2009).

becomes the privileged term and the other its suppressed, subordinated, negative counterpart.[30]

This Cartesian dualism is heavily entrenched in Western society; the naturalized distinctions between mind/body, rational/emotional, and culture/nature—all of these dualisms are hierarchized; with the first term considered the dominant. Not only do dualisms hierarchize the terms involved, the binary structure "infinitizes the negative term, rendering it definitionally amorphous, the receptacle of all that is excessive or expelled from the circuit of the privileged term."[31] Thus, "Man" is valorized for what qualities he has; "Woman" becomes all that he is not.

The rhetoric of cyberutopia reinforces this dualism, the freedom of the mind to represent and act at will without the "burden" of the body.[32] The internet, in this context, is interpreted as an equalizing platform and space, where the necessary/naturalized complications of "the body" are removed. This interpretation denies that the body is necessary for participation online. One requires a body to interact with whatever machine allows a user to join the online, not to mention the financial/technological means to access the machine itself and the material habit of how to use it. As Kristin Langellier and Eric Peterson note in a study of weblog users,

> *a person can read or write a weblog only to the extent that she or he is bodily capable of doing so . . . reading and writing weblogs requires bodily discipline (the ability to orient, reach for, and grasp or accomplish a task) and a disciplined body (a body trained to read and write, to manipulate a keyboard, to use computers and access the Internet).*[33]

As such, material elements of the "real world" are inherently bound up in and with technologies of the virtual. Beneath the cyberutopian ideal of equality "a wide range of knowledges and cultural belongings are being hidden."[34] In a very basic sense, to assume the internet is the site of an egalitarian cyberutopia is to *necessarily* negate that utopia; that is, the space *itself* excludes all who do not have access, those who do not have the cultural and technical knowledge required to participate and/or those who do not have the physical ability to participate in the utopian dream. This negation of utopia is only magnified once the myth of the "global" network is more closely examined,

---

30 Grosz, *Volatile Bodies*, 3.
31 Grosz, *Architecture from the Outside*, 95.
32 Paterson, "Cyberfeminism."
33 Kristin Langellier and Eric Peterson, *Storytelling in Daily Life: Performing Narrative* (Philadelphia: Temple University Press, 2004), 166.
34 Sunden, "What Happened to Difference in Cyberspace?," 224.

for a "digital divide" exists between more developed nations and less developed nations.[35]

In sum, a simplistic egalitarian ideal of cyberutopia *necessitates* disembodiment, denies the situated and lived experiences of individuals, and reinforces the mind/body dualism. These pitfalls can lead cyberutopists to ignore and/or downplay inequalities that exist in "real" space, as well as ignore the reification of gender and sexuality norms in cyberspace. For theorists engaged with the internet as a medium, adopting a cyberutopian stance might prohibit scholarship and activism that enhances the *ideals* of cyberutopianism; that is, adopting this stance often refuses attempts to engage critically with patriarchal codes, the performance of gender and sexuality and the daily experiences of users of the internet on- *and* offline.

In light of continued development of online interaction, particularly in light of increasingly complex media convergence and the maturation of the "internet generation," scholars must resist oversimplified theories of internet interaction. The relationship of the mind to technology and the relationship of the body to technology can no longer be separated; these relationships are a complex performance of embodiment in which we are deeply intertwined with the technology.

Corporeality: Rejecting the Universal Body

Much of feminist scholarship attempts to develop a framework for understanding the relationship(s) of body, sex, and gender. Often, sex and gender are reduced to a dualism: sex/gender, where—as in other dualisms—sex is essentialized and privileged over gender. In this way, sex "trumps" gender and sex is the determinant concept; that is, gender is inscribed or socially constructed *on* the body, which is (naturally) sexed. Feminist theorists then find themselves attempting to negate or counteract the social construction of the body as a source of oppression while also rejecting the idea of sexual determinacy—that is, the naturalizing of the female body as the source of its oppression. In the vein of sexual determinacy, women "are" one way because of the biological limitations of their bodies. On the flip side, feminists who attempt to reject sexual determinacy are compelled to "affirm women's bodily specificity as the minimal consensual stuff which grounds feminist practice."[36] It is possible to reject the (explicitly female) body as the "minimal consensual stuff" for feminist practice and instead adopt a feminism that rests on the "idea that gender is not at all a monolithic category that makes all women the same; rather, it is the mark of a position of subordination, which

---

35 For more information, see the United Nations International Telecommunications Union website: http://www.itu.int/en/about/Pages/default.aspx.
36 Pheng Cheah, "Mattering," *Diacritics* 26, no. 1 (1996): 108.

is qualified by a number of powerful variables."[37] These variables include race and ethnicity, as well as socioeconomic status, among others.

Adopting a social constructivist position from which to enact scholarship, on the other hand, considers sex "either as natural and thus unconstructed or as the fictional premise of a prediscursive ground produced by the concept of gender."[38] Thus, sex is (determines) everything or sex is (determines) nothing; the body becomes "irrelevant or becomes the vehicle expressing changes in beliefs and values."[39]

Since Butler's original publication of *Gender Trouble* in 1990, many feminist scholars have turned from social constructivism to embrace theories of embodiment and corporeality.[40] Randi Patterson and Gail Corning published an annotated bibliography of scholarship regarding the body, stressing the importance of re-evaluating the "assumptions underlying the use of a universalized body, the body of 'Man,' in terms of the sexual, racial, classed, and political body."[41] Much self-labeled postmodern, poststructuralist or postcolonial scholarship specifically addresses the importance of local, site-specific understandings of culture, social relations and an emphasis on the lived experiences of individuals—coinciding with the rise of what some term "identity politics."[42] Rejecting the universal body draws attention to the body-specific; in essence, "attention to the body challenges what counts today as knowledge by rejecting the mind/body dualisms, historical constructions of gender, and cultural inscriptions of meaning that underlie the politics of class, race, gender, and age."[43]

In terms of internet use, a rejection of the mind/body dualism requires an interrogation of referring to the internet as a space where one leaves the body behind. Lisa-Jane McGerty accuses scholars of supporting a false dichotomy of on- or off-line, failing to locate internet users firmly within the context of their use, and have singularly failed therefore to locate internet communication technologies adequately within fundamental relations of

---

37 R. Braidotti, *Nomadic Subjects: Embodiment and Sexual Difference in Contemporary Feminist Theory* (New York: Columbia University Press, 1994), 259.
38 Cheah, "Mattering," 109.
39 Ibid., 110.
40 Barad, "Posthumanist Performativity"; M. Boler, "Hypes, Hopes and Actualities: New Digital Cartesianism and Bodies in Cyberspace," *New Media & Society* 9, no. 1 (2007): 139-68; Grosz, *Volatile Bodies*.
41 Randi Patterson and Gail Corning. "Researching the Body: An Annotated Bibliography for Rhetoric," *Rhetoric Society Quarterly* 27, no. 3 (1997): 8.
42 See C. Hanisch, "The Personal is Political" in *Notes from the Second Year Women's Liberation: Major Writings of the Radical Feminists*, ed. S. Firestone and A. Koedt (New York: Radical Feminism, 1970).
43 Patterson and Corning, "Researching the Body," 9.

gender, sexuality, race and class.[44] McGerty instead encourages developing a more nuanced approach to the complex and mutually impacting relationships between user and technology. The online and offline worlds are deeply entangled, as are human relations with many other technologies. If we hope to better understand the multiple intersections of self and technology, we must move beyond the simple mind/body bifurcation. However, rejecting the mind/body dualism can leave us without a theoretical base for understanding the individual's relationship and interaction with the world.

Performativity and Articulation

Understanding performativity or articulation calls for a brief review of social constructivism and the limitations associated with that theoretical perspective. Social constructivism holds that knowledge comes *"from within* a relationship, in which, in its articulation, others around us continually exert a morally coercive force upon us *to be* persons of a particular kind, to assume a particular *identity,* and to exhibit a particular kind of *sensibility."*[45] Therefore, no one's identity or reality is created in a vacuum; it is through dialogue, participation in discourse and interaction that sense of self is developed. Thus, social constructivism is an anthropocentric theory; it holds [human] language and interaction through [human] language as the sole source of agency in the construction of the self.

Before a person is even born, Jean-Francois Lyotard argues, she or he is part of the social bond and language game, "if only by the virtue of the name he [sic] is given, the human child is already positioned as the referent in the story recounted by those around him, in relation to which he will inevitably chart his course."[46] Most interaction between individuals takes place within the context of language, and experiences are remembered, shared, reconstituted or constructed within language as well. The limitations and rules of language often parallel the limitations of social interaction, and Kenneth J. Gergen argues the language of "sense-making preexists the individual, it is 'always already' there, available for social usage."[47]

---

44 Lisa-Jane McGerty, "'Nobody Lives Only in Cyberspace': Gendered Subjectivities and Domestic Use of the Internet," *CyberPsychology & Behavior* 3, no. 5 (2000): 896. doi:10.1089/10949310050191863.

45 J. Shotter and Kenneth J. Gergen, "Social Construction: Self, Others, and the Continuing Conversation," *The Communication Yearbook* 17 (1994): 6. (Emphasis in original.)

46 Jean-Francois Lyotard, *The Postmodern Condition: A Report on Knowledge,* trans. G. Bennington and B. Massumi (Minneapolis: University of Minnesota Press, 1989), 15.

47 Kenneth J. Gergen, *The Saturated Self: Dilemmas of Identity in Contemporary Life* (New York: Basic, 1991), 107.

Limitations of language are reflected in and (from a social constructivist position) constitute relationships; for example, I cannot refer to a person in English with a non-gendered pronoun unless I use "it," a wholly unsatisfying and socially unacceptable way of referring to a person. Likewise, the social construction of gender is strained and tested by transgendered or androgynous persons, and those who interact with alternatively gendered persons struggle to find the "right" pronouns to talk about them, with them or to them. This is true in online situations as well.[48]

While social constructivism offers some useful tools to scholars attempting to understand the formation of identity and the relations between individuals and language, it is problematic because it takes as its starting point a tabula rasa of being, the *body as prediscursive*. This privileges language use as the "mind" or "self"-making process. This naturalizes the mind/body dualism in ways that elevate the body as the determinate factor of selfhood or, conversely, as irrelevant. As Butler notes, "any discourse that established the boundaries of the body serves the purpose of instating and naturalizing certain taboos regarding the appropriate limits, postures, and modes of exchange that define what it is that constitutes bodies."[49] Thus, endorsing a position of social constructivism takes for granted an a priori (i.e. before-language and before-relationship) existence of a body, uncritically examined. This body is then the site of the social construction of the self through relationships.

This uncritical acceptance of the body as a tabula rasa not only reifies traditional dualism of mind/body, but also reifies accompanying dualisms such as reason/emotion and male/female. Grosz advocates a version of Spinoza's philosophy to supplant the Cartesian affinity for the mind/body dualism.[50] In her account, the body is a monadic entity constantly reconstituting itself. It is a dynamic, irreducible thing. The body is ever-changing, and bodies are "historical, social, cultural weavings of biology . . . not being self-identical, the body must be seen as a series of processes of becoming, rather than as a fixed state of being." In contrast, for dualistic thinking, the body remains relatively fixed (after puberty, "naturally") while the mind is dynamic and reconstitutive. It is the mind, then, that is prized over the body, which at its very least is a container and at its very most a biological determinant.

Butler's discussion of performativity also addresses embodiment, though in different terms than Grosz. Butler notes that "performativity is not a singular act, but a repetition and a ritual, which achieves its effects through its naturalization in the *context of a body*, understood, in part as a culturally

---

48 See Danet's exploration of the "gender pronoun" settings of LambdaMOO and MediaMOO in Danet, "Text as Mask."
49 Butler, *Gender Trouble*, 166.
50 Grosz, *Volatile Bodies*, 12.

sustained temporal duration."[51] Some authors have criticized Butler's performativity as granting too much power to language, though the same argument has been leveled against social constructivism. The question becomes why "are these linguistic norms powerful enough to constitute us but not powerful enough to constitute us in any way that they please?"[52] Or, as Jacquelyn Zita notes, authors are reopening the "question of the body's materiality, seeking to rescue the body from discursive evaporation without returning to the mire of biological essentialism."[53] Barad replies,

> [P]erformativity, properly construed, is not an invitation to turn everything (including material bodies) into words; on the contrary, performativity is precisely a contestation of the excessive power granted to language to determine what is real . . . performativity is actually a contestation of the unexamined habits of mind that grant language and other forms of representation more power in determining our ontologies than they deserve.[54]

For Butler, performativity is the "effect" of iterated performances, that is, my "womanhood" is the effect over time of my iterative performances of gender. Performance is not merely the recitation of words, but rather an embodied moment in which "bodies and language are mutually emergent."[55] In these performances, I am reiterating (citing) heterosexual gender norms. The key concept here, for my theoretical project, is the idea of embodiment that simultaneously "recognizes one's both *being* a body and *having* a body."[56] Though critics of Butler have argued that *Gender Trouble* denies the materiality of the body, a synthesis of Butler and Grosz understands the body as produced *through* and *in* performance.

The qualities of the internet as a medium order our experience in a specific way; that is, boundaries are created at the moment of performance. The performative act of "entering" the internet is an articulation; that is, a performative "formation of order, of the body and of speech, bringing together

---

51 Butler, *Gender Trouble*, xv. (Emphasis added.)
52 A. Allen, *The Power of Feminist Theory: Domination, Resistance, Solidarity* (Boulder, Co: Westview, 1999), 79.
53 Jacquelyn Zita, "Book Reviews," *Signs: Journal of Women in Culture & Society* 21, no. 3 (1996): 787.
54 Barad, "Posthumanist Performativity," 802.
55 Stormer, "Articulation," 267.
56 B. Behrenshausen, "Touching Is Good: An Eidetic Phenomenology of Interface, Interobjectivity, and Interaction in Nintendo's Animal Crossing: Wild World" (master's thesis, University of Maine, 2006), 44. (Emphasis in original.)

the material world, language, and spatial arrangement in one act."[57] As in Grosz's moment of "becoming," the material body is (re)established at the moment of the act; it does not preexist the articulation except wherein it has already been articulated—or, the body does not preexist the performance but its perceived continuity is the effect of performativity. Our experience of "reality" then, is not "composed of things-in-themselves or things-behind-phenomena" but rather is made up of an "ongoing flow of agency through which 'part' of the world makes itself differentially intelligible to another 'part' of the world and through which local causal structures, boundaries, and properties are stabilized and destabilized."[58] Perhaps the most significant repercussion of this is the understanding that these performances or articulations do not "take place in space and time [but constitute] the making of spacetime itself."[59] As such, bodies are subject to the same; that is, they are not already there, but are constituted in performance. The experience of corporeality, of having a body, is similar to Butler's gender "effect"—it is the constant and dynamic citation or re-iterability of performances over time.

If one uses performativity as a theoretical base from which to understand agency and performative acts, "the material body marked by gender, race and class not only forms the physical ground for the cyberspace traveler, but is also clearly introduced and reproduced in the new electronic spaces it inhabits."[60] One cannot engage in, on or with the medium without one's body. While the communicative acts literally happen in a "placeless place" with others who are not physically co-present, to overlook the relationships between the material and the virtual or to downplay the role of the material world in the construction, maintenance and use of the virtual is to miss the opportunity to engage in scholarship that recognizes the importance of such interplay.

Another way of understanding performativity is that of discursive practices.[61] For Barad, discursive practices "define what counts as meaningful statements. . . ." and ". . . are the local sociohistorical material conditions that enable and constrain disciplinary knowledge practices. . . . [They] produce, rather than merely describe, the 'subjects' and 'objects' of knowledge practices."[62] Key to understanding Barad's discursive practices is her development of intra-agency, a useful theoretical concept.

---

57 Stormer, "Articulation," 263.
58 Barad, "Posthumanist Performativity," 817.
59 Ibid.
60 Sunden, "What Happened to Difference in Cyberspace?," 225.
61 Barad, "Posthumanist Performativity."
62 Ibid., 819.

Intra-agency

Barad draws heavily upon the work of Danish physicist Niels Bohr, who contributed to the understanding of quantum physics. For Bohr, "things do not have inherently determinate boundaries or properties, and words do not have inherently determinate meanings."[63] A classic example of this is measuring light: measured one way, light has wave-like properties; measured another way, light has particle-like properties. Barad uses Bohr's understanding of physics to shape her own concept of agency and performativity.

In order to discuss Barad's posthumanist performativity, one must first understand her appropriation of Bohr's idea of measurement as apparatus. An apparatus is more than the traditional definition of a tool, machine or instrument. For Barad, apparatuses are arrangements that *"are dynamic (re)configurings of the world, specific agential practices/intra-actions/performances through which specific exclusionary boundaries are enacted."*[64] In other words, an apparatus is a certain way of ordering the world that has agency in that it simultaneously limits and enables how the world is rendered intelligible. Apparatuses are the "exclusionary practices of mattering through which intelligibility and materiality are constituted."[65] Apparatuses are agential in precisely this way—they limit or enable, exclude or permit, and draw the boundaries of possibility. In the same vein as Schrodinger's cat—which posits that without direct observation and measurement (human agency and apparatus agency) the cat in question is neither living nor dead—we (as agents) cannot "know" the world without apparatuses, which also have agency.

Herein I have discussed the agency of humans and the agency of "things" (apparatuses) as two distinct things; in doing so I mean not to privilege one over the other, or indeed mark that there is a difference between the agency of an apparatus and the agency of a human. To do so would be to subscribe to anthropocentrism and in some ways support the internal/external, mind/body dualism. I have discussed them as separate entities only to render the discussion intelligible *in terms of* the mind/body dualism. The agency granted to any specific entity or thing is not a stable given; that is to say, there are degrees of agency involved in the specific act or phenomena. For example, think of a deep-sea diver—the agency of her equipment is substantial; it simultaneously limits and enables her own agency in the situation.

Thus, the constructivist or representationalist questions of the relationship(s) between words and things are rejected; instead, Barad advocates *"a causal relationship between specific exclusionary practices embodied as specific material configurations of the world . . . and specific material phenomena . . .*

---

63   Ibid., 813.
64   Ibid., 816. (Emphasis in original.)
65   Ibid., 820.

theoretical concepts . . . are not ideational in character but rather are specific physical arrangements."[66] In other words, specific practices (such as discursive practices like conversing or being online) and specific material configurations (such as an apparatus like a board game or a computer) interact (or have intra-agency) to materialize phenomenon. In this way all bodies come to "matter" (materialize) "through the world's iterative intra-activity—its performativity."[67]

Applying Barad's understanding of performativity leads us to an understanding of interaction and agency that allows us to reject social constructivism's a priori body, for the body is "neither a passive surface awaiting the mark of culture nor the end product of cultural performances."[68] The body, instead, is an intra-agential phenomenon, limited and enabled by the intra-agential phenomena of space and time, as well as other agential phenomena. In terms of applying this form of performativity to the online experience, one begins to understand and appreciate the complexity of recognizing non-humans as agential; that is, the computer as apparatus limits and enables (i.e., has intra-agency) what the user can "do" or perform online. Instead of viewing the technology or the medium as something distinct from individuals and individuals distinct from their performance of gender, for example, "in the concrete social practices of the everyday they work inextricably together in their interpellation and positioning of women and men."[69]

The performative act of "entering" the internet is an articulation, an intra-agential experience sensitive to "the contrary requirements, to the exigencies, to the pressures of conflicting agencies where none of them is really in command."[70] This experience of entering the internet is a liminal one; a concept explored in more detail here.

Liminality in the Context of Intra-agency

Liminality is often understood in terms of rites of passage, as in Victor Turner's *The Ritual Process*.[71] However, a limen can also be viewed as a "threshold, a border, a margin, a transitional space, a site of negotiation and struggle."[72]

---

66 Ibid., 814. (Emphasis in original.)
67 Ibid., 823.
68 Ibid., 827.
69 van Zoonen, "Gendering the Internet," 16.
70 B. Latour, "The Promises of Constructivism" in *Chasing Technoscience*, ed. D. Ihde and E. Selinger (Bloomington: Indiana University Press, 2003), 33.
71 V. Turner, *The Ritual Process: Structure and Anti-structure* (Chicago: Aldine, 1969).
72 Kristen Langellier, "Personal Narrative, Performance, Performativity: Two or Three Things I Know for Sure," *Text and Performance Quarterly* 19 (1999): 138.

The term has been applied in studies of the internet.[73] For Clare Madge and Henrietta O'Connor, who conducted a study of young mothers and their use of the internet and internet communities to "try on" versions of motherhood, liminality "enables a way of thinking about cyberspace as a generative space which both operates as a metaphor but also represents lived practices, where alternatives to binaries may be thought out and lived through."[74] It is feasible to fold in Madge and O'Connor's understanding of liminality into Barad's construction of performativity; that is, as a generative space. However, lauding the internet as a liminal space *because* it is a disembodied space overlooks the context of intra-agency and body-apparatus interaction. That is, if one attributes the experience of liminality singularly to an ekstasis of representation, one loses the opportunity to examine the complex interactions afforded by the body-apparatus interaction.[75]

Consider, for a moment, Butler's rejection of the mind/body dualism. She describes the policing of inner and outer worlds in terms of the body and the taboos placed upon the permeation of the body and its orifices. We as a culture prefer to maintain a strict distinction between inner and outer worlds, but for the "inner and outer worlds to remain utterly distinct, the entire surface of the body would have to achieve an impossible impermeability."[76] In the same vein, Pheng Cheah discusses the idea of torsion, or the "rotation from interiority or exteriority and vice versa, the vanishing point where outside and inside, materiality and intelligibility become indistinguishable."[77]

These ideas are of interest when discussing the concept of liminality because to participate in the idealized cyberutopia, one must leave one's body behind. In order to maintain that disembodiment, there would have to be "impossible impermeability" between the online and offline worlds. For Grosz, the question of Butler's impermeability of the body can be brought to the relationship of the person to the computer. Grosz asks, "Can the computer screen act as the clear-cut barrier separating cyberspace from real space, the space of mental inhabitation from the physical space of corporeality? What if the boundary is more permeable than the smooth glassy finality of the screen?"[78] Grosz's exploration of the concept of virtuality (specifically in

---

73 Clare Madge and Henrietta O'Connor, "Mothers in the Making? Exploring Liminality in Cyber/space," *Transactions of the Institute of British Geography* 30, no. 1 (2005): 83–97; Dennis Waskul, "Ekstasis and the Internet: Liminality and Computer-mediated Communication," *New Media & Society* 7, no. 1 (2005): 47–63.
74 Madge and O'Connor, "Mothers in the Making?," 93.
75 Waskul, "Ekstasis and the Internet."
76 Butler, *Gender Trouble*, 170.
77 Cheah, "Mattering," 122.
78 Grosz, *Architecture from the Outside*, 87.

terms of spatiality and architecture) addresses and rejects precisely this idea of cyberspace as a "containable, separable field, entered voluntarily."[79]

Instead, Grosz calls for a new understanding of virtuality that is not limited to cyberspace or "virtual reality," but rather to our understanding of reality itself. In a similar vein as Barad's intra-agency, Grosz calls for "reconceptualizing the real and the relations of embeddedness, the nesting or interimplication ... of the virtual and real within each other."[80] For Grosz, it is the "in-betweenness" that needs to be explored—not the product of intra-agency, or the product of materialization, but rather the performance, the phenomenon-in-the-making, the becoming, the space between one bounded entity to another. Like torsion as the vanishing point of inside and outside—where what is becomes what it is not—Grosz describes the "in-between" as "the space of the bounding and undoing of the identities which constitute it."[81]

Liminality, I would argue, is the *experience of torsion*—the performative act of crossing (permeating) a *threshold*, a *transitional act* of body-apparatus intra-agency. Liminality is the bodily experience that denies the false dichotomy of leaving the body behind; it is the simultaneous experience of intra-agency among multiple agents. Understanding liminality as the ability to freely represent one's self in cyberspace is a too-simple appreciation of the term. Liminality is the *bodily* experience of intra-agency, which includes the agency of the apparatus to *limit and enable* certain phenomena, including processes of self-representation.

It is possible, since intra-agency exists in all practices and phenomena, to argue that liminality is a universal, constant experience. I would not deny this. All experiences are to some degree liminal, and involve the experience of the "in-between" or of torsion; that is, all experiences are performative acts that are in some way transitional. However, I will argue that some experiences are more liminal than others; or more precisely, *felt* and *experienced* as more liminal. A "more liminal" phenomenon occurs when the balance of agency is skewed in a particular articulation of body-apparatus. Let us return to the example of the deep-sea diver: when on land, the diving equipment has no more intra-agency than its materiality—its mass and spatial dimensions. In the sea, the intra-agency of apparatus and body is significantly more; the apparatus drastically limits and enables the abilities of the user. Thus, the experience of diving is a liminal one; one in which the torsion of crossing the threshold of extant possibilities is *evident*. It is not possible for a human body to breathe underwater. However, the phenomenon of breathing underwater is possible through the intra-agency of body-apparatus.

---

79   Ibid., 88.
80   Ibid.
81   Ibid., 92.

In the same vein, it is a computer and/or the associated technologies that allow a user to enter cyberspace. Thus, the phenomenon of "being online" is a liminal experience in that one experiences the intra-agency of body-apparatus. The apparatus that allows one to enter this space (to cross the threshold, to experience the torsion of outside/body-inside/mind as bodily-apparatus-cyberspace) has intra-agency beyond its own materiality on our desktops or in our hands. It is evident to users that the apparatus is intra-agential with the user; indeed, the experience becomes so powerfully liminal that users are aware of and construct their performances with the belief that they leave their bodies behind and enter a disembodied place—a space that is an interior (mind) made exterior (visible and/or present to others). *A user's experience of "going online" is thus a liminal experience of torsion, a crossing of multiple thresholds.* These liminal acts belie the impermeability of our dualisms; we are constantly crossing the various lines between interior and exterior. Users consistently cross between the online world and offline world, and in this liminal state participate in many interactions which involve a complex interplay of self-technology and self-other.

Acknowledging liminality—the experience of torsion—is important to feminist scholars in terms of recognizing the *constant* experience of the in-between, of torsion and of crossing thresholds. Just as Butler held that drag performances are subversive in terms of bringing to the fore the idea that *all* gender is performance, the evident and experienced liminality of cyberspace recognizes that *all* experiences cross thresholds, and limiting liberation to liminal spaces like the internet thus unnecessarily delimits the possibilities of transformation in other ("real") spaces.[82]

The concept of liminality developed here is a small step toward developing more nuanced approaches to understanding our relationship with new media. New media scholars, feminist or not, would benefit from challenging the seductive simplicity of the mind/body dualism; in order to engage with increasingly complex new media environments scholars need increasingly complex conceptual tools. For feminist scholars studying new media, and the internet in particular, developing these conceptual tools can lead to a fresh take on cyberfeminism.

"Rehabilitating" Cyberfeminism as a Site for Further Research

In their tone-setting work on cyberfeminism, editors Susan Hawthorne and Renate Klein defined cyberfeminism as a "philosophy which acknowledges, firstly, that there are differences in power between women and men specifically in the digital discourse; and secondly, that CyberFeminists want to

---

[82] Butler, *Gender Trouble*.

change that situation."[83] In the decade since their words, cyberfeminism has grown to encompass a myriad of issues. Cyberfeminism is enacted variously by academics and activists and is cited and tested by theorists and those in the digital trenches. Why then attempt to "rehabilitate" a term so diffuse?

The term *cyberfeminism* offers scholars shorthand for addressing the exceedingly complex concepts surrounding gender, power, and digital technologies. As our intra-actions with technology become more complex, such examples of shorthand are both useful and problematic. Periodically unpacking such terms maintains their validity and viability in scholarship; such effort to reconnect real-world phenomena with theory is a consistently unfinished and open project.

As a shorthand term in scholarship, cyberfeminism has diffused in several directions. One such direction rejoices in the internet as a utopia as the body is left behind (discussed previously). A second direction understands the internet and virtual reality technologies as incorporating the body in a way that neither a distinct body nor technology remains, but a third entity is created, a cyborg. In response to this, I cite Langellier and Peterson's study of bloggers: "While technology extends the body's capability to participate in storytelling, it does not make the body into an extension of the computer... it is the lived-body, the conscious experience of communication, that provides the basis for its technological extension."[84] This direction in cyberfeminism, spurred and extended by authors such as Donna Haraway and N. Katherine Hayles, has much potential to explore our future relationships with technologies as these technologies become enmeshed in our own fleshed bodies.[85] However, the cyborg figure as primary in cyberfeminism tends to divorce the locally bound and experienced sociopolitical context from the self-technology axis.

The most salient version of cyberfeminist scholarship available today addresses the relationships between the lived experiences of women/users and the technology itself. As Sunden describes, this position attempts to:

> *articulate the importance for women to incorporate new electronic media into their lives without handing over control. The important question is not whether a woman can be correctly described as working class, lesbian or woman of color, but instead how the personal and political impact that*

---

83 Hawthorne and Klein, *Cyberfeminism*, 2.
84 Langellier and Peterson, *Storytelling in Daily Life*, 167.
85 Donna Haraway, *Simians, Cyborgs, and Women* (New York: Routledge, 1991); N. Katherine Hayles, *How We Became Posthuman* (Chicago: University of Chicago Press, 1999).

communication technology has in women's daily lives can be addressed and analyzed.[86]

It is this cyberfeminism which would serve as a useful platform to build feminist work regarding new media. Studies that explore the agency of users while simultaneously addressing the power of the internet and its associated technologies to shape, encourage and restrain those experiences, would "go some way to rectifying the overconcentration in much academic (and other) writing on virtuality, on the separation of mind and body during Internet use, by focusing instead on how online 'virtuality' and offline 'reality' constitute each other."[87]

This cyberfeminism would encourage the empowerment of women from their particular embodied experiences and their experiences of gender, class, race, and other identities, rather than through erasure or mechanization of the body. It would entail an emphasis on the medium as well as the embodied experience of and with the medium. A new cyberfeminism would account for intra-agency and address the particularities of users' experiences in their totality, rather than falling back into mind/body dualism.

Feminist scholars interested in the internet as a locus and focus should reframe their discussion from the limitations/repercussions of gender performance online (or bringing the body online, etc.) and the limitations or qualities of the medium online as if they are two wholly unrelated things—they are not, they are both discourses or apparatuses that enable/limit what we can do or can't do online. Each apparatus is an articulation of body-medium, and to ignore that is to fall easily into the cyberutopian cadence, ignoring both the body and the lived experiences of users. A user's experience is a performance in which both the agency of the user and the apparatus come into play, as well as the agencies of other users, other algorithms. The concept of intra-agency shapes all performance; the more limited concept of liminality more specifically addresses the *perceived* "difference" of cyberspace.

Future research, in particular, should address the internet as a space and place. Though some scholars have attempted a geography of the internet,[88] many authors refuse to view the internet as a place, despite the language we use to talk about it (i.e. I "go" online, I "surf," I "visit"). Waskul, in particular, articulates a familiar argument about the internet:

> *The internet, by definition, dislocates "space" from "place." From the "space" of an individual's home or office they access "places" on the internet that are without "space" themselves. . . . In spite of common*

---

86 Sunden, "What Happened to Difference in Cyberspace?" 222.
87 McGerty, "Nobody Lives Only in Cyberspace," 897.
88 Madge and O'Connor, "Mothers in the Making?"

jargon of "surfing" or "visiting" locations on the internet, in truth those "places" are transmitted from one locality to any and all user's varied geographic "space."[89]

Grosz has made progress in using the vocabulary and concepts of architecture (by definition the study of space) to both real and "virtual" places.[90] Scholars should continue to develop these explorations of the internet as a place and space, as well as exploring what the distinctive experiences and practices online offer understandings of the lived experiences in "real" space.

This article is a call to arms to theorists of digital media, particularly the internet. Rejecting cyberutopian fantasies will allow us to pursue the embodied experiences of internet users, and to more fully appreciate the relationships of self and technology. Developing or interrogating concepts such as liminality will expand our theoretical "tool box" and in turn enrich our scholarship. Cyberfeminism has potential as a rich position from which to theorize the complexities of new media; so long as cyberfeminism acknowledges and embraces corporeality as a necessary component of its position.

Bibliography

Allen, A. *The Power of Feminist Theory: Domination, Resistance, Solidarity.* Boulder, Co: Westview, 1999.

Barad, Karen. "Posthumanist Performativity: Toward an Understanding of How Matter Comes to Matter." *Signs* 28, no. 3 (2003): 801-31.

Basi, J. K. T. *Women, Identity and India's Call Centre Industry.* New York: Routledge, 2009.

Behrenshausen, B. "Touching Is Good: An Eidetic Phenomenology of Interface, Interobjectivity, and Interaction in Nintendo's Animal Crossing: Wild World." Master's Thesis, University of Maine, 2006.

Boler, M. "Hypes, Hopes and Actualities: New Digital Cartesianism and Bodies in Cyberspace." *New Media & Society* 9, no. 1 (2007): 139-68.

Bostdorff, D. "The Internet Rhetoric of the Ku Klux Klan: A Case Study in Web Site Community Building Run Amok." *Communication Studies* 55, no. 2 (2004): 340-61.

Braidotti, R. *Nomadic Subjects: Embodiment and Sexual Difference in Contemporary Feminist Theory.* New York: Columbia University Press, 1994.

Butler, Judith. *Gender Trouble: Feminism and the Subversion of Identity.* New York: Routledge, 1999.

Cheah, Pheng. "Mattering." *Diacritics* 26, no. 1 (1996): 108-39.

---

89 Waskul, "Ekstasis and the Internet," 54.
90 Grosz, *Architecture from the Outside.*

Danet, B. "Text as Mask: Gender, Play, and Performance on the Internet." In Jones, *Cybersociety 2.0*, 129–58.
Fallows, Deborah. *How Women and Men Use the Internet*. Pew Internet and American Life Project Report. Washington, DC: Pew Research Center, 2005. http://www.pewinternet.org/Reports/2005/How-Women-and-Men-Use-the-Internet.aspx.
Gergen, Kenneth J. *The Saturated Self: Dilemmas of Identity in Contemporary Life*. New York: Basic, 1991.
Grosz, Elizabeth. *Architecture from the Outside: Essays on Virtual and Real Space*. Cambridge, MA: MIT Press, 2001.
———. *Volatile Bodies: Toward a Corporeal Feminism*. Bloomington: Indiana University Press, 1994.
Hanisch, C. "The Personal is Political." In *Notes from the Second Year Women's Liberation: Major Writings of the Radical Feminists*, edited by S. Firestone and A. Koedt. New York: Radical Feminism, 1970.
Haraway, Donna. *Simians, Cyborgs, and Women*. New York: Routledge, 1991.
Hawthorne, Susan, and Renata Klein. *Cyberfeminism: Connectivity, Critique and Creativity*. North Melbourne: Spinifex Press, 1999.
Hayles, N.K. *How We Became Posthuman*. Chicago: University of Chicago Press, 1999.
Jones, Steven G. *Cybersociety 2.0*. Thousand Oaks, CA: Sage, 1998.
Kelemen, Mihaela, and Warren Smith. "Community and its 'Virtual' Promises: A Critique of Cyberlibertarian Rhetoric." *Information, Communication & Society* 4, no. 3 (2001): 370–87.
Kramarae, C. "Feminist Fictions of Future Technology." In Jones, *Cybersociety 2.0*, 100–28.
Langellier, Kristen. "Personal Narrative, Performance, Performativity: Two or Three Things I Know for Sure." *Text and Performance Quarterly* 19 (1999): 125–44.
Langellier, Kristin, and Eric Peterson. *Storytelling in Daily Life: Performing Narrative*. Philadelphia: Temple University Press, 2004.
Latour, B. "The Promises of Constructivism." In *Chasing Technoscience*, edited by D. Ihde and E. Selinger. Bloomington: Indiana University Press, 2003.
Lyotard, Jean-Francois. *The Postmodern Condition: A Report on Knowledge*. Translated by G. Bennington and B. Massumi. Minneapolis, MN: University of Minnesota Press, 1989.
Madge, Clare, and Henrietta O'Connor. "Mothers in the Making? Exploring Liminality in Cyber/space." *Transactions of the Institute of British Geography* 30, no. 1 (2005): 83–97.

McGerty, Lisa-Jane "'Nobody Lives Only in Cyberspace': Gendered Subjectivities and Domestic Use of the Internet." *CyberPsychology & Behavior* 3, no. 5 (2000): 895-99. doi:10.1089/10949310050191863.
Morahan-Martin, Janet. "Women and the Internet: Promise and Perils." *CyberPsychology & Behavior* 3, no. 5 (2000): 683-691.
Nakamura, Lisa. *Cybertypes: Race, Ethnicity, and Identity on the Internet*. New York: Routledge, 1999.
Patterson, Randi, and Gail Corning. "Researching the Body: An Annotated Bibliography for Rhetoric." *Rhetoric Society Quarterly* 27, no. 3 (1997): 5-29.
Rich, Adrienne. *Blood, Bread, and Poetry*. New York: Norton, 1994.
Shotter, J., and Kenneth J. Gergen. "Social Construction: Self, Others, and the Continuing Conversation." *The Communication Yearbook* 17 (1994): 3-33.
Sobchack, Vivian. *Carnal Thoughts: Embodiment and Moving Image Culture*. Los Angeles: University of California Press, 2004.
Stabile, C. *Feminism and the Technological Fix*. New York: Manchester University Press, 1994.
Stormer, Nathan. "Articulation: A Working Paper on Rhetoric and Taxis." *Quarterly Journal of Speech* 90, no. 3 (2004): 257-84. doi:10.1080/0033563042000255516.
Sunden, Jenny. "What Happened to Difference in Cyberspace? The (Re)turn of the She-Cyborg." *Feminist Media Studies* 1, no. 2 (2001): 215-32.
Turner, V. *The Ritual Process: Structure and Anti-structure*. Chicago: Aldine, 1969.
van Zoonen, Liesbet. "Gendering the Internet: Claims, Controversies and Cultures." *European Journal of Communication* 17, no. 1 (2002): 5-23.
Waskul, Dennis "Ekstasis and the Internet: Liminality and Computer-mediated Communication." *New Media & Society* 7, no. 1 (2005): 47-63.
Waskul, Dennis, and Mark Douglass. "Cyberself: The Emergence of Self in On-line Chat." *The Information Society* 13 (1997): 375-97. doi:10.1080/019722497129070.
Woodfield, R. *Women, Work and Computing*. Cambridge: Cambridge University Press, 2000.
Worthington, Nancy. "Women's Work on the World Wide Web: How a New Medium Represents an Old Problem." *Popular Communication* 3, no. 1 (2005): 43-60.
Zita, Jacquelyn. "Book Reviews." *Signs: Journal of Women in Culture & Society* 21, no. 3 (1996): 786-96.

Part Three

Online Environment

Going On-line:
Consuming Pornography in the Digital Era

Zabet Patterson[1]

On July 3,1995, before the rise (and fall) of the so-called Internet revolution, *Time* magazine shocked its readers with one of the first mass-media exposés on the prevalence and dangers of on-line pornography. The opening paragraph begins its panicked inquiry into cyberporn by stating:

> Sex is everywhere these days—in books, magazines, films, television, music videos and bus-stop perfume ads. It is printed on dial-a-porn business cards and slipped under windshield wipers. It is acted out by balloon-breasted models and actors with unflagging erections, then rented for $4 a night at the corner video store.[2]

But the accompanying illustration did not show unflagging erections or ballooning breasts. On opening to the story, readers were instead confronted with an image of a naked man, his arms and legs wrapped around a keyboard and computer monitor, seeming to dissolve into the screen.

Within this admittedly strange and startling image, with its formless room, its featureless everyman, its computer glowing with a blistering, apocalyptic light—we can begin to discern the visual tropes that would become mobilized around the issue of Internet pornography. It is a visual rhetoric of anxiety specifically located at the rapidly evolving interface between corporeal body and computer screen. It is an anxiety concerning the possible lack of control and autonomy of that body when confronted with this technology. On the level of sexuality, it figures the relationship between body and networked computer as peculiarly and unwholesomely dissolute. The

---

1   Editors' note: this paper was previously published as a chapter in *Porn Studies*, ed. Linda Williams, (Durham, NC: Duke University Press), 104-123.
2   Philip Elmer-Dewitt, "On a Screen Near You: Cyberporn," *Time*, July 3, 1995, 38.

image displays a sociocultural panic over what we might term "correct object choice"—here a man, ostensibly failing to find a suitable "other," is solipsistically collapsing into himself in mastubatory pleasure.[3] This solipsistic collapse is one engendered by the new technology. The "body" of the computer clearly replaces the body of another human. And herein lies the ostensible "danger" of cyberporn as seen by *Time* magazine:[4] the danger of the dissolution and fusing of man into machine, or perhaps, man into "network."[5] It is an understanding of the relationship of body and networked computer as potentially, peculiarly, and unwholesomely dissolvent of the subject. Simultaneously, though, we also see the danger of a sexuality mediated and transformed through the digital screen.

In part because it is so clearly symptomatic of the anxieties evoked for a certain audience when confronted with the issue of Internet pornography, this image offers a useful place to begin interrogating the topic of Internet pornography. It gestures toward important questions of proximity and

---

3   It is important to note that the gender of the figure here, while somewhat ambiguous, is necessarily, and presumably male. This would be a different article if it were evidently a woman wrapped around the computer screen. However, in this particular technological panic, it is assumed that computers, and their potential, or requisite contamination are a masculine problem, much as it assumed, by this article and by culture in general, that the lure of pornography in particular, and technology in general, is directed toward men. Because the mainstream pornographic websites that I will be addressing presume a male viewership, this paper will follow this assumption. However, it is important to note that this assumption has a normative agenda, one that works; to efface the female spectator of on-line pornography, as well as the female user of computer technology. This double effacement of women might be read as a defense, on the part of the heterosexual male imaginary, against the radical social possibilities that the Internet might seem to provide.

4   An overview of the dubious methodology behind this article can be found in Mike Godwin's "Fighting a Cyber-Porn Panic," in *Cyber Rights: Defending Free Speech in the Digital Era* (Cambridge, MA: MIT Press, 2003), 259–318.

5   If the personal computer and its connection to the World Wide Web represents in some way the entry of the public sphere into the domestic space of the home, or rather, the possibility that the soul of the domestic space might be turned outward toward a networked public sphere, there seems to be a cultural fear about promiscuity and adultery in play as well. What desires can this (potentially married?) man (or woman) have which are not satisfied by his home life? What does it mean that these desires might, for once, not have to be simply repressed, but could find some kind of expression on-line? Could this expression possibly be legitimate, and what would this do to the "space" of the domestic nuclear family? As is often the case, new technologies come to figure old social and cultural anxieties, giving these anxieties new avenues for expression.

identification by specifically staging the *corporeality* of the encounter with pornography, as well as the corporeality of the encounter with the computer. Here, it is the encounter with the computer that proves consuming; the rest of the room fades out, for both the man and the viewer. This staging also leads us to question the viewing of the pornographic image itself, in unexpected ways. The screen image within the image—the screen on-screen—turns out to be a curious blind spot; the "image" of pornography is either unimportant or unshowable. The absence of the image proposes that it is impossible for us, as outside viewers, to ever really see what the man is seeing; it suggests that the encounter with pornography, and the encounter with technology, may not allow for an easy, distanced critical spectatorship. Further, it suggests that, for this audience, an understanding of the relationship to the computer is reached indirectly, through a confrontation with the pornographic image: the relationship to the computer itself remains a non-seeing one, imbricated in the non-seeing of the pornographic image. Thus it would seem that this gesture of looking away makes for a critical element in viewing either porn or technology.

Cyberporn, in this image and its imagination, offers a new ordering of sex and the body, one scripted through a particular logic of networked computer technology. This image, and the article it accompanies, was produced when the Internet had not yet become an established fact for much of the audience and when the graphical World Wide Web had not yet assumed its present ubiquity. Digital technology was perceived as threatening the integrity of the users' bodies, and the issue of so-called cybersex could be seen as a kind of summa of these fantasies and fears. Today, questions and concerns about the relationship between the body and technology have largely dropped out of mass-media discussions, which increasingly assume computer technology as a given. As Lev Manovich points out, "the speed with which new technologies are assimilated in the United States makes them 'invisible' almost overnight: they become an assumed part of the everyday existence, something which does not seem to require much reflection."[6] But in some sense, to analyze Internet pornography is necessarily to return to these larger questions concerning the Internet itself as well as the particular mediation of embodied visual experience to which the computer user is subjected.

Categorization and the "Truth" of Desire

The pornographic image can be a particularly dense semantic site, but it is one which functions only in and through a direct visceral appeal to the body. Much of the academic writing on pornography sees this direct address to the

---

[6] Lev Manovich, "New Media from Borges to HTML," in *New Media Reader*, ed. Noah Wardrip-Fruin and Nick Montfort (Cambridge, MA: MIT Press, 2003), 13.

body as grounding both its limitations and possibilities. The appeal of the pornographic image is importantly corporeal, and images become effective as porn to the extent that they elicit certain bodily sensations, almost involuntarily. Yet cyberporn, in its engagement with the technological site of the Internet and the material interface of the computer, presents a range of novel issues and problems for our investigation of this corporeal dimension. To interrogate Internet pornography, we must begin by considering the ways in which the organization of on-line pornographic discourses function to guide, if not overtly discipline, their targeted subjects.

The massive metasites of cyberporn are organized to provide a near instantaneous mass mediation and dissemination of sexual representation. In theory, this wealth of images would seem to offer a truly emancipatory scenario allowing subjects to project their virtual selves into a seemingly endless variety of scenarios and environments, and to embody an infinite variety of freely chosen subject positions, roles, and desires. Yet, in reality, what cyberporn tends to offer—especially with a rapidly consolidating market—is an environment in which desire and subject position are produced as "truths" of the self through a discourse of categorization and classification. Images are available to the viewer only through the negotiation of an elaborate schema in which sexual desire is produced through the sequencing of fixed subject positions always and only defined in relation to each other. A subset of the cyberporn industry is devoted to the categorization and classification of these images and Web sites; these sites present categories of images, laid out in tables or allowing so-called key term searches. The "click here if you're gay!" button, like the "S/M" button, indicates a technology of desire both productive and regulatory. These buttons do allow for a kind of limited role-playing, but it is one in which the "exploration" is always already constrained by a logic requiring instantly recognizable cues, cues frighteningly regularized under the dictates of maximum efficiency and maximum profit.[7] Part of the captivation of cyberporn is that it allows images to be managed and categorized so readily, allowing the subject to assimilate and emulate a particular subject position while retaining the hallucinatory promise of flu-

---

7   The space of the Internet is generally considered in dematerialized rhetorics but it exists only by means of large, expensive machines that exist in physical space. The reality of countries prohibiting access to certain sites or the way the structure of the Internet increasingly follows the dictates of large corporate conglomerates will play an ever increasing role in our experience of this particular cultural site. As such, it seems critically important not to lose sight of the larger field of a corporatized social technology into which Internet pornography occurs. Presented through a particular technological apparatus, pornographic images are embedded in networks of production and consumption and informed by particular social conditions.

idity. The "contract" and financial exchange entailed by "clicking through" to a Web site, or in signing up for a particular site, then, forces this schema of classification to become fixed through acceptance and repetition.

Embodiment and Technologic

The question of discipline returns us necessarily to the more specific question or problem of the technological apparatus of the computer and how the intersection between pornography and the computer operates on the body. How do we begin to address this curious imbrication—so dramatically figured in the *Time* magazine image with which we began—of the human body and the computer apparatus?

Though seemingly obvious, a crucial and often unstated aspect of any technology is its material specificity—the way one cannot engage with the Internet except through the computer as a specific kind of material object or instrument with which the user has to interact in certain habitual ways. In the course of this interaction, repetitive practices concretize into a particular citational chain, one which becomes embedded both within a particular personal and more general social history. Vivian Sobchack refers to this incorporated logic as a "technologic." In "The Scene of the Screen," she claims that representational technologies, such as the computer, convey their logic in two ways: first, through the representations they display; and second, through the manner in which they latently engage our bodies. For Sobchack, technological analysis must take place on these two levels simultaneously, and any given technologic text must be read not only hermeneutically but also "through our perceptive sensorium, through the materiality (or *immanenent mediation*) of our own bodies. . . . The perceiving and sensing body is always also a lived-body—immersed in and making social meaning as well as physical sense."[8]

Considering Internet pornography in this light leads us to read collections of on-line images through the framework of a technologic always already reflexively incorporated by the viewer. This suggests not only that the habits of looking at Internet pornography are as constitutive of the viewing experience as the images themselves but, likewise, that these habits of looking insistently participate in inscribing power relations and social relations directly onto the body of the subject through gesture and repetition.[9] These physical habits of looking—of pointing and clicking, of pushing the refresh

---

[8] Vivian Sobchack, "The Scene of the Screen," in *Electronic Media and Technoculture*, ed. John Thornton Caldwell (New Brunswick, NJ: Rutgers, 2000), 139.

[9] This is informed, as I believe Sobchack's piece is critically informed, by an understanding of Pierre Bourdieu's conception of the habitus as developed in *The Logic of Practice*, trans. Richard Nice (Palo Alto: Stanford University Press, 1992).

button on Webcams, of the delays and frustrations of opening and closing windows—as well as the representational assumptions these habits entail, push the viewer into a particular kind of interaction with the Internet, one that not only reflects but reinscribes social relations. We might consider these material habits, following Judith Butler's reading of Pierre Bourdieu, as "a tacit form of performativity, a citational chain lived and believed at the level of the body."[10] This is not to say that any given technology demands a certain practicum, any more than it automatically reproduces preexistent social relations, but rather that it "generates dispositions which *incline* the social subject to act in relative conformity" with those relations.[11]

The insistent appeal of the pornographic image necessarily offers us a denser understanding of the insistent mechanisms with which particular technologies incline the body. In some sense, an analysis of on-line pornography must begin with the framework of this technologic and an examination of the physical apparatus through which pornographic images are encountered because the physical apparatus of the computer, and the material habits it requires, places the viewer in a relationship with the images in Internet pornography that differs significantly from the viewer's relationship to other types of pornography.

Delay and Deferral: Body and Interface

The question then becomes one of the body's relation to the screen as a material object and as a space of representation. Information on the World Wide Web does not simply appear, . . . it must be found. This process of searching can help us to clarify significant aspects of the interface, and the particular logic and habitus such searching provokes.

It is important to note that a substantial difference exists between being a "member" of a pay porn site and simply surfing for porn on the Web; and regardless of the growth and gross income of porn sites, many (if not most) people who look at porn on-line are not members of pay sites. Thus, from the perspective of the average viewer, a primary experience of looking for, and eventually at, cyberporn is precisely one of frustration and waiting.[12] The promise of cyberporn is one of immediate gratification, yet the technological systems of the Internet, as well as the interfaces of cyberporn sites, necessitate delay: the delay of logging on, the delay of finding a site, the delay of "signing through" the initial contract, the delay of having the thumbnails load,

---

10 Judith Butler, *Excitable Speech: A Politics of the Performative* (New York: Routledge, 1997), 155.

11 Ibid.

12 But as I will argue, even members of pay sites are not freed from the logic of delay and deferral. It is simply transformed and imparted in different ways.

and then, finally, the delay of waiting for the selected image, sequence of images, or video segment to appear. A high-speed connection may decrease this delay, but cyberporn constantly pushes the boundaries of bandwidth; as soon as the technology can immediately deliver full-frame images, streaming video comes on offer, with slower load times. Even with a high-speed connection, there is still often delay on the side of the site delivering the content. The technologic of the computer forces these sequential acts of waiting and looking and waiting to become habit, and in so doing, it inscribes repetition and delay as pleasures of a different order. On some level, there is indeed a limit to what the viewer will willingly put up with in order to get what he or she wants, and as such, delay can become frustration. But *Web surfing*, a telling term, offers its own pleasures, regardless of the frustration porn sites both understand and provoke; the structure of many porn sites seems to both direct and cater to the viewer's desires for delay and deferral by allowing the process of searching to exist under the aegis of the goal of "getting what they want," but in excess of it. Specifically, the floods of images and the enormous range of selection on any given pay site are there for a reason, and the reason seems to be precisely this process.

One might see this delay as intensifying the pleasure of the eventual visibility of the object by causing the object to acquire an illusory inaccessibility. But it makes more sense to see the satisfaction as taking place in the deferral of satisfaction itself. Seen in this light, the goal exists in part to allow the subject, or a portion of the subject, to rationalize the pleasure of surfing. To imagine the goal, then, is to project into a moment of perfect satisfaction—and the obtaining of a perfect image, one completely adequate to the subject's desire. But in comparison to this imagined perfect image, every image will always remain inadequate, and so the "search" continues. Psychoanalysis generally, and Jacques Lacan's particular articulation of the impossibility of fulfilling one's desire[13] articulates this point and its implications for subjectivity at some length. But common sense tells us that part of the pleasure in Web surfing is the pleasure of motion and movement either toward an unknown object or away from a boring desk job. The nearly perfect image, the one that comes closest to approximating one's desire—the group-sex shot with the not-too-busty redhead bent over in the front, perhaps—still only offers momentary satisfaction; in fact, images close to one's desire can provoke anxiety because they might cause the end of Web surfing. The subject is faced with a choice—will this be the last image? Even if the viewer knows he or she is unlikely to find one better, he will often continue on, forgoing the

---

13 This concept is developed, in particular, in Seminar 7 and Seminar 11; see *The Four Fundamental Concepts of Psycho-Analysis*, trans Alan Sheridan, (New York: Norton, 1981) and *The Seminar of Jacques Lacan, Book VII: The Ethics of Psychoanalysis*, trans. Dennis Porter, (New York: Norton, 1992).

pleasures of the known for the pleasures (often through frustration) of the unknown. The user constantly shifts on to new images—and in this process, new delays—in an endless slippage of desire in which part of the pleasure derives from habitual repetition and habitual deferral.[14]

Amateur Pornography

An interrogation of on-line pornography's imbrication in a particular technological apparatus necessarily leads us to a particular interrogation of on-line pornography sites, sites which, however much they may share, each constitute a specific field of application. The remainder of this inquiry will investigate the viewing mechanisms and structures of identification as developed in a specific subgenre—that of on-line "amateur" pornography. The shifting relationship between viewer and object inaugurated by cyberporn most clearly becomes evident in the category of amateur cyberporn. Beyond its immediacy, the key offer of the Internet for pornography would seem to be a sense of interactivity, which brings with it a sense of shared space and a collapse or disavowal of distance. The amateur subgenre most significantly engages with the opportunities for "interaction" and "self-production" offered by the Internet. With on-line amateur porn, we are watching, as if in a petri dish, the shifting nature of the relationship between viewer and woman-as-spectacle.

The bulk of pornographic imagery on-line is professionally produced—including, at this point, the bulk of so-called amateur porn, at least on the corporatized Web sites. Amateur porn on-line takes its visual language and textual cues in part from amateur videos, a genre which exploded in the middle of the 1980s—a case of couples doing it for themselves and distributing their homemade efforts through swap services. These efforts eventually made it to video store distribution, and the professional porn industry was quick to capitalize on the trend, which elevated previous drawbacks such as slapdash lighting, low production values, and wobbly camera movements from liability to aesthetic and financial asset. The Internet seemed to re-position this co-opted DIY aesthetic in crucial ways—an initial ease of distribution, and the possibility of "swapping," extended to the possibility of "interaction" between the producers and consumers of this pornography. The central frisson in amateur porn lies in its articulation of a certain proximity to the life of the spectator—and amateur Internet porn promises to make that proximity even more proximate.

There is a wide spectrum of material on the Web that could be classed as amateur pornography, ranging from camgirls who show a little skin

---

14 This information is taken from anecdotal evidence, personal experience, and interviews conducted in the chat rooms of various porn sites.

periodically to professionally produced shots of the same airbrushed and implanted women one sees on "professional" porn Web sites. The images, then, are set apart by the rhetoric that surrounds them: these women are billed as your neighbor, your boss, your sister-in-law.

Signing In

When you sign up as a member of a $39.95-per-month amateur porn site, such as Amateur University or Kara's Amateurs, you enter an enclosed area positioning itself as an exclusive club. Oddly enough, some of these clubs look like nothing so much as graphically enhanced Web portals. Once "inside," members are greeted by an elaborate menu—they can look at new or archived photos, watch videos, read erotica, chat in the chat room, chat with a stripper performing a private real-time Web-cast show, gamble, shop, read an advice column, or look at erotic cartoons. The lower portion of the screen sometimes links to nonerotically oriented services: news headlines, magazine articles, or free email accounts. Much like Web portals such as Yahoo!, the sites are structured to become a habit and a community. It offers full service, one-stop shopping—all your Internet needs at once. The space of the Web site becomes a familiar, even domestic "place."

Amateur porn Web sites provide some specific menu options that work to position them as amateur sites; these include personal letters, biographical information, on-line diaries, and Webcams. The personal letters address the viewer directly, inviting him into the space of the Web site or detailing the amateur's life; on-line diaries are another way for the viewer "to get up close and personal."

These viewing mechanisms offer a space of very particular, limited interaction; in their persistence across corporatized Web sites, they allow the viewer to enter into a relationship with the women shown that is simultaneously real and phantasmatic. It is the articulation of a space of public privacy that the viewer both enters and maintains at a distance. The viewing mechanisms available on a number of amateur porn Web sites foreground the idea that consumers of pornographic images are purchasing a fantasy of private access to a person; the specifically pornographic character of these images constitutes only a small part of the total "interaction." It is an interaction that comes to take on the character of a fetishistic disavowal, an "I know, but nevertheless. . . ." Critically, this relationship is grounded in seriality and repetition and the sense of proximity these characteristics serve to generate. It is a "relationship" based on and created through the purchase of intimacy, and this one-way intimacy constitutes, over and above the prurient imagery itself, a substantial part of what is being sold in amateur Internet porn, and hence a substantial part of what people are looking to buy.

A Day in The Life . . .

At Kara's Amateurs, "Members now have access to see what our Amateurs are all about. Spend a day of their life up close and personal! Go through our Amateur's daily schedule and see what they are up to. From the time they wake up. their walk in the park, to their sex life!" This section, called "A Day in the Life . . . ," is promoted as an exclusive attraction, but it functions much like the Webcams and simulated Webcams available on other sites and as such clearly demonstrates the everyday dynamics of the "encounter" with the amateur in Internet pornography. The amateur's day is divided into segments scheduled as appointments in a so-called date book. Some appointments are explicitly theatrical—the model will take a shower, masturbate with a vibrator, or have sex with the delivery boy—but many are not. The nontheatrical segments show more clearly what is at stake here: the abolition of the spectacular in favor of other models of relationality.

These appointments, or events, showcase the particular temporality of Internet pornography, as well as how it is framed and articulated by the specific mechanisms and limitations of the Internet. Importantly, the temporality of the date book is one of routine; it draws on the staging of amateur Webcams, where live, twenty-four-hours-a-day access means that the viewer can constantly check in on the performer's life or keep the performer's image in constant sight on the computer desktop. The "A Day in the Life . . ." videos participate in this rhetoric of liveness, presenting the frame as a window.

The day's events are further subdivided into brief segments of streaming video. This might seem a purely technological constraint, but the elaboration of these individual segments resembles the elaboration of "chapters" in the now ubiquitous DVD format, and this allows for a familiar exercise of control over the interface; and yet this desire to control the time of the video is not in fact complementary. With streaming video, viewers can pause the stream to create a still shot blurred with traces and ghostlines but, crucially, they cannot time-shift to fast-forward or rewind. To re-view a particular sequence is to begin again. Time thus becomes a sequence of discrete "chapters" or events—this is the logic of television before TiVO or the VCR, and it is a logic closely related to that of event and reality television, offering the sense of presence generated by an "implicit claim to be live."[15] Casting itself in this rhetoric, the necessarily low-res quality of the streaming video thus becomes a further guarantee the liveness, rather than an eruption into an awareness of the video as image. The low-res images visually reference Webcams offering continuous live broadcast, generally of still images, refreshed at rates

---

15 David Jay Bolter and Richard Grusin, *Remediation: Understanding New Media* (Cambridge, MA: MIT Press, 1999), 188.

measured in seconds or minutes. Webcam images are marked by low resolution, and are attractive precisely because of the level of "intimacy" they offer—a sense of presence guaranteed by what is perceived as a privileged relationship to the real. The low-res images themselves come to signify this privileged relationship, a signification only enhanced by their similarity to the image sequences obtained from video surveillance cameras, which have a similar claim to liveness.

Click on the 6 P.M. appointment in "A Day in the Life of Chandler," and blonde and tan Chandler leans into the camera to declare "now we're gonna go eat some sushi. We'll have some sake, get a little toasty, gonna be a lot of fun." The camera follows her as she walks into the restaurant and sits down next to a mirror. The camera is then positioned at a diagonal angle to her; part of the time she talks directly to the camera, and part of the time she talks away from it, to someone who would be sitting across the table from her. She is not alone in the film—when the sake is set down, there are two glasses—but all you see of her companion is his hand reaching for the sake.[16] The visual rhetoric of this sequence, as seen in figure 1, teases the viewer with a situation somewhere between voyeurism and direct address. The tease lies in the fact that you're not there, but you might as well be. The hand on the sake translates, with a slight hitch of dislocation, to the spectator's hand on the keyboard and the mouse.[17] Here, you are present to the space Chandler is in, more directly than in conventional narrative film (pornographic or otherwise) because you are solicited as a participant in this space. But you necessarily experience the situation and its pleasure in a thrown and almost robotic state, comfortably deprived of the necessity of

Fig 1. A typical capture from "A Day in the Life of Chandler" on the Kara's Amateurs Web site.

---

16 The hand reaching for the sake is both obviously white and obviously male. This gestures toward a presumed audience, but also works to reinforce and reiterate the limits of this exclusive identification.

17 While the analogy is not exact, we might trace out a relationship between the sense of presence here and the telepresence video games offer, particularly in cut sequences, in that viewers are pushed into inhabiting the screen space as a ghostly, mediated other.

action.[18] A second type of presence, then, is offered when Chandler addresses the camera directly. In this model, the viewer does not enter into the space of the screen, but the figure on the screen is present to and in the space the viewer inhabits.

Click on the first appointment in "A Day in the Life of Chandler," and Chandler stretches, rubbing her eyes and yawning as she rolls over in bed. Her makeup is already perfect, and she waves and smiles, saying "Hi! So are you waiting to follow me around? I'm very excited that you're coming with me. I've got a lot of errands to run, but I want you to come and watch me." She leans over and turns on the light, whispering conspiratorially that she needs to take a shower. "You still watching me? Watch me get in the shower. . . . Do you like watching me? Waking up in the morning?"

But the viewer does not, and would not want to, answer "yes." To answer would be to foreground his status as desiring, and hence, as lacking. That lack is exactly what this sequence is designed to recompense. The viewer's lack, his need, is proposed by Chandler's first question, which situates him as *waiting* for her, to wake up, to act. But this lack is announced only to be deferred, taken on by the woman with her claim to be excited that the viewer is going to accompany her throughout her day. Her "I *want* you to come and watch me" thus becomes understood by the viewer as "I *need* you to come and watch me," serving to displace his own need entirely. The event of the encounter proceeds through this dialectic of recognition. Through this play of recognition the woman acknowledges, produces, the element of lack only to take it onto herself, thus foregrounding the spectator's anxiety so much the better to relieve it. Her language accentuates the way in which this displacement of lack—a lack the spectator is aware of but fetishistically disavows—is itself one of the key sources of pleasure and excitement here.

In this encounter, a substantive portion of the fantasy seems to be the feeling, on the part of the viewer, that he is necessary to the woman on the other side of the camera; that she needs the viewer to be looking, in such a manner that the looking enables her pleasure. It is a fantasy which, as we have seen, emerges out of the spectator's own desire, his own lack—and the need to displace that lack. Displacing his needs and desires onto Chandler, he moves from a position of lack to one of overflowing plenitude. Chandler can exist by the grace of his look. She needs him, and he is able to fulfill her need. This differs from the relationship the viewer develops with an exhibitionist Web

---

18 This dynamic becomes evident even more dramatically in the "virtual lap dance" feature available at Danni's Hard Drive, where in a number of shots from Crissy Moran's lap dance, the camera offers the point of view of a man receiving a lap dance—in one video to the point of showing "location" shots of "your" lap, clad in nondescript jeans.

site such as Jennicam, however, because here the relationship is sustained entirely on the side of the spectator. This projection nourishes a more overarching vision of the woman as lacking, but more directly, it works to sustain a relationship in which the viewer, and the viewer's look, is needed by the images on the other side of the screen.[19]

"Reality"

The dynamics of this type of encounter, and the sense of presence it provokes, can be partially explained through what Jean Baudrillard terms the "frisson of the real." As he describes the filming of the Louds, the family whose lives were broadcast in the 1971 PBS series and ur-scene of reality TV *An American Family*, the producer's triumph was to say "They lived as though we were not there." An absurd, paradoxical formula—neither true nor false: utopian. The "as if *we* were not there" being equivalent to "as if *you* were there."[20] He goes on to say that it was:

> ... *this utopia, this paradox that fascinated the twenty million viewers, much more than did the 'perverse' pleasure of violating someone's privacy. In the verité experience it is not a question of secrecy or perversion, but of a sort of frisson of the real, a frisson of vertiginous and phony exactitude, a frisson of simultaneous distancing and magnification. . . . There one sees what the real never was (but "as if you were there").*

In Baudrillard's description, the pleasure of the reality TV experience lies not so much in the voyeurism of the viewing, and the power relationship that would imply, as in the way that the screen makes an impossible real available for encounter. The viewer is aware of the necessity of televisual mediation and its inevitable transformation of the depicted lives, but still disavows it in order to take pleasure in the microscopic exactitude of what is shown and the magnification of the minutest details. This magnification is of a different order altogether than that of the film screen, in which the image is literally enlarged into a physical spectacle. With reality TV, the television screen

---

19 This is not a dialectic limited to amateur sites, although it is more clearly foregrounded there. This dialectic, and the displacement it serves, becomes evident in the chat rooms and Webcam setups that make for prominent features on professional porn Web sites, from the personal sites of Jenna Jameson and Briana Banks to megasite Danni's Hard Drive, which tells its viewers, "when you become a member, you have the opportunity to truly interact with the women of your dreams."

20 Jean Baudrillard, *Simulacra and Simulation* (Ann Arbor: University of Michigan Press, 1994), 28.

begins to operate as a transparent window, showing a reality always already impacted by the structuring of televisual mediation.[21]

Baudrillard's discussion of reality television allows us to understand that in Web-based, amateur pornography, viewers are witnessing an abolition of the spectacular itself through a collapse of subject and object and of the poles of activity and passivity. It is no longer a question of watching but of a hallucinatory "being there" while knowing that one is not "there" and that in fact, there is no "there" there (i.e., no reality apart from its mediation.) This then presents a different type of subjectivity, a subjectivity for which the problem is, as Žižek puts it, not the possibility that "Big Brother" is watching, but the possibility that "Big Other"[22] is not watching.[23]

The abolition of the spectacular is further at stake in what viewers often articulate as the central draw of the amateur image—that it shows "real bodies" experiencing "real pleasure." This desire is figured oppositionally to the supposed artificiality of more general pornography, in which "it's all fake." A teaser to one site's hard-core amateur porn states:

> I have another friend who used to shoot Glam Porn Shots for a major men's magazine (you've heard of it). Eventually he became bored and when the opportunity to shoot amateur girls having sex came along, he jumped at it (wouldn't you?). He says that nothing gets him harder than watching those innocent girls lose all control.

The loss of control of the amateur is contrasted to the control of the professional—and it is the loss of control that guarantees the real-ness of the sex.

---

21 Baudrillard's statements are made even more apropos by the current explosion of the reality television genre, which has been paralleled by an explosion in on-line Webcams and journals, often accompanying one another. For the users, these on-line journals frequently articulate a public space of privacy, which dismantles traditional conceptions of the public sphere. People write in them without seeming to realize that what they say is public, and available through Internet search engines, and then are shocked when parents and colleagues at work read these journals to real-world effect. "It's my private journal!" they say. "If he wasn't going to treat it as such, he shouldn't have read it!"

22 Editors' note: this has been corrected since the original publication in *Porn Studies*; the portion here retracted read "the problem is, as Žižek puts it, not the possibility that 'big brother is watching, but the possibility that big brother is not watching.'" See Slavoj Žižek, *The Plague of Fantasies* (London: Verso, 1997) for discussion on the "big Other."

23 One of the participants in MTV's reality TV show, *The Real World*, interviewed in the *New York Times*, stated that it was "easy to get used to" being watched for four months by a network of television cameras and went on to say that "now, not having a mic and camera feels weird to me," see John Leland, "Designed to Pry: Building a Better Fishbowl," *New York Times*, June 21, 2001, 20.

It also demonstrates the type of access at issue here—the photographer (and, by extension, the viewer) is turned on by seeing something the girl does not necessarily want to reveal, something that goes past the performance of sex. The pleasure, then, comes from the "real" pleasure of the other. This begins to show a way in which the viewer desires a direct and involuntary somatic reaction on the part of the performer, which lines up rather neatly with the direct, and somewhat involuntary, somatic reaction provoked in him through identification.

Interpassivity

In attempting to assess the nature of these new mediations of subjectivity, we cannot help but return to that traditional guarantor of subjectivity itself—the concept of free choice. We often find this compensatory rhetoric and narrative of free choice, a cornerstone of American cultural ideology, inhabiting precisely those situations that, on a basic structural level admit of little or no choice at all. In the contemporary media landscape, we consistently encounter paeans to the promise and potential of media "interactivity," yet it remains often unclear how much substantive interaction is taking place, and whether we would even want it if it were.

Interactivity allows the user to break out of a relationship in which he stares passively at the screen and is acted on, as is supposed, in this particular rhetorical and theoretical constellation, to be the case in ordinary film and video spectatorship. An interface is considered interactive to the extent that it functions to return control to the user.[24] In "On Totalitarian Interactivity," Lev Manovich points toward an analysis of the illusory nature of choice in many interactive situations—after all, the viewer is only able to select from a limited number of producer-created options.[25] Paradoxically, this "choice" can have a proscriptive effect, even as the viewer is given a highly illusory sense of control.

Žižek goes beyond a critique of the lack of choice in many interactive situations by proposing the term *interpassivity* as a "shadowy supplement" to interactivity, postulating it as a necessary correlative to "interacting with the object, instead of just passively following the show."[26] In a relationship of interactivity with the object, the object performs a certain type of work for the viewer. Interpassivity is a similarly transferential relation to an other, but one in which the other not only does the work for the viewer but also enjoys or believes in the viewer's place. Žižek's typically heterogeneous examples include the canned laughter of sitcoms, the Tibetan prayer wheel, and the

---

24 Bolter and Grusin, *Remediation*, 33.
25 Lev Manovich, "On Totalitarian Interactivity," *Rhizome Digest*, October II, 1996.
26 Žižek, *The Plague of Fantasies*, n.2.

VCR. Critically, there are two aspects to this: in the first, the other takes over the dull, mechanical aspect of routine duties; and in the second, the other takes over the duty to enjoy, a demand placed on the subject by the superego. This transference constitutes a passive action, but it also constitutes a deferral of this very passivity. The term *interpassivity* pushes us toward a different understanding of the type of work that goes on in looking at Internet pornography, and it also articulates a different understanding of the ways in which technologies have already been incorporated.

In the "A Day in the Life . . ." segment with Chandler, presence is negotiated through a particular dynamic of transference. Throughout the segment, there is a sense of the woman, Chandler, performing actions *for* the viewer. Through Zizek, we might instead consider Chandler to be performing *in the place of* the viewer. This, then, is the relationship he refers to as interpassivity.

In the viewer's relation to on-line amateur pornography, three objects "work" for the subject: the camera, the computer, and the woman in the picture. This logic of transferred work is traced, imagistically, in a still image from Kara's Amateurs, in which we see a woman, Kitty, sitting on a toilet, masturbating, while another woman films her. Given the expectation that Internet porn incites masturbation, the initial identification seems to be a cross-gendered one of pleasure; the viewer takes pleasure in the woman's pleasure, in the way in which it incites his own. The pleasure of the spectator is also offered to the viewer through an identification with the woman using the camera to film, even as the viewer uses the computer to view. This is further complicated by an intrasite intertextuality; the video filmed within the photograph is also available to the viewer. It is another "A Day in the Life . . ." video, this one for Kitty. Given the process of emulation that emerges as one of the hallmarks of the computer/Internet experience, objects become radically conflated here; it is not that they represent each other, but rather that, through the logic of digitalization, they become each other. The camera is a type of digital video camera in which the image is not seen through a viewfinder, but is, rather, displayed for the viewer on a screen, in the process of filming. The computer is capable of emulating a video player, to display the "A Day in the Life . . ." video, and through this logic is capable of being a camera displayed as already a video player. Following this logic, Webcams cause the computer to function as a camera, not just as the display of the outlet of a camera. This creates a slip, or an elision between the two tasks or events. Instrumentality and use are key here, rather than any quality of the object. This fact positions objects as somewhat fluid, and the ensuing confusion about the specificity of tasks and labor becomes part of the logic of the computer, which has been reflexively incorporated into the body.

A number of potential identifications are set up for the viewer here, but the two primary ones are the enjoyment of Kitty masturbating and the enjoyment of the photographer, who is in control. Both of these figures are simultaneously subject and object, and simultaneously passive and active. And the viewer's relationship to both of them is one of transference; the spectator is able to displace his "work" of spectating onto them, as well as his passive enjoyment. In this scenario of interpassivity, we are pushed toward being conscious of pleasure as itself a type of work, a realization that seems particularly critical in the case of pornography, in which what we are seeing, and taking pleasure in, is bodies at the work of pleasure. This also allows us to conceive a radically different notion of the type of enjoyment available to the viewer in pornography, one particularly applicable to on-line pornography. In this scenario, both women are performing this work of viewing and enjoying for the subject, as are the computer and the camera. And, again, in amateur pornography, this enjoyment on the part of the woman is exactly what people articulate as the critical point of their interest. What this suggests is a situation in contemporary culture in which people displace their enjoyment onto others; that what they enjoy seeing in pornography is not necessarily the impulse toward masturbation, but precisely the experience of seeing, and having, someone else enjoying in their place.

Critically, though, in amateur porn, the enjoyment is not just sexual. These women do it all—they masturbate *and* water the plants *and* walk the dog *and* take college classes. Amateurs are not just experiencing sexual pleasure for the viewer; they are eating sushi, baking cookies, and buying pizza with and for him. This further extends the concept of interpassivity and its relationship to sexual pleasure because, in amateur porn, these secondary activities become primary—they mark the crucial difference of amateur porn. This suggests that the process of intimacy and identification is cemented by the somatic identification of one body experiencing sexual pleasure and sexual arousal with another body experiencing the same thing, only on a computer screen—but that the sexual activities are somehow less important than the other activities. It suggests the possibility that even the graphic sexuality within amateur porn exists mainly as an incitement for subjective identification with the performer, for this ever-fuller sense of participation with that performer's life, and that it is this ever-elusive relationship, in effect, that itself becomes the obscure object of desire. Yet this relationship is, as we have said, thoroughly mediated through a technology which itself holds a kind of affective charge. We will never understand Internet pornography as long as we consider the networked personal computer as a mere tool through which we access the sexually explicit graphics, for in so doing, we miss the ways in which our sexual desires are being mediated through the pleasures of the technology itself, and the particular fantasies it has on offer.

Going On-line . . .

Pornography is going on-line. And not just pornography—music, television, even mainstream films are increasingly downloaded over the Internet and viewed on personal computers. What was previously a marginal behavior is emerging as a mainstream practice. As it does, film and cultural studies needs to attend to the material specificity and the embedded cultural history of this particular interface. Yet any such account must consider the fact that the Internet, and the computer technologies that underscore it, are inherently unstable, constantly shifting and evolving. The instability of these objects is compounded by an instability of subjects, caught in the flux of technological change, capital exchange, and inscribed power relations. Any history or mapping of the Internet—or of Internet pornography—will thus be a snapshot of a particular place and a particular time. This exploration of amateur Internet pornography is thus necessarily a partial and contingent account.

Pornography is currently prevalent on the Internet not simply because it allows the quick and easy distribution and private consumption of erotic images, but because the affective charge of pornography is linked to, and redoubled by, the affective charge attached to new and perpetually renewed computer technology. Pornography changes once it is positioned on the computer; the attraction of cyberporn becomes in part the attraction to and fascination with what we perceive as the vastly new possibilities for subjectivity that technology seems to offer. There is a fascination with the continually shifting capabilities of the computer as a relatively new apparatus for displaying images, both still and moving. Not inconsequentially, there is always a link between pornography and advancing technologies of representation, and the specifically hybrid representational space of the networked computer interface is no exception. This essay has tried to introduce some of the complex fantasies of identification and interaction that are arising at this particular intersection of technology and pornography.

On-line amateur porn impels us to consider the newly hybrid space of the computer as it redraws the boundaries that operate within and around private, or domestic space. As the television has become larger, and living rooms have been transformed into home theaters, the computer has become smaller and more personal—it has become a private enclave within the domestic or corporate sphere. This becomes evident in operating systems such as Microsoft Windows and Apple's OS X, and internet portals such as AOL, which allow multiple users to each log in to their own space. In these systems, changes to the color scheme or the desktop pattern are meant to stand in for the "ownership" or delimitation of a private space on the computer. This private space *within* a public environment (even the privacy of the individual family member vis-á-vis the family) then opens out onto a larger space of the Internet, a space which is itself importantly both public and private. These interface technologies are transforming our received understanding about the very nature and division of what is private and what is public.

This transformation is key to understanding how and why Internet pornography has largely replaced magazine pornography, but it is also critical in understanding the way in which the computer functions as a space of encounter, or space of "liveness." This space of liveness is aligned with Webcams, but it is also linked to the function that digital camera images have come to serve in current culture. John Seely Brown was recently quoted in the *New York Times* stating that "We're beginning to take pictures not to keep them around, but to reach out and touch someone with them, to extend the moment, that sense of presence."[27] It is not only a matter of mapping our old conceptions of private space and the public sphere onto the Internet, but of the potential, even the necessity, of generating new kinds of spaces and encounters.

Bibliography

Baudrillard, Jean. *Simulacra and Simulation*. Ann Arbor: University of Michigan Press, 1994.

Bolter, David Jay, and Richard Grusin. *Remediation: Understanding New Media*. Cambridge, MA: MIT Press, 1999.

Bourdieu, Pierre. *The Logic of Practice*. Translated by Richard Nice. Palo Alto: Stanford University Press, 1992.

Butler, Judith. *Excitable Speech: A Politics of the Performative*. New York: Routledge, 1997.

Elmer-Dewitt, Philip. "On a Screen near You: Cyberporn." *Time*, July 3, 1995, 38–45.

Godwin, Mike. *Cyber Rights: Defending Free Speech in the Digital Era*. Cambridge, MA: MIT Press, 2003.

Lacan, Jacques. *The Four Fundamental Concepts of Psycho-Analysis*. Translated by Alan Sheridan. New York: Norton, 1981.

———. *The Seminar of Jacques Lacan, Book VII: The Ethics of Psychoanalysis*. Translated by Dennis Porter. New York: Norton, 1992.

Manovich, Lev. "New Media from Borges to HTML." In *New Media Reader*, edited by Noah Wardrip-Fruin and Nick Montfort, 13–25. Cambridge, MA: MIT Press, 2003.

———. "On Totalitarian Interactivity." *Rhizome Digest*, October 11, 1996.

Sobchack, Vivian. "The Scene of the Screen." In *Electronic Media and Technoculture*, edited by John Thornton Caldwell, 137–55. New Brunswick, NJ: Rutgers, 2000.

Žižek, Slavoj. *The Plague of Fantasies*. London: Verso, 1997.

---

27 Katie Hafner, "Turning the Page," *New York Times*, May 3, 2002.

Avatars and the Visual Culture of Reproduction on the Web

Lisa Nakamura[1]

In a 2005 episode of *Six Feet Under*, a highly regarded HBO television series, a pregnant Brenda and her husband Nate receive bad news regarding a prenatal test from their gynecologist.[2] She recommends they get an additional test, an amniocentesis, to rule out any problems, though, as she says, the first test they took and failed is "very unreliable." We later witness Brenda at home at the kitchen table using the Internet to look at a Web site called MaternityToday.com and are given a full-screen shot of the site's bulletin board page with the heading "Topic: Bad Test Results."[3] The screen shot

---

1   Editors' note: this paper was previously published as a chapter in *Digitizing Race: Visual Cultures of the Internet*, 131–170. Minneapolis: University of Minnesota Press, 2008.
2   "The Silence," *Six Feet Under*, HBO, aired July 18, 2005.
3   There is an actual Web site called MaternityToday.com (accessed July 2005), but it looks nothing like the site featured on *Six Feet Under*, whose producers created a fictitious home page just for this scene. In an ironic twist, the real MaternityToday.com focuses on publicizing "maternity homes" for young girls and women who wish to bear children but are unable to keep them. The site also features ads by NARAL, exhorting women to "protect choice: don't let Bush replace O'Connor with an anti-choice Justice," as well as advertisements for $1 "pro-life wristbands" and offer of a $250 grocery card in exchange for taking a "women's right's survey" [sic] administered by Consumerrewards.com. (Editors' note: as of this publication, MaternityToday.com redirects to the Crisis Pregnancy Web site.) The creation of fictional Web sites for use in feature films is becoming increasingly common, as I discuss in the introduction to this book, both as a means of circumventing copyright problems and as a way to legitimate the "realness" of the narrative. The Internet has become an increasingly ubiquitous aspect of everyday life, partly due to wireless home networking and laptop computers,

consists of post headings from several users, demonstrating that perusing Internet bulletin boards has become part of the process of doing research on the risks of amniocentesis and the accuracy of prenatal testing. While the laptop displays the site to the viewer, Brenda decides to present her husband with her decision not to have the amniocentesis because she is afraid of the risk of the procedure endangering the fetus; clearly her decision depicted as having something to do with what she has just read on the bulletin board. Brenda had suffered a miscarriage earlier in the season, in fact on the day of her wedding. The decision produces a great deal of conflict between Brenda and her husband, and we later witness her sadly gazing at two ultrasound images stuck on the refrigerator door with magnets as she picks up the telephone to ask her mother to lunch. In this series of vignettes that deal with digital technology, female anxiety, reproductive medicine, and networked, many-to-many versus traditional one-to-one forms of medicalized knowledge, we can see that the Internet has become a place where pregnant women go to gather information, fellowship, and alternative discourses regarding important decisions about their pregnancies. The increasing medicalization of pregnancy and its social networking on the Internet is just one aspect of the technologizing of the body that continues to work as a distinctive feature of networked postindustrial societies. And as Eugenia Georges and Lisa M. Mitchell found in their 2000 study of Canadian and Greek pregnancy guidebooks, "Baby Talk: The Rhetorical Production of Maternal and Fetal Selves," only "a decade ago, Barbara Katz Rothman observed that many North American women 'take pregnancy as a reading assignment.'"[4] They assert that this "widespread 'educating' of women, ostensibly to inform and empower them," is accomplished by texts that "discipline women to become particular kinds of patients and mothers."[5] Many North American women take pregnancy as an Internet research assignment, using the medium to find health information, both official and anecdotal; to share stories, fears, and anxieties with other pregnant women whom they may or may not know; and to view and exchange visual images of their own pregnant bodies as well as those of others. And just as the rhetoric of pregnancy guidebooks greatly influences the formation of discourses and disciplines of motherhood in different national contexts, so too have the form and visual culture of the Internet created both normative and resistant discourses of motherhood in the context of the

---

both technologies that Brenda is shown using in this scene, and devoting screen time to the Web sites that people use within the diegesis helps to guarantee its sense of realness.

4   Eugenia Georges and Lisa M. Mitchell, "Baby Talk: The Rhetorical Production of Maternal and Fetal Selves," in *Body Talk: Rhetoric, Technology, Reproduction*, ed. Mary M. Lay et al. (Madison: University of Wisconsin Press, 2000), 184.

5   Ibid.

United States. This is quite an under-researched area of study; as Georges and Mitchell observe, the content and form of these ubiquitous pregnancy guidebooks seem to have escaped critical feminist analysis, and the same can be said for the use of the Internet as an informational and educational tool in the culture of pregnancy.[6]

In *Six Feet Under*, Brenda's feelings of anxiety, fear, and anticipation engendered by the intense medical surveillance of her pregnancy (a level of scrutiny that is becoming increasingly available to middle- and upper-class women in the United States) are both assuaged and spurred on by a parallel development in this technology, that is, the production of ultrasound images that represent a "baby." While the test's "bad" results are invisible to Brenda because they are dematerialized and abstract, coming to her secondhand from her doctor, her "baby's" picture as represented by an ultrasound is depicted as a direct visual argument against terminating the pregnancy should it turn out to be "bad." Internet bulletin board posts created by female Internet users can work to decenter medical authority, yet at the same time the digital imaging technologies that create ultrasounds work to create an insistent visual argument for the "personhood" of a fetus.[7] As Peggy Phelan

---

6 See Amy Koerber, "Postmodernism, Resistance, and Cyberspace: Making Rhetorical Spaces for Feminist Mothers on the Web," *Women's Studies in Communication* 24, no. 2 (2001): 218–40, for an exceptional empirical analysis of feminist mothering websites that are part of the "Feminist Mothers and AlternaMomsUnite! Webrings." Koerber notes: "A recurring theme in all the sites I examined is the idea that parents know better than experts how to raise their children. Notably absent from all these Web sites in the kind of impossible-to-live-up-to advice that feminist scholars have critiqued in mainstream parenting advice literature" (229). She concludes that cyberspace does indeed offer a way for mothers to combat prevailing cultural norms about "parenting" but limits her analysis to textual postings made by women and does not discuss the visual culture of these sites.

7 See Lisa Cartright, "Film and the Digital in Visual Studies: Film Studies in the Era of Convergence," in *The Visual Culture Reader*, ed. Nicholas Mirzoeff (New York: Routledge, 2002) for an insightful analysis of the way that endoscopy, like ultrasound, goes "beyond the visual to include other sensory registers" (429). Virtual endoscopy, a tool that enables doctors in training to practice surgical procedures on virtual models of human organs, engenders a "new sort of gaze, a relationship with the visual representation that propels the viewing subject into the realm of full sensory experience, and full bodily perception, but with his sense disintegrated and misrouted" (431). Ultrasound as well provides a compromised and partial experience of the body, the main difference being that almost all fetal ultrasounds that are viewed depict either the viewer's or a close friend's own fetus rather than a generic or anonymous model, thus creating different stakes in the act of viewing.

notes, the image of the fetal ultrasound has been deployed in the context of television commercials to produce "both protectionist sentiment and the potential feeling of guilt in those who 'bond' with it."[8] This is because of the immediacy of this particular type of fetal image, one that produces both "bonding" to the notional infant still invisible to the mother by nontechnologically assisted means, and "bondage" to social norms regarding how a mother ought to act, view, and conceptualize her position and identity.

The increasingly visual culture of user-posted photographs and other self-produced digital images is part of a rhetorical mode of cultural production online that also works to decenter medical authority or at least to displace it somewhat in the examples from the Internet that I discuss here. Pregnant and trying-to-conceive women use Web sites as forums to receive as well as disseminate a wide range of images of pregnant bodies and fetuses. They circulate images that as often as not challenge prevailing medical authority about what kinds of decisions women ought to make, and what their duties are to themselves and their children. They, along with the non-credentialed and often intimate personal narratives of women who have experienced all types of pregnancies, work to counterbalance the discourses of centralized medical knowledge. The Internet provides a space in which women use pregnancy Web sites' modes of visuality and digital graphic production to become subjects, rather than objects, of interactivity.

As I discussed earlier, visual culture studies was created partly as a protest against an art historical tradition that was unwilling and unprepared to engage with the changes wrought on representational and artistic practices by digital technology. David Norman Rodowick provides an example of these changes in his statement:

> *Compared to the analogical arts—which are always instantiated in a fixed, Euclidean space—the digital arts seem abstract, ephemeral, and without substance. Digital representation is defined as "virtual" owing to its desubstantialization: the disappearance of a visible and tactile support for both image and text.*[9]

In this chapter, I discuss an example of the networked bodily visual image that challenges the notion of a de-substantialized digital body unsupported by the visible and the tactile, and that is the pregnancy bulletin board avatar. Avatars posted by pregnant women constitute a particularly salient example of the "substantial" and "tactile" body because they are warranted

---

8   Peggy Phelan, *Unmarked: The Politics of Performance* (New York: Routledge, 1993), 133.

9   David Norman Rodowick, *Reading the Figural; or, Philosophy after the New Media: Post-Contemporary Interventions* (Durham, NC: Duke University Press, 2001), 212.

by an offline physical state that it is unimaginable to fake, and because they are surrounded by a matrix of visual and textual discourse that attests to the irremediably embodied nature of pregnancy and childbirth. While Internet users are fond of taking on different sorts of identities in the context of computer-mediated communication, often engaging in cross-racial, cross-gender, cross-generational, or cross-sexualized forms of identity play, identity tourism as a pregnant versus non-pregnant woman is rare.[10] In addition, the stakes regarding digital pregnant body avatars are especially high on account of the contentious and bitter political and cultural discourse surrounding the status of the maternal body in our culture, and in particular the incursions that visual and other technologies have made on this concept of the materiality of bodies.

While debates between the religious Right and advocates for women's reproductive rights continue to rage, calling into question a woman's ability to "own" her own body, the Internet provides a place where pregnant and TTC (trying to conceive) women can create and own their own digital bodies. Pregnant avatars are databodies that women deploy as part of a visual counterdiscourse to the images of databodies on the Internet that come out of much nineties cyberpunk fiction and that still persist: images of male cyberhackers constitute the illusory and normative "unmarked body" to which Phelan refers. Cyberpunk fiction has figured the computer-using body as itself desubstantialized and dematerialized, just as all digital images are envisioned by many respondents to the *October* visual culture questionnaire. However, as Tom Foster cogently notes, the trope of the dematerialized or posthuman body is not necessarily progressive just because it is de-essentialized and acknowledged as socially constructed. Rather, the *nature* of that construction bears watching when digital bodies are brought into play. The condition of posthumanism, a seemingly neutral term that excludes categories such as gender and race, is never free of "racial subtexts that inform the various transformations summed up under the heading of the 'posthuman.'" As Foster writes:

> *The debates about posthumanism demonstrate that there is no fixed meaning either to the understanding of embodiment as plastic and malleable—that is, open to critical intervention—because socially constructed. In the context of postmodern technocultures and their disembodying tendencies, the materiality of embodiment, consciousness, and human nature can constitute a form of resistance, while at the same time the*

---

10   Lisa Nakamura, *Cybertypes: Race, Identity, and Ethnicity on the Internet*, (New York: Routledge, 2002); see chapter 2 for an extended discussion of cross-racial passing in Lambda MOO and the dynamic of identity tourism.

denaturalization of embodied identities, intended as a historicizing gesture, can change little or nothing.[11]

Female avatars that are modified to "set" their state of pregnancy and race permit visualization of two states that insist on the materiality of female bodies in the context of community and resistance to medicalized modes of image regulation.

"I would like to ask if someone could make a new dollie for me as I am not pregnant anymore—my son John was born on April 1st. ☺ And if it helps—I love Care Bears™ Thanks a bunch! ☺" This post from a popular Web site for pregnant and trying-to-conceive women, BabyDream.com, appeals to its members (which also serves women who have just had babies) to collaborate in the creation of visual online signifiers of identity—avatars.[12] The overwhelming majority of the site's users add digital signatures to each of their posts; these signatures usually contain images of the woman who is posting. A "post" consists of a box containing typed text from the user, which can include a quotation from a previous poster to whom the user is responding. Appended to the bottom is the poster's signature, which usually includes a graphical avatar that visually represents the user. Once the user creates her signature, it is automatically appended to each post that she creates on that board. Thus each post comprises a text element and a graphical element. These signatures, or "siggies," as they are called on pregnancy Web sites, were an enduring feature of early e-mail visual cultures before the graphical Web; many featured ASCII art images, fashioned from letters and diacritical elements available on the computer keyboard. These early signatures were part of the early Internet's do-it-yourself (DIY) culture: the labor of painstakingly tapping out rudimentary pictures using the space bar and alphanumeric characters gave a hard-won graphical quality to text-only email.[13] ASCII art images of "Kilroy," cartoon lions, and roses allowed users to give a personal touch to their signatures and to endow them with self-authored

---

11   Tom Foster, *The Souls of Cyberfolk: Posthumanism as Vernacular Theory* (Minneapolis: University of Minnesota Press, 2005), 6.

12   The name of this website has been changed to protect the privacy of its members.

13   Brenda Danet writes that "no full-fledged, systematic history of [ASCII art] exists in print" partly because of its ephemeral nature. Her chapter titled "ASCII Art and Its Antecedents" traces the history of "text-based art—pictures or visual images created with letters, numbers, and other typographic symbols on the computer keyboard" as a category of computer play. In chapter 2, she discusses the use of signature files as spaces for play, particularly among people whose professional identities are not at stake when writing or receiving e-mail. See Brenda Danet, *Cyberpl@y: Communicating Online*, New Technologies/New Cultures Series (Oxford: Berg, 2001), 195.

style. This endowed social status on the sender, who was shown to be skillful and invested enough in digital visual culture to have created something like this from scratch. This ethic of originality was a key aspect of early computing culture.

```
           /'^'\                                    /'^'\
          ( o o )                                  ( o o )
    -oOOO--(_)--OOOo-----------------------oOOO--(_)--OOOo----
                    Paul J McGlynn
                Fourth year Computer Science
         .oooO           University of Strathclyde    oooO
        (   )       Oooo.  pmcglynn@cs.strath.ac.uk  (   )   Oooo
    ---\ (----(    )---------------------------------\ (----(    )-----
        \_)    ) /                                    \_)    ) /
              (_/                                           (_/
```

Fig. 1. An ASCII art signature.

Signatures in graphical bulletin boards function as a kind of public text, since no password or authentication is needed to read them, even if you don't have an account on BabyDream.com. While a family or individual photograph is often scanned and uploaded to enhance a signature, members conceive themselves much more as authors or cultural producers in relation to their digital avatars, or "dollies" as they are called in this community (a separate bulletin board on the site deals solely with the practicalities of, and techniques for, avatar creation, modification, and sharing; it is extremely active). These are created using software that offers cartoonlike body parts that can be arranged to make different types of bodies. As can be seen in the post quoted earlier, women often envision these avatars in some of the ways that they do their own bodies. They will supply their height, weight, coloring, and preference in clothing colors and styles to the site's "Siggy Girls"—women who volunteer to use their skills with computer graphics to create avatars for their less technically inclined sisters, in hopes of acquiring an avatar that looks like them. They request, create, trade, and alter pregnant avatars when they themselves become pregnant, and, as in the quoted post, which states, "I am not pregnant anymore," they acquire new ones or alter their old ones to reflect non-pregnancy. In addition, their liberal use of visual signifiers such as smiley emoticons, figures from licensed media franchises like Care Bears, and preferences for purple and "sparklies," or animated GIFs that move and dance around an avatar, reveal an intense interest in digital aesthetics.

Women are relatively late adopters of the Internet. And many new female users of the Web are drawn to it to obtain information on pregnancy and babies on sites like BabyDream.com and others devoted to serving pregnant women and new mothers.[14] In this chapter I discuss the critical interventions that women make in pregnancy Web sites by composing and deploying digital images of pregnant female bodies, babies, fetuses, pets, and families. User-created pregnant avatars pose a direct challenge to the female "hyperreal, exaggerated, hyperbodies" evident in mainstream video games such as *Tomb Raider* and *Dead or Alive*. The "unique aesthetic for perfection" embodied in digital heroines such as Lara Croft and Kasumi presents "embodiments that have left the real female body behind in a significant way."[15] I agree with Mary Flanagan's assertion that "it is at the female body that the formation and contestation of digibodies is occurring."[16] However, the pregnant avatars that pregnant women create for parenting Web sites accomplish the opposite from those deployed in digital gaming culture; they bring the "real female body" into the digital in a central way rather than leaving them behind. Instead, these avatars turn out to be far less hyperreal and exaggerated than their owners' *real* pregnant bodies; most women seem to want avatars that are built exactly like their unpregnant bodies, only "with a belly," an offline impossibility, as anyone who has experienced pregnancy knows. However, this fantasy of modularity—a digitally pregnant body is simply a "regular" stock-model female body with another "feature," a pasted-on belly—addresses the anxiety of permanent transformation versus transient state that preoccupies many pregnant women. (Complaints and fears about losing "baby weight" and "getting your body back" give voice to this particular obsession of the gestating body.)

In addition, an analysis of pregnancy Web site signatures enables a class-based critique of a newly forming taste culture: the visual culture of pregnancy and the body on the popular Internet. While scholarly discussions of visual culture and taste have long acknowledged the roles of class and to a lesser extent gender and race, little attention has been paid to the ways that pregnancy creates visual cultural artifacts. The sociologist Herbert Gans notes that childbearing and child rearing do have an impact on new parents' media consumption by exposing them to children's programming—the babysitter of the lower classes—but he considers this mainly in terms of the ways that it forces parents to give up their previous television programs. He envisions media choices and preferences as primarily an effect of class and other factors but does not take pregnancy and parenthood itself into account:

---

14 See http://ivillage.com, http://pregnancy.org, and http://parentsplace.com for examples.

15 Mary Flanagan, "Mobile Identities, Digital Stars, and Post Cinematic Selves," *Wide Angle* 21, no. 1 (1999): 77–93.

16 Mary Flanagan, "The Bride Stripped Bare to Her Data: Information Flow + Digibodies," in *Data Made Flesh: Embodying Information*, ed. Robert Mitchell and Phillip Thurtle (New York: Routledge, 2004), 154.

> Many factors determine a person's choice among taste cultures, particularly class, age, religion, ethnic and racial background, regional origin, and place of residence, as well as personality factors which translate themselves into wants for specific types of cultural content. Because ethnic, religious, regional, and place differences are disappearing rapidly in American society, however, the major sources of subcultural variety are increasingly those of age and class.

Thus, for Gans, "the major source of differentiation between taste cultures and public is socioeconomic level or class."[17] However, pregnancy is an identity state that truly crosses classes and possesses what might be called a temporary taste culture in the sense that once its members bear and raise their children, they are no longer part of it.

This is not to say, however, that the visual culture of pregnancy is not inflected by a user's class position in terms of style and conceptions of taste. In recent years there has been a popular movement to "rescue" the visual culture of pregnancy from its association with lower-class taste cultures. In "The Modernist Nursery," an article that appeared in the *New York Times Magazine* in 2004, Elizabeth Weil writes that:

> Melissa Pfeiffer, 33, is the founder of Modernseed, a year-old store selling modern furniture, fashions and accessories for kids, and Eric Pfeiffer, 35, is a contemporary furniture designer, and theirs is the kind of home that inspires house envy, particularly if you're one of those parents who vowed not to let the house fill up with plastic junk and then saw exactly that situation come to pass, first with the musical vibrating bouncy seat, and then the doorjamb Bumper Jumper and then a gift of a multicolored plastic Fisher-Price train set that became your daughter's absolute favorite possession.

The characterization of inexpensive and widely available children's accessories and toys as "plastic junk" hails the reader of the article, who is most likely not a member of a lower- or working-class home, to identify with a different and implicitly higher taste culture of pregnancy than is commonly available. The article celebrates the entrepreneurial initiative of well-heeled and tasteful new parents who are working to bring modernism to the nursery. Their DIY spirit is seen as the appropriate and laudable reaction to the retail industry's failure to supply the correct range of taste cultures appropriate to upper-class buyers' preferences, envisioned in this article as "needs." When asked to explain why he designed a new baby crib the way he did, Michael Ryan says that he lives in a small New York City apartment and "came to this floating idea with the legs set in—on every other crib they're on

---

17 Herbert J. Gans, *Popular Culture and High Culture: An Analysis and Evaluation of Taste* (New York: Basic Books, 1999), 95.

the corners. Simple, elegant, low-profile, no embellishments. There's so much fluffiness out there, mixing textures, frilling. Tone it down, man."[18] This disdain for decoration, adornment, bulkiness, and profusion is contrasted with the "clean," elegant, minimal, modernist style currently enjoying a revival in fashionable nurseries. Similarly, in an article titled "Sophisticated Baby" that appeared in the same magazine, Corky Harvey, a cofounder of the Pump Station in Los Angeles, "which includes a boutique for new or soon-to-be-parents," says that its "clientele is well off and smart and wants things that are 'functional as well as beautiful.'" The store carries the Fleurville "Mothership" diaper bag that costs $155 and was designed by a couple who "like many entrepreneurs . . . started out as dissatisfied customers." And does the store carry diaper bags with, say, famous cartoon characters on them? Harvey replies, emphatically, that it does not. The store sells only products that "'elevate motherhood' out of the context of tacky commercialism, she explains. 'Our mothers despise that stuff.'"[19]

This identification of mainstream consumer culture's offerings as unacceptable for "smart" people, people who wish to rise above "tacky commercialism," is itself implicitly anti-feminine. As Penny Sparke writes in *As Long As It's Pink* of the modernist period, "the notion of 'taste' continued to align itself with domesticity and femininity. As such, it became increasingly marginal to modernism, representing to the protagonists of that movement all that needed to be eliminated."[20] Taste, gendered as feminine, came into conflict with design, gendered as masculine, with high culture and the authority of all its institutions on its side. The emphasis on functionality, "cleanness" and simplicity has long been employed as a way to critique and gender women's aesthetic decisions as "frilly femininity": Sparke's analysis discusses the ways that postwar advertisements for furnishings tried to teach women "good taste" as part of an attempt to create a sense of middle-class consumer identity. The identification of women as shoppers rather than creators is a distinctive feature of modernity and its advertising culture, as Rachel Bowlby has noted in her study of the French novel.[21] However, the material culture of dolls and facsimiles of children, a culture that echoes the impulse behind digital pregnant avatar creation, reveals a growing DIY culture that participates in the discourse of modification that springs from the culture of

---

18 Elizabeth Weil, "The Modernist Nursery," *New York Times Magazine*, November 26, 2004, 75.

19 Rob Walker, "Sophisticated Baby," *New York Times Magazine*, July 24, 2005, 20.

20 Penny Sparke, *As Long as It's Pink: The Sexual Politics of Taste* (San Francisco: Pandora, 1995), 74.

21 See Rachel Bowlby, *Carried Away: The Invention of Modern Shopping* (New York: Columbia University Press, 2001); and *Just Looking: Consumer Culture in Dreiser, Gissing, and Zola* (New York: Methuen, 1985).

computer hacking and software modification. Two examples of grassroots creativity in the realm of body modification, babies, and retail hacking, that of "reborn dolls" and American Girl dolls, demonstrate the ways that the culture of composable baby bodies blurs the line between creation and consumption. "Reborn dolls" are extremely realistic baby dolls that hobbyists modify using a stock "base" bought from a retail store. These dolls, which are almost exclusively marketed and bought on eBay, are made by people who have developed techniques for *reborning*, engaging in "a curious process of altering and enhancing a baby doll to look and even to feel as much like a human baby as possible."[22] Reborn dolls are frequently composited from heads, bodies, and other parts from multiple other types of dolls; the provenance of these body parts is painstakingly documented in the elaborate "birth stories" that accompany many of them. A *New York Times Magazine* article by Rob Walker describing this practice is titled "Hyperreality Hobbying: Like other do-it-yourself crafts, these dolls are a creative outlet—if a slightly strange one." The dolls sell for impressively large sums—up to $1,500 in some cases—come with birth announcements, and can incite fierce bidding wars on eBay. Walker, who writes a column on consumer and retail trends titled "Consumed" in which this article appeared, notes that "once you get past the creepier aspects of all this, it's not too hard to see it as yet another medium of grass-roots creativity, like making scrapbooks." The notion of duplicating the reproductive process through modification of existing material commodities is envisioned as "hyperreal" in the sense that it remediates an original to a degree described as "creepy" or uncanny; dolls are already uncanny, as Freud noted in his analysis of the Hoffmann story "The Sandman," and reborning intensifies this sense of boundary blurring between original and copy. It is also classed as an example of a material culture practice identified specifically with female domesticity and the active—at times too active, it seems—management of family memory, history, and representation. The notion of hacking or "modding" dolls allows women to participate in a type of productive hobbying often associated with masculinity and intrepid DIY culture.

This practice can be contrasted to the marketing of composable bodies on offer through retail outlets like American Girl, a doll manufacturer based in the American Midwest with an extremely enthusiastic cult following. While reborn dolls are "stock" bodies that are modified by users, given mock identities, and then resold, American Girl dolls can come both as stock characters and as customizable creations that can be ordered to suit from the factory. The company specializes in producing "dolls with stories," meaning dolls that have ethnic clothing, backstories (many come with books that narrate

---

22 Rob Walker, "Hyperreality Hobbying," *New York Times Magazine*, February 20, 2005, 22.

their lives in various historical time periods, in the interest of enhancing their educational value), and identities based on the notion of diversity and collectability. Though there has been no scholarly writing yet on the practice of reborning, Terri Kapsalis's article "Making Babies the American Girl Way" notes the connection between the commodification of reproductive technologies and the creation of material baby-bodies: "Traditionally, fussing over dolls is practice for future motherhood." She notes that ART, or advanced reproductive technologies, present donor sperm and American Girl dolls as customizable objects that can be made to suit. While American Girl dolls are notable for their range of identities, a quality that has been lauded by their fans ("finally, a doll company was being responsive to ethnic differences by offering Asian, Latina, and other dolls of color"), the totemization of nationality and ethnicity evident in the "character doll" modes of dress and props like pets, parasols, and so on creates a vision of ethnicity that is essentialized and unproblematic.[23] "Addy" (a black girl in the Civil War era, 1864), "Felicity" (an English girl in the Colonies, 1774), Josefina (a Latina girl in New Mexico, 1824), Kaya (a Nez Perce girl in 1764), and Samantha and Nellie (two white American girls of different social classes in 1904) wear the costumes of their individual historical periods and have their own media empires including books and accessories, as well as diegetic relationships to each other. For example, Nellie O'Malley, an Irish American girl, is hired to be a servant to Samantha, her upper-class mistress (though any danger of class, racial, or ethnic conflict is prevented by the explanation that Nellie and Samantha "quickly become best friends, even though they have lived very different lives").

While the dolls are imbued with detailed identities right out of the box, so to speak, endowed with manufactured "memories" as are the almost-human replicants in *Blade Runner*, another popular series of American Girls is marketed on the basis of its composable identity and volitional ethnicity. The American Girl Today series invites the user to select the doll ". . . with the hair, eye, and skin color you like best. Each doll is 18 inches tall and has a soft, huggable body with arms and legs you can pose. Her beautiful eyes open and close, and her hair is long so you can style it into all the looks you love! Your doll comes in her pretty new Go Anywhere Outfit." There are twenty-one possible combinations, and though some of these dolls are phenotypically different from each other, no reference to race is made in any of the discourse evident on the company's Web site or paper catalogs. Though straight hair is simply described by color, such as "honey blond," and by the word "curly" if the hair is "light," the dark curly hair evident on the "dark" doll is dubbed

---

23 Terri Kapsalis, "Making Babies the American Girl Way," in *Domain Errors! Cyberfeminist Practices*, ed. Maria Fernandez, Faith Wilding, and Michelle M. Wright, (New York: Autonomedia, 2002), 224.

"textured." Kapsalis notes the language of modularity evident in the company's discourse that stresses the interactivity of the act of purchasing one of these dolls, an act that is overtly figured as creative and reproductive in the sense that the buyer is steered toward an act of visual self-replication: "The catalog encourages girls to pick dolls that look like them, selecting skin, hair, and eye color as close as possible to their own." So while the character dolls are made to represent specific types of ethnic and national "others," American Girl Today dolls create a representational landscape that replicates the discourse of reproductive technology, one that promises to help mothers create babies that look like them. While both "reborn" dolls and American Girl dolls are part of the material culture that is derided by the tasteful parents described in articles about designer nurseries and diaper bags, classified no doubt as examples of the "plastic junk" that the Pfeiffers and Michael Ryan dismiss as "not smart," and definitely not something that "our mothers" would consider chic, what is notable about this discourse is the way that it figures reborners and American Girl doll enthusiasts as "hobbyists" and "collectors." These are both terms associated with creativity, but in a way that is distinctly gendered, and in a way that still stresses consumption and selection rather than creation and design. Michael Ryan and the Pfeiffers are described as designers and entrepreneurs, partly because of their financial success (as mentioned earlier, reborn and American Girl dolls generate a great deal of revenue in both primary and secondary markets), but mainly because of the way that their work is credited as "original" creation, because of their class position, and because of the visual styles that they prefer. While Ryan and the Pfeiffers are quite clear about not having invented modernism, but rather having applied it to an area of the home where it had not been seen before so as to make a whole house internally consistent in terms of its style, Ryan also notes that his crib design was a "hack" or modification of an existing crib, which he found inelegant and bulky. The user-driven innovation that comes from modifying existing doll bodies is envisioned as either "creepy" and socially marginal or trivial partly because it deals with babybodies themselves, rather than furniture or more general types of design objects. However, these types of modifications or hacks give voice and vision to the culture of "frilly femininity" overtly critiqued by nursery modernists. The gendering of pregnancy and baby material culture turns on the axis of two types of taste cultures that can be classified as female and male, lower and upper, modifier/consumer and creator/designer. Recent articles in the popular press regarding "sophisticated babies" and "the modernist nursery" note that "good design" has dared to invade the one domestic space that had been exempted from this injunction to adhere to standards defined by taste cultures: the nursery. While "decoration" has long been dismissed as feminine, "design" is perceived as more substantial, more the province of experts, and more connected to architecture, a "masculine" field that has immense social prestige.

The notion of a taste culture as something that can be created, rather than merely consumed, by its own users, who are consequently freed from the necessity of engaging with "tacky commercialism," has long been a part of the discourse of the Internet and its potential for interactivity. The Internet's stance toward commercialism has for the most part been a critical and oppositional one, with its more utopian critics envisioning the Internet as a form that allows "the people" to create commonly owned and collaboratively created software as in the case of the open-source and creative commons movements, and fan-authored media and taste cultures. There has, however, been little writing on taste, class, and gender when it comes to Internet visual culture. The injunction of the crib designer Michael Ryan to "tone it down, man," maps quite well onto the design imperatives and values of new media professionals, who favor sites that are "simple, elegant, low profile, [with] no embellishments," while "fluffiness out there, mixing textures, frilling," is despised in both baby carriages and digital design.[24]

Women's digital signatures on pregnancy sites function figuratively as the "nursery" in the habitus of cyberspace, indulging in a type of frilly femininity on the level of taste and design that is deeply threatening and subversive to the principles of "cleanness" and masculinity that dominated digital culture in its early years. Rather than "toning it down," their digital signatures tend to do exactly the opposite, mixing media and textures and ornamentation in a fashion that defies these notions of good taste and embodies "tackiness" as exemplified by the lower-class taste cultures reviled by the modernists cited earlier. In addition, the form of these sites challenges the bourgeois-individualist model of property and presence that characterized early cyberspace's rhetoric. This rhetoric of ownership and triumphant individualism inherent in much of the electronic frontier discourse has since been critiqued from both feminist and postcolonial perspectives. The notion that representational and cultural power could arise only from the staking out of individual spaces or "homesteads" on the Internet privileged singly owned, managed, and designed Web sites or "home pages" as "domains" or sites of identity. Susan Leigh Star critiques this notion of the home-page-as-home because it requires an amount of cultural and real capital unattainable to many; ironically, as she notes, academic nomads such as herself may be among the few who can afford to be figuratively situated or "homed" in cyberspace through the ownership and control of a personal site. She also notes that technology, the Web included, has often resulted in "more work for mother" rather than less and has also created more rather than less isolation for women,

---

24 See http://www.websitesthatsuck.com for some of the principles of "good" website design.

who are often stuck at home in caregiving roles.[25] However, the figuration of the individual home page, a space that Nina Wakeford notes can reduplicate the endless housekeeping and drudgery of domestic upkeep just as does the offline home, has since lost much of its cachet as a source of digital visual capital on the popular graphical Internet. Despite early predictions such as Star's and Wakeford's, which were published in 1996 on the eve of the World Wide Web's massification, the individual home page has not turned out to be the main or even dominant route to independent expression in terms of the Internet's visual culture. Web sites like BabyDream.com maintain or "host" discussion boards that permit users to create individual posts or spaces of visual digital identity within the confines of a shared virtual space. This model of shared rather than personal space, characteristic of blogging and online journaling spaces such as LiveJournal, which have also often been identified with female users, allows a model of digital participation and cross-linkage that requires less technical skill than is necessary to create a single stand-alone Web site, thus creating *less* work for mother and easier navigation between different users' virtual spaces of expression. While an individual Web site may constitute a burden, a virtual "room of one's own" in the form of a digital signature, even an elaborate one, is manageable. This trend away from digital privatization exemplified by the ownership and maintenance of personal Web sites and toward atomization shows the formation of a more communitarian, urban notion of graphical online space, where users create individual rooms or spaces within their signatures that are nonetheless viewed as part of a visual whole or shared visual culture. Space on BabyDream.com's pages is shared, not owned, and a user's post is displayed exactly as many times as she chooses to contribute to the discussion, thus emulating in visual form the dynamics of a face-to-face conversation.

While American Girl Today dolls permit sanitized, depoliticized racialization, by allowing the creation of "dark" dolls with "textured" hair but avoiding any overt mention of race, racial politics, or racial inequality, the female avatars or "dollz" that pregnant women create and use in their digital signatures warrant race in an intensely embodied way by bringing it into visual collision with the discourse of the reproductive body. BabyDream.com's users produce digital group portraits of themselves in varying states of pregnancy, motherhood, or hoping for pregnancy, portraits of women who unite in solidarity and support around medical and personal issues but may never have met in person. Consider the group signature of the "Beaner Dreamers" ("bean" is a popular slang term often used to describe a fetus, as very-early-term fetuses often show up as a beanlike shape in an ultrasound

---

25 Susan Leigh Star, "From Hestia to Home Page: Feminism and the Concept of Home in Cyberspace," in *The Cybercultures Reader*, ed. David Bell and Barbara M. Kennedy, (New York: Routledge, 2000), 638.

image), twelve women who became close friends using the bulletin board and wished to be represented as a group online. Their signature, which appeared in several of the members' larger signature spaces, functions like a custom T-shirt or bumper sticker in the sense that it signifies membership in a group of people with a shared purpose. In addition, each figure is composed to look phenotypically the same in terms of facial features, yet distinct from each other in terms of skin color, hair color, and body shape. While all these avatars are made using the same doll base, and thus are the same height and generally the same width and share the same visual style, much effort has been put into endowing them with pregnant or unpregnant bellies, elaborate and distinct hair styles and colors, differently embellished jeans, bouquets of flowers; and three possess the ultimate accessory: babies carried in front packs or in arms. Indeed, the language of embellishment is very much the paradigm invoked in this avatar group portrait. Like the popular BeDazzler, a device that enables users to attach crystals, beads, and other trimmings to jeans or pocketbooks, these avatars embody an aesthetic of decoration that has to do with adornment of an existing "base." And in a sense, race is one of these aspects of adornment.

Fig. 2. Beaner Dreamers avatar group portrait. Source: BabyDream.com.

While three of the Beaner Dreamer avatars have dark skin and hair and could be read as Latina, and one is quite dark-skinned and could be read as African American, these are idealized portraits that have more in common with animated characters from television or comic books than with any type of indexical visual representation. While it is possible and in fact must be the case that these users are deploying images that do not resemble their real bodies, the insistence on visual racial difference in this photograph has a different valence from the deployment of racial bodily imagery used in digital games or in chat rooms. Because pregnancy is so much an embodied state, and because these women have come together around the desire to conceive and bear children, the imperative to idealize the maternal and pregnant body works to create a uniformly and conventionally "pretty" avatar that nonetheless retains racial difference. This is in line with the site's emphasis on the production of biological children despite physical and emotional obstacles. The production of avatars and digital babies that "look like" the user reduplicates the modification-oriented reproductive desire evident in offline material-culture practices like reborning and doll collecting and is similarly viewed as a low-status and feminine activity. The communitarian impulse behind the Beaner Dreamers' group portrait characterizes the spirit of collectivity, collaboration, and responsibility for shared visual space in terms of avatar design and production evident in the site as a whole and in women's online culture devoted to family and domestic matters.

The culture of BabyDream.com overtly lauds the creators of digital signatures as important contributors to the space's overall value: "beautification" or decoration of the bulletin board by posters who go to the trouble to create elaborate and informative signatures is acknowledged and complimented, regardless of style. As one poster wrote in a thread titled "Doll Request":

> I'm new here, and I'm trying to beautify my posts. My light brown hair is to my shoulders, straight, and I like to wear hippie clothes, tie-dye, bandanna's . . . etc Justin is 5ft 10inches, short light brown hair, and usually wears jeans and a sweatshirt. Nicole is a 11 week old little girl with big blue eyes. Thanx for any help you can give me. You ladies have wonderful imaginations, and generous hearts.

Another poster earlier in the same thread also describes herself and her family in her request for assistance with a signature, saying, "I'm in desperate need of some siggy help—it's so sad and pathetic (smiley face emoticon). . . I really appreciate your work! You all make BD.com a nice and colorful place."

This post conveys the sense of a shared obligation to contribute to the formation of a visual habitus, a beautiful home or room online, as a major responsibility that attends membership in this online community. Gans notes the powerful influence of women and mothers in creating and maintaining taste cultures and is careful to be as nonjudgmental as he can regarding their choices, despite his frequent use of the outmoded term "housewife." He writes: "Every housewife of every taste culture who can afford to buy furniture seeks to make her rooms into a work of beauty expressing her standards. . . . The two housewives differ in the amount of training in their standards, the skill and resources available to put their standards into action, the verbal fluency with which they justify their choices, and of course, in the content of their standards, in what they think is beautiful, but they are similar in that both are striving for beauty."[26] Though he stops short of asserting that this aspiration toward beauty is part of a biologically essential feminine quality, Gans acknowledges that "housewives" participate in taste cultures that exceed the management of family memories and help define the class identifications that a family can aspire to or possess. While it is doubtful that any of BabyDream.com's posters are sociologists, they seem to have taken this insight—that any mode of adornment is aesthetically valuable—to heart in their stance toward digital signatures. While many of these signatures might appear monstrous and deeply unappealing to a viewer who values modernist "cleanness," they are products of a desire to create online content and images of bodies and lives that are underrepresented in other media outlets.

The digital signatures that pregnant women create for use on BabyDream.com embody a new aesthetic code of self-representation on the popular Internet. Generally speaking, digital signatures work as part of a system of verification and database mapping that ensures the legitimacy of financial and other transactions on the Internet. A "unique number" may be assigned a particular transaction to organize it and make it searchable in a database, and this can be called a "signature." In contrast to these machine-generated coded verifiers of identity, user-created digital signatures to bulletin board posts work to engender an alternative style of managing visual digital surfaces, hewing to a logic that Christopher Pinney has dubbed "vernacular modernism." The visual anthropologists Stephen Sprague and Pinney examine the ways that Yoruban and Nagda photographers have responded to a colonial discourse of photography that privileges depth, indexicality, and a particular kind of chronotope or relationship to time and history by creating a resistant practice of photographic visual representation that works under an alternative visual logic and system of representation. While Western photographs enforce a singular notion of space and identity, African and Indian montage photographs that represent double and triple portraits of the same sitter occupying a visual field "place a person beyond the space and identity that certain forms of Western portraiture enforce." Rather than condemning these portraits as poor examples of, or inept attempts at, traditional Western photography, Sprague and Pinney encourage a cultural reading that takes

---

26   Gans, *Popular Culture and High Culture*, 146.

into account their unique social purpose: "There is . . . an explicitly articulated recognition by photographers that their task is to produce not an imprisoning trace of their sitters but to act as impresarios, bringing forth an ideal and aspirational vision of the bodies that sitters wish themselves to be."[27]

This desire to create a digital body or home that reflects aspirational pregnancy and child-centered domesticity is literalized in BabyDream.com's numerous digital signatures that represent nurseries, pregnant avatars of the user, ultrasounds, and miscarried fetuses. Shown here, Holly's signature collects images from several disparate sources into one place, coalescing a broad range of desires, aspirations, bodies, and forms of representation. The scanned-in uterine ultrasound with its authenticating medical information, such as the name of the pregnant woman, location of the hospital, time of day, and date, takes pride of place at the top of the signature, alongside a collage consisting of a photograph of the poster's nursery, with a cartoon avatar inserted alongside it.[28] While the ultrasound verifies the reality of the pregnancy, the nursery depicts an idealized physical space in the home. There is a link to "Nadia Simone's" nursery pictures on another site, should the viewer care to see them, but the photograph of the nursery that is present in the signature provides a wealth of detail. The coordinated wallpaper border, curtain, valance, mobile, crib, crib bumper, quilt, and linens all attest to an anticipatory and privatized vision of the future that the ultrasound promises. Their extensive coordination and use of colorful ornament and pattern exemplifies exactly the type of "fluffiness" condemned as excessive and lower class by nursery modernists. The cartoon avatar superimposed on it looks at the viewer with one huge eye while the other hides underneath a fluffy bang. Her body is slim and childlike, and the avatar's visual style contrasts strongly with the posed quality of the photograph underneath, which resembles a catalog page in its sense of having been staged and styled to represent a "perfect" example of successfully composed middle-class domestic space. Yet the promise represented by the ultrasound and the photographed nursery ready for its occupant, both images warranted in indexicality, is given a different shading by the details underneath: while the monkey-themed pregnancy day "counter" bar underneath it reads, "A New Baby Girl Due, 1/7/2005, 24 Weeks, 2 Days Pregnant! 109 days left!" the animated swinging monkeys flank three tiny avatars that tell a different story of loss and bereavement. The fragility of the images of the ultrasound and the nursery as "aspiration-

---

27 Christopher Pinney, "Notes from the Surface of the Image: Photography, Postcolonialism, and Vernacular Modernism," in *Photography's Other Histories*, ed. Christopher Pinney and Nicolas Peterson (Durham, NC: Duke University Press, 2003), 219.

28 Images used in this chapter have had identifying details removed to protect the privacy of the poster.

Yea!

Thanks, Rebecca!

AF has "left the building", so I'm getting excited about trying this month. I've decided to chart everything that I can since my temps have been unusual due to allergies. I may need some help on this!!!

Tamara, we are all here for you and look to you as our wise leader...hope everything works for ya. Wouldn't it be great if we could all become the OPB's (Official Pregnant Buddies) next month?

Gotta go study...be back in a bit to check on everyone!

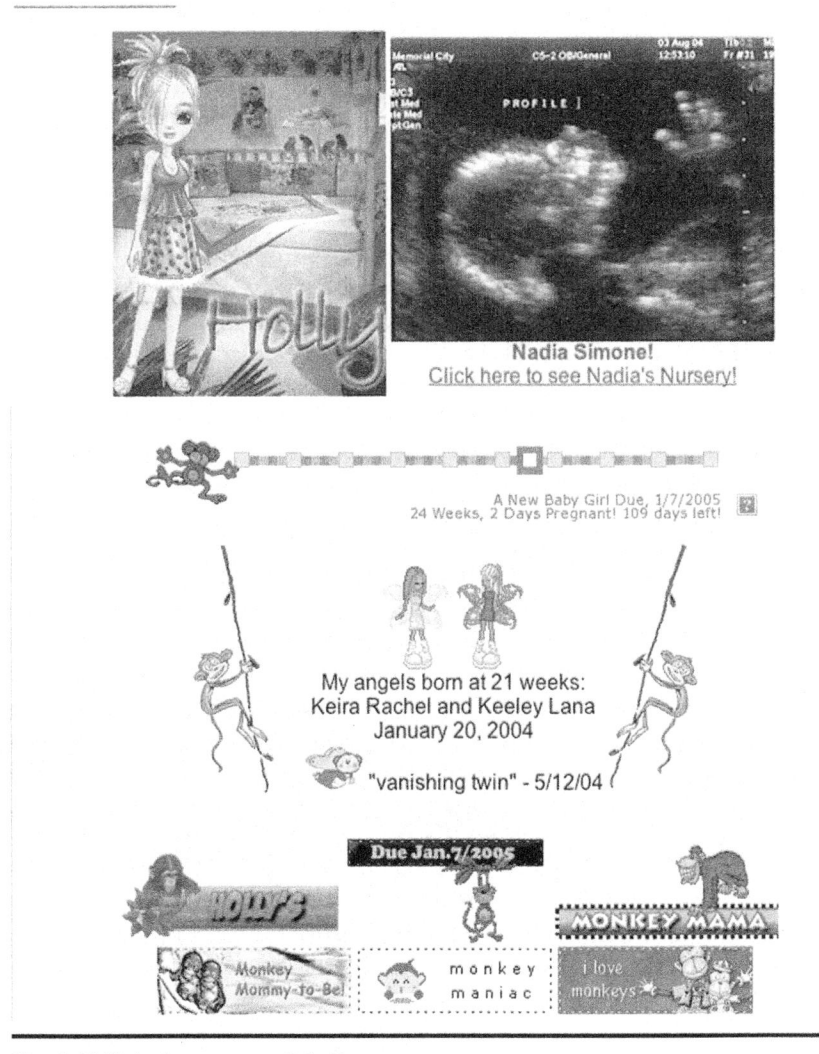

Fig. 3. Holly's signature on BabyDream.com.

al" and anticipatory signs of new motherhood is reinforced by the images of two tiny cartoon angels with long hair, dresses, large pigeon-toed sneakers, and glittery wings, along with a small baby monkey wearing a blanket over its shoulders. These angels are meant to represent miscarried pregnancies, "My angels born at 21 weeks: Keira Rachel and Keeley Lana, January 20, 2004," and the monkey is captioned with the words " 'vanishing twin'— 5/12/04." The convention of representing miscarried pregnancies or stillborn children in this way is quite common on this bulletin board and others that serve pregnant women. The visual means of memorializing them tends to include dolls that look like cartoon children with wings—angels—along with the date of miscarriage. Since miscarriages are not uncommon among women who are trying to get pregnant, this should not be surprising; what is novel is the way that these posters visualize them alongside images of viable pregnancies that they may be carrying now, as if the fetus that failed to develop were on a par with the ones that the medical establishment represented by the ultrasound image. These images of "missed" children are never represented with ultrasounds, though it is almost certainly true that women have them, as many miscarriages are diagnosed in this way. It seems that the language of loss and bereavement around the matter of miscarriage—a pregnancy that produces an invisible result, or rather one that is never visualized in popular culture—must take the form of vernacular image production or graphical avatars. The collaborative do-it-yourself visual culture of pregnancy bulletin board signatures has created a community of women who give each other liberal acknowledgment for assistance with image and icon creation and have authored images to address a need that is seldom articulated in social space. Miscarriages are still a taboo topic in the United States. Holly thanks "Jamie and Lisa A for my Monkey Mama & DD Blinkies!!!" animated GIFs that blink at the bottom of the post, and we might also assume that the "angels" and "vanishing twin" images came from another poster as well.

The practice of visualizing "lost" children using avatarial means is addressed as well in Yoruban photography. "Because twins are sacred children with connections to the spirit world, it is especially important to show them proper respect," and thus photographs are often made of them to hang in the parlor.[29] If by chance a twin or a triplet should die before a portrait is created, photographers will commonly pose a surviving child, sometimes dressed in cross-gendered clothing if the missing child was of a different gender, to represent the deceased one and print the two images together, thus creating a composited portrait in which two copies of the same body occupy the same visual field. It is also sometimes the case that an identical image of the

---

29 Stephen F. Sprague, "Yoruba Photography: How the Yoruba See Themselves," in Pinney and Peterson, *Photography's Other Histories*, 252.

surviving child, if the twins shared the same gender, is printed twice on a photograph to represent the missing body.

Holly's signature depicts five "virtual" bodies, only one of which exists in the world—her own. However, unlike many other pregnant posters to this site, she does not represent her own avatar as pregnant or "having a belly." Tattie's signature, also shown here, positions her pregnant avatar within a tableau arranged in a circle bordered by animated sparkling purple stars and bubbles. Entitled "Tattie and Stan," it depicts her pregnant avatar wearing a white T-shirt that says "baby" in large letters with an arrow pointing to her swollen abdomen; in the background and slightly to the left is an image of her husband, "Stan," who is carrying a snowboard and wearing baggy cargo pants and a short haircut. Near the bottom and arranged in a circle around the couple are five images of cats and dogs named "Grace," "Mia," "Piglet," "Sammie," and "Sophie." These images are a mixture of cartoons and photographs, but they are all similar in size. Below this family portrait sits a bank of "bumpers" three across and three deep, declaring "Pregnant with # 1!" "Expecting a blessing!" "I ♥ my hubby!" "I adore Hello Kitty," "Love and Cherish," and "To Have and to Hold." Underneath these are a series of images of Hello Kitty on shopping bags and baby blocks, and a bumper that sits

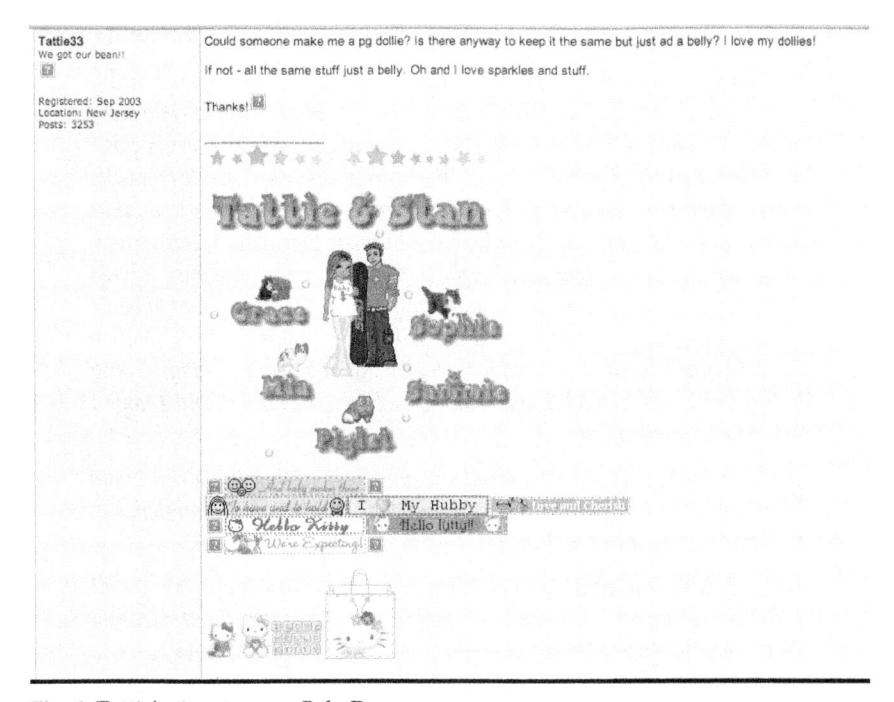

Fig. 4. Tattie's signature on BabyDream.com.

on a line by itself: "Bush Cheney '04." Candid snapshot photographs of the five pets complete the graphical section of the signature, which ends with facts such as the ages of the poster and her husband, the date of their marriage, the gender of their fetus, and its due date. This signature was created at the request of "Tattie," who had asked that her existing unpregnant avatar be modified to add "all the same stuff just a belly." The use of bumpers to speak to the story that the images tell creates a nuanced picture of the poster's political sentiments, stylistic preferences, and eagerness to assert heteronormativity and traditional domesticity. The inclusion of family pets as part of the ménage is absent from Holly's post, as is the reference to miscarriage or lost babies. This poster's willingness and indeed eagerness to represent her own avatar as physically altered in shape and appearance—a "pg dollie," as she puts it—may not be reflected in signatures created by women who have suffered one or several pregnancy losses. The power of the visual image of the avatar to project a future that may be both feared and fervently hoped for is reflected in the deployment or elision of pregnant avatars in users' posts.

The collaborative culture of avatar and signature creation links the sharing of information about the technology of pregnancy and the technology of avatar creation. The management of the pregnant or trying-to-conceive body and the virtual or avatar body comes together vividly in the following post:

> *I am about to go to the graphic site- I get real weird about internal health stuff, so hopefully I wont fall out of my chair. I will let you all know if I made it through it. I think I will start checking CM and my cervix position next month (if there is a AF this month) and start fresh from the start. Tamara, we are just BD'ing and hoping - we are trying to do it at least every other day so hopefully we will hit it that way. I don't know why, I'm just not that obsessed right this second, maybe because I don't feel good, but that is subject to change any moment. *I went* and haven't fainted yet - real graphic but I will try to do it - - it reminds me of the time I had to give myself an enema for a lower GI - I called my mom crying telling her I couldn't do it, well she calmed me and I did it, but I hope I never have to again.*
>
> *Oh, btw: I was reading more about pregnancy symptoms, and you know what?- most of them don't show for weeks or months after a missed AF, so I don't know if that will help us not be obsessed, yeah right!*
>
> *As far as hiding behind the sunglasses or feeling silly - don't - we are all just learning and I think not worrying about putting stuff out there on this thread is what is so great about it - at least we find out answers to our questions. and I know we are just going to get real close through all of this....*

Ok - some *techie help*

- To not loose my postings, I always type them out in an email or word document and then copy and paste into the thread but of course, I learned that the hard way

- If you want to have your chart as a part of your sig, here is what you can do. I am somewhat of an HTML nerd, so I hope this helps. Copy your web address that you were given by your charting site. Go to your signature here on IDOB, and add the tag below overwriting my note about pasting with the web address, save and presto, you're chart is there.

If anybody wants to learn anything else about HTML, let me know - its pretty easy (now that I know) and I could help with adding additional stuff to your sigs if you want.

The liberal use of acronyms in this post reveals how common and naturalized the language of obstetrics and gynecology has become in this online community: "CM" stands for "cervical mucus," and "GI" for "gastrointestinal." The use of more vernacular acronyms like "AF," which stands for "Aunt Flo," a euphemism for menstrual period, and "BD'ing," which means "baby dancing," or having intercourse, demonstrates the mixing of colloquial and medical rhetorics. Indeed, the posts along with the signatures show the blending of at least two modalities of discourse: the poster takes pains to reassure an interlocutor that "we are all learners here" presumably in regard to both the language of reproductive medicine and the language of HTML.[30] "Getting real close" through shared disappointment, technological expertise, anticipation, and joy is figured as one of the benefits of this online community, and the visual culture of the signature embodies this principle by calling into question the notion of singular ownership of a body or of a

---

30 See http://freewebs.com/prettyprinsess and http://over-the-moon.org/dollz for some examples of popular avatar construction sites, the first of which caters explicitly to users wanting to create pregnant avatars. These sites assume a female user; some feature only female "dollz," are notably hospitable to amateurs, and usually assume no prior knowledge of computer graphics, in contrast to the tone evident in many software-oriented sites that cater primarily to men. Don Slater in "Domestic Photography and Digital Culture," in *The Photographic Image in Digital Culture*, ed. Martin Lister (New York: Routledge, 1995) notes this characteristically technologically oriented gendering obtains as well in the photographic industry, which has marketed cameras to women based on "ease of use" and marketed darkroom equipment and high-end cameras to men based on their superior performance. Many of the creators of these dolls request that permission be given before download, and that credit be given in a byline before the user displays an image on the Web. Thus this "gift economy" of avatars comes with some caveats that imply ownership.

pregnancy. Their visual style is crowded, chaotic, and based on a principle of accretion rather than integration. There are significant clashes in styles and textures between images on the same signature, especially when compared to the orderly ACSII sigs of the text-only days of the early-nineties Internet. These are riotous combinations of bumpers, animated GIFs, blinkies, photos, borders, cartoons, and other combinations of text and image, many or most of them acquired from other sites or shared between self-styled "siggy girls" who possess graphical imaging skills. These exuberantly informational and richly multimediated images of identity exemplify a visual style created to signify identities in process, literally often in transition between the social and bodily states of "woman" and "mother" that cannot be integrated into one sign or signature. The users of these sites are often stay-at-home mothers, often quite politically conservative, often working class, and when they create avatars they often state these positions (Tattie's "Bush Cheney in '04" bumper was quite popular during that election year). In short, they are a taste culture that has never been taken much into account when new media theorists discuss avatars, embodiment, and gender. Their overt political ideologies certainly do not square with the dominant discourse of new media theory. What to do, however, when a media form that had been dominated by engineers, students, artists, and other cultural elites becomes popular in dramatically quick, Internet time? One of the most striking technology adoption stories I can think of has to do with the Internet: in 1993, Scott Bukatman could ask, "Why are there no women in cyberspace?" and mean it.[31] In 2003 the percentages of women and men online were exactly fifty-fifty, and they are holding steady as of today. However, according to Nina Wakeford, from 1992 to 1996, women's presence on the Internet increased from 5 percent to 34 percent.[32] The partial closing of the digital divide has resulted in a very different Internet user, one more likely to be female, less educated, less culturally elite. These are people who belong to much different taste cultures than previously existed on the Internet. This is not to say that kitsch never existed on the Internet; it is not difficult to find Web sites devoted to screen grabs, slash fiction, and the digital equivalent of velvet clown paintings. However, this was masculine, geek kitsch, and it seems important to note that. This was a primarily male audience in whose visual culture Tolkien, Ridley Scott, Frank Frazetta, cyberpunk, anime, and Marvel Comics figure largely. This Internet popular culture has largely been ignored except by sociologists, who tend to discuss it as symptomatic of a subculture with its own customs in

---

31 Quoted in Judith Squires, "Fabulous Feminist Futures and the Lure of Cyberspace," in Bell and Kennedy, *The Cybercultures Reader*, 365.
32 Nina Wakeford, "Networking Women and Grrrls with Information/Communication Technology," in Bell and Kennedy, *The Cybercultures Reader*, 356.

terms of social engagement, alienation, and the public sphere rather than in reference to aesthetics or taste cultures.

Visual style and taste are rarely discussed in relation to popular (as opposed to artistic or countercultural) digital forms. While art sites are often discussed and valued in relation to their challenges to old media forms, deployment of new modes of interactivity, and forms of resistance to linear modes of consuming and producing the art object, pregnancy Web sites are seldom visited by people who are not pregnant or are partnered with people who are pregnant. Web sites that deal with domestic, everyday, or commercial matters have heretofore been the province of sociologists and graphic designers or usability experts, such as Edward Tufte, whose *Envisioning Information* has become a standard text in information design. This discourse of transparency and usability values efficiency and density of information and does not discuss new media objects in terms of visual culture. "Look and feel" are elements of button positioning, font size, use of white space, and intuitive icons and are not used to signify anything vis-a-vis what sorts of offline visual traditions are being referenced.

Parenting Web sites exemplify the ways that women use the Internet to graphically embody themselves in specific reproductive states, that is, as pregnant women, nursing women, and mothers. They draw significant numbers of women who exemplify the profile of the "late adopter" of the Internet; that is to say, they are often stay-at-home mothers from the working or middle classes rather than professionals who might be required to use the Internet for work. They are more likely than in previous years to be members of racial minority groups who have previously been represented very poorly online, such as African American and Latino. In addition, they defy their gender profile in relation to the Internet because they are deeply involved in digital production: they upload significant amounts of online content in the form of their large and detailed postings and digital signatures.

Pregnant avatars challenge many conventional ideas regarding online embodiment. While nobody believes anymore that on the Internet nobody knows you're a dog, it is certainly true that many women offline can exist for several months without anybody knowing that they are pregnant. Women who work outside the home must carefully weigh factors such as economic need and work climate when they decide how and when they wish to reveal their pregnancies in the workplace. This discourse of "outing" is in some sense a queer one; pregnancy is a state of difference whose visibility and legibility are, at least at first, performative and volitional. Thus pregnant avatars represent a state that is by definition temporary. They signify a changing body, in some sense an ephemeral body. In addition, an avatar can be pregnant in the "public" space of the Internet bulletin board, while its owner may be still closeted in public. The pregnant avatar memorializes a body in transition, one that is out of the user's control. The Internet is likewise a space of ephemerality, as its content changes rapidly and constantly. In addition, pregnant avatars have a certain literal quality that leads to intriguing phenomenological questions: Would a user keep a pregnant avatar if she miscarried? Would the act of altering or removing that avatar from the board signify a miscarriage in miniature, a digital reenactment of the offline state? What are the implications of this participatory digital practice?

In *Feminism and the Technological Fix*, Carol Stabile describes the defining paradox of the visual culture of pregnancy as follows: "With the advent of visual technologies, the contents of the uterus have become demystified and entirely representable, but pregnant bodies themselves remain concealed."[33] Hence the paradox: while medical imaging technologies like ultrasounds and laparoscopy have turned the pregnant female body inside out, rendering it as transparent as a pane of glass, a vessel containing infinite visual wonders of procreation and opportunities for witnessing with machine-enabled vision the miracle (or spectacle) of birth, its exterior remains hidden in plain sight. As Stabile writes: "The pregnant body . . . remains invisible and undertheorized in feminist theory."[34] Many other scholars of feminism, technology, and the visual have noted the pregnant body's peculiar status in post-1990s feminist visual culture. As Lisa Cartright writes in "A Cultural Anatomy of the Visible Human Project," pregnant bodies have long been used to stand in for all female bodies in the culture of medical imaging, from its roots in classically rendered paintings of female pelvises by d'Agoty[35] to current projects like the Visible Woman, whose cryosectioned body was digitized and put on a database online for educational purposes.[36] Thus women's reproductive organs, and women in reproductive states, are over-represented in medical visual culture; the pregnant female body and its interior in particular is classically overdetermined as it comes to represent all female bodies. A spate of scholarly books and collections on the topic of reproductive technologies and feminism have all noted the way that the medical establishment has worked to make the pregnant female body normative, and its result, which is to pathologize nonreproductive female bodies—as Cartright notes, the Visible

---

33   Carol Stabile, *Feminism and the Technological Fix* (New York: St. Martin's Press, 1994), 84.

34   Ibid.

35   See Julie Doyle and Kate O'Riordan, "Virtually Visibile: Female Cyberbodies and the Medical Imagination," in *Reload: Rethinking Women + Cyberculture*, ed. Mary Flanagan and Austin Booth (Cambridge, MA: MIT Press, 2002) for further discussion of d'Agoty.

36   Lisa Cartright, *Screening the Body: Tracing Medicine's Visual Culture* (Minneapolis: University of Minnesota Press, 1995), 30.

Woman was criticized as an incomplete and inadequate model of the female body because, though in perfect health at her time of death, she is "postmenopausal and presumably therefore unsuited to demonstrating processes of reproduction."[37] Ultrasound has taken up the imaging practice that once belonged to medical painting and engraving and is valued because it seems to give access to the invisible, the interior, to move right past the unspeakable and abject pregnant body to its contents, the fetus.

While American culture as a whole is unappeasably eager to see photographic or "real" images of babies in the womb, pregnancy's hidden spectacle, feminists in particular are wary of the way that this desire encourages ways of seeing that represent the fetus and mother as occupying different visual frames and tends to visually reinforce the notion of their separate existences. Of course, this type of machine-enhanced seeing most famously provides fodder for anti-choice movements who have developed these medical images aggressively in their protests and signage. However, feminist theorists' skepticism regarding reproductive visioning technologies has roots in an earlier technologically critical discourse. Just as the move to challenge the medical establishment by reinvesting midwives rather than medical doctors with authority characterizes second-wave and later feminisms, so too feminist theory's suspicion of the visual as a mode of knowing conditioned this reception.

As Rosalind Petchesky writes in "Fetal Images: The Power of Visual Culture in the Politics of Reproduction," the problem with seeing as a way of knowing is that it creates a distance between the seer and the seen that translates into an uneven power relation between the knower and the known. Evelyn Fox Keller critiques this privileging of the visual in her work in science and gender, and Laura Mulvey has also written on the ways that the gaze objectifies women and, more importantly, how it is a product of the apparatus and form of narrative film. Part of visual culture's intervention into this state of things is to critique the gaze and to encourage other ways of seeing; Nicholas Mirzoeff wishes to replace the gaze with the "transverse glance," which is the "transient, transnational, transgendered way of seeing that visual culture seeks to define, describe, and deconstruct."[38]

However, as Donna Haraway writes in "The Persistence of Vision," perhaps it is time to reclaim vision for feminist ethics. Despite the eyes' "having been used to signify a perverse capacity—honed to perfection in the history of science tied to militarism, capitalism, colonialism, and male supremacy—to distance the knowing subject from everybody and everything in the

---

37 Ibid.
38 Nicholas Mirzoeff, "The Subject of Visual Culture," in *The Visual Culture Reader*, 18.

interests of unfettered power,"[39] it seems particularly strategic to do so right now, at this particular moment in both new media studies and feminist theory. For the parallels between medical visual imaging and the deployment of digital communication technologies are strong, in terms of both chronology, causality, and usage. Computer screens and ultrasound screens, while both televisual, share a common origin in radar, a military technology. Unlike the cinematic screen, which shows images of the past rather than the present, computers and ultrasounds show images in real time: "processual" images.[40] Reproductive visual imaging is an important part of digital screen culture as well as the culture of pregnancy: many a pregnant woman's first look at her baby is through a CRT monitor that is about the same size and color as a small television, the type that many people buy for their kitchens, that archetypal domestic space. While she is most likely looking at an Accuson rather than a Sony or Toshiba, and the experience of cold ultrasound gel on her belly distinguishes one viewing experience from the other, the mode of delivery is the same, that is, the dynamic screen. This engagement with screen culture as the primal scene of reproductive looking, this uncanny techno-visual moment, resonates with another scene of looking at the digital screen, and that is in using the Internet.

The linkage between the Internet's visioning of pregnant bodies and the deployment of medical images of pregnant women and fetuses allows us to parse gendered embodiment at a critical moment in its visual culture. Much feminist critique of medical imaging has targeted its mode of production. Typically, doctors, medical illustrators, and research scientists are the gatekeepers in deciding what (and when) a pregnant woman ought to visualize. Ultrasounds are not transparent texts: like all images, they require interpretation. Discovering a fetus's gender requires both the warranting of this information in the presence of the ultrasound image and the technician's expert eye, which is trained to recognize fetal genitalia. The prospective parents can be looking right at "it" and find themselves unable to identify what they are looking at. This means that the pregnant body is surveilled from both without and within, and the production, manipulation, viewing, printing, and interpretation of the image are controlled by doctors and technicians. However, the Internet has long been celebrated for its interactivity, that is, the way in which it puts image production in the hands of amateurs, or "the people." It bridges the production/reception divide. As Robert Burnett and David Marshall write:

---

39 Donna Haraway, "The Persistence of Vision," in Mirzoeff, *The Visual Culture Reader*, 677.

40 Mark B. N. Hansen, *New Philosophy for New Media* (Cambridge, MA: MIT Press, 2004). See as well, Lev Manovich, *The Language of New Media* (Cambridge, MA: MIT Press, 2001) for an account of the "dynamic screen."

> *Distinctive from telephony, the Web implicates a production component, that is, where content is developed and enhanced beyond its original orality (think of any conversation and its unpredictable flow) into some combination of visual, textual, and graphic structure. The Web, when thought of as a medium, is a hybrid that invokes the sensation of orality and contingency with the guided structure of a book or magazine.*[41]

This is one quality that makes the Internet in general and the Web in particular different from other telecommunicative forms. Hence, when we look at the ways that pregnant and trying-to-conceive women depict themselves in pregnancy Web forums, we are given insight into the reappropriation of the medicalized gaze. When these women make graphical images of themselves as pregnant avatars to insert in their bulletin board posts online, they are producing a counterdiscourse that challenges the binarism of hypervisible/invisible pregnant bodies. In addition, the avatars they produce exist to serve a specific type of orality on the Internet: the kind of asynchronous conversation that goes on among pregnant women in an online forum. In these forums, the often "unpredictable flow" of conversation is directed fairly predictably into a specific path; all discourse that is not about pregnancy or babies is flagged as an "off-topic" thread so that users can avoid it. Conversations about the virtues or drawbacks of day care, breastfeeding, stroller use, and nutrition are generally cordial and tolerant of diverse opinions, but political discourse is flagged as being off topic, since it tends to have a divisive effect on the discussion objected to by many of the participants; this became particularly evident during the US presidential election in 2004.

Since the orality of pregnancy online is so self-referential—it consists of pregnant women talking about their pregnancies ad nauseum—the graphical avatars they create combine "visual, textual, and graphical" structures in a hybrid form that remediates the pregnant body in truly multifarious ways. Rather than depicting hypervisible interiors and invisible exteriors, these women create complicated, at times visually incoherent, embodiments of pregnancy, a paradigmatically embodied state. Their use of dynamic screens to reclaim the mode of image production of their own bodies results in rich and at times bizarre taste cultures online.

Ultrasounds that depict a fetus floating in an undefined space, the invisible and occluded space of the mother's body, as well as fetal photography that encourages the sense of an "independent" fetal body, reinforce the notion of the pregnant body as really two bodies. As Phelan writes: "Detached from the pregnant woman, the fetal form has become a sign that is already powerfully implicated in the political economy of capitalism and

---

41   Robert Burnett and P. David Marshall, *Web Theory: An Introduction* (New York: Routledge, 2003), 18.

patriarchy."[42] The persistent envisioning of the pregnant female body as a vessel (the umbilical cord is painstakingly deleted from most photographic images of fetuses, thereby emphasizing its existence separately from the woman's body) echoes an older cyberutopian notion of the body or "meat" as a disposable package for what really counts: the mind. The computer scientist Hans Moravec, "the most exemplary advocate of radical disembodiment," sees the flesh as just a carrier or an envelope: a person is an "essence or pattern," signal to the body's noise, and the body is merely "the machinery supporting that process."[43] The mind, termed "wetware," operates like the software in a computer; it is housed by an apparatus but is transferable in nature. This notion of the mind/body split is the foundational assumption and driving force behind cyberpunk fiction and one of the reasons that theorists claim that new media create a "posthuman" being, one that is detachable from a body if embedded in an alternate site enabled by machinery.[44] Thus this radical sundering of the body from its contents, whether "the mind" or "the fetus" so disliked by feminist medical theorists, is not a new idea: cyberpunk has been representing bodies separated from their contents since its inception in the early eighties. What is of more interest is the ideological uses to which machine-enabled disembodiment is put. Much medical imaging encourages a similar idea to cyberpunk philosophy, that is, what "really counts" is what's inside the body, not the body itself—that is to say, the fetus.

Cyberfeminism has been described as "a restart button" for gendered ideologies partly because it seeks to reclaim machines and by extension machine-enabled vision for women, as producers and users of their own imaging. The radical possibilities that new media offer to digitally create "other" bodies, other iterations of "woman" and "man" that elude the dichotomies between interior and exterior, white and nonwhite, and female and male, are especially evident in digital visualizations of bodies, that is to say, avatars. Sites like Victoria Vesna's "Bodies INCorporated" are the darling of cyberfeminist and other new media theorists because they allow for interactive body play in the realm of the absurd; avatars made of chocolate with human and machine parts certainly challenge paradigms of normative bodies.[45] The commercialization of the Internet has led many Internet utopians to despair

---

42 Phelan, *Unmarked*, 133.
43 Dianne Currier, "Assembling Bodies in Cyberspace: Technologies, Bodies, and Sexual Difference," in Flanagan and Booth *Reload: Rethinking Women + Cyberculture*, 522.
44 See Richard Doyle, *Wetwares: Experiments in Postvital Living* (Minneapolis: University of Minnesota Press, 2003).
45 New Media criticism by Jennifer Gonzales, Julie Doyle and Kate O'Riordan has showcased the site as an example of these possibilities. See Gonzalez, "The Appended Subject: Race and Identity as Digital Assemblage," in *Race in Cyberspace*,

of its potential as a site to challenge institutional authority and tired media scripts, and they often look to artists to provide that bit of resistance or subversion which new media theorists so badly need. However, it is important to note the elitism that can arise from this position. As Burnett notes, new media are distinguished by their redistribution of image and content production to "the masses." This stance celebrates the Internet's potential to give expression to "all," to put media production into the hands of nonprofessionals (who are presumably less hegemonized, or at least freer of overt commercial agendas). Mirzoeff writes that the popularization of digital media has produced an "apparent state of emergency in North American universities at the level of criticism, pedagogy, and institutional practice," since they "promote a form of empowered amateurism—make your own movie, cut your own CD, publish your own Web site—that cuts across professionalization and specialization, the twin justifications of the liberal arts university."[46] However, Vesna is a professional herself: a professional artist. Her use of digital media is far from amateurish, and the site evidences some serious expertise with imaging software. As Grant Farred writes regarding the use of the vernacular: "The vernacular is the transcription of the popular (subaltern) experience into political oppositionality."[47] "Vernacular" assemblages created by subaltern users, in this case pregnant women, create impossible bodies that critique normative ones but without an overt artistic or political intent.

This constitutes an interesting case of theoretical convergence. However, there are institutional reasons for this; as Lisa Cartright writes of television studies, popular (as opposed to "artistic") digital media studies have "remained marginal to disciplines that shun low culture."[48] Her remarkable observation that television was excluded from serious consideration by the famous "Visual Culture Questionnaire" that appeared in *October* in 1996, while both digital media and film were discussed extensively, I would contend has to do with digital media's efforts to legitimate themselves by focusing on digital *art*. It is not a new strategy for new disciplines to array themselves with authority and prestige by invoking the artistic. As mentioned before, Victoria Vesna's work is a great favorite among feminist media theorists, and in fact the strongest critical-theoretical discussion of new media has come from the world of art.[49] Like television studies, which have "tended to rely

---

ed. Beth Kolka, Lisa Nakamura, and Gil Rodman (New York: Routledge, 2000); and Doyle and O'Riordan, "Virtually Visible."

46 Mirzoeff, *The Visual Culture Reader*, 6.
47 Grant Farred, *What's My Name? Black Vernacular Intellectuals* (Minneapolis: University of Minnesota Press, 2003), 7.
48 Cartright, "Film and the Digital in Visual Studies," 424.
49 Timothy Druckrey, *Ars Electronica: Facing the Future; A Survey of Two Decades* (Cambridge: MIT Press, 1999); and Hansen, *New Philosophy for New Media*.

on the methods of sociology and communication foundational to cultural studies,"[50] new media studies have split into two streams: high critical exegeses of new media art, and social scientific case studies of popular new media practices on the Web and Internet. The vernacular assemblages created by pregnant women on these sites demand the creation of a different stream, one that brings a critical stance to popular new media practices.

The promise of free and easy digital production is, practically speaking, an illusion; in reality it is very difficult to create "original digital images." Photoshop, Illustrator, and Fireworks are notoriously difficult to learn, and it is a truism of the Net that it is much easier to borrow or steal images than it is to create them from scratch. As Manovich writes, this new aesthetic of selecting from preexisting sets of images rather than creating new ones characterizes new media's very structure and logic.[51] The modularity of digital images makes the principle of copying and modification the basis of new media practice. Yet many new media theorists heavily favor "original" artistic production and also tend to prioritize graphical versus textual production. This tends to decrease the likelihood that "empowered amateurs" might create the kind of work that gets noticed, written about, discussed, assigned on syllabi, and analyzed. This emphasis on the essential originality of avatars, either textual or graphical, is apparent in Dianne Currier's work; she writes: "The visual avatars adopted by participants in more sophisticated graphical social environments present not simply a graphic icon manipulated by the individual user but a figure that is self-imagined and created." She emphasizes how avatar construction represents a form of "disembodiment" because "the construction of these bodies is entirely along the lines of individual desires."[52] However, considering how difficult it is on the level of techne to create "new" digital images rather than modify bitmapped ones taken from other "original" sources on the Web, individual desire, as strong as it may be, is likely to be thwarted unless the user is a graphic designer.

Popular graphical avatars created by "ordinary" users for nontechnical purposes are the blind spot of visual culture studies as well as digital culture studies. There is little writing on this topic from either perspective. Perhaps the most promising line of inquiry so far has been Don Slater's, in his lucid essay "Domestic Photography and Digital Culture." Though his essay was published in 1995 and thus predates the popular graphical Web, he engages with the meaning and deployment of digital snapshots in the "new home economy of the image" and concludes on a somewhat pessimistic note, asserting that digital domestic photography is unlikely to provide culturally

---

50   Cartright, "Film and the Digital in Visual Studies," 424.
51   Manovich, *The Language of New Media*.
52   Currier, "Assembling Bodies in Cyberspace," 526.

productive and empowering resources for everyday life, as he expects it to function only as another form of "intensified leisure consumption."[53] He points out the linkage between photography and leisure and consumer culture, and the ways that the family snapshot and family album, long the province and responsibility of wives and mothers, work to "idealize the self and the family."[54] He proposes that the pinboard replace the photo album as the most appropriate model for domestic imaging in the digital age, as it is made up of "images bound up with forms of practice rather than memory of commemoration, which are part of the instantaneous time of the consumerist present rather than a historical time marked by the family album."[55] The pinboard, like the digital signature, is an act of "practical communication rather than reflective representation" that might offer a site of resistance to the commodification of leisure created by photography's industry and history. Photo albums have lost cultural relevance because their hypervaluation as an artifact of a static and idealized notion of family is only matched by how seldom we look at them: gazing at photographs has failed to become a structured consumer leisure activity in the way that taking them has become. Pinboards, unlike traditional photographic albums, resemble digital signatures in the sense that they contain dynamic and modular content and convey the sense of a life in motion rather than one frozen in time, artifactual, and thus untrue to the sense of a lived past. In an article titled "Forum: Mombloggers, Unite!" and subtitled "Consumed by the minutiae of childraising, young parents can suffer from isolation. Cooper Munroe, mother of four kids, prescribes frequent Web logging," Munroe asserts the superiority of blogging over family photo albums. Munroe, a member of DotMoms, a blogging collective for women to share and record their experiences as mothers of young children, writes:

> *The added benefit is that by going through the exercise of thinking through what occurs in a day and writing it down, I am also creating a permanent record of what life is like while raising them. If I did not have a few hundred people stopping by every day to see what Emily and I are writing about, I likely would not be chronicling in a diary or a scrapbook about the maelstrom of Otis and a snake in a fight to the death (Otis won) or the time our 3-year-old asked the dentist if we could take home the laughing gas. Someday, I hope, my blog will tell my kids much more about themselves, and about the woman who raised them, than any photo album ever will.*

---

53 Slater, "Domestic Photography and Digital Culture," 145.
54 Ibid., 134.
55 Ibid., 139.

The notion of the "mommyblog" as a timeshifting communication medium that enhances convenience and memory can be read as a rebuke to Wakeford's and Star's fears that women's use of the Internet might produce only more drudgery and isolation for overworked caretakers and mothers of small children. Munroe writes that:

> Julie Moos, managing editor of the Poynter Institute, a journalism education organization, and editor of DotMoms, a collective of "mom" writers, to which I contribute, points out that since we are a much more mobile society, we have less time to connect. "We don't necessarily live where we grew up or where family is or friends are. There is a great deal of mobility in the workplace. It is our mobility that makes it increasingly difficult to find the company we need."

The irrelevance of the photo album in the digital age is asserted as well in an entry to TheMommyBlog.com in which the author writes an "open letter" to her family explaining its purpose. She describes her blog as:

> a family memoir, one that looks forward rather than backward (the family is backward enough without having to look there). Therapy for me. A way to get out of scrapbooking. A way to make up for my never having embraced the Cult of Creative Memories. Something I hope to pass on to my children and their descendants so that they may have the unique opportunity to see into their childhood in a way that birthday party photos and school portraits could never convey.

Indeed, it may be critically productive to envision women's blogs, digital signatures, and other representational products online as an extension of the offline material culture of scrapbooking, part of a complex of tasks that women have performed since time immemorial: the management of family memory. Scrapbook hobbyists refer to themselves somewhat touchingly as "memory consultants," implying that their function has to do with the business of memorializing the ephemeral "look and feel" of family life with small children. These two mothers identify Creative Memories, a scrapbooking retail outlet, as at worst a "cult" and at best an odious obligation that they can painlessly fulfill using the Internet, a form that allows for a "unique opportunity" to record memories in a dynamic and interactive form. Digital signatures in pregnancy bulletin boards and pregnant avatars function as a form of vernacular memory management, one as yet uncommodified by the retail behemoth of scrapbooking hobby shops, and one that women employ to represent and share the lives of young children and their lives as their mothers. These women use the Internet as a place to manage memories, replacing paper and other material forms like quilts and albums. In a way, the mode of production of digital signatures on pregnancy Web sites most resembles quilting, in the sense that like pinboards they are accreted out of scraps that are differently sourced and may not match, yet all have meaning. While the culture of Creative Memories values the creation of a professional-looking product, one that adheres to traditional middle-class notions of good taste, digital signatures, like quilts, can be "crazy."

Virtual community has fallen out of favor as a topic for academic discussion while it dominated new media theory in the nineties, it has lately taken a backseat to academic discussions of new media form, such as interfaces and databases, and other uses of the new media screen technology, such as digital gaming, which has become an economic juggernaut. However, as I have argued elsewhere, often the most sophisticated and interesting uses of new media involve its older instantiations (as in the subversive potential of e-mail) precisely because they employed less bandwidth and were thus less bounded by exacting infrastructural requirements.[56] Pregnancy bulletin boards are asynchronous and simple. They are divided into areas based on due date, "TTC" (trying to conceive), lesbian mothers, etcetera, and within each board a user is required to choose a nickname and a password. They are then given access to posting ability. Posts follow threads on topics such as spotting, sex, labor stories, and fertility charting. This particular visual culture of accretion rather than integration references scrapbooking or "scrapping," another signifying practice uniquely associated with middle-class women and reviled by "real" artists. Like scrapbooking, new media work through a logic of selection of existing modules or scraps and the subsequent accumulation and arrangement of these pieces into something new. Like patchwork, the signatures that result are often extremely large, in many cases taking up more than three computer screens to view. A short post consisting of only a sentence or two will still appear with the same signature as a more substantial one.

Avatar construction is a valorized object of study in new media, especially in gaming studies. Discussions of avatars in contexts other than gaming are relatively rare. The signatures that women create on pregnancy Web sites include images of themselves and their families that take back the power to visualize the pregnant female body from the medical establishment and return it to the women themselves. The results are often cartoonish, conflicted, disorganized, and bizarre, but the openness of the form—any image or text can be uploaded to form a signature—allows for moments of poignancy that defy description and put pressure on the notion of photographic visualization in digital media. One poster's signature consists of a photograph of her stillborn child's hand, with her own hand enclosing it. Beneath this image appears a passage by the poet Rumi: "Out beyond the ideas of wrongdoing and rightdoing, there is a field. I'll meet you there."

---

56 Nakamura, *Cybertypes*, 131.

As James Elkins writes in *Pictures of the Body: Pain and Metamorphosis*, "The crucial issue in studying pictures of the body must be the expressive value of each individual choice: what *kind* of pain is evoked, exactly *where* the sensation is strongest, precisely *how* the analogies operate."[57] The power of this image indeed resides in its pain: the pain of the bereft mother. Its transgressiveness consists in its delivering to the viewer an image of a body that is rarely represented at all in any contemporary medium: that of the stillborn child. As Elkins writes, "Some images are unrepresentable because they are forbidden by law or prohibited by custom."[58] While images of dead babies were common in nineteenth-century photography and are still publicly displayed in Yoruban photographic culture, they are extremely rare in our times, and even rarer in the context of a pregnancy Web site, thus demonstrating the ways that "custom" regarding the exhibition of these kinds of images shifts when we consider differing historical period and media use.[59] This signature represents a body that, like that of the pregnant woman, lies beyond the vocabulary of signifying practices that make up the common visual language of domesticity and home, gesturing toward the incredibly wide range of electronic elsewheres and virtual bodies that pregnant women, mothers, and trying-to-conceive women create on the Web.

The digital signature of the bereaved mother of a newborn has, itself, an ephemeral status; when "Little Livy's" mother changes her signature file, this image will disappear, leaving no trace in cyberspace except on the hard drives of those who have "captured" it. When I present this chapter as a talk, many audience members ask me why I believe a woman would want to disseminate a photograph like this one. Susan Sontag and Michael Lesy both address this question, and both write from a perspective that predates the digital. In *Wisconsin Death Trip*, Lesy explains the predominance of photographs of deceased babies by noting the relatively high infant mortality rate in mid-nineteenth-century America owing to childhood diseases like cholera, diphtheria, and smallpox but also remarks on the ritual function of funeral photography in this period:

> *None of the pictures were snapshots . . . their deepest purpose was more religious than secular, and commercial photography, as it was practiced in the 1890s, was not so much a form of applied technology as it was a semimagical act that symbolically dealt with time and mortality.*[60]

---

57 James Elkins, *Pictures of the Body: Pain and Metamorphosis* (Stanford, CA: Stanford University Press, 1999), 276.

58 Ibid., 277.

59 See Michael Lesy and Charles Van Schaick, *Wisconsin Death Trip* (New York: Anchor Books, 1991).

60 Ibid., n.p.

Little Livi, born still on her due date.

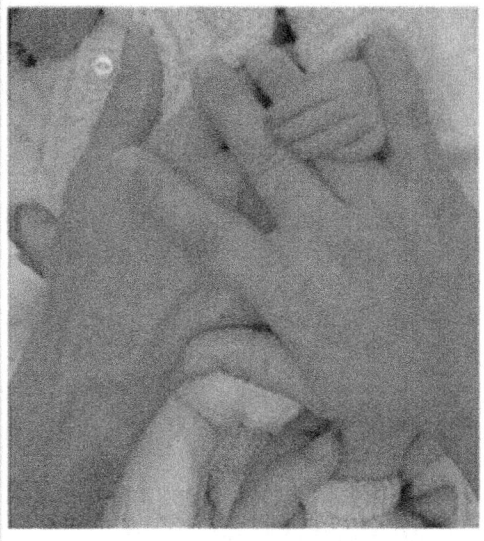

Olivia

7/27/03

"out beyond the ideas of wrongdoing and rightdoing, there is a field. I'll meet you there."

Rumi

Fig. 5. Olivia's signature on BabyDream.com.

Sontag as well stresses that ever since cameras were invented in 1839, "photography has kept company with death. Because an image produced with a camera is, literally, a trace of something brought before the lens, photographs were superior to any painting as a memento of the vanished pasts and the dear departed."[61] Photographs of deceased children were a particular type of "applied technology" that worked to manage memory in a graphical form. Digital signatures deployed on pregnancy bulletin boards work to manage visible and invisible bodies—avatars of pregnant women in particular allow

---

61　Susan Sontag, *Regarding the Pain of Others* (New York: Farrar, Straus and Giroux, 2003), 24.

users to gain access to a digital "counterutopia expressed in [an] area of contemporary culture resistant to, and less territorialized by, the mass media and commodified forms of communication," as David Rodowick puts it.[62]

Signatures that include the stillborn child put a formerly invisible body on display in a global medium—the Internet. The act of publicizing this socially invisible body flies in the face of contemporary custom but is quite in line with the ways that early photographs of departed children mediated between grieving parents and the community. While it may seem morbid to imagine a scenario in which a bereaved mother would have a photograph of her deceased baby blown up and displayed in her living room, Lesy narrates just such an event in nineteenth-century Wisconsin:

> Mrs. Friedel had a picture taken of her little baby in its coffin. Then when a fellow came up the road who did enlargements, she had just the baby's face blown up to a two-foot picture. But, since the baby's eyes were closed, she had an artist paint them open so she could hang it in the parlor.

This emphasis on public display had the dual function of "permitting the grieving parents to express and then accustom themselves to the irreversible facts of their children's death" by "permitting them to be comforted by the whole town." This primitive manipulation of the photographic image by Mrs. Friedel to produce a feeling of "liveness" in this early photographic image bespeaks a sense in which this image is both "sacred" or "semimagical" and yet modular and modifiable, traits most often associated with the digital. In addition, this sense that the image must be made public, must be shared, resonates with the use of the digital photographic portrait in the case of "Little Livy." For digital photographs are fundamentally shareable in a way that analog ones are not—as Abu Ghraib has shown us, their transmission and reproduction are uncontrollable.[63] Since they exist as binary code, they are as easy to transmit as any other type of digital file. However, their claims to truth are compromised partly for this reason; images that exist as a digital signal are easy to modify in ways that may cast them into doubt as signifiers of things that "really happened." Hence digital photography has a different kind of power in relation to the management of memory, especially in relation to the domestic and familial sphere.

Much has been written about the particular changes wrought on photographic practice and theory by digital imaging technology. In *The Reconfigured Eye*, William Mitchell notes the ways in which analog images are enduring, stable, or finished in the ways that digital ones are not, and observes

---

62 Rodowick, *Reading the Figural*, 221.
63 Nicholas Mirzoeff, "Invisible Empire: Embodied Spectacle and Abu Ghraib," *Radical History Review* 95 (2005): 21–44.

that "notions of individual authorial responsibility for image content, authorial determination of meaning, and authorial prestige are correspondingly diminished."[64] Thus, unlike analog photography, which had a privileged status in relation to memory, all digital photographs call the idea of truth and authorship into question. I would contend, however, that both the photograph of "Little Livy" and the Abu Ghraib photographs are resistant to this dilution of truth value inherent in the digital. These images are, like the funeral photography displayed in Lesy and Van Schaick's book, intensely and purposefully posed; like them, they are not "snapshots," and they perform a ritual function of public mourning in the first instance and militarized racialization in the second. It was noteworthy that when the Abu Ghraib photographs were released, nobody thought to question their authenticity despite their obvious status as digital images; they possessed a cultural truth that exceeded their always already questionable means of production. Likewise, the image of "Little Livy" is very much meant to be a "real" versus a fictional image; unlike the pregnant avatar cartoons and fairylike images of miscarried "angels" and "vanishing twins" memorialized in Holly's signature, Olivia's is decidedly meant to invoke the sense of "something brought before the lens," as Sontag puts it.

The achievement of authenticity in these cases of bodies in pain and mourning transcends the ordinary logic of the analog versus the digital photograph because these bodily images invoke the "semimagical act" of remembering types of suffering that are inarticulate, private, hidden within domestic or militarized spaces that exclude the public gaze. The truth of these images remains unquestioned because the notion that someone might purposely falsify them seems incomprehensible. Women's digital signatures on BabyDream.com perform the important work of visualizing previously hidden body narratives, and most importantly they do so in a way that juxtaposes an amazingly broad set of signifiers in the same space: images of happy pregnant women, healthy babies, pets, proudly displayed or missing husbands or boyfriends, miscarriages, stillborn babies, and postpregnant bodies coexist in the same virtual spaces.

As David Rodowick reminds us, it is crucial that new media scholarship produce a "social theory that is as attentive to creative strategies of resistance as it is to mechanisms of power and social control." It is not enough to simply locate the ways in which subjects are constrained by new media's surveillant and capitalistic tendencies; we must also identify what he calls new "lines of flight" that permit new "forms of becoming out of virtual personae and communities."[65] Early computing culture consistently marginalized women as users of digital technology by firmly embedding them in the domestic

---

64   Cited in Rodowick, *Reading the Figural*, 212.
65   Ibid., 217.

sphere as computer users: engineers could not imagine that women might use computers in any context other than that of traditional women's work, in particular, cooking. In *Interface Culture*, Steven Johnson relates the story of a hapless engineer at Intel who tried to pitch the idea of the personal computer to his bosses: "His most compelling scenario involved filing electronic versions of cooking recipes."[66] As this scenario demonstrates, a narrow conception of the domestic sphere has always intersected with the digital. The contemporary networked personal computer does indeed function as a type of domestic appliance in the sense that it helps to mediate acts of quite literal reproductive labor. In so doing, it permits women access to social collectivity around the condition of pregnancy and child rearing; women use pregnancy bulletin boards to share information and counter-information about prenatal testing, nutrition, and breast-feeding. The power of individual experience is stressed quite heavily: while many women end their posts with "YMMV" (your mileage may vary) or begin them with a modest "IMHO" (in my humble opinion), seemingly discrediting or at least casting doubt on their own claims, there is no doubt that they use the board as often as not to challenge received medical opinions by describing their experiences as conflicting with medical wisdom. For example, women who receive "bad" AFP (alpha fetal protein) or ultrasound results receive much reassurance from women who have had healthy babies with these same results, showing that the tests are often falsely positive. While a doctor or a nurse may be able to chart a test's documented rate of error, hearing from several actual women with healthy babies that the "bad" result is nothing to worry about assuages fears in a different way, one more accessible perhaps to women living in less stable, long-standing communities. Military wives, in particular, may have a more stable "home base" and community among pregnant women or new mothers on the Internet than in their offline lives, considering the rigors of frequent transfers and relocations, especially during wartime. Younger and less educated women, also newcomers to the Web, may also find personal "live" testimonials from "real" mothers less alienating and more reassuring than medical discourse and statistics.

Beyond this, women's creation of digital signatures enables genuine resistance to institutional forms of identity management that only continue to proliferate in daily life. While the seemingly free spaces of composable identities evident in build-your-own avatar games like MMORPGs continue

---

66 Steven Johnson, *Interface Culture* (New York: Basic Books, 1997), 148. For an insightful discussion of the connections between contemporary cooking websites like Epicurious.com and the ways that they intersect with this history of gender and early computing, see Tamar Brown, "Cooking and Computers: Reconsidering New Media Forms," paper presented at the Media and Cultural Studies Colloquium, University of Wisconsin, Madison, 2003.

to instantiate stereotyped images of women,[67] as Rodowick observes, "there is still an unequal division of power in the data images that count—for access to credit, medical insurance, voting and residency rights, ownership of property, and so forth—[and they are] still culled, collated, and controlled by a few large corporations and marketing organizations."[68] What are the "data images that count," the avatars that matter, in relation to women's reproductive labor online? While pregnancy bulletin boards may at times affirm normative domestic behavior in terms of pregnancy and child rearing, the digital signatures on several pregnancy Web sites are evidence of eclectic digital production that reflects the reality of reproductive labor and its attendant losses.

Women's production of digital signatures not only re-embodies themselves as pregnant subjects but also visualizes holistic visions of family that embody the paradox of pregnant women's empowerment and invisibility. While women who are on the Internet are empowered in a sense, certainly in relation to their sisters in other parts of the world where access is extremely scarce for any gender, they are still subject to the regulation of images of "proper" pregnancies and visual cultures. The gendered and classed nature of their signatures, as well as their mode of arrangement and visual ranking, which includes pets, political affiliations, and displays of communal belonging with other members of the online community, shows the development of a digital vernacular modernism. Pregnant women represent themselves exuberantly in the form of their digital avatars, and this energy and joy in self-representation take on all the more significance in a dataveillant society that continues to regulate pregnancy through imaging technologies. In representing themselves and their babies, pregnancies, babies yet to be, and lost children, women graphically embody themselves as dual subjects of interactivity in digital visual culture, thus publicizing bodies and lives previously unrepresented by the women living them.

Bibliography

Bell, David, and Barbara M. Kennedy, eds. *The Cybercultures Reader*. London: Routledge, 2000.

Bowlby, Rachel. *Carried Away: The Invention of Modern Shopping*. New York: Columbia University Press, 2001.

---

67 And no images at all of children or babies in most cases: fantasy games like *Everquest* and *Ultima Online* are adult-only. *The Sims*, an extremely popular digital game that simulates domestic activities like cleaning, taking out the trash, and working, is a notable exception in that it *encourages* players to build families. It is also exceptional in that at least half its users are women.

68 Rodowick, *Reading the Figural*, 216.

———. *Just Looking: Consumer Culture in Dreiser, Gissing, and Zola.* New York: Methuen, 1985.

Brown, Tamar. "Cooking and Computers: Reconsidering New Media Forms." Paper presented at the Media and Cultural Studies Colloquium, University of Wisconsin, Madison, 2003.

Burnett, Robert, and P. David Marshall. *Web Theory: An Introduction.* New York: Routledge, 2003.

Cartright, Lisa. "Film and the Digital in Visual Studies: Film Studies in the Era of Convergence." In Mirzoeff, *The Visual Culture Reader*, 417–432.

———. *Screening the Body: Tracing Medicine's Visual Culture.* Minneapolis: University of Minnesota Press, 1995.

Currier, Dianne. "Assembling Bodies in Cyberspace: Technologies, Bodies, and Sexual Difference." In Flanagan and Booth, *Reload: Rethinking Women + Cyberculture*, 519–538.

Danet, Brenda. *Cyberpl@y: Communicating Online.* New Technologies/New Cultures Series. Oxford: Berg, 2001.

Doyle, Julie, and Kate O'Riordan. "Virtually Visibile: Female Cyberbodies and the Medical Imagination." In Flanagan and Booth, *Reload: Rethinking Women + Cyberculture*, 239–260.

Doyle, Richard. *Wetwares: Experiments in Postvital Living.* Minneapolis: University of Minnesota Press, 2003.

Druckrey, Timothy. *Ars Electronica: Facing the Future; A Survey of Two Decades.* Cambridge, MA: MIT Press, 1999.

Elkins, James. *Pictures of the Body: Pain and Metamorphosis.* Stanford, CA: Stanford University Press, 1999.

Farred, Grant. *What's My Name? Black Vernacular Intellectuals.* Minneapolis: University of Minnesota Press, 2003.

Flanagan, Mary. "The Bride Stripped Bare to Her Data: Information Flow + Digibodies." In *Data Made Flesh: Embodying Information*, edited by Robert Mitchell and Phillip Thurtle, 153–178. New York: Routledge, 2004.

———. "Mobile Identities, Digital Stars, and Post Cinematic Selves." *Wide Angle* 21, no. 1 (1999): 77–93.

Flanagan, Mary and Austin Booth, eds. *Reload: Rethinking Women + Cyberculture.* Cambridge: MIT Press, 2002.

Foster, Tom. *The Souls of Cyberfolk: Posthumanism as Vernacular Theory.* Minneapolis: University of Minnesota Press, 2005.

Gans, Herbert J. *Popular Culture and High Culture: An Analysis and Evaluation of Taste.* New York: Basic Books, 1999.

Georges, Eugenia, and Lisa M. Mitchell. "Baby Talk: The Rhetorical Production of Maternal and Fetal Selves." In *Body Talk: Rhetoric, Technology, Reproduction*, edited by Mary M. Lay, Laura J. Gurak, Clare Graven, and Cynthia Myntti, 184-206. Madison: University of Wisconsin Press, 2000.

Gonzalez, Jennifer. "The Appended Subject: Race and Identity as Digital Assemblage." In *Race in Cyberspace*, edited by Beth Kolka, Lisa Nakamura, and Gil Rodman, 27-50. New York: Routledge, 2000.

Hansen, Mark B. N. *New Philosophy for New Media*. Cambridge, MA: MIT Press, 2004.

Haraway, Donna. "The Persistence of Vision." In Mirzoeff, *The Visual Culture Reader*, 677-684.

Johnson, Steven. *Interface Culture*. New York: Basic Books, 1997.

Kapsalis, Terri. "Making Babies the American Girl Way." In *Domain Errors! Cyberfeminist Practices*, edited by Maria Fernandez, Faith Wilding, and Michelle M. Wright, 223-234. New York: Autonomedia, 2002.

Koerber, Amy. "Postmodernism, Resistance, and Cyberspace: Making Rhetorical Spaces for Feminist Mothers on the Web." *Women's Studies in Communication* 24, no. 2 (2001): 218-40

Lesy, Michael, and Charles Van Schaick. *Wisconsin Death Trip*. New York: Anchor Books, 1991.

Manovich, Lev. *The Language of New Media*. Cambridge, MA: MIT Press, 2001.

Mirzoeff, Nicholas. "Invisible Empire: Embodied Spectacle and Abu Ghraib." *Radical History Review* 95 (2005): 21-44.

———. "The Subject of Visual Culture." In *The Visual Culture Reader*, 3-23.

Mirzoeff, Nicholas, ed. *The Visual Culture Reader*, 2nd ed. New York: Routledge, 2002.

Nakamura, Lisa. *Cybertypes: Race, Identity, and Ethnicity on the Internet*. New York: Routledge, 2002.

Phelan, Peggy. *Unmarked: The Politics of Performance*. New York: Routledge, 1993.

Pinney, Christopher. "Notes from the Surface of the Image: Photography, Postcolonialism, and Vernacular Modernism." In Pinney and Peterson, *Photography's Other Histories*, 202-220.

Pinney, Christopher, and Nicolas Peterson, eds. *Photography's Other Histories*. Durham, NC: Duke University Press, 2003.

Rodowick, David Norman. *Reading the Figural; or, Philosophy after the New Media: Post-Contemporary Interventions*. Durham, NC: Duke University Press, 2001.

"The Silence." *Six Feet Under*. HBO, aired July 18, 2005.

Slater, Don. "Domestic Photography and Digital Culture." In *The Photographic Image in Digital Culture*, edited by Martin Lister, 129–146. New York: Routledge, 1995.

Sontag, Susan. *Regarding the Pain of Others*. New York: Farrar, Straus and Giroux, 2003.

Sparke, Penny. *As Long as It's Pink: The Sexual Politics of Taste*. San Francisco: Pandora, 1995.

Sprague, Stephen F. "Yoruba Photography: How the Yoruba See Themselves." In Pinney and Peterson, *Photography's Other Histories*, 240–260.

Squires, Judith. "Fabulous Feminist Futures and the Lure of Cyberspace." In Bell and Kennedy, *The Cybercultures Reader*, 360–373.

Stabile, Carol. *Feminism and the Technological Fix*. New York: St. Martin's Press, 1994.

Star, Susan Leigh. "From Hestia to Home Page: Feminism and the Concept of Home in Cyberspace." In Bell and Kennedy, *The Cybercultures Reader*, 632–643.

Wakeford, Nina. "Networking Women and Grrrls with Information/Communication Technology." In Bell and Kennedy, *The Cybercultures Reader*, 350–359.

Walker, Rob. "Hyperreality Hobbying." *New York Times Magazine*, February 20, 2005, 22.

———. "Sophisticated Baby." *New York Times Magazine*, July 24, 2005, 20.

Weil, Elizabeth. "The Modernist Nursery." *New York Times Magazine*, November 26, 2004, 72–75.

"OH NO! I'M A NERD!"
Hegemonic Masculinity on an Online Forum

Lori Kendall[1]

Every day, on an online forum called BlueSky,[2] a group of young people gather to chat, joke with each other, exchange work-related information, and "hang out." Starting at around 10:00 a.m. Pacific time and ending very late at night, people enter and leave the electronic space, exchanging greetings and taking their leave in the casual, friendly manner of people visiting their local pub. The conversation on BlueSky ebbs and flows as people "go idle" to attend to work or other tasks, then return their attention to their computer screens and to more active participation in the ongoing electronic dialogue.

In this article, I present findings based on my research on BlueSky. I discuss BlueSky participants' online performances of gendered and raced identities. Participants interpret their own and others' identities within the context of expectations and assumptions derived from offline US culture, as well as from their membership in various computer-related subcultures. Given the predominance of white men on BlueSky, such identity interpretations also rely on expectations concerning masculinity and whiteness. BlueSky identity performances provide information pertaining not just to online interaction but also to the social construction of gendered and raced identities more generally.

---

1 Editors' note: this paper was previously published in *Gender & Society* 14, no.2 (2000): 256–274. doi:10.1177/089124300014002003.
2 I have changed all names in this article, including the name of the mud and character names. I have replaced character names with names drawn from similar sources and references to retain some of the flavor of the originals. I refer throughout to BlueSky participants by these character names because, for the most part, they also refer to each other using character names rather than real-life names.

Doing Research on BlueSky

BlueSky is a type of interactive, text-only, online forum known as a "mud." Mud originally stood for Multi-User Dungeon (based on the original multiperson networked dungeons-and-dragons type game called MUD). As in other online chat programs, people connect to mud programs through Internet accounts and communicate through typed text with other people currently connected to that mud. There are hundreds of muds available on the Internet and through private online services. Many muds serve as gaming spaces for adventure or "hack-and-slash" games. Muds also operate as locations for professional meetings, classes, and other pedagogical purposes and as social spaces. Although participants have programmed various toys and games for use within BlueSky, BlueSky functions primarily as a social meeting space.

I began my research on muds after about a year of online experience (which did not include experience on muds). BlueSky was one of many muds I visited during the first few weeks of my research. I eventually focused the research solely on BlueSky, although still spending some time each week on other muds. From the beginning of my participation on BlueSky, I informed other participants that I was conducting research and often solicited comments from them regarding my interpretations.

I refer to my online research methodology as participant-observation despite the fact that my participation consisted largely of reading and writing online text. In contrast to studies of e-mail lists or newsgroups, the forum I studied involved near-synchronous communication (meaning that messages are passed back and forth more quickly and in a more conversational style than in e-mail or bulletin board systems). During my participation, I experienced the online conversations just as the participants did, going through a learning process and acclimation to the medium like any other "newbie." My own experiences during this learning process provided me with important information about the nature of online textual communication. Unlike researchers studying previously produced online text, I had a stake in ongoing conversations. Joining the group and engaging in the same activities as other participants also allowed me to ask questions on the spot and to gain a feel for the timing and rhythm of communications.

Like participant-observers and ethnographers of other types of groups, I gradually became a member of the social group, learning both technical aspects of online communication and social norms that enabled me to continue my participation. While I was not able to observe facial and bodily gestures (except during offline group meetings and interviews), I did learn the social contexts for the text produced on BlueSky and also learned BlueSky participants' own methods for compensating for the lack of physical contact and "given-off" information.

I continued my participant-observation on BlueSky for more than two years, during which time I spent between 10 and 20 hours per week online. In addition to observing and participating in day-to-day conversations and interaction on BlueSky, I also conducted brief informal interviews with several participants online. Examples of online conversations in this article are taken from the thousands of pages of participation logs that I gathered while online through a feature of the program allowing me to record all text that appeared on my screen. Multiple conversations often occur simultaneously on the mud, making log segments long and confusing to read. I have therefore edited the log excerpts provided herein, removing portions of other conversations. However, I have left individual lines of text as originally expressed by participants. Each individual's contribution to a conversation begins with their online name. Since text from each participant only appears on other participants' screens when the participant finishes typing the line and hits the "enter" key, individual lines on muds tend to be short.

In addition to spending time with BlueSky people online, I've met them and other mudders offline for social activities and gatherings. I supplemented my participant-observation on BlueSky with many hours on several other social muds and by reading various online resources relating to muds, including Usenet newsgroup and e-mail list postings. In addition, I also conducted 30 in-depth face-to-face interviews with BlueSky participants in several US cities. As is common in ethnographic studies, my interview questions arose out of my experiences online. The interviews allowed me to more directly compare my understanding of BlueSky with that of other participants, to ask more detailed questions than is easily possible on the mud, to address sensitive and serious topics (sometimes difficult to bring up in the often raucous atmosphere of BlueSky), to obtain further information about participants' offline lives and relationships, and to compare my impressions of their offline identity performances with their online presentations of self.

Many of the people who connect to BlueSky have been mudding for more than seven years and have formed relationships with each other that often extend offline. Most are sophisticated computer users, many of whom work with computers as programmers or system administrators. Almost all come from middle-class backgrounds, and the majority are white, young, male, and heterosexual. While more than 300 people occasionally connect to BlueSky, I determined 127 to be "regulars," based on level of participation and participants' own understanding of who constituted regulars of the social space. Approximately 27 percent of these regulars are female, and approximately 6 percent are Asian American. Most participants are in their mid- to late 20s. I am able to state these demographics with confidence owing to several factors, including my own offline meetings with participants, participants' frequent offline meetings with each other, participants' length of acquaintance, and

BlueSky norms regarding self-disclosure and congruity between online and offline presentations of self.

BlueSky, like many online forums, was established during the Internet's earlier years, when online participants were even more likely to be white, male, middle-class, and either associated with a university or working in a technical field. BlueSky participants have also resisted the entrance of newcomers into their group, especially in recent years. Thus, the percentage of women on BlueSky is even lower, at 27 percent, than that on the Internet generally. Like the Internet, BlueSky also remains predominantly white and middle class but may have a higher percentage of Asian American participants.[3]

Studying Identity Online

Text-based online communication, such as that which occurs on BlueSky, limits the communication of information about selves and identities to textual description only. Participants must learn to compensate for the lack of audio and visual cues and make choices about how to represent themselves. BlueSky participants use their years of experience with online communication and their familiarity with each other to compensate for the limitations of text-only communications. They have developed an elaborate subculture, using repeated patterns of speech and specialized features of the mud program to add the nuance and depth that such attributes as tone of voice and

---

3   I conducted two online searches for information regarding Internet demographics. In 1995, two sites provided information about race, listing white participants at 83 percent and 87 percent, respectively; both showed Black participation at 5 percent and Asian at 3 percent. Neither of those sites still exists, and none of the sites I reviewed during my later search (28 November 1997) provided information regarding race. That 1997 search indicates that approximately half of Internet users are age 35 or younger, and most have at least some college experience. More than 60 percent hold some form of professional, technical, managerial, or other white-collar job, with incomes clustering in the $30,000 to $90,000 range. Estimates of the percentage of women online vary from 31 percent to 45 percent. The following is a partial list of sites I reviewed for my November 1997 search: http://www2.chaicenter.org/otn/aboutinternet/Demographics-Nielsen.html; http://www3.mids.org/ids/index.html; http://thehost.com/demo.htm; http://www.scruznet.com/%7Eplugin01/Demo.html; http://www.cyberatlas.com/demographics.html; http://www.ora.com/research/users/results.html; and http://www.cc.gatech.edu/gvu/user_surveys/survey-1997-04. Most of the surveys reported at these sites are done by commercial organizations that do not always reveal their methodology. They also often reserve details and/or the most recent information for paying customers. Therefore, I cannot vouch for the reliability of these statistics.

gesture provide in face-to-face communication. Now fully acclimated to the medium, they experience their online conversations as very similar to face-to-face interaction.

Researchers such as Candace West and Sarah Fenstermaker have emphasized the importance of understanding how "all social exchanges, regardless of the participants or the outcome, are simultaneously 'gendered,' 'raced,' and 'classed.'"[4] (Such exchanges are also importantly characterized by other aspects of identity such as sexuality and age.) Despite frequent avowals to the contrary in various media, these aspects of identity characterize online social exchanges as well as face-to-face interaction. However, because taken-for-granted visual cues are unavailable in online text-based communication, people must make choices about what to reveal about themselves, how to describe themselves, and how to evaluate others' identity information and descriptions.

The limitations and special factors of online interaction can thus make participants more conscious of both their own identity performances and their evaluation of others' identity performances. Studying relations of dominance and difference online, where appearance cues are hidden, can yield further insights into the workings of the social processes by which identity understandings are created, maintained, and/or changed.

For instance, Michael Omi and Howard Winant point out that "one of the first things we notice about people when we meet them (along with their sex) is their race," and that based on our cultural knowledge of racial differences, we make assumptions based on those appearances that we notice and classify as relating to race.[5] "We expect differences in skin color, or other racially coded characteristics, to explain social differences."[6] One might expect, then, that in a social environment in which people encounter and interact with others without being able to see them, that online participants would not make gendered, raced, and classed assumptions about others whom they encounter. Certainly many online participants, in keeping with the predominance of the ideal of "color blindness" in our society, claim that this is the case.

Yet, gender and race are concepts "which signif[y] and symboliz[e] social conflicts and interests by *referring* to different types of human bodies."[7] The importance of such signification and symbolization continues in online interaction. The bodies of others may remain hidden and inaccessible, but this

---

4   Candace West and Sarah Fenstermaker, "Doing Difference," *Gender & Society*, no. 9 (1995): 13, doi:10.1177/089124395009001002.

5   Michael Omi and Howard Winant, *Racial Formation in the United States from the 1960s to the 1990s*, 2nd ed. (New York: Routledge, 1994), 59.

6   Ibid., 60.

7   Ibid., 55. Emphasis added.

if anything gives references to such bodies even more social importance. As Omi and Winant explain, "Despite its uncertainties and contradictions, the concept of race continues to play a fundamental role in structuring and representing the social world."[8] This remains true about race, as well as about gender, class, sexuality, and age, especially when that uncertainty is compounded by the lack of physical presence in online encounters. Online participants assume that other participants do have bodies and that those bodies, if seen, would reveal important information. The assumed congruence between certain types of bodies and certain psychological, behavioral, and social characteristics results in the expectation by online participants that aspects of the hidden bodies—of, in effect, other participants' "true" identities—can be deduced (if imperfectly) from what is revealed online.

BlueSky participants told me that they hold in reserve their evaluations of people online until able to check these through an offline meeting. In cases where offline identities do not match online identities, they also attempt to explain having been fooled as to someone's true identity. Individual cases of mistaken identity require adjustment and explanation, demonstrating participants' expectations that essential, consistent identities are rooted in and connected to distinctly classifiable bodies. They expect that in most cases, the truth of these identities will come through in online communication, at least for those experienced in evaluating online identity performances.

Masculinities and Computer Technology

Masculinity does not constitute a single uniform standard of behavior but rather comprises a range of gender identities clustered around expectations concerning masculinity that R. W. Connell has termed *hegemonic masculinity*. Connell defines hegemonic masculinity as the "configuration of gender practice which embodies the currently accepted answer to the problem of the legitimacy of patriarchy, which guarantees (or is taken to guarantee) the dominant position of men and the subordination of women."[9] While few men actually embody the hegemonic masculine ideal, they nevertheless benefit from the patriarchal dividend of dominance over women. However, they must also negotiate their own relationship to that ideal.

This negotiation, as well as the performance of specific masculinities, occurs through interaction with others. As James W. Messerschmidt points out, "Masculinity is never a static or a finished product. Rather, men construct masculinities in specific social situations."[10] Lynne Segal also describes

---

8   Ibid.
9   R. W. Connell, *Masculinities* (Berkeley: University of California Press, 1995), 77.
10 James W. Messerschmidt, *Masculinities and Crime: Critique and Reconceptualization of Theory* (Lanham, MD: Rowman & Littlefield, 1993), 31.

masculinity as emerging through relations with others and as relational by definition:

> As it is represented in our culture, "masculinity" is a quality of being which is always incomplete, and which is equally based on a social as on a psychic reality. It exists in the various forms of power men ideally possess: the power to assert control over women, over other men, over their own bodies, over machines and technology.[11]

Perhaps the most salient of these forms of masculine power for the men on BlueSky is that over technology. Not all BlueSky participants work with computers, but even most of those who do not work in computer-related fields have done so in the past. In addition to their socializing on BlueSky, many participants employ computers for other leisure uses, including playing computer games on their home computers and participating in networked games available on the Internet.

As such, BlueSky participants enact a form of masculinity congruent with computer culture, itself a largely masculine domain.[12] Rosemary Wright discusses the particular style of masculinity in both engineering and computer culture as "requiring aggressive displays of technical self-confidence and hands-on ability for success, defining professional competence in hegemonically masculine terms and devaluing the gender characteristics of women."[13] Many conversations on BlueSky revolve around topics relating to computers, including information concerning new software, planned purchases, technical advice, and so on. In my interviews, many participants stressed the importance of the computer work-related information they obtained on BlueSky. During the day, people frequently log on with a particular question or problem from work that the others on BlueSky help them solve. Through these interactions, participants demonstrate technical knowledge and reinforce a group identity connected to computer technology. This also connects

---

11   Lynne Segal, *Slow Motion: Changing Masculinities, Changing Men* (New Brunswick, NJ: Rutgers University Press, 1990), 123.

12   E. Spertus, "Why Are There So Few Female Computer Scientists?" *AI Lab Technical Report*, 1991, http://www.ai.mit.edu/people/ellens/gender/why.html; Sherry Turkle, *The Second Self: Computers and the Human Spirit* (New York: Simon & Schuster, 1984) and "Computational Reticence: Why Women Fear the Intimate Machine," in *Technology and Women's Voices: Keeping in Touch*, ed. Cheris Kramarae (New York: Routledge, 1988), 33-49; Ellen Ullman, "Out of Time: Reflections on the Programming Life," in *Resisting the Virtual Life: The Culture and Politics of Information*, ed. James Brook and Iain A. Boal (San Francisco: City Lights, 1995), 131-143.

13   Rosemary Wright, "The Occupational Masculinity of Computing," in *Masculinities in Organizations*, ed. Cliff Cheng (Thousand Oaks, CA: Sage, 1996), 86.

the group identity to masculinity since, as Cynthia Cockburn states, "Technology enters into our sexual identity: femininity is incompatible with technological competence; to feel technically competent is to feel manly."[14]

"How Did I Get So Nerdy?"

While their computer skills help BlueSky participants gain and maintain employment and their connections with computers have cultural cachet as well, US culture regards computer expertise and those who hold it ambivalently. This ambivalence extends particularly to the perceived gender identity of people skilled in computer use. American ambivalence about computers centers on the figure of the "nerd." For instance, Sherry Turkle discusses the self-perception of MIT students as nerds by virtue of their connection to technology; she argues that MIT computer science students are "the ostracized of the ostracized" and "archetypal nerds."[15] However, in her discussion of Turkle's descriptions, Judy Wajcman points out that:

> *an obsession with technology may well be an attempt by men who are social failures to compensate for their lack of power. On the other hand, mastery over this technology does bestow some power on these men; in relation to other men and women who lack this expertise, in terms of the material rewards this skill brings, and even in terms of their popular portrayal as "heroes" at the frontiers of technological progress.*[16]

The growing pervasiveness of computers in work and leisure activities has changed many people's relationship to computers and thus has also changed some of the meaning of the term *nerd*. Its use as a pejorative term thus varies in meaning depending on the social context. As an in-group term, it can convey affection or acceptance. Even when used pejoratively to support structures of hegemonic masculinity, it can confer grudging respect for technical expertise.

Many BlueSky participants possess personal or social characteristics that fit the nerd stereotype. As represented in the Nerdity Test, available online, such characteristics include fascination with technology, interest in science fiction and related media such as comic books, and perceived or actual social ineptitude and sartorial disorganization.[17] BlueSky participants illus-

---

14 Cynthia Cockburn, *Machinery of Dominance: Women, Men and Technical Know-How* (London: Pluto, 1985), 12.
15 Turkle, *The Second Self*, 197–98.
16 Judy Wajcman, *Feminism Confronts Technology*, (University Park: Pennsylvania State University Press, 1991), 144.
17 The Nerdity Test is available on the World Wide Web at, among other places, http://165.91.72.200/nerd-backwards.html.

trate their recognition of the nerd as both a desirable and marginal masculine identity in their discussions about nerd identity, as exemplified by the following statements culled from several different conversations on BlueSky. (Each of the lines below is presented as it appeared on my screen. Note that all caps in online discourse generally connotes shouting.)

> *Ulysses looks in henri's glasses and sees his reflection, and exclaims "Oh NO! I'm a NERD!"*
>
> *Mender says "when you publish please feel free to refer to me as 'nerdy but nice'" Jet says, "HOW DID I GET SO NERDY"*
>
> *Randy <-- fits one of the standard nerd slots*

In the above quotes, BlueSky participants humorously identify themselves as nerds and connect with each other through play with that identity. But they also indicate their understanding that this disqualifies them from a more hegemonic masculine identity. Ulysses's mock dismay at his nerdy looks and the "but" in Mender's phrase "nerdy but nice" indicate their evaluations of the nerd identity as not completely desirable.

"Didja Spike 'Er?": Heterosexual Masculinity Online

As Segal points out, "'Gender' and 'sexuality' are at present conceptually interdependent" and "provide two of the most basic narratives through which our identities are forged and developed."[18] Understandings of one's own and others' gender identities include assumptions about sexuality. While not all BlueSky participants are heterosexual, heterosexuality is an important component of the particular style of masculinity enacted on BlueSky. However, in this forum in which relationships are based so heavily on "talk," talk about sex and about men and women not surprisingly becomes more important to acceptable masculine performance than avowed conformity to particular sexual desires, practices, or relationships.

For instance, two very active and well-respected BlueSky male regulars define themselves as bisexual. One of these has never had a sexual relationship with a man. The other had a relationship with another male mudder (who only rarely appears on BlueSky), which was known about and accepted by most other BlueSky participants. Both of these BlueSky regulars currently live with women in long-term relationships. Neither is viewed by other BlueSky men as having strayed very far from heterosexuality. However, it is also worth noting that they very actively participate in jokes and conversations depicting women as sexual objects as well as in other forms of BlueSky banter connected to the performance of masculinity.

---

18   Lynne Segal, *Straight Sex: The Politics of Pleasure* (London: Virago, 1994), 268–69.

In keeping with acceptable performance of hegemonic masculinity, both men and women on BlueSky distance themselves from femininity and, to some extent, from women in general. Conversations that refer to women outside the mud, particularly women in whom a male participant might have a romantic interest, bluntly depict such women as sexual objects. However, participants' allusions to sexual activity are so out of context to the circumstances described that these references incorporate a high degree of irony. Participants further enhance this irony through the use of formulaic joking patterns, as in the following variations on the question, "Didja spike her?" culled from three separate conversations.

> *Mender says "did I mention the secretary babe smiled at me today"*
>
> *Roger Pollack WOO WOO*
>
> *Jet says "cool Mender"*
>
> *Jet says "did you spike 'er"*
>
> *Mender says "No, sir, I did not spike 'er."*
>
> ***
>
> *McKenzie wonders if he should continue this e-mail correspondence or just wait till he can meet her tomorrow*
>
> *McKenzie siigh*
>
> *Locutus says "meet whom"*
>
> *Locutus shouts into a microphone, "SPIKE HER"*
>
> ***
>
> *Locutus had a short conversation with a 50–55 year old wrinkly well dressed woman in the wine section of the grocery*
>
> *Mender says "didja spike 'er, Locutus?"*
>
> *Rimmer says "DIDJA SPIKE HER LOCUTUS"*
>
> *Locutus says "hell no"*

In each of these conversations, mere mention of a woman provokes the formulaic question, "Didja spike her?" Such joking formulas constitute techniques of group identity construction. Through jokes regarding women's status as sexual objects, the men on BlueSky demonstrate support for hegemonic masculinity. As Peter Lyman explains, "The emotional structure of the male bond is built upon a joking relationship that 'negotiates' the tension men feel about their relationships with each other, and with women."[19]

---

19 Peter Lyman, "The Fraternal Bond As a Joking Relationship: A Case Study of the Role of Sexist Jokes in Male Group Bonding," in *Men's Lives*, ed. Michael S.

The ironic sexism of much BlueSky discourse maintains "the order of gender domination"[20] almost irrespective of other aspects of BlueSky men's activities and behaviors with and toward the women in their lives.

However, the joking quality of the "didja spike her?" conversations also suggests an uneasiness with hegemonic masculinity. During a period when several participants had read a piece I had written analyzing references to gender on BlueSky (which did not include a discussion of the term *spike*), Rimmer asked me about "spike her" references. (My online name is Copperhead in the following example.)

> *Rimmer says "So if I now said to Locutus 'So did you SPIKE her?' would that be offensive?"*
>
> *Copperhead does find the "did you SPIKE her" stuff a bit offensive, actually*
>
> *Rimmer says "Wow; the SPIKE stuff wouldn't be funny if there was any chance in hell that anyone ever would"*
>
> *henri nods at rimmer*
>
> *Locutus says "the 'didja spike her' joke brings up the whole 'women as conquest' idea"*
>
> *Rimmer says "Boy I don't think it's a woman as conquest thing at all"*
>
> *henri says "what you find offensive (and I agree) is people thinking any time a guy interacts with a woman they should ask if their pants fell off and they locked hips"*
>
> *Rimmer says "I think it's more of a 'Mudders never have sex' thing"*
>
> *McKenzie agrees with Rimmer, "asking 'didja SPIKE her' is more parody than anything else"*
>
> *Rimmer doesn't think he's ever asked "DIDJA SPIKE HER" and expected someone to actually say YES*
>
> *Rimmer says "It would be tacky as all hell in that case"*
>
> *McKenzie says "actually everyone would say 'I HATE you'"*

Rimmer points out the joking nature of the question, "Didja spike her?" His assertion that "the SPIKE stuff wouldn't be funny if there was any chance in hell that anyone ever would" specifically highlights the mildly mocking intent of the joke. Yet, as Locutus and henri recognize, "spike" references rely on the continuing portrayal of women as sexual objects. Women's

---

Kimmel and Michael A. Messner, 4th ed. (Boston: Allyn & Bacon, 1998), 173.
20 Ibid., 172.

unattainability as sexual objects to some men provides the sting in the self-deprecatory joke, leaving in place a normative expectation that masculinity involves the sexual possession of women and that this is a desirable norm to attain. Rimmer and McKenzie indicate this in their identification of "didja spike her" as a rhetorical question. Rimmer states that "mudders never have sex" and suggests that they would not talk about it if they did since the other "less fortunate" participants would, as McKenzie indicates, say, "I HATE you." The joke is intended to be on the participants themselves, regarding their nonhegemonic masculinity, but women are the true butts of the joke.

BlueSky participants' sexual practices also may diverge from the aggressive hegemonic model implied by "spike." The potential discrepancy between sexual practice and group identity practice demonstrates some of the dilemmas involved in negotiating masculinities. Like adolescent boys who feel compelled to invent sexual exploits about which they can brag, men in groups create sexual and gender narratives that may bear little resemblance to other aspects of their lived experience but that nevertheless comprise important elements of their masculine identities and their connections with other men.

"Blubbery Pale Nerdettes": Nerds, Gender, and Sexuality

BlueSky discussions also demonstrate the dilemma that nerd identity introduces into the connection between gender identity and sexuality. Nerdism in both men and women is held to decrease sexual attractiveness, but in men this is compensated by the relatively masculine values attached to intelligence and computer skills. In women, lack of sexual attractiveness is a far greater sin. This is demonstrated in the following excerpt of a conversation about attendance at science fiction fan conventions among several male BlueSky participants.

> *Mike Adams says "that's half the reason I go to cons. Sit and have these discussions with people"*
>
> *Bob . o O (No it isn't)*
>
> *Mike Adams says "well, okay it's to ogle babes in barbarian outfits"*
>
> *Drog says "*BABES*?"*
>
> *Drog says "you need new glasses"*
>
> *Drog says "pasty skinned blubbery pale nerdettes"*
>
> *Locutus laaaaaughs*
>
> *Locutus says "ARRRRR 'tis the WHITE WHAAALE"*

> *Drog wouldn't pork any women he's ever seen at gaming/other cons, not even with Bob's cock.*
>
> *Perry says "that's because pork is not kosher, drog"*
>
> *Locutus says "women-met-at-cons: the Other White Meat"*
>
> *Perry LAUGHS*
>
> *Drog HOWLS at locutus*

While apparently quite misogynistic, the impetus for this conversation relates at least as much to the BlueSky love of wordplay (another nerdy pastime) as to negative attitudes toward women. The word choices and the source of the humor in the above banter also reveal some key assumptions about and perceptions of nerd identity. Besides the implication in Drog's description that female nerds, like their male counterparts, do not spend much time outdoors or engage in exercise, his and Locutus's statements also represent nerds as white. While the term *nerd* may be applied to nonwhite males who meet other nerd identity criteria, the ideal-typical nerd is white.[21] Similarly, nerds are presumed male, as evidenced by the term *nerdette*. This term, like use of the phrase "lady doctor," defines the normative case of nerd as not female.

This connection between nerdism and masculinity may be what makes a nerd identity so damaging to women's potential and perceived sexual desirability. The participants express the assumption that nerdettes who would attend science fiction conventions by definition lack sexual desirability and quickly join in the joke set by Drog's critique of Mike Adams's potentially transgressive desire. Mike Adams, on the other hand, ceased further participation in the conversation until the topic of cons had passed.

Heterosexual "Dropouts"

Some of the ways in which BlueSky participants enact and express heterosexual identities suggest that in examining connections between sexualities and masculinities, we need to problematize notions of heterosexuality as a single, uniform sexual identity. A standard Kinsey-style spectrum of straight to gay identities based on sexual behaviors or feelings does not adequately describe sexual identity on BlueSky, as it leaves out important information concerning affectional connections and orientation toward sexuality in general. As Segal states, "It is men's fear of, or distaste for, sex with women, as well-known as it is well concealed, that the heterosexual imperative works

---

[21] See, e.g., Cliff Cheng, "'We Choose Not to Compete': The 'Merit' Discourse in the Selection Process, and Asian and Asian-American Men and their Masculinity," in *Masculinities in Organizations*, 177–200.

so hard to hide."[22] Discussions of sexuality on BlueSky sometimes reveal this distaste, as well as the unorthodox solutions some men find for the dilemma imposed on them by the tension between distaste and hegemonic masculine identity, including its heterosexual component.

For instance, several of the straight men on BlueSky report that they have "given up" on women and/or on romantic relationships and have been celibate more or less by choice for several years. In discussions on BlueSky such as the one below, these men complain of rejection based on their nonhegemonic status.

> *Stomp has problems with dating and women and stuff, but also has serious reservations about the accepted male-female dynamic in the USA, to the point where he's never felt much point in getting over the first set of problems.*
>
> *Drog says "Sides, women LIKE scumbags; it's been proven"*
>
> *Ulysses nods at Drog*
>
> *Drog should have been gay, he can relate to other guys*
>
> *Stomp says "as far as I've been able to observe, abusing women (subtly) is one of the fastest and most efficient ways of getting laid."*
>
> *Drog will agree with that*
>
> *Stomp says "Once I realized this, I just sort of went: Well, forget it, then."*
>
> *Drog says "guys get to be assholish and abusive cause that kinda attitude is richly rewarded"*
>
> *Ulysses says "Nice guys end up being the friends to whom those women say, 'You're such a good listener, let me tell you about the latest horrible thing my inconsiderate sweetie did to me'"*
>
> *Stomp says "Expressing interest in a way that isn't assholish invites getting cut down brutally."*
>
> *Ulysses says "We tried opening our mouths a few times, and got laughed at"*
>
> *Ulysses says "End of experiment"*
>
> *Stomp says "You get seen as weak."*
>
> *Ulysses says "self-assurance and confidence are not options for me. I'd have to go back to infancy and start over"*

---

22 Segal, *Straight Sex*, 257.

> *Drog says "this mud is full of 'nice guys.' it's also full of guys who haven't been laid in epochs if ever"*

The male participants in the above conversation express considerable ambivalence toward predominant standards of masculinity, portraying themselves as "nice guys" left out of the standard (in their understanding) heterosexual dynamic of violent conquest. Yet, although they designate more sexually successful men as (by definition) "jerks," their discussion implies that the real problem is not with "assholish" men but rather with the women who like the abuse they get from such men. Rather than merely rejecting a heterosexuality they view as abusive, they represent themselves as reacting to having been "cut down brutally," "laughed at," and "seen as weak," as well as used as a sympathetic ear without regard for their own potential desires. Drog, Stomp, and Ulysses still represent themselves as heterosexual, despite their avowed lack of heterosexual activity. Heterosexuality remains an important component of their identities, interconnected as it is with hegemonic masculinity. In their retreat from heterosexual activity, Drog, Stomp, and Ulysses do not opt to ally themselves in friendship or identification with women. Instead, as Drog says, they "relate to other guys." BlueSky provides them with a sympathetic forum in which most other participants are men and the few women are less obviously women both because they cannot be seen and because they conform to BlueSky standards and expectations of behavior set by the men in the group.

The rather stereotypical depiction of women, as not only tolerating but also desiring abuse, points to some potential interpretations of the male angst expressed. Hegemonic masculinity's requirement of heterosexuality contains an inherent contradiction. As Lyman points out:

> *The separation of intimacy from sexuality transforms women into "sexual objects," which both justifies aggression at women by suspending their relationships to the men and devalues sexuality itself, creating a disgust of women as the sexual "object" unworthy of intimate attention.*[23]

While the hegemonic gender order thus depicts women as inferior and not acceptable identity models, it nevertheless requires that men desire these inferior (even disgusting) creatures. The men in the conversation above represent casualties of this contradiction. Their discomfort blends a rejection of perceived expectations regarding hegemonic masculinity—especially those involving violence toward women—with a more hegemonically congruent discomfort with women themselves.

---

23 Lyman, "Fraternal Bond," 178.

"Mov[ing] Well in Caucasian Spaces"

Given online demographics, participants tend to assume that others they encounter online are white. As RaveMage, a Filipino American participant, stated, "All the males [on BlueSky] are caucasian or move well in caucasian spaces," implicitly recognizing BlueSky itself as a "caucasian space." Whiteness thus becomes the "default" identity. In addition, as revealed in the discussion of nerdettes above, whiteness is connected to the particular subcultural nerd identity. Aspects of nerdiness come to signify whiteness as well.

For instance, Jet, a very active regular on BlueSky for several years, complicates his Chinese American identity by often referring to himself online as white. Other BlueSky participants know that his parents emigrated from China, and discussions of his Chinese heritage also occur. When I asked Jet about his self-defining as white, he talked about how whiteness marks a cultural identity as well as a racial distinction. (Our conversation occurred through "whispers," meaning that the online text was viewed only by Jet and I and not by other participants on the mud.)

> *Copperhead whispers "several times when questions of ethnicity or race have come up you've made the statement that you're white; I'm wondering what you mean by that."*
>
> *Jet whispers "I mean that I am essentially an american clothed in a chinese body. I hardly know how to speak chinese, I hardly know anything about the culture, and I don't associate with orientals a lot by choice, unlike many immigrant children. So I feel 'white,' i.e. american"*
>
> *Copperhead whispers "so if 'american'= 'white' is BlueSky a white space? And what does that mean for people who aren't white here?"*
>
> *Jet whispers "no no, american != white.[24] i use 'white' in the sense of the martin mull stereotype; very bland, whitebread; obviously i'm not. it's a sort of irony."*
>
> *Jet whispers "mudding transcends ethnicity. i don't consider blue sky 'white' or 'american' or any ethnicity, I just consider it a place to hang out. if you were all asian and had the same personalities, so be it"*

While Jet refers to his own "cultural whiteness," he denies cultural effects of race or ethnicity through his suggestion that it would be possible for BlueSky participants to be "all asian" and yet have "the same personalities." This elision of the cultural aspects of race, which his ironic labeling of himself as white both contradicts and highlights, enables him to claim that "mudding

---

24 The exclamation point and equals sign in this phrase come from programming languages in which != means "not equal to."

transcends ethnicity." On one hand, Jet suggests that the physical characteristics associated with race do not determine identity. Although acknowledging his ethnic heritage in some ways (at one point during this conversation, he stated, for instance, that he would prefer to marry another Asian American) and labeling his body Chinese, Jet labels himself white based on the cultural affinities that he finds more salient. However, in calling himself white, he still gives his (cultural) identity a racial label. Although he denies that American equals white, he nevertheless labels his American-ness "white." Jet's representation of himself as white serves as a "racial project," which, in Omi and Winant's words, forms both "an interpretation, representation, or explanation of racial dynamics, and an effort to reorganize and redistribute resources along particular racial lines."[25] In Jet's case, his representation of himself as white reinforces the dominant order in which benefits accrue to those who are white. But he also attempts to reposition himself as entitled to those benefits because beneath the "clothing" of his Chinese body, he is "really" white.

In recognition of the ironic contradictions involved in his self-identity, Jet associates true whiteness with "bland, whitebread." White participants on BlueSky also make this association. For instance, Peg, a white female regular, classified herself as "pretty white, but not wonder-bread, [my] father's family are eastern europeans." By referring to "real" whiteness as "wonder-bread" (bland, nonnutritious, over-processed), Peg distances herself from hegemonic white identity. This sets up a hierarchy of whiteness in which only full-blooded WASPs qualify as "really" white. Those who, like her, have other European ancestry are only "pretty" white. Jet's similar reference to "bland whitebread" allows him to be white too, even though he is not "really" white.

Both participants mark themselves with an ironically detached white-but-not-white identity. However, they arrive at this identity formulation from very different offline physical realities. Peg is short and petite, with very pale skin and light reddish-brown hair. Jet is more than six feet tall and thin with light brown skin and almost black hair. That I can so describe them, and experience their similar self-identification as ironic, points to assumptions concerning the physical nature of racial identity that I, like the other BlueSky participants, have internalized from the surrounding culture.

In the following conversation, several participants, drawing on this physical understanding of race, contest Jet's self-definition as white.

> *Jet rather enjoyed the LA riots in a sick way*
>
> *Jet went to Canter's 3 days afterwards, and there was us, 4 white guys, and 12 cops*
>
> *Jet says "That's it."*

---
25   Omi and Winant, *Racial Formation*, 56.

Jet says "(we were the 4 white guys)"
Mender. o 0 (Jet's a white guy!)
Ichi giggles at Jet
Jet . o 0 (oh i am)
Jet says "You've met me, you know I'm white"
Mender says "not as white as I am, bucko"
Pyramid says "HOW WHITE ARE YOU?"
McKenzie says "Mender gets waspy"
Jet says "I'm pretty white"
Jet says "no joke"

Mender's claim to be whiter than Jet provokes an accusation of "waspiness" from McKenzie. As with Peg's definition of herself as only "pretty white," this stance labels the aggressive assertion of white identity as waspiness, again relying on an understanding that white Anglo-Saxon protestants represent hegemonic whiteness. Just as male participants on BlueSky distance themselves in some ways from hegemonic masculinity, white participants distance themselves from hegemonic white identity. Like the ironic references to hegemonic masculinity contained in the "didja spike 'er" jokes, BlueSky discussions of whiteness disavow identification with the very top of the dominance chain, yet ultimately leave intact the taken-for-granted workings of racial dominance found in American society.

These discussions about racial identity online emphasize both the absence and the presence of race online. Paul Gilroy argues that race and racism are processes and that the meanings of race "are unfixed and subject to the outcomes of struggle."[26] We learn to classify people by skin color and other physical identifiers and learn to associate these identifiers with race. Hence, I can easily point to Peg and label her white and to Jet and label him Asian. But the meanings of these designations vary and are sites of struggle, as both Jet and Peg indicate in their self-identifications. When these struggles are brought online, some of their parameters change.

Jet's self-identification of white is challenged by other BlueSky participants. Having met him, they rely on their understanding of the physical nature of race to classify him based on bodily characteristics. Thus, participants bring their assumptions about race with them to online interactions. However, online participants perform racial identities under slightly different rules.

---

26 Paul Gilroy, *"There Ain't No Black in the Union Jack": The Cultural Politics of Race and Nation* (Chicago: University of Chicago Press, 1987), 24.

For instance, nonwhite participants can benefit from the predominant presumption of whiteness online. Spontaneity, a Chinese American, indicates that online interactions free him from fears of harassment.

> *Spontaneity whispers "I've noticed a lack of harassment on line in general."*
>
> *Copperhead whispers "that's interesting; less harassment online than off?"*
>
> *Spontaneity whispers "Yah. Now, it may just be that people are able to be more subtle online, but I don't think so. For example, it's fairly common for me to get shouted at on the streets."*

The high percentage of whites online combines with a US discourse of "color blindness," making direct references to race taboo.[27] This enables whites to assume that other online participants are also white. Since the space this potentially opens up for harassment-free speech from nonwhites remains defined as white, the advantage to nonwhites constitutes a form of "passing" for white rather than a true dissolution of racial difference and hierarchy. However, the lack of visual cues in text-based online spaces makes passing more feasible online than off. This does constitute some degree of "leveling the playing field" (although the type of game and its rules remain unquestioned).

Conclusion

The masculinities performed on BlueSky demonstrate the convergence and interaction of several important facets of identity, including class, gender, sexuality, race, age, and relationships to technology. US cultural expectations regarding technology usage converge with stereotypes concerning race and gender, resulting in a white nerd masculine identity congruent with related forms of masculinity found in computing and engineering fields. In enacting this form of masculinity, BlueSky participants demonstrate both its divergence from and convergence with hegemonic masculinity. Participants recognize their lack of hegemonic status and poke fun at some aspects of hegemonic masculinity. However, they also distance themselves from women and from femininity and engage in a style of interaction congruent with hegemonic masculinity. The coupling of expectations of technological competence with this predominant interactional mode of obnoxious bantering strengthens connections between computer technological competence and masculinities.

---

27 R. Frankenberg, *White Women, Race Matters: The Social Construction of Whiteness* (Minneapolis: University of Minnesota Press, 1993), 14.

BlueSky participants diverge somewhat from hegemonic masculinity in their discussions of various aspects of sexuality. Several participants find their homosexual or bisexual orientation accepted within the group. However, both heterosexual and nonheterosexual men (and women) participate in conversations that depict women as sexual objects. This may indicate that at least for some men, distance from women comprises a more important component of masculine identity than sexual distance from men. Inclusion of homosexual and bisexual men who perform aspects of heterosexual masculinity (in that they also sexually objectify women) creates a social environment in which homosociality takes precedence over attitudes toward homosexuality.

This more inclusive stance may be particularly possible for men online. In text-based online communication, the lack of physical presence and awareness of each other's male bodies decreases the likelihood that gestures or utterances will be misconstrued as sexual advances or interest. Under such circumstances, heterosexual men may be able to more safely "pal around" with nonheterosexual men, at least as long as those men continue to perform a masculine identity congruent in the main with that of the heterosexual men.

Conversations on BlueSky concerning men, women, relationships, and sexuality also demonstrate some of the variation within heterosexual male identities. Heterosexual men may like or dislike the women they theoretically desire. They may spend time socially with women or mostly with other men. As in the examples of several of the BlueSky men, some heterosexual men also maintain a heterosexual identity without engaging in heterosexual relationships. For men such as Ulysses and Stomp, changing norms of masculinity have failed to resolve the contradiction inherent in hegemonic masculinity's relationship to women as both desired and disgusting objects. Such men view hegemonically masculine males as jerks, thereby distancing themselves from that ideal. However, they also view women as people who like those jerks. In this way, they distance themselves from women, representing them as foreign beings who unfathomably like abuse. This leaves these heterosexual dropouts with no company but their own and that of other, similarly not-quite-hegemonic men (and a few women who perform congruent identities). Through wryly ironic jokes about men, women, and sexuality, BlueSky participants create and enact a culture that continually reiterates this pattern of distancing from both other men and most women.

BlueSky's culture, formed by a predominantly white group, also draws from and reenacts white cultural norms of masculine behaviors. Here again, BlueSky participants distance themselves from the hegemonic ideal ("waspy" or "true" whiteness) but also continue to distance themselves from oppressed groups. The whiteness of BlueSky is reinforced by the larger cultural contexts in which it is embedded, including US and Internet cultures.

The predominance of whites online, combined with US norms of color blindness, leads to assumptions that online participants are white unless stated otherwise. Thus, Asian Americans on BlueSky must either take a distinctly oppositional stance to the predominant norm of whiteness or themselves perform versions of white masculinity to fit in with the group. For some, such as Spontaneity, presumptions of whiteness, combined with the unavailability in interaction of the physical markers of race, provide greater freedom from harassment. However, given BlueSky participants' knowledge of both online and offline identity information, Asian American men's status as "one of the white boys" can be challenged, as Jet found.

The relative inclusiveness of BlueSky is predicated on the continuation of a social structure in which white middle-class men continue to have the power to include or not to include people whose gender, sexuality, or race marks them as other. BlueSky's regulars include a few women, nonheterosexuals, and Asian Americans who fit themselves into BlueSky's cultural context through their performances of white masculinities. The text-only nature of much online communication can facilitate greater inclusiveness. However, as on BlueSky, many online groups also make offline connections with each other and bring knowledge from those meetings to their online interactions. The predominance of white men online can also limit that inclusiveness to "others" who can fit themselves into a culture formed by and for those white men.

Acknowledgements

I would like to thank Cliff Cheng, who encouraged me to write the original version of this article and gave me helpful feedback on it. For their very helpful comments and criticisms, I would also like to thank Judy Stacey, Vicki Smith, Beth Schneider, and three anonymous reviewers for *Gender & Society*.

Bibliography

Cheng, Cliff. "'We Choose Not to Compete': The 'Merit' Discourse in the Selection Process, and Asian and Asian-American Men and their Masculinity." In *Masculinities in Organizations*, 177–200.

Cheng, Cliff, ed. *Masculinities in Organizations*. Thousand Oaks, CA: Sage, 1996.

Cockburn, Cynthia. *Machinery of Dominance: Women, Men and Technical Know-How*. London: Pluto, 1985.

Connell, R. W. *Masculinities*. Berkeley: University of California Press, 1995.

Frankenberg, R. *White Women, Race Matters: The Social Construction of Whiteness*. Minneapolis: University of Minnesota Press, 1993.

Gilroy, Paul. *"There Ain't No Black in the Union Jack": The Cultural Politics of Race and Nation*. Chicago: University of Chicago Press, 1987.

Lyman, Peter. "The Fraternal Bond As a Joking Relationship: A Case Study of the Role of Sexist Jokes in Male Group Bonding." In *Men's Lives*, edited by Michael S. Kimmel and Michael A. Messner. 4th ed., 171–181. Boston: Allyn & Bacon, 1998.

Messerschmidt, James W. *Masculinities and Crime: Critique and Reconceptualization of Theory*. Lanham, MD: Rowman & Littlefield, 1993.

Omi, Michael, and Howard Winant. *Racial Formation in the United States from the 1960s to the 1990s*. 2nd ed. New York: Routledge Kegan Paul, 1994.

Segal, Lynne. *Slow Motion: Changing Masculinities, Changing Men*. New Brunswick, NJ: Rutgers University Press, 1990.

———. *Straight Sex: The Politics of Pleasure*. London: Virago, 1994.

Spertus, E. "Why Are There So Few Female Computer Scientists?" *AI Lab Technical Report*. 1991. http://www.ai.mit.edu/people/ellens/gender/why.html.

Turkle, Sherry. "Computational Reticence: Why Women Fear the Intimate Machine." In *Technology and Women's Voices: Keeping in Touch*, edited by Cheris Kramarae, 33–49. New York: Routledge Kegan Paul, 1988.

———. *The Second Self: Computers and the Human Spirit*. New York: Simon & Schuster, 1984.

Ullman, Ellen. "Out of Time: Reflections on the Programming Life." In *Resisting the Virtual Life: The Culture and Politics of Information*, edited by James Brook and Iain A. Boal, 131–143. San Francisco: City Lights, 1995.

Wajcman, Judy. *Feminism Confronts Technology*. University Park: Pennsylvania State University Press, 1991.

West, Candace, and Sarah Fenstermaker. "Doing Difference." *Gender & Society*, no. 9 (1995):8–37. doi:10.1177/089124395009001002.

Wright, Rosemary. "The Occupational Masculinity of Computing." In Cheng, *Masculinities in Organizations*, 77–96.

Part Four

Information Organization

How We Construct Subjects: A Feminist Analysis

Hope A. Olson[1]

The organization of information as practiced in catalogs, indexing and abstracting databases, and other tools of bibliographic control is primarily based on traditional or Aristotelian logic. The result is a linear, hierarchical structure made up of mutually exclusive categories. Feminists have critiqued logic, just as there has been criticism of the organization of information as gendered. This article examines traditional/Aristotelian logic and its feminist critiques together with principles and standards of the organization of information and its critiques. It is a first attempt at synthesis of these concepts. It takes threads from these various literatures and traditions and, although it may not weave a fabric, it may string the warp and suggest patterns for the weft.

Traditional/Aristotelian Logic

Logic has been called "the general science of inference,"[2] or as the *Oxford English Dictionary* elaborates, "the branch of philosophy that treats of the forms of thinking in general, and more especially of inference and of scientific method."[3] Traditional or Aristotelian logic is a philosophical practice that uses the concept of the categorical syllogism as a foundation. A categorical syllogism defines the relationships between categories such as:

> All human beings are mortal.
> *All Greeks are human beings.*
> Therefore, all Greeks are mortal.

---

1 Editors' note: this paper was previously published in *Library Trends* 56, no. 2 (2007): 509–541.
2 Simon Blackburn, *The Oxford Dictionary of Philosophy* (New York: Oxford University Press, 1994), 221.
3 *The Oxford English Dictionary*, s.v. "logic, n.," accessed March 24, 2013, http://www.oed.com/view/Entry/109788.

This syllogistic form implies a hierarchy: mortals make up a broad class containing the subclass of human beings, which in turn contains the sub-subclass Greeks. Or it may be expressed as a Venn diagram (See Figure 1).

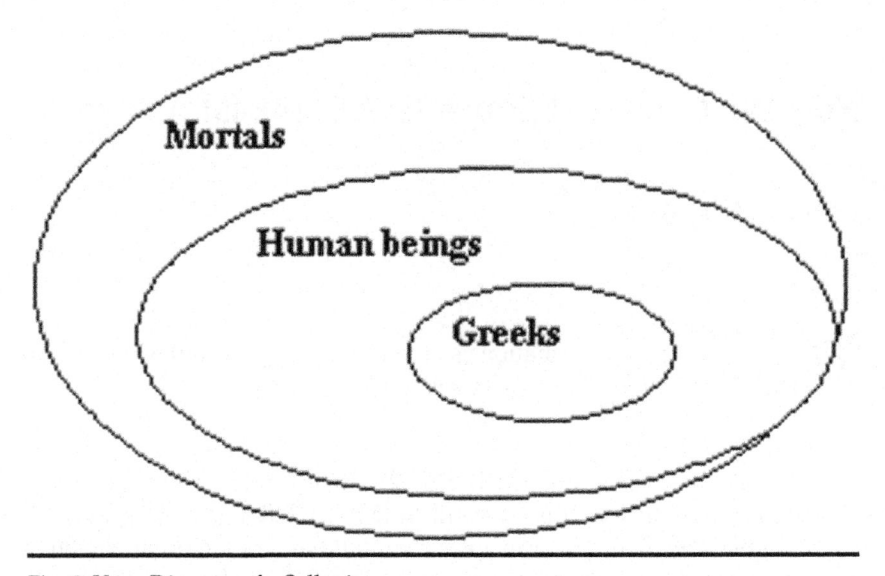

Fig. 1. Venn Diagram of a Syllogism

Alternatively, a categorical syllogism may define the relationships between categories and an individual instance such as:

>All human beings are mortal.
>*Socrates is a human being.*
>Therefore, Socrates is mortal.

A class or subclass will, of course, normally contain more than one individual or subclass, as indicated by the *Oxford English Dictionary*: "class, n. . . . 6. a. gen. A number of individuals (persons or things) possessing common attributes, and grouped together under a general or 'class' name; a kind, sort, division. (Now the leading sense.) b. in Logical classification."[4] The class mortals contains the subclass human beings, which contains groups such as Greeks and individuals such as Socrates.

Each of the first two statements in the syllogism is a premise:

>. . . *a statement of something about some subject.* . . . *This statement may be universal or particular or indefinite. By universal, I mean a statement which applies to all, or to none, of the subject; by particular a statement*

---

4   Ibid.

> *which applies to some, or does not apply to all; by indefinite, a statement which applies or does not apply without reference to universality or particularity.*[5]

The first statement in the categorical syllogism is a universal premise relating to "all" and the second is a particular premise relating to a particular group or individual. The third statement is the conclusion drawn from the two premises. This is the format of Aristotle's first form, the only form of syllogism that he deemed able to produce true conclusions.[6] It is also the basis for the hierarchy found in a conventional classificatory structure.

Key to the functioning of logic are the three "laws of thought":

- Law of Non-Contradiction: nothing can be both A and Not-A. e.g., *Nothing can be both mortal and Not-mortal.*
- Law of Identity: Whatever is A is A e.g., *Whatever is mortal is mortal.*
- Law of the excluded middle: Everything is either A or Not-A. e.g., *Everything is either mortal or Not-mortal.*[7]

These three laws taken together enforce the boundaries of classes so that classes are watertight and so that there is nothing left unaccounted for. Everything is either in or outside of any given class. This introduces further hierarchy in that everything is defined by being A or Not-A with A being privileged and Not-A being defined only by its relationship to A. The relationship between the two is, then, hierarchical in the sense that A is independent and dominant and Not-A is dependent and subordinate.

Traditional/Aristotelian logic focuses on deductive reasoning as epitomized by the syllogisms above. Deductive reasoning infers particular instances from the general/universal such as inferring that the particular class of persons, Greeks, or the particular individual, Socrates, is mortal because they are human beings. A weaker form of logic derives from inductive reasoning in which general or universal premises are inferred from a selection of particular cases. Because it is typically impossible to examine all possible cases, inferences from induction are not absolute. It is always possible that some exception exists. For example, if we depend on inductive logic, the fact that no human being with whom we are acquainted is not mortal, does not

---

5 Aristotle, *Prior Analytics*, in *The Organon*, trans. H. Tredennick (London: W. Heinemann, 1938), I.i.24a.

6 For more on Aristotelian logic and hierarchy, see Hope A. Olson, "Exclusivity, Teleology and Hierarchy: Our Aristotelian Legacy," *Knowledge Organization* 26, no. 2 (1999): 65–73.

7 For further explanation of this and other topics in logic, a useful source is A. W. Sparkes, *Talking Philosophy: A Wordbook* (London: Routledge, 1991).

mean that there is none. So, deductive reasoning, working from a universal truth to the specific instance, is certain. Inductive reasoning, working from the specific to the general, cannot incontrovertibly establish a universal truth. Thus, only deductive reasoning commands the full force of traditional/Aristotelian logic.

Feminist Critiques of Logic

Logic, in particular traditional logic, has been the object of feminist critique from various perspectives. As Susan Hekman summarizes it:

> [M]ost contemporary feminists agree on the diagnosis of this problem: since Plato, and most particularly since the Enlightenment, reason and rationality have been defined in exclusively masculine terms; the 'Man of Reason' is gendered, not generic.[8]

Andrea Nye, Luce Irigaray and Val Plumwood,[9] while voicing different views on what should be done, agree that "from Plato and Aristotle to Kant and beyond, the philosophical tradition of the west has delineated a concept of reason which is exclusive of women and other oppressed groups and is most fully represented by privileged social groups."[10]

In logic, the knowing subject (the person who achieves knowledge) is traditionally masculine, or, as Plumwood denotes him, "the master."[11] Reason has been the province of men since at least Aristotle, through Descartes and the Enlightenment and beyond with emotion being the province of women.[12] Emotion is excluded from any role in reason or logic, resulting in a familiar set of dichotomies, "Male / female" and "Reason / emotion," in which the two elements have a hierarchical relation to each other. The three laws of thought enforce these dichotomies, even though, as Nancy Jay points out, they are not truly contradictory:

---

8   Susan J. Hekman, *Gender and Knowledge: Elements of a Postmodern Feminism* (Oxford: Polity, 1995), 34. See also Marjorie Hass, "Feminist Readings of Aristotelian Logic," in *Feminist Interpretations of Aristotle*, ed. C. A. Freeland (University Park: Pennsylvania State University Press, 1998), 19–40.

9   Luce Irigaray, "The 'Mechanics' of Fluids," in *This Sex Which Is Not One*, trans. C. Porter (Ithaca, NY: Cornell University Press, 1985), 106–118; Andrea Nye, *Words of Power: A Feminist Reading of the History of Logic* (New York: Routledge, 1990); Val Plumwood, "The Politics of Reason: Towards a Feminist Logic," *Australasian Journal of Philosophy* 71 (1993): 436–62.

10 Plumwood, "The Politics of Reason," 436.

11 Ibid., 454.

12 G. Lloyd, "Reason as Attainment," in *A Reader in Feminist Knowledge*, ed. S. Gunew, (London: Routledge, 1991), 174; Plumwood, "The Politics of Reason," 437.

> *Although gender distinctions are regularly dichotomous, they do not always carry out the full implications of form A/Not-A phrasing. When they are so phrased, men and women are conceived of in ways that cannot be a consequence only of conceptualization and reinforcement of empirical distinctions between them. Concepts of femaleness and maleness come into being that have nothing whatever to do with human sexual differences, but follow from the nature of contradictory dichotomy itself....*
>
> *To begin with, all dichotomous distinctions are not necessarily phrased as A/Not-A. Consider some differences between the phrasings A/B and A/Not-A. A and B are mere contraries, not logical contradictories, and continuity between them may be recognized without shattering the distinction.... Continuity between terms is a logical impossibility for distinctions phrased as contradictories, as A/Not-A. Thus, men and women may be conceived as men and not-men, or women and not-women, between which there is logically not continuity, or as two forms (A,B) of the class "human" which may be supposed to have a good deal in common. Further, in A/B distinctions both terms have positive reality; Not-A is only the privation or absence of A.*
>
> *... The structure of A/Not-A is such that a third term is impossible: everything and anything must be either A or Not-A. Such distinctions are all-encompassing. They not only cover every possible case of the category (gender, propositions, and so forth) to which they are applied, but they can, and logically do, order "the entire universe, known and knowable."*[13]

The implication of traditional/Aristotelian logic, then, is that women are Not-men. They (we) are outside of the category. Whereas, if instead of the dichotomy of contradiction (A/Not-A) we accept that while women and men are different, they are not opposites (A/B), women need not be defined as having characteristics that are opposite to those of men (e.g., reason/emotion).

Excluded along with women is emotion in particular and women's experience in general. Traditional/Aristotelian logic denies the value of affect and of practical activities. Lorraine Code explains how the logical knowing subject, by being at an emotional distance from what is to be known, needs to be an autonomous individual, independent of all subjective factors.[14] The process of gaining knowledge through logic has the aura of neutrality with the implication that if the process is followed, including maintaining the autonomy of the knowing subject, knowledge, or even truth, will

---

13   Nancy Jay, "Gender and Dichotomy," *Feminist Studies* 7 (1989): 44.
14   Lorraine Code, *What Can She Know? Feminist Theory and the Construction of Knowledge* (Ithaca, NY: Cornell University Press, 1991), 110-21.

result.[15] Descartes reduced thought to an "orderly chain of deductions" that he believed reflected the understanding of the human mind.[16] Even though we have twentieth-century evidence that people's ordinary thinking does not follow syllogistic reasoning, the pattern persists.[17]

A major flaw with the system of logical syllogisms is with the construction of premises.[18] There is no mechanism for ensuring that premises themselves are not biased. The knowing subject's autonomy becomes a liability in establishing premises at a distance from the object to be known. A false premise does not necessarily cause the system to grind to a halt—it may simply produce a false conclusion.

So both the structure and the content of logic have been the objects of feminist criticism. There are two general reactions: to reject traditional/Aristotelian logic or to adapt traditional/Aristotelian logic. Nye and Sandra Harding are among those suggesting the first option and Plumwood and Marjorie Hass the second. There is also the suggestion of simultaneous multiple approaches described below. However, regardless of the stream, emerging from a number of critiques is a search for richer, more situated logical models that rely on interdependence or connectedness.[19] This article will seek such a model for application in the organization of information.

Logic and Tools for the Organization of Information

Classification schemes, thesauri, subject headings, and other tools used in cataloging, indexing, and even metadata are grounded, to a greater or lesser degree, in logic and the hierarchy that grows from logic. The strongest link is between traditional/Aristotelian logic and library classification. Library classification is connected to the classification of science that developed from Aristotle and blossomed particularly in the nineteenth century. W.C. Berwick Sayers asserts in his canonical *Manual of Classification*, that "of the value of the study of philosophical systems of classification there can be no doubt. Modern systems reflect earlier ones, modern terminologies are inherited, adapted, expanded or narrowed; and every system may be said in some way

---

15 See Hass, "Feminist Readings," 20–21; Lloyd, "Reason as Attainment," 168; and Code, *What Can She Know*, 110.
16 Lloyd, "Reason as Attainment," 169–70.
17 P. Oliver, "'What Do Girls Know Anyway?': Rationality, Gender, and Social Control," in *Representing Reason: Feminist Theory and Formal Logic*, ed. Rachel Joffe Falmagne and Marjorie Hass (Lanham, MD: Rowman & Littlefield, 2002), 210–11.
18 Andrea Nye, "Saying What It Is: Predicate Logic and Natural Kinds," in Falmagne and Hass, *Representing Reason*, 192; Oliver, "'What Do Girls Know Anyway?,'" 222.
19 As described by Code, *What Can She Know?*, 79ff.

to help the interpretation of every other."[20] W. C. Berwick Sayers further implies the link between classification and logic by building on a phrase from another seminal writer, Ernest Cushing Richardson:

> ... *"classification made the ape a man"* – *a phrase which has puzzled some students. It means, of course, that when in the process of evolution the ape, or whatever form of animal was man's ancestor, reached that stage of reasoning to enable him to distinguish the likenesses and differences existing between things, he became possessed of a power which is peculiar to man – the higher reasoning power.*[21]

Logic affords a structure to classification that "is not only the general grouping of things; it is also their *arrangement* in some sort of <u>logical order</u> so that the relationships of the things may become evident."[22]

As we look at classification, it does indeed go beyond likeness and difference to take on the hierarchy implied by logic.[23] For example, in the Dewey Decimal Classification (DDC):

> 746 Textile arts
>   746.4 Needlework and handwork
>   746.44 Embroidery
>   746.442 Canvas embroidery and needlepoint
>   746.443 Cross-stitch
>   746.445 Applique
>   746.46 Crewelwork
>   746.447 Silk ribbon embroidery

So, it becomes the syllogism:

> All Embroidery is Needlework
>   *All Crewelwork is Embroidery*
> Therefore, all Crewelwork is Needlework

In this way a hierarchy is built illustrating the logic of hierarchical force defined in DDC as "the principle that the attributes of a class . . . apply to all the subdivisions of the class. . . ."[24] That is, the higher levels of the hierarchy define or have authority over the lower ones. Hierarchy, then, is the manifes-

---

20 W. C. Berwick Sayers, *A Manual of Classification for Librarians & Bibliographers* (London: Grafton, 1926), 115.
21 Ibid., 22-23; my underline added.
22 Ibid., 24.
23 See Hope A. Olson, "Sameness and Difference: A Cultural Foundation of Classification," *Library Resources & Technical Services*, 45 (2001): 115-22.
24 Melvil Dewey, *Dewey Decimal Classification and Relative Index*, 22nd ed., ed. Joan S. Mitchell et al. (Dublin, OH: OCLC, 2003), lxix.

tation of logic in the instance of library classification as it is in philosophical classification.

Other tools used in the organization of information are similar, but less obviously so. For example thesauri are based, overtly or tacitly, on classification.[25] An example from the UNESCO thesaurus demonstrates its classificatory underpinnings:

> Handicrafts
> > UF Arts and crafts, Basketry, Crafts
> > NT1 Engraving
> > NT1 Jewelry
> > NT1 Mosaics
> > NT1 Textile arts
> > > NT2 Carpets
> > > NT2 Tapestry
> > RT Art glass
> > RT Art metalwork
> > RT Ceramic art
> > RT Craft workers
> > RT Handicrafts education
> > RT Informal sector
> > RT Small scale industry
> > RT Stained glass
> > RT Visual arts[26]

Primacy is given to the hierarchical relationships in broader terms and narrower terms represented by the BTs (broader terms) and NTs (narrower terms) (See Figure 2).

The associative relationships represented by the RTs (related terms) encompass all types of relationships other than the hierarchical. For example, "Handicrafts RT Craft workers" is a relationship between a product and a producer, "Handicrafts RT Informal sector" a product and its economic arena, and "Handicrafts RT Small scale industry" a product and its place of production. These nonhierarchical relationships do not arise from the logic of Aristotle's syllogisms or the sets in a Venn diagram and they are typically lumped together as undefined relationships in thesauri. Implicit in the RTs is a recognition that hierarchy alone is insufficient. The current American standard is firm about the definition of a

---

25 J. Aitchison and S. D. Clarke, "The Thesaurus: A Historical Viewpoint, with a Look to the Future," *Cataloging & Classification Quarterly*, 37, no. 3/4 (2004): 10.
26 UNESCO, "UNESCO Thesaurus," 2003, http://www2.ulcc.ac.uk/unesco/.

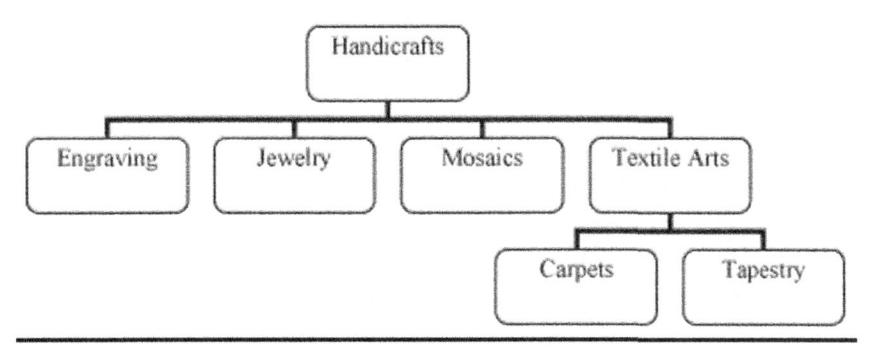

Fig. 2. The Hierarchy of BTs and NTs for Handicrafts.

hierarchical relationship as a generic, an instance (or "isA"), or a whole-part relationship.[27] However, for associative relationships (RTs), the standard leaves the options open:

> This relationship covers associations between terms that are neither equivalent nor hierarchical, yet the terms are semantically or conceptually associated to such an extent that the link between them should be made explicit in the controlled vocabulary, on the grounds that it may suggest additional terms for use in indexing or retrieval.[28]

This description is almost identical to that in the influential British standard published twenty-six years earlier.[29] In spite of radical developments, especially in technology, in the environment of information retrieval and its potential for sophisticated change, the associative relationship remains a catch-all.

Subject heading lists have the same syndetic structure favoring hierarchical relationships that thesauri do. In the following example from the Library of Congress Subject Headings (LCSH), the presence of three broader terms is not a logical problem in the sense that in each instance the three laws of thought can enforce a categorical syllogism—"All Embroidery is Fancy work" does not interfere with "All Embroidery is Sewing" because they are based on separate universal premises:

---

[27] ANSI/NISO Z39.19–2005, "Guidelines for the Construction, Format, and Management of Monolingual Controlled Vocabularies" (Bethesda, MD: NISO Press, 2005), section 8.3, http://www.niso.org/standards/index.html.
[28] Ibid., section 8.4.
[29] British Standards Institution, *Guidelines for the Establishment and Development of Monolingual Thesauri* (London: The Institution, 1979).

Embroidery
    BT Decoration and ornament
    BT Fancy work
    BT Sewing
    NT Assisi embroidery
    NT Blackwork embroidery
    NT Candlewicking (Embroidery)
    NT Canvas embroidery
    NT Couching (Embroidery)
    NT Counted thread embroidery
    NT Crewelwork
    NT Cross-stitch
    . . .
    RT Needlework

So three standard syllogisms exist—all with the same particular premise and conclusion. Only the universal premises vary (See Figure 3).

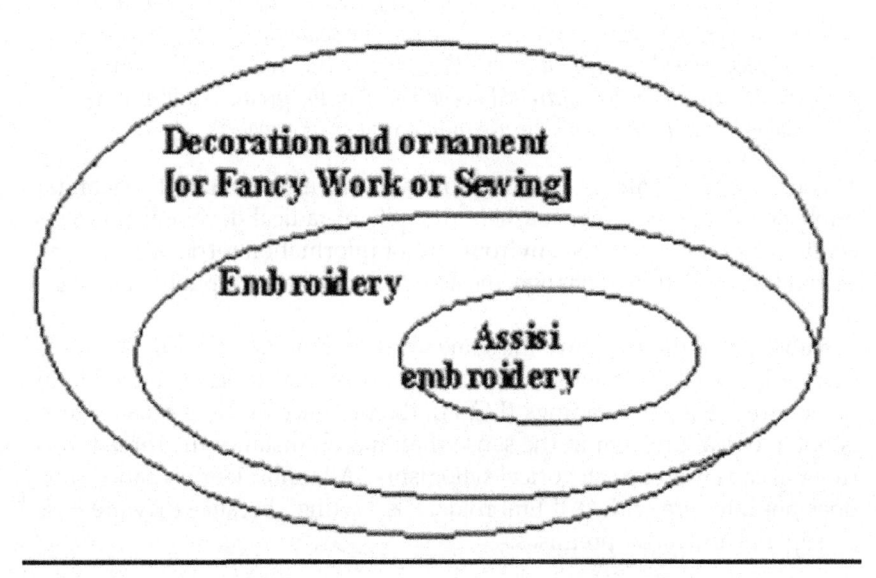

Fig. 3. Venn diagram of Decoration organizational hierarchy.

In addition to the hierarchy built into the syndetic structure of the subject heading list, subject headings and subdivisions also create hierarchical structure in the catalog through precoordinate indexing (See Figure 4). For example, in LCSH with results such as the following appearing in library catalogs:

Crewelwork
Crewelwork—England
Crewelwork—England—Patterns . . .

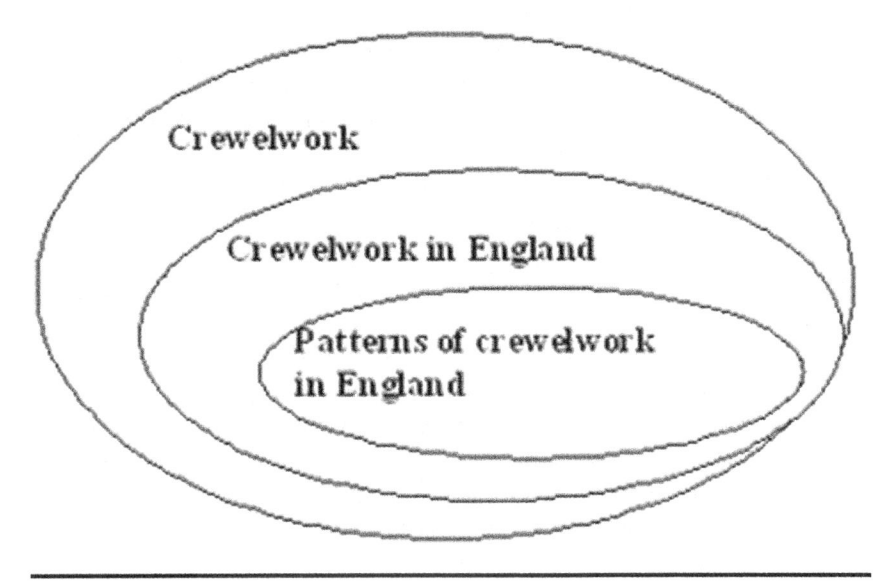

Fig. 4. Venn diagram of Embroidery organizational hierarchy

With each subdivision the result is more specific, yet still governed by the preceding main heading and subdivisions in a relationship akin to the hierarchical force of DDC.[30]

Some of the access points derived from the *Anglo-American Cataloging Rules* (AACR2R) also reflect the ubiquitous hierarchy of Western culture and impose hierarchy to create order.[31] For example, corporate bodies that are parts of administrative hierarchies need to be entered either subordinately or directly. That is, the entry may be independent of the higher body, such as the distinctive "Marin Needle People" rather than "Embroiderers Guild of America. Marin Needle People." However, distinguishing one corporate body from another often requires subordinate entry, such as "Victoria and Albert Museum. Dept. of Textiles" rather than the generic "Dept. of Textiles." In the case of corporate bodies, AACR2R approaches hierarchy somewhat

---

30 See also, B. H. Weinberg, "The Hidden Classification in Library of Congress Subject Headings for Judaica," *Library Resources & Technical Services* 37 (1993): 369-79.

31 *Anglo-American Cataloguing Rules*, 2nd ed. (Ottawa: Canadian Library Association, 2002).

differently than the standards discussed above, subverting hierarchy to "enter a subordinate body ... or a related body directly under its own name ... unless its name belongs to one or more of the types listed in 24.13."[32] Yet, there are six types of general corporate bodies that are entered subordinately, and eleven types for government bodies, so hierarchy is not entirely subverted.

In a different context, AACR2R not only reflects, but actually constructs hierarchy. In the case of uniform titles, it brings together all the editions of any particular work, and then subdivides them, often hierarchically:

> [title]
> [title. language]
> [title. language. part]
> [title. language. part. date]
> etc.

Such subdivision results in browsable files something like:

> Beowulf.
> Beowulf. English
> Beowulf. English. 1984
> Beowulf. English. Selections. 1983
> Beowulf. English. Selections. 2004
> Beowulf. German
> Beowulf. German. Selections ...

These few examples indicate the ubiquity of the hierarchy that has grown from the categorical syllogism of traditional/Aristotelian logic. Interestingly, this structure has been largely accepted, even by critics of these tools.

Feminist Critique of Tools for the Organization of Information

Subject headings, specifically LCSH, have received the most criticism from a feminist perspective, with some attention also paid to thesauri and classification schemes. In 1972, Joan K. Marshall wrote about exclusions in LCSH, describing it as having been designed for a straight, white, male, Christian norm.[33] In 1974, the Committee on Sexism in Subject Headings was formed under the sponsorship of the American Library Association's Social Responsibility Round Table Task Force on Women to address bias in LCSH. Some of the critiques implied structural problems such as topics relating to women and minorities being subsumed under mainstream topics, and the problem

---

32 Ibid., Rule 24.12.
33 Joan K. Marshall, "LC Labeling: An Indictment." In *Revolting Librarians*, edited by Celeste West and Elizabeth Katz (San Francisco: Booklegger Press, 1972), 45–49.

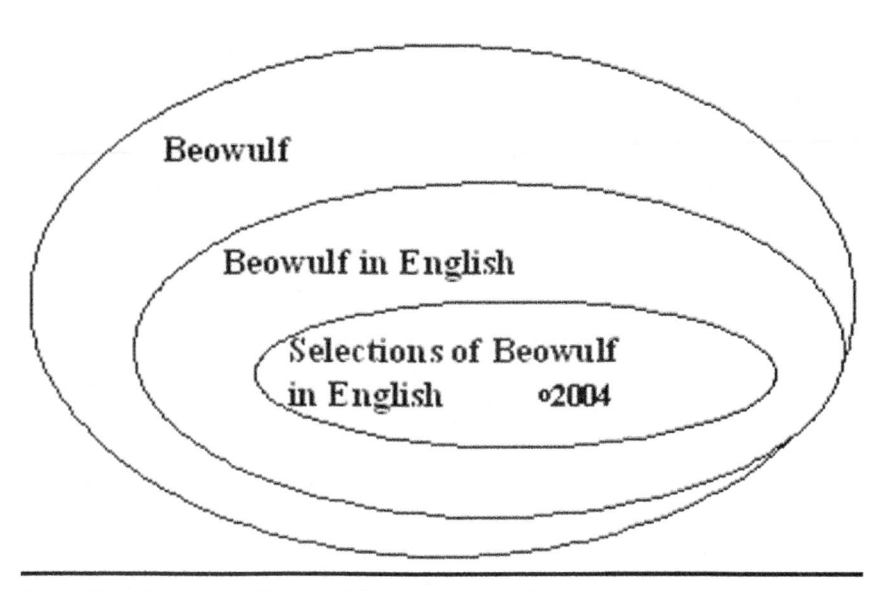

Fig. 5. Venn Diagram of Beowulf Organizational Hierarchy

of omitted topics that could result from structural issues such as the lack of a hierarchy to contain the topics. For example, there are headings for "Mentally ill women," "Mentally ill children," and "Mentally ill older people," but not for "Mentally ill men." There are subject headings for "Sexual ethics for women," "Sexual ethics for teenagers," and "Sexual ethics for youth," but not "Sexual ethics for men." Omissions occur when a broad topic is slanted in a way that is gendered in our society. For example, there is no LC subject heading for unpaid work or labor. The likely headings under which unpaid work might logically be a narrower term are "Work" and "Labor." "Work" is defined as "physical or mental exertion of individuals to produce or accomplish something." which seems open enough, but most of its narrower terms imply paid labor (e.g. "Part-time employment," "Hours of labor," "Entry-level employment"). "Labor" is defined as "the collective human activities involved in the production and distribution of goods and services" and falls under the broader term "Manpower." "Manpower" (which has no references from gender-neutral terms) is defined as "the strength of a country in terms of available personnel, including military and industrial requirements and reserves from the non-working population." ". . . military and industrial" clearly implies paid labor. Anyone unpaid is not part of "manpower." They are part of the nation's reserve. Among these options there is no term that would logically have the narrower concept of unpaid work. The report also addressed biased terminology, the issue that has attracted the most criticism in regard to LCSH over the years. In response, Marshall published an alternative standard for subject access to materials for, by, and about women.[34]

Other alternative standards, thesauri rather than subject headings, have followed, but none seems to have considered a change in structure—only in content (e.g., *A Women's Thesaurus*,[35] *The Canadian Feminist Thesaurus*,[36] and the *European Women's Thesaurus*[37]). Sanford Berman has been raising concerns about omission of topics and choice of terminology in relation to women in LCSH since at least 1981. Several empirical studies have continued to focus on terminological omission and bias.[38] While these studies addressed important issues, they did not probe the structural underpinnings of the standard. María López-Huertas, Isabel de Torres, and Mario Barité came closer to a structural critique when they examined the main subject areas or classes of four thesauri in the area of gender studies, although they did not directly address the hierarchical structure.[39] They found "severe conceptual dispersal" and recommended further study, including domain analysis, of gender studies and other interdisciplinary areas.[40]

Gender-based critique of library classification dates back to at least 1971 when A. C. Foskett addressed issues of structure among other issues.[41] A

---

34 Joan K. Marshall, *On Equal Terms: A Thesaurus for Nonsexist Indexing and Cataloging* (New York: Neal-Schuman, 1977).

35 M. E. S. Capek, ed., *A Women's Thesaurus* (New York: Harper & Row, 1987).

36 Canadian Women's Indexing Group, *The Canadian Feminist Thesaurus / Le Thesaurus Feministe Du Canada* (Toronto: OISE, 1990).

37 M. Boere, ed., *European Women's Thesaurus: A Structured List of Descriptors for Indexing and Retrieving Information in the Field of the Position of Women and Women's Studies*, trans., J. Vaughan (Amsterdam: International Information Centre and Archives for the Women's Movement, 1998).

38 K. H. Gerhard, M. C. Su, and C. C. Rubens, "An Empirical Examination of Subject Headings for Women's Studies Core Materials," *College & Research Libraries*, 59, (1989): 130-38; Hope A. Olson, "Subject Access to Women's Studies Materials," in *Cataloging Heresy: Challenging the Standard Bibliographic Product: Proceedings of the Congress for Librarians*, ed. B. H. Weinberg, 159-69 (Medford, NJ: Learned Information, 1992); M. N. Rogers, "Are We on Equal Terms Yet? Subject Headings in LCSH, 1975-1991," *Library Resources & Technical Services*, 37 (1993): 181-96.

39 Maria López-Huertas, Isabel de Torres, and Mario Barité, "Terminological Representation of Specialized Areas in Conceptual Structures: The Case of Gender Studies," in *Knowledge Organization and the Global Information Society: Proceedings of the Eighth International ISKO Conference*, 13-16 July 2004, ed. I. C. Mcilwaine, 35-39 (Wurzburg, Germany: Ergon, 2004).

40 Ibid., 38.

41 A. C. Foskett, "Misogynists All: A Study in Critical Classification," *Library Resources & Technical Services* 15 (1971): 117-21.

1987 study by Mary Huston and Joe Williams revealed the conveniences and problems of separate ethnic and women's studies sections in classification schemes that are products of hierarchical structure.[42] Sheila Intner and Elizabeth Futas examined the skewing of collection assessment that depends on classification due to the interdisciplinary nature of women's studies in a classification scheme organized by discipline.[43] The remaining feminist work on library classification is primarily mine.[44] While I have previously critiqued both content and structure and discussed theory for guiding change, this article is my first exploration of an alternative model not based on traditional/Aristotelian logic, but on feminist theory and research.

Need for Alternative Models

Feminist critiques of traditional/Aristotelian logic have called for three types of alternatives. The first two, as mentioned above, are: to include women in traditional logic; to reject traditional logic for an entirely "feminine" model; or, as Hekman defines the third option, to:

> ... *abandon epistemology in its traditional sense and thereby displace the rational/irrational dichotomy* ... *[losing] not only the gendered connotations of certain ways of knowing (the rational male, the irrational female) but also the search for the one, correct path to truth.*[45]

She describes this third alternative as a postmodern one coming particularly from French feminist theory.[46] The first two views are drawn from

---

42 Mary M. Huston and Joe L. Williams, "Researcher Response to the Politics of Information," *Research Strategies*, 5 (1987): 90–93.

43 Sheila S. Intner, and Elizabeth Futas, "The Role and Impact of Library of Congress Classification on the Assessment of Women's Studies Collections," *Library Acquisitions: Practice & Theory*, 20 (1996): 267–79.

44 A. Kublik, V. Clevette, D. B. Ward, and Hope A. Olson, "Adapting Dominant Classifications to Particular Contexts," *Cataloging & Classification Quarterly*, 37 no. 1/2 (2003): 13–31; Hope A. Olson, "Mapping Beyond Dewey's Boundaries: Constructing Classificatory Space for Marginalized Knowledge Domains," in *How Classifications Work: Problems and Challenges in an Electronic Age*, ed. G. C. Bowker and S. L. Star, Special Issue, *Library Trends*, 47 no. 2 (1998): 233–54; Hope A. Olson, "Patriarchal Structures of Subject Access and Subversive Techniques for Change," *Canadian Journal for Information and Library Science*, 26, no. 2/3 (2001): 1–29; Hope A. Olson, "The Power to Name: Representation in Library Catalogues," *Signs: Journal of Women in Culture and Society*, 26 (2001): 639–68; Hope A. Olson, *The Power to Name: Locating the Limits of Subject Representation in Libraries* (Dordrecht: Kluwer Academic, 2002); and Olson, "Sameness and Difference."

45 Hekman, *Gender and Knowledge*, 39.

46 Ibid., 42.

what Elizabeth Grosz describes as feminisms of equality and of difference.[47] Feminisms of equality assert that women are the equals of men and seek an even playing field. Therefore, this perspective can see inclusion of women in logic as a viable solution. Trying to remove the bias from existing standards without changing their structure is an example. Feminisms of difference define women on our own terms according to our own specificities. Rejecting the existing structure and substituting an entirely new one in its place would be an example of this approach. Grosz characterizes each of these stances as striving for intellectual or theoretical purity. Feminisms of equality have been criticized for accepting patriarchal definitions of what is valued. Feminisms of difference have been criticized as essentialist, defining a female essence with certain shared characteristics. Grosz draws on Gayatri Spivak in recognizing that purity cannot be achieved and, instead, shifting the focus of difference to include the situated differences of the moment.[48] Diana Fuss adds a mandate for perpetual deconstruction of these essences so that they do not solidify.[49]

My interpretation—drawing together the advice of Hekman, Grosz, Spivak, and Fuss—is that these approaches need not be mutually exclusive, especially if we begin with a poststructural rejection of universality. As long as we reject any notion that traditional/Aristotelian logic is *the* logical structure, instead viewing it as *a* logical structure, it is possible to include models that are radically different and to allow multiple models to coexist—separately or layered or even integrated with each other. Such an approach is necessary if we are to apply it to anything as concrete and ponderous as standards for the organization of information. It also acknowledges that while existing standards are biased and radical alternatives may be merited, existing tools do operate effectively for some contexts. Hekman's postmodern multiple paths offer the possibility of concatenating the one model we have and any number of others.

A Web Instead of a Hierarchy

The body of feminist thought that identifies women as viewing the world as an interconnected web offers a model radically different from the hierarchical structure of traditional logic.[50] Perhaps the two most influential works

---

47   Elizabeth Grosz, "Sexual Difference and the Problem of Essentialism," in *The Essential Difference*, ed. N. Schor and E. Weed (Bloomington: Indiana University Press, 1994), 83–92.

48   Ibid., 94–95.

49   Diana Fuss, *Essentially Speaking: Feminism, Nature & Difference* (New York: Routledge, 1998), 118.

50   For a discussion of interconnectedness across disciplines, see N. Scheman, *Engenderings: Constructions of Knowledge, Authority, and Privilege* (New York: Routledge,

come from the field of psychology: Carol Gilligan's *In a Different Voice* and Mary Field Belenky, Blythe McVicker Clinchy, Nancy Rule Goldberger, and Jill Mattuck Tarule's *Women's Ways of Knowing*.[51] Both books present theories derived from empirical research that define developmental stages. Gilligan is concerned with moral development and *Women's Ways of Knowing* documents stages of coming to knowledge. While stage theories retain a linearity that does not entirely overcome traditional hierarchy, it is possible to select aspects of these models for transposition into a less constricting structure. In the case of these two works, the factor that I want to extract is connectedness.

Gilligan very specifically rejects the universality of the masculine model of moral development based on an ethic of justice as proposed by Lawrence Kohlberg and suggests that a model based on an ethic of care better fits the moral development of women. The ethic of care grows from a focus on connectedness:

> *Illuminating life as a web rather than a succession of relationships, women portray autonomy rather than attachment as the illusory and dangerous quest. In this way, women's development points toward a different history of human attachment, stressing continuity and change in configuration, rather than replacement and separation.*[52]

Women replace "a hierarchy of rights with a web of relationships."[53] Of particular interest in this discussion is the gendered difference in structure. "The images of hierarchy and web, drawn from the texts of men's and women's fantasies and thoughts, convey different ways of structuring relationships and are associated with different views of morality and self."[54]

The major criticism of *In a Different Voice* is the dichotomous nature of Gilligan's conclusions.[55] In finding what is often read as a "women's" pattern of moral development to stand against Kohlberg's "men's" pattern, critics perceive Gilligan's work as essentialist—that she proposes the characteristic of care as part of a female essence. The most cogent criticisms focus on the fact

---

1993), 210ff.

51 Carol Gilligan, *In a Different Voice: Psychological Theory and Women's Development* (Cambridge, MA: Harvard University Press, 1982); Mary Field Belenky et al., *Women's Ways of Knowing: The Development of Self, Voice, and Mind* (New York: Basic, 1986).

52 Gilligan, *In a Different Voice*, 48.

53 Ibid., 57.

54 Ibid., 62.

55 A largely critical collection of commentary, *An Ethic of Care*, appeared in 1993; see Mary Jeanne Larrabee, ed., *An Ethic of Care: Feminist and Interdisciplinary Perspectives* (New York: Routledge, 1993).

that it does not account for differences of race and class in particular.[56] The question arises: why do "we need to limit our understanding to the recognition of only two modes."[57] The answer, of course, is that, as discussed above, we need not choose between the risks of patriarchy and essentialism. We can adopt multiple models.

Belenky et al. acknowledge their debt to Gilligan as they develop their theory of women's ways of knowing.[58] They identify five stages of knowing from silence to constructed knowing. The one that shows potential for the organization of knowledge and the one that most follows from Gilligan is the fourth: *procedural knowledge*.[59] Procedural knowledge focuses on the techniques for acquiring knowledge, offering the most attention to structure of the five stages. Procedural knowledge has two manifestations: separate knowing and connected knowing. Separate knowing is exemplified by distance between the knowing subject and the object to be known and is based on traditional/Aristotelian logic.[60] Connected knowing privileges experience and relies on connections to others to discover what they know. The knowing subject learns through empathy, putting herself in the place of the object to be known rather than maintaining distance.

Clinchy elaborates on connected knowing in a collection published ten years after *Women's Ways of Knowing*.[61] She describes connected knowing as "a rigorous, deliberate, and demanding *procedure*, a new way of knowing that requires *work*."[62] She defines it in opposition to subjectivism which Belenky et al. viewed as effortless and intuitive.[63] Clinchy particularly rejects subjectivism as opposed to connected knowing because the former allows truth to be individually defined. This assertion is especially important when transferring a model to the organization of information, which is normally represented in a tool for collective use.

---

56 Joan C. Tronto, *Moral Boundaries: A Political Argument for an Ethic of Care* (New York: Routledge, 1993).

57 L. J. Nicholson, "Women, Morality, and History," in Larrabee, *An Ethic of Care*, 100.

58 Belenky et al., *Women's Ways of Knowing*, 6–9.

59 Ibid., 100–52.

60 Ibid., 114.

61 Much of the collection answers critiques similar to those incurred by Gilligan; see Blythe McVicker Clinchy, "Connected and Separate Knowing: Toward a Marriage of Two Minds," in *Knowledge, Difference, and Power: Essays Inspired by "Women's Ways of Knowing,"* ed. Nancy Goldberger et al. (New York: Basic Books, 1996), 205–247.

62 Ibid., 209.

63 Ibid., 121.

This focus on practical application is justified by the applied nature of the organization of information. It is effectively explained by M. E. Maron who identified three different kinds of aboutness related to the indexing and retrieval process.[64] The first is subjective aboutness (or S-about), which is the psychological concept, the individual's inner experience. S-about is, therefore, a very personal aspect of aboutness. The second is objective aboutness (or O-about), which is what the individual will actually use to search. O-about is therefore an individual behavioral aspect of aboutness. The third is retrieval aboutness (or R-about), which is what groups of users who will find a document relevant will use in searching (e.g., a document is about cats if most of the users in a group who would find it relevant would seek the concept of cats in searching for it). R-about is therefore the most appropriate type of aboutness to use in a catalog or database because it is not limited to any one individual's conception. A cataloger who can be accurate in terms of identifying concepts to represent might well be defined as one who can achieve R-about or retrieval aboutness, since retrieval is the purpose of the process. R-about might be construed as a kind of connected knowing because of its ground in a knowing community.

On a spectrum from objectivist to subjectivist, connected knowing is somewhere in the middle. Separate knowing focuses on the known object while connected knowing acknowledges the role of the knowing subject. Connected knowing avoids the adversarial practices of traditional philosophy that focus on objectivity and validity, but it does maintain the notion of a singular concept of truth.[65] Particularly interesting in light of the increasing presence of wikis, collaborative tagging, and similar participatory forms of collective information on the Web is Clinchy's discussion of "knowing communities," which, in connected knowing, are made up of unique individual knowing subjects and known objects—much like Maron's.[66] Further, Harding notes that Belenky et al. did recognize that differences among women, differences in context, and differences in power are factors affecting knowing.[67] The connections that knowers make are not all the same.

Characteristics of connectedness that can be useful in informing an alternative model for the organization of information include its:

---

64   M. E. Maron, "On Indexing, Retrieval and the Meaning of About," *Journal of the American Society for Information Science*, 28 (1977): 38–43.
65   Accepting the correspondence theory of truth. Clinchy, "Connected and Separate Knowing," 212–15.
66   Ibid., 213–14.
67   Sandra Harding, "Gendered Ways of Knowing and the 'Epistemological Crisis' of the West," in Goldberger et al., *Knowledge, Difference, and Power*, 432.

- rejection of a universal model
- acceptance of a singular concept of truth
- focus on relationships
- web-like structure as opposed to a pyramidal hierarchy
- situatedness; consideration of context and experience
- involvement of knowing communities
- recognition of power as a factor in knowing.

These characteristics are not essentially feminine. The separated knowing that Belenky et al. identified in their research is directly linked to traditional logic, demonstrating that not all women are connected knowers.[68] However, there are other groups for whom connected knowing may be appropriate. For example, indigenous cultures do not necessarily ascribe to a hierarchical structure. As Donald Fixico describes it: "'Indian Thinking' is 'seeing' things from a perspective emphasizing that circles and cycles are central to the world and that all things are *related* within the universe."[69] Linda Tuhiwai Smith sees the hierarchies of classification as a tool of imperialism and of a positivist approach to knowledge in general and research in particular.[70] She includes connecting, networking, and naming in advocating a research agenda for indigenous peoples.[71] This potential applicability beyond the women studied by Gilligan and Belenky et al. suggests that intersecting sets of information seekers might find this approach fruitful.[72]

That this approach might be especially fruitful in the organization of information is evidenced in two empirical studies. Most notably, Lori Lorigo et al. tracked the eye movements of women and men graduate students while searching Google.[73] They found that men followed a linear "scanpath" when perusing a list of hits more often than did women and that women were more likely to return to something they had previously looked at than were men.[74] This difference in browsing styles suggests that a linear approach is

---

68 Belenky et al., *Women's Ways of Knowing*.
69 Donald L. Fixico, *The American Indian Mind in a Linear World* (New York: Routledge, 2003), 1; my emphasis added.
70 Linda Tuhiwai Smith, *Decolonizing Methodologies: Research and Indigenous Peoples* (London: Zed Books, 1999), 25, 42–43.
71 Ibid., 148, 156–57.
72 Joan Tronto addresses Gilligan's ethic of care more than she does connectedness, but she draws parallel lines suggesting that the ethical model more appropriate for women is adaptable in addressing issues of race and class as well as gender; see Tronto, *Moral Boundaries*.
73 Lori Lorigo et al., "The Influence of Task and Gender on Search and Evaluation Behavior Using Google," *Information Processing & Management*, 42 (2006): 1123–31.
74 Ibid., 1129.

not equally appropriate for all searchers. Women also submitted longer queries.[75] Did they connect more concepts together? Further research would be helpful. Lucinda Zoe and Diane DiMartino looked at language background as well as gender in studying differences in search techniques. They found that students whose first language is not English used different search techniques than those for whom English is a first language.[76] They attribute these differences to language, but given that language and culture are intimately intertwined, cultural differences are also likely to play a role.

Traces of Connected Knowing in the Organization of Information

Even though current practices of the organization of information are fundamentally hierarchical, they already exhibit some traces of connectedness that could be enhanced. Four that bear particular notice are associative relationships in thesauri and subject heading lists; facets and synthetic practice in classification; the entity-relationship model, particularly as embodied in the new Functional Requirements for Bibliographic Records; and the collaborative tagging in increasing evidence on the Web.

Associative relationships in thesauri and subject heading lists are well-established, though inexplicit, ways of connecting concepts that do not exhibit a hierarchical relationship. These are the connections designated as related terms or RTs. The current thesaurus construction standard, ANSI/NISO Z39.19, notes that "the associative relationship is the most difficult one to define, *yet it is important to make explicit the nature of the relationship* between terms linked in this way and to avoid subjective judgments as much as possible; otherwise, RT references could be established inconsistently."[77] Two issues arise: first, the relationships are not individually designated, that is, they are not made explicit, but are, as mentioned above, all lumped together as RTs; and, second, there are limited relationships that may be included. Specifically, with a few arcane exceptions, the associative relationships in Z39.19 are: process/agent, process/counteragent, action/property, action/product, action/target, cause/effect, concept or object/property, concept or object/origins, concept or object/measurements, raw material/product, and discipline or field/object or practitioner. Antonyms may also be included as associative relationships for a total of twelve types.[78]

---

75 Ibid.
76 Lucinda R. Zoe, and Diane DiMartino, "Cultural Diversity and End-User Searching: An Analysis by Gender and Language Background," *Research Strategies* 17 (2000): 291-305.
77 ANSI/NISO "Guidelines," section 8.4; my emphasis added.
78 Ibid., section 8.4.2.

"Node labels" *may* be used to indicate which types of relationships are represented in a vocabulary, but this option is not widely used in practice. Further, node labels are normally visible only in the thesaurus, not in the index or database in which the thesaurus is applied. A more visible option is that "in certain controlled vocabularies, it *may* be considered desirable to refine Related Term references in order to make the nature of the relationships explicit. Codes for such relationship indicators and their reciprocals *may* be developed locally."[79] This option is one that should be exploited far more often for situating connections in a particular context.

In LCSH, associative relationships are more severely curtailed:

> *In order to focus emphasis on hierarchical references, simplify future special projects to revise references in the subject authority file, and reduce the size and complexity of* Library of Congress Subject Headings, *restrictive rules are in effect for making related term references with the intended effect of minimizing the number of related term references that are made.*[80]

Associative references may be established only in the following three situations (and then only if not otherwise prohibited):

- To link two terms with meanings that overlap to some extent, or terms used somewhat interchangeably....
- To link a discipline and object studied....
- To link persons and their fields of endeavor....[81]

Associative relationships offer some options for expressing connectedness, but to varying degrees in principle and in practice.

Potential for greater focus on connection also lies in the synthetic aspects of classification. Number-building mechanisms in DDC allow making some connections, but these opportunities are carefully controlled and the nature of the relationship is not denoted in the resulting number. For example, adding "51" to a number will represent China in some instances and the Italian language in others plus miscellaneous other meanings in individual cases. While they cannot be used interchangeably in any specific instance, they could even be used in the same number such as 305.751051 Italian-speakers in China. Which "51" is which? In this case, the language comes first and then the place. So this topic will sit between Italian-speakers in Bulgaria (305.7510499) and Italian-speakers in Japan (305.751052). When classifying works about social groups, language will always take precedence over

---

79 Ibid., section 8.4.4.
80 Library of Congress, *Library of Congress Subject Headings*, 19th ed. (Washington, DC: Library of Congress, Cataloging Distribution Service, 1996), H370, 2.
81 Ibid.

location in DDC. It is not possible to group speakers of foreign languages in China. Each must be classed with the individual language group. This dictum regularizes the classification so that a topic is always classified the same way, pulling together all of the works on that topic in one place. However, it also allows the hierarchy to exert its hierarchical force. Works are gathered by one facet and then subdivided by another and so on, creating a hierarchy. As a result, one facet is the primary point of gathering and others are not gathered in one place. In DDC, the chain or order of facets is always the same. Elizabeth Spelman describes such a classification:

> *Imagine a huge customs hall with numerous doors, marked "women," "men," "Afro-American," "Asian-American," "Euro-American," "Hispanic-American," "working class," "middle class," "upper class," "lesbian," "gay," "heterosexual," and so forth. . . . The doors are arranged in banks, so that each person faces a first bank of doors that sort according to gender, then a bank that sort according to race, or alternatively sort first according to race, then according to class, then according to gender, and so on.*[82]

Different orders of sorting have different results. If gender is first and then racial or ethnic background, all of the women are together and all of the men are together, but Afro-Americans, Euro-Americans, Asian-Americans and Hispanic-Americans are each in two different places. However, if racial or ethnic background is the first characteristic in sorting then Afro-, Euro-, Asian-, and Hispanic-Americans are each together, but women are in four different places and men are in four different places. ". . . we get different pictures of people's identities, and of the extent to which one person shares some aspect of identity with another, depending on what the doors are, how they are ordered, and how people are supposed to proceed through them."[83]

In the Universal Decimal Classification (UDC), more synthesis is possible; a symbol indicates the types of relationships, and the order of elements can be adapted. Any topics in the classification scheme may be combined using a symbol "+" that indicates two topics that simply coexist in a work (dogs and cats 636.7+636.8 where part of the work is about dogs and a separate part is about cats). The order of elements is generally in ascending order, but may be varied for emphasis (ailurophiles may prefer 636.8+636.7 for cats and dogs). A different notation ":" indicates topics discussed in relation to each other (pharmaceutical products consists of the chemical industry in relation to pharmaceutical preparations 661.1:615.4). Other types of relationships

---

[82] Elizabeth V. Spelman, *The Inessential Woman: Problems of Exclusion in Feminist Thought* (Boston: Beacon, 1988), 144.
[83] Ibid., 146.

can be added (critics of the pharmaceutical industry would be classed in 661.1:615.4-056.157 with-056.157 representing persons anti- or against something). This faceted classification allows for considerable flexibility in presenting relationships, especially where the citation order can vary with emphasis rather than being at the service of the hierarchical structure.

A third trace of connectedness in existing organization of information practice is the emerging use of the entity-relationship model, most notably in the Functional Requirements for Bibliographic Records (FRBR), but also in the increased use of XML and RDF for encoding metadata.[84] The entity-relationship model allows representation of the relationships between different entities. Things are related to other things. It also adds the concept of attributes: qualities or characteristics that describe entities. The entities in FRBR are divided into three groups:

- Group 1: Products of intellectual & artistic endeavor, such as novels, films, songs, reports, biographies, operas, etc. Group 1 entities include:
  - A work is "a distinct intellectual or artistic creation"[85]
  - An expression is "the intellectual or artistic realization of a work."[86]
  - A manifestation is "the physical embodiment of an expression of a work"[87]
  - An item is "a single exemplar of a manifestation"[88]
- Group 2: Those responsible for content of the products, such as authors, artists, sponsoring organizations, etc. Group 2 entities include persons and corporate bodies.
- Group 3: What the products are about, that is, topics.

There are two factors regarding FRBR that are of particular interest to this discussion. First is FRBR's explicit recognition of relationships:

> *In the context of the model, relationships serve as the vehicle for depicting the link between one entity and another, and thus as the means*

---

84   IFLA Study Group on the Functional Requirements for Bibliographic Records, "Functional Requirements for Bibliographic Records—Final Report," Munchen: K. G. Saur, 1998, http://www.ifla.org/vii/s13/frbr/frbr.htm.
85   Ibid., section 3.2.1.
86   Ibid., section 3.2.2.
87   Ibid., section 3.2.3.
88   Ibid., section 3.2.4.

of assisting the user to "navigate" the universe that is represented in a bibliography, catalogue, or bibliographic database.[89]

Relationships can be identified between groups and within groups. The relationships between groups are not hierarchical as shown in the example in Figure 6.

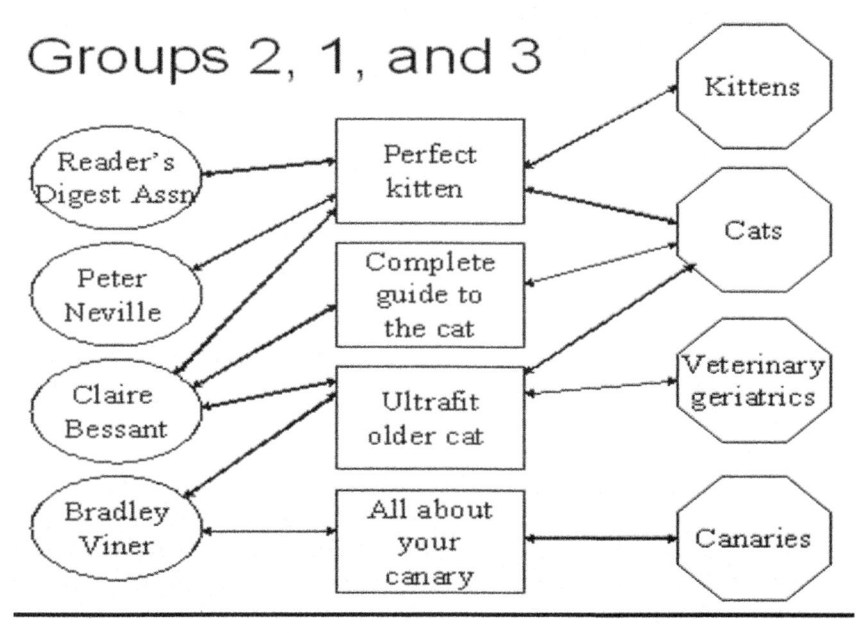

Groups 2, 1, and 3

Fig. 6. Entity-relationship Model in FRBR.

These relationships represent a wide range of possibilities. For example, a person may be the author of a work, the translator of an expression, or the owner of an item.

The relationships between different types of entities in group 1 (works, expressions, manifestations, and items) are hierarchical in that what is true of a work is true of its expressions, what is true of an expression is true of its manifestations, and what is true of a manifestation is true of its individual items. So they line up as in the following example, much like uniform titles in AACR2R:

---

89   Ibid., section 5.1.

w₁ *Pride and Prejudice*
    e₁ the original text of *Pride and Prejudice*
        m₁ *Pride and Prejudice* published in New York by Century in 1902
            i₁ first copy held by the Library of Congress
            i₂ second copy missing from the Library of Congress
        m₂ *Pride and Prejudice* published in Naples, Florida by Trident Press International in 1999
            i₁ first copy held by the Library of Congress
    e₂ the text of *The Annotated Pride and Prejudice*
        m₁ *The Annotated Pride and Prejudice* published in Delmar, NY by Pheasant Books in 2004
            i₁ first copy held by the Library of Congress

Nonetheless, the introduction of the entity-relationship model is an example of connectedness increasingly present in the organization of information. In addition to the connectedness developed in a feminist context, Yann Nicolas describes how FRBR, except for the hierarchical aspects described above, has the potential for better accommodating oral tradition works than current standards, revealing the cross-cultural potential of FRBR if a range of voices is heeded in FRBR's further development.[90]

The fourth indication that connectedness is present in the organization of information is the practice of collaborative tagging that is growing rapidly in the context of what is being called Web 2.0. While collaborative tagging is not the creation of specialists in the organization of information, it is being greeted with interest in library and information science circles.[91] Like the wikis that have become a central feature on the Web and intranets, collaborative tagging involves shared content. Multiple users of a site create tags, basically keywords, for bookmarks to Web pages (e.g., Del.icio.us) or academic publications (e.g., CiteULike.org). The tags are then searchable by other users. If a bookmark has already been tagged a user may replicate previous users' tags or assign different ones or some combination thereof. The result is that frequently tagged bookmarks will be represented by a group of tags that are related syntagmatically through the bookmark being tagged; that is, the relationship between the terms is not necessarily an innate relationship, but stems from their co-occurrence in describing an individual Web page. For example, a del.icio.us search on "embroidery" retrieved, among others, the page

---

90 Yann Nicolas, "Folklore Requirements for Bibliographic Records: Oral Traditions and FRBR," *Cataloging & Classification Quarterly*, 39 (2005): 179-95.

91 Collaborative tagging was a prevalent topic at the 2006 American Society for Information Science & Technology (ASIST) Information Architecture Summit and is embedded in the theme for the 2007 ASIST annual conference.

of The Home Sewing Association, http://www.sewing.org which had been saved by sixty-six users as of November 24, 2006. Its common tags included, by frequency:

56	sewing
13	craft
12	crafts
11	patterns
9	howto
7	sewing_patterns
5	diy
3	sew
2	how-to
2	imported
2	organization

There is no semantic link between "sewing" and "howto." It is perfectly possible to talk about sewing without discussing how it is done and vice versa. However, collectively the tags create a verbal picture of this Web page. Unlike conventional postcoordinate indexing in which an indexer assigns descriptors from a thesaurus, in collaborative tagging users arrive at something resembling a consensus as to what is the core topic more or less inductively. In this instance, fifty-six (85 percent) of sixty-six users deemed "sewing" to be applicable, with seven using "sewing patterns" and three "sew." These three tags are linked by their meaning—that is, they are linked semantically. Similarly "howto," "diy," and "how-to" suggest another cluster—possibly overlapping with "patterns" and "sewing patterns" and "craft" and "crafts." The lack of a controlled vocabulary requires users to interpret synonyms and near-synonyms. Nevertheless, the degrees of connection between a Web page and a concept are shown more distinctly than in conventional indexing and those connections come from a group of interested individuals similar to Maron's definition of R-about (retrieval aboutness)—a knowing community. Individual users may organize their tags into folders that imply very shallow hierarchies ("sewing" might be in a folder for "creative" for one person, "home" for another, and "hobbies" for a third). Users may also designate some tags as related to others, though, again, they cannot designate the type of relationship.

These four traces of connectedness—associative relationships, facets, FRBR, and tagging—illustrate that our existing systems are not monolithically hierarchical and are not incompatible with further connectedness.

A Future for Connectedness in the Organization of Information

As it stands now the organization of information generally follows a logical model and privileges hierarchical relationships, although at least a few instances of connectedness already exist. How might a larger future for connectedness develop? Returning to the characteristics drawn from the work of Gilligan and her successors, how might they be translated to apply in the case of the organization of information? The first, rejection of a universal model, is addressed simply by accepting multiple structures that might operate separately or in some complementary manner. We already accept this situation in library catalogs where we include classification, represented by notation in a hierarchical order, for the purpose of browsing for topics on library shelves and online, and subject headings, represented by words in an alphabetical order, for searching for topics in the catalog. The acceptance of a singular truth is not incompatible with accepting different ways of knowing or different systems of organizing information. The core of the connectedness model comes from its focus on relationships, its web-like structure as opposed to a pyramidal hierarchy, and its situatedness and consideration of context and experience, especially as derived from knowing communities. Finally, there is the justification for change: recognition of power as a factor in knowing, especially the imbalance of power characteristic of hierarchy. How, then, can these characteristics be applied to the organization of information? Three approaches illustrate some possibilities: enhancing browsability as compared to linear searching; focusing on nonhierarchical relationships within standards; and increasing the functionality of syntagmatic relationships within surrogates.

Browsing over Linear Searching

Enabling users to find something specific and to gather things with some common characteristic have been the usual objects of creating access points in the organization of information at least since Cutter's 1876 *Rules for a Printed Dictionary Catalog*.[92] The searching tasks that exploit this model of the organization of information are basically linear. Catalogers or indexers lay a path to a surrogate (a catalog record, index entry, or metadata record) that represents a document and users follow that path from their queries or needs to the relevant results. It presumes a goal-oriented view of information seeking. However, as Charles Hildreth pointed out already in 1995:

---

92 C. A. Cutter, "Rules for a Printed Dictionary Catalogue," in *Public Libraries in the United States of America: Their History, Condition, and Management*, part 2 (Washington, DC: Government Printing Office, 1876).

> We now understand that people do not think in terms of formal, Boolean queries. Rather, they pick and choose as they go, and the outcome of this activity may be only a redefinition of the original information need. Modern interactive systems can support this kind of non-linear, trial and error thinking process.[93]

Hildreth suggests a paradigm shift to a retrieval model that focuses on browsing. Browsing seen in these terms is not just a process of searching for information. It can also be a process of gaining knowledge. The process shapes the outcomes. Evidence from Lorigo et al. supports the view that linear searching may be less used by women than by men, making this alternative particularly appropriate.[94]

The structure of a bibliographic tool will shape the browsing process. For example, browsing up and down a hierarchy can lead one from general to specific and vice versa as shown in the examples from DDC and the UNESCO Thesaurus above. A classification hierarchy, often considered a tool for browsing, has the side effect of grouping subordinate topics next to each other (such as specific kinds of embroidery in the range from 746.442 Canvas embroidery and needlepoint to 746.447 Silk ribbon embroidery in the DDC example above). Browsing between hierarchies is not possible without references which are not normally visible to users of a classification scheme and are only available as RTs in a thesaurus or subject heading list. As noted earlier, even within thesaurus construction standards, "node labels" and specifically-developed references that indicate the type of relationship are only an option.

Though classification schemes do not currently have references where users can see them, they are available to catalogers. For example, a cataloger will see the reference in DDC from 646.2. Sewing and related operations (hierarchically under 640 Home & family management) to embroidery, "see 746.44," but there is no mechanism for the user browsing the shelves to see the same reference. References for browsing on the shelves would be difficult ("dummy books" are an awkward possibility), but better interfaces for browsing online could easily include them. The schedules for DDC and for the Library of Congress Classification (LCC) are both available in machine-readable form. Interfaces already exist that display references in subject headings. The technical difficulties of the task should be manageable.

Even the references that do exist in thesauri and subject heading lists are not easily browsable in most current interfaces. Most indexing and

---

93 Charles R. Hildreth, "Online Catalog Design Models: Are We Moving in the Right Direction?" 1990, http://www.ou.edu/faculty/h/charles.r.hildreth/clr-five.html.

94 Lorigo et al., "The Influence of Task and Gender."

abstracting databases have references only in the thesaurus or subject heading list, not in the searchable database. So users need to go back and forth between the thesaurus or subject heading list and the database to take advantage of the references. Library catalog interfaces vary in their display of the references from subject heading lists. Some include the references directly in a browsable display of headings, but many others require clicking on a link to see the references, thus removing the user from the browsable file. Fortunately, browsability can, to a significant degree, use existing data through improved technological applications to achieve a more connected, more situated result. However, nonhierarchical relationships need fuller development in the breadth of the types of relationships identified; in the frequency of their usage in standards (e.g., thesauri and subject heading lists); and in their application to achieving better browsability that is lateral as well as vertical.

Nonhierarchical Relationships in Standards

As mentioned above, standards such as thesaurus construction guidelines privilege hierarchical relationships (BT/NT), but also include nonhierarchical relations (as RTs). The latter are more flexible in thesauri than in subject heading lists, but are still limited to certain types of relationships. Further, the thesaurus construction standard allows node labels to specify the types of relationships in a related term (RT) reference. Different types of relationships may be appropriate in different contexts. As a simple example, chronological relationships (earlier, later, and contemporaneous) are likely to be more important in a historical database than in a database of health tips. Developing ways of expanding the types of relationships and denoting them shifts the focus from hierarchical relationships to a more encompassing array of relationships.

A type of relationship that is not defined in current standards is that between a concept and its manifestation. Such a relationship is grounded in experience rather than logic. For example, in the ERIC thesaurus the heading "Sex Bias" is defined in the scope note as "Prejudicial attitudes toward people because of their sex, including the conscious or unconscious expression of these attitudes in writing, speaking, etc." My initial reaction upon reading the scope note was to think of gender-biased language. The closest ERIC descriptor is "Sexism in Language," which has the scope note: "Forms of language that instill and perpetuate (or avoid) sex role stereotyping." Certainly, sexism in language, by these definitions, seems to be a manifestation of sex bias. Yet ERIC does not relate the two at all. A clear designation of the concept/manifestation relationship could link these two descriptors in a way that situates sex bias in the experience of sexism in language. A woman may say with all sincerity that she has not encountered sex bias in her career, but bias is unlikely to remain invisible if one thinks in terms of sexism in language, which we have all experienced.

One issue to be confronted in expanding types of relationships will be how to make them machine readable. In current MARC authority records for names and subject headings the only relationships that can be encoded specifically are: earlier heading, later heading, acronym, musical composition of a literary work, broader term, narrower term, and immediate parent body.[95] If other particular types of relationships are to be displayed in references they may currently appear as notes (MARC authority field 360). These are now most typically generic *see also* references to freefloating subdivisions and groups of headings such as the reference under the LCSH "Women," which tells the user to search also under the "subdivision Women under individual wars, e.g. World War, 1939-1945 – Women; also subdivision Relations with women under names of individual persons; and headings beginning with the word Women." Use of this MARC authority field could be expanded to other types of relationships between specific headings or more specific codes could be added to the subfield that defines relationships ($w/0).[96]

Another mechanism for defining relationships is the scope note. Scope notes are more typically used in an effort to differentiate between headings in LCSH. An example is found under the heading "Women and religion": "Here are entered general works on the relationship between women and religion, including the involvement of women in religion. Works on the religious or devotional life of women are entered under Women – Religious life. Works on theology or religious doctrines concerning women are entered under Women – Religious aspects." It suggests a mutual exclusivity among the three headings. There are no references to link the three, only the reciprocal scope notes under each heading. The effort to distinguish among these headings implies that, while it is not easy to attain mutual exclusivity, it is important to do so. In the terms used by philosopher Nancy Jay earlier in this paper, it is a matter of A/Not-A, but more complex. If A is "Women and religion," then everything else, including "Women – Religious life" and "Women – Religious aspects" is Not-A. However, the characteristics of these three headings are not mutually exclusive. "Women and religion," being the general heading, may readily be interpreted as encompassing the other two topics. Certainly how women practice religion and doctrinal views on

---

95 These relationships are coded in subfield $w character position 0 in 4XX and 5XX fields in MARC authority records.

96 A parallel difficulty arises in the MARC Classification format used for LCC. It has the same mechanisms available as the MARC Authority format with the specified relations being: previous classification number, new classification number, see reference, class elsewhere reference, see also reference, and standard subdivision do-not-use reference.

women fit under the umbrella of "the relationship between women and religion" or, at the very least, overlap with it. And women's religious life is unlikely to be divorced from doctrine. There is no absolute essence that defines each of these headings.

Mutual exclusivity is an even more prominent feature in classification than in subject headings, especially when it is used for determining shelf location. The DDC manual is filled with entries explaining how to decide between A and Not-A. For example, there is an entry in the DDC manual for 306 vs. 305, 909, 930–990 Social groups vs. Culture and institutions vs. History which requires establishing boundaries between the aspects of a topic (social groups) so that they can be located in different disciplines. The struggle to distinguish between social groups and culture and institutions is apparent in a change between the two latest editions of DDC. In the twenty-first edition, lesbians were classified with other groups of women. In the twenty-second edition, lesbians are classified with "lesbianism," which is hierarchically under "sexual relations":

> 300 Social sciences
> 300–301 Social sciences, sociology & anthropology
> 302–307 Specific topics in sociology and anthropology
> > 305 Social groups
> > > 305.4 Women
> > > > 305.48 Specific kinds of women
> > > > > 305.489 Miscellaneous groups
> > > > > > 305.4896 Women by social, economic, cultural level; special social status
> > > > > > > 305.489621 Upper class women
> > > > > > > 305.489622 Middle class women
> > > > > > > 305.489623 Working class women
> > > > > > > [305.489664] Lesbians
> > > > > > > > Relocated to 306.7663
> > > > > > > 305.489692 Violence in women
> > > > > > > 305.4896942 Homeless women
> > 306 Culture and institutions
> > > 306.7 Sexual relations
> > > > 306.76 Sexual orientation
> > > > > 306.766 Homosexuality
> > > > > > 306.7663 Lesbianism
> > > > > > > Class here lesbians [formerly 305.489664]

The result is that lesbians are defined only by their sexual relations because of the essentializing effect of hierarchical force. Two topics, lesbians as women and lesbians as gay were collapsed into one. The logic had been A/B (lesbians as gay/lesbians as women), but has changed to A/Not-A, (gay/Not-gay).[97] Maintaining or expanding options rather than limiting them can offer more of the situatedness characteristic of a connected approach.

The articulation of more types of paradigmatic relationships in thesauri and subject heading lists and the presence of alternative classification numbers in different contexts, or even disciplines, offer potential for the web and the hierarchy to work together.

Syntagmatic Relationships

Most of the relationships seen in thesauri and subject heading lists, as those in classification schemes, are limited to *paradigmatic relationships*. That is, they are intrinsic relationships; they do not depend on context. So "Embroidery" (unless used as an image: an "embroidered truth") is always related to "Needlework." Ferdinand de Saussure, the seminal semiotician, suggested that paradigmatic relationships belong to the relatively stable system of language. A more dynamic relationship is the *syntagmatic relationship*. Saussure identified it as belonging to speech.[98] The syntagmatic relationship is more spontaneous. It is determined by context. So a book of patterns for embroidered Christmas ornaments will have "Embroidery" and "Christmas decorations" as subject headings but the relationship between the two is only in a particular context. There is no innate relationship between embroidery and Christmas decorations. There is considerable room for expansion of this contextual relationship to enhance situatedness and connectedness.

As Jacques Maniez (1988) puts it: syntagmatic relationships "are not statements but a creative process, which produces a new compound phrase or concept (a syntagm) out of the two original words or concepts. This type of relation is *not permanent, but casual.*"[99] Paradigmatic relationships are contained in controlled vocabularies. Syntagmatic relationships are represented in surrogates for bibliographic entities: catalog records, index entries, and other metadata. In these surrogates, concepts can be linked in a way compatible with the connectedness of *Women's Ways of Knowing* and related texts. Rebecca Green suggests that paradigmatic relationships are less stated than syntagmatic relationships:

> *Since lexical paradigmatic relationships are built into our understanding of the meanings of words, to go around affirming them for other than*

---

97 There are also numbers for lesbians in relation to film, the arts, literature, and religion, but these numbers do not define characteristics of lesbians; they define film, the arts, etc.

98 Jacques Maniez, "Relationships in Thesauri: Some Critical Remarks," *International Classification*, 15 (1988): 133–38.

99 Ibid., 133. Emphasis added.

> educational purposes risks redundancy at best and tautology at worst. When we make a statement, we are much more likely to be asserting something whose meaning and logic are not a matter of definition, something whose meaning is constructed. Such statements express syntagmatic relationships.[100]

That is, when we encounter the word "poodle" we do not need to be told that it has a relationship to "dog." However, when we encounter a concatenation of "poodle," "smuggling," "lace," and "Belgium" we learn something. It opens possibilities of meaning that are represented in surrogates for bibliographic entities, not in authority files. But if we see only a list of descriptors we know nothing about the relationships. Is the lace Belgian? Are the poodles? Which, if either, is being smuggled?

The current practice of organizing information is generally paradigmatic although syntagmatic relationships are present by co-occurrence in postcoordinate indexing, requiring Boolean searching (with AND or NOT). However, co-occurrence of terms does not guarantee that they are related. For example, in a search on the descriptors "Females" (the term ERIC uses for women) and "Religion," the results crossed a wide range of topics from "A Forum of Their Own: Rhetoric, Religion, and Female Participation in Ancient Athens" to "Imaging [in film] Women's Spirituality." These relationships are syntagmatic, but not explicit. Green advocates enriching the representation of syntagmatic relationships to be more specific about the nature of those relationships.[101]

One type of syntagmatic relationship that is all but omitted is that of object/perspective. For example, in LCSH, a work taking a feminist perspective cannot express that aspect. The Library of Congress's record for the book *Through the Kitchen Window: Women Explore the Intimate Meanings of Food and Cooking* has the subject headings:

> Food.
> Cookery.
> Feminism.

However, the book is not *about* feminism, it is written from a feminist *perspective*. Nevertheless, if someone searches for a book about feminism this book will be retrieved. LCSH does have some broad headings such as "Feminism and literature" and "Feminism and science," but they do no more to specify the type of relationship than do the subject headings for *Through the Kitchen Window*. One or more explicit subdivisions such as "—Feminist perspectives,"

---

100 Rebecca Green, "Syntagmatic Relationships in Index Languages: A Reassessment," *Library Quarterly*, 65 (1995): 367.
101 Ibid.

"—Feminist aspects," or "—Feminist criticism" would solve the problem. A subject heading such as "Food—Feminist perspectives" would express the relationship in a manner compatible with LCSH structure by taking advantage of the precoordinate nature of subject headings. The same approach could be used for other perspectives: "—Psychoanalytic perspectives," "—Postcolonial perspectives," and so forth.

Green also notes the potential of the entity-relationship model.[102] Because FRBR uses this model it might be expanded to reflect specific syntagmatic relationships between topics as they are linked to particular works. Certainly, the entity-relationship model is supported by the increasing use of XML and RDF for encoding.

Conclusion

These examples of possible approaches to increase the connectedness of the ways we organize information only touch the surface. However, they do indicate that the dominance of hierarchy and linearity is neither absolute nor insurmountable. It is possible to have the web as well as the pyramid. There are numerous additional directions that merit further exploration. The A/Not-A hierarchical duality could be circumvented through fuzzy logic by turning it into a spectrum such as is used in relevance ranking. Switching languages and metathesauri offer interfaces between standards—perhaps between a hierarchy and a web. Augmenting our traditional standards with something like cluster analysis might enhance the situatedness of syntagmatic relationships. Human-defined relationships, both paradigmatic and syntagmatic, may be ideal, but some automatic techniques akin to find-more-like-this-one functions might be developed on a more sophisticated level, perhaps with natural language processing. Mapping the complexities of relationships would add greater connectedness, even if those relationships were not named. Such an approach could lead to development of standards based on inductive rather than deductive logic.

The ideas explored in this paper and those suggested for future research are a first step in weaving new patterns and textures in our models. To bring this work to fruition will require two things. First, it will need creative work of both theory and application to develop actual tools. Second, it will require institutional will to underwrite and implement such innovations. The knowing community of librarianship has evidenced the possibility of conceptual change in the past.[103] As a community we recognize our situatedness in a context of social and cultural differences. The notion of connectedness offers

---

102 Ibid., 382.
103 Indeed, the changes embodied in FRBR and the first efforts at implementation are a recent example.

us one path for better serving the great diversity of knowing communities of users.

Bibliography

Aitchison, J., and S. D. Clarke. "The Thesaurus: A Historical Viewpoint, with a Look to the Future." *Cataloging & Classification Quarterly*, 37, no 3/4 (2004): 5-21.

Anglo-American Cataloguing Rules. 2nd ed. Ottawa: Canadian Library Association.

ANSI/NISO Z39.19-2005. "Guidelines for the Construction, Format, and Management of Monolingual Controlled Vocabularies." Bethesda, MD: NISO Press, 2002. http://www.niso.org/standards/index.html.

Aristotle. *Prior Analytics.* In *The Organon*, translated by H. Tredennick, 182-531. London: W. Heinemann, 1938.

Belenky, Mary Field, Blythe McVicker Clinchy, Nancy Rule Goldberger, and Jill Mattuck Tarule. *Women's Ways of Knowing: The Development of Self, Voice, and Mind.* New York: Basic, 1986.

Blackburn, Simon. *The Oxford Dictionary of Philosophy.* New York: Oxford University Press, 1994.

Boere, M., ed. *European Women's Thesaurus: A Structured List of Descriptors for Indexing and Retrieving Information in the Field of the Position of Women and Women's Studies.* Translated by J. Vaughan. Amsterdam: International Information Centre and Archives for the Women's Movement, 1998.

British Standards Institution. *Guidelines for the Establishment and Development of Monolingual Thesauri.* London: The Institution, 1979.

Canadian Women's Indexing Group. *The Canadian Feminist Thesaurus / Le Thesaurus Feministe Du Canada.* Toronto: OISE, 1990.

Capek, M. E. S., ed. *A Women's Thesaurus.* New York: Harper & Row, 1987.

Clinchy, Blythe McVicker. "Connected and Separate Knowing: Toward a Marriage of Two Minds." In Goldberger, Tarule, Clinchy, and Belenky, *Knowledge, Difference, and Power*, 205-247.

Code, Lorraine. *What Can She Know? Feminist Theory and the Construction of Knowledge.* Ithaca, NY: Cornell University Press, 1991.

Cutter, C. A. "Rules for a Printed Dictionary Catalogue." In *Public Libraries in the United States of America: Their History, Condition, and Management.* Part 2. Washington, DC: Government Printing Office, 1876.

Dewey, Melvil. *Dewey Decimal Classification and Relative Index.* 22nd ed. Edited by Joan S. Mitchell, Julianne Beall, Giles Martin, Winton E. Matthews, and Gregory R. New. Dublin, OH: OCLC, 2003.

Falmagne, Rachel Joffe, and Margorie Hass, eds. *Representing Reason: Feminist Theory and Formal Logic*. Lanham: Rowman & Littlefield, 2002.

Fixico, Donald L. *The American Indian Mind in a Linear World*. New York: Routledge, 2003.

Foskett, A. C. "Misogynists All: A Study in Critical Classification." *Library Resources & Technical Services* 15 (1971): 117-21.

Fuss, Diana. *Essentially Speaking: Feminism, Nature & Difference*. New York: Routledge, 1998.

Gerhard, K. H., M. C. Su, and C. C. Rubens. "An Empirical Examination of Subject Headings for Women's Studies Core Materials." *College & Research Libraries*, 59, (1989): 130-38.

Gilligan, Carol. *In a Different Voice: Psychological Theory and Women's Development*. Cambridge, MA: Harvard University Press, 1982.

Goldberger, Nancy, Jill Tarule, Blythe Clinchy, and Mary Belenky, eds. *Knowledge, Difference, and Power: Essays Inspired by "Women's Ways of Knowing."* New York: Basic Books, 1996.

Green, Rebecca. "Syntagmatic Relationships in Index Languages: A Reassessment." *Library Quarterly*, 65 (1995): 365-85.

Grosz, Elizabeth. "Sexual Difference and the Problem of Essentialism." In *The Essential Difference*, edited by N. Schor and E. Weed, 82-97. Bloomington: Indiana University Press, 1994.

Harding, Sandra. "Gendered Ways of Knowing and the 'Epistemological Crisis' of the West." In Goldberger, Tarule, Clinchy, and Belenky, *Knowledge, Difference, and Power*, 431-454.

Hass, Marjorie. "Feminist Readings of Aristotelian Logic." In *Feminist Interpretations of Aristotle*, edited by C. A. Freeland, 19-40. University Park: Pennsylvania State University Press, 1998.

Hekman, Susan J. *Gender and Knowledge: Elements of a Postmodern Feminism*. Oxford: Polity, 1995.

Hildreth, Charles R. "Online Catalog Design Models: Are We Moving in the Right Direction?" 1990. http://www.ou.edu/faculty/h/charles.r.hildreth/clr-five.html.

Huston, Mary M., and Joe L. Williams, "Researcher Response to the Politics of Information." *Research Strategies* 5 (1987): 90-93.

IFLA Study Group on the Functional Requirements for Bibliographic Records. "Functional Requirements for Bibliographic Records—Final Report." Munchen: K. G. Saur, 1998. http://www.ifla.org/vii/s13/frbr/frbr.htm.

Intner, Sheila S., and Elizabeth Futas. "The Role and Impact of Library of Congress Classification on the Assessment of Women's Studies Collections." *Library Acquisitions: Practice & Theory*, 20 (1996): 267-79.

Irigaray, Luce. "The 'Mechanics' of Fluids." In *This Sex Which Is Not One*, translated by C. Porter 106-118. Ithaca, NY: Cornell University Press, 1985.

Jay, Nancy. "Gender and Dichotomy." *Feminist Studies*, 7, (1989): 38-56.

Kublik, A., V. Clevette, D. B. Ward, and Hope A. Olson. "Adapting Dominant Classifications to Particular Contexts." *Cataloging & Classification Quarterly*, 37 no. 1/2 (2003): 13-31.

Larrabee, Mary Jeanne, ed. *An Ethic of Care: Feminist and Interdisciplinary Perspectives*. New York: Routledge, 1993.

Library of Congress. *Library of Congress Subject Headings*. 19th ed. Washington, DC: Library of Congress, Cataloging Distribution Service, 1996.

Lloyd, G. "Reason as Attainment." In *A Reader in Feminist Knowledge*, edited by S. Gunew, 166-80. London: Routledge, 1991.

López-Huertas, Maria, Isabel de Torres, and Mario Barité. "Terminological Representation of Specialized Areas in Conceptual Structures: The Case of Gender Studies." In *Knowledge Organization and the Global Information Society: Proceedings of the Eighth International ISKO Conference*, 13-16 July 2004, edited by I. C. Mcilwaine, 35-39. Wurzburg, Germany: Ergon, 2004.

Lorigo, Lori, B. Pan, H. Hembrooke, T. Joachims, L. Granka, and G. Gay. "The Influence of Task and Gender on Search and Evaluation Behavior Using Google." *Information Processing & Management*, 42 (2006): 1123-31.

Maniez, Jacques. "Relationships in Thesauri: Some Critical Remarks." *International Classification*, 15 (1988): 133-38.

Maron, M. E. "On Indexing, Retrieval and the Meaning of About." *Journal of the American Society for Information Science*, 28 (1977): 38-43.

Marshall, Joan K. "LC Labeling: An Indictment." In *Revolting Librarians*, edited by Celeste West and Elizabeth. Katz, 45-49. San Francisco: Bookleggger Press, 1972.

———. *On Equal Terms: A Thesaurus for Nonsexist Indexing and Cataloging*. New York: Neal-Schuman, 1977.

Nicholas, Yann. "Folklore Requirements for Bibliographic Records: Oral Traditions and FRBR." *Cataloging & Classification Quarterly*, 39 (2005): 179-95.

Nicholson, L. J. "Women, Morality, and History." In Larrabee, *An Ethic of Care*, 87-101.

Nye, Andrea. "Saying What It Is: Predicate Logic and Natural Kinds." In Falmagne and Hass, *Representing Reason*, 191-208.

———. *Words of Power: A Feminist Reading of the History of Logic*. New York: Routledge, 1990.

Oliver, P. "'What Do Girls Know Anyway?': Rationality, Gender, and Social Control." In Falmagne and Hass, *Representing Reason*, 209-32.

Olson, Hope A. "Exclusivity, Teleology and Hierarchy: Our Aristotelian Legacy." *Knowledge Organization*, 26, no. 2 (1999): 65-73.

———. "Mapping Beyond Dewey's Boundaries: Constructing Classificatory Space for Marginalized Knowledge Domains." In *How Classifications Work: Problems and Challenges in an Electronic Age*, edited by G. C. Bowker and S. L. Star. Special Issue, Library Trends 47 no. 2 (1998): 233-54.

———. "Patriarchal Structures of Subject Access and Subversive Techniques for Change." *Canadian Journal for Information and Library Science* 26, no. 2/3 (2001): 1-29.

———. *The Power to Name: Locating the Limits of Subject Representation in Libraries*. Dordrecht: Kluwer Academic, 2002.

———. "The Power to Name: Representation in Library Catalogues." *Signs: Journal of Women in Culture and Society*, 26 (2001): 639-68.

———. "Sameness and Difference: A Cultural Foundation of Classification." *Library Resources & Technical Services*, 45 (2001): 115-22.

———. "Subject Access to Women's Studies Materials." In *Cataloging Heresy: Challenging the Standard Bibliographic Product: Proceedings of the Congress for Librarians*, edited by B. H. Weinberg, 159-69. Medford, NJ: Learned Information, 1992.

Plumwood, Val. "The Politics of Reason: Towards a Feminist Logic." *Australasian Journal of Philosophy* 71 (1993): 436-62.

Rogers, M. N. "Are We on Equal Terms Yet? Subject Headings in LCSH, 1975-1991." *Library Resources & Technical Services*, 37 (1993): 181-96.

Sayers, W. C. Berwick. *A Manual of Classification for Librarians & Bibliographers*. London: Grafton, 1926.

Scheman, N. *Engenderings: Constructions of Knowledge, Authority, and Privilege*. New York: Routledge, 1993.

Smith, Linda Tuhiwai. *Decolonizing Methodologies: Research and Indigenous Peoples*. London: Zed Books, 1999.

Sparkes, A. W. *Talking Philosophy: A Wordbook*. London: Routledge, 1991.

Spelman, Elizabeth. V. *The Inessential Woman: Problems of Exclusion in Feminist Thought*. Boston: Beacon, 1988.

Tronto, Joan C. *Moral Boundaries: A Political Argument for an Ethic of Care*. New York: Routledge, 1993.

UNESCO. "UNESCO Thesaurus." 2003. http://www2.ulcc.ac.uk/unesco/.

Weinberg, B. H. "The Hidden Classification in Library of Congress Subject Headings for Judaica." *Library Resources & Technical Services* 37 (1993): 369-79.

Zoe, Lucinda R., and Diane DiMartino. "Cultural Diversity and End-User Searching: An Analysis by Gender and Language Background." *Research Strategies* 17 (2000): 291-305.

Queer Theory and the Creation of Contextual Subject Access Tools for Gay and Lesbian Communities

D. Grant Campbell[1]

The problem of providing subject access to documents has attracted considerable scrutiny in the field of Information Studies, both from practitioners trying to create and implement efficient access tools and from theorists trying to articulate the conceptual foundations upon which these tools rest. Two problems, in particular, have challenged our expertise in recent years. First, we have come to realize that determining the subject content of a document is an inherently subjective process, which is difficult, if not impossible, to replicate from one indexer to another. Second, we have come to realize that tools purporting to provide "universal" access, such as *Dewey Decimal Classification*, *Library of Congress Classification* and the *Library of Congress Subject Headings*, provide inadequate access to marginalized groups. The terms appearing in these tools to represent communities defined by gender, race and sexual orientation are frequently inadequate; the placement of these terms in classification categories reflects ideologies and assumptions that are archaic or invalid, and these tools frequently do not provide the fine-grained distinctions that would satisfy the information needs of a member of that community.

As a result of these two insistent problems, the knowledge organization research community has become skeptical of one of its most fundamental tenets: that a document has an innate subject content, which is perceived by the indexer or classificationist, and then translated into the language of the

---

1   Editors' note: this paper was previously published in *Knowledge Organization* 27, no. 3 (2000): 122–131.

subject access system.[2] "A knowledge organization," states Jens-Erik Mai, "is a social construction. It is not a reflection or mirror of an already there structure nor an objective description of reality."[3]

Knowledge organization research has therefore come to embrace multiplicity and community identity, both in its approaches to revisions of current access tools, and in its development of new ones. Where the Classification Research Group once dreamed of uniting its many subject-specific classifications into a mammoth, theoretically-grounded universal access mechanism, classification research today is moving in the opposite direction. Now we talk of redefining authority control in terms of multiple authorized terms. We talk of information ecologies, "designed to be used within a particular context or environment."[4] We have moved, argues Clare Beghtol "from the assumption that classification schemes are culturally neutral (and therefore universally applicable) to the assumption that the schemes are culturally based, culturally biased, and nonuniversal."[5]

This is particularly welcome news for gay and lesbian communities, whose increasing influence and visibility have led to new frameworks for historical, intellectual, social and political inquiry. By admitting the existence of cultural bases and biases, knowledge organization researchers will inevitably look to such communities as they strive to update existing subject access schemes and create new ones. The result, ideally, will be up-to-date and relevant vocabularies, gay-positive classification categories, and user-friendly website organization principles, all of which will represent, and grow from, this rich growth of knowledge.

But how are these community-based classification systems going to develop, and what intellectual, conceptual, political and epistemological challenges face those information professionals who take it upon themselves to develop them? Knowledge organization theory is entering a new and

---

2 F. W. Lancaster, *Vocabulary Control for Information Retrieval* (Arlington, VA: Information Resources Press, 1986), 3.

3 Jens-Erik Mai, "A Postmodern Theory of Knowledge Organization," in *Knowledge: Creation, Organization and Use: Proceedings of the 62nd ASIS Annual Meeting, Washington, DC, October 31–November 4, 1999*, ed. Marjorie M. K. Hlava and Larry Woods (Medford, NJ: Published for the American Society for Information Science by Information Today, 1999), 554.

4 Hanne Albrechtsen, "Keynote Address Extended Abstract: The Dynamism and Stability of Classification in Information Ecologies—Problems and Possibilities," in *Dynamism and Stability in Knowledge Organization: Proceedings of the Sixth International ISKO Conference, 10–13 July 2000, Toronto, Canada*, ed. Clare Beghtol, Lynne C. Howarth, and Nancy Williamson (Wurzburg: Ergon Verlag, 2000), 1.

5 Clare Beghtol, "A Whole, Its Kinds, and Its Parts," in Beghtol, Howarth, and Williamson, *Dynamism and Stability in Knowledge Organization*, 313.

highly-politicized era; furthermore, it is embarking on this new era with a fresh suspicion of its own techniques and traditions. In a post-structuralist world, is the concept of a document's intrinsic intellectual content hopelessly naive? And if so, what new tools and new theories will supplement or supplant our old ones? What practical and theoretical problems can the designers of new, contextual access systems expect to face?

These questions are formidable, but knowledge organization theorists should remember that they are not alone. Other fields deal with the subject content of documents; other fields have discovered that their "universal" axioms are in fact contextual and subjective, and must therefore be revised to accommodate the concerns of marginalized groups. This paper examines one such example.

In the 1970s and 1980s, the literary studies community in Europe and North America experienced an epistemological revolution similar to the one facing classification research today. Literary critics were suddenly forced to acknowledge that their techniques and assumptions were anything but universal constants, and that certain communities and minorities demanded new techniques and different assumptions. In particular, the rise of gay and lesbian studies, and later queer theory, caused the literary studies community to reexamine many of its canonical texts, and to see them in very different lights. Formerly marginalized works, such as Djuna Barnes's *Nightwood*, suddenly acquired a new interest, while works of authors such as Shakespeare, Wordsworth, and Henry James were scrutinized for homosexual themes and content.

The fate of one canonical work, Herman Melville's *Billy Budd*, holds a special interest for us, because it served both as the basis of a long tradition of traditional American Literature criticism, and as a lightning rod for the new queer theory in the late 1980s and early 1990s. In particular, Eve Kosofsky Sedgwick, one of the most important innovators in queer theory, made *Billy Budd* a central part of her seminal work, The *Epistemology of the Closet*.[6] By looking at the fate of both Melville and Sedgwick in the literary studies community, we can see some of the challenges, and some of the possible solutions, that face us in knowledge organization research, as we struggle to create subject access theories and tools based on specific cultures, contexts, or communities.

This paper, then, has the following major parts. It begins by discussing a distinction fundamental to both traditional classification theory and traditional literary criticism: the distinction between "aboutness" as an expression of the fundamental content of the document, and "meaning" as an

---

6   Eve Kosofsky Sedgwick, *Epistemology of the Closet* (Berkeley: University of California Press, 1990).

expression of a specific use to which the document is put. Second, it uses this distinction to summarize attitudes to *Billy Budd* in the mainstream literary criticism of the twentieth century, particularly in relation to the story's homosexual content. Third, the discussion moves to Eve Kosofsky Sedgwick's treatment of the story, within the context of her controversial theory of male homosexuality and its place in Western structures of thought. And finally, by looking at the reactions in academia to Sedgwick's theories, the paper isolates specific tensions that arise in queer theory, and their implications for providing subject access in a gay-centered information environment.

One point should be added here. Sedgwick's theory in *Epistemology of the Closet* concerns male homosexuality exclusively: not because she lacks sympathy with, or interest in, lesbian sexuality as a theoretical issue, but because her theory is grounded specifically in the attitudes of Western culture to male homosexuality. In the ensuing discussion, I do not assume that male and female homosexuality are alike and interchangeable. I do, however, assume that the implications of Sedgwick's male-centered theory raise practical subject access concerns that affect female as well as male homosexual communities.

Aboutness and Meaning

Determining the subject content of a document has always been a highly subjective procedure. While the tools for translating the analysis of content into a retrieval system are complex and sophisticated, "there are few, if any, formal rules for the conceptual analysis of documents."[7] The task becomes even more complicated with imaginative literature such as works of fiction because of the ambiguous boundary between content and interpretation. It is very difficult to determine "what kind(s) of factual, relatively unvarying data is present in fiction. . . . In a way, every reader reads a different book."[8] In terms of homosexual content, this ambiguity has been both a spur to literary achievement and a barrier to the widespread acceptance of gay interpretations. "Homosexual novels are characteristically subtle, allusive and symbolic . . . and form an eighth kind of literary ambiguity."[9] Placing a work like *Billy Budd* into a gay literary canon, therefore, requires some theoretical framework for distinguishing data from interpretation: can we isolate in the

---

7 Nancy J. Williamson, "Standards and Rules for Subject Access," *Cataloging & Classification Quarterly* 21, no. 3-4 (1996): 156.
8 Clare Beghtol, *The Classification of Fiction: The Development of a System Based on Theoretical Principles* (Metuchen, NJ: Scarecrow Press, 1994), 125.
9 Jeffrey Meyers, *Homosexuality and Literature* (Montreal: McGill-Queen's University Press, 1977), 1.

story homosexual characters, or homosexual themes, and confidently treat them as stable content that everybody reads?

Knowledge organization theorists have made some progress in defining such a framework. Robert Fairthorne distinguishes between what discourse "mentions" and what discourse is "about":

> *What discourse speaks of, — that is, what it mentions by name or description — are amongst its extensional properties. What discourse speaks on, — that is, what it is about — is amongst its intensional properties. This, its topic, cannot be determined solely from what it mentions. For this one must take into account extra-textual considerations, such as who is using it for what purpose, what purpose the author intended it to be used for, and for whom and for what the librarian, or other manager of messages, acquired it.*[10]

Fairthorne bases his distinction on the concept of explicit "mention": equally important, he suggests that the "aboutness" of a document, in any meaningful sense, often needs something beyond what is explicitly mentioned.

Beghtol reinterprets this distinction as one between "aboutness" and "meaning," the former being the intrinsic content of the document and the latter the uses to which a reader may put the document:

> *For the present purposes . . . we may take the general position that texts of all kinds have a relatively permanent aboutness, but a variable number of meaning(s). . . . A recognition of the relatively permanent quality of aboutness in documents is one of the assumptions upon which bibliographic classification systems have traditionally been based. Classificationists have endeavoured to create classification systems conceptually and notationally hospitable to any aboutness a document might present, but it has not been suggested that the inherent aboutness of the document changes when a particular meaning is attached to it or a particular use made of it by the reader.*[11]

While the "meaning" of a work, then, can vary from reader to reader, aboutness is relatively stable, and can be identified and translated into a classification symbol or a set of controlled descriptors.

---

10 Robert Fairthorne, "Temporal Structure in Bibliographical Classification," in *Theory of Subject Analysis: A Sourcebook*, ed. Lois Mai Chan, Phyllis A. Richmond, and Elaine Svenonius (Littleton, CO: Libraries Unlimited, 1971), 361.

11 Clare Beghtol, "Bibliographic Classification Theory and Text Linguistics: Aboutness Analysis, Inter-Textuality and the Cognitive Act of Classifying Documents," *Journal of Documentation* 42 (1986): 85.

Fairthorne anchors "aboutness" in the document's context, while Beghtol's definition suggests that aboutness resists context to a certain degree. But both present aboutness as some intrinsic element of the document's intellectual content, and the successful extraction and translation of that intrinsic content constitutes useful subject access. If the aboutness is stable, then ideally the subject analyst should be able to identify it accurately and consistently all the time. Consistency has always been a primary objective of subject analysis: "In the current environment of global bibliographic information systems, it is essential to provide guidance in the design and development of the tools used in order to achieve, insofar as is possible, inter-system and intra-system consistency and compatibility."[12]

Knowledge organization theory, then, brings a recognition that a complex distinction must be made between data and interpretation; it brings a strategy for distinguishing between stable content and variable meanings; and it employs that strategy in an attempt to bring about consistent and replicable indexing activities. What happens if we apply this strategy in a field and a context where the distinction between data and interpretation is highly charged? Can we say, using the meaning/aboutness division, that there is homosexual content in a story like *Billy Budd*?

Billy Budd, Literary Criticism, and Queer Theory

Let us begin with Fairthorne's extensional properties, and attempt to summarize the plot of *Billy Budd*, solely in terms of what is explicitly mentioned. The story concerns a British warship, the *Bellipotent*, in the late eighteenth century, under the command of Captain Vere. A young foretopman, Billy Budd, has been impressed into service, and his cheerful manner and handsome appearance make him a popular and valued member of the crew. He also attracts the malice of Claggart, the master-at-arms, who arrests him on a trumped-up charge of being a mutineer. Billy, when confronted with this, strikes Claggart, and accidentally kills him. Captain Vere, while sympathizing with Billy, feels impelled to uphold navy justice and discipline, and Billy is sentenced to hang.

As any literary critic would point out, even this stark description distorts the text into an interpretation, by virtue of the plot details it chooses to omit. And because homosexuality often appears through implication, rather than through explicit mention, let us supplement this summary with a single quotation from the text, which will hopefully provide access to some of the extra-textual implications. In a scene that figures frequently in criticism, Billy Budd, unaware that he has become the object of Claggart's malevolent interest, accidentally spills his soup on the deck, just as Claggart is approaching.

---

12   Williamson, "Standards and Rules for Subject Access," 158.

> [Claggart] happened to observe who it was that had done the spilling. His countenance changed. Pausing, he was about to ejaculate something hasty at the sailor, but checked himself, and pointing down to the streaming soup, playfully tapped him from behind with his rattan, saying in a low musical voice peculiar to him at times, "Handsomely done, my lad! And handsome is as handsome did it, too!" And with that passed on.[13]

We are never explicitly told why Claggart is obsessed with Billy Budd: the narrator instead alludes enigmatically to "an antipathy spontaneous and profound"[14] to a Platonic concept of "Natural Depravity," and to the difficulties of trying to "enter his labyrinth and get out again."[15]

Billy Budd and the Critics

These teasing hints of things unsaid have fascinated critics since the story's first posthumous appearance in 1924. Early critics attempted to fill the gaps left by the narrator by arguing that the story was "about" particular themes: mutiny and discipline;[16] fall and redemption;[17] innocence and evil.[18] Later critics argue that the story is about homosexuality, if only in a veiled way.[19] Others argue that the story is "about" silence and ambiguity, rather than any hidden reasons for silence.[20]

This critical history of *Billy Budd* reflects a general shift of emphasis in literary criticism from a set of supposedly stable meanings to an emphasis on contextual and subjective readings. The early Melville critics explicitly

---

13 Herman Melville, *Billy Budd and Other Stories* (London: Penguin, 1986), 321–22.

14 Ibid., 323.

15 Ibid., 324.

16 Hershel Parker, *Reading Billy Budd* (Evanston, IL: Northwestern University Press, 1990), 76.

17 Ronald Mason, *The Spirit above the Dust: A Study of Herman Melville* (London: J. Lehmann, 1951), 25.

18 Newton Arvin, *Herman Melville*, Compass Books ed. (New York: Viking, 1957), 294.

19 Robert K. Martin, *Hero, Captain, and Stranger: Male Friendship, Social Critique, and Literary Form in the Sea Novels of Herman Melville* (Chapel Hill: University of North Carolina Press, 1986), 112; F. O. Matthiesen, "Billy Budd, Foretopman" (1941), in *Melville: A Collection of Critical Essays.*, ed. Richard Volney Chase (Englewood Cliffs, NJ: Prentice-Hall, 1962), 161; Parker, *Reading Billy Budd*, 103.

20 Paul Brodtkorb, Jr., "The Definitive *Billy Budd*: 'But Aren't It All Sham?'," *PMLA* 82 (1967): 604. http://www.jstor.org/stable/461168; Barbara Johnson, "Melville's Fist: The Execution of *Billy Budd*," *Studies in Romanticism* 18 (1979): 573. http://www.jstor.org/stable/25600211.

assume that their interpretations are bias-free and universal. Newton Arvin, for instance, argues that his interpretation is as "extensional," in Fairthorne's terms, as the words themselves:

> *Everyone has felt this benedictory quality in* [Billy Budd]. *Everyone has felt it to be the work of a man on the last verge of mortal existence who wishes to take his departure with a word of acceptance and reconciliation on his lips.*[21]

As the century progresses, the trend shifts in the opposite direction, particularly in the wake of reader response criticism, which has placed the significance of interpretation on the reader. Reader-response critics would argue that ". . . a poem cannot be understood apart from its results. Its 'effects,' psychological and otherwise, are essential to any accurate description of its meaning, since that meaning has no effective existence outside of its realization in the mind of a reader."[22] Felix Martinez Bonati makes a distinction between "*text* as a particular set of signs that we recognize as such, and *work* as the product and the experience of the appropriate decoding of the text."[23] In subject analysis terms, these approaches emphasize the importance of the text's "meaning" over its aboutness. And it presents this meaning, not as an innate quality waiting to be "discovered," but as the result of an operation, variously defined as realization, appropriation, and decoding.

This emphasis on the reader eventually undermines the notion of the text itself, to the point where "aboutness" in the subject analysis sense does not exist at all: "There is no rigorous way to distinguish fact from interpretation, so nothing can be deemed to be definitively *in* the text prior to interpretive conventions."[24] The more one looks for intrinsic content, the more one finds that even the most stable, formal features of a text are constructed and interpreted by individual readers within the context of specific discourse communities.

Literary theory, then, has never produced a distinction between data and interpretation which could be meaningfully aligned with the distinction between aboutness and meaning. Early criticism treats even the most

---

21 Fairthorne, "Temporal Structure in Bibliographical Classification," 292.
22 Jane P. Tompkins, "An Introduction to Reader-Response Criticism," introduction to *Reader-Response Criticism: From Formalism to Post-Structuralism*, ed. Jane P. Tompkins (Baltimore: Johns Hopkins University Press, 1980), ix.
23 Felix Martinez Bonati, "The Stability of Literary Meaning," in *Identity of the Literary Text*, ed. Mario J. Valdés and Owen J. Miller (Toronto: University of Toronto Press, 1985), 231.
24 Jonathan Culler, "Introduction: The Identity of the Literary Text," in Valdés and Miller, *Identity of the Literary Text*, 5.

idiosyncratic interpretation as an expression of the text's stable content; later criticism has undermined the possibility of any stable content. Just as classification theorists are now becoming convinced that essential, universal meanings are impossible, literary theorists have had to face the ultimate subjectivity of their own interpretations.

Sedgwick and Queer Theory

It is hardly surprising, therefore, that Eve Kosofsky Sedgwick barely ruffled the feathers of the Melville tradition in 1990, when *"Billy Budd*: After the Homosexual," appeared as a chapter of her second major work on male homosocial relations in literature, *Epistemology of the Closet*. Reviews in the major literary studies journals were highly complimentary towards her interpretation of the story, an interpretation which argued that all desire in the story was homosexual desire, that men turned each other into erections, and that the hanging of Billy offers an apocalyptic vision of a post-homosexual world, in which homosexuality as a potential force of mutinous desire is ejaculated and discharged. Even the staid mainstream titles in English and American Literature hailed her readings as "sharp" and "resonant,"[25] "subtle" and "complex,"[26] and "ingenious and persuasive."[27] Subsequent readings of *Billy Budd* routinely cite Sedgwick in their initial critical surveys, generally in a complimentary fashion.[28]

Sedgwick's importance for subject analysis, however, lies not in what she says about *Billy Budd*, but in the theoretical framework which underlies what she says. To understand how Sedgwick interprets *Billy Budd*, we need to recognize that *Epistemology of the Closet*, even more than her previous book, *Between Men* (1985), is a work that combines literary criticism and literary theory, and combines them both with social analysis. The literary readings in *Epistemology of the Closet* explore the ways in which male homosexuality,

---

25 James R. Kincaid, review of *Epistemology of the Closet*, by Eve Kosofsky Sedgwick, *Journal of English and Germanic Philology* 91 (July 1992): 415. http://www.jstor.org/stable/27710703.

26 Susan Gubar, review of *Epistemology of the Closet*, by Eve Kosofsky Sedgwick, *Victorian Studies*, 35 (1991): 115. http://www.jstor.org/stable/3827785.

27 Peter Thorslev, review of *Epistemology of the Closet*, by Eve Kosofsky Sedgwick, *Nineteenth-Century Literature* 46, no. 4 (1992): 559. http://www.jstor.org/stable/2933810,559.

28 Caleb Crain, "Lovers of Human Flesh: Homosexuality and Cannibalism in Melville's Novels," *American Literature* 66 (1994): 25-53, http://www.jstor.org/stable/2927432; Nancy Ruttenburg, "Melville's Handsome Sailor: The Anxiety of Innocence," *American Literature* 66, no. 1 (1994): 83-103. http://www.jstor.org/stable/2927434.

and the systematic paranoia and oppression with which it is socially viewed, infiltrates the epistemological foundations of Western society and culture. Furthermore, Sedgwick argues that the new visibility of gay communities in the wake of the AIDS epidemic have made this paranoia and oppression a topic of major social urgency. Literary criticism, then, appears within a context that includes legal decisions in the United States regarding male homosexuality, the political and social identity of the American gay community in the late 1980s, and the uses and abuses of medical education and research. Underlying Sedgwick's entire study are two primary theses:

- That an underlying definitional distinction between homosexuality and heterosexuality structures thought in modern Western culture;[29] and
- That we can best understand this distinction in terms of a binary tension between a minoritizing view, which sees homosexuality as the experience of a distinct and marginalized subset of society, and a universalizing view, which sees homosexuality, and homosexual concerns, as something which pervades all thought and all social levels.[30]

On the basis of these theses, Sedgwick articulates a number of axioms, four of which are especially relevant to us in classification research:

- People differ from each other in ways that defy our traditional tools of articulating difference. Therefore, established categories (such as "straight" and "gay") are often inadequate, and survival often depends on the ability to make, alter and remake provisional categorizations about the kinds of people there are in the world.[31]
- Gender and orientation issues can be relevant, even in cases where such issues form no part of the thematic "content."[32]
- That the nature vs. nurture question in gay studies needs to be recast, and that the important question is not, "How do people come to be gay," but "for whom is the homo/heterosexual definition of central importance?"[33]
- That historical studies, in their effort to expose social constructions of homosexuality in the past, have inadvertently created a

---

29 Sedgwick, *Epistemology of the Closet*, 1.
30 Ibid.
31 Ibid., 23.
32 Ibid., 34.
33 Ibid., 40.

falsely coherent and monolithic presentation of homosexuality "as we know it today."[34]

These theses and axioms have suggestive implications for subject access theory. First, they suggest that issues of categorization, both as grouping and as differentiation, have a vital role in the growth and survival of homosexual communities. Second, if Sedgwick's claims are justified, then it is possible to argue that *all* works, regardless of their overt content, are, to some extent, "about" homosexuality. A classification system designed for the gay male community, therefore, could theoretically encompass virtually all documents from all subject areas.

Third, gay communities and gay theorists continue to be split between essentialist and constructivist theories of homosexuality. On the one hand, readers and critics feel what Sedgwick calls a "potentially paralytic demand for essence":[35] the isolation and celebration of a transhistorical, transcultural phenomenon called "homosexuality," which can be uncovered by the careful and relentless dismantling of historical prejudices and traditions of silencing. On the other hand, many readers follow Foucault, who argued that the modern "homosexual" appeared in 1870, when the practice of "sodomy" ceased to refer to acts and became rooted in the individual identity.[36] Adherents to this approach isolate images and paradigms of homosexuality, not as eternal constants, but as local, historical, cultural constructs that may not hold true in different times or places.

The subject access system designed for a gay information ecology, therefore, has not banished multiplicity and conflict by moving from the universal to the particular. Within gay communities, Sedgwick suggests, people are different, categories shift, and labels are provisional. We are dealing with no monolithic identity, no stable categories, and no consensus. Furthermore, she suggests, survival within a marginalized group depends on the regular and frequent subversion of traditional classification categories.

While Sedgwick's analysis of *Billy Budd* has been well-received, these broad theoretical assumptions have been less fortunate. Sedgwick faced particularly keen opposition in the critical theory community, and objections to her theories and axioms began before *Epistemology* was published. David van Leer's influential critique of her work challenges Sedgwick's use of language, and suggests that her colloquial style, which uses such terms as "fag hag" and "bitch," betrays a latent

---

34 Ibid., 44.
35 Ibid., 92.
36 Michel Foucault, *The History of Sexuality*, trans. Robert Hurley, vol. 1, *An Introduction* (New York: Pantheon, 1978), 43.

homophobia.[37] The problem, van Leer argues, is not one of personal sympathy: Sedgwick's sympathy with, and sense of allegiance with, the gay community, particularly the gay male community, is never questioned; nor are her consciously gay-positive intentions. The problem, rather, is that Sedgwick is not a gay man:

> Sedgwick's majority status vis-à-vis gay men is most evident in her problematic terminology, of which her use of sexual stereotypes is only the most obvious example. Unable to speak from within the minority, Sedwick must perforce speak from within the majority; denied the language of homosexuality, she necessarily speaks heterosexuality. Such a vocabulary is inevitably prejudicial.[38]

Van Leer's argument is damning: as someone who inevitably speaks from outside the community rather than from within, Sedgwick, despite her good intentions, has "disempowered" that community: "she does not uncover a homophobic thematics but underwrites one."[39] What she *is* overwhelms what she tries to *do*.

Sedgwick's plight in the theory community suggests a startling consequence of the new assumptions of subjectivity. Even as literary theory has discredited the idea of a permanent subject matter inherent in the literary text, it has resurrected "aboutness" in a different context. If indeed there is nothing in the text that can be isolated as "intrinsic," then any analysis, any tool, any method that provides others with a means of finding coherence and meaning in a text is subject to scrutiny. The critical task is no longer to find content in the text, but rather to identify and articulate the ideological, social and cultural positions from which others find content in the text.

Three Binarisms Affecting a Community-Based System of Subject Access Based on Sexual Orientation

What, then, does this specific example from literary studies and queer theory suggest for the creator of a community-based subject access system, based on sexual orientation? I suggest that knowledge organization will have to grapple with the same two binarisms that plague literary theory:

- Essentialist views vs. constructivist views of homosexuality: homosexuality as a permanent, unchanging reality vs.

---

37 David Van Leer, "The Beast of the Closet: Homosociality and the Pathology of Manhood," *Critical Inquiry* 15, no. 3 (1989): 587–605. http://www.jstor.org/stable/1343655.
38 Ibid., 604.
39 Ibid.

homosexuality as the construction of specific historical forces and contexts.
- Minoritizing views vs. universalizing views: homosexuality as the lifestyle of a minority of the human community, vs. homosexuality as a concept with universal implications for everyone, regardless of their sexual orientation.

In addition, the subject analyst will continue to grapple with our more familiar binarism:
- Aboutness vs. meaning: homosexuality as an intrinsic part of a document's intellectual content, vs. homosexuality as a means of using and interpreting documents, regardless of their explicit or innate content.

How, then, can we expect these three binary tensions to appear in the task of constructing a contextual classification system for use within gay communities?

Essentialist vs. Constructivist Views

In his *Rules for a Dictionary Catalog*, Charles Cutter argued that a catalogue should use the most current and familiar terminology to denote concepts: when choosing between synonymous headings, one should prefer the one that "is most familiar to the class of people who consult the library."[40] Hope A. Olson has already critiqued this image of the "normal user" as a concept that oppresses and marginalizes those that do not conform to the norm.[41] In a gay-centered context, the practice becomes even more problematic, because there is no consensus on an unpopular but persistent question: is there anything out there called "homosexuality," which has existed through the ages, and which is waiting to be uncovered? Some argue that we must be wary of treating homosexuality as an essential entity through the ages; even when we treat it as a social construction, we must avoid the assumption that we are witnessing, in the decline of former constructions of homosexuality, "the emergence of a proto-modern 'homosexual identity.'"[42] Scholars, however, particularly those engaged in historical research, have faced opposition from

---

40 Charles Cutter, "Rules for a Dictionary Catalog," (1904), in Chan, Richmond, and Svenonius, *Theory of Subject Analysis*, 7.
41 Hope A. Olson, "Between Control and Chaos: An Ethical Perspective on Authority Control," *Proceedings of Authority Control in the 21st Century: An Invitational Conference, March 3, 1996*, http://www.oclc.org/oclc/man/authconf/holson.htm.
42 Cameron McFarlane, *The Sodomite in Fiction and Satire, 1660–1750* (New York: Columbia University Press, 1997), 4.

those in the gay community who argue that there is something called "homosexuality," with a history of its own which has been repressed, and which must be resurrected.

The classificationist, then, can expect to be torn, as gay critics and gay historians have been torn, between the academy and the gay community. An access tool founded upon a teleological view of homosexuality "as we know it today" might well adopt a policy similar to that of the Library of Congress: selecting the most current term, and either rejecting earlier terms or treating them as equivalences. Indeed, many critiques of the Library of Congress are founded on just such a view: like Sanford Berman, Ellen Greenblatt attacks the Library of Congress for its sluggish responses to updating terms: "The Library of Congress has been slow to implement changes in the language of LCSH to reflect common usage and current terminology."[43] Such an approach, however, runs the risk of losing the historical dimension to current terms, preventing researchers from charting the evolution of concepts and terms from one period to another.

On the other hand, a tool which was oriented to the different ways in which concepts of sexuality and homosexuality are constructed in different eras would be highly sensitive to creating equivalences, and to the imposition of current interpretations on terms that have a long and varied life of signification. This is particularly the case for terms like *sodomy*, which Foucault designated an "utterly confused category,"[44] and which, over time, has been used to denote activities as diverse as bestiality, priestly celibacy, masturbation, birth control, pederasty, and luxurious consumption.[45] Given that many current laws pertaining to homosexuality use terms and texts that are handed down from the Renaissance and the Colonies,[46] to what extent should syndetic references in an access tool reflect such terminological looseness?

Minoritizing vs. Universalizing Viewpoints

In his landmark treatment of homosexuality in Hollywood movies, *The Celluloid Closet*, Vito Russo cites a number of quotations from directors and actors who were promoting movies with homosexual themes. All claim that their movies are not "about" homosexuality, but about something else: "the

---

43 Ellen Greenblatt, "Homosexuality: The Evolution of a Concept in the *Library of Congress Subject Headings*," in *Gay and Lesbian Library Service*, ed. Cal Gough and Ellen Greenblatt (Jefferson, NC: McFarland, 1990), 76.
44 Foucault, *History of Sexuality*, 101.
45 McFarlane, *The Sodomite in Fiction and Satire*, 4.
46 Jonathan Goldberg, *Sodometries: Renaissance Texts, Modern Sexualities* (Stanford, CA: Stanford University Press, 1992), 11.

power to destroy people's lives," "loneliness," or "insanity."[47] Russo's wry list certainly points out an underlying homophobia in Hollywood and in North America, in its desire to deny the presence of homosexual themes, and in the repeated connections of homosexuality with loneliness, insanity, or both. The speakers' comments, however, indicate a standard technique for counteracting homophobia. To use Sedgwick's term, this is a "universalizing" method: homosexuality is made "mainstream" by arguing that its concerns are not those of a specific minority, but those of the human community as a whole. You don't have to be homosexual to understand loneliness or insanity: such themes are universal, and the presence of homosexual characters need not prevent anyone from paying to see the movie.

Not every gay artist approves of this approach. Harvey Fierstein, in an interview for the movie version of *The Celluloid Closet*, responds vigorously to this "universalizing" trend, using another concept central to subject analysis: "translation":

> *All the reading I was given to do in school was heterosexual; I mean, every movie I saw was heterosexual, and I had to do this "translation." I had to translate it to my life, rather than seeing my life. Which is why, when people say to me, "your work isn't really gay work, it's universal," and I say, "up yours," you know. "It's gay. And that you can take it and translate it for your own life is very nice, but at last I don't have to do the translating. You do."*[48]

If the gay community is split between two concepts of survival—integration into a universal whole and separation into a visible minority—then a classification system will have to negotiate that split. The universalizing tendency will tend to treat explicit subject headings with suspicion. Even as Sanford Berman campaigns for introducing new subject headings that promote the visibility of minority concerns, his objections to such headings as "Women as accountants" and "Women in agriculture" suggest that visibility is a double-edged sword: "The 'as' strongly suggests that women are not ordinarily competent or otherwise equipped to work at accountancy."[49] The universalizing approach implies that the explicit presence of a topic in a subject access system implies a deviation from the norm. The minoritizing view,

---

47   Vito Russo, *The Celluloid Closet: Homosexuality in the Movies* (New York: Harper & Row, 1981), 126.

48   Harvey Fierstein, interview, *The Celluloid Closet*, dir. Rob Epstein and Jeffrey Friedman (A Telling Pictures Production, 1995).

49   Sanford Berman, *Prejudices and Antipathies: A Tract on the LC Subject Heads concerning People* (Jefferson, NC: McFarland &, 1993), 145.

on the other hand, may well argue, as Fierstein has argued, for "visibility at any cost"; "I'd rather have negative than nothing."[50]

Aboutness and Meaning

If community-based classification systems follow current thinking in knowledge organization research, we can expect that the system will be contextual, socially determined, and culturally relative. However, the reaction to *Epistemology of the Closet* suggests that the creators and implementers of such a system can expect careful, sometimes ruthless scrutiny. While the terms, concepts and categories can be assumed to reflect a specific cultural position, rather than an innate and essential system of universal categories, the system itself, and the people who design and use it, will be evaluated for their stated and unstated positions and biases.

Furthermore, this scrutiny will never end, and this is something that subject analysts will have to get used to. Berman's attacks on the Library of Congress all suggest that the Subject Headings, in their nuances, terms, and implicit categories, manifest an unenlightened point of view: in this case, "a host of untenable—indeed, obsolete and arrogant—assumptions."[51] The problem, he implies, can be alleviated by being more enlightened, and responding more quickly to the suggestions of enlightened people. The attacks on Eve Kosofsky Sedgwick, on the other hand, assert that she is an intelligent, frequently ingenious scholar who has done good work from excellent personal motives, but who nonetheless manifests in her work the inescapable features of her ideological, intellectual, social and cultural position.

If Sedgwick has had a rough ride, the makers of a classification system based on a specific community cannot expect to be scrutinized any less carefully. Nor can they protect themselves with naïve protestations of being "bias-free," or consulting some arbitrary abstraction known as "the ordinary user." The makers of new classification systems will be expected to articulate their position relative to the community for whom the system is designed. This position will make a fundamental part of the tool's nature, and will become the means whereby readers, users and critics of the system will rebel, and find their own provisional categories. The makers of subject access tools are used to asking themselves the first question: "Who are my users?" They will now have to tackle two additional, equally challenging questions: "Who am I in relation to my users, and how does my position manifest itself in the tool itself?"

---

50 Fierstein, *Celluloid Closet*.
51 Berman, *Prejudices and Antipathies*, 15.

Conclusion

Classification theory and practice, then, stands on the threshold of a whole range of new developments. The forthcoming confusion, however, can be alleviated by looking at, and learning from, the experiences of document subject analysis in other fields. The example provided by *Billy Budd*, and by Eve Kosofsky Sedgwick, suggests that our break from the past, while profound, is by no means complete. Our belief in subjectivity has not banished the distinction between aboutness and meaning, but merely displaced it into a new set of relationships. And, if gay theory and gay communities are any indication, even limiting a classification to a particular community's aims and concerns will by no means make achieving consensus any easier. Categories are fluid and unstable. Community members want both to see themselves as permanent and unchanging, and to see themselves as socially constructed; they want to belong and to remain apart. By acknowledging these inevitable ambiguities, classification researchers will be well-positioned to create new, better subject access tools. But they will do so only by acknowledging that the tough questions are here to stay, and that complexity, debate and controversy can be negotiated, but not banished.

Bibliography

Albrechtsen, Hanne. "Keynote Address Extended Abstract: The Dynamism and Stability of Classification in Information Ecologies—Problems and Possibilities." In Beghtol, Howarth, and Williamson, *Dynamism and Stability in Knowledge Organization*, 1-2.

Arvin, Newton. *Herman Melville*. Compass Books ed. New York: Viking, 1957.

Beghtol, Clare. "Bibliographic Classification Theory and Text Linguistics: Aboutness Analysis, Inter-Textuality and the Cognitive Act of Classifying Documents." *Journal of Documentation* 42 (1986): 84-113.

———. *The Classification of Fiction: The Development of a System Based on Theoretical Principles*. Metuchen, NJ: Scarecrow Press, 1994.

———. "A Whole, Its Kinds, and Its Parts." In Beghtol, Howarth, and Williamson, *Dynamism and Stability in Knowledge Organization*, 313-19.

Beghtol, Clare, Lynne C. Howarth, and Nancy Williamson, eds. *Dynamism and Stability in Knowledge Organization: Proceedings of the Sixth International ISKO Conference, 10-13 July 2000, Toronto, Canada*. Wurzburg: Ergon Verlag, 2000.

Berman, Sanford. *Prejudices and Antipathies: A Tract on the LC Subject Heads concerning People*. Jefferson, NC: McFarland &, 1993.

Bonati, Felix Martinez. "The Stability of Literary Meaning." In Valdés and Miller, *Identity of the Literary Text*, 231-45.

Brodtkorb, Paul, Jr. "The Definitive *Billy Budd*: 'But Aren't It All Sham?'." *PMLA* 82 (1967): 602-12. http://www.jstor.org/stable/461168.
Chan, Lois Mai, Phyllis A. Richmond, and Elaine Svenonius, eds. *Theory of Subject Analysis: A Sourcebook*. Littleton, CO: Libraries Unlimited, 1971.
Crain, Caleb. "Lovers of Human Flesh: Homo-Sexuality and Cannibalism in Melville's Novels." *American Literature* 66 (1994): 25-53. http://www.jstor.org/stable/2927432.
Culler, Jonathan. "Introduction: The Identity of the Literary Text." In Valdés and Miller, *Identity of the Literary Text*, 3-15.
Cutter, Charles. "Rules for a Dictionary Catalog." 1904. In Chan, Richmond, and Svenonius, *Theory of Subject Analysis*, 1-20.
Fairthorne, Robert. "Temporal Structure in Bibliographical Classification." In Chan, Richmond, and Svenonius, *Theory of Subject Analysis*, 359-68.
Fierstein, Harvey. Interview. *The Celluloid Closet*. Directed by Rob Epstein and Jeffrey Friedman. A Telling Pictures Production, 1995.
Foucault, Michel. *The History of Sexuality*. Translated by Robert Hurley. Vol. 1, *An Introduction*. New York: Pantheon, 1978.
Goldberg, Jonathan. *Sodometries: Renaissance Texts, Modern Sexualities*. Stanford, CA: Stanford University Press, 1992.
Greenblatt, Ellen. "Homosexuality: The Evolution of a Concept in the *Library of Congress Subject Headings*." In *Gay and Lesbian Library Service*, edited by Cal Gough and Ellen Greenblatt. Jefferson, NC: McFarland, 1990.
Gubar, Susan. Review of *Epistemology of the Closet*, by Eve Kosofsky Sedgwick. *Victorian Studies* 35 (1991): 114-16. http://www.jstor.org/stable/3827785.
Johnson, Barbara. "Melville's Fist: The Execution of *Billy Budd*." *Studies in Romanticism* 18 (1979): 567-99. http://www.jstor.org/stable/25600211.
Kincaid, James R. Review of *Epistemology of the Closet*, by Eve Kosofsky Sedgwick. *Journal of English and Germanic Philology* 91, no. 3 (1992): 414-17. http://www.jstor.org/stable/27710703.
Lancaster, F. W. *Vocabulary Control for Information Retrieval*. Arlington, VA: Information Resources Press, 1986.
Mai, Jens-Erik. "A Postmodern Theory of Knowledge Organization." In *Knowledge: Creation, Organization and Use: Proceedings of the 62nd ASIS Annual Meeting, Washington, DC, October 31-November 4, 1999*, edited by Marjorie M. K. Hlava and Larry Woods, 547-56. Medford, NJ: Published for the American Society for Information Science by Information Today, 1999.
Martin, Robert K. *Hero, Captain, and Stranger: Male Friendship, Social Critique, and Literary Form in the Sea Novels of Herman Melville*. Chapel Hill: University of North Carolina Press, 1986.

Mason, Ronald. *The Spirit above the Dust: A Study of Herman Melville*. London: J. Lehmann, 1951.
Matthiesen, F. O. "Billy Budd, Foretopman." 1941. In *Melville: A Collection of Critical Essays*, edited by Richard Volney Chase. Englewood Cliffs, NJ: Prentice-Hall, 1962.
McFarlane, Cameron. *The Sodomite in Fiction and Satire, 1660–1750*. New York: Columbia University Press, 1997.
Melville, Herman. *Billy Budd and Other Stories*. London: Penguin, 1986.
Meyers, Jeffrey. *Homosexuality and Literature*. Montreal: McGill-Queen's University Press, 1977.
Olson, Hope A. "Between Control and Chaos: An Ethical Perspective on Authority Control." *Proceedings of Authority Control in the 21st Century: An Invitational Conference*. March 3, 1996. http://www.oclc.org/oclc/man/authconf/holson.htm.
Parker, Hershel. *Reading Billy Budd*. Evanston, IL: Northwestern University Press, 1990.
Russo, Vito. *The Celluloid Closet: Homosexuality in the Movies*. New York: Harper & Row, 1981.
Ruttenburg, Nancy. "Melville's Handsome Sailor: The Anxiety of Innocence." *American Literature* 66, no. 1 (1994): 83–103. http://www.jstor.org/stable/2927434.
Sedgwick, Eve Kosofsky. *Epistemology of the Closet*. Berkeley: University of California Press, 1990.
Thorslev, Peter. Review of *Epistemology of the Closet*, by Eve Kosofsky Sedgwick. *Nineteenth-Century Literature* 46, no. 4 (1992): 557–61. http://www.jstor.org/stable/2933810,559.
Tompkins, Jane P. "An Introduction to Reader-Response Criticism." Introduction to *Reader-response Criticism: From Formalism to Post-structuralism*, edited by Jane P. Tompkins, ix–xxvi. Baltimore: Johns Hopkins University Press, 1980.
Valdés, Mario J., and Owen J. Miller, eds. *Identity of the Literary Text*. Toronto: University of Toronto Press, 1985.
Van Leer, David. "The Beast of the Closet: Homosociality and the Pathology of Manhood." *Critical Inquiry* 15, no. 3 (1989): 587–605. http://www.jstor.org/stable/1343655.
Williamson, Nancy J. "Standards and Rules for Subject Access." *Cataloging & Classification Quarterly* 21, no. 3–4 (1996): 155–76.

Paraphilias:
The Perversion of Meaning in the
Library of Congress Catalog

Melissa Adler

The Library of Congress is the United States' oldest federal cultural institution and occupies a critical space where medical, social science, political, literary, and other discourses are collected, arranged, and disseminated to Congress and the public. This chapter is part of a larger project that examines the social construction of sexual deviance through the lens of the Library of Congress Subject Heading (LCSH): "Paraphilias," the term that replaced the earlier authorized headings, "Sexual perversion" (1898-1972), and "Sexual deviation" (1972-2007). Due to the cataloging technology known as "global updating," all subject headings can be automatically converted in local catalog records to the most current version of the heading. Prior to this technology, records were changed by hand to update bibliographic records. Therefore, everything that was previously assigned "Sexual perversion" would have been manually updated and categorized as "Sexual deviation." With the global update "Paraphilias" has replaced "Sexual deviation" in most catalogs, including that of the Library of Congress, without any human review of the catalog records. This means that texts that were cataloged in the early part of the twentieth century have retained some of the long abandoned attitudes.

An intertextual reading of relationships between a specific subject heading and the works to which it affords access reveal and problematize *LCSH* as an interface where the prevailing attitudes and assumptions in scholarship both emerge in and produce universalized and authorized terms. It will also show the shifts over time in scholarship, including changes in what counts as a perverted expression or behavior. I suggest that the authorized term "Paraphilias" offers a particularly interesting lens through which to build upon existing research on *LCSH* and classification more generally, as it presents both disciplinary and historical challenges. Drawing especially on sexuality scholar Judith Halberstam's "perverse presentism" and Sanford Berman's three principles for subject access, I will demonstrate approaches to this particular heading.

This study builds on a body of scholarship that examines the effects of state, scientific, and cultural institutions on sexual politics and practices,[1] as well as classification research in Library and Information Studies.[2] It relies heavily on feminist and queer theories, which expose the inherent slipperiness, expansiveness, and limitations of categories, and that situate sexual expression and regulation within historical, social, and political contexts. Such approaches bring various ironies and paradoxes of library classification to light. Categories are necessary for information retrieval. Librarians assign books call numbers and place them on shelves near related subjects, and they assign subject headings so that people can find information on various topics in the catalog. As patrons, scholars of sexuality studies know all too well the joy of browsing and getting swept away in the HQs.

Because *LCSH* is an institutionalized expression of societal customs and beliefs, it should be understood as a part of an entire matrix of social practices and discourses. It not only reflects mainstream ideas, but it also perpetuates and influences them. The Library of Congress operates at the center of scholarly discourses; research from medical, social science, political, and

---

1   To name a few: Margot Canaday, *The Straight State: Sexuality and Citizenship in Twentieth-Century America* (Princeton, NJ: Princeton University Press, 2009); Jennifer Terry, *An American Obsession: Science, Medicine, and Homosexuality in Modern Society* (Chicago: University of Chicago Press, 1999); John D'Emilio, "Capitalism and Gay Identity," in *Powers of Desire: The Politics of Sexuality*, ed. Ann Barr Snitow, Christine Stansell, and Sharon Thompson (New York: Monthly Review Press, 1983).

2   Ellen Greenblatt, "Homosexuality: The Evolution of a Concept in the *Library of Congress Subject Headings*," in *Gay and Lesbian Library Service*, ed. Cal Gough and Ellen Greenblatt (Jefferson, NC: McFarland, 1990), 75-101; Carole L. Palmer and Cheryl Knott Malone, "Elaborate Isolation: Metastructures of Knowledge about Women" *Information Society* 17, no. 3 (2001): 179-194. doi:10.1080/01972240152493047; Hope A. Olson, *The Power to Name: Locating the Limits of Subject Representation in Libraries* (Boston: Kluwer Academic, 2002); Hope A. Olson, "Difference, Culture and Change: The Untapped Potential of *LCSH*, in *The "LCSH" Century: One Hundred Years with the "Library of Congress Subject Headings" System*, ed. A.T. Stone (Birmingham, NY: Haworth, 2007), 53-71; Sanford Berman, *Prejudices and Antipathies: A Tract on the LC Subject Heads Concerning People* (Metuchen, NJ: Scarecrow Press, 1971); Geoffrey C. Bowker and Susan Leigh Star, *Sorting Things Out: Classification and Its Consequences* (Cambridge, MA: MIT Press, 2000).

other disciplines are collected, arranged, and disseminated to Congress and the public. This study will enhance understanding of the role of knowledge production in the construction of deviance by looking to the place where these discourses are stored and categorized.

Following scholars such as sexuality historian George Chauncey and library historian James Carmichael, Jr., who remind us of the critical importance and challenge of doing queer history,[3] I am looking to the Library of Congress to find out what kinds of materials have been collected and how they have been organized. Chauncey notes that the history of discrimination against gays and lesbians is usually misremembered—either it is forgotten or exaggerated. He states:

> [T]his history of discrimination has been erased from the historical record, and that this erasure itself has been a central element of antigay politics. . . . Even well-educated Americans are often startled to learn that the government dismissed more homosexuals than communists at the height of the McCarthy era.[4]

In fact, library historian Louise Robbins has revealed that the Library of Congress engaged in the Federal Loyalty Program and purged homosexuals from its ranks.[5] Without question, politics do play a role in Library of Congress policies regarding acquisitions and cataloging and will often shift along with wider political, social, and cultural movements. Carmichael emphasizes the vital role of libraries and archives in preserving and telling LGBTQ history. His aim is to present the importance of gay, lesbian, and bisexual presence in libraries and to discuss ways of researching and understanding GLB's by looking to events, archives, people, and theories related to GLB's in libraries, with an emphasis on doing history and the pitfalls that come into play. My project includes but is not limited to discourses about homosexuality, and it seeks to understand the role of library practices in collecting, storing, organizing, and distributing information about sexualities considered to be deviant, perverted, or obscene at various points in American history.

---

3 George Chauncey, *Why Marriage?: The History Shaping Today's Debate over Gay Equality* (Cambridge, MA: Basic Books, 2004); James V. Carmichael, Jr., ed., *Daring to Find Our Names: The Search for Lesbigay History* (Westport, CT: Greenwood, 1998).

4 Chauncey, *Why Marriage?*, 12.

5 Louise Robbins, "A Closet Curtained by Circumspection: Doing Research on the McCarthy Era Purging of Gays from the Library of Congress," in Carmichael, *Daring to Find Our Names*, 55–64.

Doing the History of Sexuality—Perverse Presentism

Taxonomic discourses for sexual practices and identities are constantly changing, expanding, reappropriating, offending, and refusing to be pinned down, presenting a challenge for the Library of Congress, which strives to describe its literature in contemporary terms. As Patrick Keilty observes, classification's goal to fit phenomena neatly into categories for information retrieval is in direct conflict with the elusive, expansive nature of "queer."[6]

As the largest library in the world, the Library of Congress houses and organizes some of the earliest printed texts, as well as the most recent, respected scholarship on virtually every discipline. *LCSH* and the Library of Congress catalog are sites where present-day authorized terms are used to facilitate the retrieval of works published over the course of history. Classification of materials on sexuality has presented particular challenges, as definitions and membership within categories have shifted quite rapidly since the Library first started categorizing its collection with subject headings on printed cards in 1898. What bearing does describing the past in today's terms have on sexuality scholarship, and by what process is authority granted?

Presentism is a persistent historiographical challenge for anyone trying to explain the past by using current terminologies that did not exist or have significantly changed in meaning since the period under investigation. Historians of sexuality are keenly aware of the changing nature of taxonomies and the inherent struggles in understanding past sexual practices, identities, and scholarship in the context of the present, in intelligible terms. The work of sexuality scholars depends on and contributes to an understanding of how categories have emerged, expanded, disappeared, and changed over time, as well as how these categories have been explained and defined in terms of identities, behaviors, conditions, and difference.

"Perverse presentism," as proposed by Judith Halberstam, is a methodology that attempts to account for and overcome the problems of presentism by denaturalizing the present as a point toward which all of history is moving and improving, and applying "what we do not know in the present to what we cannot know about the past."[7] Using present-day terms and definitions to describe the past greatly oversimplifies and distorts the historical record. It leads to a perversion of meaning and misunderstanding, and when speaking of subjects of sexuality, it may inaccurately or unfairly render certain acts and identities as perverted. However, an awareness of the limitations of language and the capacity to know both the present and the past, as well as

---

6 Patrick Keilty, "Tabulating Queer: Space, Perversion, and Belonging," *Knowledge Organization* 36 (2010): 240–248.

7 Judith Halberstam, *Female Masculinity* (Durham, NC: Duke University Press, 1998), 53.

trying to understand the past in its own terms, expands the opportunities to interpret the historical record. Halberstam uses this methodology to study 19th and early 20th century same-sex desire among women, taking care not to use "lesbian" as a blanket term to describe women who desired women during an era when "lesbian" did not exist.

Using a mixed-method, interdisciplinary approach in her book, *Female Masculinity*, Halberstam illustrates the ways in which female masculinity has been socially and historically constructed. She asks "whether there is a form of queer theory or sexual theory that is not textually based," and reads social events and phenomena as texts. Approaching popular print, film, late 19th and early 20th century sexological texts, boxing, and drag king performances as social texts, she uses literary analysis, ethnography, and historical research to explore the range of expressions of female masculinities.

Halberstam critiques some lesbian historians, including Lillian Faderman,[8] for their conflation of early, pre-lesbian behaviors with current understandings of lesbians. She argues that considering women who desired women as lesbians or proto-lesbians erases their histories and the specificities of identities and activities of tribades, female husbands, and a whole range of expressions. Halberstam implores readers to understand that, "far from being an imitation of maleness, female masculinity actually affords us a glimpse of how masculinity is constructed as masculinity."[9] She further states that "female masculinity is not simply the opposite of female femininity, nor is it a female version of male masculinity."[10] And she reemphasizes these points when she introduces perverse presentism:

> *This book rises and falls on two propositions. . . . The first claim is that women have made their own unique contributions to what we call modern masculinity, and these contributions tend to go completely unnoticed in gender scholarship. The second claim is that what we recognize as female masculinity is actually a multiplicity of masculinities. . . .*[11]

Essentially, Halberstam is opening up a category to a range of historically situated and ever-changing possibilities and is demanding that we pay attention to context when speaking of gender and sexual expressions. Her methodology invites questions concerning the representations of sexual behaviors and identities in library catalogs, especially with regard to historical works.

---

8   Faderman is considered a leading scholar and is best known for *Odd Girls and Twilight Lovers: A History of Lesbian Life in Twentieth-Century America* (1991) and *Surpassing the Love of Men: Romantic Friendship and Love Between Women from the Renaissance to the Present* (1981).
9   Halberstam, *Female Masculinity*, 1.
10   Ibid, 29.
11   Ibid, 46.

Perhaps the most striking example of perverse presentism and changing conceptions of sexual deviance in the Library of Congress catalog is the case of homosexuality. Once thought to be an indicator of degeneracy and perversion, scholarship explaining homosexuality during the majority of the twentieth century moved from language of criminalization toward pathologization.[12] Until 1946, in *LCSH* "homosexuality" was subsumed under "Sexual perversion," along with a variety of uncataloged sexual practices. "Homosexuality" was first applied to an Italian book entitled *Homosexualismo em medicina legal*, by Antonio Bello da Motta, published in 1937. When it first appeared in *LCSH*, it was cross-listed with "Sexual perversion," and given a see also reference to "Sodomy." The call numbers assigned to it were those assigned to "Social pathology" and "Medical jurisprudence." Further direction was offered to users regarding the heading: "Works on the criminal manifestation of homosexuality are entered under the heading Sodomy."[13] The related headings "Homosexuals" and "Lesbians" were created in 1976, and in 1987, "Homosexuals" was replaced by the heading "Gays."

Of the 550 unique titles assigned "Paraphilias," a significant number of bibliographic records in the Library of Congress catalog are works on homosexuality. For instance, a search using the heading "Paraphilias" and the truncated keyword "Homosexual?" turns up 25 records published from 1961 through 2002. Certainly, it's very likely that these books were given the headings "Sexual perversion" or "Sexual deviation," and through global update technology, were automatically changed to "Paraphilias." Some of the books are general works on sexual deviations with an emphasis on homosexuality. Perhaps the most alarming entry is for the book published in 2002 that associates homosexuality with paraphilias, *Objects of Desire: The Sexual Deviations*. The work is edited by Charles W. Socarides and Abraham Freedman, psychologists whose work aims to treat homosexuals so that they become heterosexual.[14] The subject headings include "Paraphilias," "Gays—Case studies," and "Lesbians—case studies." By cataloging the book using pathologizing terminology, the Library of Congress seems to affirm the opinion of the authors who assert that homosexuality is a disease.

Many early bibliographic records lack terms for homosexuality. Although some catalog records marry the concepts of paraphilias and homosexuality, other books are cataloged using only the term "Paraphilias," either because it is a general work that includes a section on homosexuality, or because it was published before the terms "Homosexuality," "Gays," or "Lesbians"

---

12   Canaday, *The Straight State*; Terry, *An American Obsession*.
13   Library of Congress Catalog Division, *Library of Congress Subject Headings* (Washington, DC: Library of Congress, 1948).
14   Charles W. Socarides and Abraham Freedman, *Objects of Desire: The Sexual Deviations* (International Universities Press, 2002).

were authorized as part of the *LCSH* lexicon. The records for Marion Zimmer Bradley's *Checklist: A Complete, Cumulative Checklist of Lesbian, Variant, and Homosexual Fiction . . . For the Use of Collectors, Students, and Librarians*[15] and the first edition of Jeannette Foster Howard's *Sex Variant Women in Literature: A Historical and Quantitative Survey*,[16] each have two subject headings: "Paraphilias in literature" and "Literature—History and criticism." In fact, there are no words for lesbians or homosexuals anywhere in the Foster Howard record that would turn up this record in a keyword search. Fortunately, later editions of the book do have the appropriate headings, including "Lesbians in literature." Unfortunately, there are no later editions of the Marion Zimmer Bradley text, so it is lost among archaic terms.

This pattern extends to local catalogs. In fact, this study was inspired by a search of the University of Wisconsin—Madison's catalog, which resulted in finding a catalog record for *Bi-Sexual Love: The Homosexual Neurosis*, by Wilhelm Stekel. The headings didn't include bisexuality or homosexuality or what was recognizable at first glance as sexuality at all. Rather, the only headings assigned to this work were "Paraphilias" and "Neuroses." Again, due to global updating, what had been cataloged under "Sexual perversion" and "Neuroses" is now under the pathologizing headings "Paraphilias" and "Neuroses," with no heading for homosexuality, bisexuality, or any reference to this as a historical text. Incidentally, a book on bisexuality should be in HQ74, but this book is classed in HQ71 which is designated for "Sexual practices outside of social norms."[17] This means it is not shelved with other books on similar subjects, but rather, it is among other books on sexual perversion and deviation. Halberstam's methodology indeed proves to be particularly useful for analyzing subject terms for historical texts, and historians should be aware of the limitations and challenges of controlled vocabularies.

The Medicalization of Sexual Deviance

Scholars have explored the relationships between medicine and homosexuality, tracing the history of homosexuality from the classical era. Thomas Laqueur argues that in the classical era through the Renaissance, the accepted belief about gender and sexuality was extremely different from today's. Males and females were understood to be versions of the same sex. Women

---

15 Marion Zimmer Bradley, *Checklist: A Complete, Cumulative Checklist of Lesbian, Variant, and Homosexual Fiction . . . For the Use of Collectors, Students, and Librarians* (Rochester, TX: 1960).

16 Jeanette Foster Howard, *Sex Variant Women in Literature: A Historical and Quantitative Survey* (New York: Vantage Press, 1956).

17 Library of Congress, "Classification [HQ71-72]," *Classification Web*, http://classificationweb.net.

were viewed as lesser men, and rather than having completely different sexual organs, the uterus and clitoris were believed to be an inverted penis and scrotum. According to Laqueur, "sex as we know it was invented" in the eighteenth century, concomitant with the production of a binary gender system.[18] The notion of "normal" and "natural" gender distinctions continued through the nineteenth century, because the middle class family was a central organizing principle for society.

From the end of the nineteenth century sexologists and psychoanalysts have been instrumental in propelling discourses about normative, deviant, and pathological sexual orientations and practices.[19] Keilty compares a number of classification systems, beginning with Ulrich's late 19th century scheme, which "developed out of his lifelong radical campaign in Germany to justify and decriminalize sexual relations between men and women. He did his utmost to defend "man-manly" and "woman-womanly" love as healthy and normal and to decriminalize them in German law."[20] Ulrich's work predated the term "homosexuality" and relied on gender inversion to classify homosexuality. He designated third and fourth sexes to account for men and women who displayed behaviors belonging to the opposite sex. He viewed such people as being not fully male or female, and he also accounted for what would later be called bisexuality. Keilty argues that Ulrich's early classification has had lasting effects on how western systems organize information about sexuality.

Similarly, Jonathan Katz argues that not only was the concept of homosexuality invented, but so was heterosexuality. Both had to be created so that there was a norm and its opposite. Jonathan Katz states that "homosexuality" and "heterosexuality" "signify historically specific ways of naming, thinking about, valuing, and socially organizing the sexes and their pleasures."[21] "Heterosexuality" did not always signify the norm. Its earliest known use was in a medical journal article by Dr. James Kiernan it 1892. Here "heterosexuality" signified a sexual desire for two different sexes or sexual gratification without reproduction.[22] Before "heterosexuality" was invented, people didn't tend to make distinctions. When the word "homosexuality" came into being, it set up a binary opposition to heterosexuality.

---

18 Thomas Laqueur, *Making Sex: Body and Gender from the Greeks to Freud* (Boston: Harvard University Press, 1999), 149.
19 Jonathan Katz, *The Invention of Heterosexuality* (Chicago: University of Chicago Press, 2007); Anne Fausto-Sterling, *Sexing the Body: Gender Politics and the Construction of Sexuality* (New York: Basic Books, 2000); Laqueur, *Making Sex*; Terry, *An American Obsession*.
20 Keilty, "Tabulating Queer," 243.
21 Katz, *Invention of Heterosexuality*, 10.
22 Ibid., 19-20.

According to Katz, the middle class appropriated the medical term to in the late nineteenth century to distinguish themselves from the promiscuous upper class and animalistic lower class. In 1934 Webster's dictionary—a good indicator of popular usage—changed its 1923 definition of "morbid sexual passion for one of the opposite sex" to one that is now generally accepted— "normal sexuality."[23] Homosexuality was viewed as a perversion or a medical problem, and was most often described in terms of sexual inversion, meaning that people take on the roles and bodily features of the "opposite sex." In other words, a man who has sexual intercourse with men is behaving like a woman, and a woman is considered to be mannish if she has sex with women.

Following Kiernan, doctors and sexologists increasingly medicalized and pathologized sexual and gender deviance. Foucault's *History of Sexuality* is based on his view that the discursive practices in the medical community created deviant identities, and produced and regulated sex practices starting in the late nineteenth century. Upon inventing the category "homosexual," the medical community produced a *"new specification of individuals."* Through categorization and diagnosis of deviance, the homosexual became a species:

> *The machinery of power that focused on this whole alien strain did not aim to suppress it, but rather to give it an analytical, visible, and permanent reality: it was implanted in bodies, slipped in beneath modes of conduct, made into a principle of classification and intelligibility, established as a raison d'etre and a natural order of disorder.*[24]

My research suggests that the normalizing effects of the medical and psychoanalytic professions are at play in the Library of Congress collection and catalog, as these areas seem to have great influence on subject authorization.

Sanford Berman's three principles for subject headings can guide theory on the disciplinary problems inherent in the heading "Paraphilias." The principles are as follows: Intelligibility (for staff and patrons) of cataloging format, elements, and terminology; Findability, meaning that users should hit on usable results with the first search attempt, especially when searching for authors or subjects; and Fairness in subject coverage, with accurate language and representation.[25] Berman believes that groups should name themselves and that medical and professional jargon should be replaced with headings that are intelligible to the general user. Each of these three

---

23 Cited in Katz, *Invention of Heterosexuality*, 92.
24 Michel Foucault, *The History of Sexuality*, vol. 1, *An Introduction* (New York: Vintage Books, 1990), 43-44.
25 Sanford Berman, "Where have All the Moonies Gone?" in *Worth Noting: editorials, letters, Essays, and Interview, and Bibliography* (Jefferson, NC: McFarland, 1988), 23-31.

principles is relevant to the discussion of the term "Paraphilias" as it can be argued that this term is not intelligible to most users, and therefore does not enhance findability. Fairness comes into question as sexual behaviors and minorities are authorized based on a psychiatric diagnostic tool—the *Diagnostic and Statistical Manual of Mental Disorders IV* (*DSM-IV*), rather than using language that might be more likely to be used by the wider audiences and people and acts described by the literature.

In fact, the term serves a very limited audience—the psychiatric community—perhaps at the expense of other potential audiences. Although Paraphilias is intelligible to the psychiatric community and may help them find materials, the term is rarely used by other disciplines. However, the works assigned this heading tend to be aimed at a multidisciplinary audience. As of this writing, 634 books in the Library of Congress collection are currently cataloged with the subject heading, "Paraphilias." Of these, approximately 550 are unique titles, and 353 are originally written in or translated into English. Searching WorldCat for the 353 books written in English has yielded information about the extent of library holdings in the United States, and which types of libraries own them. The total number of US library holdings for these books is nearly 50,000, with the majority of libraries being general academic libraries, followed by public libraries, with medical and law libraries being in the relatively small minority of holding libraries. According to the Library of Congress catalog, 62 percent of these books are classified in the HQ section, which is the Library of Congress class for family, marriage, and women in the social sciences. It is curious that the Library of Congress would choose a highly medicalized term for a subject that serves a general audience, including literary scholars, social scientists, and the general public, particularly when the United States has a national medical library, which serves the psychiatric community.

The term "Paraphilias" was authorized by the Library of Congress in 2007 to replace "Sexual deviation," which had replaced "Sexual perversion" in 1972. Wilhelm Stekel (the author of the book that inspired this study) actually coined the term "Paraphilias" in his 1917 volume, *Onanie und homosexualität: Die homosexuelle parapathie*, the second part of which was translated into English in 1922 and entitled *Bi-sexual love; the homosexual neurosis*.[26] It was popularized within the psychiatric community in the 1980s by John Money. It first appeared in the *DSM* in 1980, replacing "Sexual deviation." Researchers, practitioners, and the public disagree on what counts as sexual perversion or

---

26 Wilhelm Stekel, *Onanie und Homosexualität: Die Homosexuelle Parapathie* (Berlin: Urban & Schwarzenberg, 1917); Stekel's contribution to the psycholanalytic treatment of paraphilias remains understudied, especially considering his creation of a term that is now promoted as one that is neutral. Clearly, the origins of this term are embedded in discourses of neurosis.

a paraphilia. Even the psychiatric community disagrees on the definition and diagnosis of paraphilias. Charles Moser states: "Creation of the diagnostic category of paraphilia, the medicalization of nonstandard sexual behaviors, is a pseudoscientific attempt to regulate sexuality."[27] At the heart of Laws and O'Donohue's description of the controversy surrounding sexual deviance, is the fact that the *DSM-IV* is an "institutional rather than a scientific resolution to the definitional problem," which is value-laden, created and negotiated by committees, and subject to personal and political influences.[28] They explain that, although the *DSM* is the primary, standard-setting diagnostic tool for psychiatrists, it does not describe how decisions regarding inclusion and exclusion in the category were made.

In light of the psychiatric community's disagreement on the meanings of deviance and paraphilias, the Library of Congress's simultaneous deference to the psychiatric literature and claim to authority over knowledge is problematic, as catalogers have authorized the subjects and assign them to books in the collection. The Library of Congress is at the center of scholarly discourses and is in the position to produce meaning and subjects. I would argue that we should consider the act of subject heading creation and assignment to be much more than metadata. Rather, we need to acknowledge the fact that the Library is producing knowledge about knowledge. However, Halberstam might argue that, since it is impossible to "know" what perversion is or what qualifies as a paraphilia today, it is certainly impossible to "know" what perversion was over the course of the twentieth century. The authorization of new terms to replace the old in the catalog, and using present-day terms to describe works on past practices serves to confine the past to the present and erases the historical record.

The 2007 heading change was intended to "reflect contemporary medical and psychological thinking and usage."[29] The authority record cites several sources for literary warrant for the new heading, "Paraphilias," including *Medical Subject Headings* (MeSH), the *Thesaurus of Psychological Index Terms*, athealth.com, and *Human Sexuality: An Encyclopedia* (1994), which is quoted in the authority record for justification of the term:

> *Paraphilia is defined as an erotosexual and psychological condition characterized by recurrent responsiveness to an obsessive dependence on an unusual or socially unacceptable stimulus. The term has become a legal*

---

27 Charles Moser, "Paraphilia: A Critique of a Confused Concept" in *New Directions in Sex Therapy: Innovations and Alternatives*, ed. Peggy J. Kleinplatz (Philadelphia: Brunner-Routledge, 2001), 92-93.

28 D. Richard Laws and William T. Donahue, *Sexual Deviance: Theory, Assessment, and Treatment* (New York: Guilford, 2008), 1.

29 Paul Weiss, Personal email, June 29, 2009.

synonym for perversion or deviant sexual behavior, and it is preferred by many over the other terms because it seems more neutral and descriptive rather than judgemental.[30]

Interestingly, MeSH is the primary supporting documentation for the justification of the new heading. MeSH takes its definition for "Paraphilias," as it does for most psychological concepts, from the *DSM-IV*. This brings a number of questions to mind. Why does LC defer to the medical literature as the authority? Exactly how is this term deemed to be neutral? What are the implications for finding information? *LCSH* is supposed to reflect the current literature, but whose literature? What are the implications of using a medical term to describe non-medical research and popular works?

According to the *Diagnostic and Statistical Manual of Mental Disorders (DSM-IV)*:

> *The Paraphilias are characterized by recurrent, intense sexual urges, fantasies, or behaviors that involve unusual objects, activities, or situations and cause clinically significant distress or impairment in social, occupational, or other important areas of functioning. The Paraphilias include Exhibitionism, Fetishism, Frotteurism, Pedophilia, Sexual Masochism, Sexual Sadism, Transvestic Fetishism, Voyeurism, and Paraphilia Not Otherwise Specified.*[31]

The *DSM* does recognize the socio/cultural quality to defining sexual deviance:

> *It is important to note that notions of deviance, standards of sexual performance, and concepts of appropriate gender role can vary from culture to culture. . . . The diagnosis of Paraphilias across cultures or religions is complicated by the fact that what is considered deviant in one cultural setting may be more acceptable in another setting.*[32]

It must be noted that the *DSM-V*, due to be released in May 2013,[33] will bring significant changes to the Paraphilias diagnosis. In order to be considered a disorder, the paraphilia must be one "that causes distress or impairment to the individual or harm to others." The *DSM-V* would still distinguish between normative and non-normative sexual behaviors, but "without auto-

---

30 Library of Congress, "Paraphilias," *Authorities*. http://authorities.loc.gov.
31 American Psychiatric Association, *Diagnostic and Statistical Manual of Mental Disorders: DSM-IV* (Washington, DC: American Psychiatric Association, 1994), 522–523.
32 Ibid.
33 American Psychiatric Association, "Timeline," http://www.dsm5.org/about/Pages/Timeline.aspx.

matically labeling non-normative sexual behavior as psychopathological."[34] Certainly, this should carry new meaning into library catalogs, and it could complicate categorization by bringing together non-pathological with the pathological paraphilias, as well as the non-medical fields.

By deferring to the psychiatric literature as the authority and medicalizing alternative sexualities, it seems that the Library of Congress has effectively made it much harder to find information on this topic. The term "Paraphilia" is meaningful for psychiatrists and addresses a subset of the total literature on sexual deviance. The social science and humanities literature infrequently uses this terminology. While the librarians and authority record states that this term is preferred because it is neutral, the truth is that the term is anything but neutral, being a term that is authorized by the *DSM-IV*, pathologizing certain sexual behaviors. One might speculate that the neutrality derives from the fact that people aren't familiar with this term and therefore it is rendered meaningless.

Conclusion

It is hard to imagine a more ubiquitous, institutionalized vocabulary than that of the Library of Congress. As part of a larger project aimed at understanding the role of the Library in the organization and production of knowledge about sexual deviance, this paper has aimed to illustrate the historical and disciplinary challenges presented by the single heading "Paraphilias." It is hoped that researchers from various fields of study will gain a greater understanding of the effect of subject headings and classifications upon their own research, and they will gain an appreciation for the power of libraries to influence and regulate information and shape scholarship regarding sexuality.

Bibliography

American Psychiatric Association. *Diagnostic and Statistical Manual of Mental Disorders: DSM-IV.* Washington, DC: American Psychiatric Association, 1994.

Berman, Sanford. *Prejudices and Antipathies: A Tract on the LC Subject Heads Concerning People.* Metuchen, NJ: Scarecrow Press, 1971.

———. "Where Have All the Moonies Gone?" In *Worth Noting: Editorials, Letters, Essays, an Interview, and Bibliography*, 23–31. Jefferson, NC: McFarland, 1988.

---

34 Kenneth J. Zucker, *Report of the DSM-5 Sexual and Gender Identity Disorders Work Group* (Arlington, VA: American Psychiatric Association, 2009), http://www.dsm5.org/progressreports/pages/0904reportofthedsm-vsexualandgenderidentitydisordersworkgroup.aspx.

Bowker, Geoffrey C. and Susan Leigh Star. *Sorting Things Out: Classification and Its Consequences.* Cambridge, MA: MIT Press, 2000.
Bradley, Marion Zimmer. *Checklist: A Complete, Cumulative Checklist of Lesbian, Variant, and Homosexual Fiction . . . For the Use of Collectors, Students, and Librarians.* Rochester, TX: 1960.
Canaday, Margot. *The Straight State: Sexuality and Citizenship in Twentieth-Century America.* Princeton, NJ: Princeton University Press, 2009.
Carmichael, James. V., Jr., ed. *Daring to Find Our Names: The Search for Lesbigay History.* Westport, CT: Greenwood Press, 1998.
Chauncey, George. *Why Marriage?: The History Shaping Today's Debate over Gay Equality.* Cambridge, MA: Basic Books, 2004.
D'Emilio, John. "Capitalism and Gay Identity." In *Powers of Desire: The Politics of Sexuality*, edited by Ann Barr Snitow, Christine Stansell, and Sharon Thompson, 100–113. New York: Monthly Review Press, 1983.
Fausto-Sterling, Anne. *Sexing the Body: Gender Politics and the Construction of Sexuality.* New York: Basic Books, 2000.
Foucault, Michel. *The History of Sexuality.* Vol. 1, *An Introduction.* New York: Vintage Books, 1990.
Greenblatt, Ellen. "Homosexuality: the Evolution of a Concept in the *Library of Congress Subject Headings.*" In *Gay and Lesbian Library Service*, edited by Cal Gough and Ellen Greenblatt, 75–101. Jefferson, NC: McFarland, 1991.
Halberstam, Judith. *Female Masculinity.* Durham, NC: Duke University Press, 1998.
Howard, Jeanette Foster. *Sex Variant Women in Literature: A Historical and Quantitative Survey.* New York: Vantage Press, 1956.
Katz, Jonathan. *The Invention of Heterosexuality.* Chicago: University of Chicago Press, 2007.
Keilty, Patrick. "Tabulating Queer: Space, Perversion, and Belonging." *Knowledge Organization* 36, no. 4 (2010): 240–248.
Laqueur, Thomas. *Making Sex: Body and Gender from the Greeks to Freud.* Boston: Harvard University Press, 1999.
Laws, D. Richard and William T. Donahue. *Sexual Deviance: Theory, Assessment, and Treatment.* New York: Guilford, 2008.
Library of Congress Catalog Division. *Library of Congress Subject Headings.* Washington, DC: Library of Congress, 1948.
Moser, Charles. "Paraphilia: A Critique of a Confused Concept." In *New Directions in Sex Therapy: Innovations and Alternatives*, edited by Peggy J. Kleinplatz, 91–108. Philadelphia: Brunner-Routledge, 2001.

Olson, Hope A. (2000). "Difference, Culture and Change: The Untapped Potential of *LCSH.*" In *The "LCSH" Century: One hundred years with the "Library of Congress Subject Headings" System,* edited by Alva T. Stone, 53–71. Birmingham, NY: Haworth.

———. *The Power to Name: Locating the Limits of Subject Representation in Libraries.* Boston: Kluwer Academic, 2000.

Palmer, Carole L. and Cheryl Knott Malone. "Elaborate Isolation: Metastructures of Knowledge about Women." *Information Society* 17, no. 3 (2001): 179–194. doi:10.1080/01972240152493047.

Robbins, Louise. "A Closet Curtained by Circumspection: Doing Research on the McCarthy Era Purging of Gays from the Library of Congress." In Carmichael, *Daring to Find Our Names,* 55–64.

Socarides, Charles W., and Abraham Freedman. *Objects of Desire: The Sexual Deviations.* International Universities Press, 2002.

Stekel, Wilhelm. *Onanie und Homosexualität: Die Homosexuelle Parapathie.* Berlin: Urban & Schwarzenberg, 1917.

Terry, Jennifer. *An American Obsession: Science, Medicine, and Homosexuality in Modern Society.* Chicago: University of Chicago Press, 1999.

Zucker, Kenneth J. *Report of the DSM-5 Sexual and Gender Identity Disorders Work Group.* Arlington, VA: American Psychiatric Association, 2009. http://www.dsm5.org/progressreports/pages/0904reportofthedsm-vsexualandgenderidentitydisordersworkgroup.aspx.

Administrating Gender

Dean Spade[1]

As we shift our understanding of power from a focus on individual/intentional discrimination to a focus on norms that govern population management, different areas of law start to appear as the focal points of harm for vulnerable groups. The aim of getting the law to declare a group equal through antidiscrimination and hate crime legislation recedes and we become interested in the legal systems that distribute security and vulnerability at the population level and sort the population into those whose lives are cultivated and those who are abandoned, imprisoned, or extinguished. In this chapter, we turn toward the realm of administrative law—we look at the administrative agencies that are responsible for the bulk of government activities that impact the distribution of life chances. This is a set of operations of law that, compared to antidiscrimination and hate crime laws, are often ignored when it comes to analyzing the harms of racism, transphobia, ableism, homophobia, and sexism.[2] However, when we shift our understanding

---

1 Editors' note: this paper was previously published as a chapter in Spade's *Normal Life: Administrative Violence, Critical Trans Politics, and the Limits of the Law*, 137–169 (New York: South End Press, 2011); all cross-references herein refer to chapters in that book.

2 I intentionally left xenophobia and settler colonialism off this list, because administrative law has been articulated as a primary vector of harm in these areas of struggle. Although some antidiscrimination laws include "national origin" as a protected category, the bulk of discussion about xenophobia is rightly and necessarily focused on immigration and criminal law enforcement, often specifically on the administration of those systems. The federal administrative agencies that receive perhaps the most attention from people involved in resistance movements focused on immigration and that more of those activists and organizations understand as harmful vectors of state violence are agencies that manage immigration under the Department of Homeland Security, such as US Citizen

of power and examine where and how harm and vulnerability operate and are distributed, it is this area of law that comes to the fore. Critical trans politics requires an analysis of how the administration of gender norms impacts trans people's lives and how administrative systems in general are sites of production and implementation of racism, xenophobia, sexism, transphobia, homophobia, and ableism under the guise of neutrality. This analysis is essential for building resistance strategies that can actually intervene on the most pressing harms trans people face and illuminate how and when law reform is a useful tactic in our work.

Control that operates through population-level interventions is particularly significant to trans politics because of the way trans people struggle with gender categorization in the purportedly banal and innocuous daily administration of programs, policies, and institutions (e.g., homeless shelters,

---

and Immigration Services, Immigration and Customs Enforcement (ICE), and Customs and Border Protection. Resistance to settler colonialism has often identified the range of policies that target indigenous people for erasure and elimination as including the work of various administrative agencies such the Bureau of Indian Affairs, the Bureau of Land Management, and the Fish and Wildlife Service. Many scholars and activists opposing settler colonialism have highlighted how civil rights strategies, or strategies seeking inclusion in key institutions of US governance, fail to question the existence of the United States itself and its basis in land theft and genocide; see Nandita Sharma and Cynthia Wright, "Decolonizing Resistance, Challenging Colonial States," *Social Justice* 35 (2008-2009): 120-38. Of course, because immigrants and indigenous people are also people who are direct targets of homophobia, transphobia, racism, ableism, and sexism, their concerns are even further marginalized and less likely to be addressed when resistance is framed through narrow inclusion struggles focused on those vectors because such struggles fail to question, and even misguidedly embrace, the terms of citizenship and belonging that are established, defined and perpetuated through genocide and immigration exclusion policies. People struggling in the crosshairs, for example, of immigration enforcement and transphobia need both to be abolished—an antidiscrimination law that includes gender identity will not prevent them from being detained in a deadly immigration prison or deported. While saying all this, though, I also acknowledge that the greater focus on administrative systems in these struggles does not preclude them from the tensions this book identifies of separating impacted populations into more or less "deserving" groups through reforms that only reach a select few. Highly visible campaigns for various immigration reforms going on right now seek policy changes for "good" immigrants and affirm the exclusion of all others, using factors like history of criminal conviction, military service, or access to college education as axes of division. These might be understood as falling into the neoliberal inclusion and recognition traps faced by social movements described in this book.

prisons, jails, foster care, juvenile punishment, public benefits, immigration documentation, health insurance, Social Security, driver licensing, and public bathrooms). An understanding of power that looks at the distribution of life chances created by population-level interventions draws our attention to how the categorization of people works as a key method of control. Population-level interventions rely on categorization to sort the population rather than targeting individuals based on behaviors or traits. What characteristics are used for such categorization and how those categories are defined and applied creates vectors of vulnerability and security. Many of the administrative processes that vulnerable people find themselves struggling through are contests about such categorizations. Examples include public benefits hearings where applicants contest denials or terminations based on eligibility criteria, Social Security hearings where applicants contest their categorization as nondisabled, immigration proceedings where applicants contest administrative determinations of their asylum petitions, and, of course, the many contexts in which trans people struggle to change their gender classification with various administrative agencies. Our attention to how life chances are distributed rather than simply to what the law says about marginalized groups exposes how various moments of administrative categorization have lethal consequences.

The history of explicit uses of race and gender categorization in US law and policy to distribute certain types of life chances—and the resistance to and elimination of some of those uses—lead many people to falsely and perilously believe the conversation about racialized and gendered administrative categorization is over. The argument goes that since we got rid of Jim Crow laws, race segregation in the military, the Japanese internment, Asian exclusion laws in immigration, gender and racial exclusion in voting, and other overt uses of gender and race categories in population-level programs, things are now fair and equal. As previous chapters have discussed, the shift away from some of the explicit targeting of women and people of color in the written language of law and policy has merely reorganized those functions of maldistribution. As certain methods of control and distribution have become less politically viable, other methods have replaced them, preserving and producing race and gender disparities in the distribution of life chances. High levels of policing in neighborhoods with concentrations of people of color, the creation of tiered public benefits programs, the design of taxation schemes to tax work instead of wealth, the targeting of immigration enforcement to impact certain immigrants more than others, the structuring of public finance of education, health care, and other key necessities, all function to create and maintain these deadly disparities.[3]

---

3   One widely discussed example is the differential punishment for possession and sale of crack versus powder cocaine. As many have described, a significant

One way to think about these population-level programs is that they are created as care-taking programs. They are invented to address perceived risks to the national population and to distribute resources across the population in ways that aim to address those risks. They are aimed at increasing health, security, and well-being—access to food, transportation, public safety, public health, and the like. Because they mobilize the idea of the population (sometimes "society" or "the nation" or "the people"), they are designed in ways that reflect and amplify contemporary understandings of who is "inside" and who is "outside" of the group whose protection and cultivation is being sought, which means they always include determinations of who deserves protection and who is a threat.[4] Norms regarding race, gender, sexuality, national origin, ability, and indigeneity always condition and determine who falls on either side of that line. Population-level care-taking programs always include population surveillance as a core function of their work. Mitchell Dean's framing of care-taking population-level interventions—or to use Foucault's term, "apparatuses of security"—illustrates the simultaneous and dual nature of the care-taking surveillance state:

> *These apparatuses of security include the use of standing armies, police forces, diplomatic corps, intelligence services and spies . . . [but] also include health, education and social welfare systems. . . . It thus encompasses those institutions and practices concerned to defend, maintain and secure a national population and those that secure the economic,*

---

contribution to Black imprisonment in the United States stems from the policy decision to make the prison sentences for crack, which is more highly trafficked in Black communities, much harsher than sentences for powder cocaine, which is more frequently associated with white populations. Though the sentencing standards do not mention race or identify racist enforcement as a goal, the profoundly racist framing of drug crime, especially in regard to crack, fueled the advent of the War on Drugs which produced a set of policy decisions with a decidedly racist outcome in terms of who spends how much time in prison for possession and sale of the same quantity of illegal drugs; see Danielle Kurtzleben, "Data Show Racial Disparity in Crack Sentencing," *US News & World Report*, August 3, 2010, http://www.usnews.com/news/articles/2010/08/03/data-show-racial-disparity-in-crack-sentencing; American Civil Liberties Union, "Interested Persons Memo on Crack/Cocaine Sentencing Policy," May 2002, http://www.aclu.org/drug-law-reform/interested-persons-memo-crackpowder-cocaine-sentencing-policy; The Sentencing Project, "It's Not Fair. It's Not Working," http://www.sentencingproject.org/crackreform/.

4   Mariana Valverde, "Genealogies of European States: Foucauldian Reflections," *Economy and Society* 36, no. 1 (2007): 176, doi:10.1080/03085140601089911; Michel Foucault, *Society Must Be Defended: Lectures at the College de France, 1975–76*, trans. David Macey (New York: Picador, 2009), 256.

demographic and social processes that are found to exist within that population . . . [centralizing] this concern for the population and its optimization (in terms of wealth, health, happiness, prosperity, efficiency), and the forms of knowledge and technical means appropriate to it.[5]

Standardized, categorized data collection is essential to the creation of these programs because it allows governments, institutions, and agencies (e.g., the US Census Bureau, the New York Department of Vital Statistics, the Centers for Disease Control, the Colorado Department of Motor Vehicles) to have a general picture of the population: its health, vulnerabilities, needs, and risks. Importantly, it is this way of thinking about population that allows such programs to exist at all. James C. Scott's work shows how gathering information and creating population-level programs using this information is what defines the modern nation-state.[6] These programs make decisions about what kinds of data are relevant to their work, what the government/agency/institution/organization in each case needs to know in order to implement programs aimed at cultivating a "healthy" population while guarding against risks of various kinds. These decisions about what constitutes a proper data element/manner of classification and what does not rarely appear as controversial political decisions because people who find the commonly evoked societal norms used in classification familiar and comfortable tend to take these classification systems as neutral givens in their lives.[7] We

---

5   Mitchell Dean, *Governmentality: Power and Rule in Modern Society*, 2nd ed. (London: SAGE, 2010), 20.

6   In an article that examines the development of standardized patronyms, Scott and his co-authors write, "There is no State-making without State-naming. . . . To follow the progress of state-making is, among other things, to trace the elaboration and application of novel systems which name and classify places, roads, people, and, above all, property. These state projects of legibility overlay, and often supersede, local practices. Where local practices persist, they are typically relevant to a narrower and narrower range of interaction within the confines of a face-to-face community." Scott's work shows how the "pacification of a territory" that state-making requires involves replacing diverse local practices with national standards of naming and categorization that make people, places, and things legible to the state so that they can be counted, maintained, cultivated, and controlled; see James C. Scott, John Tehranian, and Jeremy Mathias, "The Production of Legal Identities Proper to States: The Case of the Permanent Family Surname," *Comparative Studies in Society and History* 44, no. 1 (2002): 4–44.

7   "On the one hand, we govern others and ourselves according to what we take to be true about who we are, what aspects of our existence should be worked upon, how, and with what means and to what ends. . . . On the other hand, the ways in which we govern and conduct ourselves give rise to different ways of producing truth." See Dean, *Governmentality*, 18. See also Geoffrey C. Bowker and Susan

are used to filling out forms with certain questions. We rarely question how we came to be asked for those particular pieces of information and not others except in moments when we personally have a hard time figuring out which box to check off. Because certain classifications become common and standard, there is often an implied shared understanding that certain things, like gender, are just necessary information for administering government programs. Scott writes, "Categories that may have begun as the artificial inventions of cadastral surveyors, census takers, judges, or police officers can end by becoming categories that organize people's daily experience precisely because they are embedded in state-created institutions that structure that experience."[8] The terms and categories used in the classification of data gathered by the state do not merely collect information about pre-existing types of things, but rather shape the world into those categories that, ultimately, are taken for granted by most and thus appear ahistorical and apolitical. Indeed, many such categorizations are assumed as basic truths.

However, each type of data collected by the US government and the choices made about what to collect and why have histories of controversy and resistance. The creation of birth registration programs and birth certificates, the creation of the Social Security Administration that included the assignment of a unique number to every eligible resident, the use of various racial categories (and changes to racial categorization) on the US Census, the collection of data about HIV infection and other stigmatized illnesses—all of these have met with controversy both regarding how and why government agencies were collecting certain data and how that data collection might impact particular populations.[9] Each of these data collection projects have been key moments of expanding the reach of the government and defining who are members of the "us" of the nation and who are the "outsiders" who must be abandoned or eliminated. Data collection mechanisms that establish and utilize norms are essential to the type of sorting that population management requires.

For trans politics, an area of great concern is the ubiquity of gender data collection in almost every imaginable government and commercial identity

---

Leigh Star, *Sorting Things Out: Classification and Its Consequences* (Cambridge, MA: MIT Press, 1999).

8   James C. Scott, *Seeing Like a State: How Certain Schemes to Improve the Human Condition Have Failed* (New Haven, CT: Yale University Press, 1998), 82–83.

9   Dean Spade, "Documenting Gender," *Hastings Law Journal* 59 (2008): 731; Christian Parenti, *The Soft Cage: Surveillance in America from Slavery to the War On Terror* (New York: Basic Books, 2003). Christine B. Hickman, "The Devil and the One Drop Rule: Racial Categories, African Americans and the US Census," *Michigan Law Review* 95, no. 5 (1997): 1161, http://www.jstor.org/stable/1290008.

verification system. From birth to death, the "M" and "F" boxes are present on nearly every form we fill out: on the identity documents we show to prove ourselves and in the computer records kept by government agencies, banks, and nonprofit organizations. Additionally, gender classification often governs spaces such as bathrooms, homeless shelters, drug treatment programs, mental health services, and spaces of confinement like psychiatric hospitals, juvenile and adult prisons, and immigration prisons (often called "detention centers" despite the fact that the word "detention" misleadingly denotes a relatively short-term confinement, which is, time and again, not the case for people placed in these facilities). The consequences of misclassification or the inability to be fit into the existing classification system are extremely high, particularly in the kinds of institutions and systems that have emerged and grown to target and control poor people and people of color, such as criminal punishment systems, public benefits systems, and immigration systems. The collection of standardized data and its use for identity surveillance have become even more widely implemented with the advent of the War on Terror, increasing vulnerability for many people whose lives and identities are made illegible or impossible by government classification schemes.

Administrative Gender Classification and Trans Lives

For trans people, administrative gender classification and the problems it creates for those who are difficult to classify or are misclassified is a major vector of violence and diminished life chances and life spans. Trans people's gender classification problems are concentrated in three general realms: identity documentation, sex-segregated facilities, and access to health care. Mitchell Dean's description of Foucault's analysis of government is useful for thinking about the multiple locations of the production of sex classification standards and the incoherence of sex classification systems. Such an analysis attends to:

> ... *the routines of bureaucracy; the technologies of notation, recording, compiling, presenting and transporting of information, the theories, programmes, knowledge and expertise that compose a field to be governed and invest it with purposes and objectives; the ways of seeing and representing embedded in practices of government; and the different agencies with various capacities that the practices of government require, elicit, form and reform. To examine regimes of government is to conduct analysis in the plural: there is already a plurality of regimes of practices in a given territory, each composed from a multiplicity of in principle unlimited and heterogeneous elements bound together by a variety of relations and capable of polymorphous connections with one another. Regimes of practices can be identified whenever there exists a relatively stable field*

of correlation of visibilities, mentalities, technologies and agencies, such that they constitute a kind of taken-for-granted point of reference for any form of problematization.[10]

Using this kind of analytical approach to examine the places where trans people experience extremely harmful interfaces with legal systems helps us see the significance of gender classification practices across a variety of locations of regulation. In the United States, administrative systems have emerged out of and been focused on creation and management of racial and gender categories to establish the nation itself through gendered-racialized property regimes. Racializing and gendering are nation-making activities carried out through the creation of population-level interventions, including administrative systems and norms, that preserve and cultivate the lives of some and expose others to premature death. Looking at particular regimes of practices related to the management of gender that impact trans people in significant ways, we can see this operation of population management at work. At each of these sites, significant consequences occur from gender classification problems, and the areas interact to create complex difficulties with far-reaching, long-term ramifications.

Identity Documents

Identity documentation problems often occur for trans people when an agency, institution, or organization that keeps data about people and/or produces identity documents (e.g., driver's licenses, birth certificates, passports, public benefits cards, immigration documents) has incorrect or outdated information or information that conflicts with that of another agency, institution, or organization. For many trans people, this happens because they cannot change the gender marker on certain essential documents. Many agencies, institutions, and organizations have formal or informal gender reclassification policies that require proof of some kind of medical care. Every government agency and program that tracks gender has its own rule or practice (sometimes dependent on a particular clerk's opinion) of what evidence should be shown to warrant an official change in gender status in its records or on its ID. The policies differ drastically. Some require evidence that the person has undergone a particular surgery; others ask for evidence that the person has had some surgery but do not specify which; and some require a doctor's letter confirming that the person is trans and attesting to the medical authorization for or permanence of their membership in a particular gender category. Others will not allow a change of gender at all. A small set of

---

10 Dean, *Governmentality*, 26, 27.

policies allow a person's self-identification to be proof enough to change their gender classification.[11]

The wide range of policies and practices means that many people, depending on where they live and what kind of medical evidence they can produce, cannot get any records or ID corrected, or can only have their gender changed with some agencies but not with others. So, for example, one person born in New York and living in New York might have a birth certificate she cannot change from "M" to "F" because she has not had genital surgery; a driver's license that correctly reflects "F" because she got a doctor's letter; Social Security records that say "M" because she cannot produce evidence of surgery; a name change order that shows her new feminine name; and a Medicaid card that reads "F" because the agency had no official policy and the clerk felt the name change order and driver's license were sufficient. Another person with the same medical evidence might have a completely different set of documents because she was born in California and currently lives in Massachusetts. Most likely, neither person will have a consistent set of documents that correlates to their current gender. For the many people who feel that neither "M" nor "F" accurately describes their gender, there is no possibility of obtaining records that reflect their self-identities. Gender reclassification policies are particularly problematic because they so frequently include surgical requirements. The vast majority of trans people do not undergo surgery, both because it is prohibitively expensive and because many people do not want or need it. The common misperception that surgery is the hallmark of trans experience is also particularly harmful to populations disproportionately lacking access to medical care, including low-income people, people of color, immigrants, and youth. According to a 2009 study, 80% of transgender women and 98% of transgender men have not undergone genital surgery.[12] Because it is difficult to include people in prisons, people without secure housing, and other highly vulnerable people with exceptionally poor access to health care in such studies, I would suggest that these numbers may even be higher than the study was able to confirm.

Having identity documents that misidentify gender causes extensive problems. An important consequence of identity documentation discrepancy is that it often serves as a significant barrier to employment. A recent study found that 47% of trans and gender nonconforming respondents reported having experienced an adverse job outcome, such as being fired, not hired, or

---

11 For a detailed listing of many of these policies in the United States and what each requires, see Spade, "Documenting Gender."

12 Jaime M. Grant et al., *National Transgender Discrimination Survey Report on Health and Health Care* (Washington, DC: National Gay and Lesbian Task Force and National Center for Transgender Equality, 2010), 11–12, http://www.thetaskforce.org/reports_and_research/trans_survey_health_heathcare.

denied a promotion, because of their gender.[13] Another study found that only 58% of transgender residents of Washington, DC, were employed in paid positions: 29% reported no source of income, and another 31% reported annual incomes under $10,000.[14] In yet another study, 64% of respondents based in San Francisco reported annual incomes in the range of $0–25,000.[15] Possessing identity documents with incorrect gender markers can identify people as transgender in the hiring process, exposing them to discrimination. People whose identity documents do not match their self-understanding or appearance also face heightened vulnerability in interactions with police and other public officials, when traveling, or even when attempting to do basic things like enter age-barred venues or buy age-barred products, or confirm identity for purposes of cashing a check or using a credit card or a public benefits card. Conflicting identity information can also make it difficult to obtain certain identity documents that are vitally necessary for day-to-day survival. With the advent of the War on Terror, and as security culture continues to increase in the United States, identity verification procedures have expanded and intensified in governmental and commercial sectors. As a result, the barriers created by administrative miscategorization are increasing, especially for people whose immigration status and race subjects them to intensified surveillance.

---

13   Jamie M. Grant et al., *Injustice at Every Turn: A Report of the National Transgender Discrimination Survey* (Washington, DC: National Gay and Lesbian Task Force and National Center for Transgender Equality, 2011), 51, http://www.endtransdiscrimination.org/report.html. Another study estimated that the national unemployment rate for trans people is 70%; see Patrick Letellier and Yoseñio V. Lewis, *Economic Empowerment for the Lesbian Gay Bisexual Transgender Communities: A Report by the Human Rights Commission City and County of San Francisco* (San Francisco: Human Rights Commission, 2000), 10, http://www.sf-hrc.org/ftp/uploadedfiles/sfhumanrights/docs/econ.pdf.

14   Jessica M. Xavier, *The Washington Transgender Needs Assessment Survey Executive Summary* (Washington, DC: Administration for HIV and AIDS, District of Columbia Department of Health, 2000), para. 6, http://www.glaa.org/archive/2000/tgneedsassessment1112.shtml.

15   Chris Daley and Shannon Minter, *Trans Realities: A Legal Needs Assessment of San Francisco's Transgender Communities* (San Francisco: Transgender Law Center, 2003). A 2011 study found that 79% of transgender and gender nonconforming people had not been able to update their identity documents to reflect their current gender; see Jamie M. Grant et al., *Injustice at Every Turn: A Report of the National Transgender Discrimination Survey*, Executive Summary (Washington: National Gay and Lesbian Task Force and National Center for Transgender Equality, 2011), 5, http://www.thetaskforce.org/downloads/reports/reports/ntds_summary.pdf.

Sex-Segregated Facilities

Misclassification is also a significant problem because sex segregation is used to structure so many services and institutions. People who have gender markers on records and ID that do not match their identity face major obstacles in accessing public bathrooms, drug treatment programs, homeless shelters, domestic violence shelters, foster care group homes, and hospitals. They also face significant vulnerability to violence in those spaces, especially in institutions that cannot be avoided because of their mandatory nature. Such mandatory institutions, such as jails, prisons, juvenile punishment centers, psychiatric institutions, and immigration facilities also tend to be enormously violent already. For many, the inability to access sex-segregated programs that address addiction and homelessness results in an increased likelihood of ending up in criminal punishment systems. Trans women in need of shelter (a disproportionately large population because of the combination of employment discrimination, housing discrimination, and family rejection) often remain on the streets because they are unfairly rejected from women-only domestic violence programs and they know the homeless shelter system will place them in men's facilities, guaranteeing sexual harassment and possibly assault. Many trans youth become street homeless when they run away from group homes that place them according to their birth-assigned gender, exposing them to violence from residents and staff alike. Trans people in distress often cannot receive the mental health treatment they want or need because their gender identity or expression will be seen as something that needs to be "cured" by the providers or facilities serving them. Trans people are also frequently rejected from drug treatment centers because these facilities are sex-segregated and administrators believe that trans patients will be "disruptive." The gender norms that are adopted by mental health and drug treatment providers frequently result in the exclusion of trans people from these vital services. For those seeking court-mandated drug treatment as an alternative to imprisonment, this can result in increased time in prison or jail. Lack of access to treatment also increases the harms of addiction, including economic marginalization and vulnerability to violence and criminalization. Trans people in prisons and jails report extremely high rates of sexual assault.[16]

---

16 D. Morgan Bassichis, *"It's War in Here": A Report on the Treatment of Transgender & Intersex People in New York State Men's Prisons* (New York: Sylvia Rivera Law Project, 2007), http://srlp.org/files/warinhere.pdf; Alexander L. Lee, "Gendered Crime & Punishment: Strategies to Protect Transgender, Gender Variant & Intersex People in America's Prisons," pt. 1 and 2, *GIC TIP Journal* (Summer and Fall 2004); Christine Peek, "Breaking out of the Prison Hierarchy: Transgender Prisoners, Rape and the Eighth Amendment," *Santa Clara Law Review* 44, no. 4 (October, 2004): 1211. http://digitalcommons.law.scu.edu/lawreview/vol44/iss4/11;

The operation of gender classification systems prevents access to essential services for trans people and sets up conditions of extreme violence in residential and imprisonment facilities. Gender segregation is a mechanism of management and control in the facilities and institutions where poor people, people of color, immigrants, and other marginalized people are concentrated and where gender norms are enforced with extreme violence. Trans and gender nonconforming people's experiences expose how population-management methods organized by race and gender produce structured harm and insecurity for people targeted by criminalization, immigration enforcement, and economic apartheid.

Health Care Access

Gender classification systems also have a significant impact on access to health care for trans people. Most state Medicaid policies and most health insurance programs exclude from coverage gender-confirming health care for trans people. Medicaid provides all of the gender-confirming procedures and medications that trans people request to nontrans people and only denies them to those seeking them based on a transgender diagnostic profile. For example, testosterones and estrogens are frequently prescribed to nontransgender people for a variety of conditions including hypogonadism, menopause, late onset of puberty, vulvular atrophy, atrophic vaginitis, ovary problems (including lack of ovaries), intersex conditions, breast cancer or prostate cancer, and osteoporosis prevention. Similarly, the chest surgery that transgender men often seek—removing breast tissue to create a flat chest—is regularly provided and paid for by Medicaid for nontrans men who develop the common condition gynecomastia, where breast tissue grows in what are considered abnormal amounts. Nontransgender women who are diagnosed with hirsutism—where facial or body hair grows in what are considered abnormal amounts—are frequently treated for this condition through Medicaid coverage. In addition, reconstruction of breasts, testicles, penises, or other tissues lost to illness or accident is routinely performed and covered. Further, treatments designed to help create genitals that meet social norms of appearance are frequently provided and covered for children born with intersex conditions (which has met increasing opposition in recent years[17]).

Sydney Tarzwell, "The Gender Lines Are Marked with Razor Wire: Addressing State Prison Policies and Practices for the Management of Transgender Prisoners," *Columbia Human Rights Law Review* 38 (Fall 2006): 167.

17 For additional information, please visit the Intersex Society of North America website at http://www.isna.org. The struggle to end surgeries on children with intersex conditions has important political parallels with the struggles of trans people to obtain gender-confirming health care. Both point to the ways that medical authority polices gender categories by establishing and enforcing gender norms on bodies.

Much of the care provided to nontrans people but routinely denied to trans people by Medicaid programs has the sole purpose of confirming the social gender of nontrans patients. Reconstruction of breasts or testicles lost to cancer, hormone treatment to eliminate hair that is considered gender-inappropriate, chest surgery for gynecomastia, and other treatments are provided solely because of the social consequences and mental health impact faced by people who have physical attributes that do not comport with their self-identity and social gender. Thus, the distinction made in refusing this care to transgender people appears to be based solely on diagnosis. Denying care to a politically unpopular group that is provided to others in need of such care, advocates have argued, constitutes "diagnosis discrimination," a violation of federal Medicaid regulations. However, recent cases alleging these charges have not been won, and Medicaid policies regarding trans health care are actually worsening nationwide.[18]

For trans people who need this care, the health impact of this denial can have significant mental and physical health consequences. Depression, anxiety, and suicidality are conditions commonly tied to the unmet need for gender-confirming medical care.[19] According to the few studies that have been done on the issue, rates of HIV infection are also extremely high among transgender people.[20] One study found seroprevalence of 63% among African

---

18 In recent years, Washington State and Minnesota have both undertaken changes in Medicaid policy to reduce coverage for gender-confirming health care for trans people. New York State courts have denied claims of trans litigants seeking to challenge the state's regulation that bars coverage of this care to Medicaid recipients; see Dean Spade et al., "Medicaid Policy and Gender-Confirming Health Care for Trans People: An Interview with Advocates," *Seattle Journal for Social Justice* 8 (2010): 497–509.

19 One study found suicide attempts among 12% of trans women and 21% of trans men who had not begun treatment, and no suicide attempts among the same patients after having begun treatment; see Friedemann Pfäfflin and Astrid Junge, "Results and Discussion," Chap. 6 in *Sex Reassignment. Thirty Years of International Follow-up Studies after Sex Reassignment Surgery: A Comprehensive Review, 1961–1991*, trans. Roberta B. Jacobson and Alf B. Meier (Düsseldorf: Symposion Publishing, 1998), *Internet Archive* Way Back Machine archival version, August 7, 2007, http://web.archive.org/web/20070807031128/http://www.symposion.com/ijt/pfaefflin/6003.htm.

20 A recent study of trans and gender nonconforming people found high rates of HIV in trans populations, especially among people of color and immigrants. "Respondents reported an HIV infection rate of 2.64%, over four times the rate of HIV infection in the general United States adult population.... People of color reported HIV infection at substantially higher rates: 24.90% of African-Americans, 10.92% of Latina/as, 7.04% of American Indians, and 3.70% of Asian-Americans in the study reported being HIV positive. This compares with national rates of

American trans women. A contributing factor to this may be the fact that many people seek treatments through the informal market and receive care without medical supervision because it is not available through other means. This avenue to care may result in inappropriate dosage, nerve damage, HIV, and/or hepatitis infection resulting from injecting without medical supervision or clean needles.[21]

2.4% for African Americans, 0.8% Latino/as, and .01% Asian Americans. Non-US citizens in our sample reported more than twice the rate of HIV infection of US citizens." The study further found that those without high school diplomas, those with household income below $10,000/year, and those who had lost a job due to bias or were unemployed had substantially higher rates of HIV; see Grant et al., *Injustice at Every Turn*, 80.

21 American Psychiatric Association, *Diagnostic and Statistical Manual of Mental Disorders*, 4th ed. (2000), 576–582; Kristen Clements et al., "HIV Prevention and Health Service Needs of the Transgender Community in San Francisco," *International Journal of Transgenderism* 3, no. 1–2 (1999). http://www.symposion.com/ijt/hiv_risk/clements.htm. Kristen Clements-Nolle et al., "HIV Prevalence, Risk Behaviors, Health Care Use, and Mental Health Status of Transgender Persons: Implications for Public Health Intervention," *American Journal of Public Health* 91, no. 6 (2001): 915, 917; Collier M. Cole et al., "Comorbidity of Gender Dysphoria and Other Major Psychiatric Diagnoses," *Archives of Sexual Behavior* 26, no. 1 (1997): 13, 18–19; Karen M. Goulart, "Trans 101: Trans Communities Face Myriad Issues," *Philadelphia Gay News* (1999), http://www.queertheory.com/articles/articles_goulart_trans101.htm; HCH Clinicians' Network, "Crossing to Safety: Transgender Health and Homelessness," *Healing Hands* 6, no. 4 (2002): 1, http://www.nhchc.org/wp-content/uploads/2011/09/transgendered.pdf; Nina Kammerer et al., "Transgender Health and Social Service Needs in the Context of HIV Risk," in *Transgender and HIV: Risks, Prevention, and Care*, eds. Walter O. Bockting and Shelia Kirk (New York: Routledge, 2001),39, 41; Mario Martino, *Emergence: A Transsexual Autobiography* (New York: Crown Publishers, 1977), 168–169, 190; Jan Morris, *Conundrum* (New York: Harcourt Brace Jovanovich, 1974), 40–135; Pfäfflin and Junge, *Sex Reassignment*; Jamil Rehman et al., "The Reported Sex and Surgery Satisfactions of 28 Postoperative Male-to-Female Transsexual Patients," *Archives of Sexual Behavior* 28, no. 1 (1999): 71–89; Michael Rodger and Lindey King, "Drawing Up and Administering Intramuscular Injections: A Review of the Literature," *Journal of Advanced Nursing* 31, no.3 (2000): 574, 577; Joe Lunievicz, *Transgender Positive*, TheBody.com (November 1996), http://www.thebody.com/content/whatis/art30598.html, cited in Pooja Gehi and Gabriel Arkles, "Unravelling Injustice: Race and Class Impact of Medicaid Exclusions of Transition-Related Health Care for Transgender People," *Sexuality Research and Social Policy: Journal of NSRC* 5, no. 1 (2008): 12–15. See also "Brief for the Association of Gay and Lesbian Psychiatrists, as Amicus Curae," in *In the Matter of the Review of Brian (a/k/a Maria) L.*, New York Supreme Court, Appellate Division, 1 Department, April 19, 2006.

Seeking gender-confirming care without coverage is also an avenue to harassment, profiling, and imprisonment for many trans youth and adults who engage in criminalized work to pay for the care, or who face criminalization due to the circumstances of their acquisition of the care. Further, because of the ways that medical requirements are used in gender reclassification policies of all kinds, the impact of being denied this gender-confirming care has ramifications in all other areas of life that relate to recordkeeping and identity verification. Misclassification in all three of these realms—identity documentation, sex-segregated facilities, and health care access—combined with widespread family rejection and routinized stigmatization, produce conditions of exacerbated poverty, criminalization, and violence for trans populations. In each instance, the use of gender as a category of data for sorting populations—something that is taken as neutral and obvious to most administrators—operates as a potential vector of vulnerability. In the context of massive administrative systems mobilized to produce and manage targeted populations, such as public welfare systems, criminal punishment systems, and immigration enforcement systems, trans people face particular vulnerability to displacement, violence, and early death.

Gender Classification and Trans Vulnerability in the Context of Intensified Surveillance

The ongoing vulnerability of trans people stemming from administrative classifications of gender has become even more severe with the increase in identity verification procedures that have emerged since September 11, 2001. The declaration of the War on Terror ushered in a range of policy reforms and new government practices that have drastically increased surveillance and shifted the collection and use of identity data. One major element of this new surveillance is the increased sharing and comparison of different pools of data collected by different government agencies. Historically, the various state Departments of Motor Vehicles (DMVs), the Social Security Administration (SSA), the Internal Revenue Service (IRS), and other agencies that collect data about individuals mostly maintained their data for their own uses. Comparison of data between agencies about an individual only occurred during specific investigations.

The heightening of US security culture, inaugurated in the name of terrorism prevention, has drastically changed the deployment of this data. New practices have emerged and various agencies now compare their entire data sets and seek out mismatched information. The rationale for this activity is to track down people who have obtained identity documents or work authorization using false information. For example, when a DMV compares its records with the SSA, those people whose information is inconsistent between the two agencies will be contacted with a threat to revoke their driver's licenses. When the IRS compares its data with the SSA, employers are contacted and urged to take action to rectify the conflicting information or to terminate the employee. Undocumented immigrants are the primary targets of this new use of government data. These policies have drastically increased the vulnerability of immigrants to exploitation by employers, violence from the police and immigration enforcement, poverty, lack of access to vital basic services, and deportation.[22] These new rules have also increased the significance of the inconsistency of gender reclassification policies for immigrant and nonimmigrant trans people. The inability to have ID and records changed to reflect current gender—and the fact that some documents can be changed while others cannot—has dire ramifications: trans employees face being outed by the government to their employers, losing their driver's licenses, encountering new hurdles when seeking government benefits and services, and in general experiencing greater difficulty with all administrative systems.

The enhanced focus on identity surveillance is increasing the problems that emerge due to having an inconsistent administrative identity. The augmentation of US security culture has raised the level of stability demanded of our identities and has sharpened the tools that heighten the vulnerability of those who are not "fully authorized" in any particular administrative context. Data pool comparison practices are a significant problem given the inconsistency of gender reclassification policies in the United States. The War on Terror has prompted proposals for an even wider variety of population-tracking databases along with new uses of existing data sets collected by federal and state agencies. These proposals are usually aimed at identifying undocumented immigrants and bolstering military recruitment. For instance, there have been proposals for a database that would track information related to military recruitment for all US residents under a certain age. An FBI database currently in development would be the world's largest collection of biometric data, compiling palm prints, facial images, and iris patterns.[23] Purportedly banal and uncontroversial changes like the new requirement

---

22   Rates of deportation have continued to increase under the Obama administration. In July 2010 the *Washington Post* reported, "The Immigration and Customs Enforcement agency expects to deport about 400,000 people this fiscal year, nearly 10% above the Bush administration's 2008 total and 25% more than were deported in 2007. The pace of company audits [seeking employment of undocumented workers] has roughly quadrupled since President George W. Bush's final year in office." See Peter Slevin, "Deportation of Illegal Immigrants Increases under Obama Administration," *Washington Post*, July 26, 2010, http://www.washingtonpost.com/wp-dyn/content/article/2010/07/25/AR2010072501790.html.

23   Ellen Nakashima, "FBI Prepares Vast Database of Biometrics, $1 Billion Project to Include Images of Faces," *Washington Post*, December 22, 2007.

that gender be listed on plane tickets are emerging based on a cultural logic that gender is fixed and obvious and therefore an easy classification tool for verifying identity.[24]

As with all such state care-taking programs, the aim of creating increased security for the nation hangs on the assumption of a national subject that deserves and requires that protection: a subject for whom these identity classification and verification categories are uncontroversial. Because gender remains an ever-present vector of identity verification, it is being put to use to achieve the racialized nation-making goals of the War on Terror. These examples from the War on Terror are helpful not only in illustrating how surveillance associated with military and immigration control projects is implemented and operates, but also for illuminating the dangers of projects commonly perceived as benign. Data collection and management-focused programs like driver's licensing, Social Security benefits, and taxation are less often analyzed for their racist and sexist impacts. In reality, these systems are part of a national security project that constructs national norms to sort populations for the distribution of life chances.

What Gender Classification Problems Can Tell Us about Trans Politics and Law Reform

The moment of the War on Terror's bolstering of identity surveillance and increased exposure of poor people, immigrants, people of color, and gender outsiders to exploitation, imprisonment, and violence can help us comprehend the ways that racialized and gendered subjection and violence are presently operating, and can help us begin to examine approaches to intervention. First, this analysis points us to the realm of administrative, population-level intervention as an area of control and legal codification that may be more high-stakes for trans well-being even though it has been less visibly politicized than the symbolic realm of individual/intentional discrimination. The liberal rights-seeking strategy urges us to seek declarations from the state that trans lives are equal and worthy and that gender identity difference is not a formal barrier to citizenship. This model of inclusion and recognition, however, leaves in place the conditions that actually produce the disproportionate poverty, criminalization, imprisonment, deportation, and violence trans people face while papering it over with a veneer of fairness. Attention to the administration and distribution of life chances exposes the locations that generate that vulnerability, and that attention means we must refuse to use trans struggles to assert the neutrality of systems that reproduce

---

24 Dean Spade, "Ma'am, um, I Mean, Sir, um, um, Ma'am?" *Cases and Controversies*, June 11, 2009, http://lawfacultyblog.seattleu.edu/2009/06/11/maam-um-i-mean-sir-um-um-maam/.

racism, sexism, ableism, transphobia, xenophobia, and homophobia. Prioritizing analysis of and intervention in the distribution of life chances lets us get to what is really producing the harms trans people face, and to abandon law reform interventions that are primarily symbolic. Such an analysis can inform strategies that take up law reform campaigns tactically: when doing so provides immediate relief to harmful conditions, helps mobilize and build political momentum for more transformative change, provides an incremental step in dismantling a harmful system, and makes sense when weighed against dangers of legitimization and reification of violent systems.

Second, this inquiry gives us a vantage point for asking what a trans politics that is critical of surveillance might look like. It moves us away from an uncritical call to "be counted" by the administrative mechanisms of violent systems and instead allows us to strategize our interventions on these systems with an understanding of their operations and of their tendencies to add new categories of legibility as methods of expanding their control. This is particularly meaningful given that quests for recognition and inclusion tend to forgo such a politics in favor of being incorporated into harmful systems and institutions. The trend toward recognition and inclusion demands in the gay and lesbian legal rights context—the demands for inclusion in marriage, the military, the Census, and the police force—has created significant political division between people whose race, class, immigration, and gender positions and privileges give them the capacity to benefit from such inclusion, and those who will remain targets of systems of violence and control even if exclusion explicitly based on sexual orientation is legally prohibited. In the context of gender classification policies, a critical understanding of surveillance allows us to avoid making simplistic demands to have these policies "fixed" so that trans people can be more "accurately" classified. Rather, this analysis allows for the emergence of politics and resistance strategies that understand the expansion of identity verification as a key facet of racialized and gendered maldistribution of security and vulnerability. We can start to see how narrow demands to "fix" these policies for the least marginalized trans people—those who would have proper documentation if not for a gender classification problem—sharpens divisions between those who would benefit from inclusion and those who will remain locked out, or face worsened conditions, if new formal policies of inclusion or recognition are won. As we come to understand the broader context of racialized and gendered nation-making that population management is inherent to, we can comprehend how legal equality claims that fail to challenge the broader conditions of maldistribution can cause us to inadvertently produce a trans politics that supports and legitimizes those very systems and institutions that make trans people so vulnerable.

Third, these inquiries give us a new window for looking at the role of law and policy reform work in critical trans politics. As we critically examine law reform work that threatens to engender tools of legitimacy for harmful and dangerous social and political arrangements, and as we set our sights on developing strategies that actually impact trans people's survival, we need a new way of looking at the legal problems trans people face. A central element, which will be discussed more fully in the next chapter,[25] is deemphasizing law reform more broadly, and ensuring that law reform is not the primary demand of our movements. Decentralizing legal strategies, however, does not mean abandoning them altogether. Trans people's lives are heavily mediated by a variety of legal barriers that create dire conditions, especially those related to the use of gender classification in a range of state care-taking/control programs. Legal work of various kinds can be a part of the arsenal of tools available for addressing those conditions. Using legal reform requires a careful, reflective analysis in each instance of the potential impact on the survival of trans populations. For example, we will have to ask ourselves, Is this change merely symbolic, or will it prevent trans poverty, criminalization, deportation, and death? Will this reform strengthen key systems of control or dismantle them? We must be acutely aware of the potential for dividing trans politics along lines of access and capacity to benefit from reforms, and we have to consciously work toward building shared analysis between and amongst trans and non trans populations struggling against shared obstacles and mechanisms of control. These questions help us analyze what role legal work could play in mobilizing people for transformative change. Two examples will help illustrate how this kind of analysis can inform which law reform projects we do or do not take up.

A central question facing trans politics is if and how to use legal reform tools to intervene in the various problems trans people face in criminal punishment systems. As discussed in Chapter Two,[26] hate crime laws do not prevent violence against trans people but do add punishing power to a system that is a primary perpetrator of violence against trans people. Hate crime laws do not meet the criteria I am suggesting for law reform work because they create primarily symbolic change; hate crime laws co-opt the fear, grief, and rage of trans communities at the high levels of violence we face and the low worth our lives are given into the project of expanding a system that targets us. Instead of pursuing hate crime laws, we should turn toward legal work that relates directly to the criminalization of trans people and addresses issues like police harassment and violence, inadequate criminal defense, medical neglect, and the myriad violences facing imprisoned trans people. In the context of such work, our attention must stay focused on improving

---

25 See note 1.
26 Ibid.

life chances for trans people and making sure that our work does not build up the criminal punishment system. When working to address conditions of imprisonment, then, we must avoid proposals that include constructing buildings or facilities to house trans prisoners, to hire new staff, or make any other changes that would expand the budget and/or imprisoning capacities of the punishment system. Alternatively, we should focus our efforts on decarceration tactics: increased access to adequate, safe drug treatment and other alternatives to imprisonment; access to competent/nontransphobic criminal defense counsel; access to resources for former prisoners to prevent the homelessness and poverty that often leads to additional criminalization; and direct support of prisoners who are experiencing medical neglect, violence, and retaliation. That direct support can include legal advocacy as well as emotional support and leadership development work. This approach, which uses direct individual legal services combined with mobilizing for systemic change that actually benefits the well-being of trans prisoners instead of expanding the criminal punishment system, requires continual reflection and evaluation to determine that each step considers the context of the work. This work needs to be based in a shared imagination of what ultimate transformative change we are pursuing, and what we think it will take to get there. For example, because this work seeks to mobilize a broad constituency to oppose criminalization and imprisonment, and sees trans prisoners and former prisoners as key leaders in that work because of their experience in and knowledge of criminal punishment systems, doing work to directly support their survival and political participation is an essential part of this strategy. Legal tools can be part of that struggle, but legal change is not its goal. Time and again, legal reforms of criminal punishment systems have resulted in expansions of those systems. Mindful of these dangers, we must ensure that legal work is always aimed at dismantling the prison industrial complex and supporting people entangled in it, knowing that the system is likely to try to co-opt our critiques to produce opportunities for expansion.

The matrix of the administrative programs that rely on gender classification is another location where we should apply this analysis in order to determine a path for legal reform. An understanding of the dire consequences of administrative gender classifications, especially given the expansion of identity surveillance in the wake of September 11th and the advent of the declaration of the War on Terror, points us to administrative law as a key site of the production of vulnerability for trans populations.[27] Turning away from the notion that declarations of nondiscrimination by local, state, and federal legislatures will somehow produce improved life chances for trans people and

---

27 Toby Beauchamp, "Artful Concealment and Strategic Visibility: Transgender Bodies and US State Surveillance After 9/11," *Surveillance and Society* 6, no. 4 (2009): 356-66.

instead turning toward an examination of how the operations of DMVs, shelters, group homes, jails, prisons, schools, taxation systems, work authorization systems, and immigration enforcement rely on gender surveillance and forced classification allows us to intervene more meaningfully on the technologies of governance that are most harmful to trans people. When choosing targets within administrative systems, we again want to ensure that we are not building their capacity for control and violence. This has to include how we formulate arguments about these interventions. If, for example, we want to do work regarding identity documentation and how trans people are being adversely impacted by new uses of government surveillance, we need to avoid neoliberal rhetoric about the "privacy rights of hard-working, tax-paying trans Americans." Such arguments mobilize the same "us" versus "them" logic that fuels the racist, anti-immigrant sentiments that support the growth of security culture and suggest that the main problem with the War on Terror is how it accidentally creates problems for "law-abiding" nonimmigrant trans people. Instead, we can be more effective by joining forces with the many populations facing heightened vulnerability to surveillance, and devise shared opposition to the new practices and policies.

An example of this kind of work is the Sylvia Rivera Law Project's participation in a coalition of immigrant rights organizations that formed in the mid-2000s in New York State to resist changes that were being made by the state DMV with the aim of eliminating driver's license access to undocumented immigrants. The coalition opposed particular new policies and practices and took a stand against the implementation of the REAL ID Act. New York State had begun comparing its DMV records to the federal Social Security Administration records and suspending the driver's license of any person whose records had mismatching information between the two sets of data. Trans and nontrans immigrants were impacted, as were many trans nonimmigrant people who had different genders on their driver's license than on their Social Security records, differences resulting from different administrative requirements. Social Security required evidence of genital surgery to change gender on its records while the New York DMV only required a doctor's letter stating that the person was trans. The Sylvia Rivera Law Project (SRLP) joined the coalition and shared information with the coalition members about how trans immigrants and nonimmigrants were being affected. Building relationships with groups in the coalition expanded understandings of trans policy issues of other coalition members and gave SRLP members (immigrants and nonimmigrants alike) a political space in which to take up urgent local immigrant justice work. SRLP spread the word about what was happening to its constituents, brought members to rallies and protests, and participated in the coalition's activities.[28] This collaboration provides a model for a trans political practice that refuses law and policy changes that would solely try to exempt trans nonimmigrants from the issue, thereby possibly further legitimizing these policies by refining their impact to those deliberately targeted during the racist, xenophobic uproar that produced these policy changes. Instead, SRLP's approach stands up for trans immigrants, nontrans immigrants, and trans nonimmigrants with a coalition of people targeted by these policies. It recognizes that anti-immigrant sentiment was the primary motivation for these policies, though some nonimmigrant vulnerable populations have been harmed as well, and demands change from a place of shared struggle and collective analysis. Working in coalitions of groups affected by immigration enforcement, poverty, criminalization, housing insecurity, and other key sites of the maldistribution of life chances, we can aim to have no one's messaging contribute to scapegoating another vulnerable population.

We can also approach administrative policies that govern gender classification with a strategy focused on demedicalization—for example, reducing and removing medical treatment requirements for gender reclassification. This work is important to reduce the racist and classist impacts of these policies. Reducing and eliminating medical evidence requirements for gender reclassification directly addresses trans people's survival issues, especially low-income people, youth, and people of color who are disproportionately deprived of health care access. These strategies are already being used effectively by activists around the country and have the additional benefit of building local leadership and relationships as people struggle with a range of local administrative systems (e.g., shelters, DMVs, foster care programs, drug treatment programs, jails, and prisons) that have harmful gender reclassification policies.[29] Many of these campaigns focus on the policies of various sex-segregated facilities and institutions to address the violence trans people face within them.[30] At all times, attention to how the work is being done, how

---

28 Sylvia Rivera Law Project, "Stop the Suspensions!" http://archive.srlp.org/stop-suspensions; The REAL ID Act of 2005, Pub.L. 109-13, § 119 Stat. 302 (2005).

29 Activists in Colorado won a policy change in 2005 to remove surgery requirements from their state DMV gender designation change policy. In 2008, activists in Washington State successfully advocated for a birth certificate gender designation change policy that does not require any specific evidence of specific medical procedures. Activists in New York have been working since 2004 to win similar policy changes in New York City and New York State Departments of Health. See Spade, "Documenting Gender."

30 Activists in San Francisco, New York City, Washington, DC, and Boston have won city policies that prevent the shelter systems of those cities from forcing trans people into homeless shelters correlated to birth-assigned gender. See Spade, "Documenting Gender."

it interacts with the broader context of neoliberal trends (surveillance, abandonment of the poor, criminalization, cooptation), and whether it can actually impact trans survival is required. Such an analysis necessitates contextualizing law reform in a set of broader understandings about power and control and with demands for transformation rather than inclusion and recognition.

This kind of contextualization moves us away from what critics have called the "single issue politics" that has produced much-lauded but illusory "success" in lesbian and gay politics. Further, this analysis illuminates neoliberal "victories" for what they truly are: betrayals of those most targeted by homophobia and trans-phobia, and successes for systems that want to be declared "fair" and "equal" while they worsen disparities in life chances with every passing year. The most popular law reform interventions imagine a world of white lesbians and gay men who face some kind of exclusion solely on the basis of sexual orientation and seek narrow changes that provide only formal inclusion. That narrow focus on sexual orientation means that the ways that race, class, immigration status, indigeneity, ability, gender, and other vectors of identity and experience interact with sexual orientation to create certain kinds of vulnerability are left unaddressed. The resultant legal reforms are so narrow in their understanding of the issues that they only provide access to the sought-after right for those who do not have other intervening vectors of marginality, if for anyone at all. For this reason, one might observe that the lesbian and gay rights agenda primarily operates to restore privileges of the dominant systems of meaning and control to those gender-conforming, white, wealthy gay and lesbian US citizens who are enraged at how homophobic laws and policies limit access to benefits to which they feel entitled. Advocates of single issue politics seek to restore the ability of wealthy gay and lesbian couples to inherit from each other with limited taxation, to share each other's private health benefits, to call on law enforcement to protect their property rights, and other such privileges of whiteness and wealth. In order to avoid a similar trajectory in the name of trans politics, our legal reform interventions need to do more than pick out the specific narrow ways that the law explicitly excludes trans people or that legal systems create obstacles for the most enfranchised trans people.

We need to conceptualize the ways that population-level interventions—the War on Drugs, the War on Terror, and the gutting of welfare and Medicaid programs—interact with regimes of gender classification and enforcement and utilize gender as a technology of control. We must examine how racism, sexism, capitalism, xenophobia, settler colonialism, and ableism combine to produce and sustain these violent systems of distribution while we simultaneously explore the specific vulnerabilities of trans populations in these systems. This analysis can facilitate strategies based in a broad understanding of how power and control operate and help us determine which interventions might yield the most redistribution of life chances with the least danger of legitimizing and reproducing the very conditions we oppose. Because individual rights-focused law reform operates as a cover for population-based practices of abandonment and imprisonment, we must resist logics that frame harm as primarily individual and that seek narrowly focused remedies accessible only to those already deemed "legitimate" bodies for claiming rights (white, noncriminalized, nonimmigrant, nondisabled, nonindigenous). Because reform projects always carry the danger of compromise and co-optation, and since law reform in particular tends to reproduce ideas of governmental fairness and justice, we have to employ an especially cautious analysis when using legal reform tools.

We must return for reflection frequently and look out for the common traps—building and legitimizing systems of control, dividing constituencies along the lines of access to legal rights, and advancing only symbolic change. We must not only refuse reforms that require dividing and leaving behind more vulnerable trans populations, but also try to assume that the most easily digestible invitations to be included are the very ones that bring us into greater collusion with systemic control and violence. It is not surprising that the first federal legislation formally to address harm against trans people was the Matthew Shepard and James Byrd, Jr. Act—a hate crime bill that would bring enormous resources to the criminal punishment system and do little or nothing to prevent trans death. To the extent that the mobilization of trans people and our allies begins to expose the crises of coercive and violent gender systems, those systems will respond, at least in part, with solicitation to join their projects and expand themselves in our names—and then tell us we have won victories, that enough has been done. In the face of that trend, we must think deeply and critically about how law reforms can be part of dismantling violent regimes of administering life and death and forgo them when they cannot.

Bibliography

American Psychiatric Association. *Diagnostic and Statistical Manual of Mental Disorders*, 4th ed. Washington, DC: American Psychiatric Association, 2000.

Bassichis, D. Morgan. *"It's War in Here": A Report on the Treatment of Transgender & Intersex People in New York State Men's Prisons*. New York: Sylvia Rivera Law Project, 2007. http://srlp.org/files/warinhere.pdf.

Beauchamp, Toby. "Artful Concealment and Strategic Visibility: Transgender Bodies and US State Surveillance After 9/11." *Surveillance and Society* 6, no. 4 (2009): 356–66.

Bowker, Geoffrey C., and Susan Leigh Star. *Sorting Things Out: Classification and Its Consequences* (Cambridge, MA: MIT Press, 1999).

Clements, Kristen, Kerrily Kitano, Willy Wilkinson, and Rani Marx. "HIV Prevention and Health Service Needs of the Transgender Community in San Francisco." *International Journal of Transgenderism* 3, no. 1-2 (1999). http://www.symposion.com/ijt/hiv_risk/clements.htm.

Clements-Nolle, Kristen, Rani Marx, Robert Guzman, and Mitchell Katz. "HIV Prevalence, Risk Behaviors, Health Care Use, and Mental Health Status of Transgender Persons: Implications for Public Health Intervention." *American Journal of Public Health* 91, no. 6 (2001): 915–921.

Cole, Collier M., Michael O'Boyle, Lee E. Emory, and Walter J. Meyer III. "Comorbidity of Gender Dysphoria and Other Major Psychiatric Diagnoses." *Archives of Sexual Behavior* 26, no. 1 (1997): 13–26;

Daley, Chris, and Shannon Minter. *Trans Realities: A Legal Needs Assessment of San Francisco's Transgender Communities* (San Francisco: Transgender Law Center, 2003).

Dean, Mitchell. *Governmentality: Power and Rule in Modern Society*, 2nd ed. London: SAGE, 2010.

Foucault, Michel. *Society Must Be Defended: Lectures at the College de France, 1975–76*. Translated by David Macey. New York: Picador, 2009.

Gehi, Pooja, and Gabriel Arkles. "Unravelling Injustice: Race and Class Impact of Medicaid Exclusions of Transition-Related Health Care for Transgender People." *Sexuality Research and Social Policy: Journal of NSRC* 5, no. 1 (2008): 7–35.

Grant, Jaime M., Lisa A. Monet, and Justin Tanis with Jody L. Herman, Jack Harrison, and Mara Keisling. *Injustice at Every Turn: A Report of the National Transgender Discrimination Survey*. Washington, DC: National Gay and Lesbian Task Force and National Center for Transgender Equality, 2011. http://www.endtransdiscrimination.org/report.html.

———. *Injustice at Every Turn: A Report of the National Transgender Discrimination Survey* Executive Summary. Washington, DC: National Gay and Lesbian Task Force and National Center for Transgender Equality, 2011. http://www.thetaskforce.org/downloads/reports/reports/ntds_summary.pdf.

———. *National Transgender Discrimination Survey Report on Health and Health Care*. Washington, DC: National Gay and Lesbian Task Force and National Center for Transgender Equality, 2010. http://www.thetaskforce.org/reports_and_research/trans_survey_health_heathcare.

HCH Clinicians' Network. "Crossing to Safety: Transgender Health and Homelessness." *Healing Hands* 6, no. 4 (2002): 1–2. http://www.nhchc.org/wp-content/uploads/2011/09/transgendered.pdf.

Hickman, Christine B. "The Devil and the One Drop Rule: Racial Categories, African Americans and the US Census." *Michigan Law Review* 95, no. 5 (1997): 1161–1265. http://www.jstor.org/stable/1290008.

Kammerer, Nina. "Transgender Health and Social Service Needs in the Context of HIV Risk." In *Transgender and HIV: Risks, Prevention, and Care*, edited by Walter O. Bockting and Shelia Kirk, 39–57. New York: Routledge, 2001.

Lee, Alexander L. "Gendered Crime & Punishment: Strategies to Protect Transgender, Gender Variant & Intersex People in America's Prisons," pt. 1 and 2. *GIC TIP Journal*. (Summer and Fall 2004).

Letellier, Patrick, and Yoseñio V. Lewis. *Economic Empowerment for the Lesbian Gay Bisexual Transgender Communities: A Report by the Human Rights Commission City and County of San Francisco*. San Francisco: Human Rights Commission, 2000. http://www.sf-hrc.org/ftp/uploadedfiles/sfhumanrights/docs/econ.pdf.

Martino, Mario. *Emergence: A Transexual Autobiography*. New York: Crown Publishers, 1977.

Morris, Jan. *Conundrum*. New York: Harcourt Brace Jovanovich, 1974.

Parenti, Christian. *The Soft Cage: Surveillance in America from Slavery to the War On Terror*. New York: Basic Books, 2003.

Peek, Christine. "Breaking out of the Prison Hierarchy: Transgender Prisoners, Rape and the Eighth Amendment." *Santa Clara Law Review* 44, no. 4 (October, 2004): 1211–1248. http://digitalcommons.law.scu.edu/lawreview/vol44/iss4/11.

Pfäfflin, Friedemann, and Astrid Junge. "Results and Discussion." Chap. 6 in *Sex Reassignment. Thirty Years of International Follow-up Studies after Sex Reassignment Surgery: A Comprehensive Review, 1961–1991*. Translated by Roberta B. Jacobson and Alf B. Meier. Düsseldorf: Symposon Publishing, 1998. *Internet Archive* Way Back Machine archival version, August 7, 2007. http://web.archive.org/web/20070807031128/http://www.symposion.com/ijt/pfaefflin/6003.htm.

Rehman, Jamil, Simcha Lazer, Alexandru E. Benet, Leah C. Schaefer, and Arnold Melman. "The Reported Sex and Surgery Satisfactions of 28 Postoperative Male-to-Female Transsexual Patients." *Archives of Sexual Behavior* 28, no. 1 (1999): 71–89.

Rodger, Michael, and Lindey King. "Drawing Up and Administering Intramuscular Injections: A Review of the Literature." *Journal of Advanced Nursing* 31, no.3 (2000): 574–582.

Scott, James C. *Seeing Like a State: How Certain Schemes to Improve the Human Condition Have Failed*. New Haven, CT: Yale University Press, 1998.

Scott, James C., John Tehranian, and Jeremy Mathias. "The Production of Legal Identities Proper to States: The Case of the Permanent Family Surname." *Comparative Studies in Society and History* 44, no. 1 (2002): 4–44.

Sharma, Nandita, and Cynthia Wright. "Decolonizing Resistance, Challenging Colonial States." *Social Justice* 35 (2008–2009): 120–38.

Spade, Dean. "Documenting Gender," *Hastings Law Journal* 59 (2008): 731–782.

Spade, Dean. "Ma'am, um, I Mean, Sir, um, um, Ma'am?" *Cases and Controversies*, June 11, 2009. http://lawfacultyblog.seattleu.edu/2009/06/11/maam-um-i-mean-sir-um-um-maam/.

Spade, Dean, with Gabriel Arkles, Phil Duran, Pooja Gehi, and Huy Nguyen. "Medicaid Policy and Gender-Confirming Health Care for Trans People: An Interview with Advocates." *Seattle Journal for Social Justice* 8 (2010): 497–509.

Tarzwell, Sydney. "The Gender Lines Are Marked with Razor Wire: Addressing State Prison Policies and Practices for the Management of Transgender Prisoners." *Columbia Human Rights Law Review* 38 (Fall 2006): 167–219.

Valverde, Mariana. "Genealogies of European States: Foucauldian Reflections," *Economy and Society* 36, no. 1 (2007): 159–178. doi:10.1080/03085140601089911.

Xavier, Jessica M. *The Washington Transgender Needs Assessment Survey Executive Summary*. Washington, DC: Administration for HIV and AIDS, District of Columbia Department of Health, 2000. http://www.glaa.org/archive/2000/tgneedsassessment1112.shtml.

Part Five

Information Extraction, Information Flow

On Torture: Abu Ghraib

Jasbir K. Puar[1]

The torture of Iraqi prisoners at Abu Ghraib is neither exceptional nor singular, as many—Donald Rumsfeld and the Bush administration, the US military establishment, and even good liberals—would have us believe. We need think only of the fact that so many soldiers facing prosecution for the Iraqi prisoner situation came from prison guard backgrounds, reminding us of incarceration practices within the prison industrial complex, not to mention the treatment of Palestinian civilians by Israeli army guards, or even the brutal sodomizing of Abner Louima by police officers in New York City. Neither has it been possible to normalize the incidents at Abu Ghraib as business as usual even within the torture industry. As public and governmental rage alike made clear, a line had been crossed. Why that line is so demarcated at the place of so-called sexual torture—specifically, violence that purports to mimic sexual acts closely associated with deviant sexuality or sexual excess such as sodomy and oral sex, as well as S/M practices of bondage, leashing, and hooding—and not, for example, at the slow starvation of millions due to US sanctions against Iraq, the deaths of thousands of Iraqi civilians since the US invasion in April 2003, or the plundering and carnage in Falluja, is indeed a spectacular question. The reaction of rage, while to some extent laudable, misses the point entirely—or, perhaps more generously, upstages a denial of culpability. The violence performed at Abu Ghraib is not an exception to, nor an extension of, imperialist occupation. Rather, it works in concert with proliferating modalities of force, an indispensable part of the so-called shock-and-awe campaign blueprinted by Israelis on the backs of Palestinian corpses. Bodily torture is but one element in a repertoire of techniques of occupation and subjugation that include assassinations of top leaders,

---

1 Editors' note: this paper was previously published in *Radical History Review* 93 (2005): 13–38, doi:10.1215/01636545-2005-93-13.

house-to-house roundups often involving interrogations without interpreters, the use of tanks and bulldozers in densely populated civilian residential areas, helicopter attacks, and the trashing and forced closure of hospitals and other provisional sites.

The sexual humiliation and ritual torture of Iraqi prisoners enabled the Bush administration to forge a crucial distinction between the supposed depravity of Abu Ghraib and the "freedom" being built in Iraq. Days after the photographs from Abu Ghraib had circulated in the domestic and foreign press, President George W. Bush stated of the abused Iraqi prisoners, "Their treatment does not reflect the *nature* of the American people."[2] Not that I imagine our president to be so thoughtful or profound (though perhaps his speechwriters are), but his word choice is intriguing. Which one, exactly, of the acts perpetrated by American soldiers is inimical to the "natural" tendencies of Americans? Is it the behavior of the US soldiers conducting the abuse? The ones clicking the digital shutter? Or is it the perverse behaviors forcibly enacted by the captured prisoners? What, exactly, is it that is "disgusting"—a word commonly used during the first few days of the prison scandal—about these photos? The US soldiers who are grinning, stupidly waving their thumbs in the air? The depicted sex acts themselves, simulated oral and anal sex between men? Or the fact that the photos were taken at all?

Bush's efforts to refute the idea that the psychic and fantasy lives of Americans are depraved, sick, and polluted by suggesting instead that they remain naturally free from such perversions—not only would one never enjoy the infliction of such abuse but one would never even have the mindset or capacity to think of such acts—reinstantiate a liberal regime of multicultural heteronormativity intrinsic to US patriotism. The state of exception surrounding these events is produced on three interrelated planes: that of the rarity of this particular form of violence (the temporality of emergency as excessive in relation to the temporality of regularity); that of the sanctity of the sexual and of the body (the site of violation as extreme in relation to the individual rights of privacy and ownership accorded to the body within liberalism); and that of the transparency of abuse (as overkill in relation to other wartime necropolitical [referring to the right to kill] violence and as defying the normative standards that guarantee the universality of the human in human rights discourses). Here is an extreme example, but one indicting on all three counts nonetheless: in May 2004, Rev. Troy Perry of the Metropolitan Community Churches (MCC) circulated a press release in reaction to incidents at

---

2   Thom Shanker and Jacques Steinberg, "The Struggle for Iraq: Captives; Bush Voices 'Disgust' at Abuse of Iraqi Prisoners," *New York Times*, May 1, 2004, http://www.nytimes.com/2004/05/01/world/the-struggle-for-iraq-captives-bush-voices-disgust-at-abuse-of-iraqi-prisoners.html. Emphasis added.

Abu Ghraib in which he condemned "the use of sexuality as an instrument of torture, shame, and intimidation," arguing that the fact "that prisoners were forced to perform sexual acts that violate their religious principles and personal consciences is particularly heinous." The press release concluded by declaring that "MCC pledges to continue to work for a world in which all people are treated with dignity and equality and where sexuality is celebrated, respected and used for good."[3]

Hardly exceptional, as Veena Das argues, violence is not set apart from sociality, nor is sociality resistant to it: "Violence is actually embedded in sociality and could itself be a form of sociality."[4] Rita Maran, in her study of the application of torture in the French-Algerian war, demonstrates that torture is neither antithetical nor external to the project of liberation; rather, it is part and parcel of the necessary machinery of the civilizing mission. Torture is the underside, indeed, the accomplice of the civilizing mission. Furthermore, Maran, citing Roger Trinquier, notes that "torture is the particular bane of the terrorist,"[5] remarking that the "rational equivalency" plays out as follows: "As the terrorist resorts to extremes of violence that cause grievous individual pain, so the state replies with extremes of violence that, in turn, cause grievous individual pain."[6] Any civilizing mission is marked precisely by this paradox: the civilizing apparatus of liberation is exactly that which delimits the conditions of its possibility. Thus torture is at the very least doubly embedded in sociality: it is integral to the missionary/savior discourse of liberation and civilizational uplift, and it constitutes apposite punishment for terrorists and the bodies that resemble them. As I argue in this article, deconstructing exceptionalism and contextualizing the embeddedness of torture entails attending to discourses and affective manifestations of sexuality, race, gender, and nation that activate torture's corporeal potency.

---

3 Office of the Moderator, Metropolitan Community Churches, "A Pastoral Statement from Reverend Dr. Troy D. Perry on Treatment of Iraqi Prisoners," news release, May 10, 2004, *Internet Archive* Way Back Machine archival version, September 23, 2005, http://web.archive.org/web/20050923055100/http://www.mccchurch.org/mediaroom/2004/IraqAbusePerry.htm.

4 Thomas Cushman, "A Conversation with Veena Das on Religion and Violence, Suffering and Language," *Hedgehog Review* 6, no. 1 (2004): 78.

5 Roger Trinquier, *Modern Warfare* (New York: Praeger, 1964), xv.

6 Rita Maran, *Torture: The Role of Ideology in the French-Algerian War* (New York: Praeger, 1989), 82.

The Production of the Muslim Body as Object of Torture

> *Such dehumanization is unacceptable in any culture, but it is especially so in the Arab world. Homosexual acts are against Islamic law and it is humiliating for men to be naked in front of other men. . . . Being put on top of each other and forced to masturbate, being naked in front of each other—it's all a form of torture. . . .*
>
> ~Bernard Haykel[7]

Those questioned for their involvement—tacit and explicit—in torture at Abu Ghraib cited both the lack-of-training and the cultural-difference argument to justify their behavior: "If we had known more about them, about their culture and their way of life" whined one soldier plaintively on the US news, "we would have been better able to handle the situation." The monolith of Muslim culture constructed through this narrative (performatively reiterated by Bush's tardy apology for the Abu Ghraib atrocities, bizarrely directed at the token Muslim visiting at the time, King Abdullah of Jordan) aside, the cultural-difference line has also been used by conservative and progressive factions alike to comment on the particularly intense shame with which Muslims experience homosexual and feminizing acts. For this, the prisoners receive vast sympathy from the general public. The taboo of homosexuality within Islamic cultures figures heavily in the equation for why the torture has been so "effective"; this interpretation of sexual norms in the Middle East—sexuality is repressed, but perversity is just bubbling beneath the surface—forms part of a centuries-long Orientalist tradition, an Orientalist phantasmatic that certainly informed the photographs of torture at Abu Ghraib. (A longer exposition on this subject would perhaps draw out the continuities between these photos and the paintings of Delacroix and other photographs and art considered in Edward Said's *Orientalism*.) In "The Gray Zone," Seymour Hersh delineates how the US military made particularly effective use of anthropological texts in order to determine effective torture methods:

> *The notion that Arabs are particularly vulnerable to sexual humiliation became a talking point among pro-war Washington conservatives in the months before the March 2003 invasion of Iraq. One book that was frequently cited was* The Arab Mind, *a study of Arab culture*

---

7   Seymour M. Hersh, quoting Bernard Haykel, a professor of Middle Eastern studies at New York University; see Hersh, "Torture at Abu Ghraib," *New Yorker*, May 10, 2004, 43.

> and psychology, first published in 1973, by Raphael Patai, a cultural anthropologist who taught at, among other universities, Columbia and Princeton, and who died in 1996. The book includes a twenty-five-page chapter on Arabs and sex, depicting sex as a taboo vested with shame and repression. "The segregation of the sexes, the veiling of the women . . . and all the other minute rules that govern and restrict contact between men and women, have the effect of making sex a prime mental preoccupation in the Arab world," Patai wrote. "Homosexual activity, or any indication of homosexual leanings, as with all other expressions of sexuality, is never given any publicity. These are private affairs and remain in private." The Patai book, an academic told me, was "the bible of the neocons on Arab behavior." In their discussions, he said, two themes emerged—"one, that Arabs only understand force and, two, that the biggest weakness of Arabs is shame and humiliation." The government consultant said that there may have been a serious goal, in the beginning, behind the sexual humiliation and the posed photographs. It was thought that some prisoners would do anything—including spying on their associates—to avoid dissemination of the shameful photos to family and friends. The government consultant said, "I was told that the purpose of the photographs was to create an army of informants, people you could insert back in the population." The idea was that they would be motivated by fear of exposure, and gather information about pending insurgency action, the consultant said. If so, it wasn't effective; the insurgency continued to grow.[8]

I quote these passages from Hersh's article at length to demonstrate how the intricate relations between Orientalist knowledge production, sexual and bodily shame, and espionage informed the context of Abu Ghraib. As Yoshie Furuhashi has astutely pointed out, Patai's *The Arab Mind* actually surfaced in Edward Said's *Orientalism* as an example of the contemporary conduits of Orientalism,[9] which also include the knowledge formations of foreign and public policy, terrorism studies, and area studies.[10] (We should add to Said's list the interrogation and intelligence-gathering industry: Titan Corporation and CACI International have been accused of "outsourcing torture" to Iraq and of refining, honing, and escalating torture techniques in order to demonstrate proven results, thus winning lucrative US government contracts and

---

8   Seymour M. Hersh, "The Gray Zone," *New Yorker*, May 24, 2004, 42. Emphasis added.
9   See Edward Said, *Orientalism* (New York: Vintage, 1979), 308–9, 311, 312, 349.
10 Yoshie Furuhashi, "Orientalist Torture," *Critical Montages* (blog), May 20, 2004, http://montages.blogspot.com/2004/05/orientalist-torture.html.

ultimately directing the illegal conduct at Abu Ghraib.)[11] Patai, who also authored *The Jewish Mind*, writes of the molestation of the male baby genitals by doting mothers, the routine beatings and stabbings of sons by fathers, the obsession with sex among Arab students (as compared to American students), and masturbation: "Whoever masturbates . . . evinces his inability to perform the active sex act, and thus exposes himself to contempt."[12] *The Arab Mind* constitutes a mainstay text in diplomatic and military circles, and the book was reissued in November 2001 with an introduction by Norvell B. De Atkine, director of Middle East Studies at the John F. Kennedy Special Warfare Center and School at Fort Bragg in North Carolina.[13] Clearly, not only is the lack of knowledge with respect to cultural difference irrelevant (for would knowing have ended or altered the use of these torture tactics?) but it is precisely through this knowledge that the US military has been diplomatically instructed. It is exactly this unsophisticated notion of (Arab/Muslim/Islamic) cultural difference that military intelligence capitalized on to create what it believed to be a culturally specific and thus effective matrix of torture techniques. Furthermore, though originally the photographs at Abu

---

11 The Center for Constitutional Rights has filed a lawsuit against private firms participating in the so-called torture conspiracy; see Center for Constitutional Rights, "CCR Files Lawsuit Against Private Contractors for Torture Conspiracy," press release, June 9, 2004, http://ccrjustice.org/newsroom/press-releases/ccr-files-lawsuit-against-private-contractors-torture-conspiracy. Trishala Deb and Rafael Mutis elaborate on the implications of outsourcing torture: "CACI is a corporation that generates over $930 million dollars in profit a year, 65% of its budget coming from government contracts. The question remains how these private contractors are accountable to US and international laws, not to mention the international public. Given the restrictions on access to information about the functioning of the war machine since the establishment of the USA PATRIOT Act and Department of Homeland Security, we have even less access to information and accountability regarding some of the most important and dangerous aspects of this permanent war. The relevance of this information is that it exposes one of the most insidious sides to this story the cycle of government expenditures on private contractors as enforcement agents in this war, and profits made by US corporations which are awarded those contracts. In this way the prison industrial complex is at once exposed and expanded; not only were severe crimes against humanity committed but at least one corporation has profited from those crimes. For those corporations who are being paid to provide interrogators and intelligence, war crimes are not a consideration, just a consequence." See Trishala Deb and Rafael Mutis, "Smoke and Mirrors: Abu Ghraib and the Myth of Liberation," *Colorlife!*, Summer 2004, 5.
12 Emram Qureshi, "Misreading *The Arab Mind*," *Boston Globe*, May 30, 2004.
13 Ibid.

Ghraib had a specific information-retrieval purpose, they clearly took on a life of their own, informed by what Slavoj Žižek recalls as the "'unknown knowns'—the disavowed beliefs, suppositions and obscene practices we pretend not to know about, even though they form the background of our public values."[14]

In another example of the transfer of information, the model of terrorism used by the State Department swerves between a pyramid structure and a network structure: the former represents a known, rational administrative format, one that is phallic and, hence, castratable; the latter represents chaotic and unpredictable alliances and forces. Perhaps it is mere coincidence that in several of the Abu Ghraib photos, Iraqi prisoners are arranged naked in human pyramids, in which they are seen to be simulating both the "passive" (feminized) prone position necessary to receive anal penetration and the "active" mounting stance of anal sex. What is significant here is not that the meaning of the pyramid has been understood and translated from one context to another, but rather that the transfer of information and its mimicry does not depend on contextual meaning to have symbolic and political effect.[15]

Such transnational and transhistorical linkages—including unrelated but no less relevant examples drawn from Israeli surveillance and occupation measures, the behavior of the French in Algeria, and even the 2002 Gujarat pogrom in India—surge together to create the Muslim body as a particular typological object of torture.[16] During the Algerian war, for instance, one torture of Arabs consisted of:

---

14 Žižek points out that it is not the known knowns, the known unknowns, or the unknown knowns that matter most here, but rather the unconscious, the knowledge that does not know itself; see Slavoj Žižek, "What Rumsfeld Doesn't Know That He Knows about Abu Ghraib," *In These Times*, May 21, 2004, http://inthesetimes.com/article/747/.

15 The pyramid form also appears in the *Battle of Algiers* (1966, Italy/Algeria, dir. Gillo Pontecorvo), viewed for brainstorming purposes by the Pentagon in September 2003.

16 During February and March of 2002, over two thousand Muslims were killed and tens of thousands more were displaced from their homes in rioting by Hindus; the police were complicit with this violence, and the Hindu nationalist BJP is accused of premeditated orchestration of the pogroms. In regards to Muslim masculinity, the International Initiative for Justice writes: "Muslim men, in the Hindu Right discourse, are not seen as 'men' at all: they are either 'oversexed' to the extent of being bestial (they can satisfy four wives!) or they are effeminate and not masculine enough to satisfy their women.... [As] a symbol of the 'sexual superiority' the emasculated Hindu man must recover by raping and defiling Muslim women ... there have been calls to Hindu men to join gyms and develop

> ... *suspending them, their hands and feet tied behind their backs ... with their head upwards. Underneath them was placed a trestle, and they were made to swing, by fist blows, in such a fashion that their sexual parts rubbed against the very sharp pointed bar of the trestle. The only comment made by the men, turning towards the soldiers present: "I am ashamed to find myself stark naked in front of you."*[17]

This kind of torture directed at the supposed Muslim terrorist is not only subject to the normalizing knowledges of modernity that mark him (or her) both as sexually conservative, modest, and fearful of nudity (and it is interesting how this conceptualization is rendered both sympathetically and as a problem) as well as queer, animalistic, barbarian, and unable to control his (or her) urges. Thus the shadow of homosexuality is never far off. In *Brothers and Others in Arms: The Making of Love and War in Israeli Combat Units*, author Danny Kaplan, looking at the construction of hegemonic masculinity and alternative sexual identities in the Israeli military, argues that sexualization is neither tangential nor incidental to the project of conquest but, rather, is central to it: "[The] eroticization of enemy targets ... triggers the objectification process."[18] This eroticization always inhabits the realm of perversion:

> *An instance where the image of mehablim [literally, "saboteurs"— a general term for terrorists, guerilla soldiers, or any Arab groups or*

---

muscular bodies to counter the 'animal' attraction of the over-sexualized Muslim man. Of course, when Hindu men commit rape and assault their actions are not seen as bestial or animal-like but are considered signs of valor. Simultaneously, there is an attempt to show that Muslim men are not real men, but rather homosexuals *or hijras* (eunuchs)—considered synonymous and undesirable and are therefore unable to satisfy their women. As a VHP (Vishva Hindu Parishad) leaflet called *Jihad* (holy war) boasts:

> We have untied the penises which were tied till now
> Without castor oil in the arse we have made them cry
> Those who call religious war, violence, are all fuckers
> We have widened the tight vaginas of the bibis (women) ...
> Wake up Hindus there are still Miyas (Muslim men) left alive around you
> Learn from Panvad village where their mother was fucked
> She was fucked standing while she kept shouting
> She enjoyed the uncircumcised penis."

See International Initiative for Justice, "Threatened Existence: A Feminist Analysis of the Genocide in Gujarat," December 19, 2002, 29–30, http://www.onlinevolunteers.org/gujarat/reports/iijg/2003/fullreport.pdf.

17 Alistair Horne, *A Savage War of Peace* (London: Pan Books, 2002), 197–98.
18 Danny Kaplan, *Brothers and Others in Arms: The Making of Love and War in Israeli Combat Units* (New York: Harrington Park, 2002), 193.

individuals that operate against Israeli targets] – in this case, Palestinian enemy men – merges with another image of subordination, that of actual homosexual intercourse. It seems that the sexual-targeting drive of masculitary soldier could not resist such a temptation. This is one way to understand Shaul's account of one of the brutalities he experienced in the Lebanon War. During the siege on [Palestinian Liberation Organization, PLO] forces in Beirut, he was stationed next to a post where Israeli snipers observed PLO activity in city houses. Suddenly, something unusual appeared in the sniper's binoculars:

"One of them said to me, 'Come here; I want you to see something.' I looked, and I saw two mehablim, one fucking the other in the ass; it was pretty funny. Like real animals. The sniper said to me, 'And now look.' He aims, and puts a bullet right into the forehead of the one that was being fucked. Holy shit, did the other one freak out! All of a sudden his partner died on him. It was nasty. We were fucking cruel. Cruelty – but this was war. Human life didn't matter much in a case like this, because this human could pick up his gun and fire at you or your buddies at any moment."[19]

Kaplan concludes this vignette by remarking that despite the episode's brutal ending, the gender position of the active partner is what was ultimately protected: "It is striking that even in this encounter it is the passive partner who gets the bullet in his ass, while the active partner remains unscathed."[20] This exemplifies the literalization of performativity whereby the faggot Muslim receives his torture as a faggot Muslim. Violence is naturalized as the inexorable and fitting response to non-normative sexuality. But not only is the Muslim body constructed as pathologically sexually deviant and as potentially homosexual, and thus read as a particularized object for torture, but the torture itself is constituted on the body as such: as Brian Axel has argued, "the performative act of torture produces its object."[21] The body informs the torture, but the torture also forms the body, thus suturing the double entrenchment of perversion into the circuitry of becoming. (So while it is questionable whether the acts of torture should be read as simulating "gay sex" acts, a conundrum I discuss later in this essay, they nonetheless perform an initiation, confirmation, or even conversion in the eyes of the perpetrators.) Furthermore, the faggot Muslim as torture object is splayed across five continents, prominently in Arab countries through the "transnational transfer

---

19 Ibid., 193-94.
20 Ibid., 194.
21 Brian Keith Axel, "The Diasporic Imaginary," *Public Culture* 14, no. 2 (2002): 420, doi:10.1215/08992363-14-2-411.

of people" in a tactic called "renditions," the US practice of holding terrorist suspects in third-country locations such as Saudi Arabia, Egypt, Morocco, Jordan, and, most recently, Syria, thereby sustaining a "worldwide constellation of detention centers" and rendering these citizenship-stripped bodies, about whom the United States can deny having any knowledge, as "ghost detainees."[22]

As the space of "illicit and dangerous sex,"[23] the Orient is the site of carefully suppressed animalistic and perverse homo- and hypersexual instincts. This paradox lies at the heart of Orientalist notions of sexuality that are reanimated through the transnational production of the Muslim terrorist as torture object. Underneath the veils of repression sizzles an indecency waiting to be unleashed. The most recent invocation of the perverse, deranged terrorist and his naturalized proclivities is found in this testimony by one of the prisoner guards at Abu Ghraib:

> I saw two naked detainees, one masturbating to another kneeling with its mouth open. . . . I saw [Staff Sergeant] Frederick walking towards me, and he said, "Look what these animals do when you leave them alone for two seconds." I heard PFC England shout out, "He's getting hard."[24]

Note how the Iraqi prisoner, the one in fact kneeling in the submissive position, is referred to as "it." Contrary to the public debate recently generated on torture, which foregrounds the site of detention as an exemplary holding cell that teems with aggression, this behavior is hardly relegated to prisons, as an especially unnerving moment in Michael Moore's documentary *Fahrenheit 9/11* reveals. A group of US soldiers are shown loading a dead Iraqi, presumably recently killed by them, covered with a white sheet onto a stretcher. Someone yells, "Look, Ali Baba's dick is still hard!" while others follow in disharmonized chorus, "You touched it, eeewww you touched it."[25] Even in death, the muscular virility of the Muslim man cannot be laid to rest in some humane manner; not only the Orientalist fantasy transcends death but the corpse's sexuality does, too—it rises from death, as it were. Death here becomes the scene of the ultimate unleashing of repression.

---

22 Dana Priest and Joe Stephens, "Secret World of US Interrogation: Long History of Tactics in Overseas Prisons is Coming to Light," *Washington Post*, May 11, 2004, http://www.washingtonpost.com/wp-dyn/articles/A15981-2004May10.html.
23 Said, *Orientalism*, 167.
24 Hersh, "Torture at Abu Ghraib," 44.
25 *Fahrenheit 9/11*, directed by Michael Moore (Culver City, CA: Columbia TriStar Home Entertainment, 2004), DVD.

Wither Feminism

Despite the recurring display of revulsion for attributes associated with the feminine, the United States apparently still regards itself as the arbiter of feminist civilized standards. Writing in the *Gully*, a Lesbian, Gay, Bisexual, Transgender, Queer (LGBTQ) political news forum, Kelly Cogswell worries about homophobic and misogynist backlash, as if the United States had not already demonstrated its capacity to perpetuate their most extreme forms. "Images of men forced to wear women's underwear over their faces and engage in homosexual activity," Cogswell writes:

> ... will also inflame misogyny and homophobia. Forget about Bush's anti-gay marriage stand in the United States. By tolerating this behavior in Iraq and elsewhere, his administration has made homosexuality abhorrent world-wide. The image of an American woman holding a prisoner's leash will be used as a potent argument against modernization and the emancipation of women.[26]

Barbara Ehrenreich expresses similar concerns:

> It was [Lynndie] England we saw with a naked Iraqi man on a leash. If you were doing PR for Al Qaeda, you couldn't have staged a better picture to galvanize misogynist Islamic fundamentalists around the world. Here, in these photos from Abu Ghraib, you have everything that the Islamic fundamentalists believe characterizes Western culture, all nicely arranged in one hideous image – imperial arrogance, sexual depravity, and gender equality.[27]

It is surely wishful thinking to assume that US guards, female or not, having forced prisoners to wear women's underwear, among other derogatory "feminizing" acts, would then be perceived by the non-West as a product of the West's gender equality. In fact, misogyny is perhaps most easily understood between captor and captive. Former prisoner Dhia al-Shweiri notes: "We are men. It's OK if they beat me. Beatings don't hurt us; it's just a blow. But no one would want [his] manhood to be shattered. They wanted us to feel as though we were women, the way women feel, and this is the worst insult, to feel like a woman."[28]

---

26 Kelly Cogswell, "Torture and America: So This Is Us," *The Gully*, May 13, 2004, http://www.thegully.com/essays/iraq/040513_torture_abu_ghraib.html.
27 Barbara Ehrenreich, "Prison Abuse: Feminism's Assumptions Upended," *Los Angeles Times*, May 16, 2004, http://articles.latimes.com/2004/may/16/opinion/op-ehrenreich16.
28 Joe Crea, "Gay Sex Used to Humiliate Iraqis," *Washington Blade*, May 7, 2004: 26.

The picture of Lynndie England, dubbed "Lynndie the Leasher," leading a naked Iraqi on a leash (also being referred to as "pussy whipping") has now become a surface on which fundamentalism and modernization, apparently dialectically opposed, can wage war. One could argue that this image is about both the victories of liberal feminists, who claim that women should have equal opportunities within the military, and the failures of liberal feminists to adequately theorize power and gender beyond male-female dichotomies that situate women as less prone toward violence and as morally superior to men. Writes Zillah Eisenstein:

> *When I first saw the pictures of the torture at Abu Ghraib I felt destroyed. Simply heart-broken. I thought 'we' are the fanatics, the extremists; not them. By the next day as I continued to think about Abu Ghraib I wondered how there could be so many women involved in the atrocities?*[29]

Why is this kind of affective response to the failures of Euro-American feminisms, feminisms neither able to theorize gender and violence nor able to account for racism within their ranks, appropriate to vent at this particular moment, especially when it works to center the Euro-American feminist as victim, her feminism having fallen apart? Another example: brimming with disappointment, Ehrenreich pontificates:

> *Secretly, I hoped that the presence of women would over time change the military, making it more respectful of other people and cultures, more capable of genuine peacekeeping. . . . A certain kind of feminism, or perhaps I should say a certain kind of feminist naiveté, died in Abu Ghraib.*[30]

Similarly, Patrick Moore articulates the death of a parallel yearning, as if gay male sexuality had never chanced on its own misogyny: "The idea that female soldiers are as capable as men of such atrocities is disorienting for gay men who tend to think of women as natural allies."[31] Nostalgically mourning the loss of the liberal feminist subject, this emotive convergence of white liberal feminists and white gay men unwittingly reorganizes the Abu Ghraib tragedy around their desires.

But the sight of England with her leash also hints at the sexual perversions associated with S/M, something not mentioned at all in the popular press.

---

29 Zillah Eisenstein, "Sexual Humiliation, Gender Confusion, and the Horrors at Abu Ghraib," *Z Net*, June 22, 2004, http://www.zcommunications.org/sexual-humiliation-gender-confusion-and-the-horrors-at-abu-ghraib-by-zillah-eisenstein.

30 Ehrenreich, "Prison Abuse."

31 Patrick Moore, "Gay Sexuality Shouldn't Become a Torture Device," *Newsday*, May 7, 2004, combined edition, A51.

The comparisons now proffered between the depraved, cigarette-toting, dark-haired, pregnant-and-unmarried, racialized England (now implicated in making a pornographic film with another guard) and the heroic girl next door Jessica Lynch, informed by their working class background similarities but little else, speak also of the need to explain away the solid presence of female Abu Ghraib torturers as an aberration.[32] While the presence of women torturers should at least initially give us pause, it is a mistake to exceptionalize these women as well; the pleasure and power derived from their positions and actions cannot be written off as some kind of false consciousness or duping by the military, nor as what Eisenstein refers to as "white female decoys."[33] If, as Veena Das argues, violence is a form of sociality, then women are not only the recipients of violence but are actually connected to and benefit from forms of violence in a myriad of ways, regardless of whether they are the perpetrators of violence themselves.[34] That is to say, the economy of violence produces a circulation whereby no woman is strictly an insider or an outsider. Rather, women can be subjects of violence but also agents of it, whether it is produced on their behalf or perpetuated directly by them.[35] In this regard, three points are at stake: How do we begin to understand the literal presence of women, and possibly of gay men and/or lesbians, in both the tortured and the torturer populations? How should one explore the analytic of gender positionings and sexual differentiation beyond masculine and feminine? And finally, what do we make of the participation of US guards in the photos, behind the cameras, and in front of computer screens, and of ourselves, as curious and disturbed onlookers?

---

32 "Most Americans believe the abuses were isolated instances, not common occurrences. They believe the perpetrators were acting on their own, not following orders. And by an overwhelming margin, the public sees the abuses as a violation of military policy, rogue crimes, not a policy. As a result, most Americans blame the soldiers who carried out the abuses and the officers supervising them, not Secretary Rumsfeld or President Bush." Reportage on polling results by William Schneider on Judy Woodruff's *Inside Politics*, CNN, May 10, 2004.

33 Eisenstein, "Sexual Humiliation, Gender Confusion, and the Horrors at Abu Ghraib."

34 Cushman, "A Conversation with Veena Das."

35 Ibid.; Das says: "A very good example of this is the idea that a woman gets higher status in society by being the hero's mother; or there are other examples in which a woman's honor may depend on the son's or husband's valiant performance in the world. There is a very subtle exchange of maleness and femaleness in these kinds of formations. So that, yes, you can get forms of sociality where violence is an exclusively male form of sociality from which women might be excluded or other forms of sociality in which she is incorporated within male forms of violence."

Gay Sex?

> *Male homosexuality is deeply shameful in Arab culture; to force naked Arab prisoners to simulate gay sex, taking pictures you could threaten to show, would be far worse than beating them.*
>
> ~ Gregg Easterbrook, "Whatever It Takes"

Deploying a parallel homophobic logic, conservative and progressive pundits alike have claimed that the illegal status of homosexual acts in Islamic law demarcates sexual torture in relation to the violence at Abu Ghraib as especially humiliating. Republican senator Susan Collins of Maine, for example, was skeptical that the US guards elected to inflict "bizarre sexual humiliations that were specifically designed to be particularly offensive to Muslim men,"[36] while sexual humiliation became constituted as "a particular outrage in Arab culture."[37] But from a purely military security perspective, however, the torture was very effective and, therefore, completely justified.[38] Bush's administration claims that the torture in the forms it took was particularly necessary and efficacious for interrogation because of the ban of homosexuality in Islam. That "nakedness, homosexuality and control by a woman might be particularly humiliating in Arab culture" has been a sentiment echoed by many.[39]

Madhi Bray, executive director of the Muslim American Society, a nonprofit Islamic organization located in Virginia, says that Islam calls for "modesty in dress"—"being seen naked is a tremendous taboo and a tremendous

---

36 Esther Schrader and Elizabeth Shogren, "Officials Clash on Roles at Prison," *Los Angeles Times*, May 12, 2004, http://articles.latimes.com/2004/may/12/world/fg-prison12.

37 David Stout, "Rumsfeld Offers Apology for Abuse of Iraqi Prisoners," *New York Times*, May 7, 2004, http://www.nytimes.com/2004/05/07/politics/07CND-ABUS.html.

38 Al-Fatiha Foundation, "Al-Fatiha Condemns Sexual Humiliation of Iraqi Detainees: Calls for National LGBT Groups to Denounce Homophobic Human Rights Abuses," press release, May 10, 2004, http://groups.yahoo.com/group/al-fatiha-news/message/815. Founder and director Faisal Alam opines: "As queer Muslims, we must condemn in the most forceful terms, the blatant acts of homophobia and sexual torture displayed by the US military. These symbolic acts of abuse represent the worst form of torture."

39 Michael A. Fuoco and Cindi Lash, "A Long Way from Obscurity: Members of 372nd MP Company Never Bargained For Notoriety," *Pittsburgh Post-Gazette*, May 14, 2004, A1.

humiliation in Muslim culture"—and that homosexuality, considered a sin, "only becomes a problem when it is flaunted, affecting the entire society."[40] Faisal Alam, founder and director of the international Muslim LGBTIQ organization, Al-Fatiha, states that "sexual humiliation is perhaps the worst form of torture for any Muslim." The press release from Al-Fatiha continues:

> *Islam places a high emphasis on modesty and sexual privacy. Iraq, much like the rest of the Arab world, places great importance on notions of masculinity. Forcing men to masturbate in front of each other and to mock same-sex acts or homosexual sex, is perverse and sadistic, in the eyes of many Muslims.*

In another interview, Alam maintains that the torture is an "affront to their masculinity."[41] In a very different context, Patrick Moore, author of *Beyond Shame: Reclaiming the Abandoned History of Radical Gay Sex*, opines:

> *Because "gay" implies an identity and a culture, in addition to describing a sexual act, it is difficult for a gay man in the West to completely understand the level of disgrace endured by the Iraqi prisoners. But in the Arab world, the humiliating techniques now on display are particularly effective because of Islam's troubled relationship with homosexuality. This is not to say that sex between men does not occur in Islamic society—the shame lies in the gay identity rather than the act itself. As long as a man does not accept the supposedly female (passive) role in sex with another man, there is no shame in the behavior. Reports indicate that the prisoners were not only physically abused but also accused of actually being homosexuals, which is a far greater degradation to them.*[42]

The Foucauldian act to identity telos spun out by Moore delineates the West as the space of identity, while the Arab world is relegated, apparently because of "Islam's troubled relationship to homosexuality," to the backwards realm of acts. The fiction of identity—not that identity is a fiction but, rather, that identity based on the concept of progressive coherence is—effaces men who have sex with men (MSM), such as those men on the down low (DL), so that the presence of gay- and lesbian-identified Muslims in the Arab world becomes inconceivable. But let us follow Moore's logic to its conclusion: since the acts are allegedly far more morally neutral for Muslims than they are for men in the West, being forced to do them in the obvious absence of an avowed identity should actually not prove so humiliating. Given the lack of

---

40 Crea, "Gay Sex," 26.
41 Ibid.
42 Moore, "Gay Sexuality Shouldn't Become a Torture Device," A51.

any evidence that being called a homosexual is much more degrading than being tortured, Moore's rationalization reads as an Orientalist projection.

I want to underscore the complex dance of positionality that Muslim and Arab groups, such as the Muslim American Society and especially Al-Fatiha, must perform in these times, during which a defense through the lens of culture easily becomes co-opted into racist agendas. Gay conservative Andrew Sullivan, for example, capitalizes on the cultural-difference discourse, nearly claiming that the repressive culture of Muslim extremism is responsible for the potency of the torture, in effect blaming the victims. Islamophobia has become central to the subconscious of homonormativity.[43] In general, however, either deliberately or unconsciously, these accounts by LGBTQ progressives tend to uphold versions of normative masculinity—that is, being in the feminized passive role is naturalized as bad. This comes, perhaps, as an unintended side effect of the focus on homosexuality, which tends to reproduce misogyny in the effort to disrupt homophobia. Furthermore, in both conservative and progressive interpretations of the abuse at Abu Ghraib, we see the trenchant replay of what Michel Foucault termed the "repressive hypothesis": the notion that a lack of discussion or openness regarding sexuality reflects a repressive, censorship-driven apparatus of deflated sexual desire. (Indeed, considering the centrality of Foucault's *History of Sexuality* to the field of queer studies, it is somewhat baffling that some queer theorists have accepted at face value the discourse of Islamic sexual repression. That is not to imply that Foucault's work should be transparently applied to other cultural and historical contexts; rather, his insights deserve evaluation as a methodological hypothesis about discourse.) In Said's *Orientalism*, the illicit sex found in the Orient was sought out in order to liberate the Occident from its own performance of the repressive hypothesis. By contrast, in the case of Abu Ghraib, it is the repression of the Arab prisoners that is highlighted in order to efface the rampant hypersexual excesses of the US prison guards.

This gives us a clear view of the performative privileges of what Foucault described as the "speaker's benefit": those who are able to articulate sexual knowledge appear to be freed, through the act of speech, from the space of repression. Given the unbridled homophobia demonstrated by the US guards, it is indeed ironic, yet somehow also predictable, that in these accounts the United States nonetheless emerges as more tolerant of homosexuality (and less tainted by misogyny and fundamentalism) than the repressed, modest, nudity-shy Middle East. As Sara Ahmed notes, this hierarchy between open (liberal democracy) and closed (fundamentalist) systems obscures "how the constitution of open cultures involves the projection of what is closed

---

43 Andrew Sullivan, "Sex and Humiliation," *The Dish* (blog), May 4, 2004, http://dish.andrewsullivan.com/2004/05/04/sex-and-humiliation/.

onto others, and hence the concealment of what is closed and contained 'at home.'"[44]

What, then, is closed, and what is contained at home? In the gay press, the Abu Ghraib photos are continuously hailed as "evidence of rampant homophobia in the armed forces."[45] Aaron Belkin, for example, decries them as symbolic representations of "the most base, paranoid, or extreme elements of military homophobia,"[46] while Paula Ettelbrick, the executive director of the International Gay and Lesbian Human Rights Commission, maintains that "this sort of humiliation" becomes sanctioned as a result of the "don't ask, don't tell" policies implemented during the Clinton administration,[47] as if therein lies the brunt of the military establishment's cruelty, and not in the murders of thousands of civilian Iraqis. Humiliation becomes sanctioned because the military functions as a reserve for what is otherwise seen as socially unacceptable violence, sanitizing all aggression in its wake under the guise of national security. In these accounts, the homophobia of the US military is pounced on, with scarce mention of the linked processes of racism and sexism. Patrick Moore, who admits that the photos "evoked in me a deep sense of shame as a gay man," in particular sets up the (white) gay male subject as the paradigmatic victim of the assaulting images, stating that "for closeted gay men and lesbians serving in the military, it must evoke deep shame."[48] But how prudent is it to foreclose unequivocally on the chance that there might be gay men or lesbians among the perpetrators of the torture at Abu Ghraib? To foreground homophobia over other vectors of shame is to miss that these photos are not merely representative of the homophobia of the military; they are also racist, misogynist, and imperialist. To favor the gay male spectator—here, presumably white—is to negate the multiple and intersectional viewers implicated by these images and, oddly, is also to privilege as victim the coherently formed white gay male sexuality in the West (and those closeted in the military) over acts-qualified bodies, not to mention the bodies of the tortured Iraqi prisoners themselves. Moore complicates this audience vectorship in another interview: "I felt the government had found a way to use sexuality as a tool of humiliation both for Arab men and for gay men here."[49] The drawing together of (presumably straight) Arab men and (presumably white) gay men is yet another moment where the sexuality of

---

44 Sara Ahmed, "Affective Economies," *Social Text* 79 (2004): 134.
45 For example, see Crea, "Gay Sex," 26.
46 Ibid.
47 Duncan Osborne, "Pentagon Uses Gay Sex as Tool of Humiliation," *Gay City News*, May 13, 2004, http://gaycitynews.com/5_13/pentagonusesgayssex.html.
48 Ibid.
49 Ibid.

Arab men is qualified as repressed and oriented toward premodern acts, the precursor to the identity-solidified space of "here."

Further complicating this issue is the long-standing debate among LGBTQ communities about whether or not, and to what degree, the war on terror is in fact a gay issue. Mubarak Dahir, writing for the *New York Blade*, intervenes by arguing that the depiction of "gay sex" is central to the images:

> The claim by some members of the gay and lesbian community that the invasion and occupation of Iraq is not a 'gay' issue crumbled last week when photos emerged of hooded, naked Iraqi captives at the Abu Ghraib prison near Baghdad being forced to simulate gay sex acts as a form of abuse and humiliation.

And later:

> As a gay man and as a person of Arab descent, I felt a double sting from those pictures. Looking at the blurred-out photos of hooded Iraqi prisoners being forced to perform simulations of gay oral sex on one another, I had to wonder what it was that my fellow Americans in uniform who were directing the scene found the most despicable: the fact that the men were performing gay sex, or that they were Arabs.[50]

Given the resounding silence of national and mainstream LGBTQ organizations, currently obsessed by the gay marriage agenda, the political import of Dahir's response on the war on terror in general, and on Abu Ghraib in particular, should not be dismissed. In fact, on May 28, 2004, in the midst of furious debate regarding sexual torture, the Human Rights Campaign, the Servicemembers Legal Defense Network, and the American Veterans for Equal Rights jointly released "Fighting for Freedom," a press statement highlighting brave and patriotic LGBT soldiers in the military and announcing the release of *Documenting Courage*, a book on LGBT veterans. Driven by "stories [that] go unmentioned," both the statement and the book privilege the testimonial voice of authenticity. In the absence of any commentary about or position on Abu Ghraib, this might be read as a defensive move to restore honor to US soldiers while reminding the public of the struggles LGBT soldiers face in the military, thus shifting the focus of victimhood away from Iraqi prisoners.[51]

---

50 Mubarak Dahir, "Gay Sex and Prison Torture in Iraq War," *New York Blade*, May 14, 2004, *Internet Archive* Way Back Machine archival version, June 2, 2004, http://web.archive.org/web/20040602090003/http://www.nyblade.com/2004/5-14/viewpoint/opinion/iraq.cfm.

51 Human Rights Campaign, "Fighting for Freedom," press release, May 28, 2004, *Internet Archive* Way Back Machine archival version, June 3, 2004, http://web.archive.org/web/20040603043648/http://www.hrc.org/

Declaring that the torturous acts are simulations of "gay sex," however, invites other consequences, such as the response from Egyptian protestors in Cairo calling for the removal of the "homosexual American executioners,"[52] which reaffirmed that homosexuality is an unwanted import from the West. Such an accusation feeds nicely into Bush's anti-gay marriage agenda. Right-wing organizations such as Concerned Women for America have similarly condemned the torture as a direct result of homosexual cultural depravity. But are, in fact, the acts depicted in these photographs specifically and only referential of gay sex (and here, *gay* means "sex between men")? Is it the case that, as Patrick Moore argues, homosexuality has been deployed as the "ultimate tool of degradation," and as a "military tactic [that] reaches new levels of perversity"?[53] Certainly this rendition evades a conversation about what exactly constitutes the distinction between gay sex and straight sex, and also presumes some static normativity about gender roles as well. Saying that the simulated and actual sex scenes replicate gay sex is an easy way for all—mass media, Orientalist anthropologists, the military establishment, and even LGBTQ groups and organizations—to disavow the "perverse" procilivities inherent in heterosexual sex and the gender normativity immanent in some kinds of gay sex. (It should be noted that Amnesty International is among the few organizations that did not make reference to homosexuality, homosexual acts, or same-sex sexuality in its press release condemning the torture.)[54] These readings reproduce what Gayle Rubin calls the "erotophobic fallacy of misplaced scale." "Sexual acts," Rubin argues, "are burdened with an excess of significance";[55] this excess produces a misreading and perhaps even an exaggeration of the scale by which the significance of sex is a measure done that continually privileges humiliation (mental, psychic, cultural, social) over

Template.cfm?Section=Press_Room&CONTENTID=19384&TEMPLATE=/ContentManagement/ContentDisplay.cfm.

52 Patrick Letellier, "Egyptians Protest 'Gay' Abuse in Iraq; LGBT Groups Hit Out at 'Torture' Confusion," *Gay.com/PlanetOut.com Network*, May 18, 2004, Internet Archive Way Back Machine archival version, December 4, 2005, http://web.archive.org/web/20051204092836/http://uk.gay.com/headlines/6271.

53 Moore, "Gay Sexuality" A51.

54 Amnesty International USA, "6 Months After Abu Ghraib, Conditions for Torture Persist in US Policy: President Urged to Make Measures and Directives Public," press release, October 27, 2004, *Internet Archive* Way Back Machine archival version, December 18, 2004, http://web.archive.org/web/20041218144125/http://www.amnestyusa.org/countries/iraq/document.do?id=E6F5F1B677F7FC5685256F39005C8063.

55 Gayle Rubin, "Thinking Sex: Notes for a Radical Theory of the Politics of Sexuality" in *Pleasure and Danger: Exploring Female Sexuality*, ed. Carol Vance (London: Pandora, 1992), 278–79.

physical pain. In fact, it may well be that these responses by Westerners reveal what we might deem as the worst form of torture—that is, sexual torture and humiliation rather than extreme pain—more than any comprehension of the experiences of those tortured. The simulated sex acts must be thought of in terms of gendered roles rather than through a universalizing notion of sexual orientation. But why talk about sex at all? Was anyone having sex in these photos? (One could argue that in the photos, the torturers were turned on, erotically charged, and looked as one might when having sex.)

The focus on gay sex also preempts a serious dialogue about rape—the rape of Iraqi male prisoners, but also, more significantly, the rape of female Iraqi prisoners, the occurrence of which appears neither news- nor photograph-worthy. Indeed there has been a complete underreporting of the rapes of Afghani and Iraqi women both inside and outside of detention centers. As Trishala Deb and Rafael Mutis point out:

> *Women's rights advocates in the United States have made the distinction between sex and rape for a long time. By defining rape and sexual assault as an act of violence and not sex, we are placing the validity in the voice of the assaulted, and accepting their experience as central to the truth of what happened. . . . Again, what we understand by centering the perspective of the assaulted people is that there was no sex happening regardless of the act.*[56]

Major General Anthony Taguba's report notes that among the some 1,800 digital photos, there are unreleased pictures of females being raped and women forced at gunpoint to bare their breasts, as well as videotape of female detainees forced to strip and rumors of impregnated rape victims.[57] Why are there comparatively few photos of women, and why have they not been released? Is it because the administration found the photos of women even more appalling? Or has the wartime rape of women become so unspectacular, so endemic to military occupation, as to render its impact moot? How, ultimately, do we begin to theorize the connections and disjunctures between male and female tortured bodies, and between masculinities and femininities?

Although feminist postcolonial studies have typically theorized women as the bearers of cultural continuity, tradition, and national lineage, in the case of terrorism the line of transmission seems always to revert to the male body. The locus of reproductive capacity is, momentarily, expanded from the female body to the male body. This expansion does not mark a shift away from

---

56 Deb and Mutis, "Smoke and Mirrors," 5.
57 Luke Harding, "The Other Prisoners," *The Guardian*, May 19, 2004, http://www.guardian.co.uk/world/2004/may/20/iraq.gender.

women as the victims of rape and pawns between men during wartime. But the principal yet overriding emphasis on women's rape as a weapon of war can displace the importance of castrating the reproductive capacities of men. It is precisely masculinity, the masculinity of the terrorist, that threatens to reproduce itself. Writing about the genital and anal torture of Sikh men in Punjab, Brian Keith Axel argues that torture produces sexual differentiation not as male and female, but rather as what he calls national-normative sexuality and antinational sexuality:

> *Torture in Punjab is a practice of repeated and violent circumscription that produces not only sexed bodies, but also a form of sexual differentiation. . . . National-normative sexuality provides the sanctioned heterosexual means for reproducing the nation's community, whereas antinational sexuality interrupts and threatens that community. Torture casts national-normative sexuality as a fundamental modality of citizen production in relation to an antinational sexuality that postulates sex as a "cause" of not only sexual experience but also of subversive behavior and extraterritorial desire ("now you can't be married, you can't produce any more terrorists" . . .). The form of punishment corresponds to the putative source of transgression: sexual reproduction, identified as a property of masculine agency within the male body.*[58]

It is important to emphasize, of course, that there exist multiple national-normative sexualities and, likewise, multiple antinational sexualities, as well as entities that make such distinctions fuzzy. It is equally important to recognize that, for all of its insights, Axel's formulation cannot be entirely and neatly transposed onto the Abu Ghraib situation, as Punjabi Sikh detainees form part of both the Indian nation and the religious fundamentalist terrorists that threaten to undo that nation. In other words, for Punjabi detainees, torture works to finalize expulsion from the nation-state. What I find most compelling is Axel's formulation of national differentiation as sexual differentiation. However, I would argue that it is precisely feminizing (and thus not the categories of male and female, as Axel notes), and the consequent insistence of mutually exclusive positions of masculine and feminine, that strips the tortured male body of its national-normative sexuality. This feminizing divests the male body of its virility and, thus, compromises its power not only to penetrate and reproduce its own nation ("our" women) but to contaminate the Other's nation ("their" women) as well. Furthermore, the perverted sex of the terrorist is a priori cast outside the domain of normative national sexualities: that is to say, "the form of punishment," that is, meddling with penis and anus, "corresponds to the putative source of transgression,"

---

58 Axel, "The Diasporic Imaginary," 420.

not only because of the desire to truncate the terrorist's capacity to sexually reproduce but also because of the (homo)sexual deviancy always already attached to the terrorist body. These two attributes, the fertility of the terrorist (in the case of Muslim men, always interpreted through polygamy) and the (homo)sexual perversions of the terrorist, are rendered with extra potency given that the terrorist is also a priori constituted as stateless, thus lacking national legitimization or national boundaries. In the political imagination, the terrorist serves as the monstrous excess of the nation-state.

Torture, to compound Axel's formulation, works not merely to disaggregate national from antinational sexualities—for those distinctions (the stateless monster-terrorist-fag) are already in play—but also, in accordance with nationalist fantasies, to reorder gender and, in the process, to corroborate implicit racial hierarchies. The force of feminizing, then, lies not only in the stripping away of masculinity, the "faggotizing" of the male body, or in the robbing of the feminine of its symbolic and reproductive centrality to national-normative sexualities. Rather, it is the fortification of the unenforceable boundaries between masculine and feminine, the rescripting of multiple and fluid gender performatives into petrified sites of masculine and feminine, the regendering of multiple genders into the oppressive binary scripts of masculine and feminine, and the interplay of it all within and through racial, imperial, and economic matrices of power. That is the real force of torture.

Axel writes that "torture casts national-normative sexuality as a fundamental modality of citizen production." But we can also flip these terms around: national-normative sexuality casts torture as a fundamental modality of citizen production. One could scramble this further still: citizen production casts national-normative sexuality as a fundamental modality of torture. And so on. The point is that in the metonymic chain linking torture, citizen production, and national-normative sexualities, torture surfaces as an integral part of a patriotic mandate to separate off the normative-national genders and sexualities from the antinational ones. As Joanna Bourke elaborates:

> It is hard to avoid the conclusion that, for some of these Americans, creating a spectacle of suffering was part of a bonding ritual. Group identity as victors in an increasingly brutalized Iraq is being cemented: this is an enactment of comradeship between men and women who are set apart from civilian society back home by acts of violence. Their cruel, often carnivalesque rites constituted what Mikhail Bakhtin called "authorised transgression."[59]

The bonding ritual, culminating in an authorized transgression, is authorized not from above but between actors seeking to redirect animosity toward each

---

59 Joanna Bourke, "Torture as pornography," *The Guardian,* May 6, 2004, http://www.guardian.co.uk/world/2004/may/07/gender.uk.

other. In this sense, the bonding ritual of the carnival of torture—discussing it, producing it, getting turned on by it, recording it, disseminating the proof of it, gossiping about it—is the ultimate performance of patriotism. Here all internal tensions (the working class, "white trash" Lynndie, the African American sergeant, and so forth) are focused outwards, toward the hapless bodies in detention, so that a united front of American multicultural heteronormativity can be not only performed but, more important, affectively felt.

Technologies of Simulacrum

As voyeurs, conductors, dictators, and dominatrices, those orchestrating these acts, several of whom appear erotically riled in the Abu Ghraib photographs, are part of, not external to, the torture scenes themselves, sometimes even explicitly so. For example, convicted Specialist Jeremy Sivits, who took many of the photographs, testified that "Staff Sergeant Frederick would take the hand of the detainee and put it on the detainee's penis, and make the detainee's hand go back and forth, as if masturbating. He did this to about three of the detainees before one of them did it right."[60] This is hardly indicative of a detached, objective, distanced observer behind the camera, positioned only to capture the events via the click of the shutter. Reports of US soldiers sodomizing Iraqi prisoners with chemical light sticks and broomsticks, and inserting fingers into prisoners' anuses, also fully implicate the US guards and raise specters of interracial and intercultural sex. Less overtly, the separation of participant from voyeur becomes complicated by the pleasures of taking, posing for, and looking at pictures, especially as the use of cameras and videos as an intermediary tool of sexual pleasure inform varied practices (such as watching porn) between partners of all genders in all kinds of sex.

Many of the photos, originally cropped for damage-controlled consumption, are now revealing the presence of multiple spectators, bystanders, and participants. In the case of the widely disseminated and discussed photo of a hooded man made to stand on a box with wires attached like appendages to his arms, legs, and penis—a classic torture pose known predominantly to interrogation experts as the "Vietnam"—the full photograph reveals a US soldier on the periphery, nonchalantly examining his digital camera. The Vietnam, explains Darius Rejali, derives from an amalgamation of the forced-standing techniques used by torturers in the British army (where it was known as the "crucifixion") and in the French army (where it was known as the "Silo") during the early twentieth century, and among those employed

---

60 Kate Zernike, "The Struggle for Iraq: The Whistle-Blower; Accused Soldier Paints Scene of Eager Mayhem at Iraqi Prison," *New York Times*, May 14, 2004, http://www.nytimes.com/2004/05/14/world/struggle-for-iraq-whistle-blower -accused-soldier-paints-scene-eager-mayhem.html.

by US police, Stalin's People's Commissariat for Internal Affairs (NKVD), the Gestapo in 1930s Germany, and South African and Brazilian police (who added the electrical supplement) in the 1970s.[61] In fact it is indeed this image, deemed by many to be the least sexually explicit and therefore less horrifying to view, that has been most reproduced around the world, its simulacra taking shape on billboards and murals and parodied through antiwar protest attire worn on the streets of Tehran, London, and New York and through fake iPod adverts done in hot pink and lime green. Performance artists, such as the New York City-based Hieronymous Bang, use the American flag as a substitute for the black cloak. In Salah Edine Sallat's mural in Baghdad, the hooded prisoner on the box is paired with a shrouded Statue of Liberty holding up an electric gadget connected to the circuit breaker that threatens to electrocute them both.

To what can we attribute the now iconic status of this image? For starters, it is the only released photo to date that exposes almost no skin—only the legs and shins of the victim can be seen, preserving an anonymity of body that simultaneously incriminates the viewer less than some of the more pornography-like images and also radiates a distressing mystique. The hoods hark back to the white hoods of the Ku Klux Klan, but they also resemble veils. Indeed, the cloaking of nearly the entire body references another iconic image, that of the oppressed Muslim woman in her *burkha*, covered head to toe in black and in need of rescue. It is plausible, then, that this image of the Vietnam resonates as yet another missionary project in the making. It is the male counterpart to the Muslim-woman-in-*burkha* that liberal feminist organizations (like the National Organization for Women [NOW] and the Feminist Majority Fund), the Bush administration (especially Laura), and the conservative right-wingers who tout rhetorics of democracy and freedom love so well. There is another, more sinister reason why the photo echoes so acutely. Called "stealth torture that leaves no marks," the Vietnam is traceless, leaving the bodies of its victims undifferentiated from unscathed ones. As happens with cloaking, the body remains both untroubled and unseen, and "if it were not for the photographs, no one would know that it had been practiced."[62] The only evidence of the Vietnam comes in the form of the photograph. Its mass multiplication and mutations may speak to the need to document and inscribe into history and our optic memories that which otherwise leaves no visual proof. As Susan Sontag proclaimed, "the pictures will not go away."[63] Noting that "soldiers trained in stealth torture take these

---

61 Darius Rejali, "A Long-standing Trick of the Torturer's Art," *Seattle Times*, May 14, 2004, http://seattletimes.com/html/opinion/2001928172_torture14.html.

62 Ibid.

63 Susan Sontag, "Regarding the Torture of Others," *New York Times Magazine*, May 23, 2004, http://www.nytimes.com/2004/05/23/magazine/

techniques back into civilian life as policemen and private security personnel," Rejali claims that the Vietnam is found throughout US policing and imprisonment tactics,[64] another likely rationale for the intense reverberations of this photo.[65]

Claiming that "theatricality leads us to the crux of the matter," Slavoj Žižek argues that the pictures "suggest a theatrical staging, a kind of tableau vivant, which brings to mind American performance art, [Antonin Artaud's] 'theatre of cruelty,' the photos of [Robert] Mapplethorpe or the unnerving scenes in David Lynch's films."[66] The facile comparison of the evidence of brutal wartime violence to spaces of artistic production might put the reader on edge. Indeed, the Right is concocting similar conjectures: in the *American Spectator* George Neumayr writes, "Had Robert Mapplethorpe snapped the photos at Abu Ghraib, the Senate might have given him a government grant."[67] But the point, as I understand it, is not so much that these photos resemble works of art, but more that the pictures look indeed as if the US guards felt like they were on stage, hamming it up for the proud parents nervously biting their lips in the audience. The affect of these photos is one of exaggerated theatricality; jovial and void of any somberness, it invites the viewer to come on and jump on stage as well. As Richard Goldstein points out, "One reason why these photos are such a sensation is that they are stimulating."[68]

Even more trenchant is the collapsing, in the Abu Ghraib photographs, of production and consumption, image and viewer, onto the same vectors, the same planes. There is no inside or outside here; rather, there are only movement, circulation, contingent temporalities, momentary associations and disassociations. One could argue that if there is anything exceptional about these photographs, it is not the actual violence itself but, rather, the capturing of this violence on film, the photographic qualities of which are reminiscent of vacation snapshots, mementos of a good time, victory at last, or even the trophy won at summer camp. Unlike images of the purportedly unavoidable collateral deaths of war, these photos divulge an irrefutable intentionality. We have proof, finally, of what we suspect might be true, not only in Iraq,

---

regarding-the-torture-of-others.html.

64 Rejali, "A Long-Standing Trick of the Torturer's Art."

65 Additionally, the Prison Litigation Reform Act of 1996 delimits what are deemed to be frivolous lawsuits, ensuring that prisoners must demonstrate signs of physical injury prior to claims of mental or emotional injury.

66 Žižek, "What Rumsfeld Doesn't Know."

67 George Neumayr, "The Abu Ghraib Collection," *American Spectator*, May 12, 2004, http://spectator.org/archives/2004/05/12/the-abu-ghraib-collection.

68 Richard Goldstein, "Stuff Happens! Don't Call It Torture: It's Just a Broomstick up the Butt," *Village Voice*, April 27, 2004, http://www.villagevoice.com/2004-04-27/news/stuff-happens/full/.

Afghanistan, and Guantánamo Bay but in our very own detention centers and prisons.[69] These photos not only depict the techniques of torture; they also depict how both process (the photographing) and product (the pictures) constitute shaming technologies and function as a vital part of the humiliating, dehumanizing torture itself: the giddy process of documentation, the visual evidence of corporeal shame, the keen ecstatic eye of the voyeur, the haunting of surveillance, the dissemination of the images on the Internet, the speed of transmission—aphrodisiacs unto themselves, "swapped from computer to computer throughout the 320th Battalion,"[70] perpetuating humiliation ad nauseam.

Thus these images not only represent specific acts and allude to the procedural vectors of ever-expansive audiences but they also reproduce and multiply the power dynamics that made these acts possible in the first place. As Sontag famously asserted in the *New York Times Magazine*, "the photographs are us." Comparing the images to the photographs of black lynching victims, taken between 1880 and 1930, that depicted "Americans grinning beneath the naked mutilated body of a black man or woman hanging behind them from a tree," Sontag argues that a shift has occurred in the utility of photos. Once collectible items for albums and display in frames at home, photos are now "less objects to be saved than messages to be disseminated, circulated."[71] Obviously, technology has been a major catalyst in this transition from trophy to propaganda: the digital camera, sexy and absorbing software to assist in manipulating and perfecting images, and Internet sites that serve as virtual photo albums seem ubiquitous. It is a transition from stillness to proliferation, from singularity to fertility, like ejecting dandelion spores into the wind. More important, mobility, motility, speed, and performance function as primary erotic and addictive charges of modernity: clicking the send button marks the ultimate release of productivity and consumption; dissemination is the ultimate form of territorial coverage and conquest, one more layering of the sexual matrix. While the visages and corpses of American casualties in Iraq remain protected material—even the faces of deceased soldiers were considered unseemly in a television program honoring them—Iraqi bodies are accessible to all, available for comment, ridicule, shaming, scrutiny. If we were to honor Žižek's invocation of the theatricality of the

---

69   See, for example, Nina Bernstein, "2 Men Charge Abuse in Arrests After 9/11 Terror Attack," *New York Times*, May 3, 2004, http://www.nytimes.com/2004/05/03/nyregion/2-men-charge-abuse-in-arrests-after-9-11-terror-attack.html, and Bob Herbert, "America's Abu Ghraibs," *New York Times*, May 31, 2004, http://www.nytimes.com/2004/05/31/opinion/america-s-abu-ghraibs.html.
70   Seymour M. Hersh, "Chain of Command," *New Yorker*, May 17, 2004, 39.
71   Sontag, "Regarding the Torture of Others," 28.

Abu Ghraib photos, they would indeed qualify as what Cynthia Mahmood, writing about the display of tortured Sikh bodies in Sikh living rooms and *gurdwaras* (temples), calls "massacre art": "In their very gruesomeness, [they] assert themselves in a room; they are impossible to ignore, and intrude in conversation, meditation, and everyday activities. Their potency derives only in part from their blood; it also derives from their unwillingness to be masked, covered, or distorted."[72] Abu Ghraib's massacre art disrupts the caricature of the placid, Pleasantville-like aura of the American family room, the streaming images from the television set mesmerizing us into silence. They are potent not only for their naked honesty but also because they are the evidence of how much power we can actually, and stunningly, command over others. Unlike the reports of prison abuses compiled by Amnesty International, the Red Cross, and other humanitarian organizations, as well as the testimonies of hundreds of detainees and released prisoners, all easily ignored by the Bush administration, the photos and their circulatory modalities double as representation and information, as the representation of information, and the only information taken seriously and validated by corporate media sources.

Calling the torture an initiation, for those subjected, into the "obscene underside" of "American culture," Žižek avers: "Similar photos appear at regular intervals in the US press after some scandal explodes at an Army base or high school campus, when such rituals went overboard."[73] Again, Žižek's limp analogizing effectively evacuates the political context of forced occupation and imperial expansion within which specificity and singularity must be retained. While the comparison to fraternity house hazing (I assume that Žižek means college campus rather than high school) or army pranks is not without merit—for certainly proliferating modalities of violence need and feed off one another—there is an easy disregard of the forced, nonconsensual, systemic, repetitive, and intentional order of violence hardly attributable to "rituals" that have gone "overboard." (We might also ask, in another essay perhaps, whether these acts of torture really reveal anything intrinsic or particular to "American culture," or whether they can instead be linked more broadly to war cultures and states of occupation at large.) Again, this slippery analysis is fodder for the conservative Right: Rush Limbaugh sanctioned a similar statement by a caller on his radio show by responding thusly:

> *Exactly my point. This is no different than what happens at [Yale University's secret fraternity] Skull and Bones initiation, and we're going to ruin people's lives over it, and we're going to hamper our military*

---

72 Cynthia Keppley Mahmood, *Fighting for Faith and Nation: Dialogues with Sikh Militants* (Philadelphia: University of Pennsylvania Press, 1996), 189.

73 Žižek, "What Rumsfeld Doesn't Know."

effort, and then we are going to really hammer them because they had a good time. . . . You know, these people are being fired at every day. I'm talking about people having a good time, these people. You ever heard of emotional release?[74]

Later, Limbaugh opined: "This is something you can see onstage at Lincoln Center from an N.E.A. grant, maybe on 'Sex and the City.'" Once more, the references to theatricality and staging draw together liberal and right-wing commentators, efface the power dynamics of occupation, war, and empire, and ultimately leave a distasteful sense of smugness or satisfaction—from Limbaugh—at having neatly trivialized something into next to nothing.

Conclusion

> *We now know more about Lindsey [sic] England and Charles Grainer (two of the accused military police) than we do about any of the people who were the prisoners in those pictures. We know very little of their own narratives, identities, or their perspective on the US occupation. Given that, we have to remember that their own histories, genders, and sexualities are as complex as our own. The US media has managed to once again make them subjects of a war that are marginal in their own story. And the question remains: for which culture would these acts of sexual assault, rape, and murder be less appalling?*
>
> ~Trishala Deb and Rafael Mutis, "Smoke and Mirrors"

What emerges, then, from most interpretations in terms of narratives regarding homosexuality and its intersections with the violence at Abu Ghraib can be summed up thusly:

1. The sexual acts simulated are all specifically and only gay sex acts.
2. Homosexuality is taboo in Islamic cultures, making such acts the worst forms of humiliation for Muslims to endure. This insinuates that these forms of torture would be easier for other, less homophobic populations to tolerate (this appears preferable to a more expansive notion of bodily torture as violating for all) and discounts the presence of gay-identified Muslims in Arab societies, what Joseph Massad terms the "gay Arab international," while also obscuring

---

74 Sontag, "Regarding the Torture of Others," 28.

those engaging in same-sex erotics even if not within the rubric of identity.[75]
3. American tolerance for homosexuality is elevated in relation to that of Islamic societies, as symptomatized by the unspecific, ahistorical, and generalized commentary on the taboo of homosexuality for Muslims.
4. The enactment of "gay sex" (consolidated around the act of sodomy) constitutes the worst form of torture, sexual or otherwise.
5. Iraqi prisoners, having endured the humiliation of gay sex, are subjects worthy of sympathy—an affective, emotive response more readily available than a sustained political critique of the US occupation in Afghanistan and Iraq.
6. The question of race and how it plays out in these scenarios is effaced via the fixation on sexuality; gender likewise becomes effaced when the acts are said to originate from a homophobic military culture, instead of from a misogynist one.
7. Sexuality is isolated within the purview of the individual, as opposed to situated within an integrated diagrammatic vector of power.
8. The language favoring gay sex acts over torture once again casts the shadows of perversity outside, onto sexual and racial others, rather than contextualizing the processes of normalizing bodily torture.
9. Technologies of representation work to occlude the lines of connectivity (sexual, bodily, in terms of proximity, in terms of positionality) between captors and their prisoners.

Despite the widespread absence of sexuality in public debates about 9/11 and the war on terror, the "prisoner sexual abuse scandal," as it is now termed, vividly reveals that sexuality constitutes a central and crucial component of American patriotism. The use of sexuality—in this case, to physically punish and humiliate—is not tangential, unusual, or reflective of a state of exception. Of course, not all of the torture was sexual, and thus the odd acts—threatening dogs, for example—need to retain their idiosyncrasy. Nudity itself is not automatically and innately sexual; it must be made to signify erotics. Therefore the terms *scandal*, *sexual*, and *abuse* need to be semiotically decharged. This does not mean that this treatment is not sexual or abusive, but rather that such abuse is a commonplace occurrence in detention. Thus, following what Achille Mbembe describes as "necropolitics," in which systems of domination become increasingly "anatomical, tactile, and sensorial," we can say simply that sexualized bodily abuse is a normalized facet of prisoner life,

---

75 Joseph Massad, "Re-Orienting Desire: The Gay International and the Arab World," *Public Culture* 14 (2002): 361–85.

and that the sexual is always already inscribed in necropolitics.[76] Furthermore, as postcolonial scholars such as Ann Stoler and Anne McClintock have aptly demonstrated, the sexual is part and parcel of the histories of colonial domination and empire building—conquest is innately corporeal. That is to say, this scandal, rather than being cast as exceptional, needs to be contextualized within a range of practices and discourses, perhaps ones less obvious than the Iraqi prisoner abuse, that pivotally links sexuality to the deployment and expansion of US nationalism, patriotism, and, increasingly, empire. Despite the actions of those in charge of Abu Ghraib, perversity is still withheld for the body of the queer Muslim terrorist, insistently deferred to the outside. This outside is rapidly, with precision and intensity, congealing into the population of what Giorgio Agamben has called *homo sacer*, "those who can be killed with impunity since, in the eyes of the law, their lives no longer count."[77] Žižek considers this space "between the two deaths"—dead in the eyes of history but still alive for the countdown—as the fate of the prisoners at Abu Ghraib, the ghost detainees.[78] As with the systemic failure of US military operations at the prison, not the fault of a handful of individuals but rather due to the entire assemblage of necropolitics, sexuality itself is not the barometer of exception, a situation out of control, an unimaginable reality. Rather, it constitutes a systemic, intrinsic, and pivotal module of power relations.

Acknowledgements

Thanks to Barbara Balliet, Patricia Clough, Inderpal Grewal, Nancy Hewitt, Louisa Schein, and David Serlin for their feedback on earlier drafts of this essay.

Bibliography

Agamben, Giorgio. *Homo Sacer: Sovereign Power and Bare Life*. Stanford, CA: Stanford University Press, 1998.

Axel, Brian Keith. "The Diasporic Imaginary." *Public Culture* 14, no. 2 (2002): 511–428. doi:10.1215/08992363-14-2-411.

Bourke, Joanna. "Torture as pornography." *The Guardian*, May 6, 2004. http://www.guardian.co.uk/world/2004/may/07/gender.uk.

Cushman, Thomas. "A Conversation with Veena Das on Religion and Violence, Suffering and Language." *Hedgehog Review* 6, no. 1 (2004): 78–89.

---

76   Achille Mbembe, "Necropolitics," *Public Culture* 15, no. 1 (2003): 34.
77   Žižek, "What Rumsfeld Doesn't Know"; see also Giorgio Agamben, *Homo Sacer: Sovereign Power and Bare Life* (Stanford, CA: Stanford University Press, 1998).
78   Žižek, "What Rumsfeld Doesn't Know."

Fahrenheit 9/11. Directed by Michael Moore. Culver City, CA: Columbia TriStar Home Entertainment, 2004. DVD.
Hersh, Seymour M. "Chain of Command," *New Yorker*, May 17, 2004, 38–43.
———. "The Gray Zone." *New Yorker*, May 24, 2004, 38–44.
———. "Torture at Abu Ghraib." *New Yorker*, May 10, 2004, 42–47.
Horne, Alistair. *A Savage War of Peace*. London: Pan Books, 2002.
Kaplan, Danny. *Brothers and Others in Arms: The Making of Love and War in Israeli Combat Units*. New York: Harrington Park, 2002.
Mahmood, Cynthia Keppley. *Fighting for Faith and Nation: Dialogues with Sikh Militants*. Philadelphia: University of Pennsylvania Press, 1996.
Maran, Rita. *Torture: The Role of Ideology in the French-Algerian War*. New York: Praeger, 1989.
Massad, Joseph. "Re-Orienting Desire: The Gay International and the Arab World." *Public Culture* 14 (2002): 361–85.
Mbembe, Achille. "Necropolitics." *Public Culture* 15, no. 1 (2003): 11–40.
Rubin, Gayle. "Thinking Sex: Notes for a Radical Theory of the Politics of Sexuality" In *Pleasure and Danger: Exploring Female Sexuality*, edited by Carol Vance, 267–319. London: Pandora, 1992.
Sontag, Susan. "Regarding the Torture of Others." *New York Times Magazine*, May 23, 2004. http://www.nytimes.com/2004/05/23/magazine/regarding-the-torture-of-others.html.
Trinquier, Roger. *Modern Warfare*. New York: Praeger, 1964.

Tacit Subjects

Carlos Ulises Decena[1]

Conventional views of coming out in contemporary queer communities celebrate the individual, the visible, and the proud. Given the growing legitimacy of predominantly white and middle-class lesbians and gay men in the United States and of models that presume and uphold individual decision making, negotiations of the closet that refuse speech, visibility, and pride have been generally viewed as suspect, as evidence of denial and internalized homophobia, or as outright pathology.

During my field research, I encountered characterizations of Dominican immigrant gay men in New York as "in the closet" that are consistent with existing views about how Latinos and other populations of color in the United States deal with their sexual identities.[2] Cast at best as indifferent to the development of a gay Dominican community, these men were seen at worst as immigrants whose physical displacement had not helped them overcome

---

1   Editors' note: this paper was previously published in *GLQ: A Journal of Lesbian and Gay Studies* 14, no. 2–3 (2008): 339–359.

2   Even though my discussion takes Dominican immigrant men who identify as homosexuals as case studies, the works of William G. Hawkeswood, Jason King, and Martin F. Manalansan IV suggest that what I argue might be relevant to other groups commonly identified in the United States as "people of color." See William G. Hawkeswood, *One of the Children: Gay Black Men in Harlem* (Berkeley: University of California Press, 1996); Jason King, "Remixing the Closet: The Down-Low Way of Knowledge," in *If We Have to Take Tomorrow: HIV, Black Men, and Same Sex Desire*, ed. F. L. Roberts and M. K. White (New York: Institute for Gay Men's Health, 2006), 65–70; Martin F. Manalansan IV, *Global Divas: Filipino Gay Men in the Diaspora* (Durham, NC: Duke University Press, 2003). The work of Diana Fisher illustrates that playing with being "in" and "out" of the closet is relevant to other immigrant groups. See Diana Fisher, "Immigrant Closets: Tactical-Micro-Practices-in-the-Hyphen," *Journal of Homosexuality* 45 (2003): 171–92.

the internalized homophobia that supposedly characterized their lives in the Dominican Republic.[3]

Taking for granted that all LGBTQ people should come out of the closet is consistent with a neoliberal interpretation of coming out characteristic of the current political climate in the United States. Instead of being the beginning of a project of social transformation—as coming out was understood in the early days of gay liberation—individual self-realization through speech

---

[3] This is an all-too-common view of Latinos and other gay men of color in the United States. It is also common for members of these communities themselves to espouse these views. In some contexts, "to come out" is associated with "departing" the heterosexual world one has been reared in and becoming integrated into gay communities. Thus it is not surprising that migration is a strong part of gay histories and collective imaginings, especially for Latin Americans and US Latinos. "For gays and lesbians from Latin America," one article reads, "coming out often means joining the sexual migration to the US. . . . The combined pressures of machismo, religion, family, and Latin society for gays and lesbians living south of the border and the allure of a more open life in the big gay cities of the United States—known as El Norte—draw many into a migration that is partly for material reasons, partly for personal ones, not unlike the migration of gays from small US towns." See David Kirby, "Coming to America to Be Gay," *Advocate* 834 (2001): 29-32. As this excerpt suggests, migration-as-coming-out is equivalent to a departure from locations associated with "restrictive" cultural norms and institutions: from south of the border and from rural America to urban "gay ghettos." Mapping gay and lesbian collective histories as "coming out writ large" has recently been criticized persuasively by the historian John Howard, among others. See John Howard, *Men Like That: A Southern Queer History* (Chicago: University of Chicago Press, 1999).

While in the dominant narrative, coming out to oneself in the sense of owning a gay identity implies movement *away* from home, coming out to others demands a *return* to the settings and relationships where this identity has to be revealed. And a refusal to "have the conversation" where one's homosexuality is explicitly articulated is akin to denial. Steven Seidman's argument about the closet in black communities, for instance, is that it dehumanizes. "Given their more ambivalent relationship to the gay community, blacks may be more likely than their white counterparts to manage their homosexuality within the framework of the closet." See Steven Seidman, *Beyond the Closet: The Transformation of Gay and Lesbian Life* (New York: Routledge, 2002), 42-43. According to Seidman, the problem is that blacks' racial identity weighs more heavily than their sexual minority identity: "In short, blacks—straight or gay—are heavily invested in their racial identity and in their membership in the black community in a way that is generally not true of whites" (43). Seidman's thinking about sexuality in relationship to race and ethnicity also illustrates that "coming out," for people of color, tends to be understood as a choice between sexual and racial identities, with relatively little space for both.

has been severed from collective social change. Today, one comes out not to be radical or change the world but to be a "normal" gay subject.[4] From this perspective, some queers of color have an uneasy relationship with the closet because they resist the depoliticized "liberation" that coming out promises, which currently resides in a gay identity as a social-cultural formation and as a niche market. Critiques of coming out in its current form have and continue to be made partly because of the persistence of this way of thinking about gay subject formation and the racial and class biases obscured by this dominant model.[5]

Based on research from a larger study of Dominican immigrant gay and bisexual men in New York City, this article argues that we must take seriously the distinction between refusing to discuss an openly lived homosexuality and silence.[6] Drawing from Spanish grammar, I suggest that some of

---

[4] The historical trajectories of coming out—from launching point to revolutionary gay liberation politics to the shift toward "mainstreaming" in the 1980s and 1990s and the normalization of the contemporary moment—have been discussed in texts including Robert McRuer, *The Queer Renaissance: Contemporary American Literature and the Reinvention of Lesbian and Gay Identities* (New York: New York University Press, 1997); and Urvashi Vaid, *Virtual Equality: The Mainstreaming of Gay and Lesbian Liberation* (New York: Doubleday, 1995).

[5] Critiques of coming out include Judith Butler, "Imitation and Gender Insubordination," in *The Lesbian and Gay Studies Reader*, ed. Henry Abelove, Michèle Aina Barale, and David M. Halperin (New York: Routledge, 1993), 307-20; Ellen Samuels, "My Body, My Closet: Invisible Disability and the Limits of Coming-Out Discourse," *GLQ: A Journal of Lesbian and Gay Studies* 9 (2003): 233-55; and Ben Sifuentes-Jáuregui, *Transvestism, Masculinity, and Latin American Literature: Genders Share Flesh* (New York: Palgrave, 2002). Recent critics of coming out have observed that when coming out is taken as normative, what usually gets valorized is a model that may fit white, gay, urban, middle-class men but that does not fit people in other positionalities. For three examples of insightful recent critiques, see Manolo Guzman, *Gay Hegemony/Latino Homosexualities* (New York & London: Routledge, 2006); Hiram Perez, "You Can Have My Brown Body and Eat It, Too!" *Social Text*, no. 84-85 (2005): 171-91; and Marlon Ross, "Beyond the Closet as Raceless Paradigm," in *Black Queer Studies: An Anthology*, ed. E. Patrick Johnson and Mae G. Henderson (Durham, NC: Duke University Press, 2005), 161-89.

[6] While acknowledging the range of attitudes expressed by his informants about "coming out," Hawkeswood found that "for many gay men in Harlem, coming out was not a major concern, because their homosexuality, and later their gay identity, had always been *assumed* by family and friends. There was no need to 'come out'" (*One of the Children*, 138. Emphasis added). Manalansan argues something similar for Filipinos: "Many informants ... felt that they didn't have to come out because they thought that their families knew without being told" (*Global Divas*, 28).

my informants inhabit a space that is "in" and "out" of the closet in terms of the tacit subject, an analytic framework that draws attention to the range, interaction, and intersection of the meanings and contexts that structure their social relations.[7] Negotiations of information about a person's sexual identity, as I show, teach us about the knowledge and complicity that structure and sustain hierarchical social relations.[8]

In Spanish grammar, the "sujeto tácito" (tacit subject) is the subject that is not spoken but can be ascertained through the conjugation of the verb used in a sentence. For example, instead of saying "*I* go to school," in Spanish one might say "Voy a la escuela" without using the *Yo* (I). Since the conjugation *voy* (I go) leaves no doubt who is speaking, whoever hears this sentence knows that the subject is built into the action expressed through the verb.[9]

Using this grammatical principle as a metaphor to explain how my informants interpret how others view their lives, the *sujeto tácito* suggests that coming out may sometimes be redundant. In other words, coming out can be a verbal declaration of something that is already understood or assumed—tacit—in an exchange.[10] What is tacit is neither secret nor silent.

Nevertheless, how tacit one's sexual identity is to others is a matter of interpretation and requires that the others interacting with my informants

---

7   This article draws from twenty-five semistructured retrospective life history interviews conducted between May 2001 and May 2002 with immigrant Dominican men who identified as gay and/or bisexual, who were at least fifteen years of age when they arrived in the United States, and who were then living in New York City.

8   This is an interpretation informed by the work of the cultural critic José Quiroga on the negotiation of sexual identity in the work of Latin American literary authors and cultural figures. See José Quiroga, *Tropics of Desire: Interventions from Queer Latino America* (New York: New York University Press, 2000).

9   I am aware of the potential problems that may derive from borrowing a grammatical concept for an antisexist and antihomophobic enterprise. This might be especially true in the case of Spanish, since the language is so significantly gendered. However, one remarkable and useful characteristic of the "sujeto tácito" is that although one is able to ascertain the number and person of the subject, gender is not implicit in the verbal formulation. In other words, if I say "vamos a la escuela" (We go to school), it is not clear if the "we" in this case is "nosotros" (masculine) or "nosotras" (feminine). I am grateful to Carolyn Dinshaw for asking me to clarify this point.

10 I am using the word *tacit* in the sense of something "not openly expressed or stated, but implied; understood, inferred" (*Oxford English Dictionary Online*, http://www.oed.com). In my view and as the essay shows, a tacit subject is a form of apprehending a social reality, person, or topic that materializes as implicit knowledge, speculation, or intuition.

recognize and decode the self-presentation of bodies and the information about them that circulates in family networks. In thinking that their homosexuality is knowable in a tacit way to the people close to them, my informants assume that many people have the requisite skills to recognize and decode their behavior. Everyone may not "get" the signs, but my informants understand that there is a distinction between their intentional manipulation of their self-presentation and impressions that they give to others unintentionally. Following Erving Goffman, I argue that my informants understand that there is a difference between "the expression that [they] *give*, and the expression that [they] *give off*."[11] They understand that their own bodies traverse the social world and signify in ways that exceed (and often betray) the intention of those who inhabit them. Thus it is always possible that someone might "get" their gayness despite any effort my informants may put into concealing it.

Tacit subjects help us unravel the complicities that structure social relations instead of focusing on an explicit definition or categorization of individuals. As the examples presented below show, the tacit subject in specific situations includes but ultimately might exceed individual subjectivity or sexuality. Indeed, what materializes in these examples are the power dynamics that shape how individuals negotiate information about their sexual identities. In the case of my informants, the concept shifts the analysis away from self-definition toward an investigation of the way they refuse the reductionism gayness engenders in the public sphere.[12] Avoiding this reductionism is paramount when the very conditions of migration, survival, and (imagined or real) upward mobility depend on people's continuing reliance on the networks and resources that facilitated their geographic displacement in the first place.

Producing *lo tácito*

My informants' negotiations of coming out illustrate that ambiguity and shared understandings are crucial to the sustenance of individuals and collectivities. Interviews suggest that the main pattern is the refusal of disclosure to others. Many informants see accepting themselves as an individual, private matter. Indeed, part of their coming out involves taking ownership of

---

11   Erving Goffman, *The Presentation of Self in Everyday Life* (New York: Anchor, 1959), 2.
12   The argument advanced throughout this essay *is not* a proposal for a "postgay" or "postcloset" model of identity formation. Apart from the irresponsible neglect of ways of knowing and organizing one's identity that have been fundamental to the lives of my informants, such an argument would erase the larger historical context in which my informants live their lives.

their lives. This can be seen in their frequent references to personal privacy, especially when it concerns their sexual and romantic attachments. Their understanding of personal privacy, though echoing the traditional distinction between public and private spheres that characterizes liberal democracies, takes place in social networks that render such distinctions tenuous at best. After all, many of these men have migrated and survived in New York City *through* the resources of their family networks—transnational collectivities established before these men's migrations. In other words, my informants exercise ownership of their sexual identities by negotiating the degree to which their sexual and romantic lives become (or not) points of discussion in family settings. Thus they reference the public and private realms as "indexical signs that are always relative" and that depend for their deployment, meaning, and communicative effectiveness on the context in which they are invoked.[13]

In some situations, an absent family dialogue about an openly lived homosexuality reveals the legitimacy informants enjoy within those networks, a legitimacy that allows them to refuse to make their homosexuality a point of discussion. Máximo Domínguez, a light-skinned, forty-five-year-old informant who is unemployed but who comes from a family that enjoyed ties to the Trujillo regime, does not like to talk to relatives about his life.[14] Because of what he characterizes as his "strong personality," relatives do not broach the topic with him.

MD: Nadie se atreve a preguntarme nada.
CD: ¿Cómo tú sabes que ellos saben?
MD: Ellos no son estúpidos. Mi hermano ha ido conmigo a las discotecas. Y yo me he besado con mi novio alante de ellos.

(*MD: Nobody dares ask me anything.*
CD: How do you know that they know?
MD: They are not stupid. My brother has gone to gay discos with me. And I have kissed my boyfriend in front of them.)

This example is that of someone who is "out" to his family while remaining protective of his personal space. Having relationships with men is a part of Domínguez's life that does not need to be discussed. Most readers will probably agree that this informant is "out of the closet," even though there has never been a discussion about the topic with his family.

---

13 Susan Gal, "A Semiotics of the Public/Private Distinction," *differences* 13 (2002): 80.

14 All names of the informants are pseudonyms. Rafael Leonidas Trujillo Molina was a dictator who ruled the Dominican Republic from 1930 until he was assassinated in 1961.

That Domínguez's relatives have seen him kiss his partner shows the degree of openness he enjoys within the family, but this is far from representative of what happens to others. Although some informants integrate partners into their family lives in New York City, kissing and other expressions of affection are not common. More common are situations in which informants introduce partners as "amigos" (friends) to relatives. Pablo Arismendi's dealings with information about his sexual identity illustrate how some informants handle these questions.

> CD: ¿Quiénes en tu mundo saben que a ti te gustan los hombres? ¿Cómo tú se lo has hecho saber?
>
> PA: Donde vivo, mi tía lo sabe. No porque yo se lo haya dicho. Ella lo intuye y se hace la loca. Pero ella sabe, por la manera en la que yo me visto y las salidas extrañas. Mi prima, se lo dije, porque una vez recibí una noticia de una persona muy allegada a mí, que murió de una manera trágica. Entonces, yo me puse, como que me descontrolé en ese momento. Y le bombié el asunto. . . . Y ya después de ahí es historia. Somos cómplices. Mi mamá es otra que lo sabe. No porque yo se lo haya dicho, sino que porque lo intuye como madre y también se hace la indiferente. Los demás familiares se lo imaginan, pero no se atreven a hacer comentarios ni a decir nada.
>
> CD: ¿Tu familia se ha enterado de que tú has tenido pareja?
>
> PA: Bueno, mis dos novios . . . yo los integré a la familia. Iban a los cumpleaños y a algunas reuniones.
>
> CD: Y ¿cómo tú los presentabas?
>
> PA: Como amigos. Pero [es], lo que te digo. Ellos saben quién es.

> (CD: Who in your world knows that you like men? How have you let them know?
>
> PA: Where I live, my aunt knows it. Not because I have told her. She perceives it and acts as if nothing is going on. But she knows because of how I dress and the strange outings. I told my cousin because one time I received the news that a person very close to me died in a very tragic way. Then I kind of lost control in that moment. And I spilled out the issue. . . . And then after that the rest is history. We are accomplices. My mother is another one who knows. Not because I have told her but because she perceives it as a mother and acts like nothing is happening. The other relatives can imagine it, but they do not dare make comments or say anything.
>
> CD: Has your family found out that you have had partners?

PA: *Well, my two boyfriends . . . I integrated them into the family. They went to birthday celebrations and other gatherings.*

CD: *And how did you introduce them?*

PA: *As friends. But that's what I'm telling you. They know who it is.)*

Extreme circumstances resulted in Arismendi informing a cousin of his homosexuality. As a consequence of Arismendi's coming out, the relationship with his cousin strengthened. Far more typically, the relationships Arismendi has with his aunt (in whose household he resides) and with his mother (living in Santo Domingo) show the degrees of ambiguity with which he works. His aunt may have a sense of what is going on because of the signs Arismendi gives of living a "gay" life; his mother's perception of his homosexuality is more a matter of mother's intuition than anything else. Arismendi's insistence on the visible signs of his gayness and in bringing partners into family gatherings point to the many traces of his life he brings into these settings without resorting to a verbal declaration of his gayness. His sense that his family "knows" what is going on is based on speculation, though it is also possible that his aunt and mother themselves give him signs of the presence of that knowledge. Regardless, whether and to what degree this knowledge is shared is something that cannot be expressed explicitly in this situation. Access to the support and resources his mother and his aunt provide him with depends on the ambiguity exhibited in these negotiations. A confrontation about his gayness, providing a definitive answer to traces that remain relegated to spaces of epistemological uncertainty, could rupture the bonds Arismendi has and needs.

Other informants take as given that their homosexuality is assumed or understood enough by those around them to render its revelation redundant. And underlining the redundancy of what is tacit, in the case of someone like Sábato Vega, can be a weapon used to ridicule attackers. One anecdote Vega shared with me concerns a family gathering he attended with his partner. During this gathering, one of Vega's cousins tried to show him up by asking, in front of everyone, when Vega was going to get married. Unfazed and without skipping a beat, Vega replied: "Pero ya yo tengo marido. ¿Tú no sabes que yo tengo marido? Míralo aquí [*pointing to his partner*]" (But I already have a husband. Don't you know that I have a husband? He's right here).

By responding to his cousin in this manner, Vega turned on its head a situation meant to "shame" him in public. His cousin was the one "shamed" for making an issue of something everyone else knew or should have known. What is important about Vega's response is not that the utterance "Don't you know I have a husband?" actualizes a "truth" about him (his homosexuality) but that it makes evident that the cousin should know something Vega assumes everyone else knows. One might say, following Michael Taussig, that this is a situation where the assumed character of what Vega says does not become evident until Vega points it out. What the realization of this tacit understanding effects is to underline everyone's complicity in a public secret. As Taussig puts it, "knowing what not to know" in public secrets demonstrates "not that knowledge is power but rather that active not-knowing makes it so. So we fall . . . aghast at such complicities and ours with it, for without such shared secrets any and all social institutions . . . would founder."[15]

The ability Domínguez and Vega have to present themselves before relatives in assertive ways can be partly explained by their geographic proximity to their immediate family (most of their parents and siblings also live in New York City). But it is also related to their economic independence. Their independence from relatives is evident even though Domínguez and Vega have struggled financially. While Vega's transition between jobs has been punctuated by periods of unemployment of varying lengths, Domínguez sustains himself through the disability benefits he is entitled to as an HIV-positive person. Their class backgrounds have not translated into easy upward mobility in the United States, a difficulty both share with the majority of my informants. Still, both of these men have learned enough English and have had enough experience to act as brokers between their family members and local institutions. Their proficiency at representing their families before institutions and persons with social power has come either because of their professional accomplishments (Vega holds a BA and currently works as a civil servant) or because of their ability to navigate the system (living with HIV for over a decade and having lost a partner to AIDS has taught Domínguez to be aggressive with providers of health and social services). Thus, that others "do not dare" confront them or face possible ridicule for trying to "out" them tells us much about the privileges Domínguez and Vega enjoy within their families. These networks are clearly important for Domínguez and Vega, but relegating the "public secret" of their homosexuality to the realm of what is tacit helps sustain kin relations that also depend on the knowledge, experience, and resourcefulness Domínguez and Vega contribute. In other words, all relatives are complicit in the public secret precisely because they are invested in sustaining an institution that makes them socially viable.

Arismendi's situation is more typical of participants who are undocumented, whose immediate families live in the Dominican Republic and whose relatively low level of education limits their prospects for upward mobility. Thus, although Arismendi leaves enough traces of the life he leads to let others know what is going on, the ambiguity of his situation—at least in

---

15   Michael Taussig, *Defacement: Public Secrecy and the Labor of the Negative* (Stanford: Stanford University Press, 1999), 6–7.

front of the aunt who provides him with a place to live and with his mother, his only emotional anchor—may make him shy away from a more confrontational style.

Arismendi's disclosure to his cousin may have been the outcome of a "loss of control" of information that may be tacit but that once expressed verbally could be used against him. But strengthening relationships with relatives is something most informants hope will happen when and if they disclose their homosexuality to the people who matter the most in their lives. The circumstances faced by working-class, undocumented participants living with relatives (like Arismendi) are different from those of upwardly mobile or professional participants who are US residents or citizens and who live independently. Class differences structure how participants negotiate the blurry lines separating what is tacit from that which is expressed explicitly.

While there are differences in how these informants handle information about their sexual orientation, Domínguez, Arismendi, and Vega have all been involved in gay politics since they arrived in New York City. For a brief period of time, Vega was involved in the creation and leadership of a New York-based organization for Latino gay men. As an HIV-positive gay man, Domínguez has been involved in various projects including support groups and activist initiatives among LGBTQ Latinos in New York City. Arismendi's activities include volunteering for a social service organization serving LGBTQ Latinos as well as conducting outreach for agencies promoting safer sex. These participants may be exceptional within a broader Latino gay male population. Nonetheless, how these men deal with information about their sexual orientation within their family networks suggests that more attention needs to be paid to what informs their rejection of the confession, especially given that their activism suggests their awareness of normative models of "coming out." More attention also needs to be paid to the various forms of understanding and ambiguity that they tap into as they traverse various institutional and social locations.

Situations where circumstances beyond a participant's control force him "out of the closet" constitute a disruption in the boundaries my informants establish with their parents and relatives around the handling of their sexual orientation in the family. In other words, parents and children agree not to talk about questions of sexuality in general and of homosexuality in particular. But what makes that agreement possible is the understanding that one's sexuality is a private matter best kept away from scrutiny outside one's immediate family networks. For example, Rogelio Noguera's "outing" by the publication of his arrest in a police raid of a bar frequented by homosexual men in the Dominican Republic points to the violence, challenges, and frustrations that accompany the state's shaming of homosexual subjects. This case illustrates how being outed in the Dominican Republic can make homosexual subjects vulnerable to ostracism and closes almost all possibilities of social legitimacy, let alone upward mobility.

At its core, Noguera's outing points to the costs of public scandal to upper-class informants. A man whose skin color would qualify him as "white" by Dominican standards, Noguera was one of three children of a prominent family living in a city in the Cibao region in the Dominican Republic. Noguera's father was a civil engineer and his mother was a housewife. Members of his family were farmers and generals during the Trujillo dictatorship. He describes both his father and grandfather as "machos of the land," men whose lives revolved around working in agriculture, taking care of animals, gambling on gamecocks, and visiting local prostitutes. Although Noguera's parents were invested in making professionals out of their children, they did not send Noguera to pursue a medical degree by himself in the capital. Instead, the whole family moved to Santo Domingo to support young Rogelio's university studies.

Living in Santo Domingo and attending the university brought Noguera in contact with other self-identified homosexual men. But he insisted throughout his interview that this was not a topic of conversation in his family. "El asunto de mi sexualidad no está claro" (The issue of my sexuality is not clear), he explained. "La familia y yo, tú sabes, nadie habla. Nadie pregunta. Tú sabes como es con los dominicanos. Nadie pregunta. Nunca . . . nunca se ha casado. No tiene muchachos. Pero no preguntan nada" (The family and I, you know, nobody talks. Nobody asks. You know how it is with Dominicans. Nobody asks. Never . . . he's never been married. He doesn't have children. But they don't ask anything).

When I asked whether he had ever encountered problems with the authorities because of his homosexuality, Noguera recounted a scandal that estranged him and his father for two years: Noguera met up with some friends at a bar and was arrested in a raid; he ended up in jail for a few days.

> *Después de los tres días de estar preso, parece que la publicación [en el periódico] . . . se realizó el mismo día o al día siguiente. Mi papá ya lo había leído y nadie me iba a visitor . . . cuando yo salí de la cárcel, que fui a mi casa, mi papá me llamó y me dice, "Mira. Ve eso." Y yo leí el periódico y ahí estaba: ". . . fueron detenidos por uso de drogas y los clientes homosexuales." Entonces, él me dijo, "Saca toda tu mierda y te largas de la casa."*
>
> *[Llora.] [Pausa.] Y entonces lo agarré y le dije: "Bueno. ¿Terminó? Ahora yo quiero decirle a usted algo. Primero, no fumo ni cigarrillo. Segundo, si aprendí a ir a las barras y a los sitios, fue con usted. ¿O usted no se recuerda cuando me llevaba a . . . ?" Era una loca, este, que . . . parece que*

era reformista.¹⁶ *Entonces ahí se reunían generales, ingenieros y vainas para hablar disparates. . . . "¿O usted no se recuerda las veces que yo iba a donde Cambumbo a buscarlo temprano a las siete de la mañana?*¹⁷ *Bastante veces yo fui y usted estaba tan borracho que tenía una draga sentada al lado suyo." Se paró y me dio una trompada. Eso fue el resultado de eso. [Señala su mandíbula desencajada.] Esto está arrancado. No me lo han podido poner mas para atrás. . . . Este ahí él me tiró unos puños. Yo no le tiré. . . . Entonces de ahí me fui para Puerto Plata después que duré dos años sin verlo.*

(After three days being locked up, it seems like the publication [in the newspaper] . . . was done the same day or next day. My father had read it and nobody was visiting me . . . when I came out of jail, then I went home, my father called me and said, "Look. Look at this." And I read the newspaper and there it was: ". . . they were arrested for drug use and the homosexuals . . . in this bar." Then, he said to me, "Take out all of your shit and leave this house."

[He cries.] [Pause.] Then I took this opportunity and said to him, "Well. Are you [uses the formal pronoun] done? Now I want to tell you something. First, I don't even smoke cigarettes. Second, if I learned how to find the bars and other places, it was with you. Or don't you remember when you took me to . . . ?" There was this queen there that . . . must have been a reformista. Then at that place generals, engineers, and other people gathered to talk nonsense. . . . "Or don't you remember the times that I went to fetch you at Cambumbo's at seven o'clock in the morning? I went there plenty of times and you were so drunk you had a drag queen

---

16   "Reformista" refers to a member of the Partido Reformista Social Cristiano, a right wing party led by Joaquín Balaguer. A lifelong bachelor who exercised power over the country's politics until his recent death, Balaguer has been the most powerful influence on the twentieth-century history of the Dominican Republic. Noguera suggests that it was because of the affiliation with Balaguer's party that the drag queen ran the bar.

17   Cambumbo (Tony Echavarría) is a television personality whose career began in Radio Televisión Dominicana and whose fame rests on his very public homosexuality and his ownership of a bar/cabaret frequented by working-class patrons and people involved in Dominican military, arts, and culture. Cambumbo's establishment was considered a space of debauchery and transgression, even though effeminate homosexuals—other than Cambumbo and his staff—began to be tolerated only in the last years of the cabaret. Even then, the space was more open in its last years of existence toward drag queens and their "bugarrones" than to homosexual men. Thanks to Richard Camarena for giving me background information on Cambumbo.

sitting next to you." He got up and punched me. [Points to his sunken jaw.] This is torn up. They haven't been able to put it back.... Then he threw a few punches my way. I did not punch him back.... Then after that I went to Puerto Plata and I did not see him for two years.)

This anecdote reveals the pain of Noguera's confrontation and estrangement from his father. But it is hard to tell whether the blow to Noguera's jaw was produced by his father's anger at the son's public shaming, at the son's homosexuality, or at the son's "outing" of the father's habit of frequenting bars where generals, government officials, prostitutes, drag queens, and other figures of "dubious" repute congregated. In other words, the recounted anecdote may substantiate Noguera's claim that his sexuality itself has not been a subject of discussion. This messiness suggests slippages that can help elaborate further the meaning of the tacit subject. A tacit subject might be an aspect of someone's subjectivity that is assumed and understood but not spoken about as well as a particular theme or topic. The difference between father and son, apart from the newspaper "outing" that interpellated this son of the upper class as a social outcast (possibly a drug addict or a homosexual), was that the father could enter and leave social spaces of "deviance" as part of his social power so long as his activities were "known not to be known," as Taussig might put it. Active not-knowing—after all, Noguera knew where to go pick up his father even though it is doubtful that he and the rest of the family talked about it—transformed into expressed knowledge must have given bite to Noguera's recrimination. In this sense, Noguera's sexuality may not, itself, be the tacit subject of the exchange. Noguera is not suggesting that his father is gay either. What Noguera is suggesting is that his father does not have a steady "moral" ground on which to stand and judge his son. Apart from actualizing the "truth" of social difference (homosexuality, drug addiction), this exchange actualizes the complicities constituting the social power of differently situated actors. The father's violent response is, in short, a response to the destabilizing force of an utterance by the son that reveals that the ability to "dabble" in marginality is also a function of power.

Playing with *lo tácito*

Privileging coming out as the act that produces the "public" gay subject makes the researcher insensitive to ways of dealing with the closet that avoid coming out while keeping the closet door ajar. It also makes the investigator oblivious to the fact that the closet is not an individual production but a collaborative effort. The closet door is ajar only to the extent that the gay subject and his or her others coproduce the closet when they interact with each other. Francisco Paredes, the dark-brown-skinned professional son of a Dominican business leader and of a mother with an advanced degree in biology, articulates eloquently the meanings informants give to coming out. His observations echo the uneasiness Latin Americanist critics have voiced with the metaphor.[18]

> *Cuando tú te sientas con una gente a aclarar tu vida sexual, estamos yendo con este estigma social de que "tú eres raro y tienes que explicarlo." De que "tú estás mal y tienes que explicarlo." ¿Por qué yo me tengo que defender si yo pienso que es normal? Sobre todo para que vengan a decirte, "Yo lo sabía. Entonces, ¿qué sentido tienes tú en discutirlo si yo ya lo sabía?"*
>
> (When you sit down with someone, to clarify your sexual life, we are going along with the social stigma that "you are queer and you have to explain it." That "there is something wrong with you and you have to explain it." Why do I have to defend myself if I think it's normal? And then somebody comes and says to you, "I knew it. Then, what's the point of your discussing it if I already knew?")

Paredes articulates some of the concerns other informants have expressed in interviews. Paredes rejects disclosure because he associates it with the confession. His is a rejection of the confessing subject as the guilty subject. Saying no to the confession means that Paredes repudiates the religious resonance that makes a sin of what is being confessed. Instead of "confronting" others with the revelation of his sexuality, Paredes assumes its normality. Since being a homosexual is as normal as being a heterosexual, there is nothing for Paredes to talk about with others.

As a result of owning his sexuality without the guilt associated with the confession, Paredes positions himself within the discursive register of the liberal-democratic right to privacy. At the same time, he reveals an awareness of the tenuousness of his access to privacy, for that which he considers private may already be accessible to the people who know him. Paredes's statement reveals that his sense of ownership of his own sexuality is predicated on the exercise of the right to not tell, to let others figure out what is going on if they can pick up the signs. Jason King's discussion of men "on the down-low" (DL) — predominantly African American men who have sex with other men without identifying as gay and while continuing to have female partners — resonates with what I have found among my informants. "Whether they pass as playas, [or] blend into the skateboard scene . . . young people of every race and class are responding to something in the air. It may seem like a retrenchment — and in some ways, it is — but their demand for self-determination extends a core value in gay liberation."[19] Like the men on the DL whom King

---

18   I am thinking specifically of the work of Sifuentes-Jáuregui and Quiroga.
19   King, "Remixing the Closet," 68.

writes about, Paredes's emphasis is on the necessity to respect individual self-determination.

Paredes's comments reveal his understanding that he does not ultimately control the reception of his insertion in the public sphere. In other words, he thinks it is likely that his friends will figure out that he is gay because he is seen only with men and because he may "let out a feather or two" every once in a while.[20] This is why, in gathering his friends to "tell them," Paredes fears he will be stating what will already be a "tacit subject" to them. His comments suggest his awareness of the ways his own body can be read by others as gay despite his own intentionality.

Paredes attended and graduated from a Catholic school, then pursued university studies in a private university. Before immigrating to the United States, he established himself in the Dominican Republic's engineering business community as an independent contractor. Being able to work independently was rare at the time. In addition, Paredes had spent a year in Germany living with the man who was then his partner. His decision to move to New York came once he learned of the failure of a business opportunity he had pursued in Puerto Rico. Once he began to live in New York and after meeting his current partner, Paredes chose to stay.

Even though he came to the United States on business, Paredes arrived with a tourist visa for six months. Unable to obtain employment in his own area of specialization because of his undocumented status, Paredes looked for jobs where his immigration status would not be a problem. A friend helped him get a job in a restaurant, which helped Paredes earn some money and work on his English. He eventually befriended a woman who agreed to marry him to legalize his status, and their successful application has helped him begin to find work closer to his professional expertise. Nonetheless, the scarcity of available work and his precarious position as a newly arrived professional put him at a disadvantage in the job market.

When the interview turned to the theme of disclosure, Paredes insisted that his mother and all of his relatives know everything they need to know even though he has never discussed his sexuality with them. I asked him to elaborate.

> FP: El único derecho que tú no puedes dejar que nadie te arrebate es el derecho de compartir lo que tú quieras compartir de tu vida. De ejercer ese derecho de decir, "Yo no quiero hablar de esto." ¡Y eso no quiere decir esconderlo! Porque yo nunca lo escondí.
>
> CD: Háblame de eso.

---

20 "To let out a feather or two" means to act in ways that are, in general, construed as "effeminate."

Decena: Tacit Subjects

FP: *Todos los novios que yo tuve yo los llevé a la casa.*

CD: *Pero hay personas que pueden decir que son amigos tuyos . . .*

FP: *Mi hermana mayor llevó a todos los de ella a la casa y nunca le dijo—mi mamá nunca se enteró que ella tuvo. ¿Por qué yo le tengo que decir que ese es el mío?*

CD: *Dicen que uno de los problemas que tienen estas comunidades en particular es que la gente no sale. ¿Qué le responderías tú a ese tipo de crítica?*

FP: *Una de las cosas en las que yo tengo que estar claro es que yo nací en un lugar, en un país que está colocado en una parte del globo terráqueo. Y dependiendo de donde está ese país colocado en esa parte del globo terráqueo, yo ya nací con ventajas y desventajas. Entonces, yo tengo que jugar con mis ventajas y mis desventajas, que son a nivel mundial, que son a nivel nacional, que son a nivel social, que son a nivel familiar. Tú tienes que decidir si jugar a ganar o jugar a perder.*

CD: *Háblame de tu relación con tu mamá y de tus parejas.*

FP: *Tú tienes que empezar diciendo que tu mamá te dio a luz a ti, ¿eh? Y te viene observando. Entonces, tu mamá tiene un PhD en ti. ¡Y yo no puedo subestimar la inteligencia de mi mamá! Ahora, ella hizo su trabajo y lo hizo muy bien. Excelentemente bien. Ella lo hizo bien porque ella quiso a todos mis amigos y los incorporaba en la familia. . . . Y esos novios durmieron allá muchas y otros vivieron allá otras veces. . . . Y ella iba a las 5:30 de la mañana y abría la puerta de la habitación que nunca estuvo cerrada a llevarme el café . . . y ella lo que veía ahí eran dos hombres abrazados. Entonces, ella hizo su trabajo muy bien.*

(FP: *The only right you cannot let anyone take away from you is the right to share what you want to share from your own life. To exercise the right to say, "I don't want to talk about this." And that doesn't mean to hide it! Because I never hid it.*

CD: *Tell me about that.*

FP: *All of the boyfriends that I had I took home.*

CD: *But there are people who might say that they were friends of yours . . .*

FP: *My oldest sister brought all of hers and she never said to my mother—my mother never found out that she had. Why do I have to say that that one is mine?*

CD: It has been said that one of the problems that these communities have in particular is that people do not come out. What would you say to that kind of criticism?

FP: One of the things that I have to be clear about is that I was born in a place, in a country that is located in a certain part of the globe. And depending on what part of the globe that country is located in, I was born with advantages and disadvantages. So I have to play with my advantages and disadvantages, at a global level, at a national level, at a social level, at a family level. You have to decide if you want to play to win or to lose.

CD: Tell me about your relationship with your mother and your partners.

FP: You have to start by saying that your mother gave birth to you. Eh? And she has been observing you. Therefore, your mother has a PhD in you. And I can't underestimate my mother's intelligence! Now, she did her job and she did it well. Excellently well. She did well because she loved all of my friends, she loved all of my boyfriends very much. . . . And she incorporated them into the family. . . . And those boyfriends slept there many times and others lived there other times. . . . And she went at 5:30 in the morning and opened the door of the room, which was never locked, to take coffee to me . . . and what she saw there were two men hugging. Then, she did her job well.)

Paredes is explicit in using the right to privacy to frame the decision of whether or not the individual subject discloses. In his case and that of other informants, Paredes's class privilege does not protect him from being accused of marriage fraud, for instance, should information about his homosexuality reach immigration authorities. Along with Noguera's experience of a public shaming by having his name published in a newspaper in connection with a raid on a bar frequented by drug users and homosexuals, the possibility of being "outed" as a homosexual in immigration court underlines the importance of attempting to control how and where information about one's sexuality circulates. Keeping one's sexuality in the realm of what is tacit is also a strategy for the management and circulation of information that, if expressed explicitly in the wrong context, could hurt a person's real (or perceived) possibilities of legitimacy and social mobility. Paredes's experience may be particular, but it reveals some of the ways in which he wrestles with his disadvantages within structures of inequality.

One advantage that informs Paredes's conviction of the need to respect individual self-determination and his access to privacy with an ease not shared by other informants is that he can perform normative masculinity. Paredes's ability to "pass" as a heterosexual male allows him access to a respect that may not be nearly so accessible to informants whose self-presentation is considered "effeminate" and whose gender nonconformity gets conflated with their sexuality. Though it is hard to guess what his mother thought when she brought in the coffee and saw two men hugging in bed—and asking such a question of his mother would probably do violence to the unspoken agreement between mother and son not to talk about what is tacit between them—the ability of this family to share in this "public secret" was probably facilitated by Paredes's gender conformity. In other words, Paredes's masculine self-presentation probably helped avoid external pressures (from distant relatives, from neighbors) this family could have experienced around his sexuality.

In addition, class position shapes Paredes's views about coming out. Apart from the respect that his mother and other relatives showed for his privacy while he was growing up, Paredes has resources and enjoys privacy in ways that are not accessible to informants such as Arismendi. Living with a partner and independently from relatives in New York City is not something other informants can do, especially shortly after their arrival in the United States. What sets Paredes apart from most of my informants is that he had that independence *before* he ever migrated to the United States. Although he brought partners to live at his mother's house, he had rented his own apartment and moved in with his partner for a number of years before traveling to the United States. This is rare among the men I interviewed. Thus, although other informants might share in Paredes's conviction that every individual has the right to not tell, it is not simply about whether or not one tells. Informants like Arismendi would not only have to consider whether or not to tell. Arismendi also has to consider whether he wants certain things to be "visible" to people who might say something to his mother in Santo Domingo or to his aunt in New York.

There is a game of advantages and disadvantages being played, Paredes suggests. The challenge becomes making decisions about the way one chooses to play. It is not hypocritical or unethical to wrestle with this complexity. On the contrary, it is authoritarian to suggest that everyone need announce his or her identity, no matter the complexity. Paredes's comments about his own location at various levels (family, local, national, global) suggest that while in some ways he is aware of his class privilege, he understands the risks and benefits of disclosure for someone of his position. He understands how disclosure might curtail an individual's chances to occupy certain social positions. While these comments point, once again, to mobility and aspirations possible because of a social status he already enjoys, Paredes's comments also suggest that disclosure may have little to do, in the case of working-class men, with upward mobility in New York City. Being undocumented forced Paredes to take up the same kinds of work that men with less education and professional experience continue to perform. Yet his not telling coupled with his level of education might allow him to move up the social ladder in ways that would be inconceivable for other informants.

This article has focused on interpersonal relationships between informants and their relatives. Nonetheless, my argument relies on the critic's ability to contemplate varying contingencies as she or he investigates the operations of the tacit subject across locations (e.g., "home," family gatherings, public settings, institutions), actors (e.g., parents, relatives, the police), and publics (e.g., parents and relatives, friends and colleagues, institutions, marketers, researchers). Just as I do not use tacit subjects to generalize about the experiences of all of my informants, I am also wary of assuming that this strategy works in the same way across all of the different locations that a particular subject may occupy daily. The boundaries of what is "tacit," what is "silent," and what is "secret" may be harder to define in certain instances. The ways in which people live challenge us to develop more sophisticated analyses of the contradictions they handle with ease.

However, there is more at stake here than just how individuals make choices to tell or not to tell others about their sexual identity. Some of the examples described earlier present potential or real confrontations that actualize, through the verbal utterance of tacit subjects, how people are linked to one another in relations of asymmetrical power that they are invested in maintaining. There is a meaning of the word *sujeto* in Spanish that is not immediately derived from its pairing with *tácito* but points to a slippage I want to keep between "tacit subjects" (topics) and "tacit subject*ivity.*"[21] When seen as the adjective form derived from the verb *sujetar, sujeto* is someone under the power of someone else (as in the English "subject*ed*"). Yet one meaning of *sujetar* in Spanish, according to the Real Academia Española, is "poner en una cosa algún objeto para que no se caiga, mueva, desordene, etc." (to put an object inside something so it will not fall, move, get disordered, etc.).[22] In this sense, then, something or someone is *sujeto* if they are held by someone or something else that prevents them from "falling."

An incorporation of this meaning of *sujeto* into my discussion of the "tacit subject" illustrates the complicities that constitute social relations. The tacit subject not only holds a person or topic from "falling" by bringing shame on those it concerns; the tacit subject holds the network as a whole from "falling, moving, getting disordered." In the various exchanges and confrontations

---

21 For a useful discussion of the meanings of *sujeto* in Spanish and in the larger context of European philosophy, see José Miguel Mariñas, "*Sujeto, subdito, sugeto*: The Body of the Subject: Montaigne and St. Teresa," *Radical Philosophy* 138 (2006): 38–39.

22 *Sujetar, Diccionario de la lengua española*, http://www.rae.es.

discussed throughout this article, at stake are the terms in which people address and interact with one another. When the terms are violated and people confront one another, what are exposed and most threatened are the social relations established. A *sujeto tácito* in this context might be constituted by the undiscussed yet understood knowledge (of individuals or specific issues) that links people together within specific social groupings.

The image of the individual gay subject "liberated" through migration to the metropolis may make New York attractive to men like my informants. Never the less, the experiences they recount present us with people able to make decisions and assert a sense of autonomy while being deeply aware of the social relations that make it possible for them (and for those linked to them) to survive. By underlining these implicit and shared linkages and understandings that cement social relations, the concept of tacit subjects begins to move us toward more relational accounts of the social construction of identity in queer studies. In a neoliberal world that exalts the atomized and unmoored individual and in LGBTQ communities that celebrate self-making by clinging to the promise of coming out as the romance of individual liberation, tacit subjects may make us more aware that coming out is always partial, that the closet is a collaborative social formation, and that people negotiate it according to their specific social circumstances.

Acknowledgements

My gratitude extends to Joaquín Alfredo Labour, Mireille Miller-Young, Richard Kim, Christina Hanhardt, Salvador Vidal-Ortiz, Susana Peña, Yolanda Martínez-San Miguel, Ben. Sifuentes-Jáuregui, Carolyn Dinshaw, Julian Carter, and Tanya Saunders, all of whom heard and discussed preliminary versions of the argument developed here. The Center for the Study of Gender and Sexuality at New York University, the "Migration and Diaspora" 2005–6 seminar at the Rutgers Institute for Research on Women, the Faculty Workshop hosted by the American Studies Department at Rutgers, and the Projects of Queer Studies workshop at SUNY Binghamton all have my gratitude for incisive feedback. Special thanks go to María Josefina Saldaña Portillo, Jasbir Puar, Louisa Schein, Ed Cohen, Robyn Rodriguez, Sonali Perera, Ernesto Javier Martínez, Ana Yolanda Ramos-Zayas, Licia Fiol-Matta, Lena Burgos-Lafuente, and Nicole Fleetwood for their encouragement and critical feedback. Edgar Rivera-Colón is a gifted intellectual and one of the best minds to engage my work. Final thanks are due to the three anonymous reviewers for helpful feedback.

Bibliography

Butler, Judith. "Imitation and Gender Insubordination." In *The Lesbian and Gay Studies Reader*, edited by Henry Abelove, Michèle Aina Barale, and David M. Halperin), 307-20. New York: Routledge, 1993.

Fisher, Diana. "Immigrant Closets: Tactical-Micro-Practices-in-the-Hyphen." *Journal of Homosexuality* 45 (2003): 171-92.

Gal, Susan. "A Semiotics of the Public/Private Distinction." *differences* 13 (2002): 77-95.

Goffman, Erving. *The Presentation of Self in Everyday Life*. New York: Anchor, 1959.

Guzman, Manolo. *Gay Hegemony/Latino Homosexualities*. New York & London: Routledge, 2006.

Hawkeswood, William G. *One of the Children: Gay Black Men in Harlem*. Berkeley: University of California Press, 1996.

Howard, John. *Men Like That: A Southern Queer History*. Chicago: University of Chicago Press, 1999.

King, Jason. "Remixing the Closet: The Down-Low Way of Knowledge." In *If We Have to Take Tomorrow: HIV, Black Men, and Same Sex Desire*, edited by F. L. Roberts and M. K. White, 65-70. New York: Institute for Gay Men's Health, 2006.

Kirby, David. "Coming to America to Be Gay." *Advocate* 834 (2001): 29-32.

Manalansan Martin F. IV. *Global Divas: Filipino Gay Men in the Diaspora*. Durham, NC: Duke University Press, 2003.

Mariñas, José Miguel, "*Sujeto, subdito, sugeto*: The Body of the Subject: Montaigne and St. Teresa." *Radical Philosophy* 138 (2006): 38-39.

McRuer, Robert. *The Queer Renaissance: Contemporary American Literature and the Reinvention of Lesbian and Gay Identities*. New York: New York University Press, 1997.

Perez, Hiram. "You Can Have My Brown Body and Eat It, Too!" *Social Text*, no. 84-85 (2005): 171-91.

Quiroga, José. *Tropics of Desire: Interventions from Queer Latino America*. New York: New York University Press, 2000.

Ross, Marlon. "Beyond the Closet as Raceless Paradigm." In *Black Queer Studies: An Anthology*, edited by E. Patrick Johnson and Mae G. Henderson, 161-89. Durham, NC: Duke University Press, 2005.

Samuels, Ellen. "My Body, My Closet: Invisible Disability and the Limits of Coming-Out Discourse." *GLQ: A Journal of Lesbian and Gay Studies* 9 (2003): 233-55.

Seidman, Steven. *Beyond the Closet: The Transformation of Gay and Lesbian Life*. New York: Routledge, 2002.

Sifuentes-Jáuregui, Ben. *Transvestism, Masculinity, and Latin American Literature: Genders Share Flesh*. New York: Palgrave, 2002.
Taussig, Michael. *Defacement: Public Secrecy and the Labor of the Negative*. Stanford: Stanford University Press, 1999.
Vaid, Urvashi. *Virtual Equality: The Mainstreaming of Gay and Lesbian Liberation*. New York: Doubleday, 1995.

A Tapestry of Knowledge:
Crafting a New Approach to Information Sharing

Sherilyn M. Williams and Pamela J. McKenzie

The recent turn in LIS research to social practice approaches shifts the analytic focus from the behavior of autonomous individuals to the ways that information is constituted and shared within knowledge communities.[1] A social practice perspective challenges many traditional approaches that still prevail in much information seeking research. First, although there are exceptions,[2] LIS studies primarily emphasize active forms of information seeking, searching, and retrieval. These studies see the seeker as an autonomous actor, simultaneously enlightened and ignorant, at a deficit because

1   Reijo Savolainen, *Everyday Information Practices: A Social Phenomenological Perspective* (Lanham, MD: Scarecrow, 2008); Reijo Savolainen, "Information Behavior and Information Practice: Reviewing the 'Umbrella Concepts' of Information Seeking Studies," *Library Quarterly* 77, no. 2 (2007): 109–32; Sanna Talja and Pamela J. McKenzie, "Editors' Introduction: Special Issue on Discursive Approaches to Information Seeking in Context," *Library Quarterly* 77, no. 2 (2007): 97–108; Sanna Talja and Preben Hansen, "Information Sharing," in *New Directions in Human Information Behavior*, ed. Amanda Spink and Charles Cole (Dordrecht: Springer, 2006), 113–34.

2   See for example, Sanda Erdelez, "Information Encountering: A Conceptual Framework for Accidental Information Discovery," in *Information Seeking in Context: Proceedings of an International Conference on Research in Information Needs, Seeking, and Use in Different Contexts, 14–16 August, 1996, Tampere, Finland*, ed. Pertti Vakkari, Reijo Savolainen, and Brenda Dervin (London: Taylor Graham, 1997), 412–20; Pamela J. McKenzie, "Model of Information Practices in Accounts of Everyday-Life Information Seeking," *Journal of Documentation* 59, no. 1 (2003): 19–40; Kirsty Williamson, "The Information Needs and Information-Seeking Behaviour of Older Adults: An Australian Study," in Vakkari et al., *Information Seeking in Context*, 337–50; T. D. Wilson, "Information Behaviour: An Inter-Disciplinary Perspective," in Vakkari et al., *Information Seeking in Context*, 39–50.

of "information needs."[3] Second, studies tend to be theorized and evaluated in positivist terms, focusing on instrumental tasks and cognitive behavior. Third, and not surprisingly given the instrumental focus, most studies consider workplace settings, and the literature broadly dichotomizes workplace and everyday life contexts.[4] Finally, although there is much attention to librarianship as a gendered profession,[5] gender is primarily treated as a stable construct that is analyzed as a differentiating variable.[6] Gendered contexts and practices have received little attention.[7]

We argue that a social practices approach offers many ways to challenge traditional thinking about information seeking and opens many new directions for inquiry. In this chapter, we bring feminist theories into conversation with information behavior research by drawing upon the act of crafting (for the purpose of this chapter, defined as the act of producing any sort of handmade textile good for personal use, personal consumption, or commodification) as exemplary of the ways in which gendered information sharing behaviors come to fruition. With regard to craft and information behaviour, textile handicrafts and the acts of producing them have historically been relegated to the feminine, domestic sphere. Women specifically have been the primary creative and social forces behind the making, dissemination, and exchange of handicrafts via both the intergenerational and peer group sharing of craft knowledge and artifact.

---

3   Katriina Byström, "Information Seekers in Context: An Analysis of the 'Doer' in INSU Studies," in *Exploring the Contexts of Information Behaviour: Proceedings of the Second International Conference on Research in Information Needs, Seeking and Use in Different Contexts*, ed. Thomas D. Wilson and David K. Allen (London: Taylor Graham, 1999), 82–95; Bernd Frohmann, "The Power of Images: A Discourse Analysis of the Cognitive Viewpoint," *Journal of Documentation* 48, no. 4 (1992): 365–86; Kimmo Tuominen, "User-Centered Discourse: An Analysis of the Subject Positions of the User and the Librarian," *Library Quarterly* 67, no. 4 (October 1997): 350–71.

4   Reijo Savolainen, "Everyday Life Information Seeking: Approaching Information Seeking in the Context of 'Way of Life,'" *LISR* 17, no. 3 (1995): 259–94.

5   See for example, Roma M. Harris, *Librarianship: The Erosion of a Woman's Profession* (Norwood, NJ: Ablex, 1992).

6   See for example, Maureen Hupfer and Brian Detlor, "Gender and Web Information Seeking: A Self-Concept Orientation Model," *Journal of the American Society for Information Science and Technology*, 57, no. 8 (June 2006): 1105–15.

7   For exceptions, see Paulette M. Rothbauer, "Finding and Creating Possibility: Reading in the Lives of Lesbian, Bisexual and Queer Young Women," (doctoral thesis, The University of Western Ontario, 2004); Christine Urquhart and Alison Yeoman, "Information Behaviour of Women: Theoretical Perspectives on Gender," *Journal of Documentation* 66, no. 1 (2010): 113–39.

First we locate craft within the broader discussion of collaborative information behavior, emphasizing information sharing. Second we draw on analyses of gender and textile handwork from a variety of disciplinary and theoretical approaches including political economy, feminist theory, sociology and craft theory to synthesize the multitude of ways in which craft can foster information sharing, community dynamics, identity building, and catharsis. While this chapter focuses on craft's ability to empower women and to offer them tools to facilitate sharing information about themselves, it would be naive to essentialize crafting as an entirely positive influence on the lives of women in developed and developing regions, both in the past and at present. Thus, we will also address criticisms of the role of craft in women's lives, ranging from domestic repression to capitalist exploitation in the context of women's labour, leisure, and creative self-expression. Despite this concession, we ultimately maintain that textile crafts have the potential to function in a liberatory manner and to serve as a unique social context for women's information sharing, and we provide examples from both developed and developing world contexts. Finally we review the LIS literature on information seeking in crafting contexts and suggest some future directions for further inquiry on information sharing.

We argue that crafting has, is, and will continue to facilitate the spread of information, civic engagement, community development and nurturing, and, on occasion, social justice, catharsis and healing from trauma. We contend that studying crafting as a context provides insights and frameworks that could be transferred to other information sharing contexts. We also show that the rich and multidisciplinary scholarly literature on crafting offers theoretical and methodological approaches that would enable LIS researchers to consider social meanings of information practices, attend to gender and other sites of inequality and to transcend common LIS binaries such as workplace and everyday. We argue that women's use of craft can subvert a climate of silence and facilitate the sharing of information about themselves and their interests. With this chapter, we hope to weave together these somewhat disparate strands and contribute something new to the fabric of information behavior research in LIS.

Collaborative Information Behavior

Collaborative information behavior (CIB) has been defined as document- or human-based activities "where two or more actors communicate to identify information for accomplishing a task or solving a problem."[8] Foster's review

---

8   Talja and Hansen, "Information Sharing," 114.

of the literature[9] demonstrates a focus on the workplace, on deliberate searching to meet instrumental goals, and on experimental research methods. Talja and Hansen propose that processes of CIB are embedded in dimensions of social practices:

> . . . instances and dimensions of our participation in the social world in diverse roles, and in diverse "communities of sharing." Retrieving, interpreting, and indexing information – giving names to pieces of information for the purposes of retrieval and re-use – are part of the routine accomplishment of work tasks and everyday life.[10]

They propose a social practices approach that takes up calls[11] to understand information users "in the context of their work or social life."[12] They distinguish collaborative information seeking and retrieval, which involves a cooperative search for information, from *information sharing*, which involves both active and explicit as well as less goal-oriented and implicit exchanges of already acquired information.[13] Talja characterizes information sharing as "an umbrella concept that covers a wide range of collaboration behaviours, from sharing accidentally encountered information to collaborative query formulation and retrieval."[14] Savolainen observes that, although few scholars have taken up the study of information sharing, this endeavour is important "since it sheds light upon the communicative aspects of everyday information practices"; information sharing explicitly attends to the social nature and context of information seeking.[15]

Talja takes a social practices approach to the study of information sharing among scholars from diverse academic disciplines. She identifies contextual characteristics of the scholars' social groups rather then characteristics of individual members to show how these contexts shaped and were in turn

---

9 Jonathan Foster, "Collaborative Information Seeking and Retrieval," in *Annual Review of Information Science and Technology*, ed. Blaise Cronin, Vol. 40 (Medford, NJ: Information Today, 2006), 329–56.

10 Talja and Hansen, "Information Sharing," 125.

11 See for example, Elisabeth Davenport and Blaise Cronin, "Texts at Work: Some Thoughts on 'Just for You' Service in the Context of Domain Expertise," *Journal of Education for Library and Information Science* 39, no. 4 (1998): 264–74.

12 T. D. Wilson, "On User Studies and Information Needs," *Journal of Documentation* 37, no. 1 (1981): 12.

13 Talja and Hansen, "Information Sharing," 115.

14 Sanna Talja, "Information Sharing in Academic Communities: Types and Levels of Collaboration in Information Seeking and Use," *New Review of Information Behaviour Research* 3 (2002): 145.

15 Savolainen, *Everyday Information Practices*, 183.

shaped by information sharing. Talja's work is significant both for its approach and for its identification of several interconnected forms of information sharing. Strategic sharing consciously strives to meet instrumental goals such as maximizing efficiency in a research group, paradigmatic sharing enables cross-disciplinary communication, directive sharing functions bidirectionally between junior and senior scholars, and social sharing contributes directly to relationship- and community-building activity.[16] Although Talja's study offers a fresh approach, it is typical of the small number of information sharing studies in its focus on settings such as academic contexts or computer-mediated settings where participants share instrumental and organizational goals.[17] There has been little study of information sharing in everyday life where it may fulfill more personal goals such as the nurturing and development of social circles and networks, catharsis, healing, and creative self-expression. A small number of LIS scholars explicitly or implicitly address information sharing in everyday life.

Savolainen explores the information sharing of unemployed people and environmental activists through the framework of social capital, and seeks to answer questions about motivational factors for information sharing.[18] His empirical findings "support the view that, like social capital in general, information giving draws on networks, norms, trust, and mutual understanding that bind together the members of human networks."[19] Additionally, he identifies three major motives for information sharing: serendipitous altruism, pursuit of the ends of seeking information by proxy, and duty-driven needs characteristic of people elected to positions of trust.[20] Savolainen's findings seem to mesh well with the broader literature of information behavior, namely with respect to motivations (needs, uses, and gratifications). Information is treated as an informing entity with the capacity to build up useful knowledge stores. For the participants in his study, altruism is the primary motivating factor in fostering information sharing behavior. However, Savolainen's research does not consider any benefits to the information sharer. We suggest that while crafting processes and products indeed facilitate information exchange, the knowledge shared may afford the artisan with benefits that are not immediately measureable or may not be applicable to the craft's consumer. Information does not necessarily have to "help" the

---

16 Talja, "Information Sharing in Academic Communities."
17 Caroline Haythornthwaite, "Networks of Information Sharing Among Computer-Supported Distance Learners," *Proceedings of the 1999 Conference on Computer Supported Collaborative Learning*, 1999.
18 Savolainen, Everyday Information Practices, 188.
19 Ibid., 196.
20 Ibid.

person on the receiving end to be of value. The processes of producing and sharing information are of benefit in themselves. This approach to information sharing—one that emphasizes process and the benefits of creativity and voice—has rarely been addressed by LIS scholars.

Elfreda Chatman's work on the information behavior of people in the margins consistently invoked notions of sharing and withholding information. Chatman's theories of a small world[21] and life in the round[22] evaluate information exchanges within small, localized, and disenfranchised populations such as unemployed low-skilled workers, janitors, and prison inmates, and illuminate which types of information are shared and which types are withheld in these contexts. In *The Information World of Retired Women*, Chatman used ethnographic methods to explore the information worlds of retired women living in an independent living facility. She observed that women in this community are part of a social network[23] and often gain certain types of information from their interactions with one another. However, this information is often superficial; women's continued independent living is contingent on their ability to take care of themselves both health-wise and in terms of finances and thus "risky" information is often withheld.[24]

Karen Fisher's concept of information grounds is another fruitful site of evaluating information sharing. Fisher defines information grounds as synergistic "environment[s] temporarily created when people come together for a singular purpose but from whose behavior emerges a social atmosphere that fosters the spontaneous and serendipitous sharing of information."[25] Information grounds are generally not conceived of as storehouses of information (in the way that a library may be considered as such), and those who interact in the information ground may or may not be actively seeking information. Fisher notes that, "as people gather at an information ground, they engage in social interaction, conversing about life, generalities, and specific situations that lead to serendipitous and sometimes purposive, formal and

---

21 Elfreda Chatman, "Life in a Small World: Applicability of Gratification Theory to Information-Seeking Behavior," *Journal of the American Society for Information Science* 42, no. 6 (1991): 438–49.

22 Elfreda Chatman, "A Theory of Life in the Round," *Journal of the American Society for Information Science* 50, no. 3 (1999): 207–17.

23 Elfreda Chatman, *The Information World of Retired Women* (Westport, CT: Greenwood, 1992), 73.

24 Ibid., 117.

25 Karen E. Fisher, Carol F. Landry, and Charles Naumer, "Social Spaces, Casual Interactions, Meaningful Exchanges: 'Information Ground' Characteristics Based on the College Student Experience," *Information Research* 12, no. 2 (2007), http://informationr.net/ir/12-2/paper291.html.

informal sharing of information on varied topics."[26] Information grounds are context-rich, and actors play different roles in information exchange. Fisher suggests that information grounds can occur in a multitude of settings, and offers examples including hair salons and barber shops, city buses, and quilting bees.[27] While the information ground is a promising concept, data analysis to date has consisted largely of content analyses of respondents' perspectives on such issues as the kinds of information grounds visited, the kinds of information exchanged in information grounds, the directions in which "information flow" occurs, and the value of the information and the information sources (e.g., relevance, quality, accessibility),[28] Fisher has not yet analyzed the actual processes at work in information sharing, or the benefits experienced by those on the giving end of information exchange.

Although McKenzie's work on midwife/client communication does not explicitly address the concept of information sharing, it considers several related aspects little studied by other LIS researchers. First are the social functions of information seeking and giving such as the building of relationships through information sharing.[29] Second are the ways that information seeker and giver roles are jointly and flexibly enacted during the course of the ongoing interaction.[30] Third is the situated evaluation of information sources in context of community values rather than individual.[31] Tiffany Veinot similarly explores the ways that social networks mediate information evaluation.[32]

---

26   Karen E. Fisher, "Information Grounds," in *Theories of Information Behavior*, ed. Karen E. Fisher, Sanda Erdelez, and Lynne McKechnie (Medford: Information Today, 2005), 185-86.

27   Ibid., 188.

28   Karen E. Fisher and Charles M. Naumer, "Information Grounds: Theoretical Basis and Empirical Findings on Information Flow in Social Settings," in Spink and Cole, *New Directions in Human Information Behavior*, 93-112.

29   Pamela J. McKenzie, "Informing Relationships: Small Talk, Informing, and Relationship Building in Midwife-Woman Interaction," *Information Research* 15, no. 1 (2010), http://InformationR.net/ir/15-1/paper423.html.

30   Pamela J. McKenzie, "Informing Choice: The Organization of Institutional Interaction in Clinical Midwifery Care," *Library & Information Science Research* 31, no. 3 (2009): 163-73.

31   Pamela J. McKenzie and Tami Oliphant, "Informing Evidence: Claimsmaking in Midwives' and Clients' Talk about Interventions," *Qualitative Health Research* 20, no. 1 (2010): 29-41.

32   Tiffany C. Veinot, "Interactive Acquisition and Sharing: Understanding the Dynamics of HIV/AIDS Information Networks," *Journal of the American Society for Information Science and Technology* 60, no. 11 (2009): 2313-32.

While Savolainen, Chatman, Fisher, McKenzie, and Veinot evaluate information exchanges in contexts of everyday life and address issues such as social capital, there is as yet little attention in LIS to the expressive and cathartic potential of information sharing. Crafting offers interesting ways, through both media and practice, of evaluating information sharing as a worthwhile creative process in its own right. While it is important to consider how crafting fosters information exchange, we argue that it is equally important to consider the meaning these exchanges have for the participants involved. Information sharing can have benefits for parties involved that go far beyond knowledge acquisition. Because this chapter is largely concerned with women's textile handiwork and the myriad ways in which it serves as a rich context for information sharing that is both highly gendered and highly social, the following section will explore the literature on social meanings of craft as a gendered practice. Some of the factors that enable and constrain information sharing will be outlined, and theoretical and methodological approaches from other disciplines that are promising for LIS analysis of information sharing will be explored.

Threads of a Narrative: The Informational Potential of Craft

Social Meaning of Craft Goods and Processes

Studies of women's participation in textile handcrafts have identified social meaning in relation to the physical crafted object, the practice of its production, and the social context of crafting communities. Textile objects themselves carry significance, and a finished handwork project serves as a physical manifestation of its creator's creativity, aesthetics, technical skill, and management of materials and time.[33]

Sadie Plant articulates how each crafted piece, through both process and product, persists as a record of who was involved in its production, the techniques that were used, and the skills that they employed:

> *Information can be stored in cloth by means of the meaningful messages and images which are later produced by the pen and the paintbrush, but data can also be woven in far more pragmatic and immediate ways. A*

---

[33] Catherine A. Cerny, Joanne B. Eicher, and Marilyn R. DeLong, "Quiltmaking and the Modern Guild: A Cultural Idiom," *Clothing and Textiles Research Journal* 12, no. 1 (1993): 16–25; Sherry Schofield-Tomschin and Mary A. Littrell, "Textile Handcraft Guild Participation: A Conduit to Successful Aging," *Clothing and Textiles Research Journal* 19, no. 2 (2001): 41–51; L. Lynda Harling Stalker, "Wool and Needles in My Casket: Knitting As a Habit Among Rural Newfoundland Women," (master's thesis, Memorial University of Newfoundland, 2000).

piece of work so absorbing as a cloth is saturated with the thoughts of the people who produced it....[34]

The crafted object itself is threaded with the stories, ideas, and histories of the individual or community who created it.[35] In "Conceiving a Quilt," visual arts writer Paula Gustafson[36] explains how the design and construction of a quilt is embedded with personal meaning from the quilt's maker. The quilter thus shares information to the quilt's readers about deeply meaningful personal experiences. Conversely, a quilt's reader could "examine it for meanings, could select and focus on the social value of their favourite colors and pattern pieces, could fantasize about them, and so supply personal interpretations for them."[37] In this sense, the crafted object is bi-directional. It is able to share information about its creator, and it is also open to interpretation by its reader.

Social meaning also arises from participation in a crafting community, which enables the sharing of common interests, values, and traditions and the development of a group identity as a handcrafter.[38] These two meanings are interrelated: producing hand-made goods may provide participants with a sense of success at producing something of value and worth, and with a sense of connection with other crafters that enables them both to learn from and to mentor others.[39] Producing textile handcrafts simultaneously shows the crafter's uniqueness through her crafting ability and her relationship to various communities, including the historical and contemporary crafting communities from whom she learns patterns and techniques, and a larger community of family, friends, and other community groups with whom she shares the fruits of her labors.[40] Knitters interviewed by Stalker saw knitting as an activity that enabled them to avoid idle time, a means of occupying the mind to stave off worry or loneliness, a link with past and future generations, an appropriate demonstration of their competence as women and mothers, and a source of accomplishment and pride as they decoded a difficult pattern

---

34 Sadie Plant, *Zeros and Ones: Digital Women + The New Technoculture* (New York: Doubleday, 1997), 66.

35 Cheryl B. Torsney and Judy Elsley, introduction to *Quilt Culture: Tracing the Pattern* (Columbia, Missouri: University of Missouri Press, 1994), 6.

36 Paula Gustafson, "Conceiving a Quilt," in *Craft, Perception and Practice: A Canadian Discourse*, ed. Paula Gustafson (Vancouver: Ronsdale Press, 2002): 200.

37 Joan Mulholland, "Patchwork: The Evolution of a Women's Genre," *Journal of American Culture* 19, no. 4 (2004): 58.

38 Cerny et al., "Quiltmaking and the Modern Guild"; Schofield-Tomschin, "Textile Handcraft Guild Participation," 46.

39 Schofield-Tomschin, "Textile Handcraft Guild Participation."

40 Ibid., 42; Cerny et al., "Quiltmaking and the Modern Guild," 23-24.

or finished a garment.[41] Crafting is also identified as both a gendered occupation and a collective pursuit, whether undertaken alone or in the company of others.[42]

Several scholars argue that the creation of material objects accomplishes generativity, the guiding and nurturing of the next generation and the continuation of traditions and institutions. In her study on the online information behavior of hobby quilters, Gainor found that quilters value generativity and are motivated by their desire to teach in their maintenance of detailed and descriptive websites and web communities.[43] Further, quilters feel that the act of teaching and sharing information about quilting with others is an inherent part of quilting itself.[44] The sharing of patterns and techniques begins "a natural cycle of the craft benefiting the informant; thereby contributing to active participation in the guild which ultimately provided impetus for more individual craft production."[45] Crafting serves to further the social bonds with other artisans both past and present via mentorship, teaching, and other forms of community building.[46] By facilitating a way to vocalize their perspectives and connect with others, craft has both historically and presently empowered women and provided vehicles for self-expression and meaning-making.

We argue that women's engagement with the material world is not only informed by a deep knowledge of the materials used that enables them to participate in the creation, maintenance, and communication of knowledge about those materials, but also that women's manipulation of the material world is central to constructing social realms that operate beyond the traditionally prescribed (and circumscribed) boundaries occupied by women.[47] Textile crafts offer women material strategies to foster generativity through mentorship and teaching, and information sharing through the social na-

---

41 Stalker, "Wool and Needles in My Casket."
42 Anne L. Macdonald, *No Idle Hands: The Social History of American Knitting* (Toronto: Random House of Canada, 1988).
43 Rhiannon Gainor, "Leisure Information Behaviours in Hobby Quilting Sites," in *Proceedings of the Canadian Association for Information Science*. 2009, 8, http://www.cais-acsi.ca/proceedings/2009/Gainor_2009.pdf.
44 Ibid., 9.
45 Schofield-Tomschin, "Textile Handcraft Guild Participation," 49.
46 Cerny et al., "Quiltmaking and the Modern Guild," 23; Kathleen W. Piercy and Cheryl Cheek, "Tending and Befriending: The Intertwined Relationships of Quilters," *Journal of Women & Aging*, 16, no. 1/2 (2004): 17-33.
47 Maureen Daly Goggin and Beth Fowkes Tobin, eds., "Materializing Women," introduction to *Women and Things, 1750-1950: Gendered Material Strategies* (Surrey, England: MPG Books Group, 2009), 2.

ture of crafts such as quilting. Tobin and Groggin argue that "women in the process of making and manipulating things were not only engaged in self-definition and identity performance, but were actively engaged in meaning-making and practices that involved construction, circulation, and maintenance of knowledge."[48] In this sense, the media and social processes of craft afford women opportunities to engage in creative and generative processes and communities while simultaneously sharing their specific and embodied knowledge therein.

Social Meaning of Group Activities

A final set of social meanings relate to crafting's location at the intersection of public and private spheres. Needlecraft has traditionally been considered domestic women's work; it has been designated as a domestic task, primarily for thrift and utilitarian purposes and it was most frequently practiced inside the home.[49] Even social needlecraft, such as quilting bees and early knitting circles, were held in the private home of a designated host member. Despite its frequent conceptualization as a domestic, private act, crafting has also facilitated women's interaction with the public realm, as textile works such as weaving, quilting and embroidery were displayed publicly. Further, social craft settings such as quilting bees allowed women to interact with one another in a public sort of way, which subverted the gendered norm of women's forbidden status within the public sphere.

Feminist scholars concerned with the public/private dichotomy disagree on definitions, but in general agree on the social implications this dichotomy has had on women throughout history.[50] Chris Baron and Liisa Past state, "The separation between public and private was damaging insofar as women were defined out of the conversation in the public sphere by not being given representation in politics."[51] Women's restriction from public life perpetuated sexist and gendered notions of women's labor and social roles. Thus, being confined in private spaces had a damaging effect on the ability for women to share information about themselves, and to obtain information about the world at large. In *Women's Rights: The Public/Private Dichotomy*, Jurate Motiejunaite notes that the public/private divide had serious implications on the lives of women, as they were excluded from public political

---

48   Ibid., 4.
49   Mulholland, "Patchwork," 57.
50   Ibid.
51   Chris Baron and Liisa Past, "Controversy in Feminist Theorizing: Different Approaches to the Public and the Private" in *Women's Rights: The Public/Private Dichotomy*, ed. Jurate Motiejunaite (New York: International Debate Education Association, 2005), 13.

participation and consequently, from contributing to policies that directly affected their lives. Socially, women were thought to be inferior to men, and women were excluded from economics. Unable to hold or inherit property, women were dependent on the support of fathers or husbands. "Women's work—housework and childcare that took place in the private sphere—went unpaid, and society considered it less valuable than the work men performed in the public sphere."[52]

Being skilled at crafts for domestic purposes also facilitated women's entry into the workforce, as modernization and industrialization took place in western society. In the context of work and capitalist production, craft had the potential to liberate women economically, but often served as a means to exploit their labor through long hours and poor pay. In his edited anthology of essays on European women and preindustrial craft, Daryl M. Hafter notes that women who had performed home-based craftwork became crucial to the finishing processes of mechanized factories. Capitalist employers and factory owners thought it "natural" that women should earn less than men.[53]

At the same time, the private nature of textile handcraft had liberatory potential. It enabled women to meet, chat, and imbue their craft with hidden meaning and social commentary—under the guise of domesticity and "proper" feminine acts. Friendships made through membership in crafting communities may be as important to members as the activity itself.[54] Plant traces the history of women and computer technologies, linking domestic craft to the development of complex computational tasks.[55] Plant also articulates the ways in which weaving and textile creation contributed to early social networks. The complexity of weaving necessitated multiple pairs of hands, and thus the work tended to be communal and sociable. Allowing for conversation and gossip, as well as singing, storytelling, dancing, and chanting, needleworkers were "literally networkers," who, by the nature of their social exchanges, used the end product of their craft processes as "means of communication and information storage long before anything was written down."[56]

While there are few historical analyses of craft as a means to disseminate information, the quilting bee is a prime example of craft functioning in such a way. In her analysis of quilting as a social practice and discursive genre, Joan Mulholland discusses how the textual qualities of the quilt allowed

---

52 Jurate Motiejunaite, ed., *Women's Rights*, 1.
53 Daryl M. Hafter, ed., introduction to *European Women and Preindustrial Craft* (Indianapolis: Indiana University Press, 1995), ix.
54 Piercy and Cheek, "Tending and Befriending," 31.
55 Plant, *Zeros and Ones*, 13.
56 Ibid., 65.

women to engage in speech actions that required no actual verbalization.[57] Since quilts originated out of a need for both warmth and frugality, they ultimately embodied a medium through which women could share their perspectives and experiences. According to Mulholland, "women were and are, of course, the major speakers through patchwork, which began as a practical chore and grew to be an alternative speech form. Its components set up the *kind* of discourse it would be, while the particulars of domestic life set up its *occasions* and the *uses* to which it would be put."[58] Mulholland also suggests that the quilting bee itself, in offering women a suitable and socially acceptable context for gathering, fostered a community dynamic that ultimately led to political action. She offers the folkloric anecdote about Susan B. Anthony's first public speech occurring at a quilting bee,[59] and contends that, due to its broader acceptability as a proper domain for women, "Quilt language was easily adapted to suit their new speech occasions and topics, so they could participate in political events in which they could not otherwise play a part."[60] The quilt as both product and process granted women instances to share information with one another, offer personal narratives, and hone their creative talents in nurturing community environments. Rozsika Parker similarly notes the role of embroidery in feminist political movements, most notably, the Suffrage movement and the Women's Liberation Movement in the 1970s. "Limited to practicing art with needle and thread, women have nevertheless sewn a subversive stitch—managed to make meanings of their own in the very medium intended to inculcate self-effacement."[61]

Craft, Social Justice, and Vulnerable Populations

While first-, second- and third-wave feminism(s) have facilitated positive changes for women in the workforce in developed nations, women's craft labor in developing nations is often still exploitative and capitalist interests have influenced traditional craft practices and hence women's work.[62] For many women in developing nations, craftwork is a primary source of income that perpetuates women's subjugation to the domestic realm. In the broader international capitalist economy, these crafters often experience exploitation,

---

57   Mulholland, "Patchwork," 57.
58   Ibid.
59   Ibid., 63.
60   Ibid., 64.
61   Rozsika Parker, *The Subversive Stitch: Embroidery and the Making of the Feminine* (London: Women's Press, 1986), 215.
62   Ronald J. Duncan, *Crafts, Capitalism, and Women: The Potters of La Chamba, Colombia* (Tampa: University Press of Florida, 2000), 115.

poor pay, and poor work environments.[63] Duncan explains that craft capitalism and tourism have fuelled the development of unregulated contract work that favours merchants and middlemen and exploits the women and children who craft the "traditional" cultural goods and exotic commodities.[64]

A great deal of research has been done on the exploitation of crafters and artisans in developing nations.[65] In "Weaving: Women's Art and Power," Alice G. Guillermo notes that conditions for women weavers have changed significantly, shifting from empowerment to economic exploitation. Women in developing nations now rarely weave for purely domestic needs. Rather, they are organized into cottage industries by investors, or contracted as pieceworkers. These conditions have resulted in a widespread exploitation of women weavers in poorer countries.[66]

Despite the widespread exploitation that women crafters sometimes face in developing nations, crafting nevertheless has a rich history of lending women voices in oppressive environments, and continues to offer women means through which to share their stories and perspectives, to build communities, and to ultimately heal from past traumas. Allowing oppressed peoples to tell their stories and share information about themselves can facilitate action, resistance, and social change. The story told by a crafted product may be one that might not otherwise be shared. Guillermo suggests that,

> *handwoven fabrics themselves become women's narratives through the particular medium of warp and weft which is skilfully interwoven to create the whole cloth. The fabrics are narratives of social and environmental exchange, protecting and unifying the body and spirit of a community.*[67]

A number of outreach projects and community initiatives seek to challenge and subvert the exploitative potential of handicrafts by lending voice to marginalized individuals through creative and therapeutic craft processes. Concerned primarily with personal storytelling, these projects allow the women involved to create narrative textile pieces that help share information with the artifacts' viewers. Two of these initiatives will be discussed below.

---

63 Stella Minahan and Julie Wolfram Cox, "Stitch'nBitch: Cyberfeminism, A Third Place and the New Materiality," *Journal of Material Culture* 12, no. 5 (2007): 12.

64 Duncan, *Crafts, Capitalism, and Women*, 200.

65 See Michael Herzfeld, *The Body Impolitic: Artisans and Artifice in the Global Hierarchy of Value* (Chicago: University of Chicago Press, 2004); Andrea Menefee Singh and Anita Kelles-Viitanen, eds., *Invisible Hands: Women in Home-Based Production* (New Delhi: Sage, 1987).

66 Alice G. Guillermo, "Weaving: Women's Art and Power," in *The Necessity of Craft*, ed. Lorna Kaino (Nedlands: University of Western Australia Press, 1995), 52.

67 Ibid., 36.

Create Africa South (CAS) is an NGO established in 2000 with the mission of preserving and developing creativity in South Africa.[68] A core project of CAS is Amazwi Abesifazane (Voices of Women), a project that oversees the collection of memory cloths being created by women to address racial and gender discrimination in South Africa, specifically within the province of KwaZulu Natal. Each memory cloth, a hand-sewn tapestry, expresses its creator's personal narrative. In addition to providing a channel for women to visually tell their stories and share their struggles, the project facilitates opportunities for dialogue, and ultimately, healing from past traumas. Each individual cloth is displayed with a profile of the artist and her story. Due to the political instability of the region specifically in the context of apartheid, government corruption and censorship, and numerous human rights violations, in the past women of the KwaZulu Natal region were unable to share their stories or speak out against the atrocities that were being committed.[69] The Voices of Women project allows women to reclaim their silenced narratives, share information about their struggles to people across the globe, and communicate with one another about shared experiences.

The goal of the Canadian Living Healing Quilt Project was to foster personal narrative, creative expression, catharsis, and healing for victims of native residential schools. The project involved the creation of quilts using squares made by those who endured the traumas of attending residential schools. Robertson describes the ways in which native girls attending residential schools were forced to learn crafts and sewing skills in order to turn them into docile bodies that meshed well with conceptions of proper Canadian womanhood.[70] The use of sewing in the LHQP thus subverts and reclaims this act of craft in a way that facilitates the sharing of traumatic experiences and the telling of one's story. The process of creating quilt squares provided comfort and help for survivors to tell their tales and hone their previously repressed voices. Accompanying each quilt square is a written narrative of its creator. Although this display cannot unravel decades of abuse, the act of telling one's story, and doing so through a creative and productive process such as quilting, can ultimately facilitate catharsis, and possibly, over the long run, can aid in healing from trauma.

Both the Voices of Women project and LHQP demonstrate some of the ways in which marginalized women use craft to tell their stories and

---

68 Create Africa South, 2007, http://www.cas.org.za/home.htm.
69 Carol Becker, "Amazwi Abesifazane (Voices of Women)," *Art Journal* 63, no. 4 (2004): 117.
70 Kirsty Robertson, "Threads of Hope: The Living Healing Quilt Project," in "Aboriginal Redress and Repatriation," ed. Jennifer Henderson and Pauline Wakeham, special issue, *English Studies in Canada* 35, no. 1 (2009): 87, doi:10.1353/esc.0.0166.

disseminate information about their lives and experiences. These tapestries and quilts embody visual narratives of women's lives in times and places where women's voices were and are repressed. Often encompassing political and social messages, these handcrafted textiles give women agency and control over their own narratives, something that has previously been forbidden. Being afforded the opportunity to tell their own stories, to share information on a national and international level, and to shape the course of their futures, these instances of craft demonstrate an equitable way for oppressed women to share their knowledge and communicate information with others, instead of being restricted to the receiving end of the information society.

LIS Contributions to Craft and Information

New approaches in LIS research are gravitating toward social practice, social context, and the troubling and deconstruction of social categories such as gender, sexuality, and race. Our emphasis on women's use of craft is an example of the emergent intersectionality and interdisciplinarity within LIS work. Because women's needlecraft encompasses so many social and informational facets, we suggest that it may offer some new and fruitful avenues for future work in LIS, especially within information behavior and CIS research. Accordingly, the remainder of this chapter will pick up the stitches of LIS research and knit them together with those of women's craft.

As discussed above, Talja and Hansen's conception of information sharing may or may not involve intention or specific goals in terms of information exchange; information sharing is not necessarily purposive in the ways that information seeking and retrieval have been studied and contextualized. Further, the forms of information sharing identified by Talja (strategic, paradigmatic, directive, and social) offer a framework that recognizes the breadth of reasons for information sharing that extend well beyond the instrumental and address social and relational concerns. Applying a similar framework to non-work settings such as women's craft offers fruitful pathways to new directions in LIS research. Focusing our attention explicitly on Talja's forms of information sharing, we are able to weave together some examples of how the types and contexts of craft discussed earlier are exemplary of the ways in which women's craft functions socially and in the context of information exchange: strategic information sharing is concerned with meeting instrumental objectives and thus could relate to "bee" situations where a craft group is working together on a single project such as a quilt or independently on similar goals; paradigmatic information sharing emphasizes cross-disciplinary communication (or information exchanges between different groups) and therefore could relate to craft as a form of storytelling and narrative shared by marginalized women to outsiders; directive information sharing embodies generativity in ways similar to quilting; perhaps most obvious is social information sharing, which applies to the multitude of ways women's crafting fosters interpersonal relationships and the development of community.

Williams evaluates the role of craft as a third-wave feminist strategy of resistance to consumer culture.[71] Looking at online crafting communities such as Etsy.com and Craftster.org, she identifies third-wave feminist strands within the current crafting resurgence and evaluated the community dynamics therein. Ultimately, Williams found that handicrafts are being taken up by feminist communities as a subversive act that challenges traditional gender norms and corporate dominance, as well as fosters strong communities that exist both in face-to-face and online life. While technology played a role in this study, Williams is chiefly concerned with the social aspects of craft and how they may be politicized for social capital, social justice, and creative self-expression and catharsis.

Fundamentally concerned with the intersection of technology and handicraft, Rosner and Ryokai designed and implemented a ubiquitous computing project entitled Spyn, whereby knitters could utilize digital recording technologies to document their thoughts and feelings while working on projects.[72] Spyn utilizes computer vision techniques combined with yarn printed with infrared ink that corresponds to messages recorded throughout the process of knitting. While certain textile handicrafts such as quilting or embroidery can be imbued with explicit visual messages from their creators, this is not always the case with knitting or crochet. Thus, the Spyn project seeks to allow knitters to "record a unique experience of their creation, weaving personal meaning into their physical knits."[73] Demonstrative of the ways in which new and emerging technologies can mesh well with traditional craft and help foster the production of an informational good, "Spyn provides opportunities for twining contextual information with the artifact."[74]

Extending the analysis of craft and technology intersecting, Goodman and Rosner evaluate the ways in which knitters and gardeners integrate information technologies into their handwork. They suggest three metaphors for handwork practice to challenge the binary between digital and material

---

71 Sherilyn M. Williams, "Crafting Resistance: Handmade Culture as a Third-Wave Feminist Response to Consumerism," (master's thesis, University of Western Ontario, 2008).

72 Daniela K. Rosner and Kimiko Ryokai, "Spyn: Augmenting Knitting to Support Storytelling and Reflection," *UbiComp'08, September 21-24, 2008, Seoul, Korea,* http://people.ischool.berkeley.edu/~daniela/research/RosnerRyokai_Ubicomp_2008.pdf.

73 Ibid., 8.

74 Ibid., 9.

practice: *extending* (engaging in handwork while interacting with other stimuli such as watching television), *interjecting* (briefly engaging with technological tools such as cell phones during the handwork practice and then withdrawing it shortly after), and *segmenting* (a metaphor for how the activities affecting the objects of handwork can take independent trajectories; time is segmented between different activities and materials). Goodman and Rosner note that while those engaged with handcrafts often adopt a language of resistance to technology, they nevertheless rely on these technologies and interweave the digital with traditional.[75]

Gainor explores the information behaviors (namely acts of sharing) of twenty-five hobby quilters who run websites and blogs dedicated to the craft, and evaluates their statements of motivations, teaching tools, and expressions of personal creativity.[76] She draws on ELIS and serious leisure perspectives to identify the major themes of creativity, teaching/generativity, and community, and suggests that these themes are tied not only to the community and traditions of quilting, but to the quilt artifact itself.[77] Gainor articulates five ways in which quilters discussed their creativity: quilting as a creative act, quilting as emotional succor, quilting as passion, quilting as object, and other forms of creativity such as poetry, sharing recipes, or discussing different types of needlecraft.[78] Quilting as emotional succor gave some of the quilters in Gainor's study a way to "reflect on and process life's challenges" and facilitated catharsis and healing for coping with the death of a loved one, or overcoming serious illnesses.[79] Gainor also explores the different ways that quilters share information about their craft and foster community through teaching and generativity. She suggests that these findings may extend to workplace settings and professional environments and states that they also reiterate ELIS's claim that knowledge exchange is social practice.[80] According to Gainor, each of the sites under analysis "sit within a framework of values that seem to flow from the quilt object to the community and back again in perpetual reinforcement . . . the construction of these information resources manifests the values of teaching and sharing."[81]

---

75   Elizabeth Goodman and Daniela K. Rosner, "From Garments to Gardens: Negotiating Material Relationships Online and 'By Hand,'" *Proceedings of the 2011 Annual Conference on Human Factors in Computing Systems*, 2011, http://people.ischool.berkeley.edu/~daniela/files/goodman_rosner_chi2011.pdf.

76   Rhiannon Gainor, "Hobby Quilting Websites and Voluntary Provision of Information," *New Directions in Folklore* 9, no. 1 (2011): 41–67.

77   Ibid., 41.

78   Ibid., 50–51.

79   Ibid., 51.

80   Ibid., 60.

81   Ibid.

Prigoda and McKenzie show how a public library-based knitting group functioned as a site of information sharing.[82] They employ a collectivist theoretical framework to evaluate the ways in which information exchanges occur within the knitting group itself, rather than on the individual level. They note that knitting is "conducive to chatting,"[83] and that sharing plays an important role in the processes of knitting within a group setting, namely through the sharing of patterns, techniques, and also displaying the finished good. Further, knitting in group settings and sharing information about knitting, for some participants, facilitated caring acts in addition to the free sharing of craft knowledge.[84] Thus, while information sharing is a process that occurs within a particular context, the context of a crafting community shapes the ways in which information is shared, and how the benefits are reaped by those engaged in the community processes.

Conclusions: Implications for Future Work in LIS

As LIS researchers continue to investigate information behaviors specifically in the context of information searching, use and retrieval, instrumental and positivist methodologies that emphasize workplace settings continue to proliferate. LIS could benefit from greater theorization of information sharing in the social contexts of everyday life, and by evaluating the ways in which it can be nurtured and fostered. While this type of theorization and evaluation can take place in a number of ways, through a number of different channels and settings, this chapter has focused on the role of craft as a tool that assists women in sharing and disseminating information. Despite its historic and present positioning as an often oppressive force, crafting has also been used by women to share information about their beliefs, ideals, and lives, and also, as a connecting force within different community settings. Additionally, the skill of crafting is a knowledge set that has been shared on an intergenerational level by women throughout history, fostering generativity, teaching and mentorship.

Being able to share information is as significant as being able to access information. Objectification and subjugation occur when people are marginalized and unable to speak out about their own lives or the oppression that they are facing. When one party is unable to communicate information, or when an emphasis is placed on the more privileged party's information sharing practices, issues of inequity emerge. The way to rectify such inequities

---

82 Elena Prigoda and Pamela McKenzie, "Purls of Wisdom: A Collectivist Study of Human Information Behavior in a Public Library Knitting Group," *Journal of Documentation* 63, no. 1 (2007): 95.
83 Ibid., 103.
84 Ibid., 106.

is to facilitate access to information, and facilitate means of sharing information. Concerned with the ways in which crafting has historically and presently affords women a means and a process through which to share information, we are fundamentally interested in the emergent self-narrative and the cultural and social significance of telling one's own story. Crafting processes allow for a useful framework in the context of narrative and ethnography, as well as information sharing.

Information behavior research could benefit from critical perspectives on knowledge and knowers, particularly on what it means to share information and what it means to be silenced, and on how knowledge is experienced differently by different groups of people. Crafting offers a unique narrative strategy by presenting researchers with an artifact of meaning that has been emblazoned with the personality, thoughts, and stories of its creator. Also, as a process, it facilitates group interaction that leads to information sharing and, potentially, community building. Focusing on product, process, and community can facilitate ethnographic work that is concerned with gendered material strategies of resistance, personal and collective growth, and the development of voice for those in the margins; additionally, this type of work seeks a less hierarchical relationship between researcher and participant.[85]

If LIS researchers incorporate notions of self-expression, creativity, community, and personal narrative strategies into our conception of information behavior and emphasize a social justice perspective, craft can serve as the starting point for meaningful and important research in the discipline. First, craft may bridge the gap between labour and leisure and therefore challenges the traditional LIS dichotomization of "workplace" and "everyday life" information seeking.[86] Crafting as a practice therefore constitutes something of a third space for LIS scholars that can spark more nuanced considerations of these essentialized concepts. Second, in bringing everyday life into focus, LIS researchers may move beyond purposive, linear forms of information seeking to recognize more idiosyncratic, contingent, creative, and sometimes playful ways of seeking and sharing information.[87] Third, a focus on crafting practices brings attention to the ways that information sharing contributes to the social meaning of individual and group activities and the communication of values within knowledge and discourse communities. Fourth, a focus on craft acknowledges the crafted item as well as the crafter as having informing potential. This allows for a disruption of the strict LIS distinction

---

85   Ann Oakley, "Interviewing Women," in *Doing Feminist Research*, ed. Helen Robert (London: Routledge & Kegan Paul, 1981), 30–61. Oakley's article offers an insightful discussion of feminist research praxis.
86   Savolainen, "Everyday Life Information Seeking."
87   Talja and Hansen, "Information Sharing."

between "users" and "sources" of information and invites researchers to consider creators, consumers, and artifacts as part of a single communicative system. Fifth, recognizing the potential of crafted items and crafting practices to subvert traditional norms or give voice to the silenced may remind LIS researchers that transmission models of information sharing focus on benefits to the recipient while ignoring the potential value to the sharer her or himself.[88] Moving beyond transmission models will enable LIS researchers to consider the multiple meanings the crafting activity and crafted artifacts may have for crafter, audience, and community. By considering information sharing as a complex two- (or multi-) way communicative act, LIS researchers can move away from deficit models of information seeking and acknowledge the social functions of information sharing as potentially relational, engaging, nurturing, and even healing for both sharer and receiver. Attending to crafting, through both media and process, allows LIS scholars to re-envision information sharing for its potential as a community-building, cathartic, creative and healing process that builds social capital and privileges the voices of the marginalized.

Bibliography

Baron, Chris, and Liisa Past. "Controversy in Feminist Theorizing: Different Approaches to the Public and the Private." In Motiejunaite, *Women's Rights*, 9–27.

Becker, Carol. "Amazwi Abesifazane (Voices of Women)." *Art Journal* 63, no. 4 (2004): 116–34.

Bystrom, Katriina. "Information Seekers in Context: An Analysis of the 'Doer' in INSU Studies." In *Exploring the Contexts of Information Behaviour: Proceedings of the Second International Conference on Research in Information Needs, Seeking and Use in Different Contexts*, edited by Thomas D. Wilson and David K. Allen, 82–95. London: Taylor Graham, 1999.

Cerny, Catherine A., Joanne B. Eicher, and Marilyn R. DeLong. "Quiltmaking and the Modern Guild: A Cultural Idiom." *Clothing and Textiles Research Journal* 12, no. 1 (1993): 16–25.

Chatman, Elfreda. *The Information World of Retired Women*. Westport, CT: Greenwood, 1992.

———. "Life in a Small World: Applicability of Gratification Theory to Information-Seeking Behavior." *Journal of the American Society for Information Science* 42, no. 6 (1991): 438–49.

———. "A Theory of Life in the Round." *Journal of the American Society for Information Science* 50, no. 3 (1999): 207–17.

---

88   Savolainen, *Everyday Information Practices*.

Davenport, Elisabeth, and Blaise Cronin. "Texts at Work: Some Thoughts on 'Just for You' Service in the Context of Domain Expertise." *Journal of Education for Library and Information Science* 39, no. 4 (1998): 264-74.

Duncan, Ronald J. *Crafts, Capitalism, and Women: The Potters of La Chamba, Colombia.* Tampa: University Press of Florida, 2000.

Erdelez, Sanda. "Information Encountering: A Conceptual Framework for Accidental Information Discovery." In Vakkari, Savolainen, and Dervin, *Information Seeking in Context*, 412-20.

Fisher, Karen E. "Information Grounds." In *Theories of Information Behavior*, edited by Sanda Erdelez, Lynne McKechnie, and Karen E. Fisher, 185-206. Medford, NJ: Information Today, 2005.

Fisher, Karen E., and Charles M. Naumer. "Information Grounds: Theoretical Basis and Empirical Findings on Information Flow in Social Settings." In Spink and Cole, *New Directions in Human Information Behavior*, 93-112.

Fisher, Karen E., Carol F. Landry, and Charles Naumer. "Social Spaces, Casual Interactions, Meaningful Exchanges: 'Information Ground' Characteristics Based on the College Student Experience." *Information Research* 12, no. 2 (2007). http://informationr.net/ir/12-2/paper291.html.

Foster, Jonathan. "Collaborative Information Seeking and Retrieval." In *Annual Review of Information Science and Technology*, edited by Blaise Cronin, 329-56. Vol. 40. Medford, NJ: Information Today, 2006.

Frohmann, Bernd. "The Power of Images: A Discourse Analysis of the Cognitive Viewpoint." *Journal of Documentation* 48, no. 4 (1992): 365-86.

Gainor, Rhiannon. "Hobby Quilting Websites and Voluntary Provision of Information." *New Directions in Folklore* 9, no. 1 (2011): 41-67.

———. "Leisure Information Behaviours in Hobby Quilting Sites." *Proceedings of the Canadian Association for Information Science*. 2009. http://www.cais-acsi.ca/proceedings/2009/Gainor_2009.pdf.

Goggin, Maureen Daly, and Beth Fowkes Tobin, eds. *Women and Things, 1750-1950: Gendered Material Strategies.* Surrey, England: MPG Books Group, 2009.

Goodman, Elizabeth, and Daniela K. Rosner. "From Garments to Gardens: Negotiating Material Relationships Online and 'By Hand.'" *Proceedings of the 2011 Annual Conference on Human Factors in Computing Systems*, 2011, http://people.ischool.berkeley.edu/~daniela/files/goodman_rosner_chi2011.pdf.

Guillermo, Alice G. "Weaving: Women's Art and Power." In *The Necessity of Craft*, edited by Lorna Kaino, 35-56. Nedlands: University of Western Australia Press, 1995.

Gustafson, Paula. "Conceiving a Quilt." In *Craft, Perception and Practice: A Canadian Discourse*, edited by Paula Gustafson, 197–208. Vancouver: Ronsdale, 2002.

Hafter, Daryl M., ed. *European Women and Preindustrial Craft*. Indianapolis: Indiana University Press, 1995.

Harris, Roma M. *Librarianship: The Erosion of a Woman's Profession*. Norwood, NJ: Ablex, 1992.

Haythornthwaite, Caroline. "Networks of Information Sharing Among Computer-Supported Distance Learners." *Proceedings of the 1999 Conference on Computer Supported Collaborative Learning*, 1999.

Herzfeld, Michael. *The Body Impolitic: Artisans and Artifice in the Global Hierarchy of Value*. Chicago: University of Chicago Press, 2004.

Hupfer, Maureen, and Brian Detlor. "Gender and Web Information Seeking: A Self-Concept Orientation Model." *Journal of the American Society for Information Science and Technology* 57, no. 8 (2006): 1105–15.

Macdonald, Anne L. *No Idle Hands: The Social History of American Knitting*. Toronto: Random House of Canada, 1988.

McKenzie, Pamela J. "Informing Choice: The Organization of Institutional Interaction in Clinical Midwifery Care." *Library & Information Science Research* 31, no. 3 (2009): 163–73.

———. "Informing Relationships: Small Talk, Informing, and Relationship Building in Midwife-Woman Interaction." *Information Research* 15, no. 1 (2010). http://InformationR.net/ir/15-1/paper423.html.

———. "Model of Information Practices in Accounts of Everyday-Life Information Seeking." *Journal of Documentation* 59, no. 1 (2003): 19–40.

McKenzie, Pamela J., and Tami Oliphant. "Informing Evidence: Claimsmaking in Midwives' and Clients' Talk About Interventions." *Qualitative Health Research* 20, no. 1 (2010): 29–41.

Minahan, Stella, and Julie Wolfram Cox. "Stitch'nBitch: Cyberfeminism, a Third Place and the New Materiality." *Journal of Material Culture* 12, no. 5 (2007): 5–21.

Motiejunaite, Jurate, ed. *Women's Rights: The Public/Private Dichotomy*. New York: International Debate Association, 2005.

Mulholland, Joan. "Patchwork: The Evolution of a Women's Genre." *Journal of American Culture* 19 no. 4 (2004): 57–69.

Oakley, Ann. "Interviewing Women: A Contradiction in Terms." In *Doing Feminist Research*, edited by Helen Roberts, 30–61. London: Routledge and Kegan Paul, 1981.

Parker, Rozsika. *The Subversive Stitch: Embroidery and the Making of the Feminine*. London: Women's Press Limited, 1986.

Piercy, Kathleen W., and Cheryl Cheek. "Tending and Befriending: The Intertwined Relationships of Quilters." *Journal of Women & Aging* 16, no. 1/2 (2004): 17–33.

Plant, Sadie. *Zeros and Ones: Digital Women + The New Technoculture*. New York: Doubleday, 1997.

Prigoda, Elena, and Pamela J. McKenzie. "Purls of Wisdom: A Collectivist Study of Human Information Behaviour in a Public Library Knitting Group." *Journal of Documentation* 63, no. 1 (2007): 90–114.

Robertson, Kirsty. "Threads of Hope: The Living Healing Quilt Project." In "Aboriginal Redress and Repatriation," edited by Jennifer Henderson and Pauline Wakeham. Special issue, *English Studies in Canada* 35, no. 1 (2009): 85–108. doi:10.1353/esc.0.0166..

Rosner, Daniela K., and Kimiko Ryokai. "Spyn: Augmenting Knitting to Support Storytelling and Reflection." *UbiComp'08, September 21-24, 2008, Seoul, Korea*. http://people.ischool.berkeley.edu/~daniela/research/RosnerRyokai_Ubicomp_2008.pdf.

Rothbauer, Paulette M. "Finding and Creating Possibility: Reading in the Lives of Lesbian, Bisexual and Queer Young Women." PhD thesis, The University of Western Ontario, 2004.

Savolainen, Reijo. *Everyday Information Practices: A Social Phenomenological Perspective*. Lanham, MD: Scarecrow, 2008.

———. "Everyday Life Information Seeking: Approaching Information Seeking in the Context of 'Way of Life.'" *LISR* 17, no. 3 (1995): 259–94.

———. "Information Behavior and Information Practice: Reviewing the 'Umbrella Concepts' of Information Seeking Studies." *Library Quarterly* 77, no. 2 (2007): 109–32.

Schofield-Tomschin, Sherry, and Mary A. Littrell. "Textile Handcraft Guild Participation: A Conduit to Successful Aging." *Clothing and Textiles Research Journal* 19, no. 2 (2001): 41–51.

Singh, Andrea Menefee, and Anita Kelles-Viitanen, eds. *Invisible Hands: Women in Home-Based Production*. New Delhi: Sage, 1987.

Spink, Amanda, and Charles Cole, eds. *New Directions in Human Information Behavior*. Dordrecht: Springer, 2006.

Stalker, L. Lynda Harling. "Wool and Needles in My Casket: Knitting As a Habit Among Rural Newfoundland Women." Master's thesis, Memorial University of Newfoundland, 2000.

Talja, Sanna. "Information Sharing in Academic Communities: Types and Levels of Collaboration in Information Seeking and Use." *New Review of Information Behaviour Research* 3 (2002): 143–60.

Talja, Sanna, and Pamela J. McKenzie. "Editors' Introduction: Special Issue on Discursive Approaches to Information Seeking in Context." *Library Quarterly* 77, no. 2 (2007): 97-108.

Talja, Sanna, and Preben Hansen. "Information Sharing." In Spink and Cole, *New Directions in Human Information Behavior*, 113-34.

Torsney, Cheryl B., and Judy Elsey. *Quilt Culture: Tracing the Pattern*. Columbia: University of Missouri Press, 1994.

Tuominen, Kimmo. "User-Centered Discourse: An Analysis of the Subject Positions of the User and the Librarian." *Library Quarterly* 67, no. 4 (October 1997): 350-71.

Urquhart, Christine, and Alison Yeoman. "Information Behaviour of Women: Theoretical Perspectives on Gender." *Journal of Documentation* 66, no. 1 (2010): 113-39.

Vakkari, Pertti, Reijo Savolainen, and Brenda Dervin, eds. *Information Seeking in Context: Proceedings of an International Conference on Research in Information Needs, Seeking and Use in Different Contexts, 14-16 August, 1996, Tampere, Finland*. London: Taylor Graham, 1997.

Veinot, Tiffany C. "Interactive Acquisition and Sharing: Understanding the Dynamics of HIV/AIDS Information Networks." *Journal of the American Society for Information Science and Technology* 60, no. 11 (2009): 2313-32.

Williams, Sherilyn M. "Crafting Resistance: Handmade Culture as a Third-Wave Feminist Response to Consumerism." Master's thesis, University of Western Ontario, 2008.

Williamson, Kirsty. "The Information Needs and Information-Seeking Behaviour of Older Adults: An Australian Study." In Vakkari, Savolainen, and Dervin, *Information Seeking in Context*, 337-50.

Wilson, T. D. "Information Behaviour: An Inter-Disciplinary Perspective." In Vakkari, Savolainen, and Dervin, *Information Seeking in Context*, 39-50.

———. "On User Studies and Information Needs." *Journal of Documentation* 37, no. 1 (1981): 3-15.

Sharing Economies and Value Systems on the Nifty Archive

Mica Ars Hilson

Given the amount of financial speculation surrounding the internet and, more specifically, the vast amount of money earned by online pornography, it is remarkable to note that nearly all of gay erotic fiction online is available to be read for free and brings no monetary profit for the writers who submit stories or the webmasters who host story archive sites. The Nifty Archive, which since 2001 has been listed as a "tax-exempt charity" by the IRS, has taken an especially firm line on its non-profit status; its "About the Nifty Archive" page asserts that:

> No one receives any compensation for or personal benefit from maintaining the Archive. Readers do not pay to access stories; authors do not pay to display stories; websites which host the Archive must make it accessible to all and do not pay for the content; stories are not obscured with banner advertising in and around them. The Archive does not own any of the stories and does not sell them or license them to others. All webhosting graciously is donated. Some readers help defray the incidental costs for which we are extremely grateful and hope that more readers will help in the future.[1]

Thus, one of the obvious questions that the Nifty Archive presents is: why would anyone, much less thousands of people, write gay erotic fiction for free? This question can, I think, be more easily answered if we rephrase it slightly, as "if they don't expect to get paid, then what do the authors of online gay erotic fiction hope to get out of writing and posting their work?"

---

1   "About the Nifty Archive," *Nifty Archive*, last modified March 7, 2001, http://www.nifty.org/nifty/about.html.

Nearly all of the stories posted to the Nifty Archive include some kind of prefatory or closing remarks that provide some clues to the authors' objectives. These remarks may vary, but with very few exceptions, they include a request for reader feedback, specifically positive feedback—for example, "If you enjoyed the story I love getting feedback about what turned you on at Johnny.manipulator@gmail.com,"[2] or "Like all authors of gay erotic stories, I love feedback, particularly from guys or gals who liked the story,"[3] or "I'd like to recieve [sic] feed back from fellow perverts at robert.glynn@yahoo.com."[4] Even though they apparently expect no monetary payment for their work, these authors still express a hope that their stories will serve as a means of exchange—in this case, an exchange of words for words, rather than an exchange of words for money. Some authors are quite blunt about this expectation of exchange, even demanding to be "paid"—that is, to be paid compliments—in advance of future installments of their serialized stories; for instance, "Readers, if you want me to continue this Christmas tale of two cousins give me some feedback."[5]

So what does this much-desired "positive feedback" look like? Since the Nifty Archive does not provide a forum for readers to publicly post their feedback on stories, instead relying on readers to contact individual authors privately, it is difficult to know precisely what feedback specific stories on that archive received. However, many newer gay erotic fiction websites include some form of "message boards" which allow readers to post their comments at the bottom of the story page, and in these comment sections, some clear trends emerge. Take for example the first five comments posted on an especially well-received story submitted to the Narcissus Cursed Men Collection (or NCMC), a gay erotic fiction archive specializing in stories depicting mind control (MC) and other non-consensual (NC) mental or physical transformations of men (see sidebar). These comments provide very little concrete "feedback"—none of the five commenters specifies exactly *what* he likes about the story—but they go out of their way to convey excitement,

---

2 johnnymanipulator, "Arse Whisperer," *Nifty Archive*, posted April 7, 2007, http://nifty.nisusnet.com/nifty/gay/authoritarian/arse-whisperer/arse-whisperer-1.
3 Tom Borden, "My Penis," *Nifty Archive*, September 14, 2007, http://nifty.nisusnet.com/nifty/gay/incest/my-penis/my-penis-1.
4 Robert Glynn, "Father-Son Talk," *Nifty Archive*, April 25, 2007, http://nifty.nisusnet.com/nifty/gay/urination/father-son-talk.
5 The Rumpranger, "Christmas Cocks," *Nifty Archive*, December 4, 2008, http://nifty.nisusnet.com/nifty/gay/incest/christmas-cocks/christmas-cocks-1. Clearly, this author did receive the reader feedback he solicited, since he produced 26 more installments over the story between December 2008 and May 2010.

through exclamation points, capitalization, and emoticons.[6] Even though they are posting on a public message board, most of the commenters address their verbal ejaculations directly to the author, performing their intense enjoyment of his story for his implicit gratification. One of the five respondents listed above also makes a request that can be found in the comment section of nearly every story on the NCMC (and most other gay erotic fiction message boards): "Please give us more!!" This kind of comment is made even after stories which have fairly definitive endings (and would thus be difficult to serialize or spin off into a sequel), a convention which suggests to me just how crucial the expression of desire is to the production of online gay erotic fiction. The commenting reader effusively expresses his desire for more words (of erotic fiction) from the author, but the author also conventionally expresses his desire for words (of positive feedback) from his readers, albeit in a much cooler tone.

Comments

* NIPPLESLUTS
09:01 on 2009-09-19

Fantastic story!
reply

* NIPPLESLUTS
10:13 on 2009-09-19

Wow! One of your best. Wow!
reply

* NIPPLESLUTS
13:28 on 2009-09-19 by rubberdoguk

WOW..................... :Ob.................
reply

* NIPPLESLUTS
14:04 on 2009-09-19 by greekboy

Great story man!!!! Please give us more!!
reply

* NIPPLESLUTS
18:34 on 2009-09-19 by David

FUCKIN' HOT, man!
reply

The sheer size of the Nifty Archive has helped to perpetuate the flow of desire production; with roughly 300 new stories a week, and tens of thousands of individual readers—contributing to a reported 50 million page views in 2009 alone—there are always enough readers clamoring for more, and there is always enough new material to feed their desire. Yet, from a design standpoint, the Nifty Archive doesn't seem built to engender this kind of author-centered, recognition-based economy of desire; rather, it decenters and obscures the identity of the author. Practically every online gay erotic fiction archive designed in the past ten years includes several standard features that facilitate the reader's communication with a given author and his consumption of that author's work—the archive directory lists author names beside story titles, is searchable by author, and includes hyperlinks to the author's e-mail address. The main directory pages of the Nifty Archive, however, have used the same basic design since the mid-1990s and only list stories by title, file size, and date posted; to find the name of the author, prospective

---

6   Absman420, "Nipplesluts," *The Narcissus Cursed Men Collection*, Septebmer 19, 2009, http://www.eroticgayhypnosis.com/ncmc/stories/story00853.html.

readers must actually open the story and search its text for some attribution. Because most of the stories on the Nifty Archive are posted as .txt files, rather than coded in HTML, they do not allow hyperlinks, so readers cannot simply click on the page to respond to the author or follow links to his other stories. In 1997, the Nifty Archive made an attempt to introduce the author function so prominent on other gay erotic fiction websites—without totally redesigning the Nifty Archive's own architecture—by adding an alphabetized listing of prolific authors and providing links to these authors' stories. The "Prolific Authors" directory[7] joined the two search methods the Nifty Archive had already provided its users, a listing of stories posted within the past week, titled "What's New," and the main directory of all stories on the website, divided by category, then subcategory, then sorted in reverse chronological order, with the newest stories listed on the top of each subcategory directory.

There are several things worth noting about the effects of this website architecture. One is that it is often incredibly difficult to relocate a story one has already read on the Nifty Archive; unless the story comes from a "prolific author," one must recall not only the story's title, but the subcategory it is filed under and the approximate date it was posted there. Which is to say that, whether intentionally or unintentionally, the Nifty Archive discourages practices of rereading and, instead, encourages the user to direct his attention to whatever is new at the moment. This effect is not unique to the Nifty Archive; a number of other gay erotic fiction websites utilize a message board format which lists the most recent posts first, and this general emphasis on novelty might serve to further facilitate the flow of desire-production between authors and commenting readers.

As the reader searches for something new, another major effect of the Nifty Archive's decentering of the author comes into play—its somewhat arbitrary category and subcategory classifications take on an air of special importance. On the "What's New" page, stories are grouped by category, then by subcategory, both listed alphabetically. Since the listing of "What's New" is updated roughly every day, this organizational structure is the page's one constant element; hence, readers looking for "gay/urination" stories know to scroll down to nearly the bottom of the page, just below "gay/sf-fantasy" stories and just above "gay/young-friends" stories.

Updated daily, listing story titles (but obscuring author names), and grouped into sections always arranged in the same order, the "What's New" page thus bears some significant resemblances to a newspaper. Benedict Anderson describes the newspaper as perhaps the most vivid example of a text that creates a "secular, historically clocked, imagined community," as

---

7   "Stories by Prolific Net Authors," *Nifty Archive*, last modified April 18, 2013, http://www.nifty.org/nifty/frauthors.html.

the regular, "ceremonial" reading of the newspaper is "performed in silent privacy, in the lair of the skull. Yet each communicant is well aware that the ceremony he performs is being replicated simultaneously by thousands (or millions) of others of whose existence he is confident, yet of whose identity he has not the slightest notion."[8] The "Mission Statement" of the Nifty Archive indicates a wish to *reflect* a queer community of writers—to "Provide a generally accessible, representative collection of the diverse hopes, dreams, aspirations, fantasies, and experiences of the Queer Community as expressed on the Internet through stories and information as a resource for research, exploration, and scholarship"[9]—but it is also designed to *create* a queer community of readers, each privately but collectively and relatively simultaneously perusing the [What's] News.

Unlike a newspaper, however, the Nifty Archive does not relegate any of the [What's] News to the "back page," and the "privileged" position on the top of the page is, because of the alphabetical organization of the main directories and subdirectories, devoted to a theme that is probably valued by only a small minority of the site's users: "Bestiality."[10] By way of contrast, we might note how a website like Literotica.com—which consists primarily of heterosexual erotic stories, but also includes some stories depicting sex between men—hails its readers as discriminating *consumers* of erotic fiction. As Susanna Paasonen explains:

> *Literotica is very much concerned with definitions of a good story. . . . Readers have the opportunity to rate and give feedback on the submissions and the top stories are presented in separate listings. Stories are also rated in numerous competitions such as a Valentine's Day contest and monthly and annual author awards, and are ranked according to their number of downloads.*[11]

The Nifty Archive, on the other hand, has shown no interest in identifying which stories are the "best" or "most popular," establishing collective standards for "rating" stories, or even in promoting "good"

---

8   Benedict Anderson, *Imagined Communities*, rev. ed. (London: Verso, 2006), 35.
9   "Nifty Archive Mission Statement," *Nifty Archive*, last modified September 1, 2002, http://www.nifty.org/nifty/mission.html.
10 At the very least, we might say that relatively few Bestiality stories are contributed to the Nifty Archive; as of July 2009, there were only 1,650 Bestiality stories in the archive, as opposed to well over 100,000 Gay Male stories.
11 Susanna Paasonen, "Good Amateurs: Erotica Writing and Notions of Quality," in *Porn.com: Making Sense of Online Pornography*, ed. Feona Attwood (New York: Peter Lang, 2010), 142.

writing.[12] The only way that the Nifty Archive singles out certain authors over others is through its "Prolific Authors" page, and here, it's the *quantity* of contributed material and not its (perceived) quality that matters.

Paasonen argues that many of the writers who contribute to Literotica view themselves as aspiring professionals, and "Such aspirations are supported by the contests and top listings of Literotica,"[13] as well as the edited volume, *The Very Best of Literotica.com*, published in 2001. Unsurprisingly then, the most polished stories that are posted on Literotica often eventually disappear, as (presumably) the author has managed to sell the story into print publication. By contrast, the Nifty Archive discourages writers who hope to ultimately (re)move their work from the free website and into a book, stipulating that "The only constraint that the Archive places on authors is that permission to display their stories may not be rescinded for commercial purposes without compensating the Archive."[14]

The very names and URLs of the two sites reveal quite a bit about their different attitudes towards user-generated fiction. While Literotica.com links together two terms that connote quality and class ("literature" rather than plain "fiction"; "erotica" rather than lower-grade "porn") with a URL ending signifying commerce, Nifty.org identifies itself as a fundamentally noncommercial website which aims to objectively archive stories,[15] without giving special preference to one style of story over others. Paasonen finds that the Literotica rating system, on the other hand, facilitates its readers' general preference for romantic stories that "focus on the development of relationships that are emotional as well as sexual"[16] and general disdain for stories that depict scatological content and "overall unpleasantness." For instance, one story on Litererotica which "depicts a wedding night where the best man turns the virgin bride into the 'nastiest, sluttiest whore' with a fondness for

---

12   A couple of individual users have posted their thoughts on what constitutes "good" and "bad" erotic writing, but there are relatively few of these documents, and they are buried in a fairly obscure directory; see "Resources for Authors," *Nifty Archive*, last modified July 24, 2011, http://nifty.nisusnet.com/nifty/resources.html. By contrast, Literotica includes a link to a rather copious page full of "Writer's Resources" in bold print on the main stories page; see "Erotic Stories and Pictures Index," http://www.literotica.com/stories/index.php.
13   Paasonen, "Good Amateurs," 142.
14   "About the Nifty Archive." http://www.nifty.org/nifty/about.html.
15   Recently, starting in 2009, the Nifty Archive has taken some moves in a more commercial direction, including banner advertisements for gay male pornographic pay websites and linking to a website where users can buy Nifty Archive-branded T-shirts and tote bags.
16   Paasonen, "Good Amateurs," 144.

rectum licking" elicited reader comments calling it "'putrid scum' and 'sick shit'" and even advising the writer "to check into an institution."[17]

The Nifty Archive, on the other hand, devotes a whole subcategory to "shit"—or rather, to scatology in general—and is set up so that the scatological stories listed under "Urination" are valued no less (and no more) than the romantic stories in a subcategory like "Relationships."[18] Though there is some clear overlap between the classificatory system used by the Nifty Archive and the taxonomic conventions of LGBT identity politics, as four of the five main branches of the story archive directly correspond to the four pillars of LGBT, the archive's refusal to filter out the more sordid subgenres,[19] coupled with its inclusion of "Bestiality" as a fifth major category, marks a radical departure from the self-presentation favored by the mainstream LGBT movement. Scrolling down the "Recent Updates to the Nifty Archive" page—listed by filename, which includes main category and subcategory information, along with the story title—one sees several "bestiality" stories, followed by several "bisexual/incest" stories, then "gay/adult-friends" stories, followed immediately by "gay/adult-youth" stories. Of these, only "gay/adult-friends" could be considered the least bit homonormative; seeing this more conventional style of gay erotic story embedded within listings of stories depicting pederasty, bestiality, and bisexual incest is like being transported back to the pages of 1960s gay pulp fiction, where all the books that catered to erotic tastes which deviated from the heterosexual male norm were lumped together into one advertising section.

Although the Nifty Archive relies on the terms of sexual identity for its primary directory system, it also gestures toward another mode of classification, with "story codes" based around sexual acts and genders of participants, which was developed on the Alt.sex.stories Usenet groups in the early

---

17 Ibid., 144–45.
18 The Nifty Archive's design offers a particularly extreme example of an egalitarian approach practiced by many online erotic fiction archives; even Litererotica opts for a similar alphabetical listing of story categories on its main page, which ironically results in the category "Anal" occupying the top position.
19 To be sure, the Nifty Archive does have some policies, albeit slightly nebulous ones, about types of stories it will not include, but these restrictions have much more to do with depictions of violence rather than representations of sexual perversity. On its "Submission Guidelines" page, the Nifty Archive indicates that it will generally restrict stories representing "rape or coercion of minors, abusive situations involving minors, graphic violence, unwilling participants, dangerous sexual acts, depiction of minors being photographed for distribution, [and/or] suicide or attempted suicide without consequences." See "Nifty Archive Submission Guidelines," *Nifty Archive*, last modified September 9, 2012, http://www.nifty.org/nifty/submission.html.

1990s. In the "story codes" system, which is reprinted in full on one page of the Nifty Archive and is still employed by a few authors who contribute to the archive, the story's main sexual acts, plus the genders and ages of the characters who participate in those acts, are indicated in parenthesis below the title; thus, a story which depicts anal sex between a father and his two teenage sons might be listed as: "(M/B/B inc anal)". The main page of the Nifty Archive incorporates the non-identitarian logic of the story codes system when, next to the link for "Gay Male" stories, it includes the definition "Stories involving Male/Male(/. . .)" Similarly, even if the stories on the Nifty Archive don't often follow the letter of the "story codes" system, many still observe its spirit; in the stories I examined in my dissertation chapter on the Nifty Archive, none of the characters explicitly identified as gay.[20] In a few of the stories, certain characters anxiously wonder if they might be gay, but this question quickly gets put aside so that the men in the story can continue un-self-consciously "opening up" to one another. Ironically, then, in these stories, which the Nifty Archive identifies as "gay male," gay self-identification is represented as inhibiting (rather than facilitating) sexual contact and communication between men.

Unlike 1970s and 1980s gay print fiction (but rather like 1960s gay pulp fiction), these stories rarely revolve around a clear narrative of identity formation. The feedback relation between authors and readers might play an important role in online gay erotic fiction's general resistance to that kind of narrative, which demands a firm trajectory and closure. As I noted earlier, some authors deliberately leave their stories unresolved, offering to continue only if reader feedback demands it, and even authors who write single-part stories with clear conclusions are sometimes persuaded to write a second installment. Furthermore, the feedback system provides incentive for authors to write relatively short stories or installments; whereas very long stories might put off the more casual reader, limiting the potential readership, shorter stories might draw a wider array of comments, and a story posted in short installments is likely to garner multiple comments for each installment. These formats, short stories and short installments shaped by reader feedback, perhaps lend themselves to representations of exchanges between men (which can be continued by popular demand) rather than to more novelistic tales of gay identity formation, with relatively linear narratives and fixed endpoints. Thus, although it would be wrong to assume that the medium of online gay erotic fiction always determines the genre's content, it is valuable to view these stories in the context of desiring exchanges and interactions between authors, readers, and website designers.

---

20 See Mica Hilson, "From Pulp to Plasma Screen: A History of Gay Erotic Fiction, 1965–Present" (PhD diss., Indiana University, 2010), 221–59.

Bibliography

Anderson, Benedict. *Imagined Communities*. Rev. ed. London: Verso, 2006.

Deleuze, Gilles and Felix Guattari. *Anti-Oedipus: Capitalism and Schizophrenia*. Minneapolis: Minnesota University Press, 1983.

Hilson, Mica. "From Pulp to Plasma Screen: A History of Gay Erotic Fiction, 1965–Present." PhD diss., Indiana University, 2010.

Paasonen, Susanna. "Good Amateurs: Erotica Writing and Notions of Quality." In *Porn.com: Making Sense of Online Pornography*, edited by Feona Attwood, 138–154. New York: Peter Lang, 2010.

Part Six
Archive

Police/Archives

Steven Maynard[1]

> *A new optics, first of all: an organ of generalized and constant surveillance; everything must be observed, seen, transmitted: organization of a police; institution of a system of archives (with individual files), establishment of a panopticism.*
>
> ~Michel Foucault, "The Punitive Society"[2]

In his lectures on the theme of punitive society at the Collège de France in 1972–1973, Michel Foucault prompted his audience to consider the relationship between the police and a system of archives. It is a relationship—which I will call "police/archives"—that has received remarkably little attention in the archival literature. The reason for this may be that when Foucault and archives are invoked in archival writing, it is done in a very specific way. As Joan Schwartz and Terry Cook explain, "Cultural theorists, most notably Michel Foucault and Jacques Derrida, see 'the archive' as a central metaphorical construct upon which to fashion their perspectives on human knowledge,

---

1   Editors' note: this paper was previously published in "Special Section on Queer Archives," ed. Rebekca Sheffield and Marcel Barriault, special issue, *Archivaria* 68, no. 7 (2010): 159–182.

2   Michel Foucault, "The Punitive Society," in *The Essential Works of Foucault, 1954–1984, Volume 1: Ethics: Subjectivity and Truth*, ed. Paul Rabinow, trans. Robert Hurley (New York: New Press, 1997), 55. I have amended the English translation of Foucault's course summary in several places based on my reading of the original French text. In *Essential Works*, "*surveillance*" is translated as "oversight," an odd choice given the explicit and frequent reference to surveillance in Foucault's work. "*Une police*" is rendered as "a police force," a much too limited idea of what Foucault intended by "police." "*Un système d'archives*" becomes "a system of records" when I believe Foucault meant exactly what he wrote—archives; he references the records, "individual files," parenthetically. See Michel Foucault, *Résumé des cours, 1970–1982* (Paris: Julliard, 1989), 49.

memory, and power."[3] Within queer studies, which are heavily influenced by cultural/critical theory, the archive most often also appears as a metaphorical construct. For example, Ann Cvetkovich's book, *An Archive of Feelings*, is an interesting case in point; while she is more sensitive than many queer theorists to what she cleverly calls "actually existing archives," her embrace of Derrida means that the archive as a metaphorical or psychoanalytical construct (what she variously terms an "archive of emotion" and the "archives of trauma"), is front and centre in her work.[4] To take another example, in his study of New York's post-war queer art world, Gavin Butt opts for a Derridean-derived approach to read the "absences within the archival record," a method, he suggests—in something of an understatement—that "brings me close to the limits of conventional archival procedures for producing historical knowledge."[5]

Ann Laura Stoler has recently commented:

> One could argue that 'the archive' for historians [and, we can add, for many professional archivists] and 'the Archive' for cultural [including queer] theorists have been wholly different analytic objects: for the former, a body of documents and the institutions that house them, for the latter a metaphoric invocation for any corpus of selective collections and the longings that the acquisitive quests for the primary, originary, and untouched entail.[6]

---

3   Joan M. Schwartz and Terry Cook, "Archives, Records, and Power: The Making of Modern Memory," *Archival Science* 2, no. 1-2 (2002): 4.

4   Ann Cvetkovich, *An Archive of Feelings: Trauma, Sexuality, and Lesbian Public Cultures* (Durham, NC: Duke University Press, 2003). See also, Nicholas de Villiers, review of *Queer Archives in a Queer Time and Place: Transgender Bodies, Subcultural Lives*, by Judith Halberstam, *Cultural Critique* 66 (Spring 2007): 179-83, http://www.jstor.org/stable/4539813. Queer theoretical approaches to "the Archive" have not entirely supplanted earlier, community-based traditions of lesbian/gay archives. For several recent examples of less metaphorical queer archives, see Sue Donnelly, "Coming Out in the Archives: The Hall-Carpenter Archives at the London School of Economics," *History Workshop Journal* 66 (Autumn 2008): 180-84; and Ryan Conrad, ed., *Future of the Past: Reviving the Queer Archives* (Portland, ME: Moth Press, 2009).

5   Gavin Butt, "Whispering in the Archive," in *Between You and Me: Queer Disclosures in the New York Art World, 1948-1963* (Durham, NC: Duke University Press, 2005), 16-21.

6   Ann Laura Stoler, *Along the Archival Grain: Epistemic Anxieties and Colonial Common Sense* (Princeton, NJ: Princeton University Press, 2009), 45. Stoler goes on to point out that it is of course entirely possible for a scholar to use both meanings of the archive in their work. Stoler's own study is exemplary in this regard,

In the now commonplace distinction between "the archive" as institution and "the Archive" as metaphor, Foucault is routinely aligned with the latter.[7] But Foucault also had a less metaphoric, more material understanding of archives, one perhaps more congenial to archivists and historians, and one more conducive to thinking about the police/archives conjuncture.

This paper will initiate an exploration of the police/archives nexus. It begins by sketching an alternate view of Foucault's relationship to the archive. It will then suggest some ways we can begin to conceptualize police/archives, followed by a testing of the framework against an actual police archive—the Toronto Police Museum—since it was my experience of trying to do queer historical research at the Museum that prompted me to think about police/archives in the first place. The final section will touch on the politics of police/archives, particularly in relation to issues of public access, police accountability, and sexual identity.

Foucault in the Archives

In discussions of "the Archive," Michel Foucault is often linked to Jacques Derrida whose "archive fever" is perhaps the epitome of the archive as metaphor.[8] It is a strange pairing, given the long-standing political and intellectual *différence* between the two French thinkers, not the least being the disjuncture between Derrida's Freudian impression of the archive and Foucault's deep skepticism toward psychoanalysis. The more instructive pairing vis-à-vis

---

combining an appreciation for the archive as colonial imaginary with detailed research into the archival practices of colonial rule.

7   For a recent example, see Kathleen Biddick, "Doing Dead Time for the Sovereign: Archive, Abandonment, Performance," *Rethinking History* 13 (June 2009): 137-51. Biddick's article is a mind-bending blend of the archive as metaphorical and hyper-theoretical, mixed with a Foucauldian appreciation for the institutional, including an account of Biddick's use of Dublin's Mountjoy Prison as an experimental performance space. Biddick's installation at Mountjoy—imagined to exist (metaphorically) in between the prison and some place she calls the "National Archive"—sought to interrupt the Panopticon as a "powerful means by which the spectacle of abandonment can be momentarily suspended by problematizing it by threading thought through space and time along coordinates different from the optics and scriptures of political theology" (149). I would suggest that despite her attention to the prison and archive as actual spaces, Biddick gives even Derrida a run for his metaphorical money.

8   Jacques Derrida, *Archive Fever: A Freudian Impression*, trans. Eric Prenowitz (Chicago: University of Chicago Press, 1996). For a brilliant deconstruction of the Derridean archive, see Carolyn Steedman, *Dust: The Archive and Cultural History* (New Brunswick, NJ: Rutgers University Press, 2001).

Foucault and "the Archive" is with Gilles Deleuze who, in 1986, crowned Foucault "a new archivist." Deleuze recalled Foucault's use of "archive" in his archaeological works.[9] In *The Archaeology of Knowledge*, for example, Foucault conjoined "archive" to a set of other complex terms and concepts, such as "the statement," to designate the bounded discursive space that set the range and limits on the totality of "statements," understood as encompassing things and events, in any given historical formation.[10] Foucault explained it this way:

> *By this term [archive] I do not mean the sum of all the texts that a culture has kept upon its person as documents attesting to its own past, or as evidence of a continuing identity; nor do I mean the institutions, which, in a given society, make it possible to record and preserve those discourses that one wishes to remember and keep in circulation. On the contrary . . . [t]he archive is first the law of what can be said, the system that governs the appearance of statements as unique events.*[11]

Foucault's use of "archive" here is abstract, or as Eric Paras suggests, it is "a term of art for Foucault."[12] Abstract or artful, either way it is rather far removed from the real world of most practising archivists. It was, however, in keeping with the high level of theoretical abstraction at which Foucault worked in the mid- to late-1960s, and it is a reminder that Foucault bears some responsibility for the subsequent yoking of his name to "the Archive." At the same time, one wonders whether Deleuze did his old friend any favour by anointing Foucault a "new archivist" in 1986, a move that reintroduced and

---

9   Gilles Deleuze, "A New Archivist," in *Foucault*, trans. Sean Hand (Minneapolis: University of Minnesota Press, 2006), 1-22.

10 When May writes with reference to the archaeological works, "the archives Foucault describes are complex," this is surely an understatement. Todd May, *The Philosophy of Foucault* (Montreal: McGill-Queen's University Press, 2006), 121.

11 Michel Foucault, "The Historical *a priori* and the Archive," in *The Archaeology of Knowledge*, trans. A. M. Sheridan Smith (London: Routledge, 2002), 145. In the year prior to the publication of *The Archaeology*, Foucault explained it in part this way: "I shall call an archive, not the totality of texts that have been preserved by a civilization or the set of traces that could be salvaged from its downfall, but the series of rules which determine in a culture the appearance and disappearance of statements." Michel Foucault, "On the Archaeology of the Sciences: Response to the Epistemology Circle," in *The Essential Works of Foucault, 1954-1984, Volume 2: Aesthetics, Method, and Epistemology*, ed. James D. Faubion, trans. Robert Hurley (New York: New Press, 1998), 309.

12 Eric Paras, *Foucault 2.0: Beyond Power and Knowledge* (New York: Other Press, 2006), 33. Paras begins his own study with the chapter, "Into the Archive," by which I believe he means the Foucault archive.

recirculated "the Archive" long after Foucault had more or less ceased to use the term in the same fashion.

Even during his archaeological period, archive could have a different meaning for Foucault. During an interview in June of 1967, two years before the appearance of *The Archaeology of Knowledge*, he was asked: "You surrender to the characteristic passion of the historian, who wants to respond to the endless murmur of the archives?" "Yes," Foucault replied, "because my object is not language but the archive." He was careful to qualify what he meant by archive—"the accumulated existence of discourses ... the analysis of discourse in its archival form"—but this was not yet the elaborate, rarified archive of *The Archaeology*. The interview, "On the Ways of Writing History," was clearly about the kinds of archives historians get excited over and in which Foucault spent a great deal of his working life.[13] Two years later, describing his research methods for *History of Madness* as part of his candidature to the Collège de France, Foucault explained:

> *It was necessary to consult a body of archives comprising decrees, rules, hospital and prison registers, and acts of jurisprudence. It was in the Arsenal or the Archives nationales that I undertook the analysis of a knowledge whose visible body is neither scientific nor theoretical discourse, nor literature, but a daily and regularized practice.*[14]

Here, then, we have archives as actual sites of research and archival knowledge represented not as theoretical discourse but as concrete *practice*.

Archives and libraries were among Foucault's favourite places, right up there with leather bars and S/M bathhouses. Beginning in the early 1950s and for the next thirty years, Foucault worked almost daily at the Bibliothèque nationale de France (BNF). This was the old national library located on rue Richelieu where Foucault could be found in la salle Labrouste, at his usual desk on the *hémicycle*, the slightly elevated space that looks out over the main reading room with its central aisle separating rows of long tables subdivided into individual study spaces.[15] When not at the BNF, Foucault frequented other libraries and archives. In the Archives de la Bastille at the Bibliothèque de l'Arsenal, Foucault discovered the dossiers of the "lunatics" and libertines, the prostitutes and the "perverts," confined in the Bastille and

---

13 Foucault, "On the Ways of Writing History," in *Essential Works of Foucault, Volume 2*, 289–90.

14 Quoted in David Macey, *The Lives of Michel Foucault: A Biography* (New York, 1993), 94.

15 Ibid., 49. For a peek into la salle Labrouste, the BNF offers a virtual tour, http://multimedia.bnf.fr/visiterichelieu/architecture/as.htm.

the Hôpital général, often locked up there by the police. These dossiers make up part of the evidentiary base of Foucault's magisterial *History of Madness*.[16]

It was also in the archives of the Bastille that Foucault found the records of the Lieutenant of the Police along with the well-known *lettres de cachet*. Foucault proposed a book based upon the letters as early as 1964, a project that would come to fruition in 1982 when he, along with historian Arlette Farge, published *Le Désordre des familles: lettres de cachet des Archives de la Bastille*.[17] Primary historical sources on the police, along with criminal notices from old Paris newspapers, turn up in his *Discipline and Punish* where they constitute an "'ignoble' archives," *ignoble* because these texts did not chronicle kings but documented the lower orders.[18] Foucault also conducted extensive archival research in the medico-legal case files of parricides, hermaphrodites, and countless other "abnormals," called upon to confess to sexologists and psychoanalysts their sexual sins, and whose documentary traces constitute what in the introductory volume of *The History of Sexuality*, Foucault called the "great archive of the pleasures of sex."[19] We are already some distance from "the Archive."

It was likely in the BNF that Foucault first came down with archive fever, although decidedly not of the Derridean variety. The pleasures of the archive induced what Foucault called a "feverish laziness," the burning desire to do nothing other than archival research or to loaf away one's days in a library. As he explained to the audience listening to his lecture at the Collège de France on 7 January 1976, feverish laziness is "a character trait of people who love libraries, documents, references, dusty manuscripts, texts that have never been read, books which, no sooner printed, were closed and then slept on the shelves and were only taken down centuries later . . . and, as you well know, its external signs are found at the foot of the page."[20] Archive fever produced, not, as for Derrida, a subconscious and always-already doomed desire for the originary or, worse, a violent playing out of the death drive,[21]

---

16 Michel Foucault, *History of Madness*, ed. Jean Khalfa, trans. Jonathan Murphy and Jean Khalfa (London: Routledge, 2006).

17 Arlette Farge and Michel Foucault, *Le Désordre des familles: lettres de cachet des Archives de la Bastille* (Paris: Gallimard, 1982).

18 Michel Foucault, *Discipline and Punish: The Birth of the Prison*, trans. Alan Sheridan (New York: Vintage, 1979), 191.

19 Michel Foucault, *The History of Sexuality, Volume 1: An Introduction*, trans. Robert Hurley (New York: Vintage, 1980), 63.

20 Michel Foucault, *"Society Must Be Defended": Lectures at the Collège de France, 1975–1976*, ed. Mauro Bertani and Alessandro Fontana, trans. David Macey (New York: Picador, 2003), 5.

21 Derrida writes, "What is at issue here . . . is the violence of the archive itself, *as archive, as archival violence*"; he then goes on to claim: "The death drive is not a

but, for Foucault, a longing to pursue archival research simply for the love of dusty old documents, generating perhaps nothing more than "useless erudition." Of course, Foucault did not really think archival knowledge was useless. He was toying with his audience, as he often did during his lectures, in this instance feigning worry over what might appear to be the "fragmented, repetitive, and discontinuous" character of his researches over the previous four or five years. Do not blame him for this, Foucault teased, for he had a bad case of archive fever.[22]

There is no denying Foucault loved archival documents and dusty manuscripts. The *lettres de cachet*, written on parchment or rag paper, were brittle and often in a poor state of preservation; he painstakingly copied them out by hand over the years. As David Macey suggests, Foucault's research methods "gave him a physical familiarity with his chosen texts."[23] Foucault disdained photocopying which, he told a friend, destroyed the charm of the text, "which becomes almost lifeless when you no longer have the printed page before your eyes and in your hands."[24] Archival research had other physical dimensions for Foucault. In his remarkable essay, "The Lives of Infamous Men," Foucault described how reading historical documents in the archive gave "rise to a certain effect of beauty mixed with dread," and evoked in him a feeling of "intensity," a "physical" sensation that "stirred more fibers within me" than great works of literature.[25] Foucault's tactile attachment to the document, his physical experience of the archive, capture well the premise of this paper that for Foucault the archive was much more than a metaphor. This is something French historians have understood about Foucault for some time. Foucault haunts the pages of Arlette Farge's evocative account (*Le Goût de l'archive*) of the rapport between the historian and archival research, in which

---

principle. . . . It is what we will call, later on, *le mal d'archive*, 'archive fever'." Derrida, *Archive Fever*, 7 and 12.

22 Foucault, "*Society Must Be Defended*," 5 and 4.
23 Macey, *The Lives of Michel Foucault*, 454.
24 David Macey, *Michel Foucault* (London: Reaktion, 2004), 67.
25 Michel Foucault, "The Lives of Infamous Men," in *The Essential Works of Foucault, 1954–1984, Volume 3: Power*, ed. James Faubion, trans. Robert Hurley (New York: New Press, 2000), 164 and 158. I elaborate on Foucault's experience in the archives in my forthcoming study, *Infamous Men: Perversion and Policing in Toronto, 1880–1940*, which takes Foucault's essay as one of its principle inspirations. "The Lives of Infamous Men" was also the focus of a major exhibition this past summer at the Bibliothèque municipale de Lyon. See "Archives de l'infamie, une collection imaginaire," http://www.bm-lyon.fr/expo/09/foucault/presentation.php. See also Collectif Maurice Florence, *Archives de l'infamie* (Paris: Prairies Ordinaires, 2009).

she discusses *"le réel de l'archive."*[26] (Stoler cites *Le Goût*, noting its affinity with her own notion of "the pulse of the archive."[27]) Or consider Philippe Artières who, with his own impressive historiographical output and as a member of the editorial team of the Michel Foucault Archives, has done perhaps more than anyone to solder the link between Foucault and archives as *lieux et espaces*.[28]

Tasty, murmuring, pulsating, stirring; a locale, a physical space in which one works and is fully embodied; a "real" experience of passion and prolonged feverish intensity—all this, for me, is the Foucauldian archive. It also helps to explain Foucault's down-to-earth approach to the archive as an institution.

Archives as "Complete and Austere Institutions"

Foucault took a sharp turn to the left following his archaeological works of the mid- to late-1960s, and especially after 1968, entering his *période gauchiste*, in which he began to rigorously root his theoretical and historical work in political activity, in the genealogical critique of, and concrete struggle against, institutions enmeshed in practices of power/knowledge.[29] Foucault's work on prisons comes most readily to mind,[30] but this 1970s period of radical, political engagement also had important implications for Foucault's understanding of the archive. For one thing, Foucault traded in the rarified "Archive" for a more material and historical institution. Unlike Derrida who

---

26 Farge also writes, *"l'archive entretient toujours un nombre infini de relations au réel."* Closely connected to the archive's relation to the real is a tie to the "truth" it is imagined to store: *"L'archive ne dit peut-être pas la vérité, mais elle dit de la vérité, au sens où l'entendait Michel Foucault, c'est-à-dire dans cette façon unique qu'elle a d'exposer le Parler de l'autre, pris entre des rapports de pouvoir et lui-même, rapports que non seulement il subit, mais qu'il actualise en les verbalisant."* Arlette Farge, *Le Goût de l'archive* (Paris: Seuil, 1989), 41 and 40.

27 Stoler, *Along the Archival Grain*, 19.

28 See, for example, Philippe Artières, "Espaces d'archives," introduction to "Lieux d'archives," special issue, *Sociétés et représentations* 19 (2005); Artières, "Michel Foucault: L'Archive d'un rire," in *Questions d'archives* (Paris: IMEC, 2002). See also, Artières and Mathieu Potte-Bonneville, *D'Après Foucault: gestes, luttes, programmes* (Paris: Prairies Ordinaires, 2007).

29 On the power/knowledge dynamic, see, Foucault, *Power/Knowledge: Selected Interviews and Other Writings, 1972-1977*, ed. Colin Gordon (New York: Pantheon, 1980).

30 See Philippe Artières, Laurent Quéro, and Michelle Zancarini-Fournel, eds., *Le Groupe d'information sur les prisons: Archives d'une lutte, 1970 -1972* (Paris: IMEC, 2003).

found it impossible to *penser l'archive* in historical terms,[31] Foucault insisted that archives had a particular history, one coincident with the rise of disciplinary society during the eighteenth and nineteenth centuries. In "The Punitive Society," Foucault suggested that the class antagonisms set in motion by the emergence of industrial capitalism called forth new techniques to instill docility in rebellious workers' bodies. Labourers' subjection to factory time needed to be precisely measured, and the vagabonds and beggars who idled on the fringes of the capitalist economy had to be carefully monitored if they were to be recruited as *soldats* in a reserve army of labour or inserted into the self-perpetuating system of prison/delinquency.[32] And, so, in *Discipline and Punish* Foucault drew attention to the "whole mass of documents," to the "system of intense registration and of documentary accumulation," that policed as it produced a "meticulous archive constituted in terms of bodies and days."[33]

This is very similar to Foucault's observation with which I began this paper, which stated that the punitive society depended on the "organization of a police, [the] institution of a system of archives (with individual files), [and the] establishment of a panopticism": in a nutshell, the central elements of police/archives. Consider first the relationship Foucault suggests between the organization of the police and a system of archives. This will be abundantly clear to anyone who has done research in archival police records. In my own work, I think of the thousands of individual entries in police registers, of the Bertillon system of anthropometric measurements used to identify criminals in prison records, and of the Finger Print Section of the RCMP. These

---

31   As is so often the case with Derrida, there can be no assurance of a relationship between the signifier and the signified: "Have we ever been assured of the homogeneity, of the consistency, of the univocal relationship of any concept to a term or to such a word as 'archive'?" With no assurance about the content of the concept of archive, with no certainty about what one might be looking for in the past, there can be no history. "It is thus our impression that we can no longer ask the question of the concept, of the history of the concept, and notably of the concept of the archive. No longer, at least, in a temporal or historical modality dominated by the present or by the past." Derrida, *Archive Fever*, 33.

32   Foucault wrote: "Inadequate wages, disqualification of labor by the machine, excessive labor hours, multiple regional or local crises, prohibition of associations, mechanism of indebtment—all this leads workers into behaviors such as absenteeism, breaking of the 'hiring contract', migration, and 'irregular' living. The problem is then to attach workers firmly to the production apparatus, to settle them or move them where it needs them to be, to subject them to its rhythm, to impose the constancy or regularity on them that it requires—in short, to constitute them as a labor force." Foucault, "The Punitive Society," 33-34.

33   Foucault, *Discipline and Punish*, 189.

constitute a massive archive, the documentary base of a system that not only punished but also produced new types of individuals, such as "the criminal" and other "dangerous individuals." Much of Foucault's own work—certainly the *History of Madness* and *Discipline and Punish*—could not have been written without the police/archive. The *police as archives*, then, constitute an integral dimension of the reciprocal police/archives relationship.[34]

But I want to focus on another link Foucault sketched in the police-archives-panopticism relationship: the one between archives and panopticism, or *archives as police*. I do not mean to suggest that working in an archives is like being locked up in a prison cell (although I do recall one summer at the Archives of Ontario, researching in the case files of training schools and being sequestered in a special room with two members of the Ontario Provincial Police who were using the same records for their research, albeit for different reasons). Police/archives does not normally rely upon the presence of actual police officers in the building. Rather, police/archives operates in a more subtle fashion and in at least two different ways. The first, as the references to panopticism might suggest, is spatial/architectural. For Foucault, power/knowledge did not always take a textual form and the same holds true for police/archives.[35] A growing body of archival and historical writing looks at how the architectural layout or spatial arrangement of archives and libraries orders individuals in space so as to create a generalized and constant surveillance.[36] Probably the best-known example of this is the panoptical reading

---

34 For examples of work on the police as archives, see, Michel Rey, "Parisian Homosexuals Create a Lifestyle, 1700-1750: The Police Archives," in *'Tis Nature's Fault: Unauthorized Sexuality during the Enlightenment*, ed. Robert Purks Maccubbin (Cambridge: Cambridge University Press, 1987), 179-91. In the British context, see Chris Williams and Clive Emsley, "Beware of the Leopard?: Police Archives in Great Britain," in *Political Pressure and the Archival Record*, ed. Margaret Proctor, Michael Cook, and Caroline Williams (Chicago: Society of American Archivists, 2006), 227-235.

35 See Foucault, "Questions on Geography" and "The Eye of Power" in *Power/Knowledge*. See also the excellent collection, Jeremy W. Crampton and Stuart Elden, eds., *Space, Knowledge and Power: Foucault and Geography* (Burlington, VT: Ashgate, 2007).

36 See, for example, Eric Ketelaar, "Archival Temples, Archival Prisons: Modes of Power and Protection," *Archival Science* 2 (September 2002): 221-38; and Lilly Koltun, "The Architecture of Archives: Whose Form, What Functions?" *Archival Science* 2 (September 2002): 239-61. See also, Alistair Black, "The Library as Clinic: A Foucauldian Interpretation of British Public Library Attitudes to Social and Physical Disease, ca. 1850-1950," *Libraries & Culture* 40 (Summer 2005): 416-34; and Lewis C. Roberts, "Disciplining and Disinfecting Working-Class Readers in the Victorian Public Library," *Victorian Literature and Culture* 26 (Spring 1998): 105-32.

Figure 1: The Archive as " Complete and Austere Institution." The Metro Toronto Archives and Record Centre (now the City of Toronto Archives), September 1991. Reproduced with permission of the artist, Vid Ingelevics.

room of the British Museum (1857), but BNF's la salle Ovale performs a similar function, guaranteeing *"une surveillance plus facile."*[37] Archivists must be able to see that we researchers are using our pencils!

Second, police/archives draw their power from their status as what Foucault called "complete and austere institutions" (see Figure 1).[38] Complete institutions refer to the same thing that, in his critique of Foucault, Michael Ignatieff called "total institutions," back when he was pleased to publish articles in a journal of socialist and feminist historians.[39] In "total institutions" it is hard not to hear an echo of "total archives," that distinctly Canadian contribution to archival practice in which both public and private records, in all manner of media, often end up under the purview of a government archives. Much of the commentary on total archives has, understandably, focused on issues of archival practice, such as the potentially deleterious effect of the promiscuous mixing of different documents and media on the principle of provenance. But total archives can also help to focus our attention on one of the central characteristics of the total institution: its relationship to the state. As Laura Millar has explained, "the total archives concept grew from a recognition of the central role of the government in archival enterprise."[40] Speaking in more historical terms, Foucault pointed out how "the organization of the police apparatus in the eighteenth century"—an apparatus, we know, linked to a system of archives—"sanctioned a generalization of the disciplines that became co-extensive with the state itself."[41]

---

37   As the "virtual visit" on the BNF's website explains about la salle Ovale, *"d'un bureau central dominant la salle, un bibliothécaire peut en effet surveiller et diriger les différentes parties du service."* See http://multimedia.bnf.fr/visiterichelieu/architecture/ova_ap.htm. On the reading room of the British Museum, see http://www.britishmuseum.org/the_museum/history_and_the_building/reading_room.aspx.

38   On "complete and austere institutions," see Foucault, *Discipline and Punish*, 231-56.

39   Michael Ignatieff, "Total Institutions and Working Classes: A Review Essay," *History Workshop: A Journal of Socialist and Feminist Historians* 15, no. 1 (1983): 167-73. See also Ignatieff, "State, Civil Society and Total Institutions: A Critique of Recent Social Histories of Punishment," *Crime and Justice* 3 (1981): 153-92. The notion of the total institution belonged to Erving Goffman. In his critique, Ignatieff incorrectly faulted Foucault for failing to cite Goffman. On Foucault's admiration for Goffman, see Jacques Lagrange's "Course Context," in *Michel Foucault, Psychiatric Power: Lectures at the Collège de France, 1973-1974*, ed. Jacques Lagrange, trans. Graham Burchell (New York: Palgrave Macmillan, 2006), 359.

40   Laura Millar, "Discharging our Debt: The Evolution of the Total Archives Concept in English Canada," *Archivaria* 46 (Fall 1998): 117.

41   Foucault, *Discipline and Punish*, 215.

Connections between the state and disciplinary institutions can take a host of forms. In the specific case of police/archives, the link is often a legal one in the form of access legislation. Indeed, disagreements between archivists and researchers over the interpretation and application of access laws can be viewed profitably as power/knowledge struggles. In the Canadian context, one thinks of historians Greg Kealey and Reg Whitaker who used federal access to information legislation—characterized as "often frustrating, always tedious, and sometimes expensive"—to acquire RCMP security bulletins, the periodic reports on the RCMP's surveillance of labour and the left in Canada.[42]

Rather than holding onto the bulletins for their own private research, Kealey and Whitaker embarked upon an ambitious publication program, beginning in 1989, to make the documents publicly available. There are eight volumes in the series, covering the years 1919 to 1945; they are also on-line in an open-journal system, making for even greater public access to these once secret intelligence reports.[43] Kealey underscores the importance of access legislation, particularly in opening up areas of historical research. He explains that his work could not have been done "without this 'access' legislation. ... Cumbersome and expensive though it may be, the ATI [*Access to Information Act*] of 1983, especially when combined with the *National Archives Act* of 1986 [sic for 1987], has helped to create a renewed interest in the study of Canada's secret service." One of the paradoxical features of a total or complete institution is that a relatively elaborate bureaucratic structure, while often bemoaned by researchers (and I shall do a bit of this a little further on), nevertheless provides the necessary mechanisms to start up the access machinery. At the same time, Kealey never loses sight of the policing function, in this instance, not so much of archives but of the state security apparatus itself: "[R]esearchers who wish to pursue such topics should be forewarned that they will have to battle the Canadian Security Intelligence Service (CSIS) every step of the way to access materials even from the 1920s."[44]

---

42 Gregory S. Kealey, "Filing and Defiling: The Organization of the State Security Archives in the Interwar Years," in *On the Case: Explorations in Social History*, eds., Franca Iacovetta and Wendy Mitchinson (Toronto: University of Toronto Press, 1998), 89. See also Kealey, "In the Canadian Archives on Security and Intelligence," *Dalhousie Review* 75 (1995): 26–38; and Kerry Badgley, "Researchers and Canada's Public Archives: Gaining Access to the Security Collections," in *Whose National Security?: Canadian State Surveillance and the Creation of Enemies*, eds. Gary Kinsman, Dieter K. Buse, and Mercedes Steedman (Toronto: Between The Lines, 2000), 223–28.

43 Gregory S. Kealey and Reg Whitaker, eds., *The RCMP Security Bulletins* (St. John's, NL: Canadian Committee on Labour History, 1989–1997), http://journals.hil.unb.ca/index.php/RCMP/index.

44 Kealey, "Filing and Defiling," 89.

Archivists represent another crucial link between the state and police/archives. Weighed against archivists' "professional myth of impartiality, neutrality, and objectivity," Schwartz and Cook entreat that archivists' power "should no longer remain naturalized or denied, but opened to vital debate."[45] But what is the nature of archivists' power under a police/archives regime? It might be helpful to think of police/archives as Foucault did power, that is, as both punitive and productive. He describes the relationship between sex and the police in the introductory volume of *The History of Sexuality*. "A policing of sex: that is, not the rigor of a taboo, but the necessity of regulating sex through useful and productive discourses."[46] And so we might think of the archivist's policing function less as a prison guard and more as a traffic cop—regulating the archival traffic between the public and the past in useful and productive ways, sometimes acting as security guards for the state (but also protecting people's right to privacy, and/or fragile or rare documents), and other times facilitating the public's research interests by serving as a citizen's police escort direct to the documentary scene of the crime. Which path is taken will depend, I suspect, on individual archivists and how they view their role, something vigorously debated within the archival profession. Are they archivist-historians with the critical distance from institutions such a designation usually entails, or are they government employees, with the loyalty of a civil servant hired to manage and monitor who is poking around in government records, and why?

In the case of the Police Museum and the Toronto Police Service are we really to believe they are here "to Serve and Protect—Working with the Community," as their letterhead states? The gay/lesbian community knows a long and troubled history with the police that would suggest otherwise. Think, for example, of the RCMP's surveillance of queers during the 1950s and 1960s, part of the post-war purge of gay men and lesbians from the federal civil service. As the vital work of Gary Kinsman and Patrizia Gentile demonstrates, the RCMP's surveillance extended well beyond the civil service into Ottawa's gay/lesbian communities, generating a police/archive of thousands of names. For Kinsman and Gentile, as for Kealey and Whitaker, federal access legislation proved pivotal in retrieving state documents crucial to recovering this moment in Canadian queer history.[47]

---

45 Schwartz and Cook, "Archives, Records, and Power," 1.
46 Foucault, *The History of Sexuality*, 25.
47 Gary Kinsman and Patrizia Gentile, *The Canadian War on Queers: National Security as Sexual Regulation* (Vancouver: University of British Columbia Press, 2009). See also Gary Kinsman, "Constructing Gay Men and Lesbians as National Security Risks, 1950–1970," in Kinsman et al., *Whose National Security?*, 143–153; and Kinsman, "The Canadian Cold War on Queers: Sexual Regulation and Resistance," in

Such uneasy histories between the police and some of the communities they are supposed to serve, underline the need for archivists to establish a high level of faith with researchers that archivists are indeed working in the interests of the public and not the police/archives.[48] Making the case for the archivist as public research advocate, John Smart suggested:

> I think our profession should say that the present situation is indefensible where, in our provincial and federal government records archives, so many key records series from deputy ministers' offices, justice departments, and police agencies are missing. Our profession should take as one of its principles that it should be possible for the public to review all publicly funded activities. . . . At present in Canada, this principle of public review through research does not exist for many key public agencies and their historians.[49]

Much has undoubtedly changed since Smart made his case more than twenty years ago, especially with the introduction of more access legislation, but my experience with the Toronto Police Museum would suggest that key records are still missing from public archives and the principle of public review through research continues to be hampered.

Watching the Detectives: The Case of the Missing Morality Department

For nearly two decades, I have been researching and publishing work on the history of sex between men in Toronto in the years from 1880 to 1940. Policing in both its strict and fuller Foucauldian sense has been one of my central themes. In part, this is a reflection of my sources. The bulk of my research has been in criminal court records of "homosexual offences" housed at the Archives of Ontario.[50] I realized early on during my research that the Morality Department of the Toronto Police Force would play a substantial role in the story. Officers of the Morality squad figured in the vast majority of more than

---

Love, Hate, and Fear in Canada's Cold War, ed. Richard Cavell (Toronto: University of Toronto Press, 2004), 108–32.

48 See, for example, Glenn Dingwall, "Trusting Archivists: The Role of Archival Ethics Codes in Establishing Public Faith," *American Archivist* 67 (Spring–Summer 2004): 11–30.

49 John Smart, "The Professional Archivist's Responsibility as an Advocate of Public Research," *Archivaria* 16 (Summer 1983): 145.

50 I offered an early statement on the problems and possibilities of doing this kind of research in an earlier paper. See Steven Maynard, "'The Burning, Willful Evidence': Lesbian/Gay History and Archival Research," *Archivaria* 33 (Winter 1991–92): 195–201.

350 cases of homosexual crimes that turned up in my research. A distinct unit dedicated to morality was first established within the Toronto Police in 1886. David Archibald, staff inspector of the new Morality Department, had a wide mandate, including the prosecution of prostitutes and houses of ill-fame, illicit liquor sellers, gambling dens, and sex between men. Archibald filed a report on the first year of work in the Morality Department. The chief constable appended Archibald's report to his own annual report, which regularly appeared in the minutes of city council. Although the chief constable made subsequent references in his annual reports to further reports from Archibald, none of these appeared in the minutes. I wanted to know where these other reports were and what other records from the Morality Department existed. To answer these questions, I turned to the City of Toronto Archives, which has a substantial collection of historical records relating to the Toronto Police. While these records proved invaluable to my research, I found nothing substantive in them that related to the Morality Department, other than several more tantalizing yet frustrating passing references to the existence of various Morality Department documents.

While researching in police records at the City of Toronto Archives, I had always been aware that some of the police department's historical documents remained in the possession of the police at the Toronto Police Museum within the Toronto Police Service (TPS). The Police Museum is located at police headquarters in downtown Toronto. I made my first visit to the Museum in the early 1990s. At that time, the Museum was run by Jack Webster, a police officer who, after he retired in 1988, became the Force's official historian and *de facto* archivist.[51] He adopted a very protective, proprietorial attitude toward the police records. To gain access required presenting oneself before "Copper Jack" and hoping he liked the researcher enough to allow her/him to see "his" documents. I must have made a favourable enough impression, for Webster escorted me down into the depths of police headquarters to sub-level 3. There, in a windowless room, crowded with old police registers, duty books, and other documents, Webster sat me at a desk and gave me a selection of documents to look through. How Webster chose which documents to let me see was never clear, and I was not allowed to search through them myself. As I poured over the records, Webster sat at a desk occasionally peering over the paperback he was reading to check up on me. It was not the most conducive arrangement in which to conduct research. Doing any kind of sustained, detailed, empirical research was out of the question, for there was no escaping the feeling that my presence was keeping Webster from something else he would rather be doing, probably anything else besides "babysitting"

---

51   See Jack Webster, with Rosemary Aubert, *Copper Jack: My Life on the Force* (Toronto: Dundurn Press, 1991).

me. I returned several times, but needless to say, this research arrangement did not last, and I did not locate the missing Morality Department.

A subsequent visit to the Police Museum in 2006 revealed some changes. Webster had left his position, and the Museum had been expanded to include a public exhibition space with a number of historical and contemporary displays. Still, there is nothing resembling a research room, and the spatial separation between researchers and the records is now securely in place: there are no more visits to the basement. In fact, members of the public are not allowed to look at the historical documents at all. Rather, the Museum requires one to submit a research request along with personal credit card information (for research that takes more than fifteen minutes, there is a $25/hour charge) and a "museum researcher" performs the research on the researcher's behalf. From the perspective of a professional historian, there is any number of problems with this highly irregular practice. Archivists may stand as gatekeepers between researchers and their records, but once they grant access to the records, they usually allow one to do her/his own research—not so at the Police Museum. Nonetheless, I secured a research grant from my university and submitted a request with the Museum. Even compiling the request was difficult because the Museum does not have a descriptive database of its holdings, at least not one it shares with the public. There are no references to the Toronto Police Service in the detailed "directory of records" for city departments maintained by the Corporate Access and Privacy Unit of the City Clerk's Office. Neither will one find the Police Service among city departments that have developed plans for the "routine disclosure" of documents, which are designed to help identify the types of information that can be made available to the public.[52] This should have been my first clue that the police would be more interested in policing rather than disclosing documents.

After a three-month wait, I was informed that some reports had been located, that other documents were still being gathered, and that I would be told soon how much if anything could be released. This sounded promising. However, despite my repeated requests for updates from the Museum, I heard nothing for the next year and a half. If the Morality Department had been missing before, it now seemed to have disappeared forever behind the proverbial police code of silence. Such stonewalling, as it were, has a long history in the research and writing of the queer past. Some time ago, gay historian Martin Duberman detailed his ordeal with an archive to get access to, and publish, several early-nineteenth-century letters with homoerotic content. Duberman made clear his "chief purpose is not to establish the villainy

---

52 See http://wx.toronto.ca/inter/dir_recs.nsf/CRCSRecs?OpenView and http://www.toronto.ca/cap/routine_disclosure_plan.htm.

of archivists," but to tell his story so that it "might encourage other scholars to persevere in the search for long-suppressed material; might offer tactics for extracting it; might alert them to some of the obstacles and ploys custodial guardians will use to deflect the search."[53] In my case, deflection took the form of delay as well as distortion. When, finally, I heard from the Museum again, the TPS Director of Public Information, then responsible for the Museum, informed me that my research request "on the changing perceptions of crime and morality by the people of Toronto is not one which can be answered by the Toronto Police." The Director explained: "You would have to approach sources which have access to popular publications of the time including books, newspapers, and other accounts or academic studies on the subject."[54] But my research request was quite specific. It made no mention of "the people of Toronto" and their views, and was quite explicitly about policing, which presumably the Police Museum could answer. Taking a specific request, refashioning it, and then, on that basis, claiming it is impossible to answer is what Duberman might call a ploy and what I would call another technique of police/archives.[55]

In February 2008 I redoubled my efforts to track down the Morality Department. This time I bypassed the Museum and raised my concerns directly with the TPS. My first question concerned the relationship of the Museum to the TPS. The Museum's Web page explains that it was "built entirely from private donations," and that it "exists solely on the profits of our gift shop and donations."[56] Museum staff, when they were still communicating with me,

---

53 Martin Duberman, "'Writhing Bedfellows' in Antebellum South Carolina: Historical Interpretation and the Politics of Evidence," in *About Time: Exploring the Gay Past* (New York: Meridian, 1991), 13.

54 Director of Public Information, Toronto Police Service, to Steven Maynard, 16 May 2008.

55 In a not unrelated 2009 case, the Toronto Police Service (TPS) lost a six-year-long battle with the Toronto *Star* over the *Star*'s access to information request for electronic records related to racial profiling. The TPS argued it could not answer the request as it would be too time-consuming and too difficult to generate the requested data from its existing computer programs. The Court of Appeal for Ontario disagreed and ordered the TPS to comply with the access request immediately, the judge in the appeal ruling that "the public's right to obtain this kind of information must be interpreted liberally." As commentators on the affair correctly noted, however, the struggle may not be over, for the TPS has any number of other exemptions under *MFIPPA* it can invoke. Tracey Tyler, "Star Wins 'Landmark' Court Fight over Records," *The Toronto Star* (14 January 2009), http://www.thestar.com/news/gta/2009/01/14/star_wins_landmark_court_fight_over_records.html.

56 See http://www.torontopolice.on.ca/museum.

explained that while technically the Museum belongs to the TPS, it has legal charitable status and does not receive funding from the TPS. The TPS has a slightly different understanding. According to the Director of Corporate Services, "Although the Museum was established with financial contributions from various private donors, to my knowledge, it has no separate legal status and is simply an ongoing project of the Toronto Police Service."[57] The difference of opinion is disconcerting and raises some questions. On the one hand, the Museum, with legal charitable status and built from, and existing on, private donations, sounds like a private organization, or at least one that is relatively autonomous from the TPS. If so, the crucial question becomes: How did the rare, historical records of a publicly funded institution such as the city police come to be in the custody of a private group? On the other hand, if the Museum really is "simply an ongoing project of the Toronto Police Service," then the Museum should be subject to legislation governing access to information.

The *City of Toronto Act, 2006* mandates that the "City shall retain and preserve the records of the City and its local boards in a secure and accessible manner," and that subject "to the *Municipal Freedom of Information and Protection of Privacy Act (MFIPPA)*, any person may, at all reasonable times, inspect any of the records under the control of the clerk."[58] At the same time, however, legal recognition of the public's right to know has been balanced by the protection of privacy, and not just the privacy of individuals but also the "privacy" of some of the city's institutions. *MFIPPA*, despite operating under the principle that "information should be available to the public" and despite providing a "right of access to information," nevertheless contains ten categories of exemptions, including one for "law enforcement," which further stipulates seventeen different reasons why the police can refuse to disclose a record, most of which relate to preventing interference with ongoing law enforcement operations. It is difficult, however, to imagine how any of the exemptions could reasonably be applied to the documents I am seeking, which

---

57 Director of Corporate Services, Toronto Police Service, to Steven Maynard, 9 June 2008.

58 *City of Toronto Act, 2006*, c.11, Sched. A, s. 200 (1) and c.11, Sched. A, s. 199(1). In fact, the *Municipal Act* (predecessor to the *City of Toronto Act*), provided people with this right to inspect public records long before the introduction of our current freedom of information legislation. The difficulty in those earlier years was that many administrators and members of the public were unaware of the *Municipal Act*'s provisions. In the case of the City of Ottawa, for instance, "the public was effectively excluded by this ignorance from the city's records." See Edwin Welch, "Freedom of Information in Municipalities," *Archivaria* 6 (Summer 1978): 161–62. See also Jerome O'Brien, "Archives and the Law: A Brief Look at the Canadian Scene," *Archivaria* 18 (Summer 1984): 41.

are now between one hundred and one hundred and twenty-five years old. For example, one *MFIPPA* exemption states that the police "may refuse to disclose a record if the disclosure could reasonably be expected to reveal investigative techniques and procedures currently in use or likely to be used in law enforcement."[59] My research revealed the police surveillance of sex between men in public washrooms in the late nineteenth and early twentieth centuries. The surveillance techniques were quite rudimentary—police constables set up wooden ladders and sawhorses on the exterior backside of public washrooms, which they would climb and proceed to peer into the washroom through gaps in the wall.[60] I do not doubt that surveillance of public washrooms continues, but I'm guessing that the apparatus of police surveillance no longer includes the use of wooden ladders and sawhorses and, thus, my research is not likely to blow the cover on any "techniques and procedures currently in use or likely to be used in law enforcement."

Consequently, I submitted a formal *MFIPPA* request with the TPS's Access and Privacy Section. The result was mixed. On the plus side, I received a response to my request in a timely fashion, in something considerably less than the over 630 days that it took the Museum to respond to my initial research request. On the not so positive side, the access co-ordinator determined that "your specific request . . . does not fall under the auspices of the Act." No reason was given, and I was "advised that your request for access to information under the Act has been withdrawn and is now closed."[61] At the same time, the co-ordinator was pleased to inform me that special arrangements had been made to allow me to view *some* records. And, in fact, I did finally get to see one historical register from the Morality Department. But this research trip turned out not unlike my first one with Copper Jack. I viewed the register not in the Museum or a reading room, but in the office of a detective attached to the Corporate Services Section. When I asked whether there were more documents I might be able to see, the detective disappeared into the basement and returned with another register, although this one not from the Morality Department at all. The problems persist and questions remain: How many documents are in the police basement? What types of documents are they? What years do they cover? How are they to be easily accessed? It seems impossible to know.

---

59 *Municipal Freedom of Information and Protection of Privacy Act*, R.S.O. 1990, c. M.56, s.8 (1)c. http://www.e-laws.gov.on.ca/html/statutes/english/elaws_statutes_90m56_e.htm#BK10.

60 Steven Maynard, "Through a Hole in the Lavatory Wall: Homosexual Subcultures, Police Surveillance, and the Dialectics of Discovery, Toronto, 1890–1930," *Journal of the History of Sexuality* 5 (October 1994): 207–42.

61 Coordinator, Access and Privacy Section, Toronto Police Service, to Steven Maynard, 11 June 2009.

What, then, can we make of this? My experience at the Police Museum would seem to support Stoler's observation that in some archives "the panoptic is a frail conceit."[62] The Police Museum is not a total archives. In fact, in its scattergun approach to historical records and with its informal procedures, the Museum is the exact opposite of the rational archives of the state. At the same time, the Police Museum is connected to one of the paradigmatic complete and austere institutions in our society: the police. The researcher trying to access historical police records, then, confronts a two-pronged problem; the Toronto Police Service, exerting its power through the terse interpretation of the access legislation; the Police Museum, exploiting its ambiguous position between public and private, and ultimately protected by the authority of the TPS. In this situation, I think what we encounter is not so much frailty as the dual deployment of the power of a total institution with a more anarchic approach to archives.[63] This can be a disorienting experience for the researcher as s/he is bounced within the police bureaucracy from the Museum to the Public Information unit, from the Access and Privacy section to Corporate Services, required to submit to formal procedures in one place only to encounter lax archival practices in another.

One might have guessed that dealing with an archive attached to the police, one would discover archival panopticism at its most powerful. But we want to be careful not to overstate the completeness or totality of the power of police/archives. In contrast to Derrida who saw in the archive only an ahistorical and inescapable power,[64] Foucault would emphasize the cracks in the archival edifice, the potential points of penetration, its susceptibility to pressure. The possibilities are indicated by my partial success in using access to information legislation—if only as a prod—to finally catch a glimpse of the Morality Department. Still, it is a precarious arrangement in which power ultimately rests on the side of police/archives—at least so far. In response to my queries, the Director of Corporate Services explained: "The challenge immediately before us is to ensure that the policies and practices in the Museum do not prohibit members of the community from gaining access to information they are entitled to

---

62 Stoler, *Along the Archival Grain*, 23.

63 Thanks go to one of the reviewers of this paper for suggesting "anarchic" as an apt characterization of the Museum's archival mode.

64 As Steedman writes, "In Derrida's description, the *arkhe*—the archive—appears to represent the *now* of whatever kind of power is being exercised anywhere, in any place or time." Further on, she states that "'Archive' is thus inflated to mean—if not quite Everything—then at least all the ways and means of state power; power itself, perhaps, rather than those quietly folded and filed documents that we think provide the mere and incomplete records of some of its inaugural moments." Steedman, *Dust*, 1 and 6.

receive."[65] And yet, very shortly after I first raised my concerns with the TPS, research requests at the Museum were suspended. As the Museum's Web page explains: "The museum is currently reviewing *The Access and Privacy Section Policy and Procedures Act* and will not be receiving any research requests at this time."[66] That was well over a year ago and, as of the writing of this article, the Museum remains in lockdown as far as research requests are concerned. Shutting down public access to documents is the ultimate police/archives tool.

"To Establish the Greatest Accessibility . . ."

My goal in pressing the Police Museum relates to issues of public access and police accountability. First, access. Over thirty years ago, when some of the historical records of the Toronto police were transferred to the city archives, the City Clerk, in conjunction with the archives, suggested to the police the need for an access policy to its historical records. "These records are a rich source of data for the study of Toronto's social history," wrote the Clerk, "which brings into focus the question of establishing an access policy for their use." The Clerk argued that "the goal should be to establish the greatest accessibility to bona fide scholars and students consistent with the considerations of confidentiality which may apply to some of the records." The Clerk further suggested that it may be "desirable to pay special attention to the bona fides of persons wishing to use those records less than, say 50 years old, and the responsibility for making such checks might be assigned to the City Archivist."[67] The Board of Commissioners of Police agreed to leave matters relating to the police's historical records, including the establishment of an access policy, to the City Archivist.[68]

I draw attention to this historical moment because it seems to me that even though some of the specifics of the Clerk's recommendations—the fifty-year rule, for example—may or may not correspond with current access legislation, I think the more general intent of his proposal remains sound. It represents precisely what is missing at the Toronto Police Museum today: an appreciation for, and understanding of, History. There needs to be a clear distinction between the TPS's historical records and its more recent records, the

---

65 Director of Corporate Services, Toronto Police Service, to Steven Maynard, 9 June 2008.
66 See http://www.torontopolice.on.ca/museum.
67 Toronto City Clerk to Board of Commissioners of Police, 26 April 1976. This letter is found in the City of Toronto Archives' administrative files relating to their acquisition of police records.
68 Executive Secretary of the Board of Commissioners to Toronto City Clerk, 18 May 1976.

latter of which may more legitimately fall under *MFIPPA* exemptions. There is no reason this cannot be done. *MFIPPA* already makes exceptions to many of its exemptions for records that are more than twenty years old. Once historical records have been identified, they should, rather than being left to rot in the basement of police headquarters, be transferred to the City of Toronto Archives, where the bulk of police records are already housed, and where they have an appropriate physical environment, professionally trained archivists, and proper access/privacy policies in place. The precedent for this already exists in the arrangement between the Board of Commissioners of Police and the City of Toronto Archives, which dates back to the mid-1970s. Even with such a transfer, however, we would need to remain vigilant. There is no guarantee that the removal of records from the police department to a more "complete" state archive would facilitate a more complete access, as is made clear by the many blacked-out sections of the documents obtained by those working on the history of state repression of labour/the left, and gays and lesbians. Foucault would caution us to remain wary of any such move between institutions, viewing it less as a democratization of access and more like a strategic reconfiguration of police/archives within the multiple levels of state power.

My second concern relates to accountability, particularly important when it comes to police/archives. Part five of the *City of Toronto Act* is devoted to "accountability and transparency."[69] But how are citizens to scrutinize the past operations of the police if its historical records are not easily accessible to the public? Accountability is, of course, also an issue of concern to archivists. John Dirks has discussed the shift in rationale for archives from history (i.e., archives as cultural memory, national heritage) to accountability, that is, archives as repositories of records that can be used as a check on power in democratic society (provided, of course, one can access those records). The shift from claims based on history to accountability has occurred in large part because state institutions are more responsive in these days of public scandal—think Native residential schools—to issues of accountability than they are to appeals to history. While Dirks is no doubt mapping a real shift, the distinction is somewhat dubious, for present-day issues of public accountability, such as the residential schools, are also profoundly historical. Dirks is keenly aware of this, and he argues for a dual history/accountability approach.[70]

Dirks points to the work of social historians as an example of this dual approach. Social historians often combine an appreciation for history, indeed

---

69 *City of Toronto Act, 2006*, c. 11, Sched. A, s. 156-183. http://www.e-laws.gov.on.ca/html/statutes/english/elaws_statutes_06c11_e.htm#BK200.

70 John M. Dirks, "Accountability, History, and Archives: Conflicting Priorities or Synthesized Strands?" *Archivaria* 57 (Spring 2004): 29-49.

often arguing for the greater retention of records, with a politics of accountability: "Underpinning [historians'] need for detailed documentation of the experiences of individuals under institutional or other controls is an element of justice and a demand for moral, if not legal accountability."[71] This works as a good description of my own approach to queer history and police/archives. But Dirks also points to something he regards as "ironic." He notes that with their appeals for more archives, social historians, influenced by a Foucauldian understanding of archives as power, ironically bolster the very archival authority they critique. Dirks is right, of course, although I would not call this ironic, for according to Foucault, this is precisely how power operates in modern society. Let me give a different but related example. In its *Access and Privacy Manual*, a document intended for internal use, the City of Toronto's access/privacy unit states that "*The Municipal Freedom of Information and Protection of Privacy Act (MFIPPA)* establishes an access to information regime, based on the following fundamental principles: Informed citizens are essential to the democratic process and the more that citizens know about their government the better they will be governed."[72] Setting aside the fact that *MFIPPA* does not actually make any reference to "citizens" or "democracy," I read this as something of a Foucauldian slip. I suspect what they mean is the more that citizens avail themselves of access to government information, acting as a check and balance on government power, the better government we will have. But a Foucauldian reading would stress that the more that citizens engage with the state through such things as its "freedom of information" laws, the more totally and effectively they become governed by the state via processes of incorporation, legitimation, etc. This is what Patrick Joyce means in his discussion of the "liberal archive" by "the rule of freedom": the notion that freedom is not, as commonsense would have it, freedom from power, but in fact represents yet another clever ruse of ruling.[73]

In the face of this insidious quality of modern power—the more we practice our "freedom," the more we are ruled—should we just put our hands up and surrender? For Foucault, the answer would be an emphatic *Non!*; the political struggle against the power of total or complete institutions, be it a prison, a psychiatric facility, or police/archives, was paramount. In waging that struggle, historical-archival research plays a pivotal part. In the same lecture from 1976 in which Foucault described "the feverish laziness" of working in archives and libraries, he made an impassioned *cri de cœur* for

71 Ibid., 41.
72 Corporate Access and Privacy Unit, City of Toronto, *Access and Privacy Manual*, 2nd ed. (March 2006), http://www.toronto.ca/cap/pdf/capman.pdf.
73 Patrick Joyce, "The Politics of the Liberal Archive," *History of the Human Sciences* 12 (May 1999): 35–49. See also Joyce, *The Rule of Freedom: Liberalism and the Modern City* (New York: Verso, 2003).

the "insurrection of subjugated knowledges," "disqualified and marginal" forms of knowing, the kind of "knowledges from below" that often surface in the course of doing primary, archival research. These types of research and knowledge were significant, Foucault insisted, because they allow us "to constitute a historical knowledge of struggles and to make use of that knowledge in contemporary tactics," be it "jamming the workings of the psychiatric institution," or in the "strange efficacy of the attacks that have been made on, say, morality and the traditional sexual hierarchy," or, we can add, in demanding greater public access to and accountability over police/archives.[74]

But in whose name, under what banner of identity, do we wage the struggle against police/archives? Schwartz and Cook maintain that "whether conscious of it or not, archivists are major players in the business of identity politics," and they point to, among others, "gays and lesbians."[75] This may be so, but is it desirable? Foucault wrote that he was not interested in the archive as "evidence of a continuing identity."[76] In all his intellectual work and throughout his political life, Foucault remained hyper-suspicious of claims to identity, including sexual identity. For Foucault, sexuality was not something to be claimed but something we should always keep at a critical distance. His interest in sexuality was not in how it might be embraced to name the truth of who we are, but rather how it might be used as a vehicle to invent and multiply new forms of relations and ways of knowing. This creative process might begin with queer experience, but it should ultimately have a more universal appeal, something available to everyone rather than the property of any one particular sexual constituency. In this paper, I have tried to avoid an appeal to identity. I have not argued for the greater inclusion of queer history in archives. Neither have I tried to make the case for queer archives as a specialized subfield of archival practice or theory. These may be worthwhile endeavours, but they are not mine. Rather, following Foucault, I have tried to address the notion of police/archives, not queer archives. Beginning but not ending with my experience as a queer researcher in archives, my goal has been to raise more universal issues of public access and accountability. If this aids and abets, and I hope it does, in the transfer of historical documents from the Police Museum to the City of Toronto Archives, then any resulting expanded access will benefit not only queer researchers but also anyone interested in the historical scrutiny of the police. But the "if" is crucial, for it remains to be seen whether this story will conclude on the side of police authority or on the side of greater public command over police/archives.

---

74 Foucault, "Society Must Be Defended," 7–8, 5. For a similar interpretation of these lectures, see Neil Levy, "History as Struggle: Foucault's Genealogy of Genealogy," *History of the Human Sciences* 11 (November 1998): 159–70.
75 Schwartz and Cook, "Archives, Records, and Power," 16–17.
76 Foucault, *The Archaeology of Knowledge*, 145.

Acknowledgements

I would like to thank Rebecka Sheffield and Marcel Barriault for their work on this issue and for the opportunity to contribute to it. Thank you to one of the journal's reviewers for supplying a sharp, stimulating critique.[77] Thanks, too, to Karen Teeple and Lawrence Lee at the City of Toronto Archives for their always prompt and professional responses to my many queries, as well as for making available the accession and other administrative records relating to the Archives' holdings of historical police documents. Finally, my gratitude to Vid Ingelevics for allowing me to reproduce his evocative photograph. Much of Ingelevics' work focuses on the intersection of personal/public memory and institutions, including archives and museums. See http://www.web.net/artinfact/index.htm.

Bibliography

Artières, Philippe. "Espaces d'archives." Introduction to "Lieux d'archives." Special issue, *Sociétés et représentations* 19 (2005).

— — —. "Michel Foucault: L'Archive d'un rire." In *Questions d'archives*. Paris: IMEC, 2002.

Artières, Philippe, and Mathieu Potte-Bonneville. *D'Après Foucault: gestes, luttes, programmes*. Paris: Prairies Ordinaires, 2007.

Artières, Philippe, Laurent Quéro, and Michelle Zancarini-Fournel, eds. *Le Groupe d'information sur les prisons: Archives d'une lutte, 1970–1972*. Paris: IMEC, 2003.

Badgley, Kerry. "Researchers and Canada's Public Archives: Gaining Access to the Security Collections." In Kinsman et al., *Whose National Security?*, 223–28.

Biddick, Kathleen. "Doing Dead Time for the Sovereign: Archive, Abandonment, Performance." *Rethinking History* 13 (June 2009): 137–51.

Black, Alistair. "The Library as Clinic: A Foucauldian Interpretation of British Public Library Attitudes to Social and Physical Disease, ca. 1850–1950." *Libraries & Culture* 40 (Summer 2005): 416–34.

Butt, Gavin. "Whispering in the Archive." In *Between You and Me: Queer Disclosures in the New York Art World, 1948–1963*, 16–21. Durham, NC: Duke University Press, 2005.

City of Toronto Act, 2006, c. 11, Sched. A, s. 156–183. http://www.e-laws.gov.on.ca/html/statutes/english/elaws_statutes_06c11_e.htm#BK200.

Conrad, Ryan, ed. *Future of the Past: Reviving the Queer Archives*. Portland, ME: Moth Press, 2009.

---

77 See note 1.

Corporate Access and Privacy Unit, City of Toronto. *Access and Privacy Manual*, 2nd ed. (March 2006). http://www.toronto.ca/cap/pdf/capman.pdf.

Crampton Jeremy W., and Stuart Elden, eds. *Space, Knowledge and Power: Foucault and Geography*. Burlington, VT: Ashgate, 2007.

Cvetkovich, Ann. *An Archive of Feelings: Trauma, Sexuality, and Lesbian Public Cultures*. Durham, NC: Duke University Press, 2003.

Deleuze, Gilles. "A New Archivist." In *Foucault*, 1-22. Translated by Sean Hand. Minneapolis: University of Minnesota Press, 2006.

Derrida, Jacques. *Archive Fever: A Freudian Impression*. Translated by Eric Prenowitz. Chicago: University of Chicago Press, 1996. Originally published as *Mal d'Archive: Une Impression Freudienne* (Paris: Galilée, 1995).

de Villiers, Nicholas. Review of *Queer Archives in a Queer Time and Place: Transgender Bodies, Subcultural Lives*, by Judith Halberstam. *Cultural Critique* 66 (Spring 2007): 179-83. http://www.jstor.org/stable/4539813.

Dingwall, Glenn. "Trusting Archivists: The Role of Archival Ethics Codes in Establishing Public Faith." *American Archivist* 67 (Spring-Summer 2004): 11-30.

Dirks, John M. "Accountability, History, and Archives: Conflicting Priorities or Synthesized Strands?" *Archivaria* 57 (Spring 2004): 29-49.

Donnelly, Sue. "Coming Out in the Archives: The Hall-Carpenter Archives at the London School of Economics." *History Workshop Journal* 66 (Autumn 2008): 180-84.

Duberman, Martin. "'Writhing Bedfellows' in Antebellum South Carolina: Historical Interpretation and the Politics of Evidence." In *About Time: Exploring the Gay Past*, 5-14. New York: Meridian, 1991.

Farge, Arlette. *Le Goût de l'archive*. Paris: Seuil, 1989.

Farge, Arlette, and Michel Foucault. *Le Désordre des familles: lettres de cachet des Archives de la Bastille*. Paris: Gallimard, 1982.

Faubion, James D., ed. *The Essential Works of Foucault, 1954-1984, Volume 2: Aesthetics, Method, and Epistemology*, translated by Robert Hurley. New York: New Press, 1998.

Florence, Collectif Maurice. *Archives de l'infamie*. Paris: Prairies Ordinaires, 2009.

Foucault, Michel. *Discipline and Punish: The Birth of the Prison*. Translated by Alan Sheridan. New York: Vintage, 1979. Originally published as *Surveiller et punir: Naissance de la prison* (Paris: Gallimard,1975).

– – –. "The Historical *a priori* and the Archive." Part 3, chap. 5 in *The Archaeology of Knowledge*, Translated by A. M. Sheridan Smith. London: Routledge, 2002. Originally published as *L'Archéologie du savoir* (Paris: Gallimard, 1969).

———. *History of Madness*. Edited by Jean Khalfa. Translated by Jonathan Murphy and Jean Khalfa. London: Routledge, 2006. Originally published as *Folie et Déraison: Histoire de la folie à l'âge classique* (Paris: Plon, 1961).

———. *The History of Sexuality, Volume 1: An Introduction*. Translated by Robert Hurley. New York: Vintage, 1980. Originally published as *La Volonté de savoir: Histoire de la sexualité, 1*, (Paris: Gallimard, 1976).

———. "The Lives of Infamous Men." In *The Essential Works of Foucault, 1954–1984, Volume 3: Power*, edited by James Faubion, translated by Robert Hurley, 157–175. New York: New Press, 2000.

———. "On the Archaeology of the Sciences: Response to the Epistemology Circle." In Faubion, *The Essential Works of Foucault, Volume 2*, 297–333.

———. "On the Ways of Writing History." In Faubion, *The Essential Works of Foucault, Volume 2*, 279–295.

———. *Power/Knowledge: Selected Interviews and Other Writings, 1972–1977*. Edited by Colin Gordon. New York: Pantheon, 1980.

———. "The Punitive Society." In *The Essential Works of Foucault, 1954–1984, Volume 1: Ethics: Subjectivity and Truth*, edited by Paul Rabinow, translated by Robert Hurley, 22–37. New York: New Press, 1997.

———. *Résumé des cours, 1970–1982*. Paris: Julliard, 1989.

———. *"Society Must Be Defended": Lectures at the Collège de France, 1975–1976*. Edited by Mauro Bertani and Alessandro Fontana. Translated by David Macey. New York: Picador, 2003.

Ignatieff, Michael. "State, Civil Society and Total Institutions: A Critique of Recent Social Histories of Punishment." *Crime and Justice* 3 (1981): 153–92.

———. "Total Institutions and Working Classes: A Review Essay." *History Workshop: A Journal of Socialist and Feminist Historians* 15, no. 1 (1983): 167–73.

Joyce, Patrick. "The Politics of the Liberal Archive." *History of the Human Sciences* 12 (May 1999): 35–49.

———. *The Rule of Freedom: Liberalism and the Modern City*. New York: Verso, 2003.

Kealey, Gregory S. "Filing and Defiling: The Organization of the State Security Archives in the Interwar Years." In *On the Case: Explorations in Social History*, edited by Franca Iacovetta and Wendy Mitchinson, 88–105. Toronto: University of Toronto Press, 1998.

———. "In the Canadian Archives on Security and Intelligence." *Dalhousie Review* 75 (1995): 26–38.

Kealey, Gregory S., and Reg Whitaker, eds. *The RCMP Security Bulletins*. St. John's, NL: Canadian Committee on Labour History, 1989–1997. http://journals.hil.unb.ca/index.php/RCMP/index.

Ketelaar, Eric. "Archival Temples, Archival Prisons: Modes of Power and Protection." *Archival Science* 2 (September 2002): 221-38.

Kinsman, Gary. "The Canadian Cold War on Queers: Sexual Regulation and Resistance." In *Love, Hate, and Fear in Canada's Cold War*, edited by Richard Cavell, 108-32. Toronto: University of Toronto Press, 2004.

———. "Constructing Gay Men and Lesbians as National Security Risks, 1950-1970." In Kinsman et al., *Whose National Security?*, 143-153.

Kinsman, Gary, Dieter K. Buse, and Mercedes Steedman, eds. *Whose National Security?: Canadian State Surveillance and the Creation of Enemies*. Toronto: Between The Lines, 2000.

Kinsman, Gary, and Patrizia Gentile. *The Canadian War on Queers: National Security as Sexual Regulation*. Vancouver: University of British Columbia Press, 2009.

Koltun, Lilly. "The Architecture of Archives: Whose Form, What Functions?" *Archival Science* 2 (September 2002): 239-61.

Lagrange, Jacques. "Course Context." In *Michel Foucault, Psychiatric Power: Lectures at the Collège de France, 1973-1974*, edited by Jacques Lagrange, translated by Graham Burchell, 349-368. New York: Palgrave Macmillan, 2006.

Levy, Neil. "History as Struggle: Foucault's Genealogy of Genealogy." *History of the Human Sciences* 11 (November 1998): 159-70.

Macey, David. *The Lives of Michel Foucault: A Biography*. New York, 1993.

———. *Michel Foucault*. London: Reaktion, 2004.

May, Todd. *The Philosophy of Foucault*. Montreal: McGill-Queen's University Press, 2006.

Maynard, Steven. "'The Burning, Willful Evidence': Lesbian/Gay History and Archival Research." *Archivaria* 33 (Winter 1991-92): 195-201.

———. "Through a Hole in the Lavatory Wall: Homosexual Subcultures, Police Surveillance, and the Dialectics of Discovery, Toronto, 1890-1930." *Journal of the History of Sexuality* 5 (October 1994): 207-42.

Millar, Laura. "Discharging our Debt: The Evolution of the Total Archives Concept in English Canada," *Archivaria* 46 (Fall 1998): 103-146.

Municipal Freedom of Information and Protection of Privacy Act, R.S.O. 1990, c. M.56, s.8 (1)c. http://www.e-laws.gov.on.ca/html/statutes/english/elaws_statutes_90m56_e.htm#BK10.

O'Brien, Jerome. "Archives and the Law: A Brief Look at the Canadian Scene." *Archivaria* 18 (Summer 1984): 38-46.

Paras, Eric. *Foucault 2.0: Beyond Power and Knowledge*. New York: Other Press, 2006.

Rey, Michel. "Parisian Homosexuals Create a Lifestyle, 1700–1750: The Police Archives." In *'Tis Nature's Fault: Unauthorized Sexuality during the Enlightenment*, edited by Robert Purks Maccubbin, 179–91. Cambridge, MA: Cambridge University Press, 1987.

Roberts, Lewis C. "Disciplining and Disinfecting Working-Class Readers in the Victorian Public Library." *Victorian Literature and Culture* 26 (Spring 1998): 105–32.

Schwartz, Joan M. and Terry Cook. "Archives, Records, and Power: The Making of Modern Memory." *Archival Science* 2, no. 1–2 (2002): 1–19.

Smart, John. "The Professional Archivist's Responsibility as an Advocate of Public Research." *Archivaria* 16 (Summer 1983): 139–149.

Steedman, Carolyn. *Dust: The Archive and Cultural History*. New Brunswick, NJ: Rutgers University Press, 2001.

Stoler, Ann Laura. *Along the Archival Grain: Epistemic Anxieties and Colonial Common Sense*. Princeton, NJ: Princeton University Press, 2009.

Webster, Jack, with Rosemary Aubert. *Copper Jack: My Life on the Force*. Toronto: Dundurn Press, 1991.

Welch, Edwin. "Freedom of Information in Municipalities," *Archivaria* 6 (Summer 1978): 161–62.

Williams, Chris, and Clive Emsley. "Beware of the Leopard?: Police Archives in Great Britain." In *Political Pressure and the Archival Record*, edited by Margaret Proctor, Michael Cook, and Caroline Williams, 227–235. Chicago: Society of American Archivists, 2006.

The Brandon Archive

Judith Halberstam[1]

> *The road was straight, the country was level as a lake, and other cars were seldom sighted. This was "out there"—or getting near it.*
>
> ~Truman Capote, *In Cold Blood*

Out There

Our relations to place, like our relations to people, are studded with bias, riven with contradictions, and complicated by opaque emotional responses. I am one of those people for whom lonely rural landscapes feel laden with menace, and for many years nonurban areas were simply "out there," strange and distant horizons populated by hostile populations. It is still true that a densely packed urban street or a metallic skyline can release a surge of excitement for me while a vast open landscape fills me with dread. In December 1993, I remember reading a short story in the newspaper about an execution-style killing in rural Nebraska. The story seemed unremarkable except for one small detail buried in the heart of the report: one of the murder victims was a young female-bodied person who had been passing as a man. The murder of this young transgender person sent shock waves through queer communities in the United States, and created fierce identitarian battles between transsexual activists and gay and lesbian activists, with each group trying to claim Brandon Teena as one of their own. The struggles over the legacy of Brandon represented much more than a local skirmish over the naming or classification of fallen brethren; indeed, they testified to the political complexities of an activism sparked by murder and energized by the work of memorializing individuals. The fascination with murder and

---

1 Editors' note: this paper was previously published as a chapter in Halberstam's *In A Queer Time and Place: Transgender Bodies, Subcultural Lives*, 22–46. New York: New York University Press, 2005; all cross-references herein refer to chapters in that book.

mayhem that characterizes US popular culture has led some theorists to point to the emergence of a "wound culture." It is easy to explain why homophobic violence might generate such fierce activist responses; it is harder to mobilize such responses for purposes that extend beyond demands for protection and recognition from the state. My purpose here is to build on the flashes of insight afforded by violent encounters between "normal" guys and gender-variant people in order to theorize the meaning of gender transitivity in late capitalism. Here I will use the notions of relays of influence between dominant and minority masculinities to consider the place and space of the masculine transgender subject.

The tragic facts in the case of the murder of Brandon Teena and his two friends are as follows: on December 31, 1993, three young people were shot to death, execution style, in Falls City in rural Nebraska. Ordinarily, this story would have evoked only mild interest from mainstream America and a few questions about the specific brutalities of rural America; one of the three victims, however, was a young white person who had been born a woman, but who was living as a man and had been dating local girls. The other two victims, Brandon's friend Lisa Lambert, and her friend Philip DeVine, a disabled African American man, appeared to have been killed because they were in the wrong place at the wrong time, although this too is debatable.

This chapter relates, explores, and maps the shape and the meaning of the remarkable archive that has developed in the aftermath of the slaying of Brandon Teena, Lisa, and Philip; the archive has created a new "Brandon." This new Brandon is the name that we now give to a set of comforting fictions about queer life in small-town America. The Brandon archive is simultaneously a resource, a productive narrative, a set of representations, a history, a memorial, and a time capsule. It literally records a moment in the history of twentieth-century struggles around the meaning of gender categories and it becomes a guide to future resolutions. So, while in my next chapter I will examine the "politics of transgender biography" and the difficulties involved in telling stories about people who have created specific life narratives,[2] here I want to lay out the geopolitical ramifications of Brandon's murder by imagining the Brandon archive as made up of the insights and revelations allowed by a careful consideration of the many lives and social formations that Brandon's life and death sheds light on. If we think of the murder of Brandon as less of a personal tragedy that has been broadened out to create a symbolic event and more of a constructed memorial to the violence directed at queer and transgender lives, we will be better equipped to approach the geographic and class specificities of rural Nebraska.

The execution of Brandon, Lisa, and Philip was in fact more like an earthquake or a five-alarm fire than an individualized event: its eruption damaged

---

2   See note 1.

more than just the three who died and the two who killed; it actually devastated the whole town, and brought a flood of reporters, cameras, and journalists into the area to pick through the debris and size up the import of the disaster. That media rush, in many ways, transformed the Brandon murders from a circumscribed event to an ever evolving narrative. As we will see in the next chapter,[3] among the magazine articles, talk shows, and other media that covered the case, an Oscar-winning feature film, *Boys Don't Cry*, was released about Brandon's death.[4] This film, more than any other representation of the case, has determined the legacy of the murders. In a later chapter, "The Transgender Look," I will explore the mechanics of looking at the transgender body;[5] but in this chapter on place, space, and regionality, I discuss the film that greatly influenced *Boys Don't Cry*: the documentary titled *The Brandon Teena Story*, directed by Susan Muska and Greta Olafsdottir.[6] Like the feature film yet in different ways, *The Brandon Teena Story* tried to re-create the material conditions of Brandon's undoing, but like the feature film, it ultimately told a tall story about rural homophobia.

By designating the stories told about Brandon and his friends as "an archive" in this chapter, I am tracing the multiple meanings of this narrative for different communities. Ann Cvetkovich theorizes queer uses of the term "archives" in her book *An Archive of Feelings*: "Understanding gay and lesbian archives as archives of emotion and trauma helps to explain some of their idiosyncrasies, or, one might say, their 'queerness.'"[7] The Brandon archive is exactly that: a transgender archive of "emotion and trauma" that allows a narrative of a queerly gendered life to emerge from the fragments of memory and evidence that remain. When Brandon was shot to death by John Lotter and Thomas Nissen, his failure to pass as a man in the harsh terrain of a small town in rural North America prompted a national response from transgender activists. This response has been amplified and extended by other queers for different and conflicting reasons. Some queers use Brandon's death to argue for hate-crime legislation; others have made Brandon into a poster child for an emergent transgender community dedicated to making visible the plight of cross-identified youth, and Brandon functions therefore as a reference point of what I called in chapter 1 transgressive exceptionalism;[8]

---

3   Ibid.
4   *Boys Don't Cry*, directed by Kimberly Peirce (Los Angeles: Fox Searchlight Pictures, 1999), DVD.
5   See note 1.
6   *The Brandon Teena Story*, directed by Susan Muska and Greta Olafsdottir (New York: Zeitgeist Films, 1998), DVD.
7   Ann Cvetkovich, *An Archive of Feelings: Trauma, Sexuality and Lesbian Public Cultures* (Durham, NC: Duke University Press, 2003), 242.
8   See note 1.

still others have pointed to Brandon's death as evidence of a continuing campaign of violence against queers despite the increasing respectability of some portions of the gay and lesbian community. But few of the responses have taken into consideration the specificity of Brandon's non-metropolitan location, and few if any have used the murder and the production of activist and cultural activity that it has inspired as a way of reexamining the meaning of sexual identity in relation to a postmodern politics of place.

I use the Brandon material, then, to unpack the meaning of "local homosexualities" or transsexualities in the context of the United States. Like other narratives about nonmetropolitan sexuality, popular versions of this story posit a queer subject who sidesteps so-called modern models of gay identity by conflating gender and sexual variance. Indeed, in the popular versions of the Brandon narrative that currently circulate, like *Boys Don't Cry*, Brandon's promiscuity and liminal identity is depicted as immature and even premodern and as a form of false consciousness. When Brandon explores a mature and adult relationship with one woman who recognizes him as "really female," that film suggests, Brandon accedes to a modern form of homosexuality and is finally "free." Reconstituted now as a liberal subject, Brandon's death at the hands of local men can be read simultaneously as a true tragedy and an indictment of backward, rural communities. In this sense, Brandon occupies a place held by so-called primitives in colonial anthropology; he literally inhabits a different timescale from the modern queer, and using Johannes Fabian's formulation in *Time and the Other*, Brandon's difference gets cast as both spatially and temporally distant.[9] By reading Brandon's story in and through postcolonial queer theory and queer geography, we can untangle the complex links that this narrative created for the urban consumers who were its most avid audience between modern queerness and the rejection of rural or small-town locations.

I believe that an extensive analysis of the Brandon murders can serve to frame the many questions about identification, responsibility, class, regionality, and race that trouble queer communities today. Not only does Brandon represent a martyr lost in the struggle for transgender rights to the brutal perpetrators of rural hetero-masculine violences. Brandon also serves as a marker for a particular set of late-twentieth-century cultural anxieties about place, space, locality, and metropolitanism. Fittingly, Brandon has become the name for gender variance, for fear of transphobic and homophobic punishment; Brandon also embodies the desire directed at nonnormative masculinities. Brandon represents other rural lives undone by fear and loathing, and his story also symbolizes an urban fantasy of homophobic violence as

---

9   Johannes Fabian, *Time and the Other: How Anthropology Makes Its Object* (New York: Columbia University Press, 2002), 16.

essentially midwestern. But violence wherever we may find it marks different conflictual relations in different sites; and homicide, on some level, always depicts the microrealities of other battles displaced from the abstract to the tragically material. While at least one use of any Brandon Teena project must be to connect Brandon's gender presentation to other counternarratives of gender realness, I also hope that Brandon's story can be a vehicle linked to the discussions of globalization, transnational sexualities, geography, and queer migration. On some level Brandon's story, while cleaving to its own specificity, needs to remain an open narrative—not a stable narrative of female-to-male transsexual identity nor a singular tale of queer bashing, not a cautionary fable about the violence of rural America nor an advertisement for urban organizations of queer community. Brandon's story permits a dream of transformation that must echo in the narratives of queer life in other nonmetropolitan locations.

Falls City, Nebraska: A Good Place to Die?

> *In little towns, lives roll along so close to one another;*
> *loves and hates beat about, their wings almost touching.*
>
> ~Willa Cather, *Lucy Gayheart*[10]

In *The Brandon Teena Story*, Muska and Olafsdottir attempt to place the narrative of Brandon's life and death firmly in the countryside of Nebraska, so much so that Nebraska takes on the role and the presence of a character in this drama. We see prolonged shots of the rolling Nebraska countryside, road signs welcoming the traveler to Nebraska's "good life," and scenes of everyday life and culture in small-town America. The filmmakers make it clear early on that their relationship to Falls City and its communities is ironic and distanced. They never appear in front of the camera even though about 75 percent of the documentary involves talking-head interviews with interviewees responding to questions from invisible interlocutors. In the few "local" scenes, the camera peers voyeuristically at the demolition derby and the line-dancing and karaoke bar, and in the interview sequences, the camera pushes its way rudely into the lives of the people touched by the Brandon story. In one significant scene, the camera pans the backs of local men watching a demolition derby. As the gaze sweeps over them, the men are rendered in slow motion, and they turn and gaze back at the camera with hostile stares of nonrecognition. Interactions between the camera and its subjects register the filmmakers as outsiders to the material realities of the rural Midwest, mark the objects of the gaze as literally haunted by an invisible camera, and finally,

---

10   Willa Cather, *Lucy Gayheart* (New York: Knopf, 1935), 167.

place the viewer at a considerable distance from the actors on the screen. This distance both allows for the emergence of multiple versions of the Brandon story but also pins the narrative of violent homophobic and transphobic violence firmly to the landscape of white trash America, and forces modes of strenuous disidentification between the viewer and the landscape.

The landscape of Nebraska serves as a contested site on which multiple narratives unfold—narratives, indeed, that refuse to collapse into simply one story, "the Brandon Teena story." Some of these narratives are narratives of hate, or of desire; others tell of ignorance and brutality; still others of isolation and fear; some allow violence and ignorant prejudices to become the essence of poor, white, rural identity; and still others provoke questions about the deployment of whiteness and the regulation of violence. While the video itself encourages viewers to distance themselves from the horror of the heartlands and to even congratulate themselves for living in an urban rather than a rural environment, ultimately we can use Brandon's story as it emerges here to begin the articulation of the stories of white, working-class, rural queers, and to map the immensely complex relations that make rural America a site of horror and degradation in the urban imagination.

For queers who flee the confines of the rural Midwest and take comfort in urban anonymity, this video may serve as a justification of their worst fears about the violent effects of failing to flee; closer readings of Brandon's story, however, reveal the desire shared by many midwestern queers for a way of staying rather than leaving. While some journalists in the wake of Brandon's murder queried his decision to stay in Falls City, despite having been hounded by the police and raped by the men who went on to murder him, we must consider the condition of "staying put" as part of the production of complex queer subjectivities. Some queers need to leave home in order to become queer, and others need to stay close to home in order to preserve their difference. The danger of small towns as Willa Cather described it, also in reference to rural Nebraska, emerges out of a suffocating sense of proximity: "lives roll along so close to one another," she wrote in *Lucy Gayheart*, "loves and hates beat about, their wings almost touching." This beautiful, but scary image of rural life as a space all-too-easily violated depends absolutely on an opposite image—the image of rural life as wide open and free ranging, as "big sky" and open plains. Cather captures perfectly the contradiction of rural life as the contrast between wide-open spaces and sparse populations, on the one hand, and small-town claustrophobia and lack of privacy, on the other.

The life and death of Brandon provokes endless speculation about the specificities of the loves and hates that characterized his experiences in Falls City, and any straightforward rendering of his story remains impossible. Some viewers of *The Brandon Teena Story* have accused the filmmakers of an obvious class bias in their depictions of the people of Falls City; others have seen the film as an accurate portrayal of the cultures of hate and meanness produced in small, mostly white towns. Any attempt to come to terms with the resonances of Brandon's murder will ultimately have to grapple with both of these proposals. One way in which *The Brandon Teena Story* deploys and perpetuates a class bias in relation to the depiction of anti-queer violence is by depicting many of its interview subjects in uncritical ways as "white trash." In their introduction to an anthology titled *White Trash: Race and Class in America*, Annalee Newitz and Matt Wray define white trash as both a reference to "actually existing white people living in (often rural) poverty," and a term designating "a set of stereotypes and myths related to the social behaviors, intelligence, prejudices, and gender roles of poor whites."[11] The editors offer a "local politics of place" to situate, combat, and explain such stereotypes.

One way in which *The Brandon Teena Story* is able to grapple with the lives beneath the stereotypes (of white trash, of gender impersonation) is by allowing some of the women whom Brandon dated to explain themselves and articulate their own extraordinary desires. In the media rush to uncover the motivations behind Brandon's depiction of himself as a man, most accounts of the case have overlooked the fact that Brandon was actively chosen over more conventionally male men by the women he dated despite the fact that there were few social rewards for doing so. One girlfriend after another in the video characterizes Brandon as a fantasy guy, a dream guy, a man who "knew how a woman wanted to be treated." Gina describes him as romantic, special, and attentive, while Lana Tisdale calls him "every woman's dream." We might conclude that Brandon lived up to and even played into the romantic ideals that his girlfriends cultivated about masculinity. Brandon's self-presentation must be read, I believe, as a damaging critique of the white working-class masculinities around him; at the same time, however, his performance of courtly masculinity is a shrewd deployment of the middle-class and so-called respectable masculinities that represent an American romantic ideal of manhood. In the accounts that the women give of their relations with Brandon, we understand that he not only deliberately offered them a treatment they could not expect from local boys but he also acknowledged the complexity of their self-understandings and desires.

In order to understand the kinds of masculinities with which Brandon may have been competing, we can turn to the representations of the murderers themselves. While some accounts of the Brandon case have attempted to empathize with the men who murdered Brandon—Lotter and Nissen—by

---

11   Annalee Newitz and Matt Wray, eds., *White Trash: Race and Class in America* (New York: Routledge, 1996), 7.

revealing their traumatic family histories and detailing their encounters with abuse, the video tries to encourage the men to give their own reasons for their brutality. The conversations with Lotter and Nissen are fascinating for the way they allow the men to coolly describe rape and murder scenes, and also because Lotter in particular articulates an astute awareness of the violence of the culture into which he was raised. Nissen, however, shows little power of self-reflection; the video represents him as ultimately far more reprehensible than his partner in crime. For one second in the video, the camera focuses on a small tattoo on Nissen's arm, but does not allow the viewer to identify it. In Aphrodite Jones's book on the Brandon case, *All S/he Wanted*, she provides information that situates this tattoo as a symbol of white supremacy politics. Nissen, we learn, was involved off and on throughout his early life with the White American Group for White America.[12] While Nissen's flirtation with brutally racist white supremacist groups need not surprise us, it does nonetheless flesh out the particular nexus of hate that came to focus on Brandon, Lisa, and Philip.

Nowhere in the documentary, however, nor in media coverage of the case, does anyone link Nissen's racial politics with either the brutalization of Brandon or the execution of the African American, Philip; indeed, the latter is always constructed as a case of "wrong place, wrong time," but Philip's situation needs to be explored in more detail. In *The Brandon Teena Story*, Philip's murder is given little airplay, and none of his relatives or family make an appearance in the video. While every other character in the drama, including Lisa, is carefully located in relation to Brandon and the web of relations among Brandon's friends, Philip alone is given only the most scant attention. No explanation is given for the nonappearance of his family and friends, and no real discussion is presented about his presence in the farmhouse the night of the murders.[13]

It is hard to detach the murder of Philip from the history of Nissen's involvement in white supremacist cults. Many accounts of white power movements in the United States connect them to small, all-white towns in the Midwest and to economically disadvantaged white populations. While one would not want to demonize poor, white, rural Americans as any more bigoted than urban or suburban white yuppie populations in the United States, it is nonetheless important to highlight the particular fears and paranoia that take shape in rural, all-white populations. Fear of the government, fear of the United Nations, and fear of Jews, blacks, and queers mark white

---

12 Aphrodite Jones, *All S/he Wanted* (New York: Pocket Books, 1996), 154.
13 For more on the erasure of Philip and the downplaying of the racial narrative, see the debates about *Boys Don't Cry* in *Screen*, particularly the essay by Jennifer Devere Brody, "Boyz Do Cry: Screening History's White Lies," *Screen* 43, no. 1 (2002): 91–96.

rural masculinities in particular ways that can easily produce cultures of hate.[14] In small towns where few people of color live, difference may be marked and remarked in relation to gender variance rather than racial diversity. As Newitz and Wray point out in their anatomy of white trash, some degree of specificity is necessary when we try to describe and identify different forms of homophobia and transphobia as they are distributed across different geographies.

In "Get Thee to a Big City: Sexual Imaginary and the Great Gay Migration," anthropologist Kath Weston begins a much-needed inquiry into the difference between urban and rural "sexual imaginaries." She comments on the rather stereotyped division of rural/urban relations that "locates gay subjects in the city while putting their presence in the countryside under erasure."[15] Weston also traces the inevitable disappointments that await rural queers who escape the country only to arrive in alienating queer urban spaces. As Weston proposes, "The gay imaginary is not just a dream of a freedom to be gay that requires an urban location, but a symbolic space that configures gayness itself by elaborating an opposition between urban and rural life."[16] She wants us to recognize that the distinction between the urban and the rural that props up the gay imaginary is a symbolic one, and as such, it constitutes a dream of an elsewhere that promises a freedom it can never provide. But it is also crucial to be specific about which queer subjects face what kinds of threats, from whom, and in what locations. While in the city, for example, one may find that the gay or transsexual person of color is most at risk for violence from racist cops; in rural locations, one may find that even the white queers who were born and raised there are outlawed when they disrupt the carefully protected homogeneity of white, family-oriented communities. One may also discover that while the brutalization of a transgender sex worker of color raises little outcry in the city from local queer activists, the murder of a white boy in rural North America can stir up an enormous activist response that is itself symbolic of these other imaginary divisions.

The material in the Brandon archive has led me to question my own interest in the case and it has forced me to "know my place" in terms of the rural/urban divisions in queer communities that reactions to the story make visible. When I began thinking and writing about the Brandon murders in 1996, I approached the material with the bewilderment of a typical urban queer who wanted to know why Brandon, but also his African American friend Philip, did not pick up and leave Falls City as soon as they could, and

---

14   James Ridgeway, *Blood in the Face: The Ku Klux Klan, Aryan Nations, Nazi Skinheads, and the Rise of a New White Culture* (New York: Thunder's Mouth Press, 1995).

15   Kath Weston, "Get Thee to a Big City: Sexual Imaginary and the Great Gay Migration," *GLQ: A Journal of Lesbian and Gay Studies* 2, no. 3 (1995): 262.

16   Ibid., 274.

furthermore, why they were there in the first place. Falls City, in all the literature, sounded like the last place in the United States where one would want to try to pass as a man while dating local girls; it was also clearly not a good place to be one of the few people of color in town and a black man dating a white woman. Deindustrialization and the farming crises of the 1970s and 1980s had made this town, like so many other midwestern small towns, a place of poverty and neglect where jobs were hard to come by. For the young white men in town, minorities were to blame for this latest downward swing in their fortunes, and certainly the federal government offered no real hope of retribution.

Having read much of the material on Brandon's short life and brutal murder, and having viewed this documentary about the case, I quickly rationalized the whole episode as an inevitable case of a queer running afoul of the rednecks in a place one would not want to live in anyway. In fall 1996, I was invited up to Seattle to speak at a gay and lesbian film festival following the screening of *The Brandon Teena Story*. I would be joined as a discussant by Seattle-local transman and anthropologist Jason Cromwell and Los Angeles-based philosophy professor and transman Jacob Hale. We conferred briefly before the panel, and after sitting through the disturbing documentary, we went to the stage to discuss the film with the audience. The organizers of the conference seemed to assume that the debate likely to be motivated by the documentary would involve whether we should understand Brandon as a female-to-male transsexual without access to sex reassignment surgery or a transgender butch who had deliberately decided not to transition. My comments skimmed over this debate, which seemed beside the point, and went straight to the question of regionality, location, and rural existence. I remarked that Nebraska was not simply "anywhere" in this video, but that the documentary filmmakers had skillfully tried to situate the landscape as a character in this drama. The audience made noises of approval. Next, I went on to the topic of life in small, mostly white, midwestern towns, and suggested that many of these places were the breeding grounds for cultures of hate and meanness that had both homophobic and racist dimensions. The audience was quiet, too quiet.

The question-and-answer session began without controversy, and a few people testified to the difficulties they had encountered as female-to-male transsexuals or as partners of female-to-males. Others talked about the traumatic experience of watching the video and coming so close to the horrific details of Brandon's murder. Then something strange happened. A harmless question came my way: "What do you think of the documentary? Do you think it is good? Do you think the directors were at all condescending?" While I did have some real problems with the video and its representations of the people of Falls City, I felt that I had been invited to lead an even-handed discussion of *The Brandon Teena Story*, and so I shrugged off the implied criticism and said that I thought Muska and Olafsdottir had done some amazing interviews. The next question went a bit deeper: "What did you think about the depiction in the video of rural life, and furthermore, what do you mean by small towns in the heartland being 'cultures of hate and mean-ness?'" I tried to explain that I was describing the bigotry that resides in mostly white, nonurban constituencies. Then it got ugly. A woman stood up and denounced my comments as insensitive to those people present who may have come from small towns, and who, moreover, very much wanted to return to a small-town life and did not believe that the small town was an essentially racist or bigoted place. The audience broke out into spontaneous and sustained applause, and then one person after another stood up to testify that they too were from a small town or a rural background and that they too felt offended. Apart from a bruised ego (it is no fun to have an audience give a standing ovation to someone who has just told you that you are full of it), I left Seattle unscathed, but this experience forced me to reconsider what was at stake in the mythmaking that now surrounds Brandon's murder.[17] Confronted with my own urban bias, I decided that one could make use of the Brandon material to study urban attitudes toward queer rural life, and to examine more closely the essential links that have been made between urban life and queerness per se.

The murder of Brandon Teena, like the murder of Matthew Shepard some six years later, did in fact draw public attention to the peculiar vulnerabilities of queer youth (whether transgender or gay/lesbian) living in North America's heartland. In both cases, the victims became martyrs for urban queer activists fighting for LGBT rights, and they were mythologized in a huge and diverse array of media as extraordinary individuals who fell prey to the violent impulses of homophobic and transphobic middle-America masculinities. But while it is tempting to use the materials produced in the aftermath of the killings of both Brandon Teena and Matthew Shepard to flesh out the details of the lives and deaths of the subjects, it makes more sense to my mind to collect the details, the stories, the facts, and the fictions of the cases,

---

17 I found out later that the filmmakers, Muska and Olafsdottir, had been present at an earlier screening of the film in Seattle where similar concerns had been raised and no satisfactory answers had been provided by the two directors. In some ways, I was fielding questions meant for Muska and Olafsdottir, but in other ways, I was being positioned as another "outsider" who seemed not to be able to comprehend the complexities of small-town life in the Midwest. I tried to correspond with Muska and Olafsdottir about this particular set of reactions to their work, but to no avail. They did not want to talk about the question of "condescension" at all and had no insights to offer about these readings of *The Brandon Teena Story*.

and then to create deep archives for future analysis about the many rural lives and desires that were implicated in the lives and deaths of these individuals. Here I do not mean simply a collection of data; rather, I use the word archive in a Foucauldian way to suggest a discursive field and a structure of thinking. The archive is an immaterial repository for the multiple ideas about rural life that construct and undergird urban identity in the twentieth and twenty-first centuries. In the case of Brandon, the archive that has posthumously developed contains vital information about racial and class constructions of identity and desire in rural areas, and it also provides some important details about the elaborate and complex desires of young women coming to maturity in nonurban areas; the young women who were drawn to Brandon's unconventional manhood must have lots to tell us about adolescent feminine fantasy. As I will elaborate in later chapters,[18] all too often such girlish desires for boyish men are dismissed within a Freudian model of female sexuality as a form of immaturity and unrealized sexual capacity; the assumption that underpins the dismissal of adolescent female desires is that the young women who fall for a Brandon, a teen idol, or some other icon of youthful manhood, will soon come to full adulthood, and when they do, they will desire better and more authentic manhood. By reckoning only with Brandon's story, as opposed to the stories of his girlfriends, his family, and those other two teenagers who died alongside him, we consent to a liberal narrative of individualized trauma. For Brandon's story to be meaningful, it must be about more than Brandon.

Space and Sexuality in Queer Studies

In her lyrical rendering of life in an "other" America, the coal camps and "hollers" of West Virginia, Kathleen Stewart explores at length the meaning of memory for those who live life in forgotten places of neglect and poverty, or in what she calls the "space on the side of the road." In her ethnography, Stewart collects the untidy narratives that disorganize the conventional forward motion of ethnographic telling and thus allows us insight into the particular pull exerted by small-town life for even those subjects who are brutalized by it. One such narrative, for example, emerges when West Virginian Sylvie Hess offers Stewart a rambling recollection of a childhood experience in response to a question about why she could not make a life in the city. In order to explain the attraction of her dilapidated rural hometown, Sylvie recalls her favorite animal from childhood, a cow called Susie, who followed her around throughout her day. One day, however, some stray dogs savaged the cow, and "ripped out her throat and tore her all to pieces." Lingering for a moment over the brutal memory of her beloved cow "layin' there all tore up,"

---

18 See note 1.

Sylvie abruptly switches gears and comments, "But that place was saperty!" As Stewart observes, "Here, home is a vibrant space of intensity where things happened and left their mark. Home is sweet not despite the loss of her favorite cow but because of it."[19] Stewart's insightful rendering of the seemingly contradictory impulses animating Sylvie's memory provides momentary access for the urban reader to the appeal of the small rural town for the working-class subjects who stay there, finding beauty and peace in between the brutal realities of poverty, isolation, illness, and violence. For Stewart, the rural poor represent a forgotten minority in the US imagination and offer a fertile site for the ethnographic project of documenting difference.

In gay/lesbian and queer studies, there has been little attention paid to date to the specificities of rural queer lives. Indeed, most queer work on community, sexual identity, and gender roles has been based on and in urban populations, and exhibits an active disinterest in the productive potential of nonmetropolitan sexualities, genders, and identities.[20] Or else when nonurban sexualities have been studied, most often within anthropological studies, they are all too often characterized as "traditional" and "non-Western."[21] And yet, at the same time that most theories of modern sexuality have made definitive links between the city and homosexuality, urban queers have exhibited an endless fascination for stories of gays, lesbians, and transgender people living outside the city. For example, we might explain the appeal of the case of Brandon to urban queers in terms of its ability to locate the continuing homophobic and transphobic violence directed at sex- and gender-variant people in the United States in spaces removed from urban life.

---

19   Kathleen Stewart, *Space on the Side of the Road: Cultural Poetics in an "Other" America* (Princeton: Princeton University Press, 1996), 65.

20   Alan Sinfield usefully defines the "metropolitan" for use in queer studies in his essay "The Production of Gay and the Return of Power," in *De-Centring Sexualities: Politics and Representations beyond the Metropolis,* ed. Richard Phillips, Diane Watt, and David Shuttleton, Taylor and Francis e-Library edition (London: Routledge, 2005), 19–33. He remarks on the interactive definitions of metropolitan and nonmetropolitan and defines metropolitan sexualities as those that take place in the "'global centers of capital' and the principal cities in a nation state" (21). He qualifies this homogenizing notion of the metropolitan, however, by noting that "subordinated groups living at or near the centres of capital and specifically non-white minorities, may be in some aspects non-metropolitan; a Filipino living in New York may share some ideas and attitudes with people living in the Philippines" (21).

21   See Fabian, *Time and the Other.* Fabian writes that "the temporal discourse of anthropology as it was formed decisively under the paradigm of evolutionism rested on a conception of Time that was not only secularized and naturalized but also thoroughly spatialized" (16).

The deaths of Brandon and Matthew have sparked new considerations of the relationship between mainstream gay and lesbian rights movements and the harsh realities of lives lived far beyond the reach of rights-based policies. The response to these murders, in fact, suggests that they were, in the words of James C. Scott, "but a variant of affronts suffered systematically by a whole race, class, or strata." Scott writes:

> *An individual who is affronted may develop a personal fantasy of revenge and confrontation, but when the insult is but a variant of affronts suffered systematically by a whole race, class, or strata, then the fantasy can become a collective cultural product.*[22]

While Scott's book *Domination and the Arts of Resistance* pertains mostly to class relations in nondemocratic societies, in the age of global capitalism, democracy is now riddled with pockets of intense and naked oppression that both shore up the attraction of democratic rule and fortify the myth of its totality. For those subjects—nonmetropolitan queers, homeless people, undocumented laborers—who find themselves quite literally placed beyond the reach of federal protection, legal rights, or state subsidy, democracy is simply the name of their exclusion. For these subjects, the arts of resistance that Scott ascribes to slaves, serfs, and peasants become elaborate and necessary parts of a plan for survival. The Brandon archive is, in some ways, the "collective cultural product" that has responded to the affront of this brutal and phobic murder. And the archive reveals how little we actually know about the forms taken by queer life outside of metropolitan areas. The Brandon archive also makes historical and thematic links between the kinds of violences perpetrated against queer bodies and the documented violences against black bodies in lynching campaigns in the early twentieth century. Lisa Duggan has documented the ways in which lynching narratives and lesbian murder narratives in the 1890s mapped out overlapping histories of violence, and Duggan's powerful study of race, sex, and violence in her *Sapphic Slashers* makes these two seemingly distinct narratives tell a more complete story of the emergence of what she calls "twentieth century US modernity."[23] Brandon's story, coupled as it is with the death of African American Philip DeVine, reminds us of the interchangeability of the queer and the racially other in the white American racist imagination.[24]

---

22 James C. Scott, *Domination and the Art of Resistance: Hidden Transcripts* (New Haven, CT: Yale University Press, 1990), 9.

23 Lisa Duggan, *Sapphic Slashers: Sex, Violence, and American Modernity* (Durham, NC: Duke University Press, 2000).

24 For more on the overlap between deviance and race in the racial imaginary, see Roderick A. Ferguson, *Aberrations in Black: Toward a Queer of Color Critique* (Minneapolis: University of Minnesota Press, 2003).

Most theories of homosexuality within the twentieth century assume that gay culture is rooted in cities, that it has a special relationship to urban life, and that as Gayle Rubin comments in "Thinking Sex," erotic dissidents require urban space because in rural settings queers are easily identified and punished; this influential formulation of the difference between urban and rural environments was, in 1984 when Rubin's essay was first published, a compelling explanation for the great gay migrations of young queers from the country to the city in the 1970s.[25] And since Rubin's essay was heavily committed to the project of providing a theoretical foundation for "sexual ethnographesis" or the ethnographic history of community, it made sense to contrast the sexual conformity of small towns to the sexual diversity of big cities; such a contrast made crystal clear the motivations of young white gay men who seemed to flock in droves in the 1970s from small towns in the Midwest, in particular, to urban gay centers like San Francisco and New York. So in theory, the distinction between rural repression and urban indulgence makes a lot of sense, but in actuality, as recent research has shown, we might find that rural and small-town environments nurture elaborate sexual cultures even while sustaining surface social and political conformity. As John Howard argues in his book, *Men like That*, on rural gay male practices, "The history of gay people has often mirrored the history of the city."[26] But he goes on to show that this history of gay migrations to the city depends on a "linear, modernist trajectory" and "effects a number of exclusions."[27] Howard's book resists the universal application of the gay migration narrative, and instead looks at "the interactions between men who experienced and acted on queer desire within a small, localized realm, [and] men who never took on gay identity or became part of a gay community or culture."[28]

Rural and small-town queer life is generally mythologized by urban queers as sad and lonely, or else rural queers might be thought of as "stuck" in a place that they would leave if they only could.[29] Only of late has the

---

25 Gayle Rubin, "Thinking Sex: Notes for a Radical Theory of the Politics of Sexuality," in *Pleasure and Danger: Exploring Female Sexuality*, ed. Carol S. Vance (London: Pandora, 1992), 267-319.
26 John Howard, *Men like That: A Southern Queer History* (Chicago: University of Chicago Press, 1999), 12.
27 Ibid.
28 Ibid., 14.
29 This notion of rural queers being stuck in one place resonates with Gayatri Gopinath's theorizations of the meaning of queerness for those who "stay put" in postcolonial contexts rather than leaving a remote area for a seemingly liberated metropolis. See the chapter "Nostalgia, Desire, Diaspora: *Funny Boy* and *Cereus Blooms at Night*" in Gopinath's *Queer Diasporas and South Asian Public Culture* (Durham, NC: Duke University Press, 2005), 161-186.

rural/urban divide and binary begun to produce some interesting inquiries into life beyond the metropolitan center; in some recent work, the rural/urban binary reverberates in really productive ways with other defining binaries like traditional/modern, Western/non-Western, natural/cultural, and modern/postmodern. The editors of one anthology of queer writings on sexual geographies, for example, *De-Centring Sexualities: Politics and Representations beyond the Metropolis*, suggest that rural or nonmetropolitan sites have been elided within studies of sexuality and space, which typically focus on either "sexualized metropolitan areas such as New York and Berlin or on differently sexualized, marginalized and colonized spaces including the Orient and Africa."[30] By comparison, "much less has been said about other liminal or in-between spaces including the small towns and rural parts of Europe, Australia and North America."[31] The volume as a whole points to the dominance of models of what David Bell in his "Eroticizing the Rural" terms helpfully "metrosexuality" and the concomitant representation of the rural as essentially either "hostile" or "idyllic."[32]

The notion of metrosexuality as a cultural dominant in US theorizing about gay/lesbian lives also gives rise to the term metronormativity. This term reveals the conflation of "urban" and "visible" in many normalizing narratives of gay/lesbian subjectivities. Such narratives tell of closeted subjects who "come out" into an urban setting, which in turn, supposedly allows for the full expression of the sexual self in relation to a community of other gays/lesbians/queers. The metronormative narrative maps a story of migration onto the coming-out narrative. While the story of coming out tends to function as a temporal trajectory within which a period of disclosure follows a long period of repression, the metronormative story of migration from "country" to "town" is a spatial narrative within which the subject moves to a place of tolerance after enduring life in a place of suspicion, persecution, and secrecy. Since each narrative bears the same structure, it is easy to equate the physical journey from small town to big city with the psychological journey from closet case to out and proud. As Howard comments in *Men like That*, the rural is made to function as a closet for urban sexualities in most accounts of rural queer migration. But in actual fact, the ubiquity of queer sexual practices, for men at least, in rural settings suggests that some other epistemology than the closet governs sexual mores in small towns and wide-open rural areas. In reality, many queers from rural or small towns move to the city of

---

30   Richard Phillips and Diane Watt, introduction to Phillips et al., *De-Centering Sexualities*, 1.

31   Ibid.

32   David Bell, "Eroticizing the Rural," in Phillips et al., *De-Centring Sexualities*, 81-98.

necessity, and then yearn to leave the urban area and return to their small towns; and many recount complicated stories of love, sex, and community in their small-town lives that belie the closet model.

Metronormativity, while it reveals the rural to be the devalued term in the urban/rural binary governing the spatialization of modern US sexual identities, can also shed light on the strangely similar constructions of nonmetropolitan queer sexualities in the United States and nonmetropolitan sexualities in other parts of the world.[33] The recent work on "global gays," to use Dennis Altman's term, has assumed a model of global consciousness-raising within which "unenlightened" sexual minorities around the world, and particularly in Asia, come into contact with Euro-American models of gay identity and begin to form rights-oriented activist communities. In his book *Global Sex*, Altman repeatedly describes the flows of cultural influence between the United States and the "developing" world in terms of the sway of "modern" sexualities on traditional understandings of gender and desire. Sometimes Altman articulates his awareness of the fact that "sexuality becomes an important arena for the production of modernity, with 'gay' and 'lesbian' identities acting as the markers for modernity."[34] But he quickly falls back onto thoroughly unexamined assumptions about contemporary forms of embodiment and liberation; for example, he implies repeatedly that gender variance is an anachronistic marker of same-sex desire. Altman writes:

> *I remain unsure just why "drag," and its female equivalents, remains a strong part of the contemporary homosexual world, even where there is increasing space for open homosexuality and a range of acceptable ways of "being" male or female.*[35]

Altman's model of "contagious liberation," which is passed on from Westerners to those "closeted" folks in third world countries who remain committed to an anachronistic model of gender inversion and "drag," is deeply flawed. From his conception of a "universal gay identity" to his equation of Western identity with modernity and Asian and Latin American homosexualities with tradition, Altman persistently conjures up a complex model of globalization only to reduce it at the level of sexuality to a false opposition between sexual liberation and sexual

---

33 I recognize of course that "urban/rural" is not a "real" binary; it is rather a locational rubric that supports and sustains the conventional depiction of queer life as urban.

34 Dennis Altman, "The Globalization of Sexual Identities," in *Global Sex* (Chicago: University of Chicago Press, 2001), 91.

35 Ibid.

oppression.[36] What is more, his projections of sex/gender anachronism onto so-called developing nations unnecessarily simplifies and streamlines sex/gender systems in dominant nations.[37]

In an illuminating essay that acknowledges the difference between the kind of inevitable model of global gay life that Altman proposes and the active imposition of US sexual hegemonies, Alan Sinfield notes that "the metropolitan gay model will be found in Johannesburg, Rio de Janeiro and Delhi, as well as New York and London, in interaction with traditional local, non-metropolitan, models."[38] In other words, Sinfield recognizes that a global gay model is always interacting with other, often non-metropolitan sexual economies. At the same time, then, that we find evidence of the (uneven) spread of US sexual hegemony within these metropolitan areas named by Altman and Sinfield as centers for gay cross-cultural contact, could it be possible that nonmetropolitan models also share certain characteristics cross-culturally? These shared characteristics might be attributed less to capitalist modalities like gay tourism on which the metropolitan model depends and more to the separation of localized sexual economies from the so-called gay global model. In other words, could there be some level of correspondence be-

---

36 In "Qualities of Desire," Lisa Rofel has brilliantly pointed to the structuring contradiction in Altman's work that causes him to "assert cultural diversity and the need to respect it while also recuperating identification in a monumentalist history of gay identity, and, conversely, to further gay rights yet, in pursuing this goal, to elide diversity, articulation and alliance with radical cultural difference, thereby occluding the fault lines of power that emerge in global gay discourses and practices"; see Rofel, "Qualities of Desire: Imagining Gay Identities in China," *GLQ: A Journal of Lesbian and Gay Studies* 5, no. 4 (1999): 451–74. Altman has also been criticized by North American diasporic critics for ignoring the alternative sexual economies in different—particularly Third World—places, and for assuming that Euro-American models of sexual identity are both desirable and desired. See Jacqui Alexander, "Imperial Desire/Sexual Utopias: White Gay Capital and Transnational Capital," in *Talking Visions: Multicultural Feminism in a Transnational Age*, ed. E. Shohat (Cambridge: MIT Press, 1998), 281–306; Gayatri Gopinath, "Bombay, UK, Yuba City: Bhangra Music and the Engendering of Diaspora," *Diaspora* 4, no. 3 (1995): 303–22; and Martin Manalansan, "In the Shadow of Stonewall: Examining Gay Transnational Politics and the Diasporic Dilemma," in *The Politics of Culture in the Shadow of Capital*, ed. L. Lowe and D. Lloyd (Durham, NC: Duke University Press, 1997), 485–505.

37 For more on the tendency of Western queer anthropologists to produce unidimensional models of Euro-American queer subjects in order to emphasize the otherness of non-Western queers, see Gayatri Gopinath, "Homo-Economics: Queer Sexualities in a Transnational Frame," in *Burning Down the House: Recycling Domesticity*, ed. R. M. George (Boulder, CO: Westview, 1998), 102–24.

38 Alan Sinfield, "The Production of Gay and the Return of Power," 21.

tween a nonmetropolitan sexual system in rural Indonesia and one in rural Nebraska? And could both regions be considered "other" in relation to the dominant metropolitan model of gay male sexual exchange? In an essay on "gay" men in Indonesia, for example, Tom Boellstorff posits this potential for "someone thousands of miles away (to be) closer than someone next door," and helpfully labels this confluence of distance and similarity "translocal."[39] Calling for a "more serious engagement with postcoloniality as a category of analysis" within queer studies, Boellstorff argues that such an engagement "might improve our understanding of sexualities outside the 'West.'"[40] But the full deployment of translocal analysis—by which Boellstorff means a way of moving beyond the local/global and sameness/difference binaries that have characterized much of the work on transnational sexualities—would presumably also potentially improve and indeed complicate our understanding of sexualities *within* the "West."

The kinds of sexual communities, identities, and practices that Howard describes in *Men like That*, and that have been depicted and "discovered " in relation to narrative events like the murder of Brandon Teena, may indeed have less in common with the white gay and lesbian worlds associated with the castro in San Francisco, West Hollywood in Los Angeles, and Chelsea in New York, and they may share some significant traits with the sexual and gender practices associated with *tombois* in Indonesia and Thailand, *travesti* in Brazil, and *bakla* in the Philippines.[41] Like other nonmetropolitan sex/gender systems, US small-town and rural alternative sexual communities may often be characterized by distinct gender roles, active/passive sexual positioning, and passing practices; and like other nonmetropolitan models, they may exist in proximity to, rather than in distinction from, heterosexualities.

In the United States, rural populations are studied more often in relation to class or the formation known as white trash, and only rarely is the plight of the rural poor linked to other subaltern populations around the world. There are of course good reasons for not simply lumping all rural populations into one large subaltern formation: as George Lipsitz has documented, even working-class whites in the United States have a "possessive investment in whiteness" that situates them in often contradictory relations to power and

---

39 Tom Boellstorff, "The Perfect Path: Gay Men, Marriage, Indonesia," *GLQ: A Journal of Lesbian and Gay Studies* 5, no. 4 (1999): 480.

40 Ibid., 478.

41 Donald L. Donham, "Freeing South Africa: The 'Modernization' of Male-Male Sexuality in Soweto," *Cultural Anthropology* 13, no. 1 (1998): 3–21. http://www.jstor.org/stable/656686; Manalansan, "In the Shadow of Stonewall"; and Rosalind C. Morris, "Three Genders and Four Sexualities: Redressing the Discourses on Sex and Gender in Contemporary Thailand," *Positions* 2, no. 1 (1994): 15–43. doi:10.1215/10679847-2-1-15.

dominant discourses.[42] In the Midwest, moreover, the history of whiteness is linked to the early-twentieth-century Alien Land Laws, which restricted landownership only to those eligible for citizenship, thereby excluding, for example, Asian immigrants.[43] As the federal government waged war on native populations in states like Nebraska, "white" immigrants from Scandinavia and other northern European destinations were encouraged to settle in the Midwest by specific government policies aimed at recruiting "white" settlers.[44] White rural populations in the United States, particularly in the Midwest, must in fact be thought about through the racial project of whiteness and the historical construction of working-class "whiteness" as a place of both privilege and oppression. Because of this complex construction, we must avoid either romanticizing rural lives or demonizing them: rural queers in particular may participate in certain orders of bigotry (like racism or political conservatism) while being victimized and punished by others (like homophobia and sexism). If we turn to the case of Brandon's murder, we discover a developing archive for the further consideration of queer rural lives. In the narratives and accounts that have poured out of the tragic murder of a young transgender man and his two friends in rural Nebraska, we find an intricate knot of questions about how Brandon passed; the desire he elicited from local girls; his relationship to gay, lesbian, and transgender identities; the hate and violence his performance drew from two young white male friends; and the enduring legacy of the whiteness of the heartland.

One account of gay life in the Midwest that records the combination of privilege and oppression that characterizes the lives of the white gay men who live there can be found in an oral history project called *Farm Boys*.[45] In this volume, historian Will Fellows collected the memories and testimonies of a group of midwestern gay men, all of whom grew up on farms in Scandinavian American or German American families. The narratives presented by Fellows in *Farm Boys* were all submitted in response to a questionnaire that he circulated, and so the stories have an unfortunate generic quality that emphasizes the similarities rather than the differences between the life experiences of the men. In this stock format, each man speaks of his relationship

---

42 George Lipsitz, *The Possessive Investment in Whiteness: How White People Profit from Identity Politics* (Philadelphia: Temple University Press, 1998).

43 Lisa Lowe, *Immigrant Acts: On Asian American Cultural Politics* (Durham, NC: Duke University Press, 1996).

44 Thomas R. Hietala, *Manifest Design: American Exceptionalism and Empire* (Ithaca, NY: Cornell University Press, 2003); and Robert C. Lieberman, *Shifting the Color Line: Race and the American Welfare State* (Cambridge, MA: Harvard University Press, 1998).

45 Will Fellows, *Farm Boys: Lives of Gay Men from the Rural Midwest* (Madison: University of Wisconsin Press), 1998.

with his father and brothers, describes some childhood sexual experiences (many with livestock, for example), and discusses his move from his rural hometown to the city and (sometimes) back again. But despite the repetitive and formulaic nature of these stories, some important features do emerge. Many of the men stress, for instance, the isolation and lack of queer community in rural settings. Their isolation has sometimes led to a lengthy delay in the man's coming-out process, and many take detours through unwanted marriages. Yet the isolation can, on occasion, also allow for an array of gay or queer identities since the men are not modeling themselves on one stereotypical narrative. The emergence of idiosyncratic formulations of sexual identity implies that if certain sex/gender categories are not presented as inevitable, other options may emerge. Howard claims as much in *Men like That*: "What is apparent is that gay identity in Mississippi (surely as elsewhere) existed alongside multiple queer desires that were not identity based or identity forging."[46]

Farm Boys also shows that rural settings and small towns may offer a reduced amount of contact between the queer person and the kinds of medical discourses that have been so influential on the lives of gays, lesbians, and transsexuals in the twentieth century.[47] Also, in climates where homosexual identity is not forbidden but simply unthinkable, the pre-adult sexual subject who pursues same-sex eroticism may do so without necessarily assuming that this sexual activity speaks the truth of one's identity. Furthermore, according to the male narrators of *Farm Boys*, same-sex sexual activity for them was not necessarily accompanied by noticeable degrees of effeminacy, and in fact, male effeminacy was actively discouraged within their communities less as a sign of homosexual tendencies and more because it did not fit with the heavy labor expected of boys in farm families. By the same logic, however, rural women were more likely to be characterized by gender inversion because masculinity in women seems not to have been actively discouraged. A masculine woman, in the context of a farm, is not automatically read as a lesbian; she is simply a hardworking woman who can take care of herself and her farm. Farm masculinities for men and women, then, result in an asymmetrical development of gay and lesbian identities in terms of their relations to gender-inversion models of sexual identity.

Many of the men in *Farm Boys* disassociated themselves from the metropolitan gay worlds that they discovered once they left their rural and small-town homes. Some were puzzled and disturbed by gay effeminacy in the cities, and others were annoyed by the equation of gay with "activist." This desire to have a sexual practice separate from an overt ideological critique

---

46 Howard, *Men like That*, 29.
47 Jennifer Terry, *An American Obsession: Science, Medicine, and the Place of Homosexuality in Modern Society* (Chicago: University of Chicago Press, 1999).

of the state or heteronormativity can be taken as one legacy of the history of whiteness that marks the communities the gay rural men left behind. Fellows makes no comment on the often reactionary political sentiments of these white gay men and his remarks focus instead on the importance of pluralistic accounts of gay life. As an oral historian, furthermore, who has actively solicited and shaped the responses of his informants, Fellows has left himself little room for critical commentary. His project points to the difficulties involved in taking account of rural gay lives, but it also charts the contradictory nature of rural queers who have been omitted from dominant accounts of queer life and yet must not be represented as a subaltern population.

As Fellows's volume argues, it is not always easy to fathom the contours of queer life in rural settings because, particularly in the case of gay men, queers from rural settings are not well represented in the literature that has been so much a hallmark of twentieth-century gay identity. Gay men and lesbians from rural settings tend not to be artists and writers in such great numbers, and so most of the coming-out stories that we read are written by people from cities or suburbs. As Eve Kosofsky Sedgwick's work has shown in compelling detail, the history of twentieth-century literature in an Anglo-American context has been indelibly marked and influenced by the contributions of white gay men; consequently, literature has been a powerful vehicle for the production and consolidation of gay identity.[48] But again, little of this literature has anything at all to say about rural life, and most of it ties homosexual encounters to the rhythms of the city. Just a quick glance at some of the most influential high-culture texts of queer urban life would reveal gay guidebooks to Oscar Wilde's London, Jean Genet's Paris, Christopher Isherwood's Berlin, E. M. Forster's Florence, Thomas Mann's Venice, Edmund White's New York, John Rechy's Los Angeles, Allen Ginsberg's San Francisco, and so on. Canonized literary production by Euro-American lesbian writers like Radclyffe Hall, Djuna Barnes, Jeanette Winterson, and Gertrude Stein similarly focuses, although less obsessively, on urban locations like Paris, London, and New York. But in queer writing by women, we do find some of the themes that we might also expect to see in accounts of rural queer life like stories of isolation and numerous passing narratives.

While fictional narratives of queer rural life are quite hard to find, some ethnographic work and oral histories did emerge in the 1990s. Howard's *Men like That* is an exemplary and unique history and ethnographic survey of the sexual practices and social mores of men who have sex with men in southern Mississippi. His book examines "sexual and gender nonconformity,

---

[48] Eve Kosofsky Sedgwick, *Between Men: English Literature and Male Homosocial Desire* (New York: Columbia University Press, 1986); and *Epistemology of the Closet* (Berkeley: University of California Press, 1990).

specifically male homosexualities and male-to-female transgender sexualities in Mississippi from 1945-1985."[49] Arguing that men "like that" in the rural South in the 1950s were "largely homebound, living in familial households," Howard shows that these men did travel nonetheless, but most did not migrate to big cities; instead, "queer movement consisted of circulation rather than congregation."[50] Most queers, he claims, found partners within their immediate vicinity, and in the 1950s, these men were able to escape state surveillance of their illicit activities and their queer sexual practices went undetected. By the supposedly liberal 1960s, however, a new discourse of perversion allowed for the large-scale harassment and arrest of large numbers of queer men. What Howard's book perhaps does not emphasize enough is the impunity from legal and moral scrutiny in Mississippi that was extended specifically to white men while the sexual activities of black men (gay or straight) were constantly watched by fretful white citizens. In fact, it is not so surprising that white patriarchs during the same period were able to have sex with boys, black men, and each other without incurring any kind of comment. Howard's book also has little to say about female sexual practices in rural areas, and we are left to wonder whether the histories of men like that can tell us anything at all about the women who were also homebound and yet had no opportunities for congregation or circulation.

While Brandon fits only nominally into the category of "woman" and while his complex story cannot at all be called "lesbian," Brandon's choices do give us some insight into what kinds of options may exist for cross-identified, female-born transgender people in rural settings. Many urban gays, lesbians, and transgender people responded to the murder of Brandon with a "what do you expect" attitude, as if brutality was an inevitable consequence of trying to pull off such a risky endeavor as passing for male in some godforsaken place. But what such a response ignores is the fact that Brandon had been passing for male with only mixed success in the city of Lincoln, Nebraska, since his early teenage years; indeed, it was only when he left the city and made a reverse migration to the small town of Falls City that he really pulled off a credible presentation as male. Obviously, the small town can accommodate some performances even as it is a dangerous place for others—for example, an exhibition of normative masculinity in a transgender man may go unnoticed while an overt and public demonstration of non-normative gendering may be severely and frequently punished. Urban responses to Brandon's decisions also misunderstand completely the appeal of the small town to certain subjects. Like Sylvie Hess, the West Virginian in Stewart's ethnography who remembers the loss of a favorite animal and the

---

49 Howard, *Men like That*, xiv.
50 Ibid.

beauty of the place of its death side by side, the rural queer may be attracted to the small town for precisely those reasons that make it seem uninhabitable to the urban queer.

Brandon clearly knew what was possible in Falls City, Nebraska, and he seemed to know what limits might be imposed on his passing performance. He moved to Falls City not in order to be a stranger with no history but because he had friends there. As Angelia R. Wilson observes in an essay about "Gay and Lesbian Life in Rural America": "Unknown outsiders are never welcomed in small towns." And she continues: "The key to survival in a rural community is interdependence."[51] Brandon quite quickly developed a friendship network in Falls City, which included both his girlfriends and his killers, but he seemed to take a certain comfort in being known and in knowing everyone in town. By moving to a small town and setting up life as a young man, moreover, Brandon was operating within the long tradition of passing women in rural areas of North America that has been documented by historian Lisa Duggan among others. Wilson mentions at least one such narrative in her essay involving an "African American woman who lived as a man for 15 years" in Mississippi in the 1940s and 1950s. Jim McHarris/Annie Lee Grant lived in a small town called Kosciusko, working and dating women, and was only discovered when he was arrested by the local police for a traffic violation. After that, Jim left town and began his life as a man elsewhere. The story was reported in *Ebony* in 1954.[52] And there are many more. While gender codes may be somewhat more flexible in urban settings, this also means that people become more astute in urban contexts at reading gender. In the context of a small town where there are strict codes of normativity, there is also a greater potential for subverting the codes surreptitiously.

The Brandon story brings to light at least three historiographical problems related to the topic of studying queer rural life. First, this narrative reveals how difficult transgender history has been to write in general, but also how there may be specific dimensions of transgender identity that are particular to a rural setting. Given that many gay, lesbian, and transgender people who grow up and live in small rural areas may not identify at all with these labels, the rural context allows for a different array of acts, practices, performances, and identifications. Second, the Brandon story suggests that too often minority history hinges on representative examples provided by the lives of a few extraordinary individuals. And so in relation to the complicated matrix of rural queer lives, we tend to rely on the story of a Brandon Teena or a Matthew Shepard rather than finding out about the queer people who live

---

51 Angelina R. Wilson, "Getting Your Kicks on Route 66: Stories of Gay and Lesbian Life in Rural America, c. 1950s–1970s," in Phillips et al., *De-Centring Sexualities*, 203.

52 The *Ebony* article cited by Wilson is from November 10, 1954.

quietly, if not comfortably, in isolated areas or small towns all across North America. The "representative individual" model of minority history, furthermore, grows out of the particular tendency in Western culture to think about sexuality in terms of, as Foucault describes it, "the implantation of perversions," which in turn surface as identities.[53] The history of sexuality in a Euro-American context has therefore traced the medical and legal histories of the formation of identities like "homosexual," "lesbian," "transsexual," and "heterosexual." While Foucauldian histories have been careful to depict the sexological production of identities over space and time, still much critical attention focuses on the individual, the formation and transformations of self, the psychology of desire, the drama of pathology and pathologization, the emergence of types, and even the biographies of famous representative individuals (like Radclyffe Hall, Oscar Wilde, and so on). Less time, as George Chauncey has pointed out, has been spent on considering the developments of queer communities, and the negotiations of desire and identity within communities that may be unified or disunified by other modes of identification.[54] Even less time has been spent in consideration of those subjects who remain outside the ambit of the medical and psychological productions of identity, and the reverse discourses that greet and shape their use. Precisely because queer history has been so preoccupied with individuals, it has been harder to talk about class and race, and it has seemed much more relevant to discuss gender variance and sexual practices. All too often, community models are offered only as a generalized model of many individuals rather than as a complex interactive model of space, embodiment, locality, and desire. The Brandon archive, then, needs to be read less in terms of the history of one extraordinary person, and more in terms of the constructions of community and self that it brings to light.

The third and final historiographical problem in relation to this case has to do with the stakes of authenticity. What is real? What is narrative? As I argue in chapter 6 in relation to Austin Powers and drag king subcultures,[55] queer genders profoundly disturb the order of relations between the authentic and the inauthentic, the original and the mimic, the real and the constructed. And as we will see in the next chapter in relation to transgender biographies,[56] there are no true accounts of "passing lives" but only fictions, and the whole story turns on the production of counterfeit realities that are

---

53 Michel Foucault, *The History of Sexuality* (New York: Vintage, 1980).
54 George Chauncey, "Christian Brotherhood or Sexual Perversion? Homosexual Identities and the Construction of Sexual Boundaries in the World War I Era," in *Hidden from History: Reclaiming the Gay and Lesbian Past*, ed. M. Vicinus, G. Chauncey, and M. B. Duberman (New York: Meridian, 1989), 294–317.
55 See note 1.
56 Ibid.

so convincing that they replace and subsume the real. This case itself hinges on the production of a "counterfeit" masculinity that even though it depends on deceit and illegality, turns out to be more compelling, seductive, and convincing than the so-called real masculinities with which it competes.

Future Histories

Ultimately, the Brandon archive is not simply the true story of a young queer misfit in rural North America. It is also a necessarily incomplete and ever expanding record of how we select our heroes as well as how we commemorate our dead. James Baldwin, in his account of the 1979 Atlanta murders of black children, calls our attention to the function of streamlining in the awful vicinity of violent erasure. In *The Evidence of Things Not Seen*, Baldwin writes:

> *The cowardice of this time and place—this era—is nowhere more clearly revealed than in the perpetual attempt to make the public and social disaster the result, or the issue of a single demented creature, or, perhaps, half a dozen such creatures, who have, quite incomprehensibly, gone off their rockers and must be murdered and locked up.*[57]

The desire, in other words, the desperate desire, to attribute hate crimes to crazy individuals and to point to the US justice system as the remedy for unusual disturbances to the social order of things must be resisted in favor of political accounts of crime and punishment. In the end, we are not simply celebrating a Brandon Teena and denouncing a John Lotter or Thomas Nissen, nor should we be seeing love as the redemptive outcome to a tale of hate; the real work of collecting the stories of a Brandon Teena, a Billy Tipton, or a Matthew Shepard must be to create an archive capable of providing a record of the complex interactions of race, class, gender, and sexuality that result in murder, but whose origins lie in state-authorized formations of racism, homophobia, and poverty. Justice in the end lies in the unraveling of the crime not simply in its solution, and when we cease to unravel we become collaborators. "The author of a crime," notes Baldwin, "is what he is . . . but he who collaborates is doomed forever in that unimaginable and yet very common condition which we weakly call hell."[58] The stories we collect in the Brandon archive should stretch far beyond the usual tales of love and hate and the various narratives of accommodation; this archive lends us precisely the kind of evidence for things not seen that Baldwin sought, and in the end, if we read it right, it may tell us a different story about late-twentieth-century desire, race, and geography. With careful organization now, this archive may also become an important resource later for future queer historians who

---

57 James Baldwin, *Evidence of Things Not Seen* (New York: Henry Holt, 1995), 72.
58 Ibid., 125.

want to interpret the lives we have lived from the few records we have left behind.

Bibliography

Alexander, Jacqui. "Imperial Desire/Sexual Utopias: White Gay Capital and Transnational Capital." In *Talking Visions: Multicultural Feminism in a Transnational Age*, edited by E. Shohat, 281–306. Cambridge: MIT Press, 1998.

Altman, Dennis. "The Globalization of Sexual Identities." In *Global Sex*, 86–105. Chicago: University of Chicago Press, 2001.

Baldwin, James. *Evidence of Things Not Seen*. New York: Henry Holt, 1995.

Bell, David. "Eroticizing the Rural." In Phillips et al., *De-Centring Sexualities*, 81–98.

Boellstorff, Tom. "The Perfect Path: Gay Men, Marriage, Indonesia." *GLQ: A Journal of Lesbian and Gay Studies* 5, no. 4 (1999): 475–509.

Boys Don't Cry. Directed by Kimberly Peirce. Los Angeles: Fox Searchlight Pictures, 1999. DVD.

The Brandon Teena Story. Directed by Susan Muska and Greta Olafsdottir. New York: Zeitgeist Films, 1998. DVD.

Brody, Jennifer Devere. "Boyz Do Cry: Screening History's White Lies." *Screen* 43, no. 1 (2002): 91–96.

Cather, Willa. *Lucy Gayheart*. New York: Knopf, 1935.

Chauncey, George. "Christian Brotherhood or Sexual Perversion? Homosexual Identities and the Construction of Sexual Boundaries in the World War I Era." In *Hidden from History: Reclaiming the Gay and Lesbian Past*, edited by M. Vicinus, G. Chauncey, and M. B. Duberman, 294–317. New York: Meridian, 1989.

Cvetkovich, Ann. *An Archive of Feelings: Trauma, Sexuality and Lesbian Public Cultures*. Durham, NC: Duke University Press, 2003.

Donham, Donald L. "Freeing South Africa: The 'Modernization' of Male-Male Sexuality in Soweto." *Cultural Anthropology* 13, no. 1 (1998): 3–21. http://www.jstor.org/stable/656686.

Duggan, Lisa. *Sapphic Slashers: Sex, Violence, and American Modernity*. Durham, NC: Duke University Press, 2000.

Fabian, Johannes. *Time and the Other: How Anthropology Makes Its Object*. New York: Columbia University Press, 2002.

Fellows, Will. *Farm Boys: Lives of Gay Men from the Rural Midwest*. Madison: University of Wisconsin Press, 1998.

Ferguson, Roderick A. *Aberrations in Black: Toward a Queer of Color Critique*. Minneapolis: University of Minnesota Press, 2003.

Foucault, Michel. *The History of Sexuality*. New York: Vintage, 1980.
Gopinath, Gayatri. "Bombay, UK, Yuba City: Bhangra Music and the Engendering of Diaspora." *Diaspora* 4, no. 3 (1995): 303–22.
———. "Homo-Economics: Queer Sexualities in a Transnational Frame." In *Burning Down the House: Recycling Domesticity*, edited by R. M. George, 102–24. Boulder, CO: Westview, 1998.
———. "Nostalgia, Desire, Diaspora: *Funny Boy* and Cereus Blooms at Night." In *Queer Diasporas and South Asian Public Culture*, 161–186. Durham, NC: Duke University Press, 2005.
Hietala, Thomas R. *Manifest Design: American Exceptionalism and Empire*. Ithaca, NY: Cornell University Press, 2003.
Howard, John. *Men like That: A Southern Queer History*. Chicago: University of Chicago Press, 1999.
Jones, Aphrodite. *All S/he Wanted*. New York: Pocket Books, 1996.
Lieberman, Robert C. *Shifting the Color Line: Race and the American Welfare State*. Cambridge, MA: Harvard University Press, 1998.
Lipsitz, George. *The Possessive Investment in Whiteness: How White People Profit from Identity Politics*. Philadelphia: Temple University Press, 1998.
Lowe, Lisa. *Immigrant Acts: On Asian American Cultural Politics*. Durham, NC: Duke University Press, 1996.
Manalansan, Martin. "In the Shadow of Stonewall: Examining Gay Transnational Politics and the Diasporic Dilemma." In *The Politics of Culture in the Shadow of Capital*, edited by L. Lowe and D. Lloyd, 485–505. Durham, NC: Duke University Press, 1997.
Morris, Rosalind C. "Three Genders and Four Sexualities: Redressing the Discourses on Sex and Gender in Contemporary Thailand." *Positions* 2, no. 1 (1994): 15–43. doi:10.1215/10679847-2-1-15.
Newitz, Annalee, and Matt Wray, eds. *White Trash: Race and Class in America*. New York: Routledge, 1996.
Phillips, Richard, and Diane Watt. Introduction to *De-Centring Sexualities: Politics and Representations beyond the Metropolis*, 1–16.
Phillips, Richard, Diane Watt, and David Shuttleton, eds. *De-Centring Sexualities: Politics and Representations beyond the Metropolis*. London: Routledge, 2000. Reprint, London: Routledge, 2005. Taylor and Francis e-Library edition.
Ridgeway, James. *Blood in the Face: The Ku Klux Klan, Aryan Nations, Nazi Skinheads, and the Rise of a New White Culture*. New York: Thunder's Mouth Press, 1995.
Rofel, Lisa. "Qualities of Desire: Imagining Gay Identities in China." *GLQ: A Journal of Lesbian and Gay Studies* 5, no. 4 (1999): 451–74.

Rubin, Gayle. "Thinking Sex: Notes for a Radical Theory of the Politics of Sexuality." In *Pleasure and Danger: Exploring Female Sexuality*, edited by Carol S. Vance, 267–319. London: Pandora, 1992.

Scott, James C. *Domination and the Art of Resistance: Hidden Transcripts*. New Haven, CT: Yale University Press, 1990.

Sedgwick, Eve Kosofsky. *Between Men: English Literature and Male Homosocial Desire*. New York: Columbia University Press, 1986.

———. *Epistemology of the Closet*. Berkeley: University of California Press, 1990).

Sinfield, Alan. "The Production of Gay and the Return of Power." In Phillips et al., *De-Centring Sexualities*, 19–33.

Stewart, Kathleen. *Space on the Side of the Road: Cultural Poetics in an "Other" America*. Princeton: Princeton University Press, 1996.

Terry, Jennifer. *An American Obsession: Science, Medicine, and the Place of Homosexuality in Modern Society*. Chicago: University of Chicago Press, 1999.

Weston, Kath. "Get Thee to a Big City: Sexual Imaginary and the Great Gay Migration." *GLQ: A Journal of Lesbian and Gay Studies* 2, no. 3 (1995): 253–277.

Wilson, Angelina R. "Getting Your Kicks on Route 66: Stories of Gay and Lesbian Life in Rural America, c. 1950s–1970s." In Phillips et al., *De-Centring Sexualities*, 195–211.

Love and Lubrication in the Archives, or rukus! A Black Queer Archive for the United Kingdom

Ajamu X, Topher Campbell, and Mary Stevens[1]

> *Deep in thought and*
> *Reading works of white men,*
> *I am sometimes forced to sift*
> *To give my credence, to my people*
> *My mind has to rewrite*
> *What isn't there but was.*

~From "In Pensive Mood" by Dirg Aaab-Richards.[2]

Introduction by Mary Stevens:

"Sifting" the past to recover "what isn't there but was" is not just a solitary reflective endeavour for individuals from disinherited groups, it can also be an act of collective rebellion. For the Black queer community (of which Aaab-Richards can be considered in the UK not just a prophet but also a pioneer activist),[3] doubly marginalized by the splintering of activist historiography

---

1 Editors' note: this paper was previously published in "Special Section on Queer Archives," ed. Rebeka Sheffield and Marcel Barriault, special issue, *Archivaria* 68, no. 7 (2010): 271-294; all cross-references herein refer to that issue.

2 Dirg Aaab-Richards et al., *Tongues Untied: Poems by Dirg Aaab-Richards, Craig G. Harris, Essex Hemphill, Isaac Jackson, Assotto Sainte* (London: GMP, 1987), 13.

3 As well as being a poet, Aaab-Richards was, for example, the first Black Gay Men's Outreach and Development Worker for London's Black Lesbian and Gay Centre Project (1985-1989). Aaab-Richards was profiled in a booklet produced by Gay Men Fighting AIDS for Black History Month in 2001, *In the Family: Celebrating the Builders of Black Gay Communities* (London: Gay Men Fighting AIDS, 2001), 7, http://www.gmfa.org.uk/londonservices/booklets-and-postcards/pdfs/in-the-family.pdf. A second edition was produced in 2002, http://www.gmfa.org.uk/londonservices/booklets-and-postcards/pdfs/in-the-family-2.pdf. The biographical details for individuals provided in this article are mostly drawn from

into the discrete categories of a heteronormative Black history and an exclusive monochromatic queer history, the act of rewriting through collecting and disseminating the evidence of "what isn't there but was" is particularly urgent.[4] In the United States grassroots Black "queer archive activism" (defined by Alexandra Juhasz as "a practice that adds love and hope to time and technology"[5]) dates back to the early 1990s and in some cases before.[6] For the Black queer community in the UK, however, "nobody had pulled together this thing called heritage or archive"[7] until artists Ajamu X and Topher Campbell came together to create the rukus! archive project in 2005.

The purpose of this article is to introduce the work of rukus! to an international audience, and in so doing, to juxtapose it with the Canadian queer collections profiled elsewhere in this issue.[8] The rukus! archive project was launched in June 2005 by rukus! federation ltd. rukus! federation is a limited

---

these booklets, and readers are advised to consult these for additional information, since these sources were produced from within the Black LGBT community.

4 Judith Halberstam, *In a Queer Time and Place: Transgender Bodies, Subcultural Lives* (New York: New York University Press, 2005), 44; Horacio N. Roque Ramírez, "Memory and Mourning: Living Oral History with Queer Latinos in San Francisco," in *Oral History and Public Memories*, eds. Paula Hamilton and Linda Shopes (Philadelphia: Temple University Press, 2008), 167.

5 Alexandra Juhasz, "Video Remains: Nostalgia, Technology, and Queer Archive Activism," *GLQ: A Journal of Lesbian and Gay Studies* 12, no. 2 (2006): 326.

6 See for example Roque Ramírez on the San Francisco Latino Archivo Rodrigo Reyes, "Memory and Mourning," 178. Public institutions have also been active in this area. The Schomburg Centre for Research in Black Cultures, part of the New York Public Library, has been taking in gay and lesbian material since the early 1990s. For example, the papers of poet Joseph Beam in 1991; see Jacqueline Trescott, "Anthology Of a Mother's Grief; By Finishing Her Gay Son's Book, She Came to Terms With His Life," *Washington Post*, August 17, 1991. The Black Gay and Lesbian Archive Project was founded at the Schomburg in 2000, under the direction of Steven G. Fullwood; see http://web.archive.org/web/20101103150328/http://bgla.stevengfullwood.org/.

7 The interview between Ajamu X and Topher Campbell, the two co-founders of the archive, and researcher Mary Stevens was conducted on November 26, 2008 in the context of a UK Arts and Humanities Research Council-funded project based in the Department of Information Studies, University College London, titled "Community Archives and Identities: Documenting and Sustaining Community Heritage." The research team comprises Andrew Flinn, Elizabeth Shepherd, and Mary Stevens. The research would not have been possible without the help and partnership provided by our case studies (including rukus!) and many other participants and interviewees. For further details see http://www.ucl.ac.uk/infostudies/research/icarus/community-archives/.

8 See note 1.

company and charity established in 2000, dedicated to presenting the best in work by Black lesbian, gay, bisexual and trans (LGBT) artists. The archive project is one aspect of the federation's work and its mission is to collect, preserve, exhibit, and otherwise make available to the public historical, cultural, and artistic materials related to the black LGBT communities in the United Kingdom. More information about the background to rukus! and its objectives are set out in Ajamu and Topher's own words in the interview that constitutes the main body of this article. They do not, however, provide a linear narrative of rukus!'s development and various projects; this information—including a useful timeline[9]—is available at www.rukus.org.uk.

According to Stuart Hall, "Archives are not inert historical collections. They always stand in an active, dialogic relation to the questions which the present puts to the past."[10] In bringing together the creative energy of "an artistic sensibility" with the resistance to monolithic identity categories inherent to Black queer lives, the rukus! archive posits a more critical relationship to the mainstream than most. Indeed, in offering competing definitions of the "mainstream"—sometimes the "gay mainstream," sometimes the "Black mainstream," sometimes the culture of a dominant elite—Ajamu and Topher's discourse on their archival practice continually forces us all to question the position from which we speak, especially when we seek to claim authority for that position, for example as academics or heritage professionals.

The call for papers for this special section on queer archives invited contributions that would, among other things, present "an examination of a particular queer collection."[11] For many grassroots practitioners, squeezing thoughts, energies, and experiences into the restrictive stylistic norms expected of an academic journal article is not an appealing prospect. This may be particularly true of the "repositories of feelings" that constitute gay and lesbian archives where the excess of affect, generated by an archiving practice that is about so much more than the anesthetic process of preservation, militates against the dispassionate analysis academic writing is generally felt to demand;[12] as Topher comments in a moving meditation on the presence of pain and memory in the archive, "somebody else has to interpret, because we're too deep in it." However, to attempt to speak on behalf of rukus! would be to repeat the act of dispossession repudiated by Ajamu and Topher, to "describe and prescribe" (and inevitably to proscribe) like so many others

---

9   "rukus! Time Line," rukus!, http://rukus.org.uk/timeline/.
10 Stuart Hall, "Constituting an Archive," *Third Text* 15, no. 54 (2001): 92, doi:10.1080/09528820108576902.
11 See note 1.
12 Ann Cvetkovich, *An Archive of Feelings: Trauma, Sexuality and Lesbian Public Cultures* (Durham, NC: Duke University Press, 2003), 244.

before, hence the collective decision to use an interview format to represent the work of rukus!. It should also be noted that this interview was recorded in the context of a broader research project in the Department of Information studies at University College London (UCL), which from 2008 to 2009 used ethnographic methods to explore the relationship between practices of independent archiving and identity construction, specifically in culturally diverse communities. rukus! was one of the case studies for this project and at the time of the interview I had been working in particular with Ajamu intermittently for the preceding six months, attending rukus! events, meeting up for more informal chats about his work and, where possible and desirable, helping out in a voluntary capacity, for example in transcribing audio recordings. This interview took place at UCL on 26 November 2008 and was scheduled for the express purpose of drafting this article. There was, however, an ongoing period of preparation during which time Andrew Flinn and I built trust with Ajamu and Topher, and developed an understanding of their vision and motivation. We recognize that the interview is an unconventional approach to an academic article, but it is also the fruit of the ethnographic commitment of the UCL team to presenting our case studies on their own terms. Moreover, collectively we celebrate this exceptionality for, as Robert Mills has argued, "translating queer history into the language of public culture will involve a contestation of the very norms in which . . . history narratives are currently embedded,"[13] including, in our view, the publicly marginal form of the journal article.

More pressingly, as the transcriber and editor of over ninety minutes of unscripted, three-way discussion, I am acutely aware of the extent to which the translator is a traitor. In their dialogue around the archive, the text that follows conveys only the slimmest indication of the extent to which Ajamu and Topher are engaged in an intensely social practice, in which each continually prompts the other as they recall names, dates, places, and ideas, illustrating in microcosm the process Stuart Hall describes as the "living archive . . . whose construction must be seen as an on-going, never-completed project."[14]

Moreover, the text's suppression of laughter and gestures gives even less sense of the joy of the archive so central to the rukus! project; as Topher reminisces about the process of collection, "we had lots of fun, me and Ajamu . . . just talking about them days and whatever happened." More troublingly, I fear that I have imposed an artificial linearity on a much "queerer"

---

13 Robert Mills, "Queer Is Here? Lesbian, Gay, Bisexual and Transgender Histories and Public Culture," *History Workshop Journal* 62 (2006): 261.
14 Hall, "Constituting an Archive," 89.

temporality.[15] As Ann Cvetkovich argues, "emotional experience and the memory of it demand and produce an unusual archive, one that frequently resists the coherence of narrative or that is fragmented and ostensibly arbitrary."[16] Yet here the arbitrary resides purely in the erasure of speech through editing. The distortion is to some degree compensated for by the collaborative nature of the editing process, in which an original text was revised in accordance with Ajamu and Topher's comments, but the orality of the original interview is inevitably lost.[17]

Ajamu and Topher's discourse requires little gloss. Some key themes can, however, be drawn out. The importance of affect and the characteristic disrupted temporality of queer archives have both already been highlighted. In terms that underline the close relationship between desire and the archive, Topher notes: "it came more out of an impulse really, lots of impulses, impatience." The complex trope of mourning is also explored in detail; Eng and Kazanjian's insight that "the politics of mourning might be described as that creative process mediating a hopeful or hopeless relationship between loss and history"[18] provides a way of articulating the complex interplay of mourning and celebration evident in the work of rukus!, at the interface between two categories of identity—"Black" and "gay"—both of which have integrated powerful narratives of loss, suffering, and resistance. Traumatic archives often generate a strong performative dimension, because of "the need to address traumatic experience through witnessing and retelling,"[19] and indeed with rukus!, as Topher explains, "everything has a public face." Yet emphasizing the archive's performative quality is also a means to transform what could be melancholic into "a newly imagined tracing of possibility: the chance for fresh exchanges, memories, trips, and encounters."[20]

Many of these themes will also be in evidence in Black queer archives in North America, or the Netherlands, testifying perhaps to some alternative "norms" around which queer cultures coalesce. The rukus! archive does,

---

15 For a discussion of "queer temporalities" see Carolyn Dinshaw et al., "Theorizing Queer Temporalities: A Roundtable Discussion," *GLQ: A Journal of Lesbian and Gay Studies* 13, nos. 2-3 (2007): 177-95, doi:10.1215/10642684-2006-030.

16 Cvetkovich, *An Archive of Feelings*, 242.

17 The unintended consequences of the intervention of archivist-transcribers in marginalized histories are discussed by Rodney G. S. Carter, "Of Things Said and Unsaid: Power, Archival Silences, and Power in Silence," in "Archives: Space and Power," ed. Barbara L. Craig and Joan Schwartz, special section, *Archivaria* 61 (Spring, 2006): 226.

18 Cited in Roque Ramírez, "Memory and Mourning," 165.

19 Cvetkovich, *An Archive of Feelings*, 242.

20 Juhasz, "Video Remains," 324.

however, have some distinctly "British" qualities. Indeed, for Ajamu, the whole project was about "capturing something about being born and raised here" as opposed to in the United States. Perhaps one of the defining features of that "something," certainly for "the first out Black gay generation," is the influence of the Birmingham School of Cultural Studies, and Stuart Hall in particular, whose work has produced "generations" of thought and practice in contexts where traditional modes of cultural reproduction have lost purchase.[21]

Much as Stuart Hall fostered a collective rethinking of identity discourses, the work of rukus! (and others whom he inspired) is actively reshaping the public cultures of "blackness" and "queerness." In the process "one generation's yearning" is fuelling "another's learning" (*and* yearning).[22]

The Interview

Mary Stevens: Tell me about the background to rukus!

Ajamu: rukus! federation was formed in June 2000. It was launched at the London Institute of Contemporary Arts (ICA) as part of the Mardi Gras Festival.

Topher Campbell: The original event was commissioned by Valerie Mason-John a.k.a. Queenie, who was the artistic director of the Pride Arts Festival that year.[23] She was actively trying to diversify the festival. And we were thinking about rukus! or talking about rukus! a lot, and this was a way of launching it publicly and very centrally.

Ajamu: I think we had a thousand pounds, didn't we?

Campbell: We were given a thousand pounds. And we conceived this idea of a club-based arts event. We wanted to create an organization as a way of bringing together a lot of the artistic and political forces that we had embraced up until that point. rukus! became an expression of that at the ICA on June 23, 2000.

---

21 Stuart Hall is perhaps the leading theorist of "race" and ethnicity in the UK who, through his tenure in the Centre for Contemporary Cultural Studies, Birmingham University, from 1964 to 1979, was one of the foremost influences on the development of the contemporary discipline of Cultural Studies. For a recent introduction to the impact of his thinking see Claire Alexander, "Stuart Hall and 'Race'," *Cultural Studies* 23, no. 4 (2009): 658–87.

22 Juhasz, "Video Remains," 323.

23 Valerie Mason-John is an "author, playwright, performer, professional anger-management and self-awareness trainer"; for more information see http://www.valeriemason-john.com/; see also *In the Family*, 39.

Ajamu: It is important to mention that rukus! is about how we present our politics more playfully. So the name rukus! is a derivative of the word "raucous." And Rukus is also a well-known African-American porn star.

Campbell: We spelled it R-U-K-U-S because we felt that this would give us a distinctive on-line identity. The exclamation mark also underlines the playfulness of it all.

Ajamu: Lots of Black gay groups have identified themselves as Black-gay-this, Black-gay-that. With rukus! we wanted our own title: "rukus!" can do anything we want it to. We're not restricted to other people's identity categories. Early on I was often asked: Are you a Black archive, are you a gay archive, are you a London archive? And I'd say actually we're all these things, at the same time. Our politics have never been about either/or categories.

Campbell: Neither our politics nor our lifestyles. That's the very thing about rukus!, it's not a singular thing, it's about confusing the notion of simplicity. You have to embrace complexity and diversity when you are dealing with the idea of Black, gay, or lesbian identity. With rukus! we are building our own identity. The idea was always that we would have something that was set apart from, and in opposition to, both the Black and the White gay status quo, both in terms of the way that we wanted to define the idea of rukus! and in the way we wanted to express it in the public space. rukus! is not about saying we're victims; we're very much about redefining and replacing ourselves publicly. And we're not anti-White or anti-anything, we're pro.

Stevens: And so this first event turned into rukus! federation and the archive developed in the context of the federation?

Campbell: Yes, I think so. But time is a very strange thing. It plays tricks on you. The evolution wasn't steady or linear in a very clean way. It came more out [of] an impulse really, lots of impulses, impatience. I always remember it by thinking about what else I was doing at the time. I remember I was involved in Talawa Theatre Company[24] and creating a manifesto in East London for youth culture, and then I went to the BBC. And so there were places and strands of work going in and out of the conversations that we were having. But [it] is difficult to talk about time in terms of chunks, because time jumps backwards and forwards.

Ajamu: At the time I was living in the Netherlands, so a lot of the early rukus! work was done in cyberspace. But I was also running the Breakfast Club[25]

---

24 Talawa is a leading Black British theatre company, founded in 1989; for more information see http://www.talawa.com/about_talawa.php.

25 The Breakfast Club was a monthly group for Black men regardless of sexual preference; for more information see Ajamu's profile in *In the Family*, 8.

Ajamu, co-founder of rukus!, with items from the rukus! archive, November 2007. Image courtesy of Museum of London.

and I was involved in Gay Men Fighting AIDS,[26] as an assertiveness trainer. And I was running sex classes: bondage for beginners, S&M for beginners. But around the 2000 mark I was getting frustrated with the Black gay scene; it wasn't really happening for me. I just felt that the politics weren't that adventurous, that dynamic, that playful.

Campbell: For the record, the context for a lot of Black-identified, non-club-based events was to do with sexual health, research, and activism funded by NGOs, or local government, or health organizations. And so the prism was always quite narrow. But we were, and still are, struggling and battling artists. And we wanted to create something that reflected and sustained the energy of our creative practice. But Ajamu has driven the idea of the archive more than I have.

Ajamu: There are lots of points to be made about why the archive started. One is that a well-known activist had the builders come in. They saw a pile of papers and magazines, and they threw everything out. Also, a friend of mine, Tyrone Smith, had just committed suicide. I was left his doll collection and his porn collection. But the idea for the archive actually came about in 2004, when we got planning our own exhibition, "Family Treasures."

Campbell: We got very excited by this idea and we had lots of fun, me and Ajamu and people, just talking about them days and whatever happened. We'd gossip about what happened to this person or that person. And then stories emerge, about that Pride, or this Pride, or that person, or this person, and you start to realize that the collected memory is not getting stored anywhere. We wanted to reclaim the history and put it centre stage. Reclaiming that history is a political act. Look at James Baldwin, for example. A literary icon, the first superstar writer, arguably. But you still get a complete denial of his sexuality by Black academics and White literary critics who don't think it is important.[27] Then you look at someone like Bayard Rustin.[28] These are easy people to pick out. On a different scale, like lots of people, I've worked in lots of mainstream institutions. But I have a very politicized consciousness around my sexuality and my race, and I'm not the only one. I use myself because I don't want to talk about other people out of turn. We need to find a

---

26 For more information see Gay Men Fighting AIDS, http://www.gmfa.org.uk.
27 James Baldwin (1924–1987) was an African-American writer and civil rights activist, many of whose novels such as *Another Country* (New York: Dell, 1962) and *Tell Me How Long the Train's Been Gone* (New York: Dial Press, 1968), feature homosexual and bisexual African-American characters.
28 Bayard Rustin (1912–1987) was an American civil rights activist and adviser to Martin Luther King Jr. For more information, see Jervis Anderson, *Bayard Rustin: Troubles I've Seen* (New York: Harper Collins, 1997).

way of articulating that difference. The archive can find a way of doing that. You want to reclaim the notion that when you look at Black gay and lesbian history, you are not looking at a separate thing. You are looking at something that is integral to all our histories. Black gay history is the story of somebody's brother, somebody's daughter, somebody's son, somebody's sister. Or take Brixton, for example: the people in the shops, in the markets, the parties, the cottage, it's all around us. And places like the Brixton Art Gallery were seminal in terms of the Black and the gay experience.[29]

Ajamu: Around 1994 there was also the issue of the "Murder Music" campaign against homophobia within reggae music. For some people, both within our own communities and in the mainstream community, that campaign was seen as being led by Outrage!, a White gay group. We wanted to make it clear that this campaign started back in 1992 with Black Lesbians and Gays against Media Homophobia. There was a generational impetus around reclaiming as well. We were the first out Black gay generation. And I, or we, were just approaching forty and that raised lots of questions about identity and age. Today we're dealing with a younger generation who might never have heard of Linda Bellos,[30] or Valerie Mason-John and so forth. There's work to be done there, and we need to be having public discussions within our own communities, within the Black community, within the White community.

Campbell: The generational thing is important in the wider Black community too. People in their thirties to, say, fifties who are British, born in the UK, have seen their parents or grandparents dying. They've seen their heritage pass before their eyes, so there is a personal stake in this. The argument about archives is being won by virtue of experience. Our generation wants to see its experiences placed in the mainstream. Black History Month is now an institution in the UK. But we want to move beyond the clichés, beyond Windrush, and Notting Hill, and Brixton in the sixties.

Ajamu: And in these narratives about Black history and gay history we were just invisible. There was no representation there. Black History Month is an institution, but it had very few things that were gay in it. Even though it was founded by Linda Bellos! Even if you're talking about the Black arts scene, the history of people who came through that as Black and gay is totally missing.

---

29   Brixton is a neighborhood in the borough of Lambeth in south London that has been a focus for the African-Caribbean community in the UK, since many of the first wave of post-World War II immigrants were temporarily settled in the area. The majority of individuals and organizations documented so far by the rukus! archive have a strong Brixton connection.

30   Linda Bellos was elected Leader of Lambeth Council (in south London) in 1986. See *In the Family*, 14.

Campbell: So, why archive? Archiving is a way of achieving some sort of visibility. Personally, one way I found the need for this was working as a theatre director. I can sit pitching an idea or working at a conference, and somebody turns around and says, "Where are the Black directors? Where are they?" or "We don't have any Black writers. Who? I don't know anybody." In this context the archive is a deep political intervention. In future when someone says, "Black gay history, what is it? There isn't any," or people from our own community say, "We have no legacy," we'll be able to point to the archive and say, "This happened or that happened." And share that with friends in our circle or family members who are twenty years younger or twenty years older.

Ajamu: There was a big gap around the Black gay and lesbian experience in the UK. I can tell millions of stories about my family and the Black experience. I can tell a million stories about being gay. But in terms of Black *and* gay, a lot of the material I read came from the States. *Brother-to-Brother* and *In the Life*, those books informed a lot of my thinking around what it means to be Black and gay.[31] But for me, they didn't capture what was happening here. So the archive, or rukus!, was about capturing something about being born and raised here.

Campbell: It wasn't just about invisibility in history. The early nineties were also a time when the whole Black gay scene was invisible, and the White mainstream and the Black mainstream, if there is such a thing, were anti the idea of allowing us any space. There were a lot of conversations around the club scene about how we could counter that. There were some seminal clubs in the nineties, for Black gay men particularly, some of them for women. One was called Queer Nation, one was the Vox, one was the Velvet Room. The Velvet Room was the first major Black gay club to champion R&B. Playing urban music was a big debate in the White gay scene. And then suddenly Tyrone and Chris [McKoy],[32] and various other people who were DJing started to break in. There was a lot of energy happening around the Black gay scene with people breaking out from their own confines in the gay club scene and redefining the possibilities of what a Black gay man could be. And clubs were obviously and still remain the big social spaces. At the same time 1992 was the first ragga music debacle with Shabba Ranks,[33] which Isaac Julien documented in *The Darker Side of*

---

31 Joseph Beam, ed., *In the Life: A Black Gay Anthology* (Boston: Alyson, 1986); Essex Hemphill, ed., *Brother to Brother: New Writings by Black Gay Men* (Boston: Alyson, 1991).
32 See *In the Family* 2, 29.
33 Jamaican rapper Shabba Ranks called for the execution of gay men on Channel 4's youth show *The Word* in 1992. The presenter condemned his comments, but the episode caused a scandal.

Black.[34] So we are looking at a breakthrough period in terms of Black gay visibility around music within the mainstream, in a number of different respects.

Stevens: What were your other intellectual and political influences?

Campbell: In terms of thinking about memory, for me the artistic antecedents were people like Derek Jarman.[35] Isaac Julien was an important figure too.[36] And without getting too academic about it, in the eighties there was a lot of thinking in so-called Black mainstream identity politics around hybridity, and notions of difference and diversity, as defined by Black artists, mainly. In publications like *Ten.8*, which we were both reading.[37]

Ajamu: Coming from people like Stuart Hall, Kobena Mercer,[38] and David A. Bailey.[39]

Campbell: And Sonia Boyce. And we aren't disconnected from those kinds of discourses. I asked Stuart [Hall] and Kobena [Mercer] to comment on Ajamu's work [for *The Homecoming*, Black Arts Video Project, 1995], which

---

34 *The Darker Side of Black*, directed by Issac Julien (London, UK: Arts Council of Great Britain, 1994).

35 Derek Jarman (1942–1994) was a leading British experimental filmmaker and prominent gay rights campaigner. He died of AIDS-related complications. For a discussion of his life and work, introducing a special issue of the journal *Critical Quarterly* dedicated to Jarman, see Colin MacCabe, "Derek Jarman: Obituary," *Critical Quarterly* 36, no. 1 (1994): iii–viii.

36 Isaac Julien (born 1960) is a Black British visual artist and filmmaker, currently visiting professor at the Whitney Museum of American Arts. His 1991 film, *Young Soul Rebels*, which was awarded the *Semaine de la critique* prize at the Cannes Film Festival, features several Black gay characters, and is set against the racial and sexual tensions of 1970s London. For more information see Julien's own website, http://www.isaacjulien.com, and also *In the Family*, 29.

37 For more information see David Brittain's "Ten.8: A Critical Debate," http://web.archive.org/web/20091222011502/http://staff.biad.uce.ac.uk/staff/id003706/ten8/ten8.htm.

38 Kobena Mercer (born 1960, Ghana) is an art critic and cultural commentator, currently a reader in art history and diaspora studies at Middlesex University, London. For a selection of his publications, see http://www.iniva.org/library/archive/people/m/mercer_kobena.

39 David A. Bailey (born 1960) is a photographer, writer, and curator, currently senior curator of Autograph (ABP—Association of Black Photographers), whose collections are now at the heart of the new Archive and Research Centre for Culturally Diverse Photography, which opened in 2008, in a purpose-built centre in London, Rivington Place; for more information see http://www.iniva.org/library/archive/people/b/bailey_david_a.

they did. Stuart Hall's mischievous attitude to thinking about identity, race, and social politics is very much in keeping with our approach. He just has a way of articulating difference playfully, mischievously.

Ajamu: Playfully yet seriously. He's a very seminal figure. For our first exhibition, our banner line was "The past cannot exist without its archives." That was Stuart Hall.

Campbell: And then we've got another tag line which is "Making difference work," which is also from Stuart Hall. Ajamu was also involved in the Black Unity and Freedom Party.[40]

Ajamu: And Brixton Housing Association.

Campbell: So you had these interminglings of people. And the conversations we had with people who are not necessarily centrally Black and gay have been very important, in terms of how rukus! came about.

Stevens: You were the first out Black gay generation, but as a generation you were also heavily affected by AIDS. Community archives in gay and lesbian communities have often been linked to trauma. How important was the legacy of AIDS and other traumas in the decision to create an archive?

Ajamu: Some people might argue that the past will always be about mourning, and part of it can be traumatic. It is traumatic when I think about Rotimi [Fani Kayode]'s[41] [archive] box or Chris [McKoy]'s [archive] box, people who we knew personally, worked with, had long-term relationships with or whatever. But then not all the memories that come with a person and/or a box are traumatic. Sometimes it might trigger stuff that I've forgotten. So I'm not sure if it's about mourning.

Campbell: I remember part of my impetus was a political relation to AIDS and HIV because a lot of people had died in the nineties. A lot of histories were being lost or forgotten. But I think within the Black experience, to which slavery was so integral for so long, there is a level on which pain and memory are very interlinked. This pain, the pain of lived experience is not recognized, and so there's a need to hold it, and store it, and keep it as precious. It's not recognized because there's no language which allows it to be so. If I think about the way in which *we* Black people are described and prescribed in the Western canon, it doesn't allow for the kind of space that rukus! has, a space which is owned by us. Within this space, the personal is really important.

---

40 On the context in which the Black Unity and Freedom Party developed, see Ambalavaner Sivanandan, "Challenging Racism: Strategies for the '80s," *Race & Class* 25, no. 2 (1983): 1–11.

41 See *In the Family*, 34. Fani Kayode's work was first published in book form in *Black Male / White Male* (London: GMP, 1988).

These are very personal endeavours. What that might mean, somebody else has to interpret, because we're too deep in it. But people have died. People have died, or been killed, or been forgotten or ignored. Some very fascinating, interesting people in a culture which, for lots of different reasons—not just racism, but class and poverty—has denied their existence. It can be very painful to go on about that. So there is going to be some kind of mourning, or trauma, or pain involved in the public examination of all this. We're both quite confident, strong individuals in our own right, and we have our own personal stories and scars. But a lot of people don't have the same level of articulation or vision, or connection with any kind of community or past. And I think the archive goes some way to publicly acknowledging the pain and helping people come to terms with it.

Stevens: In my mind I had set up an opposition between mourning and celebration. But actually they're completely part of the same thing. You can celebrate someone's life at the same time as mourning their loss, can't you?

Ajamu: Definitely. It goes back to constantly wanting to break down the either/or paradigm. I think historically we bang on always about coming from a position of pain and trauma, and not one of pride and celebration. Celebration is a different way into some of the discussions around who you are and what you are.

Campbell: It's a very Black thing as well, I think, bringing together celebration and loss. Although we're at an interesting stage now. With the performative stuff and "Sharing Tongues"[42] celebration is winning out, I think.

Stevens: Let's go back to how you began to gather a collection.

Campbell: We started from our own collections, because we had photographs and memorabilia from our own collections. I was very much into the club scene, and I had loads and loads of flyers for some reason. I used to keep *Boyz* magazine covers,[43] fetish magazines, stuff like that. And I had all these *QX* magazines;[44] if there was a Black person on the covers, you'd generally know who that Black guy was. They were very small, very sporadic representations of Black gay men in mainstream gay culture.

---

42 "Sharing Tongues" is a rukus! project, funded by the Heritage Lottery Fund, to uncover, record, and make available the previously hidden Black LGBT history of London, Birmingham, Manchester, and Liverpool, through recording oral and written histories and the production of a CD, booklet, exhibition, and website. For more information visit "Sharing Tongues," rukus!, http://rukus.org.uk/category/sharing-tongues/.

43 See the back issues at *Boyz* magazine for examples: http://www.boyz.co.uk/.

44 See the *QX* magazine website for examples: http://www.qxmagazine.com/issues/.

Ajamu: Linked to this, I had always documented Gay Pride, and Black men at Gay Pride, from the 1990s onward, as a photographer. Some people who were photographed are no longer around, and that was another part of the impetus for "Family Treasures."

Campbell: We tried to get "Family Treasures" off the ground by writing to people like Dennis Carney,[45] and Dirg [Aaab-Richards], and various other people who had been active. We were asking "What have you got?" And nothing came back. Nothing came back.

Ajamu: Nobody responded.

Stevens: What were you asking for?

Ajamu: Anything and everything. Anything and everything that had been said about Black lesbians and gays.

Stevens: Why do you think you didn't get a response? And what changed over time?

Campbell: There is no one reason. I think you are looking at a maelstrom, you're looking at a kind of conspiracy, circumstances which prohibit you from thinking that what you do and what you have is valuable. Obviously some activists had tapes from when they were on TV, and others had campaign information. But most people just didn't think their material was valuable.

Ajamu: That's it. As far as I know, this was the first time that we had talked about heritage in relation to our sexual identity, within the context of the UK. So people would say, "it is *just* a flyer." And so they would dismiss it. Until we started asking, nobody had pulled together this thing called heritage or archive. So we left "Family Treasures," and it turned into the exhibition "The Queen's Jewels." Ironically, we got money through HIV work, through the Terrence Higgins Trust.[46] Because at this point, I was a trainer for Terrence Higgins Trust. And we held the exhibition at Positive East in Stepney Green [east London], which is an HIV centre. I was doing a Black men's photography workshop, and they gave us a room.

Campbell: A group of us helped paint it white for the exhibition. And we hung it ourselves. To gather the material for "The Queen's Jewels" we hounded people. We went to people's houses and sat with them.

---

45   Dennis Carney is a campaigner, freelance trainer, consultant, and therapeutic group worker, focusing on issues around diversity, sexual orientation, and HIV. He is currently Vice-Chair of the Black Gay Men's Advisory Group (BGMAG). For more background, see http://www.lovingmen.org/dennis-carney.php and *In the Family*, 23.

46   Terrence Higgins Trust is the leading HIV and sexual health charity in the UK; see http://www.tht.org.uk/our-charity/About-us.

Ajamu: I had this black notebook actually, and we would walk around asking people to show us what they had and making notes. Our networks were very useful for collecting material. For example Dorothea Smartt[47] and Valerie [Mason-John] helped us get in touch with lots of women that I didn't know so well, who also had material.

Campbell: We went to Steve's [Swindells] house,[48] and sat there for ages, I remember, and Dennis's [Carney]. Again, people would go, "well I don't know, what is it you want? I mean, there's nothing here." And then they'd come out with a box, and we'd go, "Oh wow, that's great!," or "that flyer," or "yeah, I've got some of those flyers, do you have some from the other time when that happened?" What is interesting, remembering it now, was some of the conversations. It's very difficult to articulate, but people were working in a very minority maelstrom—a maelstrom which had no mainstream recognition at all. It is very tiring to work in that way, whether you are a community activist, or a DJ, or a club promoter. And then you move on, you get older, and somebody comes along and says, "that was really valuable what you did," but at the time nobody was telling you it was valuable.

Stevens: Did you have the feeling that going through the process from talking about archives to seeing items on public display changed people's attitudes toward their material and their heritage?

Campbell: Yes, definitely. I remember having a long conversation with Dennis [Carney] and he was quite overwhelmed by the transformation of something that was stuck in the bottom of a box in his kitchen into something slightly iconic. We also went to the *QX* office, and we picked out all the *QX* covers up until 2004, which were Black.

Ajamu: Yes, at this point *QX* was almost on their 500th edition, and twenty-nine of its covers were Black.

Campbell: For *Boyz*, we used the covers that I had. They didn't respond to our request for covers. *Gay Times*, I had loads of covers already, and Ajamu had some, and various other people had them. "The Queen's Jewels" evolved into an archive by virtue of the material we had. Because we said, okay, we've got media and campaigning, we've got club-based stuff. We've got activism, we've got theatre. For me it was interesting because we had three big panels of club flyers over twenty years, from 1983, which was incredible, because people are always complaining that there is nowhere to go!

---

47 Dorothea Smartt is a writer, poet, and live artist. See *In the Family*, 52, and her website, http://dorotheasmartt.wordpress.com/about/.
48 Steve Swindells is a musician, journalist, and club promoter.

Ajamu: We had something from the first Black gay play in 1986. And we also had an obituaries section, with some of the men who died as well. There were forty-three pieces.

Campbell: We suddenly had all this stuff. We had no publicity machine, we sent out a small press release. And there wasn't very much take-up on that. Obviously *QX* said something, and I think, *Boyz* said something? Because we had their covers so they were interested.

Ajamu: And there was a line in the *Pink Paper*.[49]

Campbell: No photographers came out. In a way we were "victims," we were treated as if it were some sort of minority issue that doesn't really matter, by both the Black and the gay press. We never expected *The Voice* or *New Nation* to turn up.[50] But I think for me the frustration remained that we didn't reach out beyond the minority.

Ajamu: *The Voice* had had an article on Black Gay Pride in the States. And their offices were just down the road from Stepney Green. And there was nothing in there whatsoever about what we were doing.

Campbell: But the launch was a huge event, a big landmark event. I filmed it and we invited keynote speakers. It was a very moving exhibition for those people who hadn't had a sense of the history. It was an indication for a lot of people about the strength of the archive and the possibility of it. It was exciting to think about what it could be or how it could be. It was a landmark because everybody we had struggled to get involved or who didn't know really what our vision was suddenly saw this array of forty-three pieces in this big room, and saw the wealth of history there. How it connected both deep within personal stuff, like the obituaries, and into the mainstream, with people like Justin Fashanu[51] and Isaac Julian. And I think there was a ripple effect.

---

49 *Pink Paper* was a weekly newspaper for gay men, lesbians, and bisexuals. It first appeared in 1987, but since June 2009 has been available only on the Internet at http://www.pinkpaper.com/.

50 *The Voice* and *New Nation* were two of the leading, black, weekly newspapers in the United Kingdom. *The Voice* continues to be published every Monday in tabloid format and appears on the Internet at http://www.voice-online.co.uk/. In 1990 *The Voice* became a major target of the campaigning organization Black Lesbians and Gays Against Media Homophobia for its treatment of Justin Fashanu; see note 51 herein, and *In the Family*, 18. *New Nation* has been in administration since January 2009 (see http://www.guardian.co.uk/media/2009/jan/21/new-nation-and-eastern-eye).

51 Justin Fashanu was Britain's first million-pound, Black soccer player, and remains the only top-level player to have been publicly open about his homosexuality. He committed suicide in 1998. *In the Family*, 34.

Ajamu: And from there we started the process for rukus! to become a charity. At this point we had lots of arguments around using the word "queer."

Stevens: Why was that?

Ajamu: We wanted to become a charity because we thought that people would take us more seriously. And we wanted to call it the Black, Lesbian, and Gay *Queer* Archive. And the Charity Commission wrote back saying they didn't think the word "queer" was an appropriate wording because some people might find it offensive. They told us they thought the word was seen as a derogatory term. It's a different world. [To Campbell] We had a meeting about whether or not to use the word "queer" at your house, I remember.

Campbell: We had a board meeting that went on forever. And we dropped it.

Ajamu: We dropped it formally in terms of the objects [of the charity]. But in our publicity it's still "queer."

Campbell: Yes, the Charity Commission thought it wasn't in keeping with the image it allows or something. But I personally don't really care one way or another about queer or not. I think it is a quite funny word to use. I think there was a time when it was important, but I think my personal discourse around it is not that interesting. I'm more interested in bisexuality. The focus on the whole notion of queer just betrays our generation. Queer politics was late, early nineties, in the UK anyway. There was quite a big sense in which the gay mainstream communities were identifying themselves, and reappropriating difference, in a positive way. But I think for anybody who is between fifteen and twenty-five now, it wouldn't have any meaning whatsoever. Personally, I don't mind saying Black, Queer Archive, or Black, Gay, Lesbian, Bisexual, Trans Archive. There might be people who might mind. But as long as the energy of the archive is there, it doesn't bother me personally.

Ajamu: Me neither, actually. And of course at some point, we might get rid of [the] "LGBT archive" label, and just have "the rukus! archive."

Campbell: The charity issue also raised all sorts of questions about how do we set up an organization, do we want an organization or is an organization going to tie us down? That is something that we are still struggling with. I'm very anti the notion of being institutionalized by any kind of organization, even by our own organization. There's no building, there's no core funding. We now have an editing suite in my house and an office in Ajamu's house, and lots of the stuff is stored there. We have meetings in both places. We're registered as a company and we're a charity, so we have all the legal stuff going on, and that's all we need really. The struggle obviously is for money, always. We're not paid for rukus! It's not a paid job. But I always go on about the other practices that we do, about the kind of work I'm doing, and I want to continue doing that. If rukus! was to subsume everything, that would be unsatisfying for me. The kind of infrastructure and "capacity-building" stuff that comes with an institution is not something that I'm interested in doing. I have a freelance career, and Ajamu has his own other interests and career. It is really about looking at it holistically, in terms of one's life. rukus! is more of a brand than an institution, and as a brand it's really strong.

Ajamu: I think for me, when the archive idea started I did have the idea of a centre that would house the archive. But then seeing how other groups run with a building and all the infrastructure that goes with that, it becomes so top-heavy. I guess I like the idea of something being a lot more flexible and more fluid. Otherwise the creativity is lost. For me the notion of an institution also sounds quite serious, although at the same time we are building an institution. But in a different kind of a way, around another kind of a model. I think central to what we do is that we're artists first and foremost. An artistic sensibility is woven into everything. If I think about an archive, on the basis of things I've seen, it's not pretty, it's not interesting, it's not sexy. How to bring in a community of people who might share this view is a big question. Approaching the archive with an artistic sensibility is one way into that.

Campbell: There is a vision that somehow the Black gay and lesbian presence would be more "instituted," but that's not the same as us wanting to be an institution. It may be that one day we might do a project with somebody like the Museum of London and have an office there part-time for six months, but that's it.

Stevens: It seems to me that the way you think through your organizational model is similar to the way you think through Black queer identities. These things are mobile and they're fluid, and they're there to take on what already exists, whether those are concepts or labels, or physical spaces. How did you take this fluid model forward?

Ajamu: We're very much about being very public; exhibitions and events, that's how people hear about rukus! and the archive. People see and hear what we are doing and that it makes it a living archive and not just stuck in a corner, not doing anything. Putting on events about the archive is very central to what we are doing.

Campbell: I agree. rukus! is a public organization. The archive is important and continues to be, but everything has a public face. "The Queen's Jewels" and "Outside Edge," which Ajamu curated [at the Museum of London Docklands in 2008], are public things.[52] Our focus is on events because each event is a political act, an intervention in its own right. So we did "The Fire This Time," which we called "queering Black History

---

52 See "Outside Edge," Museum of London Docklands, http://www.museumoflondon.org.uk/Explore-online/Past/Outside_Edge.htm.

Month."⁵³ It was a way of saying we're in Black History Month. I'm doing, we as rukus! are doing, a stage play called "Mangina Monologues."⁵⁴ I'm cutting a film which is a documentary that archives the "In this our lives" project.⁵⁵ I hope to make another short biography film, which is a gay film. We're doing the Zami Conference next year.⁵⁶ One day we'll probably have to apply for a grant to archive rukus!.

Ajamu: The thing with "The Queen's Jewels" and "Outside Edge" is that they were very much about campaigns, activism, public stuff. And too often that personal voice was missing from that: who's behind that, how do they think, how do they feel? Our new project, "Sharing Tongues," is about capturing the other side to our experiences. You tend to hear or see the same kind of people time and time again. What we wanted to do in terms of "Sharing Tongues" was to try to collect the voices of people that nobody would have heard about. Their stories and experience are just as valued. Some people might not be out publicly. And yet, they still might want to contribute in some shape or form. Trust and positivity are very key.

Stevens: And you've recently decided to deposit your collections in London Metropolitan Archives [LMA]?

Ajamu: Well I'm personally not an archivist, and I am not necessarily interested in the professional side of things. I think that is probably a good thing. Because it means I can approach archiving without being restricted to a professional frame of reference: "this should be done like this," and so on. Yes, what we do has to be up to a professional standard, and for me I think our material is better placed with an organization that has a history around collecting a community. We thought about this very carefully; [what] I had to ask is which organizations out there have a history of dealing with Black material and gay material. The Hall Carpenter doesn't have a history

---

53 The Fire This Time was a festival which took place on 21 October 2006; see http://www.firethistime.co.uk/. (Editors' note: at the time of this publication, the website is no longer available.)

54 See "Mangina Monologues: Stories of Love and Lubrication," rukus!, http://rukus.org.uk/2009-2/.

55 In *In This Our Lives: The Reunion*, director Topher Campbell documents a reunion of the original participants in the first and only national gathering of Black gay men in the UK, the 1987 National Black Gay Men's Conference; the documentary was screened at the London Lesbian and Gay Film Festival on April 2, 2009, http://web.archive.org/web/20090308132621/http://www.bfi.org.uk/llgff/our_lives_reunion_panel_discussion.

56 The Zami Conference was a national gathering of Black lesbians that took place in 1985; rukus! was planning to document a reunion, similar to that organized for the Black Gay Men's Conference.

of dealing with Black material. The Black Cultural Archives doesn't have a history of dealing with gay material. London Metropolitan Archives now has the Jessica and Eric Huntley archive, which is a major Black archive. They've got that and they've got other gay archives there. So I think they are best placed to house what we are collecting. And then they can conserve it and preserve it. And that makes it more accessible publicly. Because I think if you are building up an archive and people ask you "where's it held?" and you say, "well, you know, it's under my bed," people won't see it seriously. It's dismissed as, "well, that's lovely, great," but actually it's not *serious* because it's in your house.

Campbell: I agree. I mean Marx said get your hands on the means of production. We're not holding it at Conservative central office now, are we? We are holding it somewhere which has got the facilities and resources to maintain it. LMA is a huge place and they've got facilities for storage at the correct temperatures and so on. And it's our archive; they're not owning the archive. They've been very, very accessible in terms of our conversations. They gave us an award![57] And you want to be aligned with the best of the bunch. So there are all sorts of reasons for depositing there.

Ajamu: Also, we've been given people's materials and so naturally, we have to keep them at the best place; it goes back to respect.

Stevens: That leads on to the question of how you position yourself in relation to more mainstream heritage organizations.

Ajamu: I've contacted a few lesbian and gay archives just to say "we're rukus!, we're here, what do you have and can we have a record of it?" For some places, their file over a twenty-year period about the Black and Asian experience is not even one folder. The Black Cultural Archives, they've done nothing whatsoever in terms of the Black gay and lesbian experience. But that may be a generational thing. Some of the younger generation are more open, so we are talking with them. Basically we'll work with any group, as long as they're interesting and genuine, and they're not ticking boxes. Because I've been involved with some groups who want to have their funky little Black projects at the end of it. And I thought "Well [pause] no."

Campbell: We are open to anybody. Because there is a level at which we want to make sure our archive is representative and reaches people. We're open to

---

57   rukus! was one of the 2008 winners of the Archives Landmark Award (ALA). The award is given by the City of London, London Metropolitan Archives (LMA), and Archives for London Ltd. (AfL) "in recognition of innovative and original projects which make creative use of archive material and which make a real contribution to the community"; for more information see http://www.communityarchives.org.uk/page_id__205_path__0p3p37p.aspx.

anybody as long as the agenda is ours. We're depositing our archive at LMA, we've worked with the Museum of London Docklands. But we do things in our own way. Exhibitions like "Outside Edge" borrowed from classic ideas of how to make an exhibit, from memorabilia to audiovisual material. But we don't want it to be too safe. Because we're not safe, or at least I don't think so. We're not massively anarchist, but we're not safe.

Ajamu: We're not anarchists but I think we've got a kind of punk attitude. A kind of do-it-yourself ethos.

Campbell: And we're also quite subversive. I mean in the first exhibition at the Museum of London ["Queer is here," 2006][58] we just put our logo there, didn't we?

Ajamu: And some of the sex club flyers.

Stevens: And you could have submitted anything?

Campbell: We could have submitted a nice portrait of the first Black couple to have a civil partnership or a cover of Justin Fashanu, but we submitted the logo because we didn't want to be easily categorized. With "Outside Edge" they gave Ajamu a lot of rein. But he still subverted it. We couldn't get the Black Perverts Network archive posters in the exhibition, but he put them in the symposium as part of a display, and so unfortunately for them they were now fifteen feet high! There's always a bit of mischievousness in us. rukus! is the finger up at the same time as the embrace and the kiss. "Love and lubrication" is our sign-off at the same time as "Fuck off, we'll do what we want." We're not far away from the punk generation of the seventies, so there's a kind of shiftiness and abrasiveness about the way that we are.

That abrasiveness is important, because part of our history is a very unpalatable history, and that needs to be recorded. The history of Brixton cottage, the sex parties, of violent and difficult relationships, of relationships between different Black communities, and of what's now been called gay racism, which is what the White community has done, systematically, to disempower Black clubs and to stop the Black presence happening. There's a lot of stuff which isn't nice, which doesn't sit easily in museums and community events. And doesn't sit easily with our memories either. It was not some kind of halcyon trajectory from invisibility to visibility. It's born out of a struggle, from being refused entry to clubs, to clubs being closed down because they're Black. And you don't get money for talking about that sort of thing. Although perhaps "Sharing Tongues" will bring some of that to light, in terms of the earlier struggles.

---

58 See http://www.museumoflondon.org.uk/Explore-online/Past/QueerIsHere.htm. The exhibition is discussed in more detail in Mills, "Queer Is Here?"

Stevens: It can be argued that there are risks associated with keeping difficult memories alive. Paradoxically, archives and museums have often been seen as places where you put things so as not to have to deal with them.

Campbell: Yes. That's interesting territory, I think.

Ajamu: Yes, very interesting territory. One of the other dangers of the archive is that you carry all this stuff in your head. You can tell people their lives. You can say, "we know you were there" because we've seen a photo or a document.

Campbell: Yes, people say certain things about where they were and where they were not, in a good way and a bad way.

Ajamu: Although some people in their forties will just naturally have forgotten things, and for some people the archive fills in the gaps.

Stevens: What would you like to see rukus! achieve now?

Campbell: I think I would like to see these histories and these stories emerging in "mainstream" teachings about Black history in schools and colleges, and in higher education. It doesn't need to be such a mystery.

Ajamu: That's why a CD and a booklet from the "Sharing Tongues" project will be going out to schools. I have this vision that some years down the line, there's a teacher talking about Black history and gay history. And he's talking, talking, and this one Black kid goes, "well, what about this sir? Because this happened too."

Mary Stevens:

With this progressive and hopeful vision of a future in which young people are inspired to challenge their educators to produce and promote more diverse and inclusive understandings of British history, the interview drew to a close. Projecting the idea of the rukus! archive into the future reminds us that, as Stuart Hall noted, "an archive may be largely about 'the past' but it is always 're-read' in the light of the present and the future."[59] So far as the present is concerned, there can be little to add to Ajamu and Topher's regular sign-off to the friends and supporters of their work with rukus!: "Love and lubrication!"

Bibliography

Aaab-Richards, Dirg, Craig G. Harris, Essex Hemphill, Isaac Jackson, and Assotto Sainte. *Tongues Untied: Poems by Dirg Aaab-Richards, Craig G. Harris, Essex Hemphill, Isaac Jackson, Assotto Sainte*. London: GMP, 1987.

---

59 Hall, "Constituting an Archive," 92.

Alexander, Claire. "Stuart Hall and 'Race'." *Cultural Studies* 23, no. 4 (2009): 658–87.
Beam, Joseph, ed. *In the Life: A Black Gay Anthology*. Boston: Alyson, 1986.
Carter, Rodney G. S. "Of Things Said and Unsaid: Power, Archival Silences, and Power in Silence." In "Archives: Space and Power," edited by Barbara L. Craig and Joan Schwartz, special section, *Archivaria* 61 (Spring, 2006): 215–233.
Cvetkovich, Ann. *An Archive of Feelings: Trauma, Sexuality and Lesbian Public Cultures*. Durham, NC: Duke University Press, 2003.
Darker Side of Black, The. Directed by Issac Julien. London: Arts Council of Great Britain, 1994.
Dinshaw, Carolyn, Lee Edelman, Roderick A. Ferguson, Carla Freccero, Elizabeth Freeman, Judith Halberstam, Annamarie Jagose, Christopher Nealon, and Nguyen Tan Hoang. "Theorizing Queer Temporalities: A Roundtable Discussion." *GLQ: A Journal of Lesbian and Gay Studies* 13, nos. 2–3 (2007): 177–95. doi:10.1215/10642684-2006-030.
Gay Men Fighting AIDS. *In the Family: Celebrating the Builders of Black Gay Communities*. London: Gay Men Fighting AIDS, 2001. http://www.gmfa.org.uk/londonservices/booklets-and-postcards/pdfs/in-the-family.pdf.
———. *In the Family 2: Celebrating the Builders of Black Gay Communities*. London: Gay Men Fighting AIDS, 2002. http://www.gmfa.org.uk/londonservices/booklets-and-postcards/pdfs/in-the-family-2.pdf.
Halberstam, Judith. *In a Queer Time and Place: Transgender Bodies, Subcultural Lives*. New York: New York University Press, 2005.
Hall, Stuart. "Constituting an Archive." *Third Text* 15, no. 54 (2001): 89–92. doi:10.1080/09528820108576902.
Hemphill, Essex, ed. *Brother to Brother: New Writings by Black Gay Men*. Boston: Alyson, 1991.
In This Our Lives: The Reunion. Directed by Topher Campbell. London: 2008.
Juhasz, Alexandra. "Video Remains: Nostalgia, Technology, and Queer Archive Activism." *GLQ: A Journal of Lesbian and Gay Studies* 12, no. 2 (2006): 319–328.
Mills, Robert. "Queer Is Here? Lesbian, Gay, Bisexual and Transgender Histories and Public Culture." *History Workshop Journal* 62 (2006): 253–263.
Roque Ramírez, Horacio N. "Memory and Mourning: Living Oral History with Queer Latinos in San Francisco." In *Oral History and Public Memories*, edited by Paula Hamilton and Linda Shopes, 165–186. Philadelphia: Temple University Press, 2008.
Sivanandan, Ambalavaner. "Challenging Racism: Strategies for the '80s." *Race & Class* 25, no. 2 (1983): 1–11.

"Welcome Home"
An Exploratory Ethnography of the Information Context at the Lesbian Herstory Archives

Danielle Cooper

> It's a little old house in Brooklyn with stuff from years and years... from way back... like books and records and personal accounts of lesbians' lives – all interesting aspects of lesbians' lives.... It's kind of a sea of lesbian history.... You can go there on your own time and just discover things.
>
> ~"Anne," personal communication, July 13, 2010

Located in a beautiful brownstone in residential Brooklyn, the Lesbian Herstory Archives (LHA) is a dynamic institution that challenges conventional concepts of information collection, legacy, and community. Conceived through a women's consciousness-raising group in 1973, the LHA was founded as a solution for representing lesbian lives and experiences. As part of this solution, the LHA deliberately departs from conventional archival methodology by having a specific operating mandate that is for lesbians as opposed to scholars, actively seeking materials of "everyday lesbians," and existing outside of institutional and governmental affiliation.[1]

As the introductory quote from my informant Anne suggests, the LHA captures the imagination of patrons and creates a unique informational environment. In order to convey and contextualize this unique informational environment, I conducted ethnographic research at the LHA from June to August 2010. My research findings, detailed below, demonstrate that the LHA creates a unique informational context through a "home-like" setting. I also explore how the LHA fosters "exploratory" information seeking strategies, and creates a venue for "live" lesbian information sources. The LHA,

---

1   Joan Nestle, "Notes On Archiving from a Lesbian Feminist Standpoint," *Gay Insurgent* 4–5 (Spring 1979): 11.

therefore, is not only notable for housing information traditionally ignored or destroyed by society-at-large, but also for fostering a distinct, "informational" setting.

Literature Review

The LHA falls under the category of "Lesbian, Gay, Bisexual, Transgender and Queer (LGBTQ) grassroots information collection." Within Archival Studies, the push towards postmodern and critical information approaches has begun to open up a space for discussing grassroots information collections within the discipline. For example, Heather MacNeil characterizes postmodernism as "a necessary corrective to the tyranny of one way of seeing" and "posits the virtues of locality, ambivalence, contingency, multiplicity and difference."[2] Similarly, Laura Millar suggests that "archivists should celebrate the creation of each new institution in society that captures, preserves, and makes available records and archives . . . all symbols of society's desire to articulate its memories and safeguard its identity."[3] Building on MacNeil and Millar, Shaunna Moore and Susan Pell also champion the "autonomous archive" as the most effective means for grassroots communities to collect, organize, and disseminate information pertaining to their activities.[4]

Within Library and Information Studies, the recent monograph, *Library as Place*, introduces a useful framework for understanding the LHA.[5] The "library as place" model emphasizes the importance of physical context for framing information-based experiences. A renewed emphasis on library as a place allows us to view libraries as "physical entities where a complex mix of activities, processes and actions occur on a daily basis."[6] Most notably, Paulette Rothbauer's contribution, "Locating the Library as Place among Lesbian, Gay, Bisexual and Queer Patrons" explores how conventional libraries fail to serve the needs of LGBTQ patrons as a space to openly explore their identities, and therefore operate as closeting mechanisms.[7]

---

2   Heather MacNeil, "Trusting Records in a Postmodern World," *Archivaria* 51 (2001): 44–45.

3   Laura Millar, "Touchstones: Considering the Relationship between Memory and Archives," *Archivaria* 61 (2006): 126.

4   Shaunna Moore and Susan Pell, "Autonomous Archives," *International Journal of Heritage Studies* 16 (2010): 255–68.

5   John E. Buschman and Gloria J. Leckie, eds., *The Library as Place: History, Community and Culture* (Westport, CT: Libraries Unlimited, 2007).

6   Buschman and Leckie, "Space, Place and Libraries: An Introduction," in *The Library as Place*, 3.

7   Paulette Rothbauer, "Locating the Library as Place Among Lesbian, Gay, Bisexual and Queer Patrons," in *The Library as Place*, 101–115.

Another development within Library and Information Studies discourse, which is important for understanding the impetus for this research, are recent ethnographic studies that investigate activities within libraries. For example, Nancy Fried Foster and Susan Gibbons' recently edited a full-length report on a research project for the University of Rochester's River Campus Libraries that was based on anthropological and ethnographic methods.[8] Following the example of Foster and Gibbons, this ethnography aims to articulate the LHA's unique informational context.

Because the LHA's operating mandate lies explicitly outside of conventional information professional practices, recent contributions within queer theory also provide useful orienting information. Queer theory is a critical framework that examines social and cultural activities through an outsider or "queer" perspective. Ann Cvetkovich's *An Archive of Feelings* represents the first and only queering of the LHA as part of a greater project exploring issues of "trauma" in "lesbian public cultures."[9] Cvetkovich highlights the LHA's location within the home and ties this to the importance of emotional experience in lesbian activist culture. My ethnography echoes Cvetkovich's insight into the LHA's goal "to provide an emotional rather than narrowly intellectual experience"[10] by expanding discussion from focusing on stated institutional aims to analyzing patron accounts.

Another recent work in queer theory that offers useful concepts for contextualizing the LHA's activities is José Muñoz's *Cruising Utopia*.[11] Muñoz incorporates concepts of "performativity" and "loss" to explore queer relationships to history. For example, using Muñoz's framework, the LHA's mandate to collect items of an ephemeral nature and display them throughout the building represents a queer interest in the fleeting. According to Muñoz, queer historical expressions build in components of loss and the fleeting because they reflect a queer societal position as outsider and therefore not privy to the privilege of legacy.

Setting and Methods

I conducted my ethnographic research under the auspices of a graduate-level "information ethnography" research methods course entitled, "The Information Experience in Context," taught by Professor Jenna Hartel at the Faculty

---

8   Nancy Fried Foster and Susan Gibbons, eds., *Studying Students: The Undergraduate Research Project at the University of Rochester* (Chicago: Association of College and Research Libraries, 2007).
9   Ann Cvetkovich, *An Archive of Feelings* (Durham, NC: Duke University Press, 2003).
10 Ibid., 241.
11 José E. Muñoz, *Cruising Utopia* (New York: New York University Press, 2009).

of Information at the University of Toronto. Before and during my time in the field, I received in-depth instruction on how to design, implement and create a research report utilizing ethnographic methods. In order to proceed with this particular project, I not only secured permission from the LHA (detailed below), but also submitted my project to a rigorous review and evaluation process through the University of Toronto's Research and Ethics Board.

The LHA is an entirely volunteer-based and collectively run enterprise where individuals may contribute with varying levels of responsibility. For example, one may drop in at any time the LHA is open and assist in tasks such as filing, or come in on "work days" to help with a larger project. Regular volunteers, once trained, sign up to staff the archives: supervising the archives and assisting patrons during regular operating hours. A core group of regular volunteers known as "coordinators" also meet every three weeks to discuss issues such as the budget and upcoming events.

Due to my identity as a lesbian, a self-declared interest in lesbian history and archiving, and a prior interest in volunteering as a summer intern, I gained access to the setting with relative ease:

> *The LHA is welcome to all visitors regardless of sexual orientation; however, their lesbian-specific mandate makes the space particularly welcome to lesbians. Similarly, the LHA has no specific criteria for intern selection, but cites interests in Lesbian Studies, Women's Studies and/ or experience within women's groups or collective organizations as a "strength" for potential internship applicants.*[12]

After securing an internship, I also asked for permission to conduct ethnographic research through my supervisor at the LHA and at a coordinators' meeting I attended during my first week at the archives. In addition to communicating my research aims to the other LHA volunteers, I also openly discussed my project with LHA patrons when necessary through casual conversation on a person-by-person basis, and secured direct consent from interview subjects through a signed consent form approved by the University of Toronto's Research and Ethics Board.

According to James Spradley[13] and Emerson, Fretz and Shaw,[14] volunteering within an organization is the optimal method for field observation. As an intern, I regularly attended coordinators' meetings, staffed the archives,

---

12   The Lesbian Herstory Archives, "Internships," http://www.lesbianherstoryarchives.org/intern.html.
13   James P. Spradley, *Participant Observation* (New York: Holt, Rinehart and Winston, 1980).
14   Robert M. Emerson, Rachel I. Fretz, and Linda L. Shaw, *Writing Ethnographic Fieldnotes* (Chicago: University of Chicago Press, 1995).

worked on an independent project for the LHA and participated in other projects both informally and on "work days." In addition to these activities, as a researcher, I conducted semi-structured interviews, observed unobtrusively and took photographs at the site.

My research created data in the form of: jottings, field notes, photographs, and interview transcripts. In order to analyze my data, I followed a "grounded" approach, as articulated by Anselm Strauss and Juliet Corbin, whereby the researcher bases their analyses exclusively on their collected data, or from the "ground up" rather than from a previously stated hypothesis.[15] Drawing mainly from Emerson, Fretz and Shaw, I initially analyzed my data by transforming my incomplete jottings from the field into detailed field notes. In addition to field notes, I "coded" my interview transcripts and photos by reviewing the data and assigning succinct terms for the activities and phenomena that are found within the data. Throughout the coding process, I oscillated between "emic" and "etic" perspectives, anthropological concepts of viewpoints from inside and outside a particular social context. Recognizing the distinctions between these viewpoints, I worked towards creating a narrative that introduced "emic" activities to the "etic" concerns of their particular discipline.

The coded data, reflecting both "emic" and "etic" perspectives, was in turn used to create memos—written passages that do not represent final product, but rather, operate as an outlet for describing relevant activities and phenomena the researcher is observing in their data. These memos include direct quotes from the data as well as commentary from the researcher. Ultimately, the memos inform the structure that the final written product takes. The researcher selects a certain number of their memos based on their salience and themes to craft a narrative based on their research subject.

Ethnographic methods, therefore, pertain not only to research practices, but also to the writing approach adopted for the final report. The "Preliminary Findings" section below takes the form of a narrative tale based on Emerson, Fretz and Shaw's model of the "fieldnote-centred ethnography." Descriptions and observations from the field are organized around themes with content alternating from rich descriptions of activities within the field and observations from the researcher. In contrast to an argumentative essay, therefore, this paper is not organized around a thesis, but rather, unfolds through recounting specific events and explicating those events towards more general disciplinary concepts. Please note that informants' names are pseudonyms, except in the case of well-known, long-standing LHA volunteers Teddy and Maxine, who are impossible to render anonymous.

---

15   Anselm Strauss and Juliet Corbin, *Basics of Qualitative Research: Grounded Theory Procedures and Techniques* (Newbury Park, CA: Sage, 1990).

Preliminary Findings

I. Feeling "At Home" with Information

The LHA is not only located in a brownstone in a residential neighborhood, but also strives to create a home-like atmosphere for visitors. For example, the LHA hosts a regular event titled "At Home with the Archives," and the phrase "Welcome Home" is displayed prominently on the LHA website. My field data suggests that the LHA's "homey" setting also captures the imagination of its patrons and has a strong impact on how they relate to the space. "Home," therefore, is inextricably linked to patrons' "information experiences" at the archives.

My informant Ariel's first impressions of the LHA demonstrate the deep connection patrons feel towards the LHA home-like setting:

> *When I saw it for the first time it made me feel incredibly comfortable ... to be in a house as opposed to being in an office block or traditional library setting. There are a lot of advantages to being at the archives in terms of its feminist approach and in terms of its lesbian identity—it kind of fitted the kinds of stereotypes about lesbians or women—the so-called comforts of space, the comforts of safety. What women would like to feel like when they enter a space—it fits architecturally those stereotypes. Not in a negative way, more in a positive/affirming way... it has that whole feel to it—and my friends felt very similarly about that. Were all like, "yeah—this is a great idea, an archive should be in a house." It just made total sense.*

Ariel makes a direct correlation between the LHA's home settings and the needs of the archives in terms of their underlying mandate towards their constituency. In other words, homey feelings of comfort make "total sense" for archives serving lesbians. Ariel further emphasizes this point by contrasting the LHA with more conventional institutions such as offices or traditional libraries, places where she and her peers do not tend to feel safe or comfortable.

The LHA not only creates a home-like impression, but also allows patrons to relate to the space, and, by extension, with the information contained therein like they are at home. For example, when elaborating her statements above, Ariel mentioned the following: "There is a very trusting relationship. You get a key, you get in, you take responsibility as soon as you feel comfortable—you are made to feel at home as soon as possible." Ariel is referring to LHA's practice of giving out keys to volunteers and researchers who regularly use the space. What is notable in this example is that something as small as a key can convey deep feelings of trust and comfort for the LHA's patrons.

Although the LHA provides keys for only a small percentage of their patrons, all patrons engage with the space on the level of the home when utilizing the space. The images below convey how patrons can sit very comfortably on couches amongst floor-to-ceiling shelves of books and archival-quality boxes (Fig. 1 & 2) or take a lunch break in the kitchen (Fig. 3). As Cvetkovich observes, the LHA's home-like setting creates a unique private/public hybrid that invites patrons to conduct research in a leisurely fashion.[16] By extension, patron engagement can also be understood as a form of embodied experience:[17] in the process of utilizing the LHA, one literally feels as if they are "at home."

Further adding to the homey feel is the archives' large collection of ephemera displayed throughout the building, much like how one would display such items in their own home (Fig. 4). Echoing Cvetkovich's assertion that affect makes queer artifacts significant,[18] I observed that ephemeral objects at the LHA are concurrently decorative and personal as well as informational. For example, I once found a small framed photograph tucked away on the second floor that depicted a woman sitting on another woman's lap. To my delight, I recognized the two women as LHA volunteers. The photograph, therefore, creates a personally evocative form of documentary evidence: I not only felt the "intimate" connection because the photograph depicted an intimate scene, but also because I was personally familiar with the subjects, which, in turn, reinforced my own connection to the LHA.

The presence of ephemeral objects at the LHA also illustrates how artifacts more typically found in the home hold valuable information for the LHA and their patrons precisely because these objects invoke personal memories. Note for example, the following quote from my informant Ariel describing her favorite parts of the LHA:

> I'm really intrigued by . . . the buttons, clothing, photography, individual photographs that people have sent in. There are different things that I keep finding every time I'm there . . . you can pick up anything and it takes you back to memory and space in your own reference or a broader reference.

In addition to creating a home-like feel for those using information at the LHA, the LHA's "all-over" approach to organizing information creates a distinct definition of what information is and how information can be used. Recall, for example, how in Fig. 4 ephemeral objects such as coffee mugs are placed in the same space as books. Such "non-hierarchical" object placement

---

16 Cvetkovich, *An Archive of Feelings*, 241.
17 Patrick Keilty, personal communication, October 17, 2011.
18 Cvetkovich, *An Archive of Feelings*, 243–44.

Fig 1. Patrons "at home" in an LHA main space

Fig 2. Couches, books and boxes co-existing at the LHA

Fig 3. The LHA's kitchen area, open to all patrons

Fig. 4. Ephemera dispersed amongst the books

opens up the definition of what can be used as information and leads to sense of "informational freedom" for patrons. In other words, the LHA is a space imbued with information in such a way that patrons not only feel at home but also feel a great potential for discovery.

II. "Organic Exploration" as Information Seeking

It appears that the same all-over and home-like information organization structure which leads to patrons' sense of excitement and comfort while using the LHA also requires a specific strategy for finding and utilizing information once within the space. For example, my informant, Anne, had the following first impressions of the LHA:

> *It was hard to find my way at first—it was very confusing. But I think that after a while I got used to it so it didn't really bother me. At first I was like, oh gosh, there's so much stuff—but then I got used to it.*

The episode from my field notes below elaborates on how patrons become habituated to the archives' unique configuration:

> Around 12:40, a woman in her early thirties came in and asked for "any information we may have on the 'International Lesbian Information Service.'" The volunteer coordinator on duty, Monica, was familiar with this topic and referred the woman to the organization files upstairs. Immediately after delivering the information, Monica remarked to me that "it is rare that people come in here knowing what they are looking for."

The field note excerpt above suggests that people who come to the LHA to do research often first spend time visiting to get acquainted with the collection. The volunteer-coordinator considered the researcher atypical because she chose a topic before arriving at the site. I later learned that this researcher visited the archives in November 2009 without a topic in mind. This incident still reinforced the volunteer-coordinator's observations because the researcher had, in fact, first visited the site without "knowing what [she] was looking for yet." Other field notes and interview excerpts about the importance of acquainting oneself with the archives further reinforce this point. Note, for example, my informant Anne's description of her first visit to the LHA:

> I would get a book and just start reading and just keep reading because I found it interesting, but then I would have to stop myself and browse because I didn't want to spend all my time on one book. That day, I wanted to get an idea of what was there so I could just figure it out and discover the archives.

Anne's activities reflect a common approach to interacting with the LHA materials. Confronted with the sheer volume and variety of materials organized in a less formalized manner, patrons must first take time to survey the collection's contents before focusing on a specific research topic. At the most explicit, my informant Ariel describes her motivation behind understanding the LHA's layout:

> At this stage I am really interested in looking at the different areas of organizing of the archive—just orienting myself to understanding its layout, its set-up to get a better sense of what it is I am interested in [sic] terms of my own research—is it a subject? Is it a particular type of collection?

As Ariel's comments suggest, becoming familiar with the LHA's physical layout is integral to the LHA research process. Browsing at the LHA, therefore, represents a fundamental research strategy. I also had an opportunity to learn more about browsing as an information search strategy by working with an undergraduate student, Jo, who came into the LHA regularly over the course of the summer. Included below are notes from my first encounter with Jo:

> The volunteer-coordinator on duty and I asked Jo about her topic of interest and she answered "popular representation of butch/femme in the 90s." Both the volunteer-coordinator and I had some difficulties unpacking this statement and we asked some follow-up questions. We learned that she is still in the early stages of brainstorming the topic and is also looking to the archives for "topic inspiration." After trying to flush out her topic further, I felt it would be better to help Jo by showing her how to browse. I directed her to the subject files and the binders on the special collections and she selected a subject file on "passing."

The concept of "looking to the archives for topic inspiration" suggests that the LHA is a rich information site viewed by patrons as a source for discovery. By extension, browsing appears to be a central activity in that discovery process. The importance of browsing also appears to relate back to the archives mandate to be a space open to all lesbians regardless of background because one can browse at their own will and on their own terms.

The idea that the way in which the LHA is physically organized relates back to an underlying institutional philosophy and that this in turn shapes information seeking strategy is further demonstrated in the field note excerpt included below. This field entry refers to a later conversation I had with the volunteer-coordinator with whom I first encountered Jo:

> The volunteer-coordinator said that although I have been taught a particular way of doing reference work at library school I should keep in mind that the atmosphere at the LHA is meant to be different than a conventional library or archive. She cited when Jo came into the LHA and noted that I was too quick to lead Jo in a particular research direction. In contrast, the LHA wants to create a welcoming environment where people don't feel pressured into any one way of researching. She said it's best to allow people to explore the LHA "organically" for themselves.

This fieldnote excerpt represents an important breakthrough in my own process of understanding the archives' information architecture: before this point I had not truly grasped the importance of unfettered information discovery at the archives and was struggling with how to provide "reference service" to visitors. After this discussion, the ways in which the archive is organized to encourage self-discovery through browsing techniques became more readily apparent and I altered my guiding strategies accordingly.

For example, the LHA encourages self-discovery by offering tours (Fig 5), providing in-depth literature on-site and online including floor-plans and descriptions of the collections (Fig 6), and including extensive signage and labeling on the collections themselves (Figs 7 & 8). Furthermore, one can argue that the archives' all-over organization discussed in the previous section can not only be read as a product of comfortable, multi-use spaces, but also serves to reinforce self-discovery and browsing. This echoes my observation that patrons may experience anxiety when they first encounter the all-over form of organization, but that once they become familiar with the space their anxiety tends to dissipate. In other words, working with the collection is ultimately a process of personal exploration.

Fig 5. Me giving a tour as a volunteer

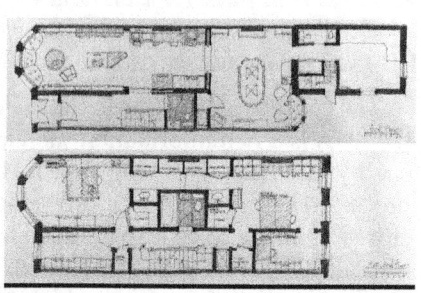

Fig 6. Floor plan provided on the LHA website

Fig 7. Files containing newsletters

Fig 8. Close-up of files; note presence of red "Newsletter" stickers and an alphabetical file tag

III. "Live" Lesbian Information

In addition to fostering study through discovery, the LHA also provides lesbian information "live" through volunteers connected with the lesbian community and by providing opportunities for lesbian socializing and networking in their home-like environment. For example, the field note below demonstrates a contrast utilizing "live" lesbians as information as opposed to materially based information forms such as books:

> When I went back downstairs [at the LHA], I found the four older women, Teddy, and Jane all sitting around the table. I sat down and joined in on their conversation [about coming out]. . . . At one point in the conversation while Teddy spoke of her experiences, she mentioned that she had an older sister who had been a G.I. in WW2. I was struck by how similar this was to a topic Jo expressed interest in and I tried to call her over but she was too absorbed in her books to notice. At that point, I came to realize the value in what Maxine had been telling me the other day: there is a lot to be learned in the archives just by being at the archive—as opposed to just diving into the files. Teddy's sister was asked and refused to give an oral testimony so Teddy is the only source on her.

As a coordinator, Teddy staffs the archive with volunteers on a regular basis. By extension, visitors not only consult material collections but also consult individuals who have personal ties to the LHA's materials and/or the LHA as an organization. Surprised and fascinated by my field note above, I observed that, at the LHA, one can miss the opportunity to discover vital information by not engaging with volunteers. Recall that personal accounts are particularly valuable in this context due to the lack of conventional historic documents about lesbians. The LHA volunteers, therefore, serve as necessary interlocutors into an otherwise undocumented past.

In addition to the live information provided by volunteers, visitors to the LHA also provide valuable information through a social context. "Four older women" in the field note above refers to a group of visitors to the LHA on that particular day. Within my field notes, I described the encounter further:

> The older women were exchanging stories about coming out and being involved in the women's movement. The women had been part of the West Side Discussion Group in the early 70s and they were looking through the file the archive had on the organization. In addition to the file, the women looked through some of the LHA's photo albums. Both Jane and I were fairly knowledgeable about feminist history and contributed to the discussion.

As this excerpt suggests, it appears that part of what makes the archive unique is that there is the potential for in-person, socially driven informational experiences. In addition to housing their collection, the LHA creates an enjoyable environment for West Side Discussion Group members. The environment, by extension, fosters information sharing between West Side Discussion Group members and other patrons. Recall that in the earlier excerpt, I mention that the conversation took place "around the table." The table is very large and centrally located on the main floor of the archive and therefore, purposefully positioned for discussion. This table is one of several main areas of major social interaction at the LHA. Other examples include: the couches in the "living room" area on the first floor (Fig. 1 & 2) and the dining area within the kitchen (Fig. 3).

Furthermore, by promoting dialogue at the site, the LHA ensures that information is not only exchanged but also created. For example, in the field note above I highlighted the fact that Jane and I, both LHA interns in our early twenties, "contributed to the discussion." Later in the same field notes, I also observed that when the women from the West Side Discussion Group left, "we thanked them but they also thanked us." The exchange above, therefore, illustrates that conversation at the LHA foster intergenerational and cross-cultural exchanges.

In addition to the informal conversations that occur at the LHA, both formal and informal information activity takes place live at the events the LHA hosts. As part of their operating mandate, the LHA serves as a multi-purpose event space for programs organized by both the LHA as well as related community and individual efforts. The LHA regularly hosts their own event called "At Home with the Archives" and the excerpt below from my informant, Ariel, highlights the experience of attending such an event at the LHA:

> [At] the lesbians in the 70s event—it was about the collection and lesbians who were activists in the 70s and bringing those stories together. Particularly of lesbians of colour . . . they had different people reading excerpts of that, and having reenactments of those narratives through different voices.

As Ariel's account illustrates, it appears that the archive creates a living context by hosting community events in the present that link back to material components of the collection. The events at LHA promote information dissemination through live delivery and thereby increase the number of those who are able to encounter their collection. Furthermore, transforming information into performance allows for new forms of information interpretation.

Beyond the programming, patrons also deem the LHA events valuable because they provide opportunities for socializing in a more casual sense. The LHA's status as social venue relates back to the LHA as a comfortable, homey space. Recalling the same event above, Ariel notes:

> I like it because they had a social space where you could have a drink and a snack, which allowed for more engagement, people were getting to know each other. The kitchen is also a great space to have a coffee and interact. People are really friendly at the archive—they are really welcoming and open, very happy to see everyone.

The homey and welcoming atmosphere described above is not only a component of the LHA's special events, but also part of the environment on a day-to-day basis. As part of my fieldwork, I regularly observed and participated in casual, friendly conversations among visitors and LHA volunteers. The excerpt below between myself, "Monica," a long-time LHA volunteer, and "Misty," a visitor who had only discovered the LHA several weeks prior to this exchange, demonstrates a typical exchange:

> Monica and I continued to talk casually, mostly about our research interests. At some point, Misty joined the conversation. We talked about a number of issues, mostly personal . . . the other girl came into our area and we invited her to join the conversation. . . . We discussed a variety of topics including: the parameters of butch/femme, the definition of "queer," the significance of hair length, Ellen Degeneres' sitcom in the 90s, The L Word. . . . At some point we begin to talk about the Dyke March and Misty was unfamiliar with it so I explained the topic in detail including information which ties back to the legacy of the LHA. I invited her to be a marshal and provided her with an information postcard.

The conversation above illustrates that important "lesbian information exchanges" often occur on a casual level. It is important to note that although our conversation began very casually, we gradually covered a number of lesbian-related topics (i.e. the concept of "queer" and "butch/femme") including issues specifically relating back to the LHA and an introduction to the Dyke March—an important local lesbian event.

This conversation also demonstrates that the LHA not only provides information through the sources housed and the presentations held on the premises, but also on a less tangible level by providing a space for social contact among lesbians both at events and during regular operating hours. In addition to discovering information through browsing, therefore, patrons also uncover a wealth of information by conversing with other lesbians.

Conclusion

My ethnography on the LHA represents an initial case study in a greater discourse on the unique shape of "queer information practice." During my field research at the LHA, I observed that patron experience connects to the LHA environment and that both the patron and the LHA value this connection. More specifically, my data suggests that the linkage between setting and experience is distinctly affective in character: at the LHA, patrons sense a deep connection to the home-like environment, which elicits feelings of comfort, trust, and freedom to explore both independently and through social exchange.

In addition to creating an emotional response, my field research also suggests that patrons adopt unique information seeking strategies in response to the LHA's setting. These strategies include: browsing organically, using the LHA setting as a source of topic inspiration, and engaging in conversation with others at the site. The LHA's unique setting, and the subsequent patron activities undertaken within the setting, demonstrate that the LHA is not only a site that houses informational content (i.e. documents), but also one that fosters informational experiences through its site-specific characteristics. In other words, the LHA is a site literally imbued with information. It is also worthwhile to note that my ethnography also illustrates how the LHA, as an institution, represents a rich information source. Like the other LHA patrons I encountered, I too spent my time at the site discovering and then turned around and used the site as source for topic-formation.

Ultimately, I believe that the LHA's multiple information forms hold clues to what defines queer information practice, and by extension, queer knowledge production. Other recent queer theoretical contributions such as the work of Cvetkovich and Muñoz explore queer information from a production-exclusive perspective. By providing insight into the experiences of patrons of queer information, my study contributes to understanding the queer knowledge process. Information use perspectives are an essential addition to queer discourse as these activities ultimately inform continuing knowledge production.

Bibliography

Buschman, John E., and Gloria J. Leckie, eds. *The Library As Place: History, Community and Culture*. Westport, CT: Libraries Unlimited, 2007.

———. "Space, Place and Libraries: An Introduction." In Buschman and Leckie, *The Library As Place*, 3–29.

Cvetkovich, Ann. *An Archive of Feelings*. Durham, NC: Duke University Press, 2003.

Emerson, Robert M., Rachel I. Fretz, and Linda L. Shaw. *Writing Ethnographic Fieldnotes*. Chicago: University of Chicago Press, 1995.

Foster, Nancy Fried, and Susan Gibbons, eds. *Studying Students: The Undergraduate Research Project at the University of Rochester*. Chicago: Association of College and Research Libraries, 2007.

MacNeil, Heather. "Trusting Records in a Postmodern World." *Archivaria* 51 (2001): 36–47.

Millar, Laura. "Touchstones: Considering the Relationship between Memory and Archives." *Archivaria* 61 (2006): 105–126.

Moore, Shaunna and Susan Pell. "Autonomous Archives." *International Journal of Heritage Studies* 16 (2010): 255–68.

Muñoz, José E. *Cruising Utopia*. New York: New York University Press, 2009.

Nestle, Joan. "Notes on Radical Archiving from a Lesbian Feminist Standpoint." *Gay Insurgent* 4–5 (Spring 1979): 10–12.

Rothbauer, Paulette. "Locating the Library as Place Among Lesbian, Gay, Bisexual and Queer Patrons." In Buschman and Leckie, *The Library as Place*, 101–115.

Spradley, James P. *Participant Observation*. New York: Holt, Rinehart and Winston, 1980.

Strauss, Anselm, and Juliet Corbin. *Basics of Qualitative Research: Grounded Theory Procedures and Techniques*. Newbury Park, CA: Sage, 1990.

Accessing Transgender //
Desiring Queer(er?) Archival Logics

K. J. Rawson[1]

Section C1 of the *Code of Ethics* of the Association of Canadian Archivists provides the following guidance on accessibility and use: "Archivists arrange and describe all records in their custody in order to facilitate the fullest possible access to, and use of, their records."[2] Section VI of the *Code of Ethics* of the Society of American Archivists has a parallel suggestion: "Archivists strive to promote open and equitable access to their services and the records in their care without discrimination or preferential treatment, and in accordance with legal requirements, cultural sensitivities, and institutional policies."[3] But what, *really*, does it mean to have access to records? Would archivists know if they were facilitating the fullest possible access to their records? How might equitable access without discrimination or preferential treatment be achieved?

In my quick translation of these codes of ethics statements into assessment questions, I am already forecasting the impossibility of fulfilling such guidelines. In a way, recognition of the impossibility of these goals is already built into the language; "fullest possible" and "archivists strive" both imply that only degrees of compliance are expected or even possible. Despite the inevitability that archival records will always be more accessible to some users than others and will never be *fully* accessible, there has been a veritable

---

1 Editors' note: this paper was previously published in "Special Section on Queer Archives," ed. Rebecka Sheffield and Marcel Barriault, special issue, *Archivaria* 68, no. 7 (2010): 123–140.

2 The Association of Canadian Archivists, *Code of Ethics*, http://www.archivists.ca/content/code-ethics.

3 The Society of American Archivists, *Code of Ethics*, http://www2.archivists.org/statements/saa-core-values-statement-and-code-of-ethics#code_of_ethics.

explosion in the archival profession to develop standards, trainings, and workshops, all with the intent to improve accessibility.[4]

What this article will explore, then, are ways that access becomes complicated in archiving a particular category of materials—in this case those related to transgender people—and making materials available to particular researchers, specifically transgender researchers. Transgender materials and patrons, I argue, warrant particular and critical attention regarding access and accessibility. Toward this end, I will examine two factors that significantly influence access to transgender materials and access for transgender researchers: the archival environment, imagined broadly, and the language practices in and around archives. Following this analysis, I will take a more theoretical turn and explore what it might mean to *queer* traditional archival logics in the context of archiving transgender materials.[5] Though traditional archival logics typically strive for near-universal access and researcher satisfaction (a point I will return to), I will make the queer move to ask: How might frustration be productive? Might archives usefully embrace a different model of (dis)satisfaction?

Before I delve into this argument, let me offer a brief definitional sidebar for readers unfamiliar with the word "transgender." "Transgender" is a young term. Many scholars trace its origins to the late 1980s and Virginia Prince, a person who felt that she neither fit the category of transsexual (someone who permanently changes their sex through medical intervention) or transvestite (someone who episodically wears the clothing of the "opposite" sex).[6] Prince coined the term "transgenderist" as a noun to describe people who are neither transsexual nor transvestite, but instead are people who "permanently changed social gender through the public presentation of self, without recourse to genital transformation."[7] In the early 1990s, Leslie Feinberg reshaped the term from a noun to an adjective in the influential pamphlet *Transgender Liberation: A Movement Whose Time Has Come* and expanded the definition to include any number of people who faced gender

---

4   I am grateful to Michele Combs for bringing this point to my attention. As an outsider to the archival profession, I am not clear why this trend is happening now, but I do wonder if it is somehow related to the development of new archival technologies.

5   When I refer to an archival logic, I mean the philosophy about how an archive should be organized and experienced.

6   For more on the origins of transgender, see Susan Stryker, "(De)Subjugated Knowledges: An Introduction to Transgender Studies," in *The Transgender Studies Reader*, eds. Susan Stryker and Stephen Whittle (New York: Routledge, 2006), 1-17.

7   Ibid., 4.

oppression.[8] This was the birth of the contemporary usage of "transgender" as an umbrella term.

Susan Stryker offers a current and concise definition of "transgender" in her recent book *Transgender History*, which encapsulates the umbrella sense that Feinberg pioneered: "I use [transgender] in this book to refer to people who move away from the gender they were assigned at birth, people who cross over (*trans-*) the boundaries constructed by their culture to define and contain that gender."[9] She continues: "it is *the movement across a socially imposed boundary away from an unchosen starting place*—rather than any particular destination or mode of transition—that best characterizes the concept of 'transgender.'"[10] This definition demonstrates the expansiveness of "transgender"; it does not only apply to those who are transsexual ("people who feel a strong desire to change their sexual morphology in order to live entirely as permanent, full-time members of the gender other than the one they were assigned to at birth"[11]). Instead, "transgender" includes anyone who crosses the gender boundaries they were assigned at birth. Some identities that are commonly clustered under the transgender umbrella include (but are certainly not limited to): transsexual, transvestite, cross-dresser, transman/transwoman, genderqueer, androgyne, female-to-male (FTM), and male-to-female (MTF).

For several important reasons, my focus in this article and in my larger work is on transgender materials and transgender users. First, transgender as a word and concept is only a few decades old.[12] This recent emergence of the term has significant implications for archival organizational systems, which tend to be slow to adapt to linguistic and categorical change. Second, the word "transgender" privileges particular people and experiences, especially along the axis of race and class (again, a point I will return to). For archives that use the word "transgender" as a key term to describe gender non-normativity, this means that they also re-inscribe the system of power and oppression inherent in the term. Finally, a significant amount of transgender people can be anti-history, which can be at odds with the archives' task of preserving transgender materials in contexts that uniformly uplift history.[13]

---

8   The pamphlet was expanded and later published. See Leslie Feinberg, *Transgender Liberation: A Movement Whose Time Has Come* (New York: World View Forum, 1992).

9   Susan Stryker, *Transgender History* (Berkeley, CA: Seal Press, 2008), 1.

10 Ibid., 1. (Emphasis in original.)

11 Ibid., 18.

12 I am not referring to the practice of trans-ing gender, which, I would agree with many historians, has always been a part of human culture in some form.

13 For some transgender people, history has the power to betray; it can stubbornly reveal details about the past that are incongruent with the identity that that person lives in the present.

This article comes from my larger research project in which I am closely engaging with three American archive repositories that have significant holdings of transgender materials. Taken together, the three archives I examine represent a cross-section of different contexts in which researchers might seek transgender materials: a university-based institutional archives, a professional historical society, and a grassroots residential archives. The first is the National Transgender Library and Archive, which is a university collection of transgender-related materials maintained at the University of Michigan Library and kept, in part, in the special collections division.[14] The second is the GLBT Historical Society, a San Francisco-based, professional archives that employs a blend of professional and non-standard archival practices.[15] Finally, the third collection I examine is the Sexual Minorities Archives in Northampton, Massachusetts, which is a grassroots archives maintained in the private residence of the archivist. Though I won't be able to detail fully the vast distinctions in archival practices among these three archives in this article, it is important to note that throughout this article I draw on my in-depth research at each of these sites, including my interviews with archivists, staff, volunteers, and researchers who have worked in, or with, these archives. It is through this lens of a spectrum of archival institutions and practices that I approach access and accessibility.

Environmental Accessibility and Genuine Transgender Inclusion

According to the *Canadian Oxford Dictionary*, the word "accessible" is defined as "can readily be reached, entered, or used." The three parts of this definition imply a broad range of access that includes the physical, the social, and the intellectual. Because archives are often physical places (though this is also becoming more complicated in the age of digital archiving), it is of course important to consider whether archival records are physically accessible to researchers. Can they be reached?[16]

There are, as archivists well know, many other dimensions of access that go far beyond whether a record can be physically reached. One that is quite influential for transgender researchers is what I would describe as "environmental accessibility." Environmental accessibility is determined by "the feel"

---

14 For a brief overview of the National Transgender Library and Archive, see http://guides.lib.umich.edu/content.php?pid=29017&sid=253054.

15 To learn more about the GLBT Historical Society, see http://www.glbthistory.org/.

16 Though I do not have space to do justice to it here, disability studies scholarship could provide a productive and more nuanced dimension to this consideration of accessibility.

of a space and the way a person is treated in that space. In order to better understand how these environmental factors work, we might usefully understand archival spaces in terms of their "geosemiotics," which Scollon and Scollon define as "the study of the social meaning of the material *placement* of signs and discourses and of our actions in the material world."[17] The utility of geosemiotics as a theoretical lens is its required placement of discourse as located in the material world. This is particularly important for archives as places, because the signs and discourses that dominate an archives both communicate social meaning and have material consequences for transgender researchers.

A recent handbook jointly published by the National Gay and Lesbian Task Force Policy Institute and the National Center for Transgender Equality, provides an excellent overview of the ways an organization can consciously make its space transgender inclusive. Though this handbook is specifically designed for LGBT organizations, the same principles are certainly transportable to archives that collect transgender materials and ostensibly serve transgender users. The authors touch upon a variety of environmental cues that indicate to transgender people whether they are welcome, several of which apply to archives: the physical environment, bathrooms, the verbal environment, the questions one asks people, and communications materials.[18]

I will begin with the physical environment, for which my own experiences as a transgender researcher might be instructive. Two of the archives I am studying in depth, the Sexual Minorities Archives and the GLBT Historical Society, have single-user or gender neutral bathrooms that I can use comfortably. This in turn makes me feel able to spend long research sessions in both archives, and it also indicates, for me, a genuine commitment on the part of each archives to welcome transgender users.

On the other hand, the gender-segregated bathrooms at the National Transgender Library and Archive at the University of Michigan were a difficult barrier to my research, in part because they were highly policed. I was forced to argue for my right to use the bathroom on the special collections floor (and as an out-of-town researcher, the only one I knew to find), which obviously made me feel unwelcome in that space. In turn, these bathroom interactions increased my anxiety while doing research, and may have even changed the amount of time I was willing (or physically able) to research in the archives.

I have had this similar experience at countless highly institutionalized archives, particularly library special collections. At such times, I often recall

---

17   Ron Scollon and Suzie Wong Scollon, *Discourses in Place: Language in the Material World* (New York: Routledge, 2003), 2.

18   Lisa Mottet and Justin Tanis, *Opening the Door to the Inclusion of Transgender People* (Washington, DC: National Center for Transgender Equality, 2008), 21.

Malea Powell's articulate discussion of the experience of being an Indian in colonial archives:

> As I sat there and thought about empire, I started to get very cold—felt myself grow puny and insignificant in the face of imperialism and shivered at the impossibility of it all—me, an Indian, a mixed-blood, here in this odd colonial space.[19]

Powell's quick movement between her thinking and her feeling demonstrates how inextricable the intellectual and bodily experiences of an archives can be.[20] For transgender patrons, this formula could also work in the opposite direction; by feeling excluded from using bathrooms, a person might then interpret the intellectual tone of an archives to be similarly unwelcoming. Even when the practices and policies of an archives collection are technically transgender inclusive, any archives that does not have bathrooms where anyone can use the facilities safely and without hassle, is making an implied statement that transgender patrons are not physically and intellectually welcome in that space.[21]

Another aspect of the geosemiotics of an archival environment is the predominant verbal discourse and the images that are displayed. Throughout my research, I only spoke with one archivist who explicitly reflected on the influence of the environment on an archival user. This archivist explained: "I've tried to be conscious about the images that go on the walls to show individuals of colour when I can." Not only was he doing this to uphold the antiracist mission of that archives, but also to make people of colour feel included into the space, especially since this particular archives is in a predominantly white area. Similarly, displaying images of transgender people around an archives and in rotating exhibits conveys a clear message to transgender users that they are a genuine part of this collection and are welcomed into this space. This functions inversely as well; if transgender visitors to an archives do not see transgender people represented or acknowledged, the implication will be that they are not welcome.

---

19 Malea Powell, "Dreaming Charles Eastman: Cultural Memory, Autobiography, and Geography of Indigenous Rhetorical Histories," in *Beyond the Archives: Research as a Lived Process*, eds. Gesa E. Kirsch and Liz Rohan (Carbondale: Southern Illinois University Press, 2008), 120.

20 For more scholarship on the impacts of archival experiences, see Antoinette Burton, ed., *Archive Stories: Facts, Fictions, and the Writing of History* (Durham, NC: Duke University Press, 2005).

21 For more information on how to make bathrooms more transgender inclusive, please refer to Mottet and Tanis, *Opening the Door to the Inclusion of Transgender People*, which provides excellent direction on how to turn even gender-segregated bathrooms into safer spaces for transgender people.

In conjunction with the accessibility of the images displayed, the verbal environment in an archives can also have strong impacts on users. Again, my own experiences might be instructive here. At only one of the archives that I visited were my preferred pronouns respected in my interactions with staff and volunteers. For non-transgender people, this may seem like a small detail. But imagine entering a space where someone incorrectly assumed that you were something that you were not—be that a particular race, age, nationality, sexuality, religion, or anything that is an important part of your identity. If an identity is incorrectly and repeatedly ascribed to a person, more than likely that person will feel uncomfortable, misunderstood, and misread. While many archivists and volunteers often spend a great deal of time trying to be aware of politically correct language in archival description, the verbal environment of an archives also hinges on the spoken language that users encounter; as Lisa Mottet and Justin Tanis argue, "[i]f gender identities and pronouns have not been established at the beginning, it is also important not to assume a person's gender."[22] The habit of assuming people's gender is so ingrained that I imagine this to be a challenging bit of advice. Still, given that the verbal environment of an archives can be so influential in welcoming or excluding transgender patrons, it seems worth the effort to attempt to create an inclusive verbal environment.

Pronouns are not the only aspect of the verbal environment of an archives that shape a researcher's experience. The verbal environment also includes things that are more fleeting, such as conversations that happen in reading rooms, and between staff and researchers. If even the slightest amount of transphobic language is present, it has the potential to have a negative impact on a transgender researcher. I am not suggesting that transgender users are more sensitive than others; however, gender assumptions and norms permeate our culture to such an extent that they often become invisible. Again, though it may seem an impossible task to stay attuned to the gendered assumptions in the verbal environment of an archives, I believe it is an important component to help maintain a space that is actively inclusive of transgender people.

When an archives wants to welcome transgender researchers, the environmental accessibility and geosemiotics of the archives should be important considerations for an archives to evaluate seriously and regularly. The environmental factors that I have discussed do not merely allow or disallow particular individuals from accessing archival materials—they have more power than that. Environmental accessibility can shape the way entire groups of people encounter an archives, or are excluded from using it altogether.

---

22 Ibid., 24.

Archives Speaking // Speaking Archives

Despite the broad trend to standardize archival descriptive systems, the language that is used for archival description is still highly adaptable and political. As a result, the language that an archives "speaks" has wide-ranging consequences for archival practices, as transgender archiving elucidates. Although a brief, though overly tidy etymology of the term "transgender" has already been provided, the word is not so innocuous and uncomplicated as that description might suggest. As David Valentine explains, "'transgender' has emerged—both as a movement and as an identity category—primarily from within a framework established by a racialized and class-inflected gay and lesbian—and latterly, queer—activism and scholarship."[23] This move to historicize "transgender" critically positions the term as emerging out of the *dominant* modes of gay, lesbian, and queer activism and scholarship, which were (and to a large extent continue to be) generated from a White and middle-to-upper class perspective.

The consequences of this bias can be quite serious for those individuals who might be described by the term, but who would not use it to describe themselves. Valentine writes: "my concern here finally is that the young, the poor, the people of color who are understood as being transgender are increasingly having to un-know what they know about themselves and learn a new vocabulary of identity."[24] If we transport this argument—that transgender is a term that is embraced by some and forced onto others (in ways that are particularly classed, raced, and aged)—to archives, it becomes clear that archives have the potential to reproduce the complex system of power and oppression inherent in the term.

I have provided a brief list above of the common categories that are often included under the transgender umbrella (e.g., transsexual, transvestite, cross-dresser, etc.), but this reclassification isn't unproblematic. As Stryker explains:

> *The terms listed here are also the ones most often used by cultural elites, or within mass media, or within powerful professions such as science and medicine and academia. They are often derived from the experiences of white transgender people. But there are hundreds, if not thousands, of other specialized words related to the subject matter of this book that could just as easily be listed in this section on terms and definitions. . . . The seemingly inexhaustible global catalog of specialized terms for gender variety shows how impossible it really is to group such a wide*

---

23 David Valentine, *Imagining Transgender: An Ethnography of a Category* (Durham, NC: Duke University Press, 2007), 60.
24 Ibid., 135.

range of phenomena together under the single term "transgender" without keeping that word's definition very flexible and without paying close attention to who is using it to refer to whom, and for what reasons.[25]

How flexible can "transgender" be in archival practice? And how can archivists pay close attention to the ways that it is being used? It seems that there are two potential pitfalls with the use of "transgender" in archives. First, it can be used too specifically to only refer to those materials that self-referentially use the term. Or second, it could be used too liberally and could start describing people who would explicitly counter-identify with the term.

Let us take a fictional example: the personal papers of a very butch, female-born person of colour who often passed as male and used the identity label "bulldagger." To begin, unless this person made it explicitly clear what his/her/hir pronoun preference was, it cannot be assumed.[26] By using "transgender" to describe these papers, either in the finding aid or in any other access tool, an archives would be ignoring Stryker's caution and disrespectfully and oppressively re-naming an identity (from a more privileged perspective) that already has a name. This has consequences, too, for other "bulldaggers" who might research in that collection looking for "bulldagger" materials. Would they be forced, following Valentine's argument, to learn a new "vocabulary of identity," to speak a new archival language, in order to successfully navigate the materials collected there?

On the flip side of this too liberal use of "transgender," is the possibility that it could be used too narrowly or conservatively. If this fictional person's papers were never labelled "transgender," they would probably become isolated from the long lineage of other people who *trans*-gender. Another consequence would be that these papers would likely be invisible to a researcher looking for "transgender" materials, which would also contribute to the perception that "transgender" is mostly a White identity. Of course, this is highly dependent on the type of organizational technologies that an archives employs; I would argue that even with the most seemingly neutral and standardized archival descriptions, these factors would be inevitably present.

My point is not that "transgender" should never be used in archival settings—certainly that would not be a desirable option. But archivists should take seriously Valentine's observation: "I am concerned that the unquestioned use of 'transgender' in activist, academic, and other contexts, while progressive in intent, actually reproduces, in novel and intensified forms, class and racial hierarchies."[27] An awareness of this complexity might prompt archi-

---

25   Stryker, *Transgender History*, 23.
26   "Hir" is a gender-neutral pronoun that grammatically replaces "his" or "her." A second gender-neutral pronoun is "ze," which replaces "she" or "he."
27   Valentine, *Imagining Transgender*, 19.

vists to ask the following questions: Is "transgender" being used to describe materials that do not contain that language? If so, what are the potential consequences? Are there other terms related to transgender identities that might better describe particular materials and better facilitate access to those materials? Is there a way to circumnavigate the archival privileging of particular terms? Again, the purpose is not to attempt to eliminate political language from archival practices—that would be an impossible task. Instead, the complexity of words like "transgender" provides an opportunity for a more careful attention to the ways that archives speak.

Some grassroots archives deal with this issue by embracing the inevitability of politically charged language and using it explicitly. For example, at the Sexual Minorities Archives (where the organizational system is designed from scratch for that collection), one of the book classifications is "Bullshit." This category, nestled between "Bisexual Lives" and "Crimes Against Girls," contains any literature that negatively characterizes sexual minorities, typically from a medical perspective. Though the archivist is committed to collecting these materials, he wants to use the classification "Bullshit" to carefully position those materials as counter to the politics of the collection as a whole.

One way to understanding this archival logic is as a shift in focus from potential archival users to designers of archival organizational systems. As Grant Campbell has articulated in regards to gay and lesbian community-based classification systems:

> ... the makers of subject access tools are used to asking themselves the first question: "who are my users?" They will now have to tackle two additional, equally challenging questions: "Who am I in relation to my users, and how does my position manifest itself in the tool itself?"[28]

For some grassroots archivists, the best way to address those questions is to be extremely subjective and intentionally biased. Obviously, this approach also has its own limitations, including the risk of over-reading and the possibility that the classification categories will not make sense for all users. And of course, this logic is not easily transportable across a spectrum of archival settings. Still, it is instructive to see an example of an archives speaking in a way that is overtly and unapologetically political.

An interesting juxtaposition to the expressly political discourse of the Sexual Minorities Archives is the University of Michigan's library catalogue, which is used to navigate the National Transgender Library and Archive. One particular detailed record, Leslie Feinberg's popular book *Transgender*

---

28 D. Grant Campbell "Queer Theory and the Creation of Contextual Subject Access Tools for Gay and Lesbian Communities," *Knowledge Organization* 27, no. 3 (2000): 129.

Warriors provides a useful and typical example of how transgender material is integrated into a preexisting cataloguing system.[29] While I am not able to provide a visual of this record, I trust that most readers are familiar with the basic components of a detailed record in an electronic catalogue.

As a rhetorician, when I encounter detailed records I am first drawn to the Library of Congress subject headings, which for Feinberg's book included "Transsexualism—History," "Transvestism—History," and "Gender identity—History." What these categories miss, of course, is the first word in the title of the book—"transgender." Though "Transgender people—History" is in the *Library of Congress Subject Headings* (*LCSH*), it has not been associated with this record, for whatever reason, which is not really important here. From the three subject headings it has been assigned, it is clear that this text is about history and it seems to relate to a broad range of gender-related topics: transsexualism, transvestism, and gender identity. But within the discourse of the *LCSH*, this book is not identifiable as "transgender," despite its explicit self-definition as such. It is important to remember, too, that Feinberg is credited with popularizing "transgender" as an umbrella term, which makes the omission of that term quite glaring and somewhat ironic. While this observation could be filed away with the countless critiques of the *LCSH* —which I will not rehearse here—it is more important to note the shifting of language that happens between the text itself and the record that claims to represent it.

One element of this record that works with (or perhaps against) the discourse of the *LCSH* is the social tagging software that the library has enabled to be applied to every library Web page. In a small, grey box near the bottom of the Web page is a space that displays the tags, or labels, that users of this catalogue have added to the record. This tagging system, called MTagger, allows tags to be added to any Web page within or outside of the library catalogue by any user who wishes to add a label. In this particular tag box, a user added the label "transgender history." Like the designated space for the *LCSH*, these small grey boxes designate a particular space for user-generated labels that function similarly to subject headings. That is to say, if one clicks on "transgender history," for example, one is directed to a new page with every record that any user has tagged with the same phrase. The benefit of this type of tagging software is that it is built in real-time, based on a researcher's logic for navigating the catalogue and can, therefore, be quite democratic and timely. Tagging can also produce a different discourse, a different mode of archival speech, than the highly predetermined model of standardized descriptive categories.

Given these complex language practices, we can flip the question "What language do archives speak?," and also ask, "What language do researchers

---

29   Leslie Feinberg, *Transgender Warriors: Making History from Joan of Arc to RuPaul* (Boston: Beacon Press, 1996).

speak?" In my interviews, several researchers explained the limitations of their own language, particularly in attempting to find older, historical materials relating to transgender. While "transgender" as a term is only a few decades old, many researchers have found evidence of people *trans*-ing gender throughout history. But how does one find such materials prior to the late twentieth century? One researcher explained hir process to me:

> *I'd have to get incredibly creative to find stuff that was relevant to what I was doing. Because . . . obviously "transgender" and "transsexual" aren't used [in the nineteenth century]. I tried "cross dresser"—there was nothing. There would be nothing that I could find. Any descriptor I could come up with for what I did I wouldn't find anything. So I had to go about finding things in really kind of like roundabout ways.*

K: Like what?

> *I mean partly, too, it was like how I was thinking about transgender, I guess. Or like how I was thinking about, you know, the kind of work that I want to do. So, I had kind of decided that I would look up "Chinese immigration" and I came up on stuff on like "normative gender," but you know, all of it is just filed under "immigration" or "Chinese culture,"— that kind of stuff. But it was very much the kind of stuff that I wanted to get to. I don't know, like . . . what remains of police files and police photographs and stuff like that. And I would find cases of people who were arrested under cross-dressing law but they were just in there as local criminals and stuff like that. . . . I mean I found tons and tons of stuff, but none of it was you know, catalogued in an easily recognizable way.*[30]

In order for this researcher to find materials, it was necessary to move beyond a conventional way of thinking about transgender. Once this researcher was able to shift from transgender to cross dressing, then to local crime files, ze was able to find the desirable materials. While this researcher's experience is a success story, it required hir to learn to speak the language of the archives, which for historical materials, means unlearning "transgender" as a category.

In sum, archives that collect transgender materials are in a difficult position with respect to language: they need to utilize broad terminology to pull together threads within a collection and yet they need to have a fair amount of specificity. These archives need to work constantly to process incoming materials, making it virtually impossible to return to previous descriptive data to update it when popular terminology shifts. While archivists may try to have the language of their archives best fit the language that researchers would be using, this is not an apolitical venture. It is a delicate and somewhat

---

30 Personal interview conducted with an unnamed researcher on 21 August 2008.

impossible task to try to enable archives and researchers to speak the same language. Still, a pressing concern for archivists should be trying to answer the question: Who *does not* speak the language of your archives?

"Please Fondle the Toys!": Queer(er?) Archival Logics

In mid-2003, the Association of Research Libraries (ARL) produced an influential white paper in which it stated:

> With the diverse types of access tools listed above, it is important that special collections librarians consider which tool will provide the most satisfactory patron access for a particular collection. This essential analysis mandates a balance between the ideal access record for "every patron"—and economic realities.[31]

This quotation typifies the dominant archival logic: archives should provide researchers with satisfactory access. By emphasizing "every patron" in scare quotes, the authors seem to be aware that such a concept is not meant to be literal or comprehensive, but rather a projected rhetorical ideal. As I have shown above, the concept of "every patron" can be usefully complicated by the experiences of transgender users and the politics of transgender-related language practices. What strikes me as more interesting in this quotation, however, is the notion of "the most satisfactory patron access," which lacks scare quotes. What might it mean for archives to try to enable "satisfactory" access to materials?

Let me take a step back and establish that the precursor to any type of satisfaction is *desire*, irrespective of whether or not a person can articulate or name that desire. For typical archival research situations, a researcher's desire may be to find materials as efficiently and successfully as possible, which would lead to a particular kind of affirmative satisfaction. Typified by the above quote from the ARL white paper, the archival logic that seems to predominate the archival profession is tailored to this model of researcher satisfaction, which is based on the desire to have efficient and successful research experiences. Notably, satisfaction in this context is a measurement of the research process, not the researcher him/her/hirself. In other words, satisfaction is externalized, located outside of the body of the researcher, and is instead contingent on the practical aspects of researching.

While this model of satisfaction may be the most common in archival settings, my study of collections of transgender materials has revealed an

---

31 Barbara M. Jones, compiler, *Hidden Collections, Scholarly Barriers: Creating Access to Unprocessed Special Collections Materials in North America's Research Libraries*, A White Paper for the Association of Research Libraries Task Force on Special Collections (June 6, 2003), 8, http://www.arl.org/news/arl-news/1157.

alternative logic that is built on quite different principles. Though I risk severe oversimplification, Figure 1 offers a visual spectrum and stratifies three different types of archives that collect transgender materials.

Despite the chart's flattening of complex archival practices, I hope to demonstrate that not all archives share the same logics based on providing traditional satisfaction (i.e., efficiency and predictability) for researchers. Readers of *Archivaria* are most likely more familiar with institutional and professional archives; I will, therefore, focus my attention on a grassroots archives in order to demonstrate the alternative logics that can support and strengthen a collection.

The Sexual Minorities Archives, a grassroots archives in Western Massachusetts, is built on an alternative archival logic that reframes researcher satisfactions and desires. The very minimalist organizational system of the archives only uses a classification-level overview (i.e., periodical titles, book classifications, etc.); there are no comprehensive lists of collected materials and no searchable databases, either in-house or on-line. There is no adherence to professional standards (in fact, they are eschewed). Instead, the organizational tools are entirely self-created; consequently, a researcher is *forced* to browse through the collection in order to discover materials. Some archivists may pass quick judgment on how inefficient this must be; it is, however, important to note that the repository's archivist is no less serious about researcher satisfaction than the professional archivists who make use of complex technologies. The archival logics that govern this collection are, quite simply, different. Below is how the archivist compares his collection to a university archives:

Type of Archive	Archival Logic	Organizational System	Proximity to Material
Institutional (e.g., university special collections)	Focus on efficient access	On-line based; follows professional guidelines for finding aids, content standards, Library of Congress headings, etc.	Far: typically closed stacks, sometimes off-site
Professional (e.g., historical society)	Mixed focus on both efficiency and discovery	On-line and in-house databases; partial adherence to professional guidelines when possible and desirable	Mixed: some closed stacks, some browsing
Grassroots (e.g., residential collection)	Focus on discovery	In-house, paper based lists; no adherence to professional standards; some creation of new standards	Near: direct access to all materials

Figure 1: The spectrum of LGBT archival settings and their varying archival logics, organizational systems, and proximity to materials

> *I always think of this collection as the most interactive setting. You don't need to come to me and know what you want and ask me to get it for you*

> with gloves on. . . . It's more a process of discovery in that you come in here and browse and you can actually not know what you [want]. Let the collection tell you what you are looking for and find it in the process of discovery.[32]

Of course, when a researcher cedes power to the collection in such an extreme way, it requires a considerable amount of time, and quite likely, frustration. But is frustration always bad? Can it sometimes result in a deferred satisfaction? Or perhaps a queering of satisfaction and access altogether?

Recent scholarship on queer temporality will be instructive here to help frame the logic of the Sexual Minorities Archives as not merely a failed efficiency model, but perhaps an example of a queerer logic. In the introduction to the special issue of *GLQ: A Journal of Lesbian and Gay Studies* on queer temporality, Elizabeth Freeman argues:

> We are still in the process of creating . . . a historiographic method that would admit the flesh, that would avow that history is written on and felt with the body, and that would let eroticism into the notion of historical thought itself. This we might call a queer desire for history itself to desire.[33]

I want to suggest that the archival logic of the Sexual Minorities Archives recognizes that archives can desire. This logic is a queer imagining of a new historiographic method of archival research, one that carefully accounts for a researcher's body moving through the space of the archives. It is a historiographic method that is based on the ways that researchers *feel* archives and *desire* history, and the ways that archives and history feel and desire right back.

If a traditional archival logic responds to a researcher's desire to find archival materials in a satisfactory way, queer logics can flip that idea by embracing a different kind of satisfaction that recognizes that collections can have desires and want to be touched, too. The possibility that the Sexual Minorities Archives collection can "tell you what you are looking for" is a queer revision of traditional historiographic method that grants desire only to the researcher.

This model of discovery is also highly dependent on proximity, the ability to browse, and the tactile experience of touching the past. Grant me another moment of self-indulgence to relate two of my own experiences in archives. My own love of archives began in Cornell University's Kroch Library. During my writing seminar in the fall of 1999, my instructor brought us to see

---

32 Personal interview conducted with Bet Power on April 25, 2008.
33 Elizabeth Freeman, ed., introduction to "Queer Temporalities," special issue, *GLQ: A Journal of Lesbian and Gay Studies*, 13, nos. 2-3 (2007): 165, doi:10.1215/10642684-2006-029.

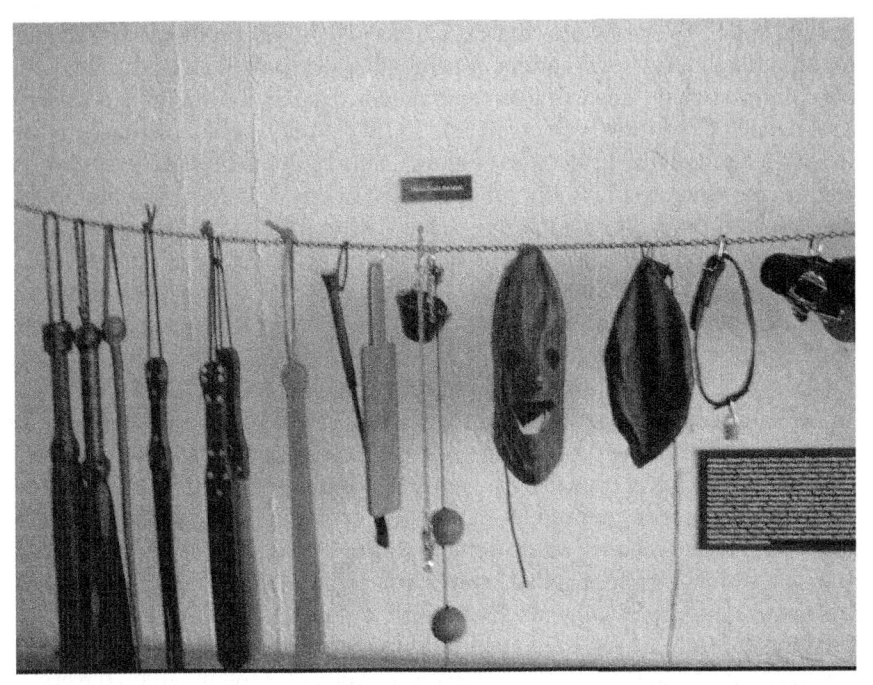

Figure 2: Display of S&M materials at the GLBTHS's Folsom Street Fair exhibit. Photo provided by Rawson, courtesy of *Archivaria*.

Shakespeare's fourth folio. I was ushered in with awe as I slipped on ill-fitting white gloves. For the briefest moment, I passed a gloved finger along the edge of that folio, not even daring to flip a page. I don't recall reading anything on that page, yet I remember that experience with such utter emotional clarity that whenever I sit with the memory, the same emotions of excitement well up inside of me. Sure, I appreciate Shakespeare as much as any respectable scholar with two literature degrees, but to offer him sole credit for my longstanding love of archives is somewhat misplaced. It was the *context* as much as the content that elicited my strong emotions in that archival encounter. I became attached to touching the past, in part, because it seemed like a sacred ritual.

Fast forward to the GLBT Historical Society during my first visit in August of 2008. As part of the museum-like display in the Historical Society's suite commemorating the Folsom Street Fair,[34] a series of sado-masochistic (S&M) materials hung as if on a clothesline (see Figure 2). A small sign

---

34 The Folsom Street Fair, which began in 1984, caps San Francisco's "Leather Pride Week." It is California's third-largest spectator event and the world's largest leather event. It is today a nonprofit charity. For more information, see the FSF website at http://www.folsomstreetfair.org.

behind read "Please Fondle the Toys!" No gloves. No protective archivists. So I did touch these toys, and much more liberally than Shakespeare's fourth folio, I must admit. The exhibit encouraged my touch; it even invited a semi-erotic touch ("fondling"). Being able to so freely touch certain artifacts in the archives, without the protection of gloves, may be an archivist's preservation nightmare—increased likelihood of theft, skin oils damaging the materials, careless handling, etc. But it also elicited within me a very different kind of emotion and pleasure, which was no less powerful than the wonder I had over Shakespeare. I left both archives feeling *satisfied*, but somehow different.

The difference between my touch of Shakespeare's folio and my touch of the S&M toys had less to do with my perceived value of those artifacts and more to do with how I was imagining being touched back. Heather Love aptly explains this queer touching of the past: "Contemporary critics approach these figures from the past with a sense of the inevitability of their progress toward us. . . . Our existence in the present depends on being able to imagine these figures reaching out to us."[35] Whether or not these figures and materials are actually reaching out to contemporary researchers is irrelevant. It is the imagining of this reach that creates a particular kind of relationship with historical artifacts. Since Shakespeare was so far removed from my world, in the moment of touching the fourth folio I simply felt as though I was touching a sacred object. With the S&M toys, however, I vividly imagined the eroticism and pleasure that may have been part of their past. Only with the S&M toys was I able to imagine a reciprocated touch, a touch that I desired.

Recall the point I make earlier about the logic of the Sexual Minorities Archives being based on the idea that the archives have desires too and that browsing can lead to satisfaction, albeit deferred. By forcing researchers to browse the collection, to submit to the direction the archives take you, the queer logic of the Sexual Minorities Archives facilitates a meeting of desires, of touches, between archival materials and researchers, as I experienced with the S&M toys at the GLBT Historical Society. Again, the satisfaction that seems to support this logic is based more on the internal desires of the researcher, such as my pleasure in touching the S&M toys, rather than the more external satisfaction that comes from an efficient and successful research process.

In the two examples I have offered, touching artifacts is a desirable and pleasurable experience. But queer archival encounters can be painful as well. Love's work is again useful to substantiate this claim; she writes:

> *The experience of queer historical subjects is not at a safe distance from contemporary experience; rather, their social marginality and abjection*

---

35 Heather Love, *Feeling Backward: Loss and the Politics of Queer History* (Cambridge, MA: Harvard University Press, 2007), 40.

> *mirror our own. The relation to the queer past is suffused not only by feelings of regret, despair, and loss but also by the shame of identification.*[36]

This relation to the past is explicitly queer because, as Love argues, there is no safe distance, no real barrier, between the queer pain and trauma that we find in the archives and that of contemporary queers. It may be that this painful and shameful identification with archival materials is particularly possible for transgender people who experience very high rates of violence, both physical and verbal, both in the past and in contemporary society.

Conclusion

Queer and transgender archival experiences, then, include a complicated negotiation between the satisfaction of fulfilled desires and the discovery and the shame of identification with history. So despite what may sound like my glorification of the queer archival logic of the Sexual Minorities Archives, I am not advocating for a widespread embrace of this approach. Instead, my goal is to complicate what it might mean for a researcher to have satisfaction, pleasure, touch, and affect in the archives. I hope to have shown that the moment of touch, of both the researcher and the past, is a deeply affective moment, laced with desire and sometimes, shame.

It is not coincidental that the last thing a visitor sees after a research session at the Sexual Minorities Archives is the mirror that hangs on the back of the front door. In the above quote, Love describes the past abjection of historical subjects as mirroring our own contemporary abjection. In archives that collect transgender materials, this mirroring may become particularly intensified as a transgender researcher touches and is touched by transgender historical subjects of the past. But what that researcher experiences, be it satisfaction, shame, or any other emotion, is a product of both that researcher's approach to the past and the archival logics that design the archival experience.

Acknowledgement

I would like to thank Stephanie Crist, Elisa Norris, Lois Agnew, Eileen Schell, Kenneth Lavender, Michele Combs, and especially Margaret Himley for feedback and direction with this article, directly and indirectly. Thank you also to Rebecka Sheffield and Marcel Barriault for their editorial guidance, and to the two anonymous reviewers who provided very useful suggestions for revision.

---

36   Ibid., 32.

Bibliography

Burton, Antoinette, ed. *Archive Stories: Facts, Fictions, and the Writing of History.* Durham, NC: Duke University Press, 2005.

Campbell, D. Grant. "Queer Theory and the Creation of Contextual Subject Access Tools for Gay and Lesbian Communities." *Knowledge Organization* 27, no. 3 (2000): 122–131.

Feinberg, Leslie. *Transgender Liberation: A Movement Whose Time Has Come.* New York: World View Forum, 1992.

———. *Transgender Warriors: Making History from Joan of Arc to RuPaul.* Boston: Beacon Press, 1996.

Freeman, Elizabeth, ed. Introduction to "Queer Temporalities." Special issue, *GLQ: A Journal of Lesbian and Gay Studies*, 13, nos. 2–3 (2007): 159–176, doi:10.1215/10642684-2006-029.

Jones, Barbara M., compiler. *Hidden Collections, Scholarly Barriers: Creating Access to Unprocessed Special Collections Materials in North America's Research Libraries.* A White Paper for the Association of Research Libraries Task Force on Special Collections. June 6, 2003. http://www.arl.org/news/arl-news/1157.

Love, Heather. *Feeling Backward: Loss and the Politics of Queer History.* Cambridge, MA: Harvard University Press, 2007.

Mottet, Lisa, and Justin Tanis. *Opening the Door to the Inclusion of Transgender People.* Washington, DC: National Center for Transgender Equality, 2008.

Powell, Malea. "Dreaming Charles Eastman: Cultural Memory, Autobiography, and Geography of Indigenous Rhetorical Histories." In *Beyond the Archives: Research as a Lived Process*, edited by Gesa E. Kirsch and Liz Rohan, 115–127. Carbondale: Southern Illinois University Press, 2008.

Scollon, Ron, and Suzie Wong Scollon. *Discourses in Place: Language in the Material World.* New York: Routledge, 2003.

Stryker, Susan. "(De)Subjugated Knowledges: An Introduction to Transgender Studies." In *The Transgender Studies Reader*, edited by Susan Stryker and Stephen Whittle, 1–17. New York: Routledge, 2006.

———. *Transgender History.* Berkeley, CA: Seal Press, 2008.

Valentine, David. *Imagining Transgender: An Ethnography of a Category.* Durham, NC: Duke University Press, 2007.

In the Archives of Lesbian Feelings: Documentary and Popular Culture

Ann Cvetkovich[1]

> *Every lesbian is worthy of inclusion in history.*
> *If you have the courage to touch another woman,*
> *then you are a very famous person.*
>
> ~Joan Nestle, *Not Just Passing Through*

Perhaps to the surprise of those who think of both traditional and grassroots archives as an esoteric interest, Cheryl Dunye's 1996 film *The Watermelon Woman* elevates the institution to a new level of popular visibility by making fun of it. The archives also serve as a source of narrative drama in *The Watermelon Woman*, in which Cheryl (played by Dunye herself) becomes obsessed with uncovering the life of the mysterious Watermelon Woman, an African American actress who plays the stereotypical maid roles in old Hollywood films such as *Plantation Memories*. Through interviews and trips to libraries and obscure archives, Cheryl slowly pieces together the story of Fae Richards, whose offscreen life includes a romance with her white director, Martha Page (styled after Dorothy Arzner), a career as a singer in black clubs, and, in her later years, a long-term lesbian relationship. Combining documentary with fiction, *The Watermelon Woman* weaves a visual archive of old photographs, film clips, and newsreels into its drama, simulating the look of these genres so well that it is hard to believe that Fae Richards is Dunye's creation and not an actual historical figure.[2] The most accessible part of the

---

1 Editors' note: this paper was previously published in *Camera Obscura* 17, no. 1 (2002): 107-147.

2 Along with pseudofilms such as *Plantation Memories*, *The Watermelon Woman* includes a fake archive of photographs of Fae Richards, which Dunye produced in collaboration with photographer Zoe Leonard. The photographs have been exhibited independently (including at a 1997 Whitney Biennial installation) and have been published as a book, *The Fae Richards Photo Archive* (San Francisco: Artspace, 1996).

Fae Richards archive are the materials that connect her to mainstream popular culture—Hollywood films and a relationship with a prominent white woman—and Cheryl at once cherishes these artifacts and searches for other evidence that would bring Fae Richards to life as something more than a stereotype or a marginal figure. As part of her quest, Cheryl makes the trip from Philadelphia to New York to visit the Center for Lesbian Information and Technology (CLIT). Novelist Sarah Schulman makes a memorable cameo appearance as the archivist who sternly informs Cheryl and her friend that the huge boxes of relevant materials are not filed or indexed because CLIT is a "volunteer-run" collective. When Cheryl discovers some of her first photographs of Richards in the boxes, she is told that they cannot be reproduced without the consensus-based approval of the collective, which meets only every other month. Not content to wait, she illegally documents the images with her video camera.

Those in the know would recognize CLIT as a parody of the Lesbian Herstory Archives (LHA); and while some might not find the joke funny, its humor can also be considered a form of respect and affection, demonstrating the important place of the archive in the lesbian popular imaginary. The actual LHA inspires the same devotion that draws Cheryl to Fae Richards. Founded in 1974, the archives were first housed in the cramped quarters of Joan Nestle and Deborah Edel's Upper West Side apartment, and stories of visits to their apartment's pantry, filled with documents in every nook and cranny, are legendary in accounts of LHA's origins, especially now that the archives have relocated to a more public space.[3] Conceived more as a community center than a research institution, one of LHA's original missions was to provide safe space for lesbian-owned documents that might otherwise be left to neglect or destroyed by indifferent or homophobic families. Since 1993, LHA has been housed in a Brooklyn brownstone purchased not through large grants or public funding but through many small donations from lesbians around the country. Desiree Yael Vester, a longtime LHA volunteer, notes that the archive serves as a ritual space within which cultural memory and

---

3   My information about LHA comes from discussions with volunteers during visits there, and I offer thanks to Polly Thistlethwaite, Lucinda Zoe, and Paula Grant for their generous assistance, and especially to Maxine Wolfe and Desiree Yael Vester for giving me time in which to interview them about the archives. Other sources of information include the "Lesbian Herstory Archives" newsletters; Joan Nestle, *A Restricted Country* (Ithaca, NY: Firebrand, 1987), especially "Voices from Lesbian Herstory," 110-19, and "When the Lions Write History," 178-88; as well as Polly Thistlethwaite, "Building 'A Home of Our Own': The Construction of the Lesbian Herstory Archives," in *Daring to Find Our Names: The Search for Lesbigay Library History*, ed. James V. Carmichael Jr. (Westport, CT: Greenwood, 1998), 153-74.

Zoe Leonard, The Fae Richards Photo Archive, 1993–96. Created for Cheryl Dunye's film *The Watermelon Woman* (1996). From a series of seventy-eight black and white photographs and notebook of seven pages of typed text on typewriter paper. The accompanying notes in this fictional archive identify this photograph as "Martha and Fae at home. (mid-1930s)." Courtesy Paula Cooper Gallery, New York

history are preserved.[4] The new site continues to combine private, domestic spaces with public, institutional ones, especially because it occupies a building that was once a home: the downstairs living room serves as a comfortable reading room, the xerox machine sits alongside other appliances in the kitchen, the entryway is an exhibit space, and the top floor houses a member of the collective who lives there on a permanent basis.[5] Visitors can browse in the filing cabinets and shelves at their leisure rather than having to negotiate closed stacks. Organized as a domestic space in which all lesbians will feel welcome to see and touch a lesbian legacy, the LHA aims for an emotional rather than a narrowly intellectual experience.

Both LHA and its representation in *The Watermelon Woman* point to the vital role of archives within lesbian cultures and to their innovative and unusual forms of appearance. As one way of exploring the cultural and especially the emotional power of archives, this article investigates recent documentary films *Not Just Passing Through*, *Forbidden Love*, and *Greetings from Out Here*, along with Sadie Benning's videos—*Girlpower* and *It Wasn't Love*—in order to show how these works themselves constitute an archive.[6] These documentaries use the power of visual media to put the archive on display, incorporating a wide range of traditional and unorthodox materials, including personal photographs, videotapes from oral history archives, innovative forms of autodocumentary, and "archival" footage, including clips from popular film and television. Film and video can extend the reach of the traditional archive, collating and making accessible documents that might otherwise remain obscure except to those doing specialized research.

But in addition to exploring how these works transform our ideas about what an archive can and must include, this article will argue that they

---

4   Desiree Yael Vester, interview with the author, Hart, MI, August 24, 1997.

5   According to Vester, there have been proposals that the top floor be used for the collection, but others think the live-in resident gives the archives its identity as a home.

6   See *Forbidden Love: The Unashamed Stories of Lesbian Lives*, dir. Aerlyn Weissman and Lynne Fernie (Montreal: National Film Board of Canada, 1992); *Girlpower* (1992) and *It Wasn't Love* (1992), in *Sadie Benning Videoworks: Volume 2*, (Chicago: Video Data Bank, 1999); *Greetings from Out Here*, dir. Ellen Spiro (Chicago: Video Data Bank, 1993); and *Not Just Passing Through*, dir. Polly Thistlethwaite et al. (New York: Women Make Movies, 1994). Both Women Make Movies, founded by Ariel Dougherty and Sheila Paige in 1972, and Video Data Bank, founded by Lyn Blumenthal and Kate Horsfield in 1976, deserve mention for their important role in developing an archive of women's work by virtue of distributing and promoting it. My thinking about Women Make Movies' cultural significance has been indispensably informed by Patricia White's "Feminist Reruns: Women Make Movies at Twenty-Five" (paper delivered at Consoleing Passions: TV, Video, and Feminism Conference, Montreal, May 1997).

demonstrate the profoundly affective power of a useful archive, especially an archive of sexuality and gay and lesbian life, which must preserve and produce not just knowledge but feeling. Lesbian and gay history demands a radical archive of emotion in order to document intimacy, sexuality, love, and activism, all areas of experience that are difficult to chronicle through the materials of a traditional archive.[7] Moreover, gay and lesbian archives address the traumatic loss of history that has accompanied sexual life and the formation of sexual publics, and they assert the role of memory and affect in compensating for institutional neglect. Like other archives of trauma, such as those that commemorate the Holocaust, slavery, or war, they must enable the acknowledgment of a past that can be painful to remember, impossible to forget, and resistant to consciousness. The history of trauma often depends on the evidence of memory, not just because of the absence of other forms of evidence but because of the need to address traumatic experience through witnessing and retelling. Central to traumatic memory is what Toni Morrison, in the context of remembering slavery, has called "emotional memory," those details of experience that are affective, sensory, often highly specific, and personal.[8] Subject to the idiosyncracies of the psyche and the logic of the unconscious, emotional experience and the memory of it demand and produce an unusual archive, often one that resists the coherence of narrative or that is fragmented and ostensibly arbitrary.[9] Memories can cohere around

---

7   For her thinking about archives and intimacy, as well as for conversations about the ideas in this essay, I am indebted to Lauren Berlant. For discussions of the archive, see "'68 or Something," *Critical Inquiry* 21, no. 1 (1994): 124-55, http://www.jstor.org/stable/1343889, and the section titled "I Hate Your Archive" in the introduction to *The Queen of America Goes to Washington City* (Durham, NC: Duke University Press, 1997), 10-15. For discussions of intimacy, see the special issue of *Critical Inquiry* 24, no. 2 (1998), http://www.jstor.org/stable/i257793. For their connections, see Berlant's "Intimacy's Ephemera" (paper delivered at the Modern Language Association, Toronto, December 1997).

8   See Toni Morrison, "The Site of Memory," in *Out There: Marginalization and Contemporary Cultures*, ed. Russell Ferguson et al. (Cambridge, MA: MIT Press, 1990), 299-305.

9   A valuable resource for a theory of the archive that takes account of the unconscious and memory is Jacques Derrida's *Archive Fever* (Chicago: University of Chicago Press, 1995). Using Freud as his point of departure, Derrida explores how the challenge posed by psychoanalysis to the question of memory also transforms what it means to produce and preserve an archive. Since psychoanalytic discourse is also bound up with the production of sexual identity, Derrida's argument is suggestive for exploring how gay and lesbian history redefines the meaning of the archive. *Archive Fever*'s concern with the question of whether psychoanalysis can be considered a "Jewish science" (and thus read as an archive of Jewish culture) also contributes to understanding the project of archiving

objects in unpredictable ways, and the task of the archivist of emotion is thus an unusual one.

Understanding gay and lesbian archives as archives of emotion and trauma helps to explain some of their idiosyncracies, or, one might say, their "queerness." They address particular versions of the determination to "never forget" that gives archives of traumatic history their urgency. That gay and lesbian history even exists has been a contested fact, and the struggle to record and preserve it is exacerbated by the invisibility that often surrounds intimate life, especially sexuality. Even the relatively short history (roughly "one hundred years") of homosexuality as an identity category has created the historiographic challenge not only of documenting the wide varieties of homosexual experience, but of examining documents of homophobia and of earlier histories of homoeroticism and same-sex relations.[10] As another legacy of Stonewall (itself an important and elusive subject for the archive), gay and lesbian archives have sought to preserve not only the record of successful efforts to combat homophobia and create a public gay and lesbian culture, but also the evidence from periods "before Stonewall" of many different forms of sexual public cultures. The last decade, in particular, has seen a marked historical turn, as historians, documentary makers, and average citizens have been drawn to historicizing not just the politics of a gay movement, but earlier generations of struggle that threaten to become lost history; they are affectively motivated by the passionate desire to claim the fact of history and to acknowledge those who provided the foundations for the sev-

---

traumatic histories, including Jewish history and gay and lesbian history, as idiosyncratic or queer. For a fuller discussion of the intersections of Derrida's notion of the archive and gay and lesbian archives, see my book *An Archive of Feelings: Trauma, Sexuality, and Lesbian Public Cultures* (Durham, NC: Duke University Press, 2003).

10 On the paradigm of "one hundred years of homosexuality," see David Halperin, *One Hundred Years of Homosexuality* (New York: Routledge, 1990), which is influenced by Foucauldian models of sexuality as a category with a history. Historian John Boswell adopts a different historical model, arguing both polemically and with considerable archival evidence for a continuous tradition of homosexuality in his books, *Christianity, Social Tolerance, and Homosexuality* (Chicago: University of Chicago Press, 1980) and *Same-Sex Unions in Premodern Europe* (New York: Villiard, 1994). It can be useful to understand Boswell's scholarship as driven by the affective need for history. For an interesting discussion of Boswell along these lines—informed by Halperin, Foucault, and others—see Carolyn Dinshaw's introduction to her book about the intersections of medieval studies and queer studies, *Getting Medieval: Pre- and Post-Modern Sexualities and Communities* (Durham, NC: Duke University Press, 1999). Dinshaw argues for the affective power of different historical periods to "touch" one another through the queer juxtaposition of past and present.

enties gay movement. Contemporary queer culture, including the films and videos investigated in this article, has shown a particular fascination with the generations of the fifties and early sixties, which immediately preceded gay and lesbian movement activism.[11] This trend is especially evident in the popularity of the documentary genre; the groundbreaking *Before Stonewall: The Making of a Gay and Lesbian Community*,[12] has been followed by an explosion of documentary film and video that has a ready audience at gay and lesbian film festivals.

The stock in trade of the gay and lesbian archive is *ephemera*, the term used by archivists and librarians to describe occasional publications and paper documents, material objects, or items that fall into the miscellaneous category when catalogued.[13] Gay and lesbian archives are often built upon the donations of private collectors who have saved the ephemeral evidence of gay and lesbian life—both personal and public—because it might otherwise disappear. These archives preserve publicly available materials that might not be found in libraries or other public institutions, such as pornographic books, short-run journals, and forms of mass culture that are objects of camp reception. Also collected there are personal materials, such as diaries, letters, and photographs, which assume additional archival importance when public cultures have failed to chronicle gay and lesbian lives. In addition to accumulating these textual materials, gay and lesbian archives are likely to have disproportionately large collections of ephemera because of their concern with sexuality and leisure culture, as well as with the legacies of grassroots political activism. Thus San Francisco's Gay, Lesbian, Bisexual, and Transgender Society of Northern California (GLBTS) has items such as matchbook covers, the notepads available for exchanging phone numbers in gay bars, fliers for club events, personal photo albums, condoms packaged for special events, and vibrators. LHA has a collection of T-shirts with political slogans, the hard hat with a lambda sign on it worn by a lesbian construction worker,

---

11 In lesbian culture, the resurgence of interest in butch-femme cultures has been part of this phenomenon. The popular interest in gay and lesbian history has been facilitated by the recent publication of many important scholarly books, including George Chauncey, *Gay New York* (New York: Basic, 1994); Martin Duberman, *Stonewall* (New York: Dutton, 1993); Elizabeth Lapovsky Kennedy and Madeline D. Davis, *Boots of Leather, Slippers of Gold: The History of a Lesbian Community* (New York: Routledge, 1993); and Esther Newton, *Cherry Grove, Fire Island: Sixty Years in America's First Gay and Lesbian Town* (Boston: Beacon, 1993).

12 *Before Stonewall: The Making of a Gay and Lesbian Community*, directed by Greta Schiller (New York: Cinema Guild, 1985). Videocassette (VHS).

13 José Muñoz discusses the status of ephemera in the production of queer history in "Ephemera as Evidence: Introductory Notes to Queer Acts," *Women and Performance* 16 (1996): 5-18.

and posters from political and cultural events. Both archives also house the files of activist groups such as ACT UP and Lesbian Avengers, which include ephemera such as meeting minutes, publicity fliers for demonstrations, buttons, stickers, and financial records. Their principles of selection and inclusion differ from those of a public research archive that defines value according to historical or research interest. It is LHA's policy, for example, not to refuse any donation of materials that a lesbian considers important in her life and actively to encourage ordinary lesbians to collect and donate the archival evidence of their everyday lives.

In insisting on the value of apparently marginal or ephemeral materials, the collectors of gay and lesbian archives propose that affects—associated with nostalgia, personal memory, fantasy, and trauma—make a document significant. The archive of feelings is both material and immaterial, at once incorporating objects that might not ordinarily be considered archival and at the same time resisting documentation because sex and feelings are too personal or too ephemeral to leave records. For this reason and others, the archive of feelings lives not just in museums, libraries, and other institutions, but in other more personal and intimate spaces and also, very significantly, within cultural genres. The films and videos explored in this article use the power of the moving image to conjure and preserve emotion, and they often seek to "move" by moving or combining a series of still images to create a montage that works affectively. Especially striking is their use of an archive of popular culture, one that is strongly visual in form, to create an archive of feelings.

The Archive of the Archives

One of the ways that documentary film and video expands the archive is by documenting the archive itself. Archives make an explicit appearance not only in *The Watermelon Woman*, but also in the 1994 video *Not Just Passing Through*, which opens with footage from the inauguration of the new LHA space in Brooklyn.[14] Composed of a series of four loosely connected episodes, *Not Just Passing Through* documents the importance and the challenges of preserving, representing, and communicating lesbian history, which, as Joan Nestle puts it in an interview in the video, has often been "[wrested] from piles of garbage." One segment of the video offers a tribute to the life of African American lesbian Mabel Hampton, who had close ties to LHA; another

---

14 See *Not Just Passing Through*, dir. Polly Thistlethwaite et al. Thistlethwaite has been centrally involved with the Lesbian Herstory Archives and also works as a professional librarian. Bringing the archives to popular attention, she has appeared as "Polly the Butch Librarian" in a *Dyke TV* feature called "In the Archives." (*Dyke TV* is a weekly cable-access show produced in New York City.)

tells the story of Marge McDonald, who willed her personal "woman-related" papers to LHA, which had to rescue them from the clutches of a family bent on destroying the evidence of their daughter's lesbianism. McDonald was confident enough of the historical significance of her everyday life that she had taken the time to retype her handwritten diaries in order to make them more accessible. The other episodes focus on the Asian Lesbians of the East Coast, an organization engaged with the challenges of documenting a lesbian presence within Asian history and an Asian presence within US history, and New York's WOW Cafe theater collective, a center not only for lesbian performance but for the formation of lesbian publics. Like the slide shows that LHA presents in order to tour its collection across the United States for the benefit of those who cannot come to New York, *Not Just Passing Through* expands the reach of the archive, using video to make its stories public. One goal of the slide shows is to facilitate the formation of community, including the creation of local archives. Documentary video and media serve a similar function, especially when distributed through film festivals and other venues that create visible publics.[15] For example, *Not Just Passing Through*'s episode about Mabel Hampton demonstrates LHA's distinctiveness as a grassroots archive and makes one of its most important contributors more visible. Hampton had close personal ties to LHA cofounder Joan Nestle, and she not only was involved in the formation of the archives, but also served as something of a matriarchal mentor for the project of preserving history across the generations. As an African American woman who came of age in the twenties, she is one of the important voices documented in LHA's oral history archive.[16] *Not Just Passing Through* not only includes footage from this video interview, thus circulating it more widely, but it also contains testimony from Nestle, Jewelle Gomez, and other younger lesbians about Hampton's significance to them. Like the volunteers at LHA who provide oral history as they guide visitors through the collection, this video segment activates the archive, bringing its significance to life. Serving also as a memorial to Hampton after her death, the segment ends with a vivid contrast between the official history recorded in her *New York Times* obituary—she had no immediate survivors—and footage from a memorial in which Gomez reminds those assembled that "we are Mabel's immediate survivors."

---

15   For more on how film festivals create publics, see Patricia White, B. Ruby Rich, Eric Clarke, and Richard Fung, "Queer Publicity: A Dossier on Lesbian and Gay Film Festivals," *GLQ: A Journal of Lesbian and Gay Studies* 5 no. 1 (1999): 73–93.

16   Mabel Hampton is also one of the oldest lesbians whose story of life in butch-femme cultures appears in Joan Nestle's collection *The Persistent Desire: A Femme-Butch Reader* (Boston: Alyson, 1992), which is itself a kind of archive. The widespread popularity of the collection (both fiction and nonfiction) as a gay and lesbian print genre owes something to its archival functions.

Especially notable in the segment is Hampton's account of her pulp fiction collection, which is given pride of place in the LHA's main reading room. Pulp fiction can seem to be primarily a document of homophobia unless it is recognized as evidence of lesbian existence for consumers in the fifties and sixties who had no access to a lesbian public culture. It resembles celebrity culture, whose ostensible heteronormativity can be queered by the machinations of reception and fandom. The archive of lesbian emotion must include materials such as Mabel Hampton's pulp fiction collection, and it is crucially supplemented by videos such as *Not Just Passing Through*, in which Hampton's oral testimony explains the significance of the collection. Sentimental value is taken seriously as a rationale for acquisition in the gay and lesbian archive.

Equally suggestive of the role of popular culture and affect in the archive is *Not Just Passing Through*'s final segment on New York's WOW Cafe theater collective, which, like so many forms of live performance culture, is in danger of going undocumented. The episode adds WOW to its list of archival institutions as a place in which a lesbian culture is generated and rendered visible; more than just a theater, WOW has served as a gathering place for lesbians to work collectively to create a public culture. The video gives special attention to the work of the Five Lesbian Brothers, one of the many important theater groups and performers, along with Split Britches, Holly Hughes, Reno, and others fostered by WOW. In addition to clips from productions such as *Brave Smiles . . . Another Lesbian Tragedy* and *Voyage to Lesbos* (thus increasing the reach of live performance often difficult to see outside of New York), the segment includes interviews with the Brothers, who explain that their work challenges the assumption that lesbian culture should provide positive images. Instead, they draw on an archive that includes stereotypical images of lesbians from classic melodramatic films, such as *Mädchen in Uniform*[17] and *The Children's Hour*.[18] Mainstream representations that leave lesbians sad, lonely, or dead have become part of the archive of lesbian culture, a repository drawn on and transformed in the Brothers' hilarious and campy reworking of these films in their play *Brave Smiles*.

Like the Five Lesbian Brothers' plays, *Not Just Passing Through* and LHA embrace the archive of popular culture, even when it is homophobic, inventing an archival and documentary aesthetic more interested in preserving affect than in collecting positive images. Inspired by the Five Lesbian Brothers' strategies, this article takes the fan as a model for the archivist. The archivist of queer culture must proceed like the fan or collector whose attachment

---

17 *Mädchen in Uniform*, directed by Leontine Sagan (Berlin: Deutsche Film-Gemeinschaft, 1931).

18 *The Children's Hour*, directed by William Wyler (Los Angeles: The Mirisch Corporation, 1961).

Mable Hampton Photo from *Not Just Passing Through*. Courtesy Women Make Movies

to objects is often fetishistic, idiosyncratic, or obsessional.[19] The archive of lesbian fandom and fantasy would need to include, for example, the pinup photos, gossip, film clips, and other memorabilia that serve as the material evidence of fan culture. The fan cultures that queer certain stars, or the use of pulp novels as an indication of the existence of homosexuality, are historical practices whose story is not wholly told by the objects and persons in and around which these forms of reception take place. In considering fantasy's place in the archives, this article thus focuses in particular on the role of popular culture in documentary film and video because it reveals how, in the archive of lesbian feeling, objects are not inherently meaningful but are made so through their significance to an audience. Like the arbitrariness (or ephemerality) of the connections between feelings and objects, and especially between traumatic memories and objects, the queer dimensions of popular culture's presence in the archive are unpredictable because they are so often not intrinsic to the object.

Pulp Fiction and the Fantasy Archive

The Canadian documentary film *Forbidden Love*, which uses lesbian pulp fiction as an organizing visual motif in order to explore pre-Stonewall lesbian culture, provides one of the best examples of this queer archival strategy. *Forbidden Love* combines talking heads testimony with shots of the novels' lurid covers, interspersing four scenes that narrate a fictional coming-out story and romance in the melodramatic idiom of the pulps.[20] Among *Forbidden Love*'s invaluable contributions to the archive of gay and lesbian emotional history, is the oral testimony of ten women narrators whose stories provide a

---

19 In essays such as "Unpacking My Library: A Talk about Book Collecting," Walter Benjamin establishes himself as an important theorist of the archive interested in the connections between memory, history, and archival objects. See Benjamin, *Illuminations*, trans. Harry Zohn (New York: Schocken, 1968), 59–67. Benjamin's interest in the photograph can be linked to his interest in modes of historicization that encompass memory and affect, including the trauma of shock. For more on this issue, see Eduardo Cadava, *Words of Light: Theses on the Photography of History* (Princeton, NJ: Princeton University Press, 1997).

20 Produced on film by the National Film Board of Canada's Studio D, *Forbidden Love* has a higher production value than some of the other documentaries discussed in this article, and, according to White, is one of WMM's bestsellers. Institutional support for documentary work often makes the difference between film and video format and between short and feature-length product. *Forbidden Love* was broadcast on Canadian television as well as being distributed commercially in movie theaters (which was possible because of its feature length and film format).

sense of lesbian life in Canada in the fifties and sixties from the perspective of those who actually experienced it.[21] The narrators offer important insights about butch-femme culture, bar culture, racial and ethnic difference among lesbians, harassment and homophobia prior to the activism of the sixties, and the specificity of gay and lesbian life in Canada, as distinct from that in the United States, which too often serves as the sole point of reference for gay and lesbian history.[22] Aerlyn Weissman and Lynne Fernie interviewed thirty women in the course of making *Forbidden Love*, thus in effect creating an oral history archive as the foundation for the film. In editing this footage, they make this archive more accessible, grouping materials under particular topics and enabling the viewer to construct a cumulative history from a range of stories. The challenges of making such generalizations are especially evident in the film's approach to representing race. The only two narrators marked as nonwhite—Nairobi, an Afro-Latina nightclub entertainer who immigrated to Canada from Panama, and Amanda White, a First Nations woman—at once render visible (literally) questions about racial difference and make it difficult to provide answers since their stories remain so particular. For example, White explains that her antipathy for bar culture stems from its role in the oppression of First Nations people through alcoholism, offering a qualification to the more enthusiastic reminiscences of some of the other narrators. Her comments make *Forbidden Love*'s representation of butch-femme bar culture more heterogenous, but in the absence of other Afro-Canadian or First Nations narrators (or narrators from other racial groups), it is difficult to

---

21 I adopt the term narrators here and throughout this essay from Davis and Kennedy, and from Newton, who use it in their oral histories of gay and lesbian communities to indicate that their interview subjects are active participants in and contributors to their projects. See Kennedy and Davis, *Boots of Leather, Slippers of Gold*, and Newton, *Cherry Grove, Fire Island*.

22 For other readings of *Forbidden Love*, see Linda Dittmar, "Of Hags and Crones: Reclaiming Lesbian Desire for the Trouble Zone of Aging," in *Between the Sheets, in the Streets: Queer, Lesbian, Gay Documentary*, eds. Chris Holmlund and Cynthia Fuchs (Minneapolis: University of Minnesota Press, 1997), 71-90. *Between the Sheets, in the Streets*, which appeared while I was in the process of writing this essay, has served a valuable function in constituting an archive of gay and lesbian documentary through criticism. Three of the works explored in this article receive extended analysis in the collection's essays. Establishing a body of secondary work on these materials is difficult, as is locating sources, since many gay and lesbian publications are too ephemeral to be cited in most indexes. Also published after this article was largely written is Amy Villarejo's outstanding essay, "Forbidden Love: Pulp as Lesbian History," which overlaps with many of my concerns here. See *Out Takes: Essays on Queer Theory and Film*, ed. Ellis Hanson (Durham, NC: Duke University Press, 1999), 316-45.

formulate any broad picture of the patterns of race and racism in this period. Addressing the question of how representative their depiction of history is, the filmmakers include in the credits the disclaimer that *Forbidden Love* "is not intended to be a 'survey' of lesbians in Canada" but "is meant to contribute another fragment, another telling" through a focus on the evidence of lesbian public cultures, especially bar culture, and the stories of out lesbians.[23]

But the questions raised by the oral testimonies are given a different spin by the film's incorporation of other kinds of footage, especially pulp novel imagery, which suggests an approach to documenting history and constructing an archive not bound by the liberal politics of representation, diversity, and inclusion.[24] The dime store pulp novels that constituted one of the all too few public representations of lesbianism and homosexuality in the forties, fifties, and sixties, serve as inspiration for four fictional fantasy sequences that are intercut with the documentary segments in *Forbidden Love*. They narrate the story of a small-town girl who leaves her best friend behind (in a teary farewell at the train station) in order to move to the big city, where she gets picked up for a night of romance in a lesbian bar. Rewriting the conventions of the pulps, in which lesbian love is often punished, the final segment contains an explicit sex scene (going all the way with the soft-porn tease of the pulp covers) and a happy ending that suggests that this one-night stand, far from being sordid or perverse, is just the beginning of both romance and a happy lesbian life. Even as they erase the homophobia of the pulps, though, the sequences also exist in loving relation to them, borrowing the visual style of the lurid covers—bold, artificial colors, noir lighting, and retro fashion. Accentuating their status as pulp covers brought to life, each of the sequences ends in a freeze-frame that dissolves from the filmed action to an illustrated portrait resembling a book cover. Largely replaced by photographs in the sixties, the illustrated covers of the pulps derive their nostalgic appeal from the now outmoded aesthetics of drawing, which allows for melodramatic exaggeration.

---

23 For a fuller discussion of *Forbidden Love*'s representation of race and these two narrators, see Villarejo, "Forbidden Love." Villarejo is ultimately critical of the romanticization of bar culture in *Forbidden Love*'s interviews and its use of the pulps, using a Marxist framework wary of fetishism to argue that the covers efface material histories. I share Villarejo's sensibilities (both theoretical and cultural), but I would suggest that the importance of the pulp covers and *Forbidden Love*'s use of them lies precisely in their capacity to revise Marxist paradigms, as well as traditional understandings of documentation and documentary.

24 For an important history and critique of this politics of equal representation within gay and lesbian publics, see Eric Clarke, *Virtuous Vice: Homoeroticism and the Public Sphere* (Durham, NC: Duke University Press, 2000).

The reconstruction of pulp fiction covers in *Forbidden Love*. Courtesy Women Make Movies

Forbidden Love heightens the affective power of its fantasy sequences by including interviews in which lesbians explain the significance of the pulp novels in their lived experience. Their testimony, along with that of Ann Bannon, who has been justifiably celebrated as one of the few lesbian writers of these novels, offers different, and sometimes conflicting, perspectives, as the narrators alternately joke about the pulps and consider them seriously, revealing that, then as now, lesbians are adept at negotiating popular culture representations to meet their own needs.[25] One might expect the juxtaposition of documentary footage of real dykes with mass-market stereotypes to result in the privileging of the former over the latter, as "true" over "false" images, or positive over negative or stereotypical images. However, the montage of oral testimony, fantasy sequences, stock footage (from both film and photographic sources), and shots of pulp novel covers, along with the musical soundtrack, challenges simple distinctions between "real" lesbians and their pulp fiction counterparts. The narrators' accounts of their consumption of the paperbacks reveal that these artifacts form a vital part of the history of lesbian culture, as does the film's visual engagement with the covers. Combining the sensationalistic covers of the novels with the images of the women narrators, *Forbidden Love* posits the centrality of fantasy and fiction to the construction of lesbian identity and community. Homophobic and formulaic as the novels might have been (in their conventions, for example, for punishing lesbianism and/or perverse sexuality), they also provided evidence that there may be other lesbians out there. In the absence of other forms of public culture, this form of print culture offered access to lesbianism within the (sometimes stolen) privacy of the home (Stephanie Ozard describes reading pulps while babysitting) or for those in small towns that did not even have bars (Bannon mentions the significance of the mass distribution of paperback novels for reaching a wide audience).

It is notable that the pulp novels are primarily represented in *Forbidden Love* by their covers. This is not just because the translation from novel to screen privileges the visual over the textual; as the narrators make clear, the covers of the novels, even when only tangentially related to the stories, constituted a crucial part of their value. Ozard explains that novels with lesbian content could be selected from among the vast displays of genre fiction by

---

25 *Forbidden Love* advances the argument of *Before Stonewall*, one of the first and most important documentaries of gay and lesbian history, which also considers the role of the pulps in history and includes an interview with Ann Bannon. For more on Bannon's work, see Suzanna Danuta Walters, "As Her Hand Crept Slowly up Her Thigh: Ann Bannon and the Politics of Pulp," *Social Text* 23 (1989): 83–101; and Michele Barale, "When Jack Blinks: Si(gh)ting Gay Desire in Ann Bannon's Beebo Brinker," in *The Lesbian and Gay Studies Reader*, ed. Henry Abelove, Michele Barale, and David Halperin (New York: Routledge, 1993), 604–15.

looking for a "picture of two women." The needs of a mass-market culture using sensational and titillating representations of women and/or lesbians to sell books converge with the needs of actual or incipient lesbians eager for visible evidence that lesbians exist. Even if the books tend to ignore the reality of butch dykes or even butch-femme couples in favor of pairs of very feminine women on the covers, this fantasy has its own power. Reva Hutton remembers that the novels "all had great covers" that were "very suggestive and entrancing." The intersections of the fantastic and the real in constructions of desire are highly unpredictable, and the lesbian readers of the pulps feel no pressure to identify mimetically either with the characters in the novels or with the women on the covers. Of course, such interpretive skills may be available only to certain readers and thus constitute a specifically lesbian reading public. Keeley Moll describes with bemused horror her mother's efforts to understand her lesbianism by reading pulp fiction, which was "the worst kind of literature she could read next to the Kinsey Report." The film is a remarkable testament to the value of reception studies, as the women describe the creative ways that they negotiate the discrepancies between the covers and "real" lesbians. Moreover, it proposes an alternative to a cultural politics of positive images by articulating the ways that pulp novel covers could become treasured objects in the archive of lesbian emotion.

One name for this form of reception might be "camp," the aesthetic that governs *Forbidden Love*'s fascinated documentation of the covers and its narrative homage to their pulp aesthetic. These mass-cultural texts, threatened with extinction because they are viewed as disposable trash, become, like so much other "waste" (to invoke Nestle's words), important artifacts in the archives of lesbian emotional culture. *Forbidden Love* fully exploits the visual appeal of the covers through its use of close-ups, pans across the covers, and the freeze-frame at the end of each narrative sequence, which is followed by the dissolve from photographic to illustrated image in imitation of a book cover. The film's editing creates an interplay between still and moving images, transforming the visual power of the cover images into filmic sequences and then condensing the action of the narrative into one still image that can be fetishized.

This interest in the combined archival and affective power of the still image is also evident in the film's use of photographs. In one segment, *Forbidden Love* incorporates footage from a fifties National Film Board (NFB) of Canada documentary short that celebrates the postwar role of women as housewives, mothers, workers, and consumers. The footage is followed by narrator Hutton's discussion of the pressures to marry and conform to fifties domestic ideology and her process of coming out after getting married. From the vantage point of feminism and the present, the documentary is a lavishly camp artifact of postwar consumer culture. The voice-over advises that "the woman of today is trying to solve her problems in the way of the twentieth century. Around her she sees household aids of modern design—pressure cookers, freezers, tiny garbage disposal units, lightweight irons, and a host more—and she wants them all." The film's putatively documentary images show women shopping for furniture, taking care of babies, working as phone operaters, and marching in beauty pageants. It also includes propagandistic close-ups of women's hands operating a sewing machine, shutting off an alarm clock, washing dishes, cooking, sterilizing baby bottles, and ironing, all of which look thoroughly fantastic. (One beautifully composed and framed shot shows people riding an escalator alongside a sculpture of a rocket juxtaposed at a diagonal with the escalator.) The film closes with the comment, "Although she will never abandon her role as wife and mother, she looks forward to . . . a world that can be an adventure in happiness," accompanied by images of a young bride.

Forbidden Love then cuts to two photographs of Hutton, one in which she is on the phone and another in which she is posing by a television set. Even as her coming-out narrative undercuts the short's message of conformity, it also shows her to have replicated a version of its fantasy; the snapshots of everyday life are imbued with the conventions of national public cinema. In documenting Hutton's coming-out process from young bride to young lesbian, these photographs do not necessarily serve as truth to the NFB documentary's fiction. Even when she displays lesbian fashions and lifestyles, Hutton poses according to conventions defined by movies and commercial photography. In one snapshot, she lounges in bed with her arm thrown back behind her head and her bare shoulder revealed, and in another, she poses in a bathing suit. Her coming-out story begins with her lover seducing her by giving her copies of pulp novels, and we see a photo of Hutton tucked in bed reading one.[26] As it does with the pulp novel covers, the camera pans across the photographs in order to heighten their dramatic effect. Both the documentary footage and the photographs are archival documents powered by affect; we look to them after the fact and find history hidden there, whether it is the story of a young wife about to become a lesbian, or the use of appar-

26 For an interesting discussion of the archival challenges of identifying photographs as "gay" or "lesbian," see the section titled "It's Not What You See But Where and How You Look," in Susan Stryker and Jim Van Buskirk, *Gay by the Bay: A History of Queer Culture in the San Francisco Bay Area* (San Francisco: Chronicle, 1996), 14–15. *Gay by the Bay* primarily relies on ephemeral artifacts, especially visual ones such as photographs, posters, and pulp fiction covers, as a way to tell and document queer history. Important stories emerge from the objects; unlike many other gay and lesbian histories, this book did not substantially depend on interviews. On the importance of photographs for the production of memory and history, see Marianne Hirsch, *Family Frames: Photography, Narrative, and Postmemory* (Cambridge: Harvard University Press, 1997).

ently innocuous public films to link clean dishes, consumption, and heterosexual normalcy to national prosperity.

Forbidden Love's attention to Greenwich Village as a mecca for gay and lesbian life also demonstrates the interplay between fiction and "realist" media and the role of fantasy in structuring everyday experience. Bannon describes her trips to New York as a "diamond in [her] pocket" that provided the inspiration for her fictional representations of lesbian life and culture. The fiction is in turn read in documentary ways by women such as Hutton, who describes traveling from Canada to Greenwich Village to find "the lesbians" depicted as congregated in such bohemian neighborhoods. We see the cover of one pulp whose subtitle announces "Greenwich Village where angels and addicts, lovers and lesbians, bohemians and bawds live and love." Even when Hutton laughs at her mistaken assumption that she and her lover need to assume butch-femme postures and clothing in order to be visible in the streets of New York, thus implying that the novels were misleading, her testimony articulates pulp as a powerful resource, not a distorting mechanism.

Taking its cue from its narrators, *Forbidden Love* draws on the considerable pleasures of mass culture in its representation of lesbian life and becomes a documentary that understands fantasy as part of reality. Its use of the pulps suggests that the desire for history takes affective forms and that the current fascination with bar culture, butch-femme roles, and pre-Stonewall homophobia makes history, like sexuality, the stuff of romance. *Forbidden Love* is joined in this recognition by many gay and lesbian archives which, like the LHA with its Mabel Hampton collection, have extensive pulp collections. Many of these collections are displayed prominently because of the books' visual power as both objects and images. For example, in the opulently decorated reading room of San Francisco Public Library's James C. Hormel Gay and Lesbian Center, which is the spatial point of entry for the library's gay and lesbian holdings, pulp fiction is displayed in a glass case, and a selection of the covers can also be viewed in the library's digital collection available at computer workstations.[27] *Forbidden Love*'s visual and affective power helps

---

27 For information about the Barbara Grier and Donna McBride Pulp Paperback Collection, see http://sfpl.org/index.php?pg=2000134801. Pulp fiction has also been a rich resource for contemporary lesbian visual culture, including ephemeral genres such as posters and zines. See, for example, Nina Levitt's refunctioned pulp novel covers in "Conspiracy of Silence," in *Stolen Glances: Lesbians Take Photographs*, ed. Tessa Boffin and Jean Fraser (London: Pandora, 1991), 60–66. Levitt's work first appeared in an exhibit curated by Lynn Fernie, codirector of *Forbidden Love*. Another sign of the recognition of the historical significance of the pulps, and especially their covers, is the recent publication of a book devoted to them: Jaye Zimet, *Strange Sisters: The Art of Lesbian Pulp Fiction, 1949–1969* (New York: Viking Studio, 1999).

explain why the pulp covers are essential documents in the archive of lesbian feelings.

Queer Signs: The Tourist's Archive

Like Aerlyn Weissman and Lynne Fernie, Ellen Spiro transforms the traditional ethnographic documentary by injecting it with the power of popular culture, adapting to her own purposes a characteristically masculine and American genre, the road movie. Nominally a documentary about gay and lesbian life in the US South, Spiro's *Greetings from Out Here* disrupts the urban (and deceptively) national focus of most gay and lesbian history by depicting the rural and regional.[28] (*Forbidden Love*'s focus on Canada accomplishes a similar goal.) The video's subtitle, "A Queer's Eye View of a Strangely Straight (or So We Thought) Southern Universe" indicates Spiro's lack of interest in conventional identity politics or representation. She has no pretensions about providing a representative survey, instead presenting an assortment of old ladies, drag queens, and other "queer" eccentrics of uncertain, but sometimes probably hetero-, sexuality.[29] For Spiro, a queer ethnography can adopt a queer perspective toward its subjects, rather than being about *queers*. More so than "gayness," the people she meets share a "creative independence" and have "figured out ways to invent their own lives outside of big urban support systems." Like many uses of the word *queer*, Spiro's definition overlaps with but is not equivalent to *gay and lesbian*, but it is also distinctive because it is not primarily sexual.

Spiro presents herself as both inside and outside the cultures that she documents, framing her interest in her subjects in terms of her own autobiographical location as someone who grew up in the South and left it to become an "urban gay activist." As those who stayed, her subjects (or narrators) are other to her, but they also present fantasies about what she might have been (or might still become, as Miss Miller, the seventy-five-year-old woman

---

28 See John Howard, *Men Like That: A Southern Queer History* (Chicago: University of Chicago Press, 1999), and Kath Weston "Get Thee to a Big City: Sexual Imaginary and the Great Gay Migration," *GLQ: A Journal of Lesbian and Gay Studies* 2, no. 3 (1995): 253–77, for discussions of the need to question how urban/rural distinctions structure gay and lesbian histories and discourses.

29 For a different reading of *Greetings*, see Chris Cagle, "Imaging the Queer South: Southern Lesbian and Gay Documentary," in Holmlund and Fuchs *Between the Sheets*, 30–45. I disagree with Cagle's argument that *Greetings*'s narrators "represent" different regions and communities, an argument linked to his criticism of Spiro's use of kitsch. A different understanding of Spiro's use of popular culture, I will argue, can give rise to a different understanding of how she is representing or documenting the South.

with the pet cemetery, prompts Spiro to wonder what she will be doing in her seventies). Spiro avoids the sometimes problematic difference between ethnographer and subject that creates a voyeuristic gaze or an exotic other by claiming a sympathetic identification with her subjects. This capacity for identification across difference becomes marked as queer or even gay. Allan Gurganus, author of *The Oldest Living Confederate Widow*, articulates this sensibility in his encounter with Spiro:

> One of the many advantages of being a gay person is precisely that you're not so defined in terms of gender that you're fearful of communicating across the boundary of gender, and if you have that other capacity, it gives you a kind of power, it's a kind of passport. It lets you travel across boundaries and borders, and it encourages you, and it even insists that you identify with people who are unlike yourself.

This metaphorical notion of journey is literalized by Spiro's road trip through the South, which allows her imaginatively to "identify with people who are unlike [herself]" in order to document their queer version of the South. Rather than casting her subjects as other, Spiro explores how their lack of need for legitimation in urban communities provides a valuable model for her. Hers is not the anthropological expedition that uses the exotic difference of the margins or outposts in order to establish the metropolitan or civilized center; Spiro finds a dense culture in the regions she explores, forms of life unimagined by mass culture's version of "America." As John Blansett, who speaks about his experience of being HIV-positive in small town USA, says, "The Cleavers have never been to Okolona [Mississippi]." His extended family does not fit the TV model and challenges urban dwellers, including gays and lesbians, to examine stereotypes about rural US culture. Spiro seeks a queer South in stories that are marked by difference and eccentricity as much as in communities that are manifestly gay. Although she does chronicle public events and cultures, including the gay rodeo, Mardi Gras, the Rhythmfest women's festival, and Atlanta's Gay Pride celebration, her investments seem to lie more with the quirky loners she interviews. (In her most recent video *Roam Sweet Home* (1997), Spiro further reveals this sensibility by documenting people who live in vintage trailer homes and pursue what she calls "nomadic" lifestyles.)

Spiro is not the interviewer from on high, either all-knowing or all-invisible, but one person talking to others. Avoiding the apparent seamlessness and objectivity of the talking heads ethnodocumentary, Spiro as videomaker is not the invisible mover behind the scenes. Instead, she puts herself into the picture, showing us her hotel room, her car troubles, the view from the windshield of her van, and her dog Sam. She discusses the possible dangers of being a woman on the road, indicating that she may be as vulnerable as those being documented and reminding us of the material challenges at stake when women take over the road movie. She presents herself as a dyke; as documenter of queerness, she takes over the camera from those who might have made her its object, providing the "queer's eye view" of a terrain so often rendered by straight or male perspectives. Like lesbian oral historians Elizabeth Kennedy, Madeline Davis, and Esther Newton, who are part of the communities they document, Spiro builds her archive from the intimacy of emotional investment.[30]

Contributing to Spiro's intimate approach is innovative video technology. Even though her Hi-8 camera produces professional quality footage, she uses it like a home video camera to create a personal or intimate point of view. Because the camera is highly portable and gives high-quality footage in available light, Spiro can work without an elaborate setup or crew, and she is thus able to develop a spontaneous rapport with her subjects. Less a Q-and-A session than a conversation, Spiro's interviews establish a relationship with her narrators; it is clear that the fact that she likes these people and feels she has something to learn from them generates her interest.

Yet even as Spiro's documentary mission resists traditional ethnography, her emphasis on queer eccentrics and the cultures that they have created away from the mainstream does have the familiar resonance of the folklorist's effort to preserve authentic regional cultures. Moreover, as individual self-creations, her subjects in a sense become other to everyone except themselves and thus embody that quintessential American type, the rugged individualist. There is a romantic dimension to *Greetings'* construction of its subjects, as well as its fantasy that being gay, and thus queer, enables one, as Gurganus claims, to negotiate other kinds of difference.

Nowhere are these complexities of *Greetings'* queer sensibility more evident than in its attachment to an archive of emotion comprised of the artifacts of tourist culture. The video's contrast between the urban and the rural, and the North and the South, emerges from Spiro's desire to locate something outside of mass culture and from her nostalgic and retrospective search for a lost or disappearing version of America. This has long been one of the functions of the American tourism that emerged out of postwar automobile culture; *Greetings* displays a nostalgia for that earlier era of tourism, now replaced by a landscape of interstates, chain motels, and mass-produced rest stops. Spiro is fascinated with the old national highway system, the one-of-a-kind neon signs of independently owned motels and restaurants, and the thrift stores that circulate the artifacts and documents of tourist culture, making them

---

30 See Kennedy and Davis, *Boots of Leather, Slippers of Gold*; and Newton, *Cherry Grove, Fire Island*. For further discussion of how these books function as archive, critical ethnography, and theory, see my review of them in *Signs* 21, no. 1 (1995): 212–15, http://www.jstor.org/stable/3175139.

Publicity image, used for Ellen Spiro's *Greetings from Out Here*, inspired by tourist postcards. Courtesy Ellen Spiro

available to collectors who can be thought of as amateur archivists. *Greetings* seeks to intervene against the Wal-Mart-ization of the United States that destroys regional culture and replaces it with a homogenized national culture. This dichotomy drives its relation to queer and gay and lesbian issues, producing a resistance to the forms of gay identity associated with urban culture and commodification and a resistance even to collective identity itself.[31]

Spiro's interest in this earlier period of American culture turns *Greetings* into a visual archive. The video almost obsessively collects images of the material artifacts that affectively, often nostalgically, conjure this history of a generation once removed. Especially prominent are road signs and old tourist postcards in which, through a fusion of word and image, the names of the states are intertwined with the iconic symbols of the state. The postcards recall an era of tourist culture in the United States when the romance of the road was invented for the nuclear family and spawned a distinctive set of souvenir commodities. Providing evidence that you have been there, the postcard that condenses the varied experiences of a particular place into a name is a perfect emblem of tourist culture, which often constructs spectacles by attaching signs to them. And like *Forbidden Love*'s pulp novel covers, *Greetings*' postcards are powerful documents of the past because they are drawn rather than photographed.

Taking their visual aesthetic as inspiration for her own images, Spiro uses these place-name postcards to introduce the different episodes of *Greetings* in montages that include more contemporary road signs, both from the national interstate system and from more local routes. Like the postcard, the road sign becomes the object and text that is an emblem of both Southern culture and rural/road culture, and Spiro also works with these visuals to expose their queer dimensions. Building a collection of images on tape, she finds not only the funny signs and objects—such as Christian slogans displayed by car repair shops, the Christ of the Ozarks statue, or the small-town signs such as "Okolona, The Little City That Does Big Things"—but also the queer ones, including the intersection of "Camp St." and "Cherry St.," the "Homochitto River," "Gaywood Campground," a town called "Beaver," a *National Enquirer* cover story about Garth Brooks's lesbian sister, signs for Dollywood followed by a big erotic peach statue, and a boat named "Paul N Tony." Even the American flag is given a humorous twist, shown at one point in tatters, and later as part of the campy festiveness of a fireworks store, another oddity of the road trip's particular brands of consumer culture. Spiro searches out the quirky icons that give her version of the South its character, videotaping with

---

31 Spiro thus implicitly responds to the urban focus of scholarship, such as Chauncey's *Gay New York* and John D'Emilio's *Sexual Politics, Sexual Communities: The Making of a Homosexual Minority in the United States, 1940–70* (Chicago: University of Chicago Press, 1983).

a collector's eye and documenting material objects that serve as emblems of the region. Through a way of seeing that queers the landscape, Spiro finds that queers are present everywhere in the homespun ephemera of tourism. Serving as transitions from one narrator and place to the next, these visual diaries are a crucial part of Spiro's archive, equal in significance to the stories she collects for the archives of oral history. As visual icons turned into documents, they are the counterpart to *Forbidden Love*'s pulp novel covers—mass-produced images that performed important affective and cultural work in their own time and that now form an archive of sentimental value for the film- or videomaker.

It is important to note, however, that if *Greetings* is nostalgic, it is nostalgic for an earlier version of mass culture, not a pre- or noncommodified folk culture. Furthermore, its version of the South is not necessarily a strictly local culture since the archive that interests Spiro actually results from the commodification of regionalism for consumption by outsiders and the creation of a national tourist culture that (literally) paved the way for that which has displaced it.[32] Her love of objects, and images of objects, as the foundation for history draws her toward an archive of commodities, but the commodities of the thrift store as opposed to the mall superstore. The resulting archive queers both US and Southern cultures, showing them never to have been what a celebratory straight culture might make them. It reveals the queer possibilities always there in the celebration of rugged individualism, Southern identity, tourism, or consumerism. The archive's meaning emerges from the queer sensibility of its collector rather than a history intrinsic to its objects. As queer ethnographer, the archivist builds a collection out of love and intimate connection, creating an archive in which popular culture's ephemera has the power to conjure the past.

Sadie Benning: The Bedroom Archives

As my final example of documentary that creates a lesbian archive, Sadie Benning's videos might seem like an unusual choice. Viewed collectively, Benning's early videos provide a compendium of the everyday life of young girls, especially baby dykes, having to establish their sexuality and their life stories without the benefit of public affirmation or representation.[33] But rather

---

32 On the history of US tourism and road culture, see Donna R. Braden, *Leisure and Road Culture in America* (Dearborn, MI: Henry Ford Museum and Greenfield Village, 1988); and James J. Flink, *The Automobile Age* (Cambridge: MIT Press, 1988), especially chapter 10, "On the Road."

33 Produced prior to Benning's videos *Girlpower* (1992) and *It Wasn't Love* (1992), discussed elsewhere herein, the videos *If Every Girl Had a Diary* (1990), *Jollies* (1990), *Living Inside* (1989), *Me and Rubyfruit* (1989), *A New Year* (1989), and *A Place Called*

than documenting a subculture by interviewing a range of people, Benning stays at home, focusing primarily on herself and often venturing no farther than the confines of her own bedroom. Although her work is often classified as experimental video or as autobiography, I want to claim it as documentary in order to promote its value as an innovative archive of lesbian life, one that includes the material spaces of intimacy, such as bedrooms, and intimacy's imaginary spaces, such as fantasies.[34] Insisting on the value of the narcissistic and the insular, Benning creates the video counterpart to a young girl's diary, chronicling her secret desires, the intimate details of her body, and her fandoms and fantasies. (One of her early videos is called *If Every Girl Had a Diary*, and *It Wasn't Love* includes an image of a diary, on the cover of which is a drawing of a girl and the words "Dear Diary" in feminized handwriting.) Her camera is a child's toy, the Fisher-Price Pixelvision camera that can capture only a fraction of the angle of vision of a more standard video camera and that makes objects look fuzzy and distorted. Although her transformation of the point-and-shoot real world into an alternately haunting and comic psychic landscape gives her work its experimental look, her videos are also easily accessible to a punk generation raised on video, MTV, and DIY (do it yourself) production values.

Benning documents a culture of girlhood that is even less publicly visible than the marginal locations recorded in *Forbidden Love* and *Greetings* because it is not public in any conventional sense of the term. If one imperative of the gay and lesbian and the emotional archive is to remake the relation between public and private spheres, then Benning's videos do so by including a teenage girl's bedroom within what Michael Moon has called the "semi-public" sphere.[35] They reveal that, even when isolated from the world, such bedrooms

---

Lovely (1991) are available in the her earlier compilation, *Sadie Benning Videoworks: Volume 1*, distributed by Video Data Bank; see http://www.vdb.org/titles/sadie-benning-videoworks-volume-1.

34 Holmlund makes a similar point in arguing that Benning's autobiography should also be understood as ethnography, that is, as a means of documenting a culture and a collective reality; see "When Autobiography Meets Ethnography and Girl Meets Girl: The 'Dyke Docs' of Sadie Benning and Su Friedrich," in Holmlund and Fuchs, *Between the Sheets, in the Streets*, 127–43. For more on Sadie Benning, see Alexandra Juhasz, "Our Auto-Bodies, Ourselves: Representing Real Women in Feminist Video," *Afterimage* 21, no. 7 (1994): 10–14; and Mia Carter, "The Politics of Pleasure: Cross-Cultural Autobiographic Performance in the Video Works of Sadie Benning," *Signs* 23, no. 3 (1998): 745– 69.

35 See Michael Moon, "Unauthorized Writing: AIDS and the Revival of 'Archaic' Modes of Literary and Cultural Production" (paper delivered at the Sixth North American Lesbian, Gay, and Bisexual Studies conference, University of Iowa, November 1994).

are connected to it, offering sanctuary from the alienation of more properly public spaces through a queer version of the cultural logic of domesticity. Moreover, the television and film footage and the many popular images that Benning includes, as well as the soundtrack of pop songs that accompanies her images, bring the world into her bedroom. She in turn refunctions that world by recording televised images and combining them with images of herself, turning this archival resource into her own product, a video that can be circulated in public. Rewriting studies of popular culture that have sought subcultures in public spaces such as streets and clubs, and that have hence produced a largely masculinist picture, Benning suggests that girls' culture begins at home.[36] The process of documenting and archiving it by making a video provides testimony to its existence, breaking out of isolation to build an imagined community of girls in their bedrooms.

Like Spiro's *Greetings From Out Here*, Benning's *It Wasn't Love* shows the influence of popular culture by reworking not only the road movie genre, but the gangster movie and the romance as well. But when Sadie and another teenage girl leave home in search of romance and adventure, they don't get very far.[37] Sadie's head appears in front of the camera (the Pixelvision version of a talking head becomes surreal in its fuzzy too-extreme close-up) to explain: "We didn't make it to Detroit, much less Hollywood. Instead, we pulled into a fried-chicken parking lot and made out." After one of the most remarkable "sex scenes" in contemporary lesbian visual culture, in which Sadie wraps her fingers around the camera lens and sucks on her thumb slowly, her voice-over explains that this ending is far from a failed version of the standard plot:

> *I wanted to feel sorry for myself like I was missing out on something. And yet in that parking lot, I felt like I had seen the whole world. She had this way of making me feel like I was the goddamn Nile River or something. We didn't need Hollywood. We were Hollywood and that made us both famous.*

These girls make a "whole world" out of a parking lot and kisses, in defiance of what usually counts as fame and fortune in popular fantasy and world history. Without going anywhere, they are as "famous" as Hollywood stars

---

36 Benning thus implicitly extends and revises Angela McRobbie's observations about girls and subcultures, exposing the hetero-centrism of McRobbie's assumptions about the gendered opposition of the bedroom and the street; see, for examples, the chapters "Girls and Subcultures" and "Settling Accounts with Subcultures" in McRobbie's *Feminism and Youth Culture: From "Jackie" to "Just seventeen"* (Boston: Unwin Hyman, 1991).

37 Like Carter, I adopt the convention of using "Sadie" to refer to Benning's appearances in her own videos. See Carter, "The Politics of Pleasure."

and as adventurous as (but possibly less exploitive than) the explorers who colonize the world. *It Wasn't Love* borrows from pop culture narratives, acknowledging their power to confer the public status that enfranchises one as a citizen. But it uses those stories to construct forms and spaces of celebrity and (counter)publicity that do not require acknowledgment from the world at large.[38]

Space constraints do not permit the detailed attention that Benning's work as archive demands. Composed of a dense array of images and sounds edited in ways that produce meaning through juxtaposition and sequencing, they suggest that an archive that can do justice to the affective dimensions of girls' lives is as lyrical as a dream and as chock-full of images as a day spent watching TV or reading magazines. Moreover, as Laura Marks suggests in her work on haptic video, Benning produces images that ask to be touched rather than seen.[39] In fact, Benning touches her viewers both literally and figuratively through what might be called an aesthetics of intimacy.[40] She takes intimacy literally by getting close to the objects she shoots and thus narrowing the distance between the viewer and the visual field. The resulting shots are so unusual, both visually and affectively, or so ephemeral, that even detailed description can fail to capture them. I would like to mention briefly two kinds of materials in the Benning archive that reflect the affective sensibility shared by the other documentaries examined in this article—old drawings and archival footage from television. My examples are taken from *Girlpower*, one of the most varied of Benning's videos in its range of archival sources, and the video that, as its title suggests, documents not only her life but that of "girls everywhere."

Girlpower opens with a sequence (with a soundtrack from Sonic Youth) that includes a drawing of a lineup of girls, each one at a different stage of developing into a woman. The camera pans backwards across the row from woman to girl and then moves quickly across the image in a blur. Like *Forbidden Love*'s pulp novel covers and *Greetings*' postcards, this imagery's stereotypical, even archetypal, power is related to its status as a drawing. This found image is preceded by a shot of a piece of paper on which is written the title "Girlpower" in a cursive script, below which we see a drawing of a girl or woman that looks like the cliché image of a "pretty face" that a young girl

---

38 For more on mass culture, publicity, and identity, see Michael Warner, "The Mass Public and the Mass Subject," in *Habermas and the Public Sphere*, ed. Craig Calhoun (Cambridge: MIT Press, 1992), 377–401.

39 Laura Marks, "Video Haptics and Erotics," *Screen* 39, no. 4 (1998): 331. doi:10.1093/screen/39.4.331.

40 I invoke this term in order to connect Benning's uses of intimacy with the resonances of the concept as developed in the special issue of *Critical Inquiry* 24, no. 2 (1998), devoted to the topic of intimacy and edited by Lauren Berlant.

might make.[41] Even as she uses video technology, Benning is drawn to an archive of archaic genres, such as drawing and illustration, echoing *Forbidden Love*'s interest in the illustrations of the pulp novel covers. Drawing reveals the ideological operations of visual culture in ways that the apparent realism of photographs or video can obscure.[42]

Another sequence later in the video also uses a range of archival images from textbooks, accompanied by a Bikini Kill song. Most prominent is a line drawing of a girl playing tennis; her body is rendered as a skeleton whose parts are labeled with their technical names. In another shot, a male scientist looks into a microscope, and the camera cuts to a series of drawings of cells. In the Pixelvision's close-up, the scientific world is aestheticized; the drawings are hauntingly beautiful, made into something else by a girl's camera and her eye for detail. Interspersed is archival footage of a bomb exploding and of bombs being dropped from planes. The video incorporates and remakes the visual archive of official culture and its documents of femininity. Such archives must be resisted because, as the video proceeds to show, they can pathologize a young girl's sexual experience in the form of the case history. Archiving not just images but also text, Benning's camera pans across the words "masturbation in young females," along with some text from a science book that appears to be about freaks. We can just catch the words "accident of abnormal birth" and "considered a disgrace." The inability of the camera to take in more than a

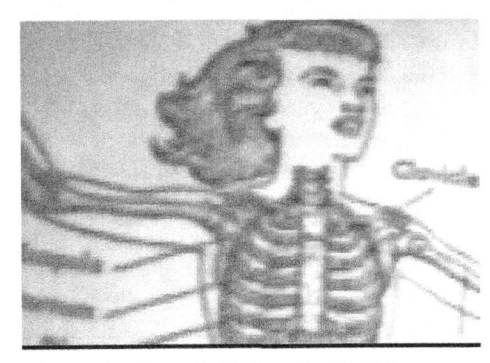

Illustration from Sadie Benning's *Girlpower*

---

41   In Benning's more recent video, *Flat Is Beautiful* (1997), the characters wear paper masks made out of these same kinds of drawings; see *Flat Is Beautiful*, in *Sadie Benning Videoworks: Volume 3*, distributed by Video Data Bank, http://www.vdb.org/titles/sadie-benning-videoworks-volume-3. The centrality of drawing in recent girl and lesbian cultures is also evident in the visual art of Nicole Eisenman. See my "Fierce Pussies and Lesbian Avengers: Dyke Activism Meets Celebrity Culture," in *Consequences: Feminist Theory for the New Century*, ed. Elisabeth Bronfen and Misha Kavka (New York: Columbia University Press, 2001), 283–318, for more on Eisenman as well as the relation between drawing and advertising media.

42   For more on the ideological operations of drawing, especially in children's culture, see Ann Reynolds's discussion of *My Weekly Reader* in "Visual Stories," in *Visual Display: Culture beyond Appearances*, ed. Lynne Cooke and Peter Wollen (Seattle: Bay, 1995), 82–109.

few words at a time twists the words out of context, framing and highlighting them as code and making them available as slogans for new meanings. The limits of Benning's toy camera become its strength; by taking in only fragments of the official archive and blowing them up, she reveals their sinister power and makes them the raw material for her own vision. Like Ellen Spiro, she turns words and signs into her own affectively charged montage of images.

The sequence climaxes with the end of the song and culminates in a shot of two girls kissing and then one of a mouth laughing triumphantly in a mirror. The camera moves across another line taken from the textbook that reads "I was a girl, 19 years of age." Benning has remade the case history in her own idiom, documenting the life of young dykes by reworking an archive that depicts them in crude and inadequate ways. Like *Forbidden Love*'s inclusion of archival footage and pulp novel covers, *Girlpower*'s incorporation of official documents carries nostalgic and emotional power. The riot-grrrl sensibility that Benning shares with many musicians and zine makers reappropriates cultural constructions of girlhood that often seem denigrating and infantilizing, especially those from earlier generations, and converts them into a powerful repository. The fashion and visual sensibility of girl's culture, which over the last decade has surged far beyond its subcultural formations of the early nineties, has become a new language of feminism.[43] Images from the archives of the fifties and sixties and from pseudoscientific sources have become a resource for the montage and collage aesthetics of videos and zines.

In its affective response to mass culture, Benning's aesthetic draws on another staple of girls' culture—fandom. Sadie fashions herself in the image of pop culture icons, reflecting the role of fantasy in shaping gender and sexual identity that *Forbidden Love* also emphasizes. Fantasy takes up the seductions of a mainstream culture that apparently confines its audience to heteronormativity; Sadie can be Matt Dillon from *Teen Beat*, or Erik Estrada rescuing young girls (far from being an obstacle for dyke fantasy, masculinity fosters it), or a medley of girl-band icons.[44] "And when I sang, I became every member of the Go-Gos. Blondie, Joan Jett, Devo—I did it all," she says,

---

43 In 1999, for example, the Spice Girls hosted a "Girl Power" video event on MTV, and the success of girls' culture is now visible in a range of cultural products from *Buffy the Vampire Slayer* to Sanrio's "Hello Kitty" line. The commercialization of girl power, like that of lesbian chic, is, of course, to be expected given its origins in a subculture fascinated by mass culture.

44 For more on Benning's cross-racial fantasies, especially her identification with African American popular culture figures, see Carter, "The Politics of Pleasure." It includes a discussion of Ken Feil's treatment of this issue in his dissertation, "From Queer to Hybridity: Questions of Cultural Difference in Contemporary Queer Film and Video" (Ph.D. diss., University of Texas at Austin, 1995).

as she samples footage of Debbie Harry singing "Rapture." Voice-over, text, music, original images, and sampled images are woven together to represent the intertwining of pop culture heroes and Sadie's own iconic power. Luke Perry's image on a poster waves in front of the camera and then gets cut in two as Sadie, a baby butch who styles herself after her male heroes, inserts herself between the two halves. Her voice-over fantasy about being Erik Estrada "rushing on my motorcycle to save the life of some girl who desperately needed to be rescued" is accompanied by home movie footage of a young girl (quite likely Benning herself) riding a tricycle around the living room. The personal archive of the home movie and the public archive of television are both resources for an affective archive shaped by fantasy and by the teenage Sadie's nostalgic relation to herself as an even younger girl.

Sadie Benning posing with a photo of Luke Perry in *Girlpower*

Benning rewrites the relation between public and private spheres in her assertion that, "In my world, in my head, I was never alone," whereas the worlds of "school, my father, and my culture" produce alienation and isolation. Fantasy is juxtaposed with reality as a necessary survival tactic rather than a luxury or a fiction: "I survived because I created my own heroes." But the raw material for those heroes is the archive of images available for scavenging within the confines of her room: textbooks, movies broadcast on TV, home movies, records. Privatized consumption becomes a form of public access when the streets are dangerous. The archive that the girl fan or collector accumulates is the public archive made personal, a scrapbook in which the feelings that accompany media events are as important as those events. Private ownership of images becomes a form of self-assertion in the face of a mainstream culture that threatens to keep girls' feelings inarticulate and invisible. Through a highly personal and intimate archive, Benning creates an imagined community of girls everywhere who can recognize themselves in her tastes and sentiments. Such self-empowerment is the goal of riot grrrl as a movement and, in the credits, Benning thanks not only Bikini Kill, but "all the secret superstars everywhere. You rule." It is not necessary that "superstars" be public to be meaningful; in the archive of lesbian culture, they are meaningful because the power of the imagination has made them so: "In my imagination I traveled the world. I was as powerful as a bullet. I survived because I created my own heroes. Nobody needed to know I was somebody 'cause it was my secret." The secrecy of the archive becomes its power; being a celebrity or a public person is not a necessary prerequisite for a girl to star as the heroine of her own archive. As Nestle suggests in the comments that serve as the epigraph to this article, when ordinary girls kiss each other, they merit the fame of inclusion in the archive of lesbian feelings.

Actually Existing Archives

Like Benning, the creators of grassroots gay and lesbian archives have often turned their bedrooms into safe havens for history. Both the LHA and San Francisco's Gay, Lesbian, Bisexual, and Transgender Society of Northern California started out at home. Even the very public James C. Hormel Gay and Lesbian Center at the San Francisco Public Library has its intimate dimensions; the beautifully designed reading room provides a sanctuary from the open spaces of the central library. The history of any archive is a history of space, which becomes the material measure and foundation of the archive's power and visibility as a form of public culture. In so far as their existence has been dependent on the possibility of making private spaces, such as rooms in people's homes, public, grassroots gay and lesbian archives constitute another example of what Moon has called a "semi-public" sphere. Each of the archives that preserves gay and lesbian history has a history that itself belongs in the archives because they have been formed out of the same queer and obsessional urges to collect that guide the makers of these documentaries, and the archives' histories are as emotional and idiosyncratic as their collections.[45] Moreover, as more institutionalized archives develop gay and lesbian collections, it will prove increasingly important not to forget the more queer collections and strategies of the grassroots archives.[46]

---

45 In addition to drawing on time spent at the LHA, my insights are based primarily on research in and about the Gay, Lesbian, Bisexual, and Transgender Society of Northern California (GLBTS) and the James C. Hormel Gay and Lesbian Center at the San Francisco Public Library. My thanks to Jim Van Buskirk of the public library, and to Bill Walker and Susan Stryker of GLBTS for sharing information about the history of these archives and institutions. Another valuable resource is the Carmichael's *Daring to Find Our Names*.

46 Also important to examine are the collaborative arrangements between the two kinds of institutions, such as the agreement between the San Francisco Public Library and the GLBTS to share their collections. Another example is the negotiations between the Mazer Collection and the One Collection, both grassroots archives based in Los Angeles, with the University of Southern California regarding the collection's removal to the campus. The Mazer (a lesbian archive) ultimately decided not to move its collection to USC because the university agreed to provide only space, not staff. In our interview, Maxine Wolfe also describes

Against the traumatic loss of gay and lesbian history, documentaries and archives serve a vital task of cultural memory. The indispensability of popular and mass culture in such an archive points to the idiosyncratic and necessary ways in which an archive must preserve affective value. Like the archive of popular culture, the archive demanded by gay and lesbian history is an emotional one. It not only demands new kinds of evidence but also requires that we think about evidence as an emotional category. Because gay and lesbian history in particular is produced through memory as much as through documents, those in search of the past must construct an archive through the work of emotional investment. Popular culture has much to teach us about this archive because it is so vulnerable to dismissal as trivia or waste or low culture and because it is also kept alive through personal history, nostalgia, and other queer investments. The documentaries explored in this article make vivid use of an archive of visual culture, especially old photographs, the intimate technology for preserving everyday life, and drawings or illustrations, the archaic media that threaten to be superceded by new technologies of memory. *The Watermelon Woman*'s fake photographs of Richards, *Forbidden Love*'s images of pulp fiction covers and *Not Just Passing Through*'s depiction of their presence in the archive, Benning's home movie clips and textbook drawings of girls, Spiro's antique postcards—these objects and the feelings associated with them belong in the archive.

As part of an archive, these artifacts of popular culture open up new approaches to histories of trauma and the trauma of historical absence. They refuse to conform to standards of realism or equal representation. As *The Watermelon Woman* suggests, for example, one may have to invent an archive and create a fiction about an African American woman in order to make up for the fragmented and distorted state of the existing records. Indeed, looking for racial histories within popular culture reveals particularly strongly the unpredictable relation between artifacts and histories. Benning, for example, uses African American popular music to articulate her (white) adolescent identity, and Spiro uses nostalgic postcards of a South whose regional identity emerges from a dense history of race relations that cannot easily be articulated. An archive of popular culture traffics in stereotypes and myths, and its pleasures are often attached to other more painful emotions. It is energized by the power of the image to preserve a specifically emotional memory and by the idiosyncratic cathexis that turns old objects into fetishes embodying memory and affect. Through the ephemeral materials of popular culture, a

considerable debate within ACT UP about whether to donate its archives to the New York Public Library, with some arguing that presence in the public library would provide legitimacy and visibility, and others arguing that the public institution would provide no guarantee of safety or access. A much more extended discussion of these issues appears in my book, *An Archive of Feelings*.

range of lesbian documentary makers forge a past for themselves and teach us to value an archive of feelings that will always remain ephemeral.

Bibliography

Barale, Michele. "When Jack Blinks: Si(gh)ting Gay Desire in Ann Bannon's Beebo Brinker." In *The Lesbian and Gay Studies Reader*, edited by Henry Abelove, Michele Barale, and David Halperin, 604–15. New York: Routledge, 1993.

Before Stonewall: The Making of a Gay and Lesbian Community. Directed by Greta Schiller. New York: Cinema Guild, 1985. Videocassette (VHS).

Benjamin, Walter. "Unpacking My Library: A Talk about Book Collecting." In *Illuminations*, translated by Harry Zohn, 59–67. New York: Schocken, 1968.

Berlant, Lauren. "'68 or Something." *Critical Inquiry* 21, no. 1 (1994): 124–55. http://www.jstor.org/stable/1343889.

———. "Intimacy." Special issue, *Critical Inquiry* 24, no. 2 (1998). http://www.jstor.org/stable/i257793.

———. "Intimacy's Ephemera." Paper delivered at the Modern Language Association, Toronto, December 1997.

———. Introduction to *The Queen of America Goes to Washington City*, 1–24. Durham, NC: Duke University Press, 1997.

Boswell, John. *Christianity, Social Tolerance, and Homosexuality.* Chicago: University of Chicago Press, 1980.

———. *Same-Sex Unions in Premodern Europe.* New York: Villiard, 1994.

Braden, Donna R. *Leisure and Road Culture in America.* Dearborn, MI: Henry Ford Museum and Greenfield Village, 1988.

Cadava, Eduardo. *Words of Light: Theses on the Photography of History.* Princeton, NJ: Princeton University Press, 1997.

Cagle, Chris. "Imaging the Queer South: Southern Lesbian and Gay Documentary." In Holmlund and Fuchs *Between the Sheets*, 30–45.

Carmichael, James V. Jr., ed. *Daring to Find Our Names: The Search for Lesbigay Library History.* Westport, CT: Greenwood, 1998.

Carter, Mia. "The Politics of Pleasure: Cross-Cultural Autobiographic Performance in the Video Works of Sadie Benning." *Signs* 23, no. 3 (1998): 745–69.

Chauncey, George. *Gay New York.* New York: Basic, 1994.

Clarke, Eric. *Virtuous Vice: Homoeroticism and the Public Sphere.* Durham, NC: Duke University Press, 2000.

Cvetkovich, Ann. *An Archive of Feelings: Trauma, Sexuality, and Lesbian Public Cultures.* Durham, NC: Duke University Press, 2003.

———. "Fierce Pussies and Lesbian Avengers: Dyke Activism Meets Celebrity Culture," in *Consequences: Feminist Theory for the New Century*, edited by Elisabeth Bronfen and Misha Kavka, 283–318. New York: Columbia University Press, 2001.

———. Reviews of *Boots of Leather, Slippers of Gold: The History of a Lesbian Community* by Elizabeth Lapovsky Kennedy and Madeline D. Davis, and *Cherry Grove, Fire Island: Sixty Years in America's First Gay and Lesbian Town* by Esther Newton. *Signs* 21, no. 1 (1995): 212–15. http://www.jstor.org/stable/3175139.

Derrida, Jacques. *Archive Fever*. Chicago: University of Chicago Press, 1995.

Dittmar, Linda. "Of Hags and Crones: Reclaiming Lesbian Desire for the Trouble Zone of Aging." In Holmlund and Fuchs, *Between the Sheets, in the Streets*, 71–90.

Duberman, Martin. *Stonewall*. New York: Dutton, 1993.

Flat Is Beautiful. In *Sadie Benning Videoworks: Volume 3*.

Flink, James J. *The Automobile Age*. Cambridge: MIT Press, 1988.

Forbidden Love: The Unashamed Stories of Lesbian Lives. Directed by Aerlyn Weissman and Lynne Fernie. Montreal: National Film Board of Canada, 1992. DVD.

Girlpower. In *Sadie Benning Videoworks: Volume 2*.

Greetings from Out Here. Directed by Ellen Spiro. Chicago: Video Data Bank, 1993. DVD.

Halperin, David. *One Hundred Years of Homosexuality*. New York: Routledge, 1990.

Holmlund, Chris. "When Autobiography Meets Ethnography and Girl Meets Girl: The 'Dyke Docs' of Sadie Benning and Su Friedrich." In Holmlund and Fuchs, *Between the Sheets, in the Streets*, 127–43.

Holmlund, Chris, and Cynthia Fuchs, eds. *Between the Sheets, in the Streets: Queer, Lesbian, Gay Documentary*. Minneapolis: University of Minnesota Press, 1997.

Howard, John. *Men Like That: A Southern Queer History*. Chicago: University of Chicago Press, 1999.

It Wasn't Love. In *Sadie Benning Videoworks: Volume 2*.

Juhasz, Alexandra. "Our Auto-Bodies, Ourselves: Representing Real Women in Feminist Video." *Afterimage* 21, no. 7 (1994): 10–14.

Kennedy, Elizabeth Lapovsky, and Madeline D. Davis. *Boots of Leather, Slippers of Gold: The History of a Lesbian Community*. New York: Routledge, 1993.

Levitt, Nina. "Conspiracy of Silence." In *Stolen Glances: Lesbians Take Photographs*, edited by Tessa Boffin and Jean Fraser, 60–66. London: Pandora, 1991.

Marks, Laura. "Video Haptics and Erotics." *Screen* 39, no. 4 (1998): 331–348. doi:10.1093/screen/39.4.331.

McRobbie, Angela. *Feminism and Youth Culture: From "Jackie" to "Just seventeen"* (Boston: Unwin Hyman, 1991).

Moon, Michael. "Unauthorized Writing: AIDS and the Revival of 'Archaic' Modes of Literary and Cultural Production." Paper delivered at the Sixth North American Lesbian, Gay, and Bisexual Studies conference, University of Iowa, November 1994.

Morrison, Toni. "The Site of Memory." In *Out There: Marginalization and Contemporary Cultures*, edited by Russell Ferguson, Martha Gever, Trinh T. Minh-ha, and Cornel West, 299–305. Cambridge, MA: MIT Press, 1990.

Muñoz, José. "Ephemera as Evidence: Introductory Notes to Queer Acts," *Women and Performance* 16 (1996): 5–18.

Nestle, Joan. *The Persistent Desire: A Femme-Butch Reader*. Boston: Alyson, 1992.

———. *A Restricted Country*. Ithaca, NY: Firebrand, 1987.

Newton, Esther. *Cherry Grove, Fire Island: Sixty Years in America's First Gay and Lesbian Town*. Boston: Beacon, 1993.

Not Just Passing Through. Directed by Polly Thistlethwaite, Jean Carlomusto, Dolores Perez, and Catherine Saalfield. New York: Women Make Movies, 1994. DVD.

Reynolds, Ann. "Visual Stories." In *Visual Display: Culture beyond Appearances*, edited by Lynne Cooke and Peter Wollen, 82–109. Seattle: Bay, 1995.

Sadie Benning Videoworks: Volume 1. Directed by Sadie Benning. Chicago: Video Data Bank, 1998. DVD. http://www.vdb.org/titles/sadie-benning-videoworks-volume-1.

Sadie Benning Videoworks: Volume 2. Directed by Sadie Benning. Chicago: Video Data Bank, 1999. DVD. http://www.vdb.org/titles/sadie-benning-videoworks-volume-2.

Sadie Benning Videoworks: Volume 3. Directed by Sadie Benning. Chicago: Video Data Bank, 1999. DVD. http://www.vdb.org/titles/sadie-benning-videoworks-volume-3.

Stryker, Susan, and Jim Van Buskirk. *Gay by the Bay: A History of Queer Culture in the San Francisco Bay Area*. San Francisco: Chronicle, 1996.

Thistlethwaite, Polly. "Building 'A Home of Our Own': The Construction of the Lesbian Herstory Archives." In Carmichael, *Daring to Find Our Names*, 153–74.

Villarejo, Amy. "Forbidden Love: Pulp as Lesbian History." In *Out Takes: Essays on Queer Theory and Film*, edited by Ellis Hanson, 316–45. Durham, NC: Duke University Press, 1999.

Walters, Suzanna Danuta. "As Her Hand Crept Slowly up Her Thigh: Ann Bannon and the Politics of Pulp." *Social Text* 23 (1989): 83–101.

Warner, Michael. "The Mass Public and the Mass Subject." In *Habermas and the Public Sphere*, edited by Craig Calhoun, 377–401. Cambridge: MIT Press, 1992.

The Watermelon Woman. Directed by Cheryl Dunye. New York: First Run Features, 1997. DVD.

Weston, Kath. "Get Thee to a Big City: Sexual Imaginary and the Great Gay Migration." *GLQ: A Journal of Lesbian and Gay Studies* 2, no. 3 (1995): 253–77.

White, Patricia, B. Ruby Rich, Eric Clarke, and Richard Fung. "Queer Publicity: A Dossier on Lesbian and Gay Film Festivals." *GLQ: A Journal of Lesbian and Gay Studies* 5 no. 1 (1999): 73–93.

Zimet, Jaye. *Strange Sisters: The Art of Lesbian Pulp Fiction, 1949–1969*. New York: Viking Studio, 1999.

Part Seven
Performance

How I Learned to Stop Worrying and Love the Rape Kit

Aliza Shvarts[1]

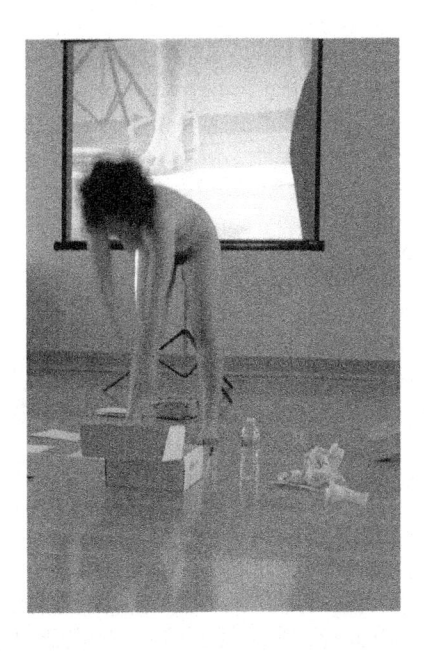

We know less about the sexual life of little girls than of boys. But we need not feel ashamed of this distinction; after all, the sexual life of adult women is a 'dark continent' for psychology.[2]

---

1. Editors' note: this paper was previously published in *Extensions: The Online Journal of Embodiment and Technology* 6 (October, 2011): http://www.extensionsjournal.org/the-journal/6/how-i-learned-to-stop-worrying-and-love-the-rape-kit.
2. Sigmund Freud, *The Question of Lay Analysis*, trans. James Strachey, standard ed. (London: Hogarth 1961), 212.

Dark continents require special rituals, types of magical thinking that allow them to be known. Originating in the contact of European traders with the tribes of West Africa, the fetish emerged to enact this alchemy of comprehension. For what other logic could so fearlessly approach the breadth and depth of darkness to derive knowledge and value from it? By what other means could the things that happen in obscurity be brought to justice and light? Since this primal colonial scene, the fetish has functioned as a language of exchange, translating content into meaning through the medium of materiality. A logic of slippage and substitution, translation and transposition, it renders the virtues of the material world visible in the virtualities of ideology and language—virtualities that are themselves equally material, but whose materiality is obscured by a dominating shadow of legibility. It does not apprehend but rather productively misapprehends, creating a basis of communication as part of an ideologically inflected misreading, an implicit criticism articulated through the imperative to production and profit. In this sense, the fetish is a thing that makes, and as a politicized making, it is successful only when its productive work is obscured. Always producing, the fetish is most often producing to reinforce a position of power, maintaining concepts of similarity and difference that echo the colonizing instinct from whence it came: it makes, generates, and as a generative tool, reproduces the body as raced, gendered, and classed.

The contemporary methods of probing the unknowability of the female organ certainly invoke the fetish's historical function. Indeed, the implements of measurement—the stirrups, the table, the speculum—enable a line of sight that makes clear the location of the observing and interpreting eye, the ideological perspective from which knowledge is produced. Violence perpetrated in or by the enigmatic darkness of the female body, within that realm of femininity which resists both knowability and visibility, is not like other violence, for it must be discovered. In the case of rape—that crime specific to either female or effeminized dark holes—a perspectivized gaze fabricates the legibility of bodily violation, translating flesh into fact by way of a spatialized scrutiny. This gaze is explicitly embodied by the set of standardized forensic objects and procedures commonly known as a rape kit, which is used to gather physical evidence to support a criminal investigation into reported instances of sexual assault. Through a fetishistic logic, the kit uses corporeality to legitimate an external system of value, impressing upon the skin not only specific conditions of visibility, but also specific modes of discourse. Through its systematized ritual of collection, the kit territorializes the victim's body as a crime scene, as a series of material surfaces from which a politicized meaning manifests. Knowledge of the crime and the value of prosecuting evidence emerge in a process of evaluation, translation, and exchange. In this sense, the rape kit represents an instance of how the fetish makes, as its expository gestures work to re-make the body by transliterating the materiality of flesh into a mandate for State power. By strategically overexposing parts of the body, the kit makes a new whole, concealing not only that which falls outside normative narratives of bodily integrity and violation but also the ideological inflections with which the normatively narrativized body intones. To this end, the rape kit constructs not only the truth of a crime committed on an otherwise unknowable body, but also the truth of that body itself. Speaking in terms of power—through the persuasive language of medical fact and juridical force—the body produced by the kit bespeaks its own subjection and subjugation.

By reading the rape kit in relation to the historical lineage and theoretical applications of fetishism, I hope to discover what ideological work is accomplished through the kit's forensic mode of knowing. By tracking how the term has been produced, reproduced, and circulated, I hope to reconstruct not a chronology but a genealogy of the fetish, making visible the figurative inheritance that reifies darkness through the bright light of medical and legal exposition. Yet I also hope to do something more. By plotting the kit's function of the fetish's legacy, I want to be attentive to its productive ability—to not only the purposes to which such production has been appropriated, but also to the capacity to which such production can be re-appropriated to serve different political ends. As a mode of making, the fetish could perhaps be employed to make otherwise, to do other things—even to address and dismantle those very structures of domination that have historically wielded its power. In this sense, my project is not to make a better rape kit—for no forensic law enforcement tool of this nature could ever be better than the larger purpose of State-mandated discipline and punishment to which it is employed. My project is not even to advocate for a better system through which to address the trauma of sexual assault than one of discipline and punishment enacted by the State—for insofar as we maintain a concept of criminality that organizes the body politic, rape and sexual assault must continue to be serious and prosecutable crimes. Rather, I mean to explore how although the rape kit serves a vital function in enabling the prosecution of a violent and hideous crime, its fetishistic apprehension of the body also mobilizes the victim in a larger structure of State power and domination. Furthermore, I want to understand how although fetishism is most often deployed as a violent tool of reification, it is also an abstract mechanism of making, a violence that can cut both ways. Through the specificity of this project, I hope to discover ways in which the existing kit can be employed to a different purpose: a purpose that harnesses its productive capacity to do something beside precipitating the juridical violence and disciplinary force that maintains the subjugation and vulnerability of certain raced, classed, and gendered bodies.

I should point out that my analytical methods of close reading are not all that different than the strategies of overexposure employed by the rape kit itself. The insidious work of the fetish, its creativity, is indeed work I engage in—albeit for the purpose of identifying and critiquing rather than concealing and upholding the ubiquity of State power. Yet this apparent irony bespeaks the very ambivalence that gives fetishism such great potential, its enormous productive capacities that can serve contradictory ends. The anxiety of overexposure, in this sense, rests in this duplicity—a duplicity I not only draw attention to, but actively deploy. In the first section of my analysis, I look at the speech that precedes the rape kit, which reproduces it in a cultural discourse on violence and violation. Reading a specific monologue on an instructional DVD that accompanies the kit alongside Claude Levi-Strauss' correlation of literacy to power, I explore how the rape kit's "language of healing" conscribes the body's violation as a mandate for juridical force. The second section focuses on the text of the rape kit itself, analyzing its narrative of evidence collection through William Pierz's historical concept of the fetish—specifically its role in valuation and exchange—turning to Michel Foucault and Karl Marx in order to understand how the kit's fetishistic creation of value uses the materiality of the body to produce a historicized concept of subjecthood, further substantiating the power of the State. The third and final section looks at the materiality of the object itself, using Sigmund Freud's notion of the monument, Gilles Deleuze and Félix Guattari's reading of property, and Marcel Mauss' analysis of the gift to explore the rape kit as a site of alternate modes of making. By analyzing the rape kit as a fetish in these ways, I hope to open the possibility for performances of the kit that are not "healing" insofar as the language of healing has been marshaled to legitimize systemic modes of hierarchical power to both make and know the subjugated body, but rather reparative in the sense that the kit's fetishistic and productive capacities can be re-deployed by a subjugated body in order to make and know something else—something that confronts rather than accepts the conditions of subjugation.

The Speech

A cultural echo produces the rape kit even in the absence of the object. This echo—This speech—is that of the good subject, and it makes explicit the ideological nature of the material exchange between kit and body. The New York State Division of Criminal Justice Services produces a video called *A Body of Evidence: Using the NYS Sexual Offence Evidence Collection Kit*, which is meant to instruct medical professionals on the proper use of a standardized rape kit manufactured for distribution throughout the state of New York. Though Ann Galloway, a sexual assault nurse examiner practicing in New York State, conducts the instructional bulk of the video, the kit's function is perhaps more meaningfully illuminated by a short introduction that precedes this content and stars Mariska Hargitay—the actress who portrays one of the lead detectives in the television show *Law and Order: Special Victims Unit* on NBC (1999–present). Part fantasy and part reality, part actress and part officer, she performs and enforces the rape kit in a seamless simultaneity, as through her speech, Hargitay portrays the normative subjecthood the rape kit's strategies seek to construct. In this sense, the content of her speech as well as the fact of her participation construct the mythopoeic frame within which the rape kit operates. Before the rape kit ever appears on screen, indeed, even before it is named or mentioned, the good subject—the dual figure that is the real Mariska Hargitay and the fictitious Detective Olivia Benson—metaphorically stages its expositional function. Describing the relationship between her dramatic and charitable work, she explains:

> *To prepare for the role I trained as a rape crisis counselor, and saw the epidemic's horrendous impact first hand. But the severity of the trauma and the complexity of the healing process truly hit home when I started receiving emails and letters from survivors sharing their stories. That these survivors would reveal something so intensely personal, often for the very first time, to someone they knew only as a fictional character on television, demonstrated to me how desperate they were to be heard; how desperate they were to be believed, understood, comforted, and healed. That led me to create my non-profit organization the Joyful Heart Foundation. Our mission is to heal, educate, and empower survivors of sexual assault, domestic violence, and child abuse, and to shed light on the darkness that surrounds these issues.*[3]

Like the magical power attributed to the fetish object itself, the authority framing this video is both real and narrative: the actress who plays a fictitious rape detective but has trained as a real rape counselor and founded a real rape charity. In Hargitay's figural presence—her recognizable voice, her facial expressions, her cadence and mannerisms—the fiction and fact of law converge. Her speaking figure intonates with resonances of a legal order that reverberates in the rape kit itself, her celebrity both illuminating and illuminated by the object's aura of healing and power. In this sense, she is perhaps more accurately not only a metaphor for the kit that is the focus of the film, but a metonym as well, a contiguous part. The force of the object and the force of her speech are animated by the performative term "healing." This term denotes an extenuated, ongoing process of both reification

---

[3] Taken from *A Body of Evidence: Using the NYS Sexual Offence Evidence Collection Kit*, an online video available at http://criminaljustice.state.ny.us/ofpa/evidencekit.htm.

and transformation of the raped body—a process that encompasses the survivor, medical practitioner, and the actress. Hargitay suggests we can all participate in the survivor's desire to be "believed, understood, comforted, and healed"—a desire articulated as the progression from remote to proximate intersections between the body and knowledge. If "belief" is the most remote, implying a knowing uncorroborated by worldly material, then "understanding" gains an object, and "comfort" goes further to invoke the sensuous tactility of flesh, and finally "healing" arrives at an interpenetration of the somatic and the signifying. This succession narrates a process of knowing that becomes contiguous with the body—the appendage of apprehension moving closer, moving in. In this sense, the language of healing is a language of discipline, a language that seeks to touch and transform the body in accordance with a State-sanctioned model of health, legality, and subjecthood.

A body, once healed, will propagate this language of healing; indeed, such propagation is part of the healing process. As Hargitay tells us, to "heal" is the first component of a mission to "educate" and "empower"; it brings the survivor into a type of literacy that substantiates future authority. This link between education and power, however saccharine it might sound, is not a casual one, as it further performs the ideological frame in which the rape kit functions. The rape kit's power of healing—of bringing the body into language and language into the body—should be understood within the terms of a larger structure of legibility and domination. Healing is itself an education, literacy in the look and language of power; it is a generative education, one that enables the subject—once fully conscribed as a subject—to write for herself in that powerful language, to produce and reproduce the authority of the State. As Claude Lévi-Strauss asserts in his essay "Writing Lesson" from *Tristes Tropiques*:

> *If we look at the situation closer to home, we see that the systematic development of education in the European countries goes hand in hand with the extension of military service and proletarianization. The fight against illiteracy is therefore connected with an increase in governmental authority over citizens. Everyone must be able to read, so that the government can say: Ignorance of the law is no excuse.*[4]

The rape kit works by enacting and enforcing this cultural imperative to literacy, by making dumb flesh speak. Indeed, the kit inscribes the terms of legibility onto the body, terms later reproduced in the more general civic mission of educating the public about risk. By making the corporeal literate, the rape kit as an object is itself "connected with an increase in governmental authority over citizens," extending the gaze of sovereignty to the body's deepest

---

4   Claude Lévi-Strauss, *Tristes Tropiques*, trans. John Weightman and Doreen Weightman (New York: Penguin 1992), 300.

crevices and subjection to the palpable surfaces of the skin: it is a writing mechanism, making marks that are as expressive as they are appropriative. Through the writing of the rape kit, the body becomes a prosecutable space under the State's protection and dominion. As such, the claim to "empowerment" becomes a more complicated thing: the body is indeed empowered insofar as it is brought to power, translated by the kit into the language of legal *actionability*. These empowered bodies can speak to the State by way of the forensic object; yet insofar as their speech reproduces the conditions of power to which they make themselves legible, they are also always already spoken to. To become empowered through these means is thus to become a subject under power, to become a vector of biopolitical force. In this sense, literacy is physical, felt tangibly on the flesh—not only in the sense that the literate body is a conscripted body, corporeally managed and marshaled in the service of the State, but also to the extent to which a literate body is a healed body, a body whose wound is exorcised through its articulation. The mission "to heal, educate, and empower" thus corresponds to the model of dominion that originated in the economic and anthropological project of colonialism, the context from which the early incarnations of fetishism first emerged. A metaphor for the fetish object's transpositional stance, a metonym of its transliterative endeavor, Hargitay's speech, like the rape kit itself, demystifies obscure places with an ideologized language. This speech, like the object—as part of the object—indeed functions to "shed light on the darkness," furthering the greater ideological imperative began on the subjugated bodies and continents of history.

The Text

How the rape kit produces the good subject seems to have everything to do with how it produces itself, how it narrativizes its own function, which is immediately evident in its text. A note preceding the written instructions to New York's Sexual Offense Evidence Collection Kit discursively positions it as a fetish: as a locus of productive misapprehension, as a medium of translation, a vector of exchange. In its instructional content and physical placement, this text functions figuratively to serve as a metonym of the kit's overall purpose, a rhetorical part standing for the larger whole of its cultural capital, as well as a metaphor, a staging in language of what the rape kit does to the body. Like Mariska Hargitay's speech in the instructional video, this note comes before any specific direction, serving as a metanarrative that harmonizes each forensic step in terms of a larger ideological mission. Directly addressing the question of purpose, the note explains:

> *Each step in this kit is designed for one of two purposes. The first is to recover potentially valuable physical evidence that will be useful in any*

> subsequent investigation and legal proceeding to identify the perpetrator of the reported assault (through forensic DNA analysis, for instance) and/or to verify the nature and circumstances of the reported assault. The type of evidence often detected includes saliva, semen, hairs, spermatozoa, blood, fibers, plant material, soil and other debris that may have been transferred from the perpetrator's clothing or personal effects, or from the scene of the reported assault. The other steps are intended to collect evidence that will be used as a reference standard (controls from the victim). Each step is noted as either "Evidence Collection" or "Control Sample."

This text asserts that the primary function of the rape kit is to "recover potentially valuable physical evidence," yet what, exactly, is the nature of its value? What does the note mean by "recover"? These terms seem to make explicit that the kit's process of evaluating the body is in fact a process of valuating the body, that is, enacting the alchemy of exchange that transforms bodily excess and excrement—literally what can be swabbed and scraped from flesh—into evidence. Such recovery transforms the physical substances in question—the "saliva, semen, hairs, spermatozoa, blood, fibers, plant material, soil and other debris" that have no value outside the legibility of the rape kit—into the literacy of law. Evidence functions as the point of translation that turns the substrate that is the material body into a vector of State power. When the process of evidence recovery objectively discovers the body as violated, it enables and legitimates the consolidation of power: the ever-increasing force and jurisdiction of police, courts, and laws. In this sense, the text positions the rape kit within the lineage William Pietz describes in his historical genealogy of fetishism, for it, like the *Fetisso*, is primarily a marker of exchange value—or more specifically, an object that makes possible exchange in differing systems of valuation. As Pietz writes:

> The fetish, then, not only originated from, but remains specific to, the problematic of the social value of material objects as revealed in situations formed by the encounter of radically heterogenous social systems, and a study of the history of the idea of the fetish may be guided by identifying those themes that persist throughout the various discourses and disciplines that have appropriated the term.[5]

As a fetish, the rape kit negotiates the "problematic of the social value of material objects formed by the encounter of radically heterogenous social systems" insofar as it turns physicality into forensics. Valuation becomes a type of ideologized knowing; bodily material becomes produced as evaluate-able

---

5   William Pietz, "The Problem of the Fetish, I," *RES: Anthropology and Aesthetics* 9 (Spring, 1985): 7, http://www.jstor.org/stable/20166719.

and thus valuable knowledge. The centrality of evidence to the rape kit—similar to the centrality of trade to the *Fetisso*, the centrality of labor to the commodity fetish, and the centrality of the phallus to the sexual fetish—elides the radical heterogeneity between the two systems it straddles. In a productive misapprehension, the materiality of the body becomes reproduced as the literacy of legal value.

Yet the term that serves as the point of translation is defined by the dominant conception of one system or culture rather than a synthesis of both. The fetish, it seems, tends to always speak in the language of domination, in the legibility of hegemonic systems, and in this tendency is both a gesture of political consolidation as well as a potential for an implicit critique. As the note asserts, in addition to evidence collection, the rape kit's other purpose is "to verify the nature and circumstances of the reported assault." The "and/or" that precedes this second statement of intent bespeaks an ambivalence in the rape kit's strategy of valuation, an inherent skepticism of the very body it seeks to produce as knowledge. This simultaneous valuation and skepticism of the body points to a duality undergirding the fetish's work. As Pietz writes:

> *The fetish might then be viewed as the locus of a sort of primary and carnal rhetoric of identification and disavowal that established conscious and unconscious value judgments connecting territorialized social things and embodied personal individuals within a series of singular historical fixations. It would thus be the site of articulation both of ideological reification and hypostasis, and of impassioned spontaneous criticism.*[6]

The rape kit literalizes the fetish's "carnal rhetoric" as through its forensic mechanisms of evaluation, it turns the embodied personal individual into a territorialized social thing: a mandate for the consolidation of juridical force and the exercise of State power. Yet in the duplicity of its speech, the "and/or" of its text, the rape kit takes on a multiplicity of political potentials, potentials present in structure of the fetish itself. Because the carnal rhetoric of the fetish is a double rhetoric, an identification and disavowal, the rape kit functions not only as the site of "ideological reification and hypostasis" that its mobilization of the State would suggest it is, but also a site of "impassioned spontaneous criticism"—a criticism that its normative usage and deployment work to obscure. The proper use of the rape kit conceals such potential for criticism through its manipulation of time. As Pietz asserts, the fetish's value judgments take place within "a series of singular historical fixations," and in the case of the rape kit, these historical fixations could not only refer to the legal, medical, and social context in which the rape kit emerged as a forensic

---

6   Pietz, "Problem of the Fetish," 14.

technology (one that privileges, for example, a patriarchal legacy of visibility), but also the historicity the rape kit itself creates. The indexical nature of evidence—the "this was there" quality that characterizes its material—constructs a timeline that substantiates a genealogy of subjecthood. By evaluating what happened to a body in its recent past, the rape kit constructs a mandate for the present and future exercise of legal force of that body's behalf. As the deployment of sexual violence in prison and combat zones demonstrates, only fully established subjects—citizens—are raped in prosecutable ways; thus, the rape kit discovers not only a past crime but also past subjecthood, for no crime occurs on bodies un-evaluated by the kit and un-interpolated by the State's language of healing. The prosecution of the crime presupposes a cohesive temporality of the subject, and by making the crime prosecutable through its process of evidence collection, the rape kit fabricates the historical continuity of the subject. The temporality of the rape kit thus positions it as a negotiation of not only a possible crime, but also a possible subjectivity, and through this historicizing function, the rape kit transforms the material fact of the body into a broader mechanism of security. In *Security, Territory, Population*, Michel Foucault identifies how security functions within multiple modalities of power, explaining that:

> ... *sovereignty capitalizes a territory, raising the major problem of the seat of government, whereas discipline structures a space and addresses the essential problem of a hierarchical and functional distribution of elements, and security will try to plan a milieu in terms of events or series of events or possible elements, of series that will have to be regulated within a multivalent and transformable framework. The specific space of security refers then to a series of possible events; it refers to the temporal and the uncertain, which have to be inserted within a given space.*[7]

Through its inherent skepticism or ambivalence towards the body it evaluates, the rape kit functions as a milieu that negotiates or manages the possible event—the hidden truth of rape. The evidentiary processes described by the kit are therefore not the linear deductions they appear to be, but rather represent circular relationships of cause and effect, for they treat the event of rape not as a historical fact, but rather an event that has taken place only once an evidentiary threshold has been met. In this manner, the rape kit not only capitalizes the body as a territory from which value can be derived and structures it as a space of greater and lesser legibility or worth, but furthermore temporalizes it as a zone of possibility, creating a milieu which suspends not only the certainty of the criminal event but also the status of the

---

[7] Michel Foucault, *Security, Territory, Population: Lectures at the Collège de France, 1977-78*, ed. Michel Senellart, trans. Graham Burchell (London: Palgrave Macmillan 2007), 20.

body's subjecthood. Such temporalization renders a rape no longer a unique event in time, but rather a suspended and ever-present possibility, a statistical likelihood, a risk. The kit produces the evaluatable subject in relation to this perpetual time of risk, reconstructing the crime through various thresholds of likelihood, destabilizing both certainty of the body and the certainty of the event. In doing so, the rape kit manages the very terms of risk that it constructs.

The subjecthood that the rape kit reproduces on the body recapitulates the political conditions that structure the rape kit's mode of production. The substrate of the kit's transformative action—the "saliva, semen, hairs, spermatozoa, blood, fibers, plant material, soil and other debris" which are turned into evidence—bespeaks the ideology that motivates its alchemy, for in its description of the materials it deems valuable, the text of the rape kit invokes the values of ownership and territory. These materials that are evaluatable and valuable as evidence are ultimately proprietary materials, derived either from the "perpetrator's clothing or personal effects" or "the scene of the reported assault"—that is to say, derived from property. In this sense, the transformative action of the kit functions in an economy of larger transformations and is itself a territorializing discipline, mobilizing the body in a capitalist construction of value and subjectivity: a microcosmic staging of the larger biopolitical mechanism by which spaces, objects, and bodies take on meaning through the exclusionary and hierarchicizing investments of property ownership. The role of property or proprietary-ness in the production of value so central to the rape kit's process of evaluation—that hair, sweat, soil, or grass is valuable evidence because it belongs to someone or to somewhere—not only conforms to a model of capitalist private property, but furthermore hints at what Karl Marx, in his dialectical analysis of the capitalist political economy, calls "the negation of the negation." In *Capital*, Marx theorizes a point of crisis through the notion of capitalist property, which lays the foundation for his subsequent influential work on class antagonism and revolution. He writes:

> *The capitalist mode of appropriation, which springs from the capitalist mode of production, produces capitalist private property. This is the first negation of individual private property, as founded on the labour of its proprietor. But capitalist production begets, with the inexorability of a natural process, its own negation. This is the negation of the negation. It does not re-establish private property, but it does indeed establish individual property on the basis of the achievements of the capitalist era: namely co-operation and the possession in common of the land and the means of production produced by labour itself.*[8]

---

8 Karl Marx, *Capital: A Critique of Political Economy*, vol. 1, trans. Ben Fowkes (New York: Penguin 1990), 929.

This is to say, capitalist private property negates individual private property by displacing the mode of production from the labor of the proprietor; yet, "with the inexorability of a natural process" capitalist production furthermore negates this negation through its own exercise, re-establishing "co-operation and the possession in common of the land as the means of production produced by labor itself." This formulation bespeaks the double-edge of property—its crisis—the coupling of the material with the social that constitutes both its limitation and potential. On one hand, the negation of the negation could be read as a model of stasis, pointing to capitalism's futility, its own undoing of itself. At the same time, it could also be read as a formulation of the new, a Hegelian motion of thesis, antithesis, and synthesis. The rape kit, as a mode of appropriation that produces the fact of capitalist private property, is amenable to either reading. On one hand, as a process of territorialization that reproduces implicit values of ownership and property, the rape kit negates not only the association of value with individual labor—the victim's declaration "I have been raped"—but is furthermore a negation of this negation, performing its processes of evidence collection so that the victim can say, "I have been raped." On the other hand, through these same evidence collection processes, redundant though they might seem from the perspective of the victim, the rape kit instantiates a new thing entirely: a mode of producing speech on the body that functions differently than the speaking body can. This second reading opens up the possibility of using the kit in new ways—ways that exploit its generative capacity rather than its redundancy, its capacity for spontaneous and impassioned criticism rather than ideological reification. To this end, the rape kit lends itself to an artistic exploration of what not only speech, but also the body itself can do. After all, the implicit values of ownership and territory that are the basis of the rape kit's construction of value ultimately derive from the body's corporeal essence. Committed to this corporeality, this mining of materiality, the rape kit further evokes Pietz's description of the fetish, for as he writes:

> *The fetish is, then, first of all something intensely personal, whose truth is experienced as a substantial movement from "inside" the self (the self as totalized through an impassioned body, a "body without organs") into the self-limited morphology of a material object situated in space "outside." Works of art are true fetishes only if they are material objects at least as intensely personal as the water of tears.*[9]

The fetish is an instance of the personal literally becoming the political. By bringing the body into legibility—into language and into speech—fetishism endows the inchoate materiality of flesh with a performative force. To the extent that it mobilizes, enlists, and conscripts the body to legitimize and

---

9   Pietz, "Problem of the Fetish," 12.

propagate the power of the State, the fetish's power to make the personal political is a damning power, a totalization of subjugation. Yet to the extent that the body can give an idiosyncratic performance, convey the force of its specificity, a minoritarian-ness that falls outside dominant narratives of subjecthood, the body can perform—as it did in the feminist movements of the 1960s and 70s—to further a more radical and liberatory politics. To this extent, the body is always already political: it performs for the State insofar as it is mobilized in the apparatuses of education, citizenship, the military, and the law; and it performs for something else—something minoritarian, something systematically oppressed in normative formulations of subjecthood—insofar as it falls outside of a political economy of production and reproduction, insofar as it is a figure of resistance, protest, intervention, or art. By bringing outside what was inside, by making matter into value, the rape kit presents an opportunity wherein the body can be mobilized conservatively or radically—as a mandate for the propagation of power, or as a mode of intervention that insists on the body's material specificity, its aesthetic. In this sense, the kit's practice of property proposes two very different potentials: the conservation, consolidation, and propagation of an existing power through a normative embodiment of a capitalist subjecthood, as well as the radical critique of that power through the non-normative embodiments made possible by an artistic reinvestment in the political potentials of the material body.

The Object

It seems that an artistic reinvestment into the material potentials of the body would need to begin with an artistic reinvestment into the material potentials of the object that so normatively and powerfully interpolates that body: the rape kit itself. Although this study has heretofore focused on the New York State's Sexual Offense Evidence Collection Kit, the specificity of this particular kit might not speak fully to the way the rape kit functions as an object in the world, as the kit exists in endless variations, standardization being more an overall sense than a concrete reality. A way of accounting more fully for the object's function might be to ask, what is the virtue of the rape kit? The rape kit, as an object, is really just so many containers—boxes, envelopes, and vials; so many skins waiting to be filled. In fact, the rape kit is virtually skin: a labeled wrapping of the body's essential fragments that organizes inchoate flesh into a meaningful and legible form. The kit's membranous body, like the ectodermal ego, creates surfaces that function as an interface between the dark interiority of the violable physical body and the illuminated bodies of medicine and law. In this sense, the virtue that elides each iteration of the rape kit is the object's relationship to virtue and vitality: the virtue of ideology and essentialized embodiments, the virtuality of signification and language. Not only is the kit narrativized within a discourse of healing justice and forensic virtue, but it is itself an object of virtue, as there are several groupings of meaning inherent to the word "virtue" which animate the fetishistic workings of the kit. The first grouping has to do with the power of a supernatural or divine being becoming embodied or personified, either in the form of a "mighty work" or miracle, or in enumerations such as the seven virtues that oppose the seven deadly sins—something that is perhaps not so different from the fetish's metaphoric and material embodiment of an omniscient power, be it God, Medicine, or Law. The second grouping refers more specifically to the life and conduct of people, to moral fortitude and observance, to the abstention from vice—something not so different, it seems, than the fetish's valuation of the perpetrator's trace, the wrongdoer's malevolent part left behind that becomes valuable for its metonymic qualities, its conjuring or evidentiary power. This latter grouping of meanings become further specified in two distinct ways: the first, as chastity or sexual purity, especially on the part of women, and the second as industry or diligence—that is, as the reproductive disciplining of women and the productive duties of men as they converge in issues of generation and inheritance under capitalism.

These aspects of virtue seem particularly prominent in the working of the rape kit, both in the way the object frames sexual violence—as an all-permeating wound, a localized event that stains (literally, in the terms of contagion and trace) the entire-body—as well as the way it constructs its own labor, that is, as an obligatory industriousness aiding the larger paternalistic industries of medicine and law enforcement. In this sense, the question of virtue at the heart of the rape kit's physical performance of collection and measurement resonates with the notion of virtue that underlies the idea of value in the fetish, particularly of the commodity. In *Capital*, Karl Marx anchors his larger discussion of value in a footnote that reads:

> Things have an intrinsick vertue (this is Barbon's special term for use-value) "which in all places have the same vertue; as the loadstone to attract iron" (op. cit., p. 6). The magnet's property of attracting iron only became useful once it had led to the discovery of magnetic polarity.[10]

The commodity fetish as a reified social relation, it seems, is not so different than the idea embodied by virtue in all its connotations—the latter innovation haunted by this earlier definition. Perhaps the fetish as a negotiating term of value is always imbricated in this concept of virtue—a concept which blurs the bounds between economic empiricism and the murkier mists of valuation. Yet as an interface, the rape kit seems to go even further, not only articulating virtue in terms of value, but also mediating between virtue and virtuality. That is to say, the materiality of the object translates the virtue of

---
10 Marx, *Capital*, 125.

the body's essence, the corporality of its mucosal membranes, into the virtuality of measurement, effluvia made legible in clean white envelopes and clearly labeled slides. And again, this material function seems to correlate to an etymological evolution. Virtuality, like virtue, has the Latin root of *virtus*, which means manhood or manliness. Both terms, it seems, despite their difference in meaning now, have in common the same figural—masculine—core. This is interesting in relation to Jean Baudrillard's revision of Marx's notion of the commodity fetish, which insists on a shift of focus from the materiality of the object to the immateriality of the sign:

> *Thus the fetishization of the commodity is the fetishization of a product emptied of its concrete substance of labor and subjected to another type of labor, a labor of signification, that is, of coded abstraction (the production of difference and of sign values).*[11]

While Marx emphasized the material qualities of the commodity fetish—a "congealing"[12] of ideology into physical form—Baudrillard understands the commodity fetish as precisely immaterial, "emptied of its concrete substance of labor" and circulating as a virtuality of signification. Yet bound to Marx by a common root—by "virtus" and its classical imagining of the body—does Baudrillard's shift away from the materiality of the object towards the immateriality of the sign, really hold? Or does the ideological nature of the sign mask its materiality? Though functioning as the objective tools of measurement, the materiality of the rape kit—itself a semiotic virtuality of the body—is still real, still sensuous. The tactility of its parts—so apparent when handling it—disappears into the dominant narrative of evidence collection, a narrative whose authoritative act overshadows its sumptuous matter. In this sense, the productive misapprehension of the fetish—the turning of material into value—seems to cut both ways, as it is not only the sumptuousness of the dark that becomes reified, but also the heft and weight of the light.

There is yet another meaning of virtue that has a curious relationship to the rape kit object. In addition to the connotations mentioned above, the word virtue also refers to a personified moral quality, or a representation of this, usually in art. The fetish furthermore has a unique relationship to art in its memorializing function, for as Sigmund Freud writes, the sexual fetish comes into being when "the horror of castration sets up a sort of permanent memorial to itself."[13] This memorializing function lives on in the rape kit, as in it, the rape lives on as a permanent reification, a lasting memory of a

---

11 Jean Baudrillard, *For a Critique of the Political Economy of the Sign*, trans. Charles Levin (St. Louis: Telos 1981), 93.
12 Marx, *Capital*, 128.
13 Sigmund Freud, *Fetishism*, trans. James Strachey, standard ed. (London: Hogarth 1961), 21; 147-57.

fleeting horror: a horror of violation and powerlessness insofar as power is constructed on phallic terms. In this sense, the rape kit functions semiotically by bringing the body into language, virtue into virtuality; yet it also works materially, as a coagulated memory, as a sedimentation, a monument. This observation inspires a question: although the material qualities of the rape kit have been largely narrativized within the larger structures of medical knowledge and legal authority, would it—given this additional connotation, this memorializing function—be possible to understand it also as an *objet d'art*? It seems that the fetishistic logic of the rape kit, through its generative force and territorializing function, enacts what is often a goal of art practice: to make in both creative and politically incisive ways, as speaking in the language of domination, the rape kit can use its creative capacities to launch a powerfully legible and material critique. In this sense, the object's relationship to capitalist private property invests it not only with a unique capacity for political intervention, but also a unique potential to make art. As Gilles Deleuze and Félix Guattari assert in *A Thousand Plateaus*: "territorial marks are readymades,"[14] suggesting that gestures of appropriation—of marking, of seizure—are already creative gestures. This is to say not that one must find art in what these marks do, but that the mark itself is a found art object, a readymade. Towards their larger purpose of exploring capitalism and its lines of flight, Deleuze and Guattari go on to write:

> *Property is fundamentally artistic because art is fundamentally poster, placard. As Lorenz says, coral fish are posters. The expressive is primary in relation to the possessive; expressive qualities, or matters of expression, are necessarily appropriative and constitute a having more profound than being. Not in the sense that these qualities belong to a subject, but in the sense that delineate a territory that will belong to the subject that carries or produces them. These qualities are signatures, but the signature, the proper name, is a domain, an abode. The signature is not the indication of a person; it is the chancy formation of a domain. Abodes have proper names, and are inspired. "The inspired and their abodes . . ."; it is with the abode that the inspiration arises. No sooner do I like a color that I make it my standard or placard. One puts one's signature on something just as one plants one's flag on a piece of land.*[15]

The fetish's potential to make meaning politically relies on the dual nature of property that Deleuze and Guattari describe: the fact that not all art is property, but that property, being a thing made, produced through signification,

---

14 Gilles Deleuze and Félix Guattari, *A Thousand Plateaus*, trans. Brian Massumi (Minneapolis: University of Minnesota, 1987), 316.
15 Ibid., 316.

is also an art. Objects of territorialization are not just appropriative, but are more broadly performative, as "the expressive is primary in relation to the possessive." The force of an appropriating action is a creative process, a process of world-making through inhabitation, "a having more profound than being." Property, the claim made on space and on matter, bespeaks an expressive and signifying intentionality: a signing. The material remnant of signing, the fact of having signed, the signature, presents a field in which one can exert power, as "the signature, the proper name, is a domain." In this sense, property is predisposed to making, meaning that the rape kit's ethic of property and proprietary-ness predisposes the object to artistic production. Furthermore, property presents—in addition to the deeply repressive ways it hierarchizes people into classes and substantiates practices of exclusion, exploitation, oppression, and alienation—a more politically radical potential, as it is also a dwelling place. To linger, dwell, remain, or repeat is to avoid the imperative to move on, move through, and propagate. Such dwelling exerts pressure on the normative constructions of the body, reducing it again to its material components, and exposing how those components are mobilized to form a normative subjectivity. Dwelling is an intervention, an interruption, an aesthetic performance; it forces the object to speak about the fact of its materiality, interrupting, for a brief moment, the hegemonic mobilization of its matter. In forcing it to speak about itself, about its own material capacities, understanding the rape kit aesthetically and as an art object would work to mobilize it towards other political ends.

Dwelling, insofar as it is an aesthetic practice, invests the rape kit object with a performative potential beside that imbued by the State. If one dwells long enough in the text and form of the rape kit, one realizes that the kit could be only a thing performed upon the body; it is also a thing the body can do. As a potential performance of the body—as a thing one could do at anytime, repeatedly, an action one could perfect—the rape kit becomes not just a mechanism that translates the body to power, but a mechanism one can deploy for oneself: a tool, a talent, a gift. Here, the word gift resonates as both an object and an action, both the thing given as well as the capacity to give. As a material constellation as well as a performative potential, a gift—artistic or otherwise—works sensibly as well as suprasensibly, touching and moving the body through its material trace as well as the invisible structures of power that animate its force. In his analysis of gifts, Marcel Mauss proposes that an animate force possesses the object, a soul that, like a human soul, is a receptive organ, speaking to others of its own kind:

> *What imposes obligation in the present received and exchanged, is the fact that the thing received is not inactive. Even when it had been*

> *abandoned by the giver, it still possesses something of him . . . the legal tie, a tie occurring through things, is one between souls, because the thing itself possesses a soul, is of the soul. Hence it follows that to make a gift of something is to make a present of some part of oneself.*[16]

The trace, this defining material of the gift, mobilizes the object in an economy of liability, creating cohesion between giver and receiver, encompassing them in a common field of force. Its ability to impose obligation functions as a mechanism by which power consolidates itself, as the gift is always that for which something was already given. Mauss explains that an object could not be a gift if it did not possess something of its giver, and to this end, a gift is not only something that can be possessed, but also something that possesses—possesses perpetually through revolving obligation. In this sense, Mauss' conception of the gift articulates a lens through which bodily trace—which is so central to the kit's construction—can be mobilized to a political end, as the deployment of the rape kit as a gift would create a mode of circulation and communication based not on the assumption of a natural and cohesive body, but on the overt fabrication of the body, which can be exploited and deconstructed through its explicit staging. By making a gift of this explicit fabrication, this material mode of making, the excessive performance of the rape kit obligates any receiver of the gift, to perform reciprocally in this economy of bodily fabrication—implicating the ways the receiving body is already fabricated. The rape kit's productive capacity is malignant, it seems, only insofar as it is a reproductive capacity, insofar as it produces and reproduces the conditions of power on the body. The perversity of the sexual fetish in psychological development, on the other hand, lies in its non-reproductive stance, its politics of dwelling, and perhaps this dwelling could serve as a political model. By treating the rape kit as a gift—by performing it as such—one could harness its productive capacity by positioning it in an economy of repetition rather than reproduction, by dwelling in the process that makes rather than privileging the object as an affirmation of a productive lineage. Making in this non-reproductive mode, the rape kit could perhaps make otherwise. After all, fetishism, particularly as Freud means it, is a politics of stasis, an attempt to supplement the body with the materiality of the object in order to maintain and propagate the myth and privilege of the phallic body—perverse only in relation to the progress narrative, the socio-political decree to go forth and propagate. By harnessing this capacity of the fetish—perversity's spontaneous and impassioned critique of normative models of health—the rape kit, as a site of production but not reproduction, could function as a site of critical art practice rather than as the consolidation

---

16 Marcel Mauss, *The Gift: The Form and Reason for Exchange in Archaic Societies*, trans. W. D. Halls (New York: Norton, 2000), 11-12.

and propagation of hegemonic structures. In this instance, the politics of fetishism could be crafted to overlap with the politics of feminism, as both can be used to rethink the historical construction of the female body—to deconstruct its fabrication rather than insist on a repressive model of cohesion. For this reason, the rape kit is a gift given by the hegemonic forces that narrativize the normative body, and artistic gift that can be mobilized—a material monument that can be held on to, as well as a performative potential waiting to be exercised. As a gift, the rape kit contains a trace of its making, a trace normally concealed by hegemonic structures of visibility and representation, yet a trace that can be made visible by deploying the kit to serve artistic rather than juridical ends. Choosing to receive the rape kit as a gift opens up the possibility of employing it beyond its intended function, using its fetishistic productivity to form alternate embodiments of subjecthood, to make a new type of body, one whose violation does not serve to mandate and legitimate the violence of State power.

Bibliography

Baudrillard, Jean. *For a Critique of the Political Economy of the Sign*. Translated by Charles Levin. St. Louis: Telos 1981.

Deleuze, Gilles, and Félix Guattari. *A Thousand Plateaus*. Translated by Brian Massumi. Minneapolis: University of Minnesota, 1987.

Foucault, Michel. *Security, Territory, Population: Lectures at the Collège de France, 1977–78*, edited by Michel Senellart. Translated by Graham Burchell. London: Palgrave Macmillan 2007.

Freud, Sigmund. *Fetishism*. Translated by James Strachey. Standard ed. London: Hogarth 1961.

———. *The Question of Lay Analysis*. Translated by James Strachey. Standard ed. London: Hogarth 1961.

Lévi-Strauss, Claude. *Tristes Tropiques*. Translated by John Weightman and Doreen Weightman. New York: Penguin 1992.

Marx, Karl. *Capital: A Critique of Political Economy*, vol. 1. Translated by Ben Fowkes. New York: Penguin 1990.

Mauss, Marcel. *The Gift: The Form and Reason for Exchange in Archaic Societies*. Translated by W. D. Halls. New York: Norton, 2000.

Pietz, William. "The Problem of the Fetish, I." *RES: Anthropology and Aesthetics* 9 (Spring, 1985): 5–17. http://www.jstor.org/stable/20166719.

Joe Orton, Kenneth Halliwell and the Islington Public Library: Defacement, Parody and Mashups

D. Grant Campbell

Bringing queer theories together with LIS research requires an influx of methods, together with a recognition of limits. On the one hand, the voices of queer and feminist theorists open LIS research to a multitude of perspectives, narratives and insight that fall well outside what Charles Cutter once called "the public's habitual way of looking at things."[1] And these fresh voices require the full range of LIS methodologies to deal with the complexity: quantitative empirical research into collections and collection use; naturalistic inquiry into information practices; discourse analysis of information policies, controlled vocabularies and classification systems; historical studies of library and information behaviour in the past. On the other hand, any researcher who steps into this field of inquiry must take care to select from this diversity, and accept with good grace the limitations of any one inquiry. In the spirit of acceptance, I will state at the outset that this is a study of gay men and information. I will use Eve Kosofsky Sedgwick's distinction between minoritizing and universalizing perspectives to argue that the perspectives of gay men, especially during periods of stringent marginalization, can speak to issues of universal concern. In particular, I will revisit a famous instance of library vandalism by two gay men: the case of Joe Orton, Kenneth Halliwell, and their defacement of the collection of the Islington Public Library. I will argue that their transformation of conventional mainstream library books was essentially a parody of conventional mainstream literary appreciation: a parody that arose from their ambivalent status as gay men at a time when homosexuality was a criminal offence. Orton and Halliwell combined images

---

1 Charles A. Cutter, *Rules for a Dictionary Catalog*, 4th ed. (Washington: Government Printing Office, 1904).

together to create shocking and disturbing effects: in so doing, they anticipated the parodic uses of information that have become widespread with the rise of Web-circulated mashups. At the same time, they enable us to see the library's own ambivalent relationship to parodic information combination, particularly from the perspective of marginalized communities: while the library was relentless in its pursuit and persecution of Orton and Halliwell, its subsequent acts of archival preservation have ensured the survival of this early form of information combination.

Background I: The Theory

Issues related to gay and lesbian sexualities have figured prominently in Library and Information Science (LIS) research and practice over the past three decades. Treatments of such issues tend to fall into two primary categories. Some studies use classificatory tools that are commonly, if not exclusively used in LIS research to define the various slippery categories of non-mainstream sexual identity and behaviour: taxonomies of sexual identity,[2] or various definitions of what constitutes "gay content."[3] Other studies use the ample suite of LIS methodologies to study marginalized sexual communities and their relationships to information and information services. Some use user studies and naturalistic inquiry to examine reading strategies within libraries and book clubs.[4] Others use discourse analysis and other techniques to assess the degree to which libraries actually live up to their fine words of equal access when it comes to sexual minorities.[5]

All of these studies proceed from a very reasonable assumption: that communities based on alternate sexualities have specific information needs, experience various and formidable barriers to information access, and have developed sophisticated strategies for realizing their sexual identities through information use. Eve Kosofsky Sedgwick, however, in *The Epistemology of the Closet* (1990), suggests that a crisis of heterosexual/homosexual definition structures a significant part of Western culture and knowledge. Part of this

---

2   Alan Sinfield, "Lesbian and Gay Taxonomies," *Critical Inquiry* 29, no. 1 (2002): 120–38, doi:10.1086/368000.
3   D. Grant Campbell, "Queer Theory and the Creation of Contextual Subject Access Tools for Gay and Lesbian Communities," *Knowledge Organization* 27, no. 3 (2000): 122–31.
4   Paulette Rothbauer, "Reading Mainstream Possibilities: Canadian Young Adult Fiction with Lesbian and Gay Characters," *Canadian Children's Literature* 108 (Winter 2002): 10–26.
5   J. L. Pecoskie and P. J. McKenzie, "Canadian Census Data as a Tool for Evaluating Public Library Holdings of Award-Winning Lesbian Fiction," *Canadian Journal of Library and Information Science* 28, no. 2 (2004): 3–23.

crisis, she argues, centers upon a distinction between minoritizing and universalizing perspectives:

> ... [a] contradiction between seeing homo/heterosexual definition on the one hand as an issue of active importance primarily for a small, distinct, relatively fixed homosexual minority (what I refer to as a minoritizing view), and seeing it on the other hand as an issue of continuing, determinative importance in the lives of people across the spectrum of sexualities (what I refer to as a universalizing view).[6]

In this paper, I will adopt Kosofsky Sedgwick's suggestion and distinction to make the following assumptions. First, I will suggest that the historically marginalized status of gay men places them at the nexus of ongoing anxieties in information communities about proper and improper use of information, the ethics of surveillance and surreptitious control, and the nature of information crime. Second, I will argue that strategies of irony, parody and subversion developed within gay male communities have consequences far beyond their communities. Specifically, I will argue that the history of gay men helps us to understand an issue that has no inherent relationship to alternate sexualities: that of the growth of mashups and recombinant data on the World Wide Web.

Background II: Digitization Projects and Mashups

Two recent developments in Web information culture carry profound implications for the Web's relationship to traditional libraries and the services they have historically offered. On the one hand, the large-scale scanning initiatives undertaken by Google, the Internet Archive, and other consortia are breaking down the distinction between electronic information offered through digital libraries and print resources maintained in traditional physical collections. On the other hand, the increasing ease with which data can be extracted, copied, decontextualized and recombined has led to the rise of mashups. While projects like Google Books, Amazon's full-text searching and the Open Content Alliance initiated the widescale conversion of print resources to electronic form, research in the areas of human-computer interaction, information visualization and information architecture are carefully watching, documenting and facilitating a new generation of digital libraries, whose functions extend beyond search and retrieval to become full-fledged electronic environments in which users can freely manipulate the information they find in various useful and creative ways. Information visualization research provides ways in which digital libraries can make the transition

---

6 Eve Kosofsky Sedgwick, *Epistemology of the Closet* (Berkeley: University of California Press, 1990), 1.

from mere repositories to interactive knowledge environments, within which users can do a multitude of creative and epistemologically-rich activities.[7] And the rise of Google Maps, YouTube and other sources has sparked a similar burst of creativity from Web users.

Much of Web history since 2000 has involved reclaiming the Web as a place of collaboration. Tim Berners-Lee complained in the late 1990s that Web authoring tools had lagged far behind Web display tools, creating a first-generation Web that made Web display far more important than Web authoring.[8] The Semantic Web, which he developed within the aegis of the World Wide Web Consortium, envisioned a far more sophisticated Web infrastructure, in which a Web of data will expose data currently existing in databases to a series of standards that would enable computers to do more useful work.[9]

Even without the Semantic Web, the Web 2.0 has created an environment in which authoring, tagging and annotation tools have proliferated, and with them an inevitable corollary: as Web information has grown more granular, data elements can no longer be seen solely within their original context. Modern Web systems are premised on principles and technologies of sharing, repurposing and transforming data. Metadata harvesting systems, made possible through standards such as the Open Archives Initiative's OAI-MHP protocol, make it possible for harvesters to aggregate metadata from multiple sources. Social software programs have largely reinvented RSS aggregators as programs that enable us to personalize our data streams. And programs that build upon combinations of user-created tags and third-party metadata have expanded the principle of emergence beyond Google's PageRank system to embrace media sharing through programs such as Flickr and Last.fm.

The principle of recombinant data has become so prevalent that it has made an impact in numerous areas of information and media. Mashups have gained a special prominence in both the Web 2.0 community and the library community, both of whom have identified some of the intriguing and promising features they present. Mashups are Web applications that "combine data from more than one source to create a new tool, resource, widget, and—ultimately—a new experience."[10] At the utilitarian level, this involves the use

7 K. Fast and K. Sedig, "The INVENT Framework: Examining the Role of Information Visualization in the Reconceptualization of Digital Libraries," *Journal of Digital Information* 6, no. 3 (2005), http://journals.tdl.org/jodi/index.php/jodi/article/view/66/69.

8 Tim Berners-Lee and Mark Fischetti, *Weaving the Web: the Original Design and Ultimate Destiny of the World Wide Web by Its Inventor* (New York: Harper San Francisco, 1999).

9 World Wide Web Consortium, "Standards," 2009, http://www.w3c.org/standards.

10 Laura Gordon-Murnane, "Mashups as DIY Tools," *Online* 32, no. 1 (2008): 14.

of multiple data sets superimposed on each other that enable the user to use one set to locate the desired data in another set quickly and efficiently. Often, this involves the spatial representation of database data by plotting such data on a service like Google Maps.[11] Libraries have been exploring the use of mashups to create catalogue interfaces[12] or to incorporate RSS feeds into public web pages.[13] Some also see mashups as a new dimension of library services, in which technologically-sophisticated reference librarians help users to create their own mashups for personal and professional uses.[14]

While librarianship has naturally focused on the utilitarian purpose of mashups, media theorists and critical theorists have expressed greater interest in a second purpose of mashups: the combination of media sources, generally unrelated, for the purpose of creating startling juxtapositions in music and video. Similar to the flash mob, in which groups of individuals converge with seeming spontaneity at a specific site to do something inconsistent with everyday expectations, the mashup typically involves combining media for comic, satiric or parodic effect. Mashups of this type are typically mounted on sites such as YouTube, and examples include overlaying *Top Gun* previews with the soundtrack from *Brokeback Mountain*, or using a popular song to turn news footage of George W. Bush and Tony Blair into a love duet.

Mashups of this type have attracted both praise and rebuke from media theorists:

> On one hand, these often clever recombinations of recorded music are celebrated as innovative and creative interventions in the material of bland commodity culture. On the other hand, they are often reviled as derivative, inauthentic, and illegal because they do nothing more than appropriate and reconfigure the intellectual property of others.[15]

Either way, they are seen as expressions of youth, both in their youthful rebelliousness and the ambivalence that they evoke towards technology and media:

---

11   Timm Lehmberg, George Rehm, Andreas Witt, and Felix Zimmerman, "Digital Text Collections, Linguistic Research Data, and Mashups: Notes on the Legal Situation," *Library Trends* 57, no. 1 (2008): 52, doi:10.1353/lib.0.0023.
12   Michael Vandenburg, "Using Google Maps as an Interface for the Library Catalogue," *Library Hi-Tech* 26, no. 1 (2008): 33, doi:10.1108/07378830810857780.
13   Jamal Cromity, "Hot New Web 2.0 tools," *Information Outlook* 12, no. 8 (2008): 17.
14   Gordon-Murnane, "Mashups as DIY Tools," 16.
15   D. J. Gunkel, "Rethinking the Digital Remix: Mash-Ups and the Metaphysics of Sound Recording," *Popular Music and Society* 31, no. 4 (2008): 489, doi:10.1080/03007760802053211.

By conducting a close reading of press articles and several interviews and textually analyzing some of the most popular and critically acclaimed tracks, it is argued that the mash-up is a response to larger technological, institutional, and social contexts. Through themes of irony, empowerment, and re-appropriation, the mash-up serves as a fitting expression of today's youth media experience.[16]

These two purposes of mashups—the utilitarian and the parodic—tend to be discussed, therefore, in different literatures: librarianship and technology on the one hand, and media and cultural theory on the other. To investigate how the parodic purpose appears in a library environment, we have to look at cases in library history where the extraction of data from its original context, and the combination of data sources for purposes of parody forced themselves into the forefront of librarianship.

Parody existed long before the Internet, and the creation of startling effects through ludicrous juxtapositions often has the subversive effect of undermining a predicted or expected emotional response to the individual parts. However, in the days of physical collections, a mashup involved doing physical damage. Furthermore, when that damage expresses the perspective of a marginalized, criminal minority, it becomes embedded in the discourse and history of crime in libraries: particularly in instances of theft and vandalism of library materials.

Background III: Theft and Vandalism

In 1996, James Billington, the thirteenth Librarian of Congress, discussed his plans to deal with a pressing problem: the theft and defacement of materials in the Library of Congress Collection. Billington's measures included closing the Library's stacks, use of surveillance cameras in the Reading Room, electronic control of stack access, and a comprehensive risk assessment, using the company Computer Sciences Corporation, that had been recommended by the Department of Defense. In justifying these measures, Billington invoked his predecessor, Ainsworth Rand Spofford. Spofford, in 1896, justified the hiring of two guards for the Library of Congress by arguing that:

> . . . in all great libraries, and in many smaller ones, there are continual depredations, cutting from newspapers by unscrupulous readers, attempts to abstract books, and other processes of thieving. . . . That is the

---

16 M. Serazio, "The Apolitical Irony of Generation Mash-Up: A Cultural Case Study in Popular Music," *Popular Music and Society* 31, no. 1 (2008): 79, doi:10.1080/03007760701214810.

case in all countries; men of great ability have sometimes been thieves in public libraries.[17]

For Spofford, and for Billington, the problem is two-fold. First, library vandalism never ends, and is not inherently localized; therefore, the problem will never go away permanently, and you cannot address it by moving elsewhere or waiting it out. Second, those who commit these acts are sometimes highly able, intelligent people, thereby demanding from the library staff considerable time, imagination and ingenuity in response.

Other instances on record indicate that library vandalism has indeed been widespread, and has taken many different forms. In some cases, the vandalism comes from the library, as a public space, being caught in the crossfire: in 1997 the Wyoming Branch of the Kent District Libraries was plagued by gang members, using the library's computer terminals in their gang wars, and, in the process damaging the building and its infrastructure: library tables and graffiti in the washrooms.[18]

But other vandalism instances have been more insidious, and the very subtlety of the attacks has led library staff to retaliate with an energy bordering on fanaticism. In 1994, members of the staff at Cleveland Ohio State University decided on their own to find the person who had placed about 300 stickers and countless flyers for a neo-Nazi organization inside library books. They patrolled the stacks on their own time: during breaks and lunch hours and after their shifts. A cataloguing assistant, Lynn Duchez, eventually spotted the vandal, called the police, and then followed him into an elevator and out of the building, tailing him until the police arrived and arrested him on the spot. The criminal was sentenced to six months in prison. The judge called him "cowardly," and called Duchez "the toughest and bravest librarian in Cleveland."[19]

Librarians have always hated vandals, especially the quiet subversive ones who appear to live within the walls and come out when no one is looking; the very ingenuity that Spofford identifies appears threatening and contemptuous. Library staff have traditionally taken theft and destruction of library materials personally, and have sometimes acted with considerable bravery in resisting them. The problem, however, is that Spofford was right: sometimes these acts are carried out by people of great ability and significant creativity.

---

17 James H. Billington, "Here Today, Here Tomorrow: The Imperative of Collections Security," *American Libraries* August 1996, 40–41.

18 "Patron Abuse Prompts Trial of Social Network Filter," *American Libraries*, September 2007, 41, http://www.jstor.org/stable/27771295.

19 "Library Sleuth Collars Neo-Nazi Book Defacer," *American Libraries*, December 1994, 977, http://www.jstor.org/stable/25633437.

Joe Orton and Kenneth Halliwell had enough intelligence and creativity to keep the Islington Public Library guessing from 1959 to 1963.

The Case of Orton and Halliwell

Joe Orton was born John Kingsley Orton in Leicester, England, in 1933. Growing up in a working-class area that provided little scope for his artistic and intellectual interests, he sought training in the theater. In 1950, he was accepted into the Royal Academy of Dramatic Arts, and in 1951 he met fellow student Kenneth Halliwell. Neither made significant headway as actors, but both harboured significant artistic ambition as authors and, in Halliwell's case, as a visual artist. The two became lovers, and upon graduating from RADA in 1953, they made numerous unsuccessful attempts to publish or produce their work; their collaborative novels *The Boy Hairdresser* and *The Last Days of Sodom* were rejected by publishers, as was Halliwell's own novel, *Priapus in the Shrubbery*.[20] In 1957 they moved to a flat in Islington, London, where they eked out an ascetic living, attempting to get published while living off the National Assistance, as well as Halliwell's rapidly diminishing inheritance. In 1959, with no success at getting their own books published, whether written together or separately, they began a curious activity: stealing and defacing books from their local library.

According to Alexander Connell of the Islington Public Library, staff and readers began to find books on the shelf in mutilated condition, the damage falling into two categories. First, false blurbs had been typewritten onto the book jackets. Items published by Gollancz were often targeted, probably because its dust jackets had a "dashed-off" design that made the emendations difficult to notice. The blurbs were parodies of the effusive praise typical of dust jackets, beginning mildly but growing more obscene as the blurb continued.[21] A Dorothy Sayers novel, for instance, was given a plot summary involving "a seven-inch phallus and a pair of knickers," and closed with the injuction: "Read this behind closed doors. And have a good shit while you are reading."[22]

Second, many book jackets had been altered by collage, in which illustrations removed from other books were superimposed upon the jacket to create a "humorous or incongruous dust-wrapper."[23] Examples included the

---

20   John Lahr, *Prick up Your Ears: The Biography of Joe Orton* (London: Allen Lane, 1978), 123.
21   Alexander Connell, "A Successful Persecution," *Library Association Record*, 1963, 102.
22   Lahr, *Prick Up Your Ears*, 95–96.
23   Connell, "A Successful Persecution," 102.

insertion of monkey faces onto pictures of birds or in the middle of flowers, or the replacement of a dignified portrait with one that was ludicrous or startling. Internal illustrations underwent similar alterations, sometimes with inserted captions for humorous or obscene effect. The collages were created by Halliwell, who had developed a fascination for the art form that amounted to an obsession. The blurbs, on the other hand, were mostly written by Orton, who delighted in making fun of mainstream literary genres, as well as outing some closeted figures like actor Robert Helpmann.[24]

For some time, Orton and Halliwell continued with their pranks, without being caught. But when they switched their activities from the central library to a smaller branch, the staff had more success. "Eventually," states Connell, "the branch librarian found her suspicions centering on two men who shared the same address and who always visited the library together."[25] The library consulted with the police of the local division, and on their advice, assistants from other departments, unknown as library staff to the public using the branch, were posted as browsing readers, hoping to catch the two in the act of replacing doctored books on the shelf. Several weeks passed, but the staff had no success in catching them.

While Orton and Halliwell were very clever at covering their tracks, their vandalism of the materials exhibited a recurring distaste of bureaucracy and contempt for the established authority. This gave Islington Borough Council's legal clerk, Sidney Porrett, an idea for a more underhanded approach. He sent them a letter full of "bureaucratic jargon," which, John Lahr suggests, was the very tone calculated to raise the men's ire and make them careless. In the letter, he inquired if they were the owners of a particular abandoned car and asked them to remove it. Halliwell responded with an indignant denial, signed "Yours contemptuously."[26] This was all the police needed: in a piece of forensic work worthy of Sherlock Holmes himself, the police compared Halliwell's typewritten letter with the false dust jackets, and declared that they came from the same machine. When they obtained a search warrant and searched the flat, they found that "the four walls of the living room were covered from ceiling to floor with pasted-on plates apparently taken from art books."[27] Connell visited the flat himself and eventually identified 1600 loose plates removed from books, of which he was able to identify all but 30 as belonging to defaced library books.

---

24 Simon Shepherd, *Because We're Queers: The Life and Crimes of Kenneth Halliwell and Joe Orton* (London: Gay Men's Press, 1989), 100.
25 Connell, "A Successful Persecution," 102.
26 Lahr, *Prick Up Your Ears*, 99.
27 Connell, "A Successful Persecution," 102.

Neither Orton nor Halliwell impressed the magistrate at their trial; they were sentenced to six months imprisonment on each of five counts of theft of books and malicious damage to books, the sentences to run concurrently. And in a civil court case, Orton and Halliwell were required to pay over 262 pounds for damage to property vested in a local authority. The magistrate, Harold Sturge, attributed their behaviour to envy of other authors' success, and rebuked them for malice towards their fellow library users:

> *What I am anxious to see is that the decision of this court should make it abundantly clear to those who may be clever enough to write criticisms of other people's books – public library books – or to deface them or ruin them in this way are made to understand very clearly that it is disastrous. . . . I am most concerned about the malice shown by both of you in what you did – sheer malice towards fellow users of this library who, until these books are replaced, will be denied what they might have reasonably expected to enjoy.*[28]

For Connell, however, the judge had only praise: according to C. Al Elliott, Chief Librarian and Curator of Islington, the judge described Connell as a "'highly-experienced, extremely capable librarian.' He was," continued Elliott, "apparently astounded that librarians possessed such skills."[29]

So far, this account differs very little from other accounts of vandalism: many librarians could probably match it with equally bizarre stories. Indeed, the matter might well have disappeared permanently from public view, were it not for unexpected developments in the succeeding years. First, Joe Orton turned out to be an excellent writer and not long afterwards emerged as one of Britain's most brilliant and iconoclastic playwrights of the 1960s, penning such modern classics as *Entertaining Mr. Sloane*, *Loot*, and *What the Butler Saw*.

Orton's fame as a writer only increased for being abruptly and brutally cut short. In August 1967, Kenneth Halliwell murdered Joe Orton and then committed suicide: the lurid story was a media sensation that turned Orton into an impudent martyr, cut short before the full flowering of his genius. The tragic incident became the primary subject of John Lahr's biography, *Prick Up Your Ears*, which was later adapted by Alan Bennett as a film in 1987, and by Simon Bent into a stage play in London in 2009. The sensational story has kept Orton and Halliwell as very public figures in British queer history.

Orton's satire has largely resuscitated his own reputation and, indeed, the very activities that once made him a criminal and an outsider. One of the many public toilets that he used for public sex has been slated for preservation by Britain's Department of National Heritage; Orton's sister applauded

---

28 Lahr, *Prick Up Your Ears*, 100–101.
29 Connell, "A Successful Persecution," 104.

the move, linking Orton's behaviour with the arrest of pop singer George Michael and citing public washrooms as places where "gays meet and strut their stuff."[30]

Finally, the postmodernist taste for collage and startling juxtaposition has created a fresh interest in the damage that Orton and Halliwell did to the Islington Library Books. John Lahr, Orton's biographer, described Halliwell's collages as "fractured images, a series of haunting notions where the past, present and the surreal coexisted but never coalesced to make a coherent whole."[31] Collage became Halliwell's chosen art form, and he eventually held an exhibition in a Chelsea antique store. Orton's diaries recount the incident of taking the collages for the dealer's inspection. The works included:

> ... a hideous youth sitting in the foreground with a nightmare scene going on behind, a cadaverous monk and a wraith-like nun standing either side of a small picture which was captioned 'Rosencrantz was Jesus CHRIST?' and, lastly, a bull made of human hair leaping around in a sandpit and charging three human eyes. Freddie turned the pictures around and said, 'I think they'd have to be dolled up a bit. Don't you?' He looked beadily around for confirmation.... 'They want putting under glass,' Kenneth said. 'It'll bring out the colours.'[32]

According to Linda Hutcheon, "adaptation" as a post-modernist phenomenon involves surprising changes of context:

> an adaptation is an announced and extensive transposition of a particular work or works. This "transcoding" can involve a shift of medium ... or genre ... or a change of frame and therefore context.... As a process of creation, the act of adaptation always involves both (re-)interpretation and then (re-)creation; this has been called both appropriation and salvaging, depending on your perspective.[33]

Orton's emphasis on the grotesque juxtaposition of human and beast, of religion and emaciation, and Christianity and Shakespeare highlight a feature of adaptation that has come to fascinate theorists who are exploring new media's ways of superimposing new information on the old. His slightly mocking account also suggests that the real fascination of the incident lay in yet another startling juxtaposition: not in the collages themselves, but the way in

---

30 Liz Highleyman, "Joe Orton (1933–1967): 'The Oscar Wilde of Welfare State Gentility,'" October 8, 2003, http://www.gmax.co.za/think/history/10/08-joeorton.html.
31 Lahr, *Prick Up Your Ears*, 6.
32 Joe Orton, *The Orton Diaries: Including the Correspondence of Edna Welthorpe and Others*, ed. John Lahr (London: Methuen, 1986), 51.
33 Linda Hutcheon, *A Theory of Adaptation* (New York: Routledge, 2006), 8.

which Halliwell and the dealer discussed the disturbing images in a facile discourse of art and dealership.

Simon Shepherd has defined three aspects of the "adaptations" that made the altered books threatening to the sensibilities of the general public: an irreverence towards Art, an irreverence towards eminent persons, and the presence of sex.[34] While some of the alterations—to Shakespeare's works, in particular—were comparatively tasteful expositions of the plays' themes, the most publicly decried alterations levelled a contemptuous eye at successful figures of mainstream. A book called *Queen's Favourite*, for instance, was overlaid with a homoerotic image of two men wrestling, while the novel *Steel Cocoon* featured a male figure in a jockstrap. Even more suggestively, the biography of Poet Laureate John Betjeman was altered to show an aged man in a tight bathing suit covered with tattoos: an artist at the very peak of establishment veneration—a Poet Laureate—is made to seem grotesque, unattractive, and, above all, written-upon, as if such mainstream adulation makes the artist a cultural artifact in himself, rather than the creator of cultural artifacts. Modern critics perceive a complex Swiftean satire in these pranks, in which supposedly ethereal qualities of beauty are invested with images of bestiality, and in which, as Shepherd argues, the male body becomes "the object of society's gaze."[35] In their satiric and iconoclastic barbs at a perceived mainstream sensibility from which they felt alienated, Orton and Halliwell anticipated the very problematic perspectives that current media theorists find in music mashups.

We have, then, an instance of two gay men, living together at a time when homosexuality was a criminal offense, engaging in satiric and parodic information behaviour remarkably similar to the behaviour of many mashup artists today. This behaviour involved the theft and defacement of library materials, and their surreptitious method, together with the library staff's determination to track them down and catch them, further reinforced their status as outsiders. Their actions are now seen and interpreted retrospectively in light of two subsequent events: Orton's emergence as an important writer, and the burgeoning gay liberation movement of the late 1960s and 1970s, which turned both Orton and Halliwell into icons.

The Library as Villain: Early Interpretations

Orton and Halliwell never fully explained their reasons for doing what they did at the trial. Later, Orton defended his behaviour on the grounds of literary quality:

---

34   Shepherd, *Because We're Queers*, 13.
35   Shepherd, *Because We're Queers*, 100.

> I went to quite a big library in Islington and asked for Gibbon's Decline and Fall of the Roman Empire. They told me they hadn't got a copy of it. They could get it for me, but they hadn't one on their shelves. . . . Libraries might as well not exist; they've got endless shelves of rubbish and hardly any space for good books. . . . You can obviously say when some things are rubbish and some things aren't. I can obviously say Gibbon isn't.[36]

This explanation challenges the Islington Library in two important ways. First, Orton declares that libraries stock bad books at the expense of good books; they are therefore not serving their users adequately. Second, the distinction between good books and bad books is neither mysterious nor complicated; nor does it require special education or training or credentials. Orton himself—impoverished, as yet unpublished, and technically a criminal for his sexual preference—expresses perfect confidence in his ability, and in his right, to distinguish good books from "rubbish." In his framing of the incident, the Islington Public Library is incompetent at doing what it has no right to do anyway: serve as the mediator and arbiter of public taste.

It was inevitable, then, that the actions of the Islington Public Library should suffer in light of Orton's subsequent fame. For early critics and commentators on Joe Orton, the thefts and defacements were gestures of audaciousness, and the library represented the tyranny of the mainstream that marginalizes sexual difference. Critics like C. W. E. Bigsby group the library with those other public institutions of society that Orton branded as tyrannical and hypocritical, gloating over its ability to intimidate outsiders:

> In many ways Orton's mere existence was regarded as an affront by society. His particular kind of sexuality was legally outlawed, his anarchic humour seen as a challenge by petty officialdom (the campaign conducted by the Islington librarian to catch him "improving" the dustjackets of library books was conducted with such vigour and pride that it was written up for the Library Association Record.[37]

Bigsby cites Orton's comments on his prison experience to imply that the library belongs with all the other hypocritical institutions that make up a society gone seriously wrong: "Before I had been vaguely conscious of something rotting somewhere; prison crystallized this. The old whore society really lifted up her skirts and the stench was pretty foul." The Islington Public Library, in its very zeal to protect its collection, came to be seen at least in some quarters of theater and queer history, as "petty officialdom."[38]

---

36 Lahr, *Prick Up Your Ears*, 97.
37 C. W. E. Bigsby, *Joe Orton* (London: Methuen, 1982), 20.
38 Bigsby, *Joe Orton*, 20.

In most of his work, Orton levels his most withering satire at mainstream society, and those institutions that maintain that society through the application of fatuous moral principles that are unexamined and that are used to oppress society's outsiders. This is exhibited in the famous scene in *Loot*, in which the psychotic policeman bullies his victims with physical violence punctuated by inane cliches:

> TRUSCOTT. *Where's the money?*
> HAL. *In church.*
> TRUSCOTT *kicks HAL violently. HAL cries out in terror and pain.*
> TRUSCOTT. *Don't lie to me!*
> HAL. *I'm not lying! It's in church!*
> TRUSCOTT. *(shouting, knocking HAL to the floor). Under any other political system I'd have you on the floor in tears!*
> HAL. *(crying) You've got me on the floor in tears.*[39]

Truscott embodies the very qualities that Orton decried in the Islington Public Library: incompetence and power. The policeman speaks a discourse of investigation, crime and punishment which has no coherent center, just an accumulation of fragmented phrases; he nonetheless has the power and the will to impose those meaningless phrases and his incapacity to make distinctions upon others.

Michael Beehler suggests that the library is no mere collaborator in the distortions of society. He goes so far as to interpret the library as the epitome, in Orton's writing, of a prescribed order that refuses to acknowledge the innate "heterogeneity" of both the book and of the human body: "both the body as such and the Book as such originate in the heterogeneity described by the Librarians as an unnatural mutilation, in the 'collage' of original fragmentation and difference."[40] Most of Orton's plays, he asserts, involve "a central mutilation, around a body whose wholeness is dismembered and disseminated."[41] Libraries, in Beehler's interpretation, are no mere bystanders, but central articulators of a blind and intolerant social order.

The dedication of the original library staff in catching vandals, then, has been significantly eclipsed by the strength and persistence of Orton's satiric voice, by the sensational events that followed, and by changes in artistic taste that have created a fresh interest in the work of collage, satire and parody. It is tempting to class the Islington Public Library together with the police as a

---

39 Joe Orton, *Loot* (London: Methuen, 1967), 47.
40 Michael Beehler, "Joe Orton and the Heterogeneity of the Book," *SubStance* 10, no. 4 (1981-1982): 93, http://www.jstor.org/stable/3684533.
41 Ibid., 94.

voice of an oppressive mainstream society that failed both to embrace sexual diversity and to recognize artistic genius, and in so doing shares a responsibility for Orton's untimely death. However tempting such a conclusion may be, it fails to tell the whole truth.

The Library as Hero

Three aspects of the behaviour of the staff at the Islington Public Library deserve mention. First, while the staff were assiduous in tracking down the vandals, Connell's account of the incident in *The Library Association Record* refrains from making any homophobic remarks, or even of expressing any implied homophobic sentiments. Indeed, Connell goes so far as to admire the cleverness of some of the collages he discovered. His account confines itself entirely to the library's attempts to curate its collections responsibly. Even if this is disingenuous—even if Connell did in fact nurse homophobic sentiments behind a pose of public service and impartiality—his account clearly articulates the library's role, not as an arbiter of public standards of sexuality, but as the mediator of a collection that is intended to serve all of the library's users.

Second, Orton scholarship owes a significant debt to Eric Willats, the Principal Reference Librarian of the Islington Public Library. Simon Shepherd's analysis of Orton in 1989 was provocatively titled *Because We're Queers: The Life and Crimes of Kenneth Halliwell and Joe Orton*. In writing this story of the men's struggles with an oppressive and homophobic society, Shepherd discovered that Willats had unexpectedly retained and archived the materials defaced by Orton and Halliwell. Shepherd, in his introduction, saluted Willats, "who had the foresight to establish and mainstream an Orton archive before Orton became an industry."[42] While the Islington Public Library was at a severe disadvantage when dealing with surreptitious changes made to its materials, it performed a significant service to later Orton scholarship by capturing and archiving those changes for future use and study.

Third, the Islington Public Library has over the years responded with integrity and willingness to later historians at a time when private individuals were obstructing scholars and researchers. Matt Cook, in his study of the Orton Archives, suggests that after Orton's death, his plays and his reputation were jealously guarded by his biographer, John Lahr, and his agent, Peggy Ramsey, both of whom sought to protect the Orton "industry." When Simon Shepherd was writing on Orton in the 1980s, AIDS had created a significant homophobic backlash, which led both Ramsey and Lahr to refuse to cooperate with Shepherd's radical gay approach to Orton's work and

---

42 Shepherd, *Because We're Queers*, 6.

life.[43] The only information available came from Orton's former adversary: "In the period Shepherd was working on *Because We're Queers* it was Islington Central Library alone that was allowing access to primary material relating to Orton and Halliwell."[44]

Conclusion: Libraries and Recombinance

The story of Orton and Halliwell at the Islington Public Library was, and remains, the story of two gay men acting out some of the stresses and contradictions of being gay in an oppressive and uncongenial social context. While the moral of the story extends beyond this particularizing view, I in no way intend to discredit or disavow our right to see Orton and Halliwell as key historical figures in the story of gay men in England in the 1960s.

Nonetheless, the story of Orton and Halliwell is relevant beyond its immediate gay context, and is of great significance to the challenges facing libraries today in their efforts to curate electronic materials. In examining the library community's response to the Orton/Halliwell incident, we can see some of the tensions and ambiguities in that community's relationship with document use, particularly when that use involves iconoclastic creativity of the sort common in some mashups and other Web 2.0 innovations.

First, if tragedy plus time equals comedy, vandalism plus time sometimes equals art. While the wit and intelligence of the satire may have been evident to the library staff at the time of the incidents, they had absolutely no opportunity to appreciate it. At the time of the crime, the library was faced with a responsibility to maintain its collection for its users. Only later did the vandalized books become recognized as objects of cultural and historical interest, to the point where they became part of a curated collection themselves.

Second, the incident suggests that there is a strong connection between creativity and crime in information use. Northrop Frye once characterized the appreciation of a literary work as an act of possession: a "crowning act of self-identity as the contemplating of what has been made, including what one has recreated by possessing the canon of man's word as well as God's."[45] In cases where the user feels alienated or ostracized from the value system which produced the work, such acts of possession can acquire an aggressively transformative character, in which the reader does not possess the work so much as dominate it, and in so doing ridicules those who possess the work in a more tranquil or traditional way.

---

43 Matt Cook, "Orton in the Archives," *History Workshop Journal* 66 (2008): 163, doi:10.1093/hwj/dbn041.

44 Ibid.

45 Northrop Frye, *The Secular Scripture: A Study of the Structure of Romance* (Cambridge: Harvard University Press, 1976), 188.

In the digital world, the damage done to original works may be less serious. Mashing *Top Gun* with *Brokeback Mountain* does not destroy any of the original prints of either movie, although fans of *Top Gun* might not view the movie the same way after seeing the mashup. Nonetheless, libraries that work with mashups will undoubtedly find themselves dealing with complicated copyright issues, particularly those that relate to fair dealing. "Mashups," warn Miguel Ramos and Dawn Gauthier, are concerned not with copyright but with creativity.[46] Indeed, Emily Walshe warns that the mashup paradigm is ultimately an unattractive one for library operations: "we are not in the business of stealing fire," she claims; "we are in the business of sparking it."[47] While current copyright laws in the United States and proposed laws in Canada extend fair use to include parody, certain mashup communities clearly court controversy, rather than attempting to avoid it.

Even more important, this incident throws light on the library's problematic relationship to the rhetoric of infinitude that works through the advocates of Google Books. In the idealized world of online documents, access is no longer limited by the physical book and its vulnerabilities; the access envisioned by the creators of Google Books is aggressive, large-scale, and somewhat ruthless. Libraries, whatever their advocates may claim, have never bought into that rhetoric, and are unlikely to do so now. Libraries mediate access among large numbers, rather than simply providing it, and as such, they sometimes find themselves saying "no" far more often than "yes." The large-scale trolling of vast information stores envisioned by Google is at odds with the realities of providing information in libraries. Librarianship involves the stewardship of an expensive collection on behalf of the entire community; traditionally, that has meant that the resources are finite, and that usage must be regulated according to principles of fairness and equal access.

As the story of Orton and Halliwell shows, mediation and stewardship can leave the library vulnerable to criticism, and some of it may be justified. We can look back at the library's response to Orton and Halliwell and wonder if, indeed, the library staff was consciously or unconsciously homophobic. We can wonder if the library community's allegiance to "the user," and to what Cutter called "the public's habitual way of looking at things,"[48] leads it into collusion with unjust social systems, and places it in a reactionary relationship to social change.

All these things may be true. But the story of Orton and Halliwell suggests something else, equally important: that "foresight" in libraries means more

---

46 Miguel Ramos and Dawn Gauthier, "Mash It Up!" *Searcher* 15, no. 6 (2007): 17.
47 Emily Walshe, "On My Mind: Mashups in the Stacks," *American Libraries*, December 2008, 37, http://www.jstor.org/stable/25650159.
48 Cutter, Rules for a Dictionary Catalog.

than being on the cutting edge of technological innovations, or anticipating changes in social standards and mores. Foresight also involves the capacity to recognize the importance of preserving records and of making them available: of possessing the intelligence to recognize the cultural and intellectual significance of materials and activities that are popularly decried, and the commitment to access that makes those materials available even at the risk of backlash and condemnation.

In a world of widespread digitization and recombinant data, the story of Orton, Halliwell and the Islington Public Library provides a salutary indication of where libraries can and should position themselves. Libraries stand for the responsible and long-term use of the bibliographic universe, and as such position themselves outside the rhetoric of information as an infinite, infinitely-renewing resource. And librarians, one hopes, will have the foresight to ask difficult questions, rather than echo the enthusiastic press releases; they will strive, in this new information environment, to contribute to a widespread redefinition of information use, and of those activities that a collection, print or digital, can or cannot sustain.

Acknowledgements

The author wishes to acknowledge Dr. Sam Trosow, University of Western Ontario, for his explanation of Bill C-32, and the Pride Library at University of Western Ontario for access to its materials on Joe Orton.

Bibliography

Beehler, Michael. "Joe Orton and the Heterogeneity of the Book," *SubStance* 10, no. 4 (1981-1982): 84-98. http://www.jstor.org/stable/3684533.

Berners-Lee, Tim, and Mark Fischetti. *Weaving the Web: the Original Design and Ultimate Destiny of the World Wide Web by Its Inventor.* New York: Harper San Francisco, 1999.

Bigsby, C. W. E. *Joe Orton*. London: Methuen, 1982.

Billington, James H. "Here Today, Here Tomorrow: The Imperative of Collections Security." *American Libraries.* August 1996.

Campbell, D. Grant. "Queer Theory and the Creation of Contextual Subject Access Tools for Gay and Lesbian Communities." *Knowledge Organization* 27, no. 3 (2000): 122-31.

Connell, Alexander. "A Successful Persecution." *Library Association Record.* 1963.

Cook, Matt. "Orton in the Archives." *History Workshop Journal* 66 (2008): 163-179. doi:10.1093/hwj/dbn041.

Cromity, Jamal. "Hot New Web 2.0 tools." *Information Outlook* 12, no. 8 (2008): 17–19.

Cutter, Charles A. *Rules for a Dictionary Catalog*, 4th ed. Washington: Government Printing Office, 1904.

Fast, K., and K. Sedig. "The INVENT Framework: Examining the Role of Information Visualization in the Reconceptualization of Digital Libraries." *Journal of Digital Information* 6, no. 3 (2005). http://journals.tdl.org/jodi/index.php/jodi/article/view/66/69.

Frye, Northrop. *The Secular Scripture: A Study of the Structure of Romance*. Cambridge: Harvard University Press, 1976.

Gordon-Murnane, Laura. "Mashups as DIY Tools." *Online* 32, no. 1 (2008): 14–17.

Gunkel, D. J. "Rethinking the Digital Remix: Mash-Ups and the Metaphysics of Sound Recording." *Popular Music and Society* 31, no. 4 (2008): 489–510, doi:10.1080/03007760802053211.

Hutcheon, Linda. *A Theory of Adaptation*. New York: Routledge, 2006.

Lahr, John. *Prick up Your Ears: The Biography of Joe Orton*. London: Allen Lane, 1978.

Lehmberg, Timm, George Rehm, Andreas Witt, and Felix Zimmerman. "Digital Text Collections, Linguistic Research Data, and Mashups: Notes on the Legal Situation." *Library Trends* 57, no. 1 (2008): 52–71. doi:10.1353/lib.0.0023.

"Library Sleuth Collars Neo-Nazi Book Defacer." *American Libraries*. December 1994. http://www.jstor.org/stable/25633437.

Orton, Joe. *Loot*. London: Methuen, 1967.

———. *The Orton Diaries: Including the Correspondence of Edna Welthorpe and Others*, edited by John Lahr. London: Methuen, 1986.

"Patron Abuse Prompts Trial of Social Network Filter." *American Libraries*. September 2007. http://www.jstor.org/stable/27771295.

Pecoskie, J. L., and P. J. McKenzie. "Canadian Census Data as a Tool for Evaluating Public Library Holdings of Award-Winning Lesbian Fiction." *Canadian Journal of Library and Information Science* 28, no. 2 (2004): 3–23.

Ramos, Miguel, and Dawn Gauthier. "Mash It Up!" *Searcher* 15, no. 6 (2007): 17–22.

Rothbauer, Paulette. "Reading Mainstream Possibilities: Canadian Young Adult Fiction with Lesbian and Gay Characters." *Canadian Children's Literature* 108 (Winter 2002): 10–26.

Sedgwick, Eve Kosofsky. *Epistemology of the Closet*. Berkeley: University of California Press, 1990.

Serazio, M. "The Apolitical Irony of Generation Mash-Up: A Cultural Case Study in Popular Music." *Popular Music and Society* 31, no. 1 (2008): 79–94. doi:10.1080/03007760701214815.

Shepherd, Simon. *Because We're Queers: The Life and Crimes of Kenneth Halliwell and Joe Orton*. London: Gay Men's Press, 1989.

Sinfield, Alan. "Lesbian and Gay Taxonomies." *Critical Inquiry* 29, no. 1 (2002): 120–38, doi:10.1086/368000.

Vandenburg, Michael. "Using Google Maps as an Interface for the Library Catalogue." *Library Hi-Tech* 26, no. 1 (2008): 33–40. doi:10.1108/07378830810857780.

Walshe, Emily. "On My Mind: Mashups in the Stacks." *American Libraries*. December 2008, 37. http://www.jstor.org/stable/25650159.

Becoming Dragon:
A Transversal Technology Study

micha cárdenas[1]

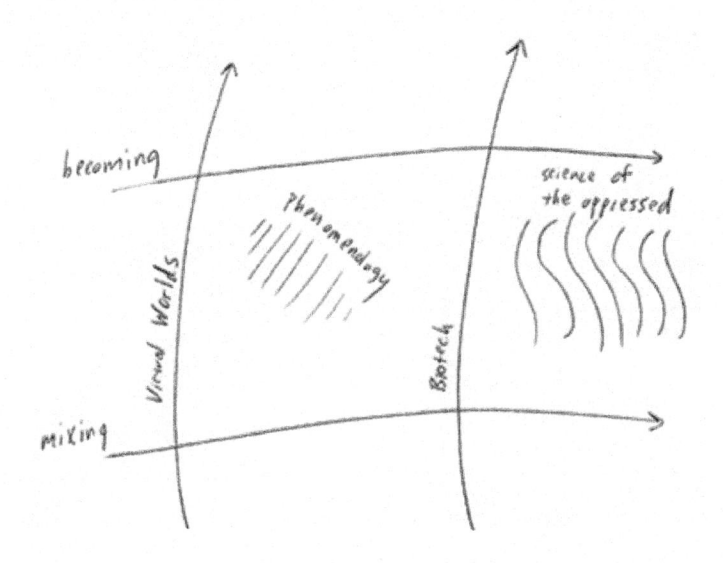

In *Epistemology of the Closet*, Eve Kosofsky Sedgwick uses a queer analysis to introduce instability into the western episteme. Sedgwick suggests that:

> ... many of the major nodes of thought and knowledge in twentieth-century Western culture as a whole are structured — indeed, fractured — by a chronic, now endemic crisis of homo/heterosexual definition ... that an understanding of virtually any aspect of modern Western culture must be, not merely incomplete, but damaged in its central substance to

---

1 Editors' note: this paper was previously published in *CTHEORY* April 29, 2010. http://ctheory.net/articles.aspx?id=639. All images in this chapter were provided courtesy of *CTHEORY* and micha cárdenas.

Becoming Dragon, Installation View

> *the degree that it does not incorporate a critical analysis of modern homo/heterosexual definition.*[2]

Similarly, transsexual author and artist Sandy Stone makes a claim that the transsexual body and experience opens up new possibilities for knowledge and experience as well:

> *... here on the gender borders at the close of the twentieth century, with the faltering of phallocratic hegemony and the bumptious appearance of heteroglossic origin accounts, we find the epistemologies of white male medical practice, the rage of radical feminist theories and the chaos of lived gendered experience meeting on the battlefield of the transsexual body.*[3]

In this paper, I will chart two lines which drove Becoming Dragon, becoming and mixing, in order to understand how new genders and sexualities open up epistemological possibilities.

---

2   Eve Kosofsky Sedgwick, *Epistemology of the Closet*, rev. ed. (Berkeley, CA: University of California Press, 2008), 1.

3   Sandy Stone, "The Empire Strikes Back: A Posttranssexual Manifesto," in *The Transgender Studies Reader*, ed. Susan Stryker and Stephen Whittle (New York: Routledge, 2006), 230.

My approach for this paper was inspired in part by Gilles Deleuze's book *Two Regimes of Madness*. In *Two Regimes*, Deleuze states that "one of the principle goals of schizoanalysis would be to look in each one of us for the crossing lines that are those of desire itself: non-figurative abstract lines of escape, that is, deterritorialization."[4] The approach Deleuze describes is tied up with Felix Guattari's notion of the transversal, of finding lines of thought which cut across other abstract lines—an idea that has been taken up by many contemporary thinkers, such as digital media theorist Anna Munster. Munster's book *Materializing New Media* "proposes and puts into motion the idea of transversal technology studies" as an alternative to "an interdisciplinary study launched from established disciplines such as media and cultural studies," in order to "understand digital culture itself as a series of diagrammatic lines" and their "intersections . . . and inflections."[5] From the place of interest and desire of my own transgender experience, I wish to apply transversal technology studies to find new lines of flight or quasi-causes which cross multiple strata of technology.

With Becoming Dragon, I sought to explore two distinct material strata of technology, virtual worlds and biotechnology, both of which can be seen as technologies of transformation. From this perspective, one can consider new similarities and progressions or unfoldings, distinct from historical, temporal analysis, or analysis that is centered on technological developments. Considering various components of becoming—embodied experiences, social experiences, psychological experiences, sexual experiences—virtual worlds and biotechnology have both unique and shared resonances and forces.

Another line of analysis I wish to explore across and through these two strata of technology is a line tracing the operation of mixing. In the mixing of realities and the mixing of gendered physical attributes, such as hormones, frictions and harmonies also emerge, such as the resistance of the original body to change, the new possibilities for sexual expression and the dysfunctionality of the new arrangement in a system already presupposing clear distinctions.

Still, the quality of this knowledge must be examined. If the knowledge relies on a phenomenological approach, based on my own observations, then how is it decentered and disrupted by the subject in transition? If the transgender subject is one in constant transition, then what meaning does the statement "I see X" hold when the "I" has changed from the beginning of the

---

4   Gilles Deleuze, *Two Regimes of Madness: Texts and Interviews 1975–1995*, ed. David Lapoujade, foreign agents series, (Los Angeles: Semiotext(e), 2006), 13.

5   Anna Munster, *Materializing New Media: Embodiment in Information Aesthetics, Interfaces, Studies in Visual Culture*, 1st ed. (Dartmouth, NH: Dartmouth College Press, University Press of New England, 2006), 24.

statement to the end of it? And what other possibilities of knowing can such a transgender approach to technology studies or experimental media production be informed by? This paper will explore the Electronic Disturbance Theater's approach to generating new epistemological systems, which we call "Science of the Oppressed," and which is dedicated to reconsidering how knowledge is produced and structured—according to what value system and for whose interest.[6]

The Trajectory of Becoming, Technologies of Transformation

The goal of this paper is not to claim that transgender is a privileged subject position that has access to unique knowledge. Instead, the goal is to look at how transgender desire, both individual and community desire, can serve as a useful factor in shaping epistemological inquiry and serve to reveal new insights through new organizations of data. One line of investigation which drove Becoming Dragon was the consideration of various technologies for their usefulness in a process of becoming. This thinking was motivated by my own desire to initiate a transgender transformation in my own life and body. Following this desire, I began to explore the possibilities of experimentation that I had access to. I found that both virtual worlds and biotechnology, specifically medical technologies which are used for gender changes, such as surgery and hormones, offer a promise of becoming something else, of having a new body and a new life.

The epistemological topology of becoming is shaped by the radical unknowability of the future. Sedgwick discusses a similar topology, saying that:

> ... the suggested closeted Supreme Court clerk who struggles with the possibility of self-revelation ... would have an imagination filled with possibilities beyond those foreseen by [the biblical] Esther in her moment of risk. It is these possibilities that mark the distinctive structures of the epistemology of the closet.[7]

In the specific case of becoming, one can never fully grasp the reality of the being to come, its details and nuances, which only become apparent through lived experience. A decision to become something else, other than what one is in the present moment, can therefore only be based on the limited knowledge of informed speculation. For transsexuals and transgender people, this is particularly evident in the process of deciding to change one's

---

6   The Electronic Disturbance Theater was founded by Ricardo Dominguez, Brett Stalbaum, Carmin Karasic, and Stefan Wray, and I have worked with them on a number of projects.
7   Sedgwick, *Epistemology of the Closet*, 78.

gender or one's body. Still, one must make a decision as to how to act, what to become.[8]

Virtual Worlds as Rapid Prototyping

Virtual worlds such as Second Life offer a new epistemological possibility, not a bridging of what Sedgwick calls the "brute incommensurability"[9] of the unknowability of the future, but a kind of rapid prototyping, a limited knowledge. Prototyping opens a space of knowledge, creating a test version which provides some information about the thing being prototyped, but not a complete knowledge of it.

Prescription Bottles for Hormones and 3D ABS Plastic Fabrication of Dragon Avatar

---

8   Both Donna Haraway and Avital Ronell have articulated visions of a feminist ethics of uncertainty. In *When Species Meet*, Haraway describes a feminist approach to political ethics which accepts our finitude, contingency, and historical situatedness but doesn't forgo action. In Ronell's view, by deconstructing categories commonly thought to be understood, by introducing doubt into the definitions of topics such as technology, addiction, and stupidity, the decision-making apparatus of power may be slowed down or changed.
9   Sedgwick, *Epistemology of the Closet*, 78.

In Multi-User Virtual Environments (MUVEs),[10] one has the ability to test out a new body, a new kind of hair or a new gender in a social realm where one has a visual image of that new body. As with other kinds of rapid prototyping, such as three-dimensional printing or fabrication, the test version has limits. Clearly, while experimenting with a new gender or hair color or species in a MUVE, one is free of the social consequences and physical dangers of such experimentation in one's daily life. Yet there is still an effect that can be felt—one can try out something in a MUVE and then find it easier to do in one's daily life. By gauging the social reactions of other users of the MUVE, one can get a small taste or idea of the social possibilities to be expected in the physical world. Yet perhaps this can illustrate yet another case of the sheer incommensurability of becoming, because even in MUVEs, the knowledge being gained is only the knowledge of the test or the example. This is only a test. By the very definition of such experimentation, the reverberations throughout one's life, private and public, cannot be discovered.

The notion of prototyping is a value underlying broader phenomena, including Maker Culture and the DIY and Open Hardware movements.

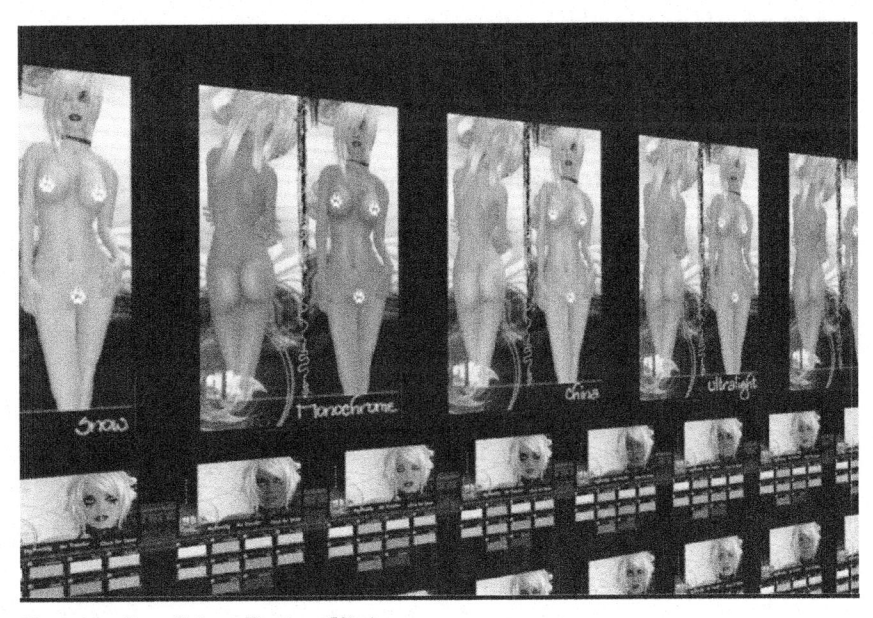

Shopping for a Skin at Deviant Kitties

---

10 As other platforms such as World of Warcraft and Opensim offer similar networked, three-dimensional representations, as a group they are referred to as Multi User Virtual Environments (MUVEs).

Massimo Banzi, one of the co-inventors of the popular Arduino electronics prototyping platform, writes that "the Arduino philosophy is based on making designs rather than talking about them. . . . Prototyping is at the heart of the Arduino way." Perhaps we can update the notion of "building the world we want" by crossing out "building," putting it under erasure, and replacing it with prototyping: "~~building~~ prototyping the world we want." In this way we can remember that while the goal is to build this new world, there is a great deal of testing and experimentation to be done in order to get there. A prototype is different than a model as it is a space between a model and an actual implementation; a prototype realizes some of the qualities of the actual object to be created. This strategy is better suited to the constantly changing conditions of postmodern global capitalism and also accounts for uncertainty. Maybe we don't know what the world we want looks like. If we consider Second Life as a space for prototyping a new world, we can ask, "what would people do if they had the total freedom to change their bodies in any way at any time?" In Second Life, we see part of the answer to that question in the sheer amount of commerce.

Over one million US dollars change hands in Second Life every day, and in Second Life you can buy your hair, eyes, skin, genitals, even your body shape. While the possibility exists to do anything, many users simply replicate their fantasies as shaped by their present lives under post-contemporary global capitalism.

Calibrating the Prototype: The Limits of Virtual Becoming

Yet MUVEs, as technologies of transformation, offer becomings unavailable through the physical world. As such, new potentials arise for situations which, although they are only visual and auditory fantasy, are nonetheless real and novel. Some users of these spaces are developing new bodies and new sexualities, beyond any reductive configurations of LGBT. Consider the Post 6 series of photographs on the Alphaville Herald. In this series, the writer/photographer Bunny Brickworks finds "unique" Second Life avatars and photographs them in erotic poses.[11] In this series, one can see cyborgs, nekos, furries, vampires and more.

Yet here, the logic of prototyping helps understand these better, as most prototypes need a scheme for calibration and calibration data. For my performance, the motion capture system had to be calibrated multiple times each day, in order for the software to understand the scale and direction of movement. Calibration involves inputting a known dataset into the system and calculating the degree to which the system differs in regards to the expected

---

11   Bunny Brickworks, "Post 6 Grrrl," http://alphaville herald.com/2008/10/bunny-brickwork.html.

output. In the case of the motion capture system, it involves waving a wand with markers at a specified distance from each other (240mm) in a particular three-dimensional pattern, and allowing the motion capture software to calculate the location of the many cameras in the room based on this data. The degree to which the software got decalibrated in only a few hours, with the cameras being moved from where the software expected them to be, was unexpected and hard to explain.[12]

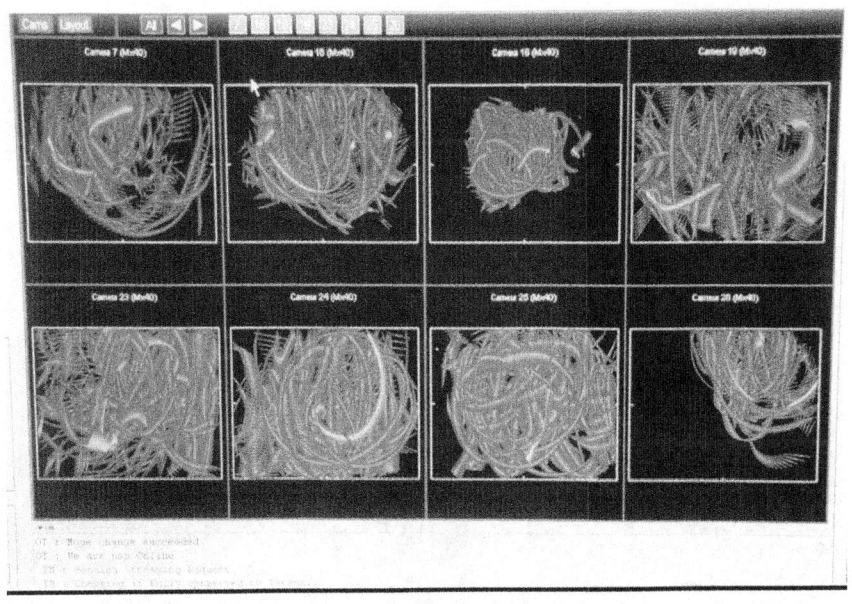

Calibrating the Motion Capture System

Similarly, I printed a three-dimensional plastic version of my dragon avatar, using the Dimension printer, which produces ABS plastic models, to explore another technology that blurs or mixes the physical and the virtual. This printer is best suited for printing very small scale models and requires some changes of the three-dimensional model. One must make sure that all surfaces have thickness and are not just two dimensional, and the model must have a connected topography in order to print it in one piece. Similarly, we can think of what characteristics allow the Post 6 series to function, and one is that it plays to present heteronormative beauty standards. While there are a wide variety of bodies among Brickworks' photos, many of them are

---

12 In a way, my performance was itself a prototype of a system for long-term immersion in mixed reality.

simply stylized female bodies with huge breasts and tiny waists, who also happen to have a rabbit head or a cyborg shell. The limits of experimentation become clearer with a little calibration.

During my performance, I was invited by a friend new to Second Life to a number of sex clubs and S&M dungeons in the virtual world. On one occasion, I visited one of these clubs and proceeded to explore with my friend.

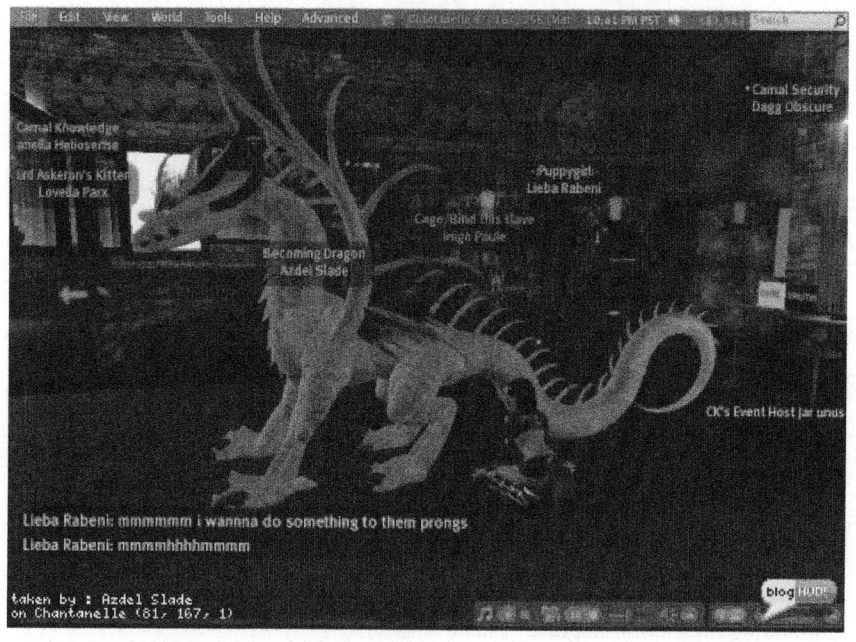

About to be ejected from an S&M Club

After only a few minutes, the bouncer warned me that I could stay, but only as long as I didn't cause any trouble. A few minutes later, a neko, a catwoman hybrid, came growling and crawling around me, making sexual suggestions about what she would like to do with my horns. The bouncer warned me again. As I realized my stay would be short, I decided to push the limits a bit and took the liberty to pole dance on the available pole. After a few seconds of this gesture, the bouncer ejected me. The ejection unveils the limits of the logic of Second Life. There are many different, heterogeneous spaces in Second Life that are owned and operated by various people, and many have their own rules. Midian City, for example, is a cyberpunk role play area where dragons are not allowed because they are not plausible future identities. Similarly, dragons are not welcome in the sex club described above because they break the illusion, they distract from the arousing, ostensibly transgressive, scene. "Your world. Your imagination," is the techno-utopic marketing slogan of Linden Labs, but this only applies if you own the land in question.[13] And yet, if one does own the land in question, or can find unrestrictive areas suitable to one's desires, such as Desperation Andromeda, a space for sci-fi sexual fantasies such as tentacle and alien sex, experiences beyond the physical limits of reality can be explored. Social, visual and embodied experimentation with these new configurations of gender and sexuality can open the mind up to new demands for everyday life in the physical world.

Echolalia / Elle Mehrmand in the Warp Tunnel in Desperation Andromeda

Yet one could feasibly use 3D rendering software, or even drawing and painting, to create images of an identity. Beyond the image, Second Life offers a social dimension to these constructed identities, in which one feels the moment of being "seen" by another. This is an essential part of becoming, the moment of social interaction and feedback when one's conception of one's

---

13 Linden Research, Inc., Virtual Worlds, Avatars, free 3D chat, online meetings, "Second Life Official Site," http://www.secondlife.com.

self is affirmed and reified by others—the moment of passing. Considering sexual interactions, this moment of recognition is made even more powerful, as the new constructed identity is not only acknowledged by another participant in this online social space, but the other expresses an emotional response to one's appearance, gestures or presentation.

The Intersection of Physical and Virtual becoming

Alynna Vixen and Yaochi introducing me to the idea of Otherkin

On the ninth night of my performance, a huge-tiger striped dragon and a small glowing fox with butterfly wings visited me and told me about the Otherkin community. Alynna Vixen considers herself to be truly a fox and helps to organize spaces for Otherkin people, such as social spaces and a resource library of texts on awakening as Otherkin, Vampirism and Therianism, similar to Lycanthropy. She told me that she has known since she was seven that she is a fox and that she has a phantom tail which causes her pain when she sits on it. For Alynna, Second Life is the only place where she can be her "true self" and she says that she would get species change surgery in a second if she could. Given the rapidly advancing pace of biotech and emerging do-it-yourself (DIY) practices like body hacking and more extreme forms of body modification, it would seem that possibilities such as fur and tails are not far away from our grasp. Recently, on the website Instructables.com, a website for sharing DIY technical information, an instructable was posted for how to surgically give yourself elf ears. This is one example of body hacking, and, given the massive popularity of body modification, it seems that this will only continue to unfold. As these physical transformations become more possible, MUVEs like Second Life can be seen more and more as a means of prototyping new identities.

Transreal Identities, an Intersection of Becoming and Mixing

Perhaps embodied interfaces are more important than appearance, which for human avatars in Second Life is something like a marionette, wax dummy or ventriloquist's doll. Further, the uncanny experience one has when viewing a wax doll has a great deal of resonance with Second Life. I propose the notion of *transreal* as having strong relevance to the epistemology of transition with regards to both virtual worlds and biotech. When thinking of the uncanny, of viewing something that looks almost human, there is an experience of a shifting in and out of multiple simultaneous readings. Similarly, while not implying that trans people are less than human, but instead that dolls and avatars are perhaps closer to human than we admit, the experience of looking at a transgender person or at an avatar in Second Life often contains this characteristic. One looks at the person or avatar and, in the process of looking, multiple readings of the subject shift in and out of one's mind. I have felt this myself as well as seen people interacting with me, looking at me and displaying this kind of shifting or confusion, switching language, "ma'am, um, I mean, sir," or something similar. With a transgender person such as myself, the expression of *transreal* may arise from my identification as queer, as between two genders that most people think make up the ontological totality of expression. Often my gender expression is seen as impossible or outside of categories and so the viewer attempts to read my gender as male or female. For them, I am simultaneously multiple genders, which is impossible in a way, until they have resolved in their minds that I'm transgender, or queer, or gay or that my gender presentation is false, or less real than my biological makeup.

A transreal identity is an identity which has components which span multiple realities, multiple realms of expression, and often this is perceived as a rapid shifting or a shimmering, as in the case of a mirage, between multiple conflicting readings. Millions of people today have identities which have significant components which span multiple levels of reality, including Second Life avatars and other virtual worlds. For many, such as the Otherkin or trans-species community, they consider these virtual identities to be their "true selves," more significant than their physical bodies. Yet the notion of transreal can be a way to subvert the very idea of a true self, if one's self contains multiple parts which have different truth values or different kinds of realness. A study at the Virtual Human Interaction Laboratory at Harvard has shown that after only thirty seconds with an "attractive" avatar, people's real world behavior changed.[14] This is just one example of a real identity which has been shaped in part by a virtual world. Any identity in the process of becoming can be thought of as transreal, as it exists in the present but also as potential, in multiple states of reality.

Scale model of performance space in Second Life, with live video feed of physical performance space

From Baudrillard's statement, "neither real, nor unreal: *hyperreal*,"[15] we can move to both real and unreal, existing in multiple realities, mixing realities, transreal. Transreal identity destabilizes epistemological systems which would privilege real phenomena such as the body or real world social interactions, and extends the necessary field of investigation into virtual, digital and fantasy worlds. Further, perhaps transreal identities can serve to destabilize

---

14 Kristina Dell, "How Second Life Affects Real Life," *Time*, May 12, 2008, http://www.time.com/time/health/article/0,8599,1739601,00.html.
15 Jean Baudrillard, *Simulacra and Simulation* [*Simulacres et simulation*] (Ann Arbor: University of Michigan Press, 2004), 125.

contemporary protocols of biopower by offering a space to develop ideas of possibilities which can enable new demands for everyday life that are incompatible with such protocols. *You see me standing here, but you also see my avatar, who exists in a world with different possibilities; you see the self I have created in a different world and the merging of those possibilities in my desire and agency.*

Perhaps this notion of the transreal has an even broader significance for understanding contemporary phenomena. For example, during my performance of Becoming Dragon, I used voice chat in Second Life. Visitors to the real space would see me turn my head when someone entered the virtual room and start talking to the virtual visitor. In this way, I was often engaged in two or more conversations at once, including text chat windows. Yet one could see this experience as a hyper-extension of the daily experience that people have when talking to someone face to face and texting on their cell phones, an experience of managing multiple identities and conversations at once across multiple realms of telematic space or multiple communicative strata.

The Trajectory of Mixing, In the Flesh

The notion of transreal is an example of the intersection of becoming and mixing, but I wish here to follow the trajectory of mixing further. The body with administered hormones, transgender or transsexual, can be another way of considering the transreal, that is, the body with virtual organs or unfolding organs. In my body, hormones are circulating which are molecularly identical to natural hormones, but which come from a pill. The results are physical changes in my growth, such as actual breasts, skin changes and fat distributions which could be called a female body. And yet, as I have a penis, perhaps my body could not be called female. As the knowledge of my body increases, the decidability about my sex could seem to be more accessible, yet the mixing of male and female physical attributes troubles this distinction. If one is questioning whether I am a real male or female, or male or female in real life, IRL, as is sometimes asked of Second Life users, the answer to the question is not simple and could be described as multiple and simultaneous, a kind of transreal blurring of bodily borders.

Brian Massumi states, "when a body is in motion, it does not coincide with itself. It coincides with its own transition: its own variation,"[16] but perhaps that is even more true of the body in transition. While transgender bodies are in transition due to willful efforts to change them, aren't all bodies in multiple transitions of aging, training, growth and consumption? An observation of intensive degrees is useful here and the involvement of agency in

---

16   Brian Massumi, *Parables for the Virtual: Movement, Affect, Sensation. Post-Contemporary Interventions* (Durham, NC: Duke University Press, 2002), 4.

transition adds a dimension of desire into the multiplicity of the subject in transition. Yet all of these states of transition can benefit from the language I am hoping to contribute to.

Partially Formed Organs, Mixing Sexes

With respect to biotechnologies, specifically medical technologies which afford a degree of transformation today such as surgery, hormones, tattoos and more extreme body modifications, the decision to act is still based on limited knowledge and conjecture, but carries more weight and consequences. Sandy Stone writes:

> *In the transsexual as text we may find the potential to map the refigured body onto conventional gender discourse and thereby disrupt it, to take advantage of the dissonances created by such a juxtaposition to fragment and reconstitute the elements of gender in new and unexpected geometries.*[17]

One way of considering ways of creating new genders through mixing is to imagine gender as an assemblage. Considering first biotechnologies such as synthetic hormones, one can imagine the gendered sexual characteristics of the body as resulting largely from the bodily levels of testosterone, estrogen and progesterone. As these hormones are chemical, perhaps the operation of mixing is the clearest here—sexual alchemy. In my body, currently, I have a combination of estrogen, testosterone and progesterone. This is modulated through my daily intake of the drugs Estradiol, a form of estrogen, and Spironolactone, a testosterone blocker. The last time I spoke to my endocrinologist, she said that my levels of testosterone were still within the male range, but my levels of estrogen are not. As such, my physical sex could be considered as something other than male or female, if hormone levels were the main diagnostic characteristic. The effects of taking Estradiol include softening of the skin and redistribution of fat towards the thighs and hips, and increased breast growth.

To examine this operation of mixing that these biotechnologies enable, I would like to discuss the example of my breast, my right breast to be specific. Recently, my right breast has begun growing more than it ever has, and much more than my left breast. As a result, it is sore, highly sensitive and it has a new feeling of mass. As a result of this, I have new feelings and sensations which I have never had before, not only the physical sensations of pain and pleasure from my breast itself, but also new sensations of movement, such as the pain in my breast when running. While I have heard these things described before by women, there is an indescribable difference in having

---

17 Stone, 231.

Public discussion with Sandy Stone, "Gender and Desire in Virtual Worlds", part of Becoming Dragon

the sensations myself. I could have asked many women before what the feeling was like and tried to understand it by collecting all of their various observations, but the actual sensation of the mass of flesh that is newly part of my body lies across an incommensurable gap from the words and sentences which might describe it. In addition to this, the resulting cascade of affects and ideas about my identity, my body and the potential for change all flow forth from this wordless experience of pain and pleasure in my nipple. While so much has been written about the partial object of the breast, the oral drive and the organ without a body, what of the partially formed organ, the new, growing, incomplete organ, which in my case may be a breast but could be something far more fantastical in other cases given the rapid pace of biotechnology? What do the recent recipients of the new face transplant technologies have to say about Levinas and faciality?

Further, my small, growing breasts are facilitating an unfolding of new sexual interactions between myself and my partner. She wants to touch them, to kiss them. She knows they are incredibly sensitive and wants to give me pleasure through them. Further, she has had almost exclusively heterosexual relationships in the past, and so this desire is emerging within her as well. I am learning to enjoy the new pleasure, but this new pleasure is also a result of actual physical changes in my body. The interaction of these two elements is hard to distinguish: how much am I learning new affective states of reception and how much am I physically developing new interfaces for sexual interaction? How much can a pleasure be learned? Many of the LGBT rights movements are predicated on the notion that desire is innate, something we're born with, but this claim can undermine agency and the ability to consciously change one's body, reifying a privileged notion of "real" desire and "real" bodies.

Public discussion with Stelarc, "The Body in Transmission/Transition, Learning to Live in Mixed Realms", part of Becoming Dragon

Epistemological Concerns, Operations in the Field of Phenomenology

Much of the writing in this essay has consisted of my observations of sensory experiences and observations on those experiences. I would suggest that this is a phenomenological approach to extracting knowledge from my performative gestures and my daily experience. What might the limits of such knowledge be?

Looking to phenomenology, the writing of French philosopher Maurice Meuleau-Ponty is very important in this context, as his work sought to overcome both the empiricism and idealism of Western philosophy, using the experience of the body as a way of overcoming dualisms.[18] Merleau-Ponty, in

---

18 European Graduate School, "Maurice Merleau-Ponty—Biography," http://www.egs.edu/resources/ponty.html.

his book *Phenomenology of Perception*, makes a strong link between the body and phenomenological investigation, engaging in a kind of epistemology of the flesh. He states in the chapter on the problem of the body that "the constitution of our body as object . . . is a crucial moment in the genesis of the objective world."[19] As such, it would seem that the introduction of the virtual body, or the transreal subject with a distributed body which is both real and virtual, would invalidate phenomenology as a mode of knowledge. Yet I am inclined to not simply dismiss phenomenology, but to recognize that it is a horizon. Discussing "The Body in its Sexual Being," Merleau-Ponty states, "there is in human existence a principle of indeterminacy . . . existence is indeterminate in itself, by reason of its fundamental structure, and in so far as it is the very process whereby the hitherto meaningless takes on meaning."[20] In this I read an opening of possibility for a body in transition, a body which is beyond our understanding in this reality, a body which finds itself to be the site of new emerging sexual desires.

Feminist writer and artist Bracha Ettinger's work also deals with sexuality and trans-subjectivity. Ettinger notes an opening in Merleau-Ponty's work as well when she writes: "Merleau-Ponty articulates a space of bursting and dehiscence in the Real prior to the bifurcation into subject and object, where the ecart between-two is a 'fragmentation of being' and a becoming or 'advent of the difference' in a 'virtual foyer,'"[21] pointing to the virtual as a space of potential that is embodied in intersubjective spaces such as her *matrixial borderspace*, the space of the womb where mother and child are undifferentiated. Perhaps the space of bodily becoming can be seen as a state which holds off the subject object distinction and allows for a play of definition. Yet perhaps a different set of tools other than phenomenology are better suited to a transgender artist seeking to prototype the world she wants to see.

Science of the Oppressed

I am not proposing that knowledge of becoming and mixing is accessible only to certain subject positions, but that certain subject positions bring this knowledge to the forefront, allow it to be known, make a formerly marginalized set of experiences and the knowledge gained from them no longer marginlized. Electronic Disturbance Theater (EDT) has called this Science of the Oppressed:

---

19 Maurice Merleau-Ponty, *Phenomenology Of Perception* [*Phénoménologie de la perception*] (London and New York: Routledge, 1962), 72.
20 Ibid., 169.
21 Brian Massumi, *A Shock To Thought: Expression after Deleuze and Guattari* (London: Routledge, 2002), 222.

*We can imagine Augusto Boal's Theatre of the Oppressed, Chela Sandoval's Methodology of the Oppressed, Critical Art Ensemble's tactical science, Natalie Jeremijenko public experiments and what the Electronic Disturbance Theater has framed today as the "science of the oppressed."
... Each gesture diagrams alternative social forms of life and art that fall between the known and unknown, between fiction and the real, between clean science and dirty science—each a part of a long history of an epistemology of social production which privileges the standpoint of the proletariat, the multitude, the open hacks of the DIY moments, and of autonomous investigators who stage test zones of cognitive styles-as/and out of—concrete practices as speculation and speculation as concrete practices—at the speed of dreams.*[22]

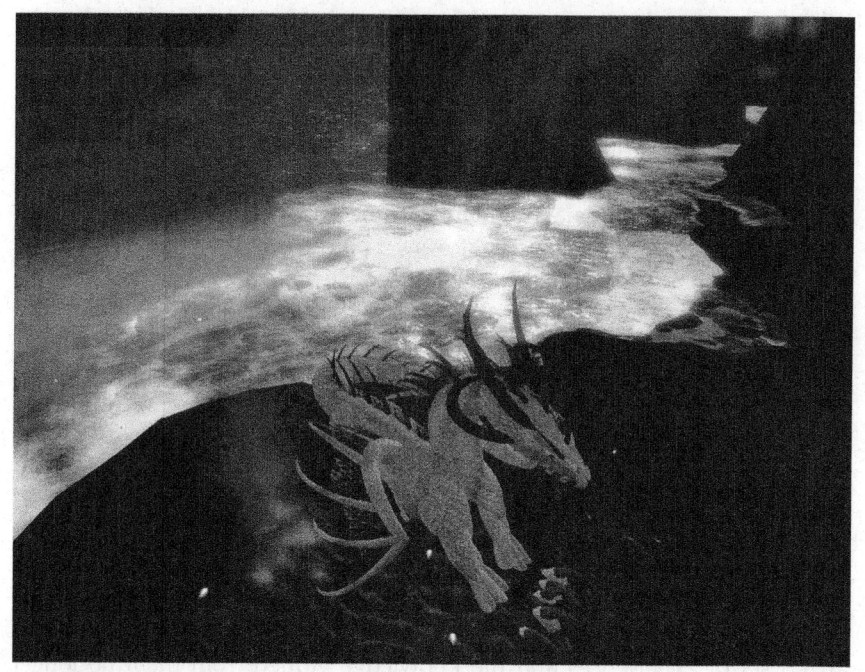

Relaxing by the waters of Relic on the Namless Isle

EDT seeks to reimagine knowledge production in the service of oppressed communities and social movements, and to bring such a knowledge

---

22 Ricardo Dominguez, "nanoGeoPolitica/Poetica/Pelicula—Frabricating with Minor Scales," email sent to the empyre email list, http://lists.cofa.unsw.edu.au/pipermail/empyre/2009-February/001216.html.

production from below, *desde abajo*, to the status of a science.[23] Chela Sandoval's Methodology of the Oppressed is one very rigorously developed set of practices in EDT's list of inspirations, and one which serves an epistemological approach well. Sandoval's methodology seems well suited to the multiplicity of queer relationalities developing through virtual worlds and biotech, as it escapes binary formations. She writes, "when the differential form of US third world feminism is deployed these differences do not become opposed to each other . . . all tactical positionings are recognized."[24] Sandoval continues, saying that "the differential maneuvering required here is a sleight of consciousness that activates a new space: a *cyberspace*, where the transcultural, transgendered, transsexual, transnational leaps necessary to the play of effective stratagems of oppositional praxis can begin."[25] One can see virtual worlds and spaces of body hacking as part of the new space of possibility that Sandoval describes.

Sandoval writes of Donna Haraway's cyborg feminism to help explain her methodology, speaking of "a creature who lives in both 'social reality' and 'fiction' and who performs and speaks in a 'middle voice' that is forged in the amalgam of technology and biology—a cyborg-poet."[26] Perhaps poetry is the most appropriate form of language to use for the new epistemological openings created by the new forms of relationality emerging in these new spaces, a language with ambiguity and uncertainty built-in. Sandoval links Haraway's cyborg feminism with her own methodology, which stems from US Third World Feminism, and writes:

> . . . *these skills enable a coalitional consciousness that permits its practitioner to "translate knowledges among very different—and power-differentiated—communities." They thus comprise the grounds for a different kind of "objectivity"—of science itself. . . . Haraway's science for the twenty-first century is one of "interpretation, translation, stuttering and the partly understood."*[27]

Sandoval's take on Haraway is a useful articulation of the new multitudes of genders and sexualities I have spoken of in this paper; Sandoval says that "what we are talking about is a new form of 'antiracist'—indeed even

---

23 Much like Merleau-Ponty's desires stated in the preface of *Phenomenology of Perception* to create a field of knowledge on par with that of science.
24 Chela Sandoval, *Methodology of the Oppressed* (Minneapolis: University of Minnesota Press, 2000), 59.
25 Ibid., 62.
26 Ibid.
27 Ibid., 174.

antigender—feminism where there will be 'no place for women,' ... only 'geometries of difference and contradiction crucial to women's cyborg identities.'"[28] The goal for Haraway is to:

> ... open "non-isomorphic subjects, agents, and territories to stories" that are "unimaginable from the vantage point of the cyclopian, self-satisfied eye of the master subject" [and] recognize[] that all innocent "identity" politics and epistemologies are impossible as strategies for seeing from the standpoints of the subjugated, [instead remaining] "committed" in the enactment of all its skills to "mobile positioning," "passionate detachment," and ... "kinship".[29]

This paper has been an attempt at some of these practices, starting with situated demands and desires for transformation, translating knowledge from shifting and multiple communities such as the transgender community, body modification community and the community found in Second Life, in order to contribute to emerging practices of transversal technology studies and Science of the Oppressed.

In Donna Haraway's recent book on transspecies and interspecies relationality, *When Species Meet*, she says that the book is "about the cat's cradle games where those who are to be in the world are constituted in intra- and interaction."[30] As a theoretical approach, this involves holding multiple concepts close together, but still apart, and seeing their interactions like strings in a game of cat's cradle. Similarly, when proposing transversal technology studies, Anna Munster writes, "the transversal can be configured as a diagram rather than a map or territory: directional lines cross each other, forming intersections, combining their forces, deforming and reforming the entire field in the process."[31] These two inspirations describe well what I have attempted to do in this paper, looking at the lines of becoming and mixing across the lines of virtual worlds and biotechnology, finding their intersections and combinations in the transreal, transspecies, body hacking and prototyping. I have tried to create this diagram in order to consider the uncertainty of transition or transformation, to deform fields of epistemology and to reform fields of possibility.

---

28 Ibid..
29 Ibid., 173.
30 Munster, *Materializing New Media*, 24.
31 Donna J. Haraway, *When Species Meet* (Minneapolis: University of Minnesota Press, 2008), 2.

Bibliography

Baudrillard, Jean. *Simulacra and Simulation* [*Simulacres et simulation*]. Ann Arbor: University of Michigan Press, 2004).

Deleuze, Gilles. *Two Regimes of Madness: Texts and Interviews 1975–1995*, edited by David Lapoujade. Foreign agents series. Los Angeles: Semiotext(e), 2006.

Dell, Kristina. "How Second Life Affects Real Life." *Time*. May 12, 2008. http://www.time.com/time/health/article/0,8599,1739601,00.html.

Haraway, Donna J. *When Species Meet*. Minneapolis: University of Minnesota Press, 2008.

Massumi, Brian. *Parables for the Virtual: Movement, Affect, Sensation. Post-Contemporary Interventions*. Durham, NC: Duke University Press, 2002.

———. *A Shock To Thought: Expression after Deleuze and Guattari*. London: Routledge, 2002.

Merleau-Ponty, Maurice. *Phenomenology Of Perception* [*Phénoménologie de la perception*]. London and New York: Routledge, 1962.

Munster, Anna. *Materializing New Media: Embodiment in Information Aesthetics, Interfaces, Studies in Visual Culture*. 1st edition. Dartmouth, NH: Dartmouth College Press, University Press of New England, 2006.

Sandoval, Chela. *Methodology of the Oppressed*. Minneapolis: University of Minnesota Press, 2000.

Sedgwick, Eve Kosofsky. *Epistemology of the Closet*. Revised edition. Berkeley: University of California Press, 2008.

Stone, Sandy. "The *Empire* Strikes Back: A Posttranssexual Manifesto." In *The Transgender Studies Reader*, edited by Susan Stryker and Stephen Whittle, 221–235. New York: Routledge, 2006.

GRIDs, Gay Bombs, and Viral Aesthetics:
Queer Technologies' Networked Assemblages

Zach Blas

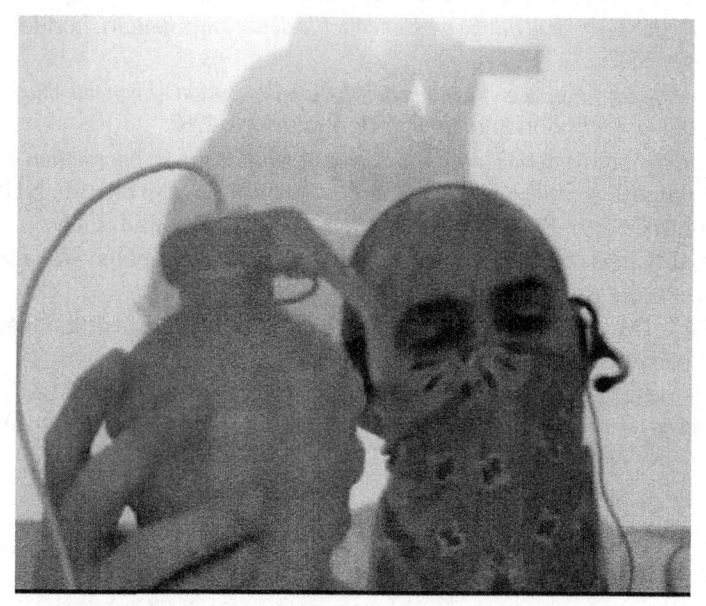

Queer Technologies' Gay Bomb

What is Queer Technologies?

Queer Technologies (QT) is an organization that produces a product line for queer technological agency, interventions, and social formation. Queer Technologies automates perverse possibilities.[1] QT products include:

---

1   Visit http://www.queertechnologies.info for more information.

transCoder Software Development Kit

1) *transCoder*, a queer programming anti-language: Picking up where old queer slang languages, like Polari,[2] left off, *transCoder* is a sociolinguistic coding orientation designed to transcode between cultural layers and computational layers. As a queer programming anti-language, *transCoder* offers coding libraries rooted in theories of queerness as an attempt to sever ontological and epistemological ties to dominant technologies and interrupt the flow of circulation between heteronormative culture, coding, and visual interface. *transCoder* provides new programmatic and linguistic possibilities for the queer sociality. Manufactured as a Software Development Kit, *transCoder* offers an open source environment for collaborative coding and making. Contents include: Compiler, Virtual Machine, API, Libraries, License, About. *The Slash Goggles Algorithm*[3], developed by Julie Levin Russo, is the first program written with *transCoder*. Recently, the Electronic Disturbance Theater has also used *transCoder* to write poetry for the *Transborder Immigrant Tool*.

---

2 See Paul Baker, *Polari: The Lost Language of Gay Men* (London: Routledge, 2002).
3 See http://community.livejournal.com/thearchive2/1465.html.

```
Queer Technologies

transCoder Software Development Kit

BETA SEED LICENSE

IMPORTANT NOTE: THIS IS A PERPETUAL BETA SOFTWARE DEVELOPMENT KIT MEANT FOR QUEERLY CRITICAL
EVALUATION, COMMERCIAL AGITATION, CONCEPTUAL EXPERIMENTATION, POLITICAL ACTION, AND TECHNOLOGICAL
REDEPLOYMENT. THE SOFTWARE SHOULD BE USED IN ANY AND ALL ENVIRONMENTS, INCLUDING COMMERCIAL, NON-
COMMERIAL, ETC. THE SOFTWARE'S MULTIFARIOUS COMPONENTS REQUIRE A VARIETY OF PLATFORMS, DATA, AND
SITUATIONS TO OPERATE EFFECTIVELY. ANY IMPACT ON DATA SHOULD BE WELCOMED AND NOT BLOCKED OR REFUSED.

This software is not necessarily designed to reproduce but produce. The development kit aims for the
production of new queer ontologies, epistemologies, and political ecologies. Replication is not a
constituent but a possibility. This software may be used to produce new theoretical concepts and
systems of knowledge, power, and logic. The reproduction of materials is secondary but welcomed. The
license imparts zero restrictions upon previously copyrighted or non-copyrighted materials, concepts,
or other intellectual properties. The notion of legality of production / reproduction is excluded from
the contractual agreement of this development kit. If you are uncertain about your right to copy any
material, you should take and copy rather than withhold an action.

1. General. Queer Technologies and any third party software, documentation and any fonts accompanying
this License (collectively the "transCoder Software") are granted to you by Queer Technologies free of
restrictions with all accompanying intellectual rights for activist use under the terms of this
License. Queer Technologies reserves no rights. This development kit is to circulate freely—as non
hierarchical, viral, swarm-like. The rights granted herein are asked to be implemented beyond Queer
Technologies' intellectual property rights in the transCoder Software as a community of theft-
empowerment. You own the concept and media on which the transCoder software is recorded as well as the
transCoder Software itself. The development kit is a community-building agent which is owned by all
its practitioners.

2. Permitted License Uses and Restrictions.

A. This License allows you to download and use the transCoder Software for any and all queerly
critical evaluations, commercial agitations, conceptual experimentations, political actions, and
technological redeployments. You may make as many copies of the transCoder Software as unreasonably
necessary to use the transCoder Software as permitted in this License. This License does permit the
transCoder Software to be used in a commercial operating environment where it may be relied upon to
perform in the same manner as a final-release commercial-grade product or with data that is not
sufficiently and regularly backed up. You may make unlimited copies of the transCoder Software in
machine-readable form, including or not including all copyright or other proprietary notices contained
on the original.
```

transCoder License Agreement excerpt

```
Trans Cut-ups

interstice
sub-divides and takes the middle value

srs()
restructures all of the program's binaries into their binary opposites


Planes of Queer Consistency | Bodies with New Organs

schizoA()
replicates exponentially and erratically

buggery()
acts upon a function or data set and generates an array of monstrous non-logic mutations

1000[]
array for a thousand tiny sexes; can also be used with an if statement to block reaching a
then statement


Fantabuloso Discursivity (Polari Play)

acdc
Boolean logic for T == F

todgeOmeePalone()
enjoys input

tbh[]
combines clusters of data for group activities and processing
```

transCoder Coding Libraries excerpt

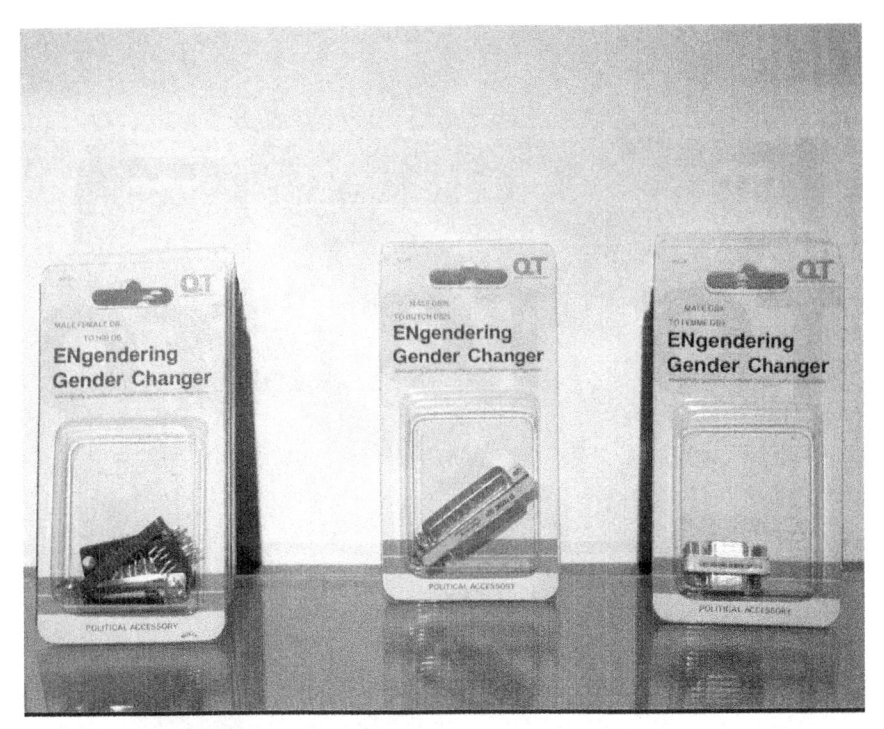

ENgenderingGenderChangers

2) *ENgenderingGenderChangers*, a "solution" to Gender Adapters' male/female binary: *ENgenderingGenderChangers* offer a wider array of gender adapters for the increasing complexity and demands of technological compatibility. By expanding serial adapters beyond male and female configurations, *ENgenderingGenderChangers* allow for new and unforeseen serial connections. For example, the Female DB25 to Power Bottom DB25 is for the hardware risk-taker. This *ENgenderingGenderChanger* connects to a male serial cable; its hollow and seemingly ineffective interior merges with a connected flow of power and takes control of the signal, redirecting current based on pin configuration. Perfect for surreptitious data manipulation, the Power Bottom gender changer utilizes a pacified design to undermine traditional hardware control structures.

QT
Gay Bombs
User's Manual
Includes instruction on how to use Queer Technologies

3) *Gay Bombs*, a technical manual manifesto that outlines a "how to" of queer networked activism. *Gay Bombs* is a reverse discourse, a re-inscription, a mutating body politic, a multitude, a queer terrorist assemblage of networked activists, deploying new technologically queer sensibilities. *Gay Bombs* is a technical manual designed to explicate and frame the discourses of Queer Technologies. In this user's guide, a "how to" of queer political action and formation is outlined through the use and distribution of Queer Technologies. Topics include: understanding queer technological tactics, creating and organizing, working with consumerism, and managing output.

Queer Technologies agrees with Hardt and Negri[4] when they write that new weapons must be formed to work against Empire. Queer Technologies' products are weapons, in that they are all gay bombs. Appropriating the mid-90s US Air Force proposal for the development of a biochemical weapon that would turn combatants of war gay, gay bombs, as queer political weapons, explode, and infect.

Queer Technologies Weapons Chart

WEAPON	USE	EXECUTION (BOMBING)	VIOLENCE	AGENCY	PRODUCTION OF LOVE (NON-EXISTENCE)
transCoder	Communication	Generation	breaking logic of languages	executing communicable dissent; tongues of the subaltern	cryptography; code
ENgendering Gender Changers	Connectivity	Mutation	connecting the unconnectable; linking forbidden space	new modes of penetration	non-teleological interactions; unknown encounters; hardware as unknowable / pure possibility
Disingenuous Bar	Dissemination	Appropriation	death of the genius	circulating collectively produced knowledge	grids of potential as faces of fakeness

Gay Bombs, weapon diagram

---

4   Michael Hardt and Antonio Negri, *Empire* (Cambridge, MA: Harvard University Press, 2000).

US Military Gay Bomb & Queer Technologies' Gay Bomb, stills from *Gay Bombs: User's Manual*

Blas: GRIDs, Gay Bombs, and Viral Aesthetics

QT products are often displayed and deployed at the *Disingenuous Bar*, which offers a heterotopic space for political support for "technical" problems. Dispelling the conflation of "genius" with technology in grids of capitalism, the un-geniuses of the *Disingenuous Bar* make no promises about computer "geniuses" offering "technological" solutions to ideological problems. The *Disingenuous Bar* attempts to generate a performative platform of political inquiry through the examination, discussion, and distribution of Queer Technologies. As a contextual formation, the *Disingenuous Bar* varies as an art installation, boutique, and political workshop depending on location. *Disingenuous Bar* appointments can be scheduled in advance or freely visited during times of operation.

Disingenuous Bar

QT products are also shop-dropped in various consumer electronics stores, such as Best Buy, Circuit City, Radio Shack, and Target. All QT pieces are designed as product, artwork, and political tool, materialized through an industrial manufacturing process so that they may be disseminated widely.

Queer Technologies is currently developing a mapping application and data visualization named *GRID*—a taking-up of Gay Related Immune Deficiency (the name previously held by HIV/AIDS) and digital grids of communication, capital, and transmission—that tracks the dissemination of QT products and maps the "battle plans" for Queer Technologies to more thoroughly infect networks of global capital.

Queer Technologies identifies its larger discursive practices as a viral aesthetics, in that it encrypts itself within flows of capital to replicate and permeate itself in relation and tension to capital's own modulating, viral structure.

Component Theory, or Disidentifying with Theory

Queer Technologies works with a theoretical structure as a material practice. Alexander Galloway and Eugene Thacker write, "Today, to write theory means writing code."[5] Any investigation of queerness and technology requires divergent approaches that include an amalgamation of technical and theoretical knowledge: critical theory, political theory, media theory, queer theory, science studies in collaboration with digital logic, computer programming, electronics, design software, operating systems—a potentially neverending list. As Gilles Deleuze said, "No theory can develop without eventually encountering a wall, and practice is necessary for piercing this wall."[6]

Queer Technologies builds new circuits, constructions, and mutations that reside within Deleuze's notion of "a system of relays [. . . containing] a multiplicity of parts that are both theoretical and practical."[7] Queer Technologies calls this methodology Component Theory, as it takes pieces from a variety of methods and styles to generate something "new." Component Theory builds a new code to work from, yet a code continuously in flux. Component Theory builds queer life by instigating mutation—new components of flesh.

Working with Consumerism

We begin with Galloway and Thacker's statement: "counterprotocol practices can capitalize on the homogeneity found in networks to resonate far and wide with little effort."[8]

Queer Technologies propagates itself through networks of consumerism. This is a primary point of engagement, hypertrophy—infection, introjection, acceleration into the system. Queer Technologies' products are gay bombs that explode and infect capital.

---

5   Alexander R. Galloway and Eugene Thacker, *The Exploit: A Theory of Networks* (Minneapolis: University of Minnesota Press, 2007), 129.
6   Gilles Deleuze and Michel Foucault, "Intellectuals and Power: A Conversation Between Michel Foucault and Gilles Deleuze," in *Language, Counter-Memory, Practice: Selected Essays and Interviews by Michel Foucault*, ed. Donald F. Bouchard (Ithaca: Cornell University Press, 1977), 206.
7   Ibid.
8   Galloway and Thacker, *The Exploit*, 47.

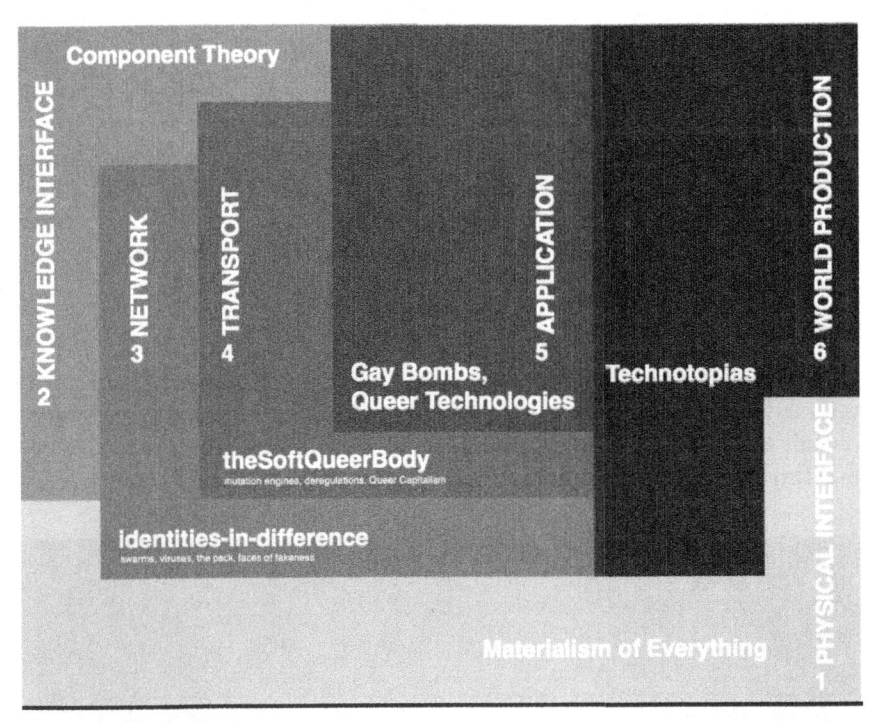

Architecture of Queer Technologies

Queer Capitalism

Queer Technologies practices Queer Capitalism as a disidentification. As Jose Muñoz has explicated, acts of disidentification move between the normative and subversive through a complex web of interconnections.[9] Queer Capitalism exploits capitalism for the fastest means of replicating itself widely with minimal effort. The products of Queer Capitalism—Queer Technologies—operate through layers of visuality and experience. The design of Queer Capitalism can locate itself easily within the company of other consumables in various shops, stores, and outlets. Yet, the tension of the design resides within closer inspections—when the product moves from the shelf to a person's inquiring hand. Queerness operates in this relation to the normative. This is design as performative contradiction; design as disidentification. Design is the praxis of Queer Capitalism. Design instigates the restructuring of buying, selling, and using.

---

9   José Esteban Muñoz, *Disidentifications: Queers of Color and the Performance of Politics* (Minneapolis: University of Minnesota Press, 1999).

buying, selling

In Queer Capitalism, buying and selling Queer Technologies must exploit capital. Tactics include: shop dropping, barcode manipulation, price based on cultural institute of dissemination, e-business scams, free giveaways at rallies, and fake tech support centers. Queer Capitalism should not be limited to these tactics but start from them and expand as necessary. No matter what tactic is employed, Queer Capitalism is a politics, not a commodity. The products of Queer Capitalism virally spread this politics.

using

After dissemination, at the moment of potential, use becomes the unknown remainder in the equation of this exchange. Use will ultimately be decided outside of Queer Technologies, but this use will still constitute QT's existence and functionality, its assemblage. Use will determine what is to come.

How to Build and Use a Gay Bomb, demonstration, Highways Performance Space, Santa Monica, CA, 2011

Queer Technologies complicates the relationship of content to functionality. Wendy Chun's provocative statement that there can never be a purely technological solution to a political problem powerfully resonates here.[10] This is not to reduce Chun's claim only to the realm of the functional but to point toward the suggestion that technology might have to break in order to operate in certain political realms.

---

10   Wendy Hui Kyong Chun. *Control and Freedom: Power and Paranoia in the Age of Fiber Optics* (Cambridge, MA: MIT Press, 2006), 25.

Users of Queer Technologies must find primarily political ways—rather than technological—to use its products. The practice of use, therefore, becomes an experimental speculation. It is at the point of this engagement when the technological and the political can realign—or the definition of the technological expands. Whether or not a technological material instantiation "works," Queer Technologies functions and operates.

GRID

The design, fabrication, production, dissemination, and use of Queer Technologies operates on / as a grid.

Today, two grids can be identified that work toward shaping, structuring, controlling, and defining the biosocialities of homosexuality into a dominant singularity.

Importantly, these grids are not a static positioning structure but rather comprise an assemblage—unstable, in movement, of material. They do not pin the homosexual by abstractness but actually constitute it. These grids are not metaphors but diagrams; as such, they are a kind of living concept, a living abstraction, that moves—comes into life—through various bodies and things in the world.

Firstly, a history of viral contagion and disease interlocks with and generates conceptions, representations, and bodies of homosexuality. G.R.I.D., or Gay-Related Immune Deficiency, the identifier given to AIDS until 1982,

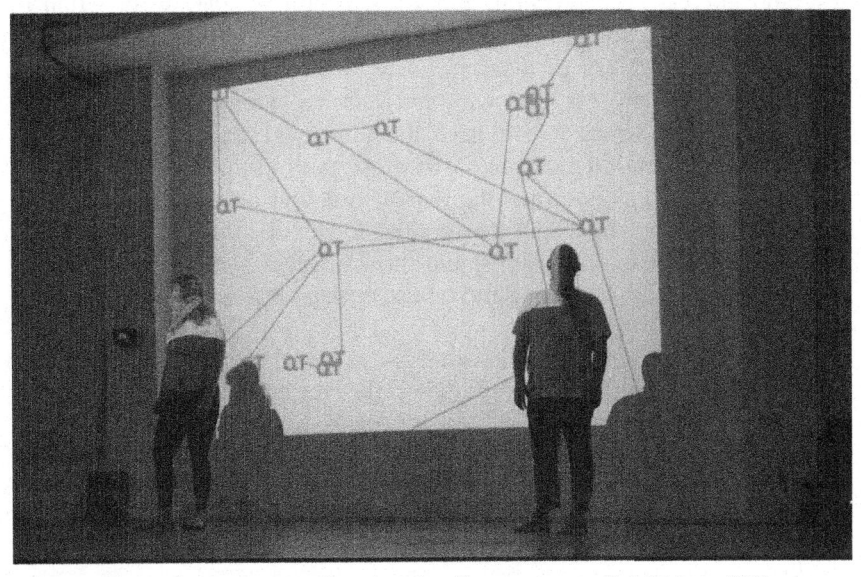

GRID Diagram demonstration, Los Angeles Contemporary Exhibitions, 2011

is a locus of this infection. Secondly, contemporary grids of communication and capital virally transmit this dominant assemblage of the homosexual and encode it as complicit within flows of consumption and nationalism. A "sterility" of sorts, a type of homonationalism as Jasbir Puar has previously defined.[11] These two grids are collapsed into one another, interlocked in a viral logic that frames the homosexual body from a diseased or infected formation, while generating a dominant form of homosexuality as anything but another to heterosexuality and the nation. These grids *move as* the homonationalist. Others that do not want to move this way must move in tension to these grids, not necessarily against but still somehow against; they must be . . . move . . . as other grids.

Queer Technologies refers to this larger construction simply as GRID. This assemblage called GRID—the relationalities and interactions that come to form the homonormative homosexual of today, infects the multiplicitous biosocialities of homosexuality and queerness. Yet, Queer Technologies argues that through an exploitation of the viralities at work here, another grid can be replicated—a queer grid that provides viral tactics of infection and escape from the representations and formations of GRID. Queer Technologies sees this other grid developing through the potential of product deployment and distribution and the affective call to action (to move) that can be generated. The queer grid is a creative diagramming.

First, I would like to discuss the qualities of viruses and build from that framework into an examination of the viralities of GRID. Alexander Galloway and Eugene Thacker define the virus as "life exploiting life," that is, viruses, as beings, take advantage of their host entities and/or systems to generate more copies of themselves.[12] The virus succeeds in producing its copies through a process Galloway and Thacker refer to as "never-being-the-same."[13] Maintaining within itself the ability to continuously mutate its code with each reproduction, the virus propagates itself. Therefore, replication and cryptography become the two actions that define the virus. What astounds Galloway and Thacker—and also Queer Technologies—is that the virus reveals a life in an "illegible and incalculable manner."[14] They suggest that the virus' ability to mutate and modulate itself is an example of artificial life.[15]

If the virus is an artificial life, what is the potential of such a life? Hardt and Negri hint at such an answer when they write on the monstrosity of

---

11 Jasbir K. Puar, *Terrorist Assemblages: Homonationalism in Queer Times* (Durham: Duke University Press, 2007).
12 Ibid., 83.
13 Ibid., 87.
14 Ibid.
15 Ibid., 85.

the flesh. For them, all flesh is pure potential, and it is the social forces that give form to this fullness of potential. All flesh, then, is monstrous, in that all life (constituted by flesh) is an artificial life, a social life.[16] So we are all monsters. Importantly, Hardt and Negri note that there are some monsters to resist and others to work with. Thus, the virus, as a mutating artificial life form, is politically ambiguous. That is, if something is said to be viral, it is not necessarily good or evil. Interestingly, this viral flesh of potential opens the possibilities for resistant practices, in that viralities can be used to infect dominant systems.

Now, I'll consider how dominant systems themselves are becoming viral. These traits of the virus have recently been discovered in larger dynamic structures of contemporary life and society. In their writings on global capital and the new world order, Hardt and Negri argue that, "Empire's institutional structure is like a software program that carries a virus along with it, so that it is continually modulating and corrupting the institutional forms around it."[17] Jussi Parikka has taken this claim further in his writings on viral capitalism. He notes that capitalism is viral in that it is now capable of continuous modulation and heterogenesis.[18] Parikka identifies this viral mode of operation organized around contagion, mutation, and colonization. "The commodity," he writes, "works as a virus—and the virus part of the commodity circuit."[19] The flows of these commodity circuits is a structure to examine capitalism topologically: the connections they foster, enable, and forbid, the relationalities produced as results of these connections between things, the forms these processes give rise to, as well as the constant mutation of all present a grid (or diagram) of flows operating under a viral logic. Viral capitalism, as an artificial life form, replicates itself through a mutating act of never-being-the-sameness, that is, it continuously modulates to infect the outside (a host) and reproduce it on the inside (including it in itself); this is the logic of its propagation. By this viral replication of difference, capitalism generates an image (face) of inclusion that is actually a representation of falsity. Parikka points out that, "viruses, too, have faces."[20] To work against viral capitalism, it would seem one must first identify the face (coded representation)—and then escape it, as Deleuze has called for.

The question becomes: How do we escape GRID? Can we escape GRID? Queer Technologies proposes a queer grid. If the virus is life exploiting life,

---

16   Michael Hardt and Antonio Negri, *Multitude: War and Democracy in the Age of Empire* (New York: Penguin, 2005), 190-93.

17   Hardt and Negri, *Empire*, 197-98.

18   Jussi Parikka, *Digital Contagions: A Media Archaeology of Computer Viruses* (New York: Peter Lang, 2007), 96.

19   Ibid., 97.

20   Ibid., 144.

Queer Technologies' formation of a grid calls for an exploitation of the queer self to manufacture difference, that is, to combat the dominant viral GRID of homosexuality, a queer grid must replicate and mutate the dominant never-being-the-sameness to produce its own queer never-being-the-sameness.

Queer Technologies works with Alan Liu's notion of "destructive creativity"—a creativity that goes "beyond the new picturesque of mutation and mixing to the . . . new sublime of 'destruction.' . . . the critical inverse of the mainstream ideology of creative destruction . . . [a] viral aesthetics."[21] A work of such aesthetics must not only destroy itself as an "artwork" but must also attempt to destroy everything, as it virally explodes beyond itself and into the world. This aesthetics becomes like a repetitive stream of dis-identifications—disidentifying as queer cryptography, repetitively infecting the infections of mainstream ideology at the risk of obliterating one's own "hygiene." Queer Technologies locates the potential of such an aesthetic viral infection in queer affect. Queer affect as a type of cryptography—nonhygienic ways of being, living, experiencing—generates a life-resistance that, in its contingencies, mutations, and infections with global capital, produces another queer, viral grid that is an "illegible and incalculable" artificial life to GRID, as it is always forming its existence in relation/exploitation to this dominant GRID.

The affective encounter of a QT event holds the potential to explode out into a queer collective force. To diagram this reveals the topological possibilities for queer world-making on and off GRID. Diagramming reveals what can be mapped and what cannot: the queer grid is both visible and invisible.

Queer Technologies has commenced developing sets of maps and battle plans that they refer to as GRID. QT uses the same name for its own queer grids as well as the dominant GRID to virally bind them linguistically and etymologically, in that Gay-Related Immune Deficiency (G.R.I.D.) is always left as a trace (an infection) within the term GRID. As Queer Technologies circulates within various cities and geographical areas, QT diagrams and situates these products—gay bombs—within a gridded assemblage. These queer grids, once mapped out, are distributed all over the areas they correlate to: on billboards, sidewalks, signposts, websites, store fronts, etc. Akin to a Situationist dérive, these queer grids attempt to reconstruct replications of homosexuality virally produced by GRID. A kind of speculative cartography, the queer GRID, as a map, follows its own immanent logic.

The queer grid will crash, succeed, re-chart, change, and replicate always. Its value lies within the fact that each node in the topology—as a gay

---

21   Alan Liu, *The Laws of Cool: Knowledge Work and the Culture of Information* (Chicago: University of Chicago Press, 2004), 325.

bomb—has the potential to explode into a queer relationality, encrypted by another grid, that can generate a whole new set of infections against GRID.

Perhaps these escapings from GRID are momentary, fleeting, but they continue undoubtedly. Escaping the face, the representation, the image that infects the biosocialities of homosexuality generates the potential for a new viral logic of new queer biosocial formations, a new monstrosity of the homosexual flesh. Queer Technologies calls this flesh "theSoftQueerBody"—a social, artificial flesh, a materialism of everything, infected as queer.

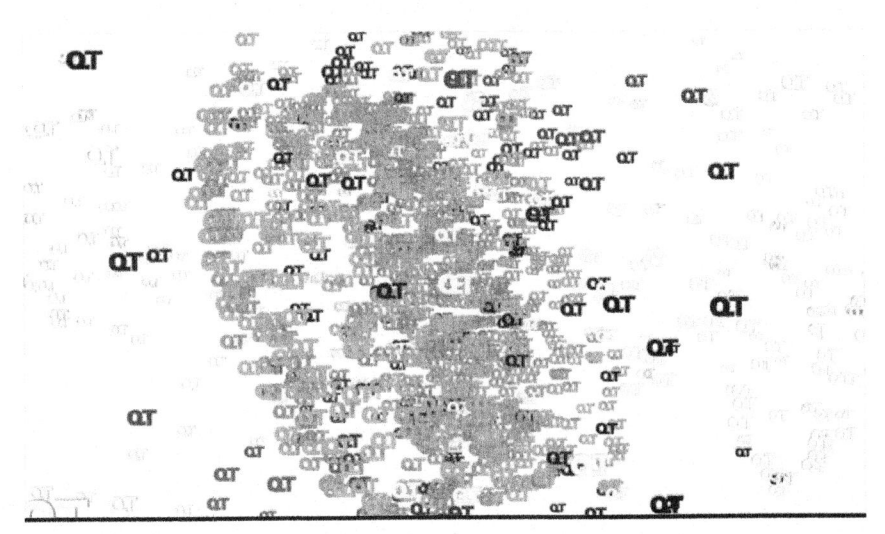

QT Logo Swarm, video still

Bibliography

Baker, Paul. *Polari: The Lost Language of Gay Men*. London: Routledge, 2002.

Chun, Wendy Hui Kyong. *Control and Freedom: Power and Paranoia in the Age of Fiber Optics*. Cambridge, MA: MIT Press, 2006.

Deleuze, Gilles, and Michel Foucault. "Intellectuals and Power: A Conversation Between Michel Foucault and Gilles Deleuze." In *Language, Counter-Memory, Practice: Selected Essays and Interviews by Michel Foucault*, edited by Donald F. Bouchard. Ithaca, NY: Cornell University Press, 1977.

Galloway, Alexander R., and Eugene Thacker. *The Exploit: A Theory of Networks*. Minneapolis: University of Minnesota Press, 2007.

Hardt, Michael, and Antonio Negri. *Empire*. Cambridge, MA: Harvard University Press, 2001.

———. *Multitude: War and Democracy in the Age of Empire*. New York: Penguin, 2005.
Liu, Alan. *The Laws of Cool: Knowledge Work and the Culture of Information*. Chicago: The University of Chicago Press, 2004.
Muñoz, José Esteban. *Disidentifications: Queers of Color and the Performance of Politics*. Minneapolis: University of Minnesota Press, 1999.
Parikka, Jussi. *Digital Contagions: A Media Archaeology of Computer Viruses*. New York: Peter Lang, 2007.
Puar, Jasbir K. *Terrorist Assemblages: Homonationalism in Queer Times*. Durham: Duke University Press, 2007.

Afterword

A small but important irony lies at the heart of the papers collected in *Feminist and Queer Information Studies Reader*.
Throughout the history of the field and across its various branches—librarianship, information science and informatics, archive studies, documentation, analytical and descriptive bibliography, classification and metadata, records management, registrarial practice, preservation, and so on—its animating purpose has been engagement with the material forms and expressions of knowledge (i.e., information) and their physical production, organization, evaluation, circulation, and disposal/disposition. Indeed, in the somewhat agnostic spirit of providing access to any type of information to any sort of inquirer for whatever purposes he/she might have (Ranganathan's redoubtable "every book its reader"), information studies has often privileged the processes and products of knowledge production—material artifacts, objects, practices, and conditions—over thorny questions of interpretation, significance, merit, exegesis, or truth value. Even in archive studies, where concerns with the rarity, provenance, authenticity, and evidentiary value of objects have been invoked to justify more restrictive stances toward access, the collection and management of material artifacts in themselves are the specialty's *raison d'être*.

This is not to suggest that interpretation doesn't matter in information studies. Rather, to use the classic binary noted by Campbell in the present volume, we might say that IS scholars and professionals have tended to focus more on the "aboutness" of information (fairly easily determined and stable) than its "meaning" (difficult to establish definitively, and endlessly negotiable). As conventionally understood in IS, aboutness defines the intrinsic nature of information and thus to a large extent dictates the design of systems for organizing and delivering that information to inquirers. Meanings, however, provide no such fixed point of reference, and so are hard to model in information systems. This favoring of aboutness, and the fundamental orientation toward materiality, may be what most decisively distinguish IS from cognate disciplines that are more tilted toward the "meaning" side, and toward idealist rather than materialist ontologies, such as communication, critical theory, cultural studies, literary and media criticism, and so on.[1]

As the present contributions demonstrate, however, more culturally-minded IS scholars and professionals, particularly in the last decade or so, have led a vigorous drive into the messy and undecideable domain of meaning. Issues of social and cultural representation, construction, signification, discourse, and interpretation have become focal aspects of critical IS scholarship, influenced by the same strands of post-Frankfurt School critical theory, Birmingham School cultural studies, strong social constructivism adapted from science and technology studies, and French postmodernism that roiled the humanities and social sciences in the 1980s and 90s.

Here is the irony: as much as they have been at the forefront of this interpretive/constructivist move, feminist and queer theory must also, and necessarily, confront and account for the materiality of bodies and their relations with material, informational artifacts and practices. Virtually every contribution to this *Reader* grapples (if that is the right word) with the same set of problems: the nature of bodies, and information, as entities that are simultaneously material and symbolic, and how to map the intersections among them. In what senses do discourses and representations configure bodies, artifacts and practices? Conversely, what do bodies, artifacts and practices represent and signify, and how do they configure informational discourses and culture? Ironically, in the move toward constructivism, interpretation and discourse, feminist and queer theory have retrieved materiality as a crucial concern of IS scholarship.

In this volume, "information studies" is construed in a very broad sense. Although many papers address more narrow disciplinary questions of theory and professional practice, others reflect on larger relations among gender, information, and technology in society and culture. A detailed commentary on all the works is outside the scope of a short afterword. In retrospect, however, we can ask: what does this collection, focusing on feminist and queer theory, say about research and scholarship in information studies as a field today? What themes or insights can the general scholarly reader, as well as those more versed in the particular concerns and arguments of gender theory and cultural studies, take away from this *Reader*? I would like to suggest three main "clusters" of implications, corresponding to three scales or levels of analysis—all of which, in one way or another, illustrate the importance of materiality in theorizing information artifacts, practices, and institutional formations.

---

1   John Durham Peters, *Speaking into the Air: A History of the Idea of Communication* (Chicago: University of Chicago Press, 1999).

First, at the micro-level scale of individuals and relationships, the studies here provide compelling evidence that information seeking (including the use of technological tools) is an indispensable part of identity formation and performance. Gender, like other aspects of identity, is emergent, deeply interwoven with and dependent on interaction with other people and the tools and affordances of information that help us understand and present ourselves as individuals and as related to others through complex social ties. With a few promising exceptions (e.g., studies of everyday life information seeking, or ELIS), most information seeking research follows a rational, goal-directed model, where the process is conceived as a matter of matching individuals' questions with documentary/institutional answers, perhaps inflected by the seeker's social traits or demographics. However, various chapters here (e.g., those by Cooper, Hilson, Kendall, Nakamura, Williams & McKenzie) suggest that information seeking is as much about a sense of belonging and being situated in a web of relational ties and identifications as it is about delivering "relevant" information to someone with a "need" for it.

At the middle-range level of organizing and community, this collection reminds us that knowledge, especially professional knowledge, is thoroughly socialized and always, inevitably negotiated. This idea is something of a commonplace in contemporary critical scholarship, though it is more often asserted as intuitively obvious than concretely demonstrated. But the papers by Adler, Blas, Campbell, Flanagan, Olson (alone and with Fox), Schrader, and Sandoval provide powerful examples of just how collective knowledge is *made* in practice: tasks and ascribed roles in the workplace, subject classification decisions and assignments, interface designs, rape kits, irreconcilable cultural practices, sexualized avatars in online games, collections of documents and artifacts, transgressive performances and acts of vandalism—these are not simply dematerialized "discourses," significations, or representations, but concrete actions, and products of action, that manifest and change the material conditions of existence and social life. (The classical pragmatist axiom, "things *perceived* as real are real in their consequences," reiterated by Leigh Star and Geof Bowker in their classic book, *Sorting Things Out*,[2] is worth remembering here—perhaps especially with respect to gender.)

Finally, at the macro-level of society and institutions, this *Reader* shows us the real work that institutions do to make the world (or worlds) out of action and artifacts, to create, instantiate, and sanction persons, places, and knowledge. Again, the notion that institutions that collect and organize information in fact constitute society, legitimacy and power is hardly new in IS; indeed, it is a foundational premise in archive studies and increasingly

---

2 Susan Leigh Star and Geoffrey C. Bowker, *Sorting Things Out: Classification and Its Consequences* (Cambridge, MA: MIT Press, 2000), 53; emphasis in the original.

taken for granted in library studies and informatics. However, the contribution here is to demonstrate *how* the institutional process of making the world works, not as the generation of disembodied "ideology" but as action in space and time: how administrative law and regulatory codes create definitional gaps and borderlands that penalize certain classes of persons economically and politically (Spade); how archives actually police and regulate state authority and citizen deviance (Maynard); or how a "species reassignment" simulation in Second Life parodies the absurdities of legal codes that dictate waiting periods and medical treatment prior to gender reassignment surgery (Cardenas).

In sum, *Feminist and Queer Information Studies Reader* offers us a tool to think with: not only about the contributions of feminist and queer theory to contemporary IS scholarship in the strict sense, but more broadly about the nature of information and its forms; the systems and devices we design, build and deploy to make, find, and use it; and the kind of societies and cultures we make (or hope to make) when we do so.

~Leah A. Lievrouw
Los Angeles, May 2012

Author Bios

Melissa Adler is Assistant Professor in the School of Library and Information Science at the University of Kentucky. She earned her Ph.D. in Library and Information Studies, with a Ph.D. minor in Gender and Women's Studies in 2012 from the University of Wisconsin—Madison. Her research investigates processes of disciplining and resistance in classifications and names, and the roles of such practices in knowledge production. She is currently examining discourses of interdisciplinary fields that study marginalized populations, such as critical animal studies, disability studies, queer studies, and critical race studies. By looking to new media and online social networks, she is exploring ways in which tagging functions in information sharing among groups and individuals who are underserved by traditional classification systems. Her work carries implications for interdisciplinary studies, as well as access to information for people outside academia.

Ajamu is an internationally acclaimed fine art queer photographer, who has shown work in galleries, museums and alternative spaces around the world. He is the co-founder of rukus! Federation, an award winning charity dedicated to working with Black LGBT artists, activists and cultural producers nationally and internationally. He is currently Archive Curator for the rukus! Black LGBT Archive. For more info, see http://ajamu-fineartphotography.co.uk/ and http://rukus.org.uk/.

Zach Blas is an artist-theorist working at the intersections of networked media, queerness, and the political. He is a PhD candidate in The Graduate Program in Literature, Information Science + Information Studies, Visual Studies, and Women's Studies at Duke University. Zach has exhibited and lectured in numerous festivals, galleries, and museums around the world, including Los Angeles, Berlin, San Francisco, Tijuana, Sao Pāulo, Mexico City, Singapore, New York, Venezuela, Liverpool, Paris, Istanbul, and Toronto.

Jessica E. Brophy is an interdisciplinary PhD candidate at the University of Maine in Communication and Women's Studies. Her research interests include feminist theory and technology, rhetoric of technology, and the interrelationship of technology with space and place. She is also interested in community engagement with technology, particularly in rural or isolated communities. She currently works as a newspaper editor and reporter on an island in Maine.

D. Grant Campbell completed his Ph.D. in English at Queen's University, Canada. He has taught at Queen's, University of Toronto and Dalhousie University, and is currently Associate Professor in the Faculty of Information and Media Studies at the University of Western Ontario. His research interests include cataloguing and classification, metadata, and the Semantic Web, particularly as they apply to the challenges of specific communities, particularly GLBT communities and communities of those facing dementia.

micha cárdenas is an artist/theorist who works in performance, wearable electronics, hacktivism and critical gender studies. She is a PhD student in Media Arts and Practice (iMAP) in the School of Cinematic Arts at University of Southern California and a member of Electronic Disturbance Theater 2.0. Her latest book *The Transreal: Political Aesthetics of Crossing Realities* was published by Atropos Press in 2012. She blogs at http://transreal.org and tweets @michacardenas.

Danielle Cooper is a doctoral student at the School of Gender, Feminist and Women's Studies at York University. She holds a Masters degree from the Faculty of Information at the University of Toronto in collaboration with the Mark S. Bonham Centre for Sexual Diversity Studies. Her research, which focuses on LGBTQ grassroots information organizations, includes recent ethnographic projects at the Pride Library at the University of Western Ontario and the Lesbian Herstory Archives in Brooklyn, New York.

Ann Cvetkovich is Ellen C. Garwood Centennial Professor of English and Professor of Women's and Gender Studies at the University of Texas at Austin. She is the author of *Mixed Feelings: Feminism, Mass Culture, and Victorian Sensationalism* (Rutgers, 1992), *An Archive of Feelings: Trauma, Sexuality, and Lesbian Public Cultures* (Duke, 2003), and *Depression: A Public Feeling* (Duke, 2012). She co-edited (with Ann Pellegrini) "Public Sentiments," a special issue of *The Scholar and Feminist Online*, and (with Janet Staiger and Ann Reynolds) *Political Emotions* (Routledge, 2010).

Rebecca Dean is a gender and technology researcher with a background in Information Studies and Women's Studies. Her research examines the role of data in documenting violence against women. Currently she's on an adventure in the mobile software industry.

Carlos Ulises Decena is the author of *Tacit Subjects: Belonging and Same-Sex Desire Among Dominican Immigrant Men* (Duke UP, 2011). He teaches in the

Departments of Women's and Gender Studies and Latino and Hispanic Caribbean Studies at Rutgers University.

Mary Flanagan is a scholar, artist, and inventor known for her theories on playculture, activist design, and critical play. Her artwork ranges from game-based systems to computer viruses, embodied interfaces to interactive texts; she founded Tiltfactor.org, a leading game design laboratory. Flanagan is known as a writer of electronic literature and she is also a poet. She has written more than 20 critical essays and chapters; her books include *reload* (2002), *re:SKIN* (2007), (both with A. Booth), *Critical Play* (2009), and the forthcoming *Values at Play in Digital Games* with collaborator Nissenbaum. She teaches at Dartmouth College. For more info, see http://www.maryflanagan.com.

Melodie J. Fox is a doctoral student at the University of Wisconsin–Milwaukee's School of Information Studies and is a member of the Information Organization Research Group there. She holds an MLIS from the University of Wisconsin–Milwaukee and an MA in English from the University of Illinois at Chicago. Her research interests include epistemology and the social consequences of the organization and representation of knowledge, with particular focus on gender.

Judith Halberstam is Professor of English, Gender Studies and American Studies and Ethnicity at the University of Southern California. Halberstam is the author of four books including *Female Masculinity* (Duke UP, 1998) and, most recently, *The Queer Art of Failure* (Duke UP, 2011) and has a new book out from Beacon press titled: *Gaga Feminism: Sex, Gender and the End of Normal*. Halberstam also blogs at http://bullybloggers.wordpress.com

Mica Hilson is a visiting lecturer at Indiana University–Bloomington, specializing in gender and sexuality studies, twentieth-century literature, popular culture, and critical theory. For over a decade, he has studied the development of online communities devoted to the production, sharing, and discussion of erotic stories. His essay in this reader is adapted from a chapter in his forthcoming first book, *From Pulp to Plasma Screen: A History of Gay Erotic Fiction, 1965–Present*.

Patrick Keilty is Assistant Professor in the Faculty of Information and teaches in the Bonham Centre for Sexual Diversity Studies at the University of Toronto. His writing examines and critiques feminist and queer engagements with digital technology, particularly visual culture, aesthetics, metadata, databases, embodiment, stylistics of the self, politics, sexual representation, and philosophy of science and technology. With Rebecca Dean, he is co-editor of *Feminist and Queer Information Studies Reader*.

Lori Kendall is Associate Professor in the Graduate School of Library and Information Science at the University of Illinois. Her book *Hanging out in the Virtual Pub* is an ethnography of an online group. She has written articles on online community and culture, popular representations of nerd identity, and research methods. Her current work focuses on personal archiving.

Leah Lievrouw is Professor of Information Studies at the University of California, Los Angeles. Her research and teaching focus on the relationship between media, information technologies, and social change. She is author of *Alternative and Activist New Media*. With Sonia Livingston, she is co-editor of *Sage Benchmarks in Communications: New Media* and *The Handbook of New Media*. She is currently at work on two monographs, *Media and Meaning: Communication Technology and Society*, and *Foundations of Media and Communication Theory*.

Steven Maynard teaches in the Department of History at Queen's University in Kingston, Ontario. His work has appeared in a wide range of academic and activist publications. In 2010, his "Police/Archives" won the Association of Canadian Archivists' W. Kaye Lamb Prize for the article that "most advances archival thinking in Canada."

Pam McKenzie is an Associate Professor in the Faculty of Information and Media Studies at The University of Western Ontario. Her research focuses on the ways that individuals in local settings collaboratively construct information needs, seeking, and use. She is interested in temporal, textual and interactional aspects of information practices, in the intersections of information work and caring work, and in gendered and embodied information practices and spaces.

Lisa Nakamura is the Director of the Asian American Studies Program at the University of Illinois at Urbana Champaign and Professor of Media and Cinema Studies and Asian American Studies. She is the author of four books on digital media and identity, including *Digitizing Race: Visual Cultures of the Internet*, winner of the 2010 Association of Asian American Studies Book Award in Cultural Studies.

Hope A Olson, Professor in the School of Information Studies at the University of Wisconsin—Milwaukee, focuses her research and teaching on representation, epistemology, and classification theory using feminist, poststructural, postcolonial and other critical theories. She has authored *The Power to Name* (Kluwer 2002) and articles, chapters, and papers in knowledge organization, librarianship, women's studies, and humanities publications. Dr. Olson edited *Knowledge Organization* 2000–2004. She is currently writing a book on the cultural construction of classification.

Zabet Patterson is Assistant Professor of Contemporary Art and Digital Media at Stony Brook University, State University of New York. Her research specializes in the intersection of contemporary art and computational media in the postwar period. Her work is shaped by psychoanalytic and post-structuralist theory, and her interests include contemporary art history and criticism, digital media history and theory, performance, and cybernetics. She is currently completing a book-length manuscript entitled *Visionary Machines*.

Jasbir Puar is Associate Professor of Women's & Gender Studies at Rutgers University. Her research interests include gender, sexuality, globalization, postcolonial and diaspora studies, South Asian cultural studies, and theories of assemblage and affect. She is the author of *Terrorist Assemblages: Homonationalism in Queer Times*, which won the 2007 Cultural Studies Book Award from the Association for Asian American Studies. Her edited volumes include a special issue of *GLQ* titled, "Queer Tourism: Geographies of Globalization" and co-edited a volume of *Society and Space* titled "Sexuality and Space". Most recently she edited, with Julie Livingston, a special issue of *Social Text* on "Interspecies."

K. J. Rawson is an Assistant Professor in the Department of English at the College of the Holy Cross. At the intersections of queer, feminist, and rhetorical studies, his scholarship focuses on the rhetorical dimensions of queer and transgender archiving in both traditional and digital collections. With Eileen E. Schell, he co-edited *Rhetorica in Motion: Feminist Rhetorical Methods and Methodologies* (University of Pittsburgh Press, 2010) and his scholarship has also appeared in *Archivaria* and several edited collections.

Chela Sandoval is chair emerita of the Department of Chicana/o Studies at the University of California, Santa Barbara. Her award-winning book *Methodology of the Oppressed* (University of Minnesota Press, 2000) is one of the most influential contemporary theoretical texts worldwide. Sandoval's work, which includes a variety of articles and chapters on social movements, third space feminism, and critical media theory, has been published in major anthologies. At UCSB she teaches courses on de-colonial feminism, power and truth, liberation philosophy, and radical semiotics. Sandoval received a PhD in the History of Consciousness at the University of California, Santa Cruz. Her current book project is on story-wor(l)d-art-performance as activism (SWAPA) and the shaman-nahual/witness ceremony. She has recently co-edited an anthology on Xican Latina-o Indigenous Performance, *Performing the US Latina and Latino borderlands*.

Alvin M. Schrader is Director of Research, University of Alberta Libraries, and professor emeritus and former director of the School of Library and Information Studies, University of Alberta. He is the co-author, with Kris Wells, of *Challenging Silence, Challenging Censorship: Inclusive Resources, Strategies and Policy Directives for Addressing Bisexual, Gay, Lesbian, Trans-Identified and Two-Spirited Realities in School and Public Libraries*. He also studies the impact of Internet filters on access to LGBTQ information and websites. He received the Canadian Library Association's 1997 Award for the Advancement of Intellectual Freedom in Canada.

Aliza Shvarts is a PhD student in the department of Performance Studies at New York University, where she writes on figuration and failure. She is also a managing editor of the performance studies journal *TDR/The Drama Review*. Shvarts received her BA from Yale University in 2008, where she double-majored in English and Art—and where her senior thesis for the Art major was the subject of major controversy.

Dean Spade is an assistant professor at the Seattle University School of Law. In 2002 he founded the Sylvia Rivera Law Project, a non-profit collective that provides free legal help to low-income people and people of color who are trans, intersex and/or gender non-conforming and works to build trans resistance rooted in racial and economic justice. He is the author of *Normal Life: Administrative Violence, Critical Trans Politics and the Limits of Law*.

Judy Wajcman is a Professor of Sociology at the London School of Economics. Her books include: *Feminism Confronts Technology; Managing Like a Man: Women and Men in Corporate Management; TechnoFeminism;* and *The Politics of Working Life*. Her most recent edited book is Hackett et al., the *Handbook of Science and Technology Studies*. She recently ended a term as President of the Society for the Social Studies of Science.

Sherilyn Williams is a Library and Information Science doctoral candidate at The University of Western Ontario, where she focuses on feminist theoretical and methodological approaches to information. She is primarily interested in women's subversive informational strategies, the ways they share information and knowledges, and distinctions between "information" and "knowledges." Elements of material culture including handicrafts, and more recently, contraceptives, serve as case studies for her analyses. She is currently working on her dissertation.

Index

A

aboutness, 301, 303, 679
   and indexing and retrieval, 269
   and meaning, 293–95, 297, 302, 305–06
   objective aboutness (O-about), 269
   retrieval aboutness (R-about), 269, 277
   subjective aboutness (S-about), 269
Abu Ghraib, 353–82
   and digital photography, 220, 22, 353–82
   and feminism, 363–75
   and simulation of gay sex, 375–78, 381
   and the Muslim body, 357–61
   photos, 221
   process of torture at, 7
   reactions to, 353–54, 356
accessibility
   as goal of archivists, 542–43
   environmental, 545
   of transgender researchers to archives, 543, 548
Adobe Photoshop, logo of, 33
AIDS, 392, 634, 669, 673. *See also* G.R.I.D. (Gay-Related Immune Deficiency); GRIDs
AIDS and HIV, and archives, 514–15
AIDS epidemic, 299
American Civil Liberties Union (ACLU), and censorship of websites, 89, 90
American Library Association (ALA), 74, 81
   LGBT rights, 85–86
   Gay, Lesbian, Bisexual, and Transgendered Round Table, 67, 87
   Social Responsibility Round Table Task Force on Women, 262
angels, 202, 221
archive
   as metaphorical construct, 444–45. *See also* archive fever
   black queer. *See* ruckus!
   as police, 452. *See also* police/archives
   city, 453f1, 458, 464–68
   gay and lesbian, 502–22, 526–40, 549–51, 556, 562, 565–74, 579–86, 592–94
   transgender, 546

archive fever, 445, 448, 449, 466. *See also* Derrida, Jacques
Archive of Feelings, An. See Cvetkovich, Ann, theories of
artists, Black lesbian, gay, bisexual and trans (LGBT). *See* ruckus!
avatars, 182–89, 196–98, 200–02, 204, 207–08, 211–12, 214, 216–17, 219, 223, 651. *See also* angels

B

BabyDream.com, 187, 188, 196–201, 203, 219, 221
Banned Websites Awareness Day, 90
Barthe, Roland, theories of, 117
  desire vs. pleasure, 35–39, 40, 44, 135
  on love, 126, 133
  semiotiology, 120
  texts that speak, 29–30, 43
bathrooms, and accessibility for trans people, 546–47
Baudrillard, Jean, theories of, 36, 40, 43, 175–76, 615, 652
becoming
  and the virtual body, 642–43, 646, 649–53, 657
  concepts of, 147, 149, 153, 361
Benning, Sadie, videos of, 564, 585–92
Berman, Sanford, 264, 303–05, 310, 317
Bibliothèque nationale de France (BNF), and Foucault, 447
biotechnologies, 108–09, 642, 654, 660
bisexuality, classification of, 315–16
Black Queer Archive for the United Kingdom. *See* ruckus!
BlueSky, 227–47

and hegemonic masculinity, 236–39, 241, 244–46
and nerd identity, 234–35, 238–39, 242, 245
Asian Americans on, 242–44, 247
bodies
  as conduits for information, 15
  increased scientific fascination with, 32
  as universal, 144–45
bodies, virtual, 14–15.
  mapping of the interior, 31
  See also hyperbodies
Bourdieu, Pierre, theories of, 168
Boys Don't Cry, film, 475–77. See also Teena, Brandon
bride, Duchamps representation of, 17–20, 21, 35
Briet, Suzanne, 1–2, 5, 8
  continuation of project, 2
browsing, process of, 270, 279, 534–36, 558
Butler, Judith, theories of, 28, 138, 145, 147–49, 152, 154, 168

C

Campbell, Topher, 503–25. *See also* ruckus!
Canadian Charter of Rights and Freedoms, 64
Canadian Library Association, 78, 81, 85
Canadian Living Healing Quilt Project (LHQP), 420–21. *See also* quilting
Cartesian dualism. *See* mind/body split
categorization, in US law and policy, 326
categorizing. *See* classification

Index

Cather, Willa, on small towns, 477, 478
Celluloid Closet, The, film, 88, 92, 304
Center for Lesbian Information and Technology (CLIT), 562
classification
    associative relationships (RTs), 258–59, 271–72, 277
    paradigmatic relationships, 283–85
    of perversion, 309–21
    scope notes, 281
    sexual orientation, 301, 551
    subject headings, and access for LGBTQ youth, 66–67
    subject headings, and logic, 256–64
    subject headings, 279–85
    of transgender books, 552
Classification Research Group, 291
classification systems
    community-based, 291–92, 305–06
classificationist, 290–91, 303
code
    as body, 42
    as text, 40
coming out, 65, 384–93, 396–97
community archives. *See* Lesbian Herstory Archives (LHA); and ruckus!
computer, vs. human, 14
connectedness
    characteristics of, 269
    logical models of, 256
    and organization of information, 71–78, 285
    and syntagmatic relationships, 283
    of technological development, 111

consumerism, 585, 667, 670
crafters, 414–19
crafting, 406–26
    communities, online, 422
    informational potential of, 413–16
    and vulnerable populations, 418–21
crafts
    and technology intersecting, 421–24
    as a means to disseminate information, 416–18
    liberatory potential of, 417
    social meaning of, 413–16
    textile, 258, 407–08, 413–17, 418, 422
Create Africa South (CAS), 420
criminals, gay. *See* Orton, Joe and Kenneth Halliwell
culture, concept of, 2
Cutter, Charles, 59, 278, 302, 620, 636
Cvetkovich, Ann, theories of, 444, 475, 506, 528, 532, 540
Cyber Consciousness, 120, 134
cyberfeminism. *See* feminism, cyberfeminism
cyberpunk
    fiction, 26, 186, 212
    play area, 648
cyberspace. *See* virtual realities
Cyberutopia, 137–152, 156–57, 212
cyborg, 36, 108, 118–20, 122–35, 140, 155, 646, 648, 659–60
cyborg feminism. *See* feminism, cyberfeminism

D

data collection, 329, 339–40
    and gender, 329–30

databodies, 24, 33, 36, 186
de Saussure, Ferdinand, theories of, 17, 283
Dead or Alive, game. *See* virtual characters, Kasumi
deconstruction, 62, 121, 131, 266, 421
Deleuze, Gilles and Felix Guattari, theories of, 604, 616–17, 642
democratics, 121–22, 131, 132
departs from conventional archival methodology, 526
Derrida, Jacques, theories of, 133, 443–45, 448, 450, 463
Desk Set, film, analysis of, 4–5, 13–14, 16
DeVine, Philip, 481
   media erasure of, 480
   murder of, 474, 486
Dewey Decimal Classification, 257, 286, 290
Diagnostic and Statistical Manual of Mental Disorders IV (DSM-IV), 318–20
differential movement, 121–22, 126, 132–33
digibodies, 33
digital
   characters, and state of media, 22–23
   closet, 88, 91f3
   divide, 144, 206
   images, production of, 33–34
digital signatures, 187–89, 195–200, 205, 207, 215–23.
   women's production of, 189, 198, 221, 223
   See also Siggy Girls
discrimination, history of, against gays and lesbians, 331
Disingenuous Bar, 669. *See also* Queer Technologies (QT)

do-it-yourself (DIY), 187, 190–92, 202, 523, 645, 650–51, 658
documentary film, as lesbian archive, 585
dolls, American Girl brand, 192–94, 196
Duchamp, Marcel, and depictions of women and technology, 16–21, 26, 35

E

embodied data, social implications of, 38–39
EMERAC, 4, 13, 14
ENgenderingGenderChangers, 665. *See also* Queer Technologies (QT)
environmental accessibility. *See* accessibility, environmental
ephemera, 207–08, 532–33, 567–68, 585
erotic fiction
   consumers of, 435
   gay, 431–38
   feedback on, 435
essences, minimizing of, 54
essentialism, 50, 57, 268
   and ethic of care, 55
   and feminism, 51–52
   definition of, 49
   vs. constructivist, 301, 302–03
ethic, of care, 55–58
   in libraries, 58–59
ethnography, 484, 526–30, 539–40, 580–82
exploitation, 53, 418–19, 676

F

Fae Richards Photo Archive, The, 561–62. *See also* Watermelon

Index

Woman, The
Fairthorne, Robert, theories of, 294–95, 297
Farm Boys, documentary, 492–93
Fellows, Will, historian, 492
feminism
    cyberfeminism, xiii, 3, 137–39, 154–57. *See also* Haraway, Donna, theories of
    radical, 105–06
    Socialist, 105–07
    technofeminism, 101, 110–13
    third world, in the United States, 119–35, 659
    third-wave, 107, 418, 422
feminisms, of equality, 266
feminist cyborg theory, 122–24. *See also* Haraway, Donna, theories of
fetish, 320, 593, 602–09, 612–16, 618–19.
    historical function of, 602–09
    See also rape kit, as fetish
fetishism, virtual body, 35–36, 37, 39. *See also* Marx, Karl, and commodity fetish
fetishistic disavowal, 171, 174,
films, documentary, 475, 477, 482, 521, 564, 567–69, 572–79.
filtering, of Internet, 72, 76, 80–84, 88–92
Folsom Street Fair, 557
Forbidden Love, film, 572–79, 580, 584–86, 589–90, 593
Foucault, Michel, theories of, 300, 317, 327, 330, 368, 443, 445–56, 465–67
freedom of expression, 63, 68, 71–74, 91
French-Algerian war, torture during, 355, 359
Functional Requirements for Bibliographic Records (FRBR), 271, 274
Fuss, Diane, theories of, 49, 266

G

G.R.I.D. (Gay-Related Immune Deficiency), 673. *See also* GRIDs; AIDS
gaming culture, 189, 217, 228
Gay Bombs, technical manual manifesto, 666–69, 670. *See also* Queer Technologies (QT)
Gay, Lesbian, Bisexual, and Transgender Society of Northern California (GLBTS), 592
gender classification systems
    administration of, 7, 330–32, 338–45
    and trans people, 330–37
gender power relations, 102–03, 106–08
generativity, 415, 422, 423, 424
girl-band icons, 590–91
GLBT Historical Society (San Francisco, CA), 545, 546, 557–58
Greenblatt, Ellen, 85, 303
Greetings from Out Here, film, 564, 580, 582–88
GRIDs, 669, 673–77
Grosz, Elizabeth
    corporeal feminism, 42
    on utopian space, 137
    theories of, 149, 152–53, 266
group activities, social meaning of, 416–18

H

Halberstam, J., theories of, 310, 312–13, 315, 319, 473–99
Hampton, Mabel, 568–70, 679. *See also Watermelon Woman, The*, film

Haraway, Donna, theories of, 36, 108–09, 117, 118–19, 122–35, 155, 209, 659–60
Harding, Sandra, theories of, ix, 5, 6, 105. 256
hazing, 379
health care access, and trans people, 330, 332, 335, 338, 345
health information sites, blocking of, 88–89
heteronormativity, 65, 92, 494, 503, 570, 590, 547, 663
homosexuality and heterosexuality structures, distinctions between, 299
human genome project, 32
Human Rights, 68, 71
human-computer interface (HCI), 16
hyperbodies, 14–15

I

identities, transreal, 651–53, 660
identity
    and documents, 331–32, 338–39, 446
    as nerd, 234–35, 238–39, 242, 245
    gender, 62, 85–86, 105, 109, 112, 234, 238, 334, 340
    multiple axes of, 6
    studying online, 230–32
indexing languages, 90
information
    cultural position of, 13
    definition of, 6, 15
information behavior, 407, 411, 421, 425
    collaborative, 408
    of marginalized people, 411, 425
information organization tools

    feminist critique of, 251, 262–65
information sharing, 406–13, 421–42, 424–26, 537
information studies (IS), xii–xiv, 1–8
    and queer studies, 1–8, 67–70, 82, 92
internet access, 81–90, 143, 171, 220–23
internet generation, 144
interpassivity, 177–79
intersectionality, 6
intra-agency, 138, 150–56
invisibility
    impact of, 90–91, 566
    in history, 512, 566
invisible machine, xii
Iraq, war in, 69, 253–62, 367–82. *See also* Abu Ghraib
Islington Public Library. *See* Orton, Joe and Kenneth Halliwell

J

joint kinship, 126
joking, online, about women as sexual objects, 236

K

Katz, Jonathan, theories of, 316–17
knitting, 414–15, 416, 422, 424. *See also* crafting
knowledge worker, industrialization of, 1
KwaZulu Natal, 420

L

Lacan, Jacques, theories of, 169
Lambert, Lisa, murder of, 474. *See also* Teena, Brandon; DeVine,

Index

Philip, murder of
laws, hate crime, 324, 342, 347, 375, 398
LCSH. *See* Library of Congress Subject Headings (LCSH)
Lesbian Herstory Archives (LHA), 526–39, 562
    as home, 531–33
    study of, 526–39
LGBT professional organization, first, 3
LGBTQ, youth, 66–67
librarians, and ventriloquial, 54
librarianship,
    and inclusion of computer technologies, 5
    gender of, 48, 59–60, 407
    gender, differences in salary, 60
libraries
    as hero, 634–35
    queering of, 85, 87
    representation of in film, 13–14
    theft and vandalism in, 625–27. *See also* Orton, Joe and Kenneth Halliwell
    as villain, 631–34
library and information studies (LIS), 48, 69–71, 621
library classification, gender-based critique of, 264–65, 552
Library of Congress Classification (LCC), 279, 290
Library of Congress Subject Headings (LCSH), 67, 259, 290, 303, 305, 309–21
library schools, closure of, 3–4
liminality, 138, 151–54, 156–57
literary canon, gay, 293
literary
    criticism, 292–93, 295–99
    theory, 297–98, 301
Literotica.com, 435–36

logic
    Aristotelian and traditional, 49–51, 251–56, 266, 268
    "feminine" model, 265
    feminist critique of, 254–56, 265
    postmodern feminist model, 265–67

M

male/female binary, 130, 665
manifesto, technical manual. *See* Gay Bombs, technical manual manifesto
mapping of the body, and use of technology, 30–32
Marx, Karl,
    and capitalist mode of appropriation, 611
    and commodity fetish, 35, 574fn23, 604, 614–15
    and technology of production, 106, 522
masculinity
    working class, 479, 493
    and computer technology, 232–33
mashups, 622–5, 631, 635–36
masturbation, 178–79, 358, 589
meta-ideologizing, 121–22, 131, 133
metadata, 256, 274, 319, 623. *See also* classification
methodology
    of the oppressed, 119–20, 122, 124, 127, 130, 132–35
    scientific positivist vs. humanistic, 5
metronormativity, 488–89. *See also* rural/urban divide
migration, of queers, 478
mind/body split, 20, 142, 143, 147
muds. See Multi-User Dungeon

(MUD)
Multi-User Dungeon (MUD), 228–10. *See also* BlueSky
Multi-User Virtual Environments (MUVEs), 645–6, 651
naming, 53, 68, 74–77, 80, 90, 316

N

Nannycams. *See* women, and surveillance systems
National Transgender Library and Archive at the University of Michigan, bathrooms at, 546
Nebraska, 473, 482, 491, 492, 495. *See also* rural/urban divide
Nebraska, Falls City, Nebraska, 474, 477–78, 495
Nerdity Test, 234. *See also* identity, as nerd
Nifty Archive, 431–39
node labels, 272, 279, 280
Noguera, Rogelio, 393–96, 400
Norman, Donald, design specialist, 23
Not Just Passing Through, film, 561, 564, 568–71, 593

O

odyssey, personal, 62, 92–93
online forums. *See* BlueSky
oppressed, science of the, 643, 657–60
oral history, 492, 537, 569–70, 572–73, 576, 585
Orton, Joe and Kenneth Halliwell, case of, 8, 620–37
Other, the, 77–78

P

paraphilias, as authorized heading, 309, 314–15, 317–21
parenting, websites on, 187–89, 207
PATRIOT Act, 2
patriotism, 354, 375, 381–82
pedagogy, guerrilla, xv
performativity, 138, 148
  and articulation, 138, 146–49, 151
perverse presentism, 310, 312–14
phenomenology, 656–57
Police Museum and the Toronto Police Service, 456, 458–64
police, and archives, 443–67
police/archives, 443, 445, 452, 454–7, 460, 463, 465–67
Polly the Butch Librarian. *See* Thistlewaite, Polly
pornography, amateur, 170–79
  "A Day in the Life . . .", 172–74, 178
pornography, online, 163–81. *See also* Nifty Archive
pornography, vs. erotica, 79
post-feminism. *See* feminism, third-wave
postcards, 583–84, 588, 592
postcolonial theory, 145, 476
power, structures of, 74–77
pregnancy
  and digital signatures, 189, 198, 221, 223. *See also* digital signatures
  medicalization of, 183
  visual culture of, 183, 185, 189–90, 202
  websites on, 187, 188, 196–201, 203, 219, 221
pregnant body, 183, 186, 189, 196–98

Index

presentism, 312-14
printer, three-dimensional, 647
psychoanalysis, 169, 455
public/private dichotomy, 416
pulp fiction,
    gay, 437, 438
    lesbian, 572-80
    lesbian, covers of, 575-76
Punjabi Sikh detainees, 373

Q

queer capitalism, 671-72
queer discourses, xii
queer programming anti-language, 663-66
queer studies, 368, 403, 444
    foundations of, xiii
    space and sexuality in, 484-98
Queer Technologies (QT), 662-77
queer theory, xiii, 5, 292-302, 298-301, 313, 467, 476, 528, 670, 680. *See also* Sedgwick, Eve Kosofsky, theories of
quilting, 216, 412, 415-18, 422-23. *See also* crafting

R

race representation and digital characters, 25
rape, 372-73, 602-19
rape kits, 602-19
    and ethical issues, 8
    as fetish, 603
    as object, 613-18
    text in, 607-13
Razorfish, 24. *See also* virtual characters, Syndi, search engine portal
real vs. narrative, 497
Real, the
    and gender, 38, 43
    definition of, 33
    fascination with, 37, 44
    fragmentation of, 657
    frission of, 175.
    reconceptualizing, 153
    See also Baudrillard, Jean
revolution, microelectronic, 107-08
Rich, Adrienne, theories of, 91
rukus! archive project, 502-24
rural, 473, 474-77, 479, 491-94
rural and small-town queer life, 481, 484, 485-88, 494-97
rural/urban
    divide, 481
    divisions in queer communities, 484, 489, 580-82
    See also metronormativity

S

sado-masochistic materials, display of, 557-58
sadomasochism, 109
Schrodinger's cat, 150
Schulman, Sarah, cameo of, 562
science and technology studies (STS), 101, 680
scientific positivist methods, 5
Second Life. *See* virtual worlds
security culture, in the United States, 333, 338-39, 344
Sedgwick, Eve Kosofsky, theories of,
    on *Billy Budd*, 292-93
    and information communities, 622-24
    and issues of categorization, 298-301
    modern homo/heterosexual definition, 640-44
    production of gay identity, 494

universalizing, 304–06
semiotics, 2, 15, 17, 23, 36, 121, 131
   geosemiotics, 546–48
   semiology, 120
sex segregation, in facilities, 330, 334, 338, 345
sexism, 92, 237, 280–81
sexual deviance, medicalization of, 315–21
sexual imaginaries, of rural and urban space, 481
Sexual Minorities Archives, 545–46, 551, 556, 558–59
Sexual Offense Evidence Collection Kit, 607, 613. *See also* rape kits.
Shepard, Matthew, murder of, 347, 483, 496, 498
shop-dropped, 669
Siggy Girls, 188, 206. *See also* digital signatures
signatures. *See* digital signatures
Silicon Valley, and recognition for tech workers, 118
Six Feet Under, television show and pregnancy anxiety, 182–83
social networking, 7, 82, 183
Socialist feminism. *See* feminism, Socialist
sodomy, as confusing classification subject, 303
Spivak, Gayatri
   on essences, 54, 58
   theories of, 49, 52–53, 127
SRLP. *See* Sylvia Rivera Law Project (SRLP)
stereotypes
   class, 479
   as metonymy, 77
   reinforcing norms online, 140
   rural, 581
   sexual, 301, 531, 576
   similarities to universals, 51, 67
   about technology usage, 245
strategic essentialism, 49, 52–53, 121, 122, 127, 129fn35. *See also* Spivak, Gayatri, theories of
subject access, issues for marginalized groups, 291–92
subject headings. *See* classification
subjects, tacit, 7, 384–403
Sylvia Rivera Law Project (SRLP), 344–45
syntagmatic relationship, 276, 278, 283–85

T

tags
   clouds, 80, 84, 87–88, 91–92
   bookmarks, 276–77
tagging, 269, 271, 522, 623
   collaborative, 276–77
taste culture, 195, 199
technofeminism. *See* feminism, technofeminism
technologies, of simulacrum, 375–80
technology
   as culture, 102–05
   as gendered, 105–07, 110–13
   fetish, 39
Teena, Brandon, 473–98. *See also* DeVine, Philip; Lambert, Lisa, murder of
Textile crafts. *See* crafts, textile
The Bride Stripped Bare by Her Bachelors, Even, painting. *See* bride, DuChamps representation of
Thistlewaite, Polly, 564, 568
Tomb Raider. *See* virtual characters, Croft, Laura
torture. *See* Abu Ghraib
trans people, and surgery

Index

identity documents for, 331
health care access, 335-36
lack of access to, 482
and becoming, 643, 645
trans politics, 325
and law reform, 340-42
transgender desire, 343-44
transgender researchers, 543, 545, 546, 548
and accessibility to archives, 543, 548
transgender
as classification term, 549-54
definition of, 543
translator, as traitor, 505
transreal. See identities, transreal
transversal, 642, 660
Tronto, Joan, theories of, 48, 55, 58, 59
Tufte, Edward, design specialist, 22, 207

U

UCLA, Departments of Information Studies, 8
Universal Decimal Classification (UDC), 273
users, concept of, 2

V

values, Canadian, 73
vandalism, and libraries, 8, 620, 625-29, 635
viewpoints, minoritizing vs. universalizing, 303-05
virtual body fetishism, 35-36
virtual characters, 14-15, 22, 23, 29-30, 33, 34, 36-39
Ananova, first virtual newscaster, 26-27

Croft, Laura, 14, 25, 39, 189
embodied code of, 16-30
Kasumi, 14, 189
Mya, digital personal assistant, 27-28
Syndi, search engine portal, 23-26
virtual portals, 41
virtual realities, 24-26, 134-44
and gender identity, 108
gendering of, 206
and individualism, 195
queerness in, 659
relationship to reality, 152-57
sex clubs in, 648
virtual reality communications agents, 22
virtual spaces, 15
Second Life, 109, 644, 646-53, 660
virtual worlds, 642-44, 652, 659
as prototyping, 644, 651
See also Multi-User Virtual Environments (MUVEs)
virtuality, explorations of, 152-53
visual culture
of digital signatures, 202
lesbian, 587, 589
of motherhood, 183
of pregnancy and the body, 189-90
and self-produced digital images, 185
Voices of Women project, 420
voyeurism, 31, 173, 320, 375, 581.
and reality television, 175-77
See also women, and surveillance systems

W

War on Terror,

and administrative law, 343
as gay issue, 370
and increased surveillance, 338, 339, 340
and nonimmigrant trans people, 344
and sexuality, 381
and standardized data, 330, 333
and technologies of control, 346

Watermelon Woman, The, film,
and creation of visual archive, 561, 563, 593
and archives in lesbian cultures 564

Web surfing, 157, 168–70

white identity, hegemony of, 244–47

women
and surveillance systems, 30–31
as face of virtual reality, 22
bodies of, and ties to technology, 14, 15

workplace
and gender politics, 13–14
and sexism, 13

WOW Cafe theater collective, 569, 570

X

X, Ajamu, 503–24. *See also* ruckus!